Dreamers and Opportunists

Dreamers and Opportunists
Polish–Swedish relations during the Second World War

Paweł Jaworskpi

Södertörns högskola

Author: Paweł Jaworski (ORCID: 0000-0001-5256-1238)

Attribution 4.0 International (CC BY 4.0)
This publication is licensed under a
Creative Commons Attribution 4.0 License

First published 2009 by Instytut Pamięci Narodowej, Poland
Original title: Marzyciele i oportuniści. Stosunki polsko-szwedzkie w latach 1939–1945

 **NARODOWY PROGRAM ROZWOJU HUMANISTYKI**

Translation: Katarzyna Hussar
The translation of this volume was financed by
the Polish Ministry of Science and Higher Education.
Narodowy Program Rozwoju Humanistyki, Project: 31H 13 0148 82

Södertörns högskola
(Södertörn University)
Library
SE-141 89 Huddinge

www.sh.se/publications

Cover: Jonathan Robson (Illustration by Paweł Jaworski)
Graphic form: Per Lindblom & Jonathan Robson

Södertörn Academic Studies 73
ISSN 1650-433X
ISBN 978-91-88663-35-1 (print)
ISBN 978-91-88663-36-8 (digital)

Contents

Abbreviations 7
Introduction 11

PART 1
In the Circle of Politics and Propaganda 21

1. On the Eve of War 23

2. Aggression of Germany and the Soviet Union Against Poland from
the Swedish Perspective 35
First reactions 35
Reports from the front 44
The picture of total war 51
The attack from the East 56
The final phase of the campaign 65
The fate of Swedish diplomats in Warsaw 71
Representation of Polish interests by Sweden in Germany 74

3. In the Face of Consequences of the Ribbentrop-Molotov Pact 93
Following the defeat of Poland 93
During the Winter War 107

4. Consolidation of German Hegemony in Europe – Polish Strategy
of Maintaining Relations and Swedish Dodging 121
A freeze in relations following Hitler's invasion of Scandinavia 121
Operation Barbarossa and the apparent improvement
in Polish–Swedish relations 144
Polish and Swedish federalist concepts for post-war Europe 166
Overcoming stagnation in bilateral relations following
Hitler's defeat in Moscow 177

5. Revival of Bilateral Relations Following the Battle of Stalingrad 191
Polish diplomatic activity in the period of the Wehrmacht's failures ... 191
Swedish public opinion on the situation in occupied Poland and
Polish–Soviet relations 197
Swedish discussion on Katyń 216

6. Sweden's Return to Strict Neutrality and the Normalisation of
Relations with the Polish Government 231
The visit by the Minister of Industry, Trade and Shipping
Jan Kwapiński to Stockholm 231
Change in the policy of the Swedish government 242

Sweden's position on the Polish matter (January–July 1944) 246
Swedish reactions to the birth of the Lublin Committee 268
Activity of the Union of Polish Patriots (ZPP) in Sweden 272

7. The Double Game of Swedish Diplomacy 287
   The rising in Warsaw from a Swedish perspective 287
   The propagandist campaign for the recognition of Poland's right
   to sovereignty and territorial integrity 302
   Diplomatic chess 315
   Around Yalta 325
   Sweden's break-up of diplomatic relations with
   the Polish government in exile 355

PART 2
Economic Issues 361

8. Swedish Presence in Occupied Poland 363

9. Plans of Polish–Swedish Post-War Economic Cooperation 391

10. The Mission of Brynolf Eng 439

PART 3
Humanitarian Mission of Sweden 447

11. The Fate of Polish Refugee 449

12. Swedish Humanitarian Aid for Poland 473
    Humanitarian activity 1939–44 473
    The plans for providing post-war humanitarian aid 491
    The mission of Sven Hellqvist in the General Government 498
    Swedish transports of humanitarian aid to the
    Lublin Committee Poland 503
    Final negotiations regarding humpanitarian aid in the post-war period ..508

13. The Problems of Polish Soldiers Interned in Sweden 513
    Submarine crews 513
    Aviators 540
    Soldiers of the 1940 Norwegian Campaign 546

Conclusion 547
Bibliography 553
Index 571

Abbreviations

AAN	Archiwum Akt Nowych (Central Archives of Modern Records in Warsaw)
AK	Armia Krajowa (Polish Home Army)
AMSZ	Archiwum Ministerstwa Spraw Zagranicznych (Archive of the Ministry of Foreign Affairs, Poland)
ARAB	Arbetarrörelsens arkiv och bibliotek (Swedish Labour Movement's Archive and Library)
AA	Auswärtiges Amt (Federal Foreign Office of the German Empire)
BBC	British Broadcasting Corporation
ČTK	Československá tísková kancelář (Czech News Agency)
FO	British Foreign Office
FRA	Försvarets Radioanstalt (Swedish National Defence Radio Establishment)
IAfÅ	Internationella Arbetslag för Återuppbyggnad (International team for reconstruction)
KA	Krigsarkivet (Military Archive in Stockholm)
KBN	Komitet Badań Naukowych (State Committee for Scientific Research in Poland)
KMW	Kierownictwo Marynarki Wojennej (Polish Navy leadership)
KRN	Krajowa Rada Narodowa (State National Council or Homeland National Council in German-occupied Poland)
LO	Landsorganisationen (Swedish Trade Union Confederation)
MUST	Militära underrättelse- och säkerhetstjänsten

	(Swedish Military Intelligence and Security Service)
NA	National Archives (London)
NSDAP	Nationalsozialistische Deutsche Arbeiterpartei (National Socialist German Workers' Party or Nazi Party)
PAT	Polska Agencja Telegraficzna (Polish Telegraphic Agency)
PCK	Polski Czerwony Krzyż (Polish Red Cross)
PKWN	Polski Komitet Wyzwolenia Narodowego (Polish Committee of National Liberation or the Lublin Committee)
PPS	Polska Partia Socjalistyczna (Polish Socialist Party)
PRL	Polska Rzeczpospolita Ludowa (Polish People's Republic)
PRM	Prezydium Rady Ministrów (Prime Minister of Poland)
RA	Riksarkivet (National Archives of Sweden)
RAF	Royal Air Force
RGO	Rada Główna Opiekuńcza (Central Welfare Council, Kraków)
RP	Rzeczpospolita Polska (Second Polish Republic)
SAE	Sveriges Allmänna Exportförening (Swedish Export Association)
SAP	Sveriges socialdemokratiska arbetareparti (Swedish Social Democratic Party)
SIH	Svenska kommittén för internationell hjälpverksamhet (Swedish Committee for International Assistance)
SIS	Statens Informationsstyrelse (Sweden's Board of Information)

SISU	Studentförbundet för internationellt samhällstudium och uppbyggnadsarbete (Student Union for International Society Study and Construction)
SKP	Sveriges kommunistiska parti (Communist Party of Sweden)
SPP	Studium Polski Podziemnej (Polish Underground Movement Study Trust)
SRK	Svenska Röda Korset (Swedish Red Cross)
SSU	Sveriges socialdemokratiska ungdomsförbund (Swedish Social Democratic Youth League)
TASS	Tielegrafnoje Agientstwo Sovietskogo Sojuza (Russian News Agency)
TRJN	Tymczasowy Rząd Jedności Narodowej (Provisional Government of National Unity)
TT	Tidningarnas Telegrambyrå (TT News Agency/Swedish Telegraphic Agency)
UD	Utrikesdepartementet (Swedish Ministry of Foreign Affairs)
UNRRA	United Nations Relief and Rehabilitation Administration
ZPP	Związek Patriotów Polskich (Union of Polish Patriots)
ZPPwSz	Związek Patriotów Polskich w Szwecji (Union of Polish Patriots in Sweden)
ZPPwZSRR	Związek Patriotów Polskich w ZSRR (Union of Polish Patriots in the Soviet Union)
ZŻP	Związek Żydów Polskich (Union of Polish Jews)

Introduction

Having restored its independence in 1918, Poland did not prioritize Scandinavia in its foreign policy. The Swedes were also wary of their new partner on the international arena. Both sides lacked motivation to set up a closer political or economic cooperation. There was some revival in the mid-1920s, when Polish coal appeared on the Swedish market, but only the Polish minister Józef Beck attempted to develop the mutual relations. Their foundation became economic relations and cooperation under the League of Nations. Common commercial interests and efforts to uphold peace in Europe were the cornerstones of good Polish–Swedish relations in the 1930s.[1] The Swedish Envoy to Warsaw, Eric von Post, on summing 1934, emphasized 'the interest of the Polish side with Sweden was striking and certain plans of economic and cultural cooperation were starting to crystallize. It may be said that the development of Swedish–Polish relations is currently by no means a significant issue in Poland.'[2] The subsequent Swedish Envoy to Warsaw, Erik Boheman, commented on the breakthrough in Polish foreign policy involving the balancing of Poland's two powerful neighbours and avoiding multilateral commitments, as well as its wait-and-see attitude towards international developments. He continued to submit his positive assessments of former and current Polish policy to his headquarters. He stated: 'Over the long period of time that passed from the conclusion of the war, numerous circumstances have allowed us to distinguish Poland among the countries

---

[1] For more information on Polish–Swedish relations in the interwar period see i.e.: J. Szymański, *Stosunki gospodarcze Polski ze Szwecją w latach 1919–1939*, Gdańsk 1978; idem, *Polsko-skandynawska współpraca w zakresie żeglugi w okresie międzywojennym (1919–1939)*, Gdańsk 1988; idem, 'Problemy polityki Polski wobec Skandynawii w okresie międzywojennym (1919–1939)', *Zapiski Historyczne* 1993, iss. 1; idem, 'Z genezy stosunków Polski ze Szwecją w latach 1919–1925', *Zeszyty Naukowe Wydziału Humanistycznego UG, Studia Scandinavica* 1978, iss. 1; idem, 'Wybrane aspekty kwestii rozbrojenia w stosunkach polsko-skandynawskich w okresie międzywojennym', *Acta Universitatis Lodziensis, Folia Historica* 1991, iss. 42; briefly in: *Historia dyplomacji polskiej*, vol. 4: 1918–1939, ed. P. Łossowski, Warszawa 1995; mostly based on printed sources: P. Jaworski, *Polska niepodległa wobec Skandynawii 1918–1939*, Wrocław 2001; A. Staniszewski, Po dwóch stronach Bałtyku. Polityczno-gospodarcze stosunki polsko-szwedzkie w latach 1918–1932, Toruń 2013; P. Jaworski, 'Polish experiences with Scandinavian activity in the League of Nations', *Scandinavian Journal of History*, 2015, Vol. 40, No. 5.
[2] RA, UD 1920 års dossiersystem, HP 1, vol. 482, quarterly report for the period 1 October20 December, 1934 by E. von Post, Warsaw, 21 XII 1934.

whose foreign policy stance is marked by the desire to preserve and reinforce its territory and maintain the political status quo established by the peace treaties.'³ Therefore, he was not surprised by Poland's alliance with France, which supported Polish territorial claims at a conference in Paris and later joined an anti-German alliance. He did not consider this consensus to be purely opportunistic, but the result of cultural and historical tradition. At the same time, he highlighted that the decision-makers of the Second Polish Republic (*Rzeczpospolita Polska*) were acting solely in the interests of the Polish state.⁴

Although the atmosphere for developing bilateral relations was favourable, their activation required overcoming barriers both in Stockholm and Warsaw. Michał Sokolnicki, who served as Polish envoy to Copenhagen 1931–36, on judging the situation from the perspective of his subsequent resident mission in neutral Turkey, stated that economic cooperation schemes could create a chance for Poland to develop its foreign relations, also with Scandinavia. He also noted the following: 'I have observed that efforts in this direction were obstructed by […] bureaucratic obtuseness in Warsaw, political strife, squabbles and discrepancies between offices, excessively detailed regulations instead of programmes and inability to see the wood for the trees.'⁵ At the same time the Swedes' attachment to neutrality, reaching back to the close of the Napoleonic era, required them to show restraint even when it came to discussing the subject of cooperation with Poland.

It is worth mentioning the friendly connection established at the time between the head of Swedish diplomacy, Rickard Sandler, and Józef Beck. Equally good relations were maintained between the Polish Minister of Foreign Affairs and Envoy Boheman. Beck showed his trust to the Swedish representative in Poland, for instance by secretly briefing him on the content of talks with Anthony Eden during his visit to Warsaw.⁶ It was not a coincidence that Beck made Boheman, Secretary-General at the Swedish Ministry

---

³ RA, UD 1920 års dossiersystem, HP 1, vol. 483, letter by Swedish Envoy to Warsaw E. Boheman to UD, Warsaw, 4 III 1935.

⁴ RA, UD 1920 års dossiersystem, HP 1, vol. 483, letter by Swedish Envoy to Warsaw to UD, Warsaw, 16 IX 1936. In his memoirs, apart from a critical picture of Polish internal relations in the interwar period, Boheman also evaluated Polish foreign policy. His conclusion was that had Sweden found itself in a similar situation to Poland, 'it would have most probably acted in a similar way', and 'Poland could have not been rescued by any other policy.' See E. Boheman, *På vakt. Från attaché till sändebud. Minnesanteckningar*, Stockholm 1963, pp. 208, 212, 221.

⁵ M. Sokolnicki, *Dziennik ankarski 1939–1943*, London 1965, p. 50.

⁶ RA, UD 1920 års dossiersystem, HP 1, vol. 483, letter by Swedish Envoy to Warsaw E. Boheman to UD, Warsaw, 5 IV 1935.

of Foreign Affairs from 1938, a guardian of his 'Final Report' manuscript, which he wrote following his internment in Romania during the Second World War. The manuscript was handed to the Swede by Beck's widow close to the end of the war.

It may be said that the interwar period was also when the distrust of the Swedes towards Poland was overcome, and most importantly of anti-Polish stereotypes promoted by German propaganda. At the same time fragile economic links and personal contacts paved the way for more intensive bilateral international relations. The final months of peace and the subsequent years of war put both countries under severe pressure.

Sweden, in the face of political tensions across Europe, hid behind the policy of neutrality, drawing from experiences gathered during the First World War. Poland, however, became the main target of aggression and was forced to find powerful allies.

Polish–Swedish relations during the Second World War are yet to be covered by a synthetic study. Although, the subject is examined on numerous occasions in academic literature. The most valuable and available resources are monographs by Andrzej Nils Uggla and Józef Lewandowski. Uggla, a Polish philologist and literary scholar at the University of Uppsala, presented the problems of Polish refugees in Sweden.[7] He also briefly discussed the question of the presence of Polish literature in Swedish publishing and the question of Poland-related themes in the Swedish press.[8] Lewandowski in turn was a historian who became known in the 1960s for his papers devoted to the Piłsudskiite movement. Following his move to Sweden he established a cooperation with Uppsala University where he began his investigation of the arresting of a group of Swedes in Warsaw (1942), who cooperated with

---

[7] A. N. Uggla, *Polacy w Szwecji w latach II wojny światowej*, Gdańsk 1997; the Swedish edition: idem, *I nordlig hamn. Polacker i Sverige under andra världskriget*, Uppsala 1997.
[8] A. N. Uggla, *Den svenska Polenbilden och polsk prosa i Sverige 1939–1960: två studier i reception*, Uppsala 1986. Uggla is also the author of several papers devoted to subjects mentioned in this book (see: Bibliography). Yet, his primary research focus was literary studies. He authored, among others, the polonica bibliography, discussed below.

the Polish resistance movement.[9] The same subject discussed by Swedish historian Staffan Thorsell.[10] The Swedish researchers were also interested in former Polish prisoners from German concentration camps who reached Sweden in the last weeks of the war as a result of the "white buses" action.[11]

The question of Polish–Swedish relations was mentioned in the periphery of source literature, mostly as side threads of larger works. The fate of Polish seamen interned in Sweden, however was thoroughly examined,[12] as was the Poles' chances of escaping from the occupied territories across the Baltic Sea on Swedish ships.[13] Based on Polish sources attempts have been made to describe the activities of Polish intelligence in Scandinavia and the activity of the communication headquarters in Stockholm, which provided contact between London and the Polish resistance movement.[14] Polish issues were mentioned

---

[9] Initially, the results of his preliminary research were published: J. Lewandowski, *Swedish Contribution to the Polish Resistance Movement during World War Two, 1939–1942*, Uppsala 1977; and later the amended and supplemented version: *Węzeł stockholmski. Szwedzkie koneksje polskiego podziemia IX 1939–VII 1942*, Uppsala 1999; the Swedish edition: *Knutpunkt Stockholm: den polska motståndsrörelsens svenska förbindelser från september 1939 till juli 1942*, Stockholm 2006. Apart from this, he also translated and compiled an excerpt from the diary of the Swedish diplomat Sven Grafström, and later, in cooperation with A. N. Uggla, prepared an extended Polish edition of J. Lewandowski, 'Polski dziennik Svena Grafstróma', *Zeszyty Historyczne* 1982, iss. 60, pp. 158–207; S. Grafström, *Polskie stronice. Dziennik od 5 lipca 1938 do 6 grudnia 1939 roku*, selected, translated and compiled by J. Lewandowski, A. N. Uggla, Warszawa 1996. See also: J. Szymański, 'Polska–Szwecja. W cieniu wydarzeń europejskich XIX i XX wieku' [in:] *Szwecja–Polska. Lata rywalizacji i przyjaźni. Polen och Sverige: År av rivalitet och vänskap*, ed. J. Niklasson-Młynarska, Stockholm 1999, pp. 50–67; idem, 'Skandynawia–Polska 1918–1945–1989' [in:] *U progu niepodległości 1918–1989*, ed. R. Wapiński, Gdańsk 1999, pp. 194–214.
[10] S. Thorsell, *Warszawasvenskarna: De som lät världen veta*, Stockholm 2014.
[11] W. Bogatic, *Exilens dilemma. Att stanna eller att återvända – beslut i Sverige av polska kvinnor som överlevde KZ-lägret Ravensbrück och räddades till Sverige 1945–1947*, Växjö 2011; L. Olsson, *På tröskeln till folkhemmet. Baltiska flyktingar och polska koncentrationslägerfångar som reservarbetskraft i skånskt jordbruk kring slutet av andra världskriget*, Lund 1995.
[12] This issue has been discussed in both Polish and Swedish historiography. See chapter 13, "Submarine crews", footnote 1.
[13] B. Chrzanowski, 'Organizacja sieci przerzutów drogą morską z Polski do Szwecji w latach okupacji hitlerowskiej (1939–1945)', *Zeszyty Muzeum* (Stutthof) 1984, iss. 5; B. Chrzanowski, A. Gąsiorowski, K. Steyer, *Polska Podziemna na Pomorzu w latach 1939–1945*, Gdańsk 2005.
[14] A. Pepłoński, *Wywiad Polskich Sił Zbrojnych na Zachodzie 1939–1945*, Warszawa 1995; L. Gondek, *Na tropach tajemnic III Rzeszy*, Warszawa 1987; L. Kliszewicz, 'Baza w Sztokholmie', *Zeszyty Historyczne* 1981, iss. 58, pp. 44–174; idem, 'Baza w Sztokholmie', Warsaw–London 2000; A. Pepłoński, 'Skandynawia i republiki bałtyckie' [in:] *Polsko-brytyjska współpraca wywiadowcza podczas II wojny światowej*, vol. 1: *Ustalenia Polsko-Brytyjskiej Komisji Historycznej*, eds. T. Dubicki, D. Nałęcz, T. Stirling, Warszawa 2004, pp. 342–349; G. Bennett, 'Skandynawia i republiki bałtyckie' [in:] *Polsko-brytyjska...*, pp. 337–341. See also: B. Chrzanowski, 'Ekspozytura *Północ* Oddziału II Sztabu Naczelnego Wodza na terenie

several times in the book by Klas Åmark that concluded discussions in the recent years about the Swedish policy during the Second World War.[15]

Nevertheless, we lack a study with the diplomatic and political relations as its point of departure, where particular attention is paid to propaganda carried out by Poles in Sweden.[16] The primary research objective of this book is to answer the three following questions: 1. Where and when, despite the unfavourable circumstances, did the authorities of Poland and Sweden develop their common interests and how were they manifested? 2. Did the both sides feel co-responsible for the Baltic Sea region? 3. What was the attitude of the Swedes towards the 'Polish matter' (a complex of all issues connected with Poland during the War) and how was Swedish policy evaluated by the Poles?

This study is divided into three parts presenting the covered research problems in chronological order. The first and most extensive part examines the changes in political relations between Poland and Sweden as well as the evolution of the attitude of the Swedish society towards the Polish matter based on diplomatic sources and newspaper content published during the Second World War. There will be a detailed discussion of the visit to Stockholm in 1943 by Jan Kwapiński, Minister of Industry, Trade and Shipping for the Polish government in exile. From the Polish perspective this visit was considered a breakthrough in bilateral relations. Important in this context is the reaction of

---

Szwecji' [in:] *Polski wywiad wojskowy 1918–1945*, eds. P. Kołakowski, A. Pepłoński, Toruń 2006, pp. 480–493. It is worth to become familiar with the extensive paper: T. Potworowski, 'The Polish Legation's undiplomatic activities, Stockholm September 1939–July 1942', *Acta Sueco-Polonica* 2001–2002, iss. 10–11, pp. 5–93. Sweden is mentioned in a paper devoted to the activity of the Continental Action, which used the members of Polish emigrant community for anti-German activity in Scandinavia, see: E. Kruszewski, *Akcja Kontynentalna w Skandynawii 1940–1945*, Copenhagen 1993.

[15] K. Åmark, *Att bo granne med ondskan. Sveriges förhållande till nazismen, Nazityskland och Förintelsen*, Stockholm 2011; 2nd edition: Stockholm 2016.

[16] Only the final period of the war was of greater interest to historians, where attempts were made to reconstruct the process of establishing relations between the Swedish government and the Polish PKWN government, which later became the Provisional Government of the National Unity. This subject is directly addressed in the book from the field of political science, see: J. Dorniak, *Stosunki polsko-szwedzkie w latach 1944–1974*, Słupsk 1978. The author based his work exclusively on published academic papers and Polish daily newspapers; this can constitute a starting point to further archival study. An academic paper was published in Sweden on economic negotiations between the so-called Lublin Committee Poland and Sweden during the final stage of the war (based on Swedish sources), see: S.-O. Olsson, 'Swedish-Polish Trade Negotiations at the End of the Second World War and Their Results', *Scandinavian Economic History Review* 1988, iss. 2. For a valuable work on this subject, based only on Polish source material, see: A. Kłonczyński, *Stosunki polsko-szwedzkie w latach 1945–1956*, Gdańsk 2007. The author opens his lecture by discussing July 1944, and the final months of the Second World War are treated by him as a point of departure to the essential part of the lecture.

the Swedes to the disclosure of the Katyń Massacre, to which here a great deal of attention has been devoted. The key issue of 1944–45 became the two-way policy of Sweden and its concurrent contacts with the Polish Legation in Stockholm and the representatives of the Polish Committee of National Liberation (PKWN), which was later transformed into the Provisional Government and finally the Provisional Government of National Unity (TRJN).

The second part of the book presents two fundamental plots of Polish-Swedish economic relations. Much interest has been devoted to the presence of Swedish business enterprises in occupied Poland, and inter alia, to the role of the Swedish Chamber of Commerce in Warsaw, which sought to continue the activity of the Polish-Swedish Chamber of Commerce despite the unusual conditions presented by the Second World War. Another crucial issue addressed in this book is the recovery of mutual financial claims between Polish and Swedish partners. Negotiations on such matters (especially regarding advance payments from the Polish for military equipment from the Bofors company) continued throughout the war and remained unresolved. An entirely separate issue was the re-establishing of trade following the war, initiated by negotiations as early as in 1943. Their continuation in 1944 was conducted by Swedish representatives in Moscow and the final stage took place in Warsaw (Brynolf Eng's mission). The negotiations were no longer with the representatives of the Polish government in exile but with representatives of the Provisional Government.

The third part of the book covers the fate of Polish refugees as well as seamen and soldiers interned in Sweden. It also focuses on the issues of humanitarian aid for Poland. Insofar as the commonly known facts about the interned Poles were only supplemented by some new and detailed findings, the issue of humanitarian aid is presented in a broad political context based on so-far unexamined Swedish archival resources. This extensive source base allowed for a comprehensive presentation of the activity of the Swedish Red Cross (*SRK*) in Poland, especially during 1944 and 1945, when humanitarian actions were carried out both in the General Government (Sven Hellqvist's mission) and in the territory of the so-called Lublin Committee Poland.

For the study, collections of both Polish and international archives have been examined.[17] Fortunately for this investigation, the New Acts Archive (AAN) in Warsaw now contains, aside from an incomplete collection of documents from the Polish Legation in Stockholm, copies of documents

---

[17] Since not all investigated collections were paginated, in the case some of the quoted documents' page numbers are not mentioned in the footnotes.

issued by the Polish Ministry of Foreign Affairs during the war, held in the Hoover Institution Archive (Stanford University). Another important supplementation were documents from the economic departments of the Polish government in exile. These collections helped create a complete picture of Swedish policy, as well as expectations towards Sweden and plans to reactivate Polish–Swedish relations. A separate group of archival materials consists of documents devoted to the activity of Polish communists in Sweden (the Union of Polish Patriots in Sweden headed by Jerzy Pański) and their attempts to initiate official relations with the Swedish government. Motivation which accompanied the leaders of the Lublin Committee Poland on the establishment of relations with the Swedes can be examined based on the PKWN protocols, the documents from the Union of Polish Patriots (*ZPPwZSRR*) in the Soviet Union and the collection of the Polish Ministry of Foreign Affairs of the Provisional Government (Political Department, Polish Embassy in Moscow).

Archival collections of ministries and military authorities, contained in the archives of the Polish Institute and Sikorski Museum in London proved to be of great significance for this study. Primarily they made it possible to put Polish–Swedish relations in a broader context. The documents of the Ministry of Congress Work have confirmed the presence of Sweden in the agenda for political cooperation in the post-war period (federalist concepts). Materials from private collections, however, have revealed the secrets behind many political and propaganda actions in Sweden. This is especially true of the collections of socialist Adam Ciołkosz, which documents the activity of the Polish Socialist Party (*PPS*), and of minister and socialist activist Jan Kwapiński, which contains a detailed description of his visit to Stockholm. Some documents were found at the Polish Underground Movement (1939–45) Study Trust (*Studium Polski Podziemnej*) in London.

The research largely focused on materials found at *Riksarkivet* (National Archives of Sweden) in Stockholm. This archive held documents produced by *Utrikesdepartementet* (*UD*, Sweden's Ministry of Foreign Affairs), much of which reflected the content of the Polish documentation, but also descriptions of matters lacking in Polish collections.

Documents from the Foreign Office (FO) held in the National Archives in London presented the British perspective on Polish activity in Sweden and detailed the Swedish attitude towards Polish interests. These were a meaningful complement to the Polish and Swedish sources. Results of investigations at *Krigsarkivet* (*KA*, the Military Archives in Stockholm) and *Arbetarrörelsens arkiv och bibliotek* (*ARAB*, Swedish Labour Movement's Archive and

Library, Stockholm) were of similar help, so too were the division of manuscripts at Uppsala University Library (*Carolina Rediviva*) and the difficult to access archive of *Militära underrättelse- och säkerhetstjänsten* (*MUST*, Swedish Military Intelligence and Security Service).

A crucial element of the study was the analysis of newspaper commentaries, mostly from Swedish dailies. This represents a separate subject. The review of a wide spectrum of newspapers, books and political brochures allowed for a general evaluation of the presence of Polish affairs in the Swedish public debate. What has been particularly helpful during the examination of the Swedish newspapers was the polonica bibliography compiled by Andrzej Nils Uggla[18] and press reports from a private collection of the Polish Press Attaché in Stockholm during the war, Norbert Żaba. When researching for the Polish edition of this book, Dr Janusz Korek granted me access to the documents, which he was in possession of. At present, these documents can be found in the New Acts Archive in Warsaw. The character of the materials collected during research of the Polish newspapers published in exile were slightly different. These newspapers addressed Swedish issues very rarely. Nevertheless, some articles have proven very helpful in becoming familiar with Polish views on Swedish policy.

This book is a result of my long-term stays abroad and in Warsaw thanks to scholarships from the Swedish Institute (*Svenska Institutet*) in Stockholm (a two-month stay in 2001 on the invitation of *Centrum för multietnisk forskning* at Uppsala University and a six-month stay in 2005 at the Centre for Baltic and East European Studies at Södertörn University, Stockholm), the Lanckoroński Foundation (a one-month stay in London in 2001 and a two-month stay in London in 2003). The subject has been studied under the KBN 2 H01G 004 23 project.

To conclude, I would like to thank everyone who supported me in the process of creating this book. I am very grateful to the late Professor Józef Lewandowski for numerous meetings and discussions and to Tomasz Potworowski for giving me a copy of his father's private writings and a mention about him in a letter. I owe my sincere thanks to two Professors who were my guardians during my visits to Sweden: Professor Andrzej Nils Uggla, who was always ready to offer me his useful advice, support and granted me access to his extensive collection of press cuttings, and Professor David Gaunt. I would like to thank Dr Andrej Kotljarchuk for bibliographical data, Ludomir Garczyński-Gąssowski from Stockholm for granting me access to

---

[18] A. N. Uggla, *Polen i svensk press under andra världskriget: En bibliografi*, Uppsala 1986.

copies of documents on the Katyń Massacre, and Philip Mallet for allowing me to quote the unpublished memoirs of his father.

I would also like to thank the staff at all of the archives I have visited, who made it possible for me to conduct this extensive (due to the specificity of the subject) study efficiently, and especially Ewa Berndtsson from *Riksarkivet*, Catharina Hammarström from MUST, the staff at Carolina Rediviva and of the division of the *Riksarkivet* in Arninge, Captain Jerzy Milewski and Andrzej Suchcitz from the Polish Institute and Sikorski Museum in London, the staff at the New Acts Archive (including the reprographics department). I would like to thank the Head of the Section of Polish History and Contemporary History of the 19th and 20th Centuries at the Institute of History at the University of Wrocław Professor Teresa Kulak for her help in all organisational matters and her constant willingness to support me in my academic research. I am grateful for all the critical input given by the reviewer of the Polish edition of this book, Professor Wojciech Materski. The first edition of this book was published in Polish by the Institute of National Remembrance in Warsaw in 2009. This edition has been updated, shortened and revised. The revision of the text would not have been possible without help of Marta and Arthur Sehn (Stockholm), Per Nilsson (Hässleholm) and, finally, Iwona Sakowicz (Gdańsk).

The translation was possible thanks to a grant from the Polish Ministry of Science and Higher Education under the NPRH programme (*Narodowy Program Rozwoju Humanistyki, 0138/NPRH3/H31/82/2014*). The application for the translation of this book into English was supported by Professor Anthony Kemp-Welch and Dr Piotr Wawrzeniuk, for which I am deeply grateful to both. I am thankful for all the critical remarks made by the reviewers of the new English edition Professor emeritus Klas Åmark and Professor emeritus Kent Zetterberg both of Stockholm University.

PART 1
In the Circle of Politics and Propaganda

1. On the Eve of War

In April 1939, the Polish Envoy to Stockholm, Gustaw Potworowski,[1] reported to his headquarters that the Swedish government claimed: 'the policy conducted by Poland contributes to the stabilization of relations in the Baltic Sea region, which is in line with the interests of Sweden.'[2] Some time later, in July 1939, the envoy informed Deputy Minister of Foreign Affairs Jan Szembek on the Swedish 'great recognition, understanding and admiration of our attitude.' The speech delivered by Polish Minister for Foreign Affairs Józef Beck on 5 May, where he categorically rejected Hitler's claims towards Gdańsk (Danzig), met with an exceptionally positive reaction from Stockholm. According to Potworowski, Secretary-General at the Swedish Foreign Ministry Erik Boheman 'exhibited a strongly pro-Polish attitude' and Minister Rickard Sandler was 'very effusive towards us.' What needs to be highlighted, however, is that these views, which continued the good atmosphere of mutual relations over the past several years, in fact only illustrated the positive personal relations between the diplomats. According to Potworowski, the attitude of the Swedish government was the following: 'The Swedes are afraid of war, they do not feel sufficiently safe and are afraid of being dragged into a military conflict.'[3] During the interwar period, the policies of the Scandinavian countries were dominated by a spirit of pacifism, self-armament and keeping away from all possible alliances. It could hardly be expected then that in the face of Hitler's expansion, Sweden, which had

---
[1] Gustaw Potworowski (1889–1951), Polish Envoy to Stockholm 1936–42, held a diplomatic post from 1921. In the years 1921–24, he worked in the General Commissariat of the Free City of Danzig and 1928–35 he served as secretary of the Polish Embassy in Paris. Potworowski participated in several delegations to the sessions of the League of Nations in Geneva. His son Tomasz said: 'he was famous for his interest in economic issues, his socialist sympathies, as well as for skillful handling of relations with leftist journalists in Paris. All the above elements combined with the highest social refinement of both of my parents only confirmed the appropriateness of their appointment as diplomatic representatives in a country where the royal court coexisted with the socialist government based on a firm leftist majority' (letter by T. Potworowski to the author, Kensington, California, 15 November 2002). From 1943 Potworowski resided in Lisbon, where he served as head of the Polish Legation until his death.
[2] *Polskie dokumenty dyplomatyczne 1939 styczeń–sierpień*, S. Żerko (ed.), in cooperation with P. Długołęcki, Warsaw 2005, doc. 224, p. 373 and doc. 227, p. 381.
[3] *Diariusz i teki Jana Szembeka (1935–1945)*, vol. 4, compiled by J. Zarański, London 1972, p. 668. Potworowski noticed that Swedish society was gradually reviving its former pro-German sympathies.

not been involved in any military conflict since the Napoleonic era, would suddenly change its policy and join forces with Poland and its Western Allies, France and Britain, in a war with Germany. In May 1938, Swedish Prime Minister Per Albin Hansson claimed that in the event of a pan-European conflict, Sweden should choose 'the right side' and, if keeping away from military activity proved impossible, fight against totalitarian regimes. Nevertheless, following the conference in Munich, which exposed the powerlessness of the democratic countries of Europe, Sweden confirmed its former political course and its will to maintain strict neutrality.[4]

In the spring of 1939, in the face of growing tensions in Polish–German relations and British promises to provide Poland with support in the event of, among other things, Hitler's aggression, Swedish diplomats from the Berlin mission were convinced that war would break out. Military Attaché Colonel Curt Juhlin-Dannfelt, Attaché of Aviation Colonel Harald Enell and Naval Attaché Commodore Anders Forshell, in a joint report prepared for Minister of Defence Per Edvin Sköld, confirmed this opinion, backing it up with the following arguments: 'numerous events that have taken place over the past year prove that German leaders are not acting rationally and responsibly.'[5] In mid-1939, the Swedish military diplomats were submitting possible outcomes of the unfolding international situation to their headquarters, and judged the chances of maintaining peace as rather slim and considering the result of the Polish–German clash to be foregone. Juhlin-Dannfelt, in July 1939, suspected that if it came to a conflict with Poland, the German army would probably conduct a brisk offensive. He claimed that Poland's position was critical both in the northern and southern section. Pomerania was to be cut off right away by two strikes, from the west and from East Prussia. Polish diplomats residing in Berlin passed him the news that the line of defence was being prepared along the Vistula and Narew rivers. In the south, also during the initial stage of the war, Upper Silesia was to be annexed by the Germans owing to their unquestionable superiority. In the circles of representatives of the Baltic States apprehensions were growing that the outbreak of a Polish–German conflict could lead to an agreement between Hitler and Stalin and to the division of the Baltic Sea region and Poland into their spheres of influence.[6] At the beginning of August it was

---

[4] A. W. Johansson, *Per Albin och kriget*, Stockholm 1984, p. 22.
[5] K.-R. Böhme, *Tysklands expansion börjar. Österrike 1938, Tjeckoslovakien 1938–1939* [in:] *Stormvarning. Sverige inför andra världskriget*, B. Hugemark (ed.), Luleå 2002, p. 54.
[6] RA, UD 1920 års dossiersystem, HP 2, vol. 717, an overview of military preparations of Germany in July 1939, report by Swedish Military Attaché to Berlin Colonel C. H. Juhlin-Dannfelt, Berlin, 4 VII 1939.

clear that the Germans were at their peak combat readiness both in the military and economic sense. The Germans reached in to their deepest reserves and in no time mobilized all types of military and paramilitary formations. These discernible actions showed, according to Juhlin-Dannfelt, clear signs of preparations for the so-called *blitzkrieg*, that is, the rapid crushing of Poland, the weakest opponent of Germany. Taking these preparations into account, the Swedish attaché suspected that the critical period would be at the turn of August and September. The only thing missing was the declaration of war.[7] As Juhlin-Dahnfelt reported in the last days of August, Polish Military Attaché Colonel Antoni Szymański did not believe Germany would attack. He explained that the preparations were merely a bluff.[8]

At the outset of July, at an international congress of trade unions in Zurich, August Lindberg, head of the Swedish Trade Union Confederation (LO), did not support the resolution favouring the conclusion of the agreement with Germany. On the other hand, Minister of Foreign Affairs Rickard Sandler, in a speech delivered on 30 July 1939, refused the idea that Sweden should back the initiative of pledging support to the countries of the Baltic Sea region by the Soviet Union, France and Great Britain. Both Lindberg and Sandler excused their decisions with the need for maintaining the policy of strict neutrality, which allegedly did not permit participation in official resolutions regarding international affairs. Sandler also did not approve of the fact that the European powers, who joined forces in the name of peace by pledging their support to smaller countries, at the same time granted themselves the right to interfere in these countries' affairs.[9] The Swedes considered only the possibility of cooperation within the Nordic States, which were equally interested in defending their neutrality.[10]

Apprehensively following the process of German preparations for the aggression against Poland, both the diplomats, who were knee deep in political problems, and the press commentators, who were divided in their sympathies, predicted that the upcoming war would be a total war, much more gruesome than the First World War, and a threat to the well-being of European culture. That is why some individuals considered that categorical rejection of Hitler's claims was impossible, as it would lead to war. But others

---

[7] RA, UD 1920 års dossiersystem, HP 2, vol. 717, an overview of military positions of Germany at the outset of August 1939, report by Swedish Military Attaché to Berlin Colonel C. H. Juhlin-Dannfelt, Berlin, 5 VIII 1939.
[8] S. Thorsell, *I hans majestäts tjänst. En berättelse från Hitlers Berlin och Stalins Moskva*, Stockholm 2009, p. 75.
[9] W. M. Carlgren, *Svensk utrikespolitik 1939–1945*, Stockholm 1973, p. 18.
[10] Ibidem, p. 16.

claimed that war would be a better solution than surrendering to the gradually growing pressures from the Nazis.[11] It ought to be highlighted that Hitler's expansion more often than not was met with understanding by Swedish journalists. Even the opinion of journalists working for social-democratic daily newspapers claimed that the right of nations to self-determination was a traditional Marxist principle and for that reason they accepted German claims against Austria and Czechoslovakia. The influential editor of *Social-Demokraten*, Rickard Lindström, was of a similar opinion, though he did not approve of 'detestable gangster political methods' employed by Hitler.[12] In general, the ruling elites of Sweden adopted the position of passive observers, which brought hope that war could be avoided.

At the meeting of the ministers of the Nordic States on 13 August 1939, Minister Sandler highlighted that one war fathers another war, and lasting peace may be reached only as a consequence of war, provided that the foreign policy of Sweden would be limited only to the territory of northern Europe, to which the war, as he said, was not a threat. He also said: 'our greatest concern, both at the moment and in the very near future, is that peace and honour – and, shielded by this honour, also our proud freedom – be maintained in the North and for the North.'[13] A joint manifestation of will to maintain strict neutrality was the meeting of the diplomatic heads of Sweden (Rickard Sandler), Norway (Halvdan Koht), Denmark (Peter Munch) and Finland (Eljas Errko) in Oslo on 30–31 August 1939.[14]

In August 1939 the Polish–German conflict was the number one story in all Swedish newspapers. Breaking news from Berlin and Warsaw were anxiously awaited. What became a sensation was the unexpected news about the conclusion of the agreement between the Soviet Union and Germany which, despite being vividly commented on, did not change the course of Swedish foreign policy. Instead, speculation emerged on the possibility of a Soviet attack and the division of Poland between Stalin and Hitler.[15] Johannes Wickman, a famous opinion journalist for *Dagens Nyheter*, who specialized

---

[11] K. Åmark, *Makt eller moral. Svensk offentlig debatt om internationellpolitik och svensk utrikes- och försvarspolitik 1938–1939*, Stockholm 1973, pp. 59, 67, 71.
[12] Ibidem, pp. 43–44.
[13] ARAB, Rickard Sandlers samling, vol. 5a, speech by R. Sandler at the Nordic meeting, 13 VIII 1939.
[14] W. M. Carlgren, *Svensk utrikespolitik...*, p. 22.
[15] K. Åmark, *Makt eller moral...*, pp. 113–117. Erik Boheman did not give any credence to Aleksandra Kollontai when she explained to him that the agreement between the Soviet Union and the Germans was averting the threat of war, see: A. Kollontai, *Diplomaticeskie dnevniki 1922–1940*, vol. 2, Moscow 2001, p. 447 (a conversation from 24 VIII 1939).

in foreign policy, suspected that the pact entailed a secret agreement to the detriment of Poland. He claimed Hitler was no longer focusing only on Gdańsk, but on all the territories, at the very least, which had been taken away from Germany under the Treaty of Versailles. It was obvious to Wickman that the situation for Poland following such a Hitler–Stalin pact would be disastrous.[16] Two public discussions, devoted to the Soviet–German agreement, took place in Stockholm on 31 August and 5 September. Officials speculated whether this was an alliance or simply a pact of non-aggression and, if so, had the outbreak of war already been determined by this point. Activists belonging to the Communist Party of Sweden (*SKP*), who participated in both of these meetings, rejected claims that Stalin intended to spark a pan-European conflict. They claimed instead, that the arrangement had been concluded only because Poland did not accept the Soviets' offer of assistance in the event of external attack, and the arrangement with the Soviet Union was rejected both by France and Great Britain.[17]

During the following days, further information came to light from various sources on the secret agreement regarding the division of Central and Eastern Europe,[18] but faced with the prospect of an alternative arrangement between the Soviet Union, Great Britain and France, under which Stalin demanded extensive concessions from the Baltic States, officials in the Swedish government could breathe a sigh of relief. They believed that the threat of Sweden being pulled into the war was, as a result, considerably diminished. Swedish diplomats claimed that during the British–French–Soviet negotiations, conducted in Moscow, bargaining on the future of the Baltic States was on the agenda and, perhaps, even of Poland. Swedish Military Attaché to Moscow Carl Vilhelm Birger Vrang was informed by a German source that the French had allegedly already decided to sacrifice the Baltic States and Finland, but that the British disagreed. He doubted that there was such an opposition: 'the independence of these countries was of no significance to the Empire.'[19] Prime Minister Hansson expressed the view that the Soviet–German arrangement did not worsen the situation in Europe, because it had been very difficult for many preceding months, and so the outbreak of the war was

---

[16] Wickman's articles were published 22 and 25 August 1939. See also: J. Torbacke, *Dagens Nyheter och demokratins kris 1937–1946. Genom stormar till seger*, Stockholm 1972, pp. 16–17.
[17] E. Karlsson, 'Två diskussionsmöten', *Ny Dag*, 7 IX 1939.
[18] W. M. Carlgren, 'Den stora överraskningen. Regeringen och Moskvapakten' [in:] *Stormvarning. Sverige inför andra världskriget*, B. Hugemark (ed.), Luleå 2002, p. 155.
[19] RA, UD 1920 års dossiersystem, HP 2, vol. 716, secret letter by Swedish Military Attaché to Moscow C. V. B. Vrang to the head of intelligence, Moscow, 16 VIII 1939.

unavoidable.[20] According to the Swedish Ministry of Foreign Affairs, the agreement between Hitler and Stalin led to the calming of situation in the Baltic Sea region, limited the number of incidents and virtually eliminated military operations there. After the Soviet Union had started exporting natural resources to Germany, German pressures on Sweden regarding trade diminished. Minister Sandler, among other things, in a conversation on 29 August with Envoy Potworowski, was sceptical regarding the value of the German–Soviet pact.[21] In short, Stockholm showed great disregard towards the pact, convinced that it was of little importance for northern Europe. It was considered that the fate of Sweden was not dependent on the fate of Poland. What was sought for instead of the actual threats were positive aspects of the rapprochement between the two dictators.[22] The Swedish king Gustaf V even claimed that this agreement would actually prevent war.[23] If war were to break out, Sandler convinced Potworowski that Sweden would be in a better situation than during the First World War when it had to battle against economic isolation: 'Firstly, because in such a case the transit of resources to Russia on a massive scale will be out of the question, and secondly because – due to the position of the Soviet Union – the isolation of Germany may be not as severe as then.'[24]

Meanwhile, reassuring reports were pouring in from Poland. The Swedish Military Attaché to Warsaw, Colonel Erik de Laval, in a conversation with Colonel Józef Englicht, First Deputy of Division II of the General Staff, heard that Poland had rejected all support offered by the Soviet Union and that the pact was beneficial for the Baltic States. This was because it averted the looming danger of the German preventive war in this region, whereas for Stalin the status quo meant the creation of a buffer zone separating him from Germany.[25] Attaché de Laval noted that the Poles were mostly focusing on the conflict with Germany, against which a press campaign had been launched.[26] Numerous articles described, among other things, the might of the German army. According to de Laval, it could not be denied that it was larger and

---

[20] A. W. Johansson, *Per Albin...*, p. 60.
[21] *Polskie dokumenty dyplomatyczne 1939 styczeń...*, doc. 497, p. 834.
[22] W. M. Carlgren, 'Den stora överraskningen. Regeringen och Moskvapakten' [in:] *Stormvarning...*, p. 151.
[23] Ibidem, p. 156.
[24] *Polskie dokumenty dyplomatyczne 1939 styczeń...*, doc. 497, p. 835.
[25] E. Norberg, 'Det militära hotet. Försvarsattachéernas syn på krigsutbrottet 1939' [in:] *Stormvarning...*, pp. 74–75.
[26] RA, UD 1920 års dossiersystem, HP 2, vol. 725, letter by Swedish Military Attaché to Warsaw Colonel E. de Laval to Minister of Defence, Warsaw, 6 VII 1939.

better armed than its Polish counterpart, and for those reasons what was emphasized about the Polish soldiers were the virtues of patriotism, persistence and readiness to make sacrifices:

> It is undeniable that so far this strategy has brought a positive response and broad masses of the public are anticipating war with Germany peacefully and strongly convinced that Poland would secure a military victory over Germany. Whether this largely exaggerated and biased press campaign brings only advantages may be naturally called in to question – the breakdown in the face of the grim reality may turn out to be massive.

To name an example, de Laval presented the situation of France in 1870. In light of the Swede's report, Polish society was, psychologically, fully prepared for the approaching war, 'certain of their national strength, manifested mostly by the army, and united in the will of armed defence of their freedom.'[27] On the verge of the outbreak of war, however, de Laval, while discussing the condition of Polish armed forces in his report from 28 August, established that the Polish army was, in most cases, equipped with modern weaponry. With some inconsistency he pointed out that the Poles were second to the Germans in the air as well as artillery, but agreed with the view that the Poles disdained death, which, as he explained, was a consequence of their 'Slavonic determinism'. Polish individualism could turn out to be unfavourable when conducting efficient operation of the army. And yet: 'Owing to the national character and military training we may say that the standards of the Polish army are high: the soldiers are brave, insensitive to losses and adversities of fate, [...] feature high marching skills.' His final evaluation was far from critical:

> Although in the event of war with Germany, the Polish army would have to fight in highly unwelcoming strategic conditions and although there exist many arguments that allow us to suspect that the support of first-line military units would be performed in particularly difficult conditions, this army may prove to be a difficult opponent. For one thing, it is indeed possible that the faith in the Poles' military superiority over the Germans (the quality of six Germans said to equal one Pole), encouraged by the public and by the press, may be shattered during the initial battle, and another – also the expectations of the Germans,

---

[27] RA, UD 1920 års dossiersystem, HP 2, vol. 725, letter by Swedish Military Attaché to Warsaw Colonel E. de Laval to Minister of Defence, 6 VII 1939.

expressed, among other things, in official speeches, that Poland will be defeated in a couple of weeks, may become a dangerous delusion.[28]

Following the reports of the Swedish Chargé d'affaires to Warsaw Sven Grafström, the stance of Polish diplomacy in the frenzied days of August 1939 was also optimistic: '"The thesis" of the Polish government, as I have already allowed myself to say, is a conviction that the Germans will not dare to risk flaring up a world war and therefore the probability of war between Poland and Germany is low.'[29] At the same time, Grafström reported from Warsaw that views were heard among the Poles that war was inevitable, because 'Hitler's standing requires a quick solution on the question of Gdańsk.' He added that he had heard such statements from many influential officials, 'yet not in the Ministry of Foreign Affairs.' Besides, Grafström confirmed de Laval's view that Polish society had a firm belief in victory over Germany, which was consolidated continuously by the press. According to Grafström, naive military arguments were used such as German tanks would prove useless when confronted by the potholed roads of Poland. Nevertheless, he would soon add that the authorities have achieved an unquestionable success, namely the internal national consolidation around the idea of independence.

It was Grafström's personal conviction on Europe being threatened by Hitlerism that encouraged him to take unconventional steps. On the evening of 18 August, he met with Minister Beck, intending to warn him of the impending German attack which had been confirmed by various Swedish sources. To his surprise, Beck's views on the matter were quite different. He claimed that Germany was putting on the line its final arguments in a battle of nerves with Poland. According to Beck, Hitler started to hesitate when it transpired that Poland's position on the question of Gdańsk was unyielding. He did not give credence to the concept of 'the new Munich'. He was convinced that if Poland entered combat its Western Allies would rush forward to help. Beck estimated the chances of maintaining peace were 50 percent, which was very similar to the view of Swedish Envoy to Warsaw Joen Lagerberg. Beck confirmed the press reports on the withdrawal of the Soviet army

---

[28] RA, UD 1920 års dossiersystem, HP 1, vol. 725, report by Swedish Military Attaché to Warsaw Colonel E. de Laval, Warsaw, 28 VIII 1939.

[29] RA, UD 1920 års dossiersystem, HP 1, vol. 485, letter by Swedish Chargé d'affaires to Warsaw S. Grafström to Prime Minister P. A. Hansson, Warsaw, 15 VIII 1939.

from the Polish border, which was additionally reassuring.[30] Meanwhile, Swedish Envoy to Berlin Arvid Richert on 21 August reported of news from independent sources that it could take two days for the German army to be at full combat readiness and that the outbreak of the war was most probably very close.[31]

The day after, Envoy Lagerberg informed his headquarters that the announcement regarding the German–Soviet pact of non-aggression broadcast by German radio as early as in the evening of 21 August, came as a total surprise to Warsaw, but the consternation of the Ministry of Foreign Affairs lasted only a moment. Beck's secretary Ludwik Łubieński continued to convince Lagerberg that Poland's position would not change and that news of the pact with the Soviet Union was another bluff used by Hitler to apply pressure to Great Britain and France. And, by the same token, his estimate for maintained peace remained at 50 percent. An anonymous informer of the Swedish Legation, however, received news that Gauleiter Albert Forster revealed to one of his co-workers that the question of Gdańsk would be solved between 24 and 28 August.[32] Similar news was passed on to Stockholm by Swedish Consul to Gdańsk Knud Lundberg, who had earlier discussed these rumours, considering them likely to be true, with High Commissioner of the League of Nations Carl Burckhard. This was because Lundberg had heard from a high official of the German Ministry of Foreign Affairs that following the conclusion of the agreement with Stalin, the question of Gdańsk and the Corridor could be settled within a couple of days.[33]

In the face of the looming war, the Polish government expected Sweden to maintain its Poland-friendly neutrality. Initially, there even existed plans to transport military equipment from the west across Sweden, the Baltic Sea and Gdynia. Eventually, fearing the isolation of Pomerania, Polish staff officers chose a route across Romania.[34] In addition, the Swedes were reluctant to the idea of a Polish transit route running through Sweden. When asked about this matter by Envoy Potworowski two days before the outbreak of the

---

[30] RA, UD 1920 års dossiersystem, HP 1, vol. 485, letter by Swedish Chargé d'affaires to Warsaw S. Grafström, to Minister K.G. Westman, Warsaw, 18 VIII 1939. See also: J. Lewandowski, 'Polska przygoda Svena Grafströma' [in:] *S. Grafström, Polskie...*, pp. 7–44.
[31] RA, UD 1920 års dossiersystem, HP 1, vol. 485, note by A. Croneborg, Stockholm, 21 VIII 1939.
[32] RA, UD 1920 års dossiersystem, HP 1, vol. 485, letter by Swedish Envoy to Warsaw J. Lagerberg to S. Söderblom, Warsaw, 22 VIII 1939.
[33] RA, UD 1920 års dossiersystem, HP 1, vol. 485, note by A. Croneborg, Stockholm, 23 VIII 1939.
[34] *Diariusz...*, p. 691.

war, Sandler 'brushed it off by talking in general terms, making everything conditional on the actual situation which might take place but which was impossible to predicted. He seemed sceptical about the transit route across the Baltic Sea, claiming that the route through Romania will be of greatest importance.'[35] Polish diplomats limited themselves to issuing a request to the Swedish authorities on 26 August 1939 in which they asked them to represent the interests of Polish citizens staying in Germany in the event of war.[36]

At the time, the Poles had no idea about the secret activity of Swedish diplomats conducted in the guise of Birger Dahlerus' mission. In the final days of peace, this Swedish industrialist, believing in the friendly intentions of Hermann Göring, took part in a German game, the purpose of which was to present Germany as a country striving to maintain peace at any price. It is clearly visible that the Swedes had ambitions to, if such an opportunity arose, play the role of 'peace-broker'.[37] Though the government in Stockholm was cautious about the mission of Dahlerus, its context highlighted the major principle of the Swedish state of reasoning: the stabilization of the political situation in Europe was of greater importance than the fate of Poland, which was to pay the price for maintaining, at least for some time, peace in Europe. Prime Minister, and leader of Swedish Social Democrats, Per Albin Hansson, in a conversation with Dahlerus on 10 July 1939, expressed a view that war would not be declared and that Polish-German disputes would end. Despite this, Sandler, with whom Dahlerus met on 13 July, thought that any participation by the Swedish government in the negotiations between Great Britain and Germany aimed at preventing the war would be unreasonable,

---

[35] *Polskie dokumenty dyplomatyczne 1939 styczeń...*, doc. 497, p. 835.

[36] AAN, MSZ 1918–1939, 6509, the issue-related correspondence, pp. 33–35. The issue is also mentioned by S. Grafström, *Anteckningar 1938–1944*, p. 72, the record from 26 VIII 1939: 'The Polish government, partially represented by minister Potworowski in Stockholm, partially by Lagerberg in Sweden, requested Sweden to represent Polish interests in Germany and Italy in the event of war'. The note from 27 August 1939: 'In the face of the feverishly reissued Szembek's inquiries to Lagerberg, about whether he finally received the answer from Stockholm, we were able, having received the coded messages from UD, to inform you today that the government of Sweden is willing to represent Polish interests in one of these two countries, depending on Poland's choice. I am satisfied with the answer. A negative answer would put us here in Poland in a very difficult situation. Luckily it turned out that Poles were most probably the first ones to submit such request in Stockholm. Had it been done by any of "the Axis Powers" we would be forced, as I understand, to accept their claim. Choosing another solution would be a violation of the policy of strict neutrality, which (for how much longer?) we are striving to maintain.' The efforts made by Poland are also confirmed in the journal, *Diariusz*, by Jan Szembek p. 698: the note about a conversation on August 26 with Envoy Lagerberg, whom he asked to expedite the decision.

[37] K. Åmark, *Makt eller moral...*, p. 175.

since such behaviour would be perceived by the world, and most certainly by Poland, as a departure from the policy of neutrality. At the same time, he assured the disappointed Dahlerus that he personally had nothing against efforts to initiate peace talks, but it was nevertheless only possible for him to make such request as a private person and on his own initiative. A secret preliminary meeting of negotiators in Germany on 7 August, at the Sonke Nissen Koog estate owned by Dahlerus' German-born wife, ended with no specific arrangements. Both sides simply promised to continue convincing their governments as well as those of France and Italy to organize a conference on a neutral ground (most probably in Sweden) aimed at solving all the disputes. Göring gave assurances that Germany was interested in a rerun of the Munich agreement. The Swedish authorities, in line with their announcements, did not participate in these events, but on 9 August Dahlerus met with Hansson, who was constantly underestimating the threat of war in Europe, in order to update him on the talks in Germany. The Prime Minister of Sweden maintained that Dahlerus, even in a non-official capacity, was forbidden to do anything that might compromise the interests of his homeland. What is worth noting is that despite the ostentatious reserve of the Swedish government towards the matter, Dahlerus remained in contact with the Swedish Legation in Berlin and systematically prepared detailed reports of the events he witnessed and took part in.[38] At Göring's request he came to Berlin on 24 August. Following a meeting with the Marshal of the Third Reich he flew to London, where Minister of Foreign Affairs Lord Halifax assured him that the agreement was possible. Urged by Göring, he asked the British to present a concrete offer to the German government. On 26 August, supplied in a letter from Prime Minister Neville Chamberlain and Minister Halifax, Dahlerus visited Berlin once again. The meeting with Hitler strengthened his conviction that war could be avoided. Subsequent runs between Berlin and London were a smokescreen for the predetermined German aggression against Poland.[39]

---

[38] B. Dahlerus, *Sista försöket. London–Berlin sommaren 1939*, Stockholm 1945, pp. 45–75, 84, 134.

[39] Accompanied by Forbes, advisor to the Embassy of Great Britain, on 31 August Dahlerus participated in a meeting in Berlin with Polish Ambassador Józef Lipski and as a 'neutral mediator enjoying the trust of the [British] cabinet, the [British] Embassy and the German government' he read out the 16 points of the German demands towards Poland. He ensured the participants that the Germans wanted to limit themselves only to the annexation of Danzig and the so-called Corridor. He was disappointed to meet with a reserved reaction of Lipski, who stated that accepting these proposals would be tantamount with 'the violation of Poland's sovereignty' and: 'their acceptance is out of question.' Quoted after J. Karski, *Great Powers and Poland 1919–1945. From Versaille to Yalta*, Lanham 2014, pp. 226–228.

According to Boheman, Dahlerus was 'daring and utterly naive in his grand political game.'[40] He thought that Swedish authorities had no option other than to make it easy for him to carry out his entire mission. At the same time though, Boheman admitted much later on that at the outbreak of the Second World War he was relieved that the period of uncertainty was finally over and 'that it was good that the process of the downfall of European civilization was finally stopped.' He also stated: "It was clear that this would entail great sacrifices, but was it not worth these sacrifices?" Aware that certain sentiments, however, would not result in any consequences for his homeland, Boheman added: "It was perhaps easier to think that it was not necessary at all to take sacrifices of Sweden into account."[41]

According to Dahlerus' account, Lipski was also to add that in the case of war riots would take place in Germany, and the Polish army would easily capture Berlin. See: B. Dahlerus, *Sista...*, p. 175. For more extensive information on the role of Dahlerus, see: H. Batowski, *Agonia pokoju i początek wojny (sierpień–wrzesień 1939)*, Poznań 1979. See also: J. Lipski, *Diplomat in Berlin 1933-1939. Papers and Memoirs of Jozef Lipski, Ambassador of Poland*, ed. W. Jędrzejewicz, New York–London 1968, p. 573 (correspondence with the Ministry of Foreign Affairs where Lipski considered Dahlerus' mission to be another phase of pressures from the Germans), pp. 595–609. Ambassador of Great Britain to Berlin Neville Henderson did not make an explicit reference to Dahlerus in his memoirs. Without mentioning his name, he described him as 'a source of information close to Göring [...], yet unofficial', see: N. Henderson, *Failure of a Mission. Berlin 1937–1939*, New York 1940.

[40] E. Boheman, *På vakt. Kabinettssekreterare under andra världskriget*, Stockholm 1964, pp. 69–70. Dahlerus' attitude was more bluntly summed up by the controversial British historian David Irving, who describing him as 'gentle and courteous Swedish manufacturer of machine tools' who was 'stupefied and as pure as the driven snow' and 'by no means understood the treacherous complexities of great diplomacy,' see: D. Irving, *Reichsmarshall Hermann Göring 1893-1946. Biography*, chapter: *With hope for a new Munich*.

[41] E. Boheman, *På vakt...*, p. 70.

2. Aggression of Germany and the Soviet Union Against Poland from the Swedish Perspective

First reactions

According to the reports of the Swedish press, the inhabitants of Stockholm reacted to the news of the outbreak of war with 'quiet dejection' (*lugn beklämning*).[1] People crowded around shop windows, where the latest issues of newspapers were displayed, and read them with interest.[2] Some passers-by were even taking souvenir photos. A frantic search for essential items began. Suddenly the city was without sugar, whilst the authorities assured the population that there was no reason to panic as there was plenty.[3] Worse still was the supply of petrol, where restrictions on its distribution were expected to be introduced at any moment. In a few locations around Stockholm yellow posters appeared announcing partial military mobilization. Nobody was under the illusion that this would be a war between Poland and German. The dispute over Gdańsk was compared to the Serbian–Austrian tensions at the outset of the First World War. It was clear that a system of alliances would be initiated and a confrontation between countries of continental Europe would take place.[4]

On the first day of the conflict, 1 September 1939, King Gustaf V announced that Sweden would maintain strict neutrality (*fullständig neutralitet*) in the war between Poland and Germany.[5] At the same time, partial military mobilization was ordered.[6] On the same day Prime Minister Per Albin Hansson, announced on the radio: 'for Swedes, this means that we should firmly and unanimously focus on one serious task: keeping our country out

---

[1] 'Kö till bensin och socker. Tyst och lugnt Stockholm avstod från diskussioner', *Dagens Nyheter*, 2 IX 1939. See also H. Dahlberg, *I Sverige under 2:a världskriget*, Stockholm 1983, p. 13.
[2] Radio news was usually broadcast only three times a day – at 12:30, 19:00 and 22:00. See: K. Lindal, *Självcensur i stövelns skugga. Den svenska radions roll och hållning under andra världskriget*, Stockholm 1998, p. 30.
[3] Thanks to rich harvests in 1938 the government was able to put aside considerable stocks of grain, but liquid fuels were still in short supply. See: A. W. Johansson, *Per Albin...*, pp. 61–62.
[4] 'Krigsutbrottet', *Dagens Nyheter*, 2 IX 1939.
[5] *Svensk utrikespolitik under andra världskriget. Statsrådstal, riksdagsdebatter och kommunikéer*, Stockholm 1946, p. 7.
[6] W. M. Carlgren, *Svensk utrikespolitik...*, p. 23.

of the war, defending and nursing our indispensable national values, as well as trying to manage the current difficult situation in the best possible way. The will to maintain strict neutrality, which fills and unites our nation, was today announced by the government in agreement with the representatives of parliament in the Commission of Foreign Affairs. Nobody should doubt the honesty and firmness that are behind this statement. Nevertheless, I would like to remind you strongly once more about the duties obliging all of us and every single one of us in the face of our solemn promise to maintain cautiousness and good tone in all we say. We value our right to freedom of speech and it is nobody's intention to restrict it. For this reason, we are even more entitled to expect those who make use of this precious gift to do it with sense of responsibility and self-discipline.'[7]

From Hansson's talks with his ministers it follows that he constantly hoped that an agreement would be reached and that Hitler's aggression towards Poland would not evolve into a pan-European conflict.[8] The Ministry of Foreign Affairs received news of the outbreak of war in an undramatic manner. Zenon Przybyszewski-Westrup, who was of Polish descent, spoke Polish and had fond memories of his childhood in Poland prior to the First World War, arrived at work outraged and cursing the Germans. Gunnar Hägglöf, who described Westrup's reaction in his journal, claimed to understand his reaction, for the Germans had invaded 'his beloved Poland.' He also added, showing little regard, that nothing had in fact happened that was not expected. For Sweden, as he stated, the most important task in this case was to sign commercial arrangements with both sides of the conflict as quickly as possible to secure food provisions. A couple of days later Minister Sandler came out in support of his view.[9]

Commentaries published in the daily newspapers were largely varied and sympathies were mostly determined by political profile. The communist *Ny Dag* drew attention to the fact that Poland too, like Germany, had a fascist government that participated in the partition of Czechoslovakia. At the same time *Ny Dag* assured its readers that anti-fascists would still side with Hitler's next target, Poland, and that Sweden needed to do everything possible to

---

[7] *Svensk utrikespolitik...*, p. 8.
[8] A. W. Johansson, *Per Albin...*, p. 61.
[9] G. Hägglöf, *Möte med Europa. Paris–London–Moskva–Genéve–Berlin 1926–1940*, Stockholm 1971, pp. 190–191. In his memoirs, Westrup, son of a Polish writer Stanisław Przybyszewski and Norwegian Dagny Juel, admitted that he was raised to be a Polish patriot. Nonetheless, after he had moved to Sweden at the age of 10 and was adopted by his late mother's family, his contacts with Poland were only occasional, see: Z. P. Westrup, *Jag har varit i Arkadien*, Stockholm 1975, pp. 10–15, 86–93, 131–132.

2. AGGRESSION OF GERMANY AND THE SOVIET UNION

help. Rumours that the Soviet Union, together with Germany, was to assume the role of aggressor following the agreement concluded on 23 August were denied. This option was completely ruled out, and efforts were undertaken to prove that the Soviet Union, having earlier signed a pact of non-aggression against Poland, 'maintains the policy of providing peace to all countries and nations.' The daily added that the Communist Party of Sweden supported neutrality. A couple days later their leader, Sven Linderot, delivered a public speech at *Folkets hus* in Stockholm where he presented a more aggressive position on the matter of the on-going war. Quoting prolifically the statements of the leaders of the Third International, Dmitriy Manuilsky and Vyacheslav Molotov, he said that the war was imperialist and came about because Western Allies had rejected the peace-building policy of the Soviet Union. He asked rhetorically: 'Is it not the Soviet Union that has always tried to issue guarantees to prevent war? All those who have not lost their temper and clarity of mind recognize that it has been so. They recognize that the Soviet Union has been consequently conducting its peace-building policy and fighting in defence of collective security at all times.'[10] Linderot explained that the pact of 23 August was not a treaty of alliance or aid, but an agreement of non-aggression. He described Poland as a link in the imperialist English–French block conducting a war with Germany, the ambitions of which were also imperialist. Linderot presented the position of the Communist Party of Sweden on the politics of the Swedish government: 'We support the government that wants to keep Sweden away from the on-going war, but we are not neutral when it comes to fighting against an imperialist power, we are not neutral towards Fascism, Nazism and other anti-popular forces in the world. Against them we must fight even more strongly.'[11] On 7 September news broke about the mobilisation of reservists in the Soviet Union.[12] The next day, Military Attaché for the Baltic States Major Karl Lindquist informed Swedish staff about the continuing preparations of the Soviet army for a military intervention in Poland.[13]

---

[10] 'Kamp mot imperialisternas krig skydda Sveriges folk och frihet. Sven Linderots tal', *Ny Dag*, 9 IX 1939.
[11] 'Kamp mot imperialisternas krig skydda Sveriges folk och frihet. Sven Linderots tal', *Ny Dag*, 11 IX 1939.
[12] 'Sovjet i Polen', *Sydsvenska Dagbladet Snällposten*, 26 IX 1939.
[13] E. Norberg, 'Det militära hotet. Försvarsattachéernas syn på krigsutbrottet 1939' [in:] *Stormvarning...*, p. 79.

Illustration 1: *Germanias nya axel* ['Germania's New Shoulder']. The caption reads "As long as the others don't feel replaced, dear Stalin". By Blix, *Göteborgs Handels- och Sjöfarts-Tidning*, 9 September 1939.

On 9 September, the Berlin correspondent of *Svenska Dagbladet*, Bertil Svahnström, published an article with the ominous title: 'Berlin reckons with a looming Russian invasion of Polish Ukraine.' In this article he heralded a partition of Poland with the co-participation of Lithuania and Slovakia.[14] At the same time a report in *Svenska Dagbladet* announced that one million Soviet soldiers were waiting at the border with Poland.[15] A commentator for the newspaper, on analysing the foreign policies of the neutral states, claimed that in the case of Italy and the Soviet Union this was 'provisional neutrality.' He predicted that Stalin's policy could bring many surprises in the future, and he did not rule out his collaboration in the partition of Poland.[16] On September 9, the daily newspaper *Göteborgs Handels- och Sjöfarts-Tidning*

---

[14] B. Svahnström, 'Berlin räknar med snar rysk inmarsch i polska Ukraina', *Svenska Dagbladet*, 9 IX 1939.
[15] 'Redan en million ryssar vid gränsen till Polen', *Svenska Dagbladet*, 11 IX 1939.
[16] 'Olika neutralitet', *Svenska Dagbladet*, 14 IX 1939.

2. AGGRESSION OF GERMANY AND THE SOVIET UNION

published a suggestive and original satirical drawing (Illustration 1, previous page) presenting Stalin and Germany as allies.[17] Also alarming were early reports from the Soviet TASS news agency on the Ukrainians' uprising against the Poles.[18]

In the first days of the war there also flared up a discussion on who was to blame for its outbreak. It manifested itself mostly in exposing the defamatory German accusations towards Poland on its rejection of Hitler's restrained demands.[19] The Berlin information service operated more efficiently than the Polish Telegraphic Agency (PAT), however. German propaganda in Stockholm was more dynamic than that of the Allies. News of the alleged Polish attack was spread on the radio in Gliwice and dramatic photographs were distributed of German refugees from Poland, whose dire situation confirmed that Hitler's demands were legitimate.[20] Pro-German newspaper *Aftonbladet* justified Hitler's attack with his intention to forestall Polish aggression.[21] The presented views of Edmund Urbański, editor of the Polish bulletin *Handel i Transport Morski (Trade and Sea Transport)*, explained that the Germans were afraid of the economic dominance of Poland in the Baltic Sea region and for this reason committed this act of aggression. Urbański claimed, however, 'this is nothing new because Scandinavians, and Swedes in particular, are frequent visitors to Gdynia and Gdańsk and they know that the two cities specialize in maritime foreign trade.'[22]

On 3 September, after Great Britain and France had declared war on Germany, Gustaf V announced another declaration of neutrality.[23]

In the third year of the war Prime Minister Hansson stated that the policy of neutrality was an obvious one for the Swedish government and that Sweden was not obliged to make any choices, as it traditionally rejected the option of participating in alliances. He said: 'The declaration of neutrality we

---

[17] 'Germanias nya axel', *Göteborgs Handels- och Sjöfarts-Tidning*, 9 IX 1939.
[18] 'Hitler hotar', *Arbetaren*, 14 IX 1939.
[19] 'Tyska kraven offentliggjorda', *Social-Demokraten*, 1 IX 1939; 'Polen vägrade förhandla förklarar Berlin', *Göteborgs Handels- och Sjöfarts-Tidning*, 1 IX 1939.
[20] See for example, 'Allting beror på om Polen i sista stund kommer att ge vika', *Sydsvenska Dagbladet Snällposten*, 1 IX 1939.
[21] Already from the first day of the war even the dailies which tried to maintain objectivity were put to a serious test of evaluating contradictory information which was breaking from Berlin and Warsaw. See: J. Torbacke, *Dagens Nyheter och demokratins kris 1937–1946. Genom stormar till seger*, Stockholm 1972, p. 77.
[22] 'Polens utrikeshandel oroade Tredje Riket', *Göteborgs Handels- och Sjöfarts-Tidning*, 5 IX 1939.
[23] *Svensk utrikespolitik under andra världskriget. Statsrådstal, riksdagsdebatter och kommunikéer*, Stockholm 1946, p. 9.

announced in September 1939 was an expression of our practical actions, unanimous views and our nation's will.'[24]

A vivid expression of his attitude towards the war was provided by Tage Erlander, who in the 1930s was an official at the Ministry of Social Affairs (*Socialdepartementet*). After the war he became a long-term Prime Minister of Sweden. In his memoirs he contended: 'Sweden had no enemies. Neither did she have any friends who would be ready to spill even a drop of their blood for our sovereignty. We were left to our own devices, which in turn left us with little room for political manoeuvring.'[25] According to Erlander, Sweden adopted the role of terrified spectator and helpless participant.[26] The pro-German daily newspaper *Stockholms-Tidningen* presented the neutral countries with the task of preventing the war from spreading outside of the countries that were already involved and saving Western civilization from destruction. Quite grandiloquent were Erlander's predictions that even the winners of the war would end up its losers and that Sweden's role was to provide humanitarian aid to all the victims of the catastrophe.[27] The suggestively titled article 'Responsibility and duty' in *Svenska Dagbladet* stated optimistically that Sweden was outside of the powers' line of fire, and therefore only the Swedes would decide whether to stay away from the struggle. The possibilities of coping with a war-related economic crisis were described as satisfactory, but a certain scarcity of food and restrictions on civil rights were assumed.[28] The same newspaper also examined the policies of the Soviet Union and Italy. It was highlighted that although the situation in the Baltic Sea region, despite its proximity to the battlefield, was simple and obvious, the situation in the Mediterranean Sea region was hazy.[29]

In early September 1939 Stockholm still believed that Sweden's political and economic situation was better than in 1914. Gustaf V, during a meeting with the government, mentioned that at the outset of the First World War virtually all countries could have been dragged into the conflict. He said he remembered the summer of 1914 as being a continuous series of conferences with foreign diplomats trying to convince him to participate in the war. Consequently, his opinion was that the danger of becoming engaged in the conflict had been

---

[24] P. A. Hansson, *Vår neutralitetspolitik*, Stockholm 1942, p. 6.
[25] T. Erlander, *1901–1939*, Stockholm 1972, p. 266.
[26] T. Erlander, *1940–1949*, Stockholm 1973, pp. 262–263.
[27] 'Efter det nya krigets inledningsdag', *Stockholms-Tidningen*, 2 IX 1939.
[28] 'Ansvar och plikt', *Svenska Dagbladet*, 2 IX 1939.
[29] 'Första krigsdagen', *Svenska Dagbladet*, 2 IX 1939. W. M. Carlgren, *Svensk utrikespolitik…*, p. 24.

greater then than at that moment.[30] Sweden demanded warranties from both sides that they would respect its sovereignty and territorial integrity. Germany granted Sweden such warranty on 2 September and Great Britain one week later. Both declarations were announced in the Swedish press and turned out to be a well-regarded basis for the arrangement of commercial relations with the powers. As predicted by Gunnar Hägglöf, negotiations on the issue of trade with Germany and Great Britain during the Second World War became the most important task of the Swedish diplomacy.

The Swedish government always highlighted that its actions were in line with the will of Swedish society, and even that there was harmony between the position of the authorities and public opinion.[31] At the same time they insisted repeatedly that society cannot become involved in the propagandist rivalry between the powers and must remain self-restrained in voicing their opinions. Such an appeal was made to the Swedes by Prime Minister Hansson in the second chamber and by Minister Sandler in the first chamber of parliament on 12 September 1939. In accordance with these appeals leading Swedish daily newspapers stated with utmost certainty that Sweden had adopted the policy of neutrality and that the Swedish nation supported its government.[32] The newspaper *Sydsvenska Dagbladet Snällposten* pointed out on 6 September that neutrality placed demands not only on the government but also on society, including the press: 'The press are most of all obliged to fulfil an unconditional requirement to provide the public with objective information. [...] One cannot serve only one side and treat failure as victory and the other way round.' It was also added: 'To feel sympathy or aversion towards others is an inalienable human right which cannot be refused to anyone. [...] Nonetheless, both showing one's feelings and discussion should take a worthy form and should be performed with moderation and dignity.'[33] The journalist Hans Eric Holger, in turn, in the *Nya Dagligt Allehanda* newspaper protested the interference of the Swedish diplomacy in the content of press announcements.[34] *Stockholms-Tidningen* had no illusions that the neutral countries were also showing an inclination towards favouring one side or the other and that people too had preferences. This daily nevertheless

---

[30] W. M. Carlgren, *Svensk utrikespolitik...*, p. 24.
[31] P.A. Hansson, *Vår neutralitetspolitik*, p. 22. The Allies were counting on the support from the neutral states. French General M. Weygand maintained that these countries were supporting the Allies, though these sympathies were not 'shown openly.' See: M. Sokolnicki, *Dziennik ankarski 1939–1943*, p. 23.
[32] 'Vart neutrala Sverige och kriget', *Stockholms-Tidningen*, 2 IX 1939.
[33] 'Neutralitetens förpliktelser', *Sydsvenska Dagbladet Snällposten*, 6 IX 1939.
[34] H. E. Holger, 'Pressen och UD', *Nya Dagligt Allehanda*, 9 IX 1939.

supported the position of the government: 'Even though everyone enjoys freedom of thought, it is to be expected from the opinion-forming circles in a neutral country that this neutrality be manifested also in words and deeds, and that ideas and feelings or likes and dislikes do not clash with the common interest of the citizens expressed by the state in the proclamation of neutrality. [...] This requires not only observing the demanded caution and moderation in the interests of one's own country, but also showing an honest spirit of neutrality in all information activities directed towards society.' This explains the suggestion that the press should collect news from both sides of the conflict and allow readers to evaluate it themselves.[35] Many daily newspapers published both German and Polish announcements, but sometimes commentaries attached to these mostly short news items, to a large extent, compromised their impartiality and revealed the true attitude of their editors. A small breakthrough in the understanding of press neutrality occurred on 17 September. A commentator for *Stockholms-Tidningen* readdressed the issue of impartiality of Swedish dailies in the context of Poland's fate: 'It is us, the neutral states, who are obliged to understand and evaluate the motifs and conduct of the countries who are participating in the war as impartially as possible. It is our duty and our privilege. But we are human beings and we have a nationality. Let us defend ourselves against the suffering which is inflicted by the war upon the citizens of both sides. We are also strongly hoping that peace would not have to be gained at the cost of any of the nations losing its liberty.'[36]

Stockholms-Tidningen and *Aftonbladet*, which were part of the press company owned by Torsten Kreuger, brother of Ivar (the famous financier), showed a clear sympathy towards Nazi Germany from the beginning.[37] How can one generally evaluate the Swedish dailies in terms of the objectivity of the content of their reports from the front? In the first days of the war Envoy of Great Britain to Stockholm Edmund Monson, in the face of Germany's wide-ranging propaganda offensive, had serious doubts as to whether the British would be able to maintain their prestige in Sweden. The Swedish press became practically cut off from the English information service which only reached Sweden with a significant delay, whereas the broadcast from Berlin

---

[35] 'Pressens neutralitet', *Stockholms-Tidningen*, 9 IX 1939.
[36] 'Polens fjärde delning som krigsmål', *Stockholms-Tidningen*, 17 IX 1939.
[37] A quite different image of Torsten Kreuger from the 1920s was recorded in the memoirs of Alfred Wysocki, Polish Envoy to Stockholm in the years 1924–1928, who highlighted his merits for the Polish foreign policy in Sweden. See: A. Wysocki, *Na placówce dyplomatycznej w Sztokholmie 1924–1928. Wspomnienia*, edited by P. Jaworski, Toruń 2004, pp. 85–99, 127–128, 137, 167–169.

was transmitted perfectly. As a result, there appeared many more German announcements in the Swedish press than were received from the Allies. This, in spite of the fact that from the beginning of the war both the press and radio endeavoured to maintain a balance in their selection of news. Difficulties in maintaining impartiality by the Swedish press were highlighted by a commentator for *Sydsvenska Dagbladet Snällposten*, who blamed the British for their lack of imagination and willingness to cooperate with journalists from other countries. The journalist noted that the Germans provided exhaustive information on a regular basis, whereas the British excused themselves with war censure, preferring to remain silent.[38] The attitude of the British press service contrasted the Polish Legation, which started distributing its own news bulletin based on radio reports. Drawn up by a correspondent for the PAT, Jan Otmar-Berson, the so-called *zielonek* (from the Polish for the colour green '*zielony*,' which was the colour of the printing paper used), was distributed by the legation's chauffeur amongst individual editorial sections of dailies and periodicals, as well as government institutions and diplomatic missions of other countries.[39]

The situation was exceptional for the Swedes. The news services were much more active; for the first time ever, the radio began broadcasting morning news. When the highest priority news items came in, regular programming was interrupted. This occurred only once, on 17 September 1939, when the Soviet Union invaded Poland. The Swedes were always at risk of being reprimanded by the warring parties. For the first time in history, the head of the Swedish Telegraphic Agency (*Tidningarnas Telegrambyrå* or TT), Gustaf Reuterswärd, received a complaint from the German Consul to Malmö, Alexander Bogs. In a telephone conversation, Bogs claimed the evening radio news had expressed hostility towards Germany.[40]

---

[38] 'Svårigheter for neutralpress', *Sydsvenska Dagbladet Snällposten*, 4 X 1939.
[39] A letter by Tomasz Potworowski to the author, 15 XI 2002 r. See also: T. Potworowski, 'Zapiski do pamiętnika: Sztokholm, wrzesień–grudzień 1939', *Acta Sueco-Polonica* 2003–2005, iss. 12–13, pp. 191–204. Report by Gustaw Potworowski from 16 October 1939, see: *Polskie dokumenty dyplomatyczne 1939 wrzesień–grudzień*, W. Rojek (ed.), Warsaw 2007, p. 202, where the Envoy calls for setting up special press-news unit in Paris for the needs of Polish propaganda in Sweden.
[40] K. Lindal, *Självcensur i stövelns skugga. Den svenska radions roll och hållning under andra världskriget*, Stockholm 1998, pp. 31.

Illustration 2: 'Världen har intet val' ['The World has no choice'], The captions on the uniforms translate to 'Hitler's understanding of war' and 'Hitler's understanding of peace'. By Low, *Göteborgs Handels- och Sjöfarts-Tidning*, 12 September 1939.

Reports from the front

From the first day of the war the Swedish press had published regular reports about military operations on the Polish–German front. The ambition of many daily newspapers was to provide professional explanations of the combat based on situation maps and present probable scenarios of the forthcoming military actions.[41] *Dagens Nyheter* offered its pages to Colonel Axel Gyllenkrok, who on 1 September presented his analysis with the characteristic title: 'Military opportunities for Poland',[42] which had been prepared before the German aggression took place. The Swedish officer made an accurate prediction that principal German blows would be directed at the so-called abdomen of Poland, from Lower Silesia to Kalisz and Łódź, as well as from East Prussia to Warsaw and from Slovakia to Dęblin. He also correctly predicted that Pomerania and Upper Silesia would be cut off quickly from the rest of the country. According to Gyllenkrok the Germans would annex provinces which were formerly theirs within a week. He neither excluded guerrilla warfare at the rear of the German army nor doubted that the Allies would be unable to provide direct support to Poland, except for the air force.

---

[41] J. Torbacke, *Dagens…*, p. 81.
[42] A. Gyllenkrok, 'Polens chanser vid krig', *Dagens Nyheter*, 1 IX 1939.

2. AGGRESSION OF GERMANY AND THE SOVIET UNION

He maintained that the Polish–German war would be a good opportunity for Soviet aggression. Gyllenkrok presumed too that such an attack was unlikely during the initial stage of the war, but at the same time did not deny that the Soviet army would await the opportunity to make use of German successes, thereby conserving its efforts. He estimated that the Polish chances for success were relatively slim, even if the Western Allies eventually achieved victory over Germany. Opinion journalists reacted to the news of the decision of London and Paris to join the war with understanding. On 12 September, *Göteborgs Handels- och Sjöfarts-Tidning* published a drawing (Illustration 2, previous page) suggesting that the world had no other choice than to take up arms against Hitler, and beat him.[43]

After the Western Allies had become engaged in the conflict, Swedish opinion journalists started to wonder if the Allies could provide support to Poland, and with clear doubt expected that a major offensive would be launched in the West. What was considered improbable at the same time was the conclusion of the war after the breaking of the Polish army's resistance by the Germans as the conflict was perceived as a fight between powers for hegemony in Europe. Starting on 4 September, the title of a famous novel by Erich Maria Remarque *All Quiet on the Western Front* was repeated continuously and a rhetorical question about how long would there be peace on the French–German border and what would happen there was asked time and time again.[44] This quiet on the western front made a ghastly and unrealistic impression on the Swedes.[45] Commentators in the Swedish press doubted that the Western Allies had long to consider whether they wanted to do something for Poland. They also made the Swedish public aware of how impossible it was to offer Poland immediate help. Having compared the current situation with that of the Polish army in 1920 during the war with Soviet Russia, Colonel Sune Bergelin, a commentator for *Göteborgs Handels- och Sjöfarts-Tidning*, argued that sending French staff officers to the front was unnecessary in that case, as Poles were well-qualified and it was impossible to transport weapons and ammunition there. The heavy military equipment of the French army would not improve the chances of overcoming the German defence on the western front. The only way to provide help, as suggested by Bergelin, was to launch an air raid on Germany, but at the same time he claimed that this would not take place, because, as he put it: 'A terrorizing air

---

[43] 'Världen har intet val', *Göteborgs Handels- och Sjöfarts-Tidning*, 12 IX 1939 (Illus. 2).
[44] K. A. B., 'Från västfronten intet nytt', *Dagens Nyheter*, 5 IX 1939; 'Lugnet på västfronten', *Dagens Nyheter*, 7 IX 1939.
[45] T. Erlander, *1940–1949*, p. 44.

battle, which would probably give the quickest results, is contrary to the Western Allies' general democratic approach towards war.' Besides, 'a terrorizing air battle – from a moral perspective – could in fact prove to be a double-edged sword.' Nonetheless, according to Bergelin, the Western Allies were obliged to take some pro-active measures on the western front for the sake of maintaining their prestige. He also comforted the Poles by mentioning the case of Belgium and Serbia, which despite being conquered during the First World War, were liberated and territorially enlarged right after its conclusion, but at the same time he also noted that in the case of Poland the circumstances were quite different and similarities rather small.[46] A commentator for *Svenska Dagbladet* argued that the situation on the western front-line certainly may not be described as 'somewhat idyllic', the evidence of which was to be the sinking of the passenger ship *Athenia*.[47] By 14 September *Göteborg Handels- och Sjöfarts-Tidning* had published Gunnar Cederschiöld's article from 3 September, where he accepted the ultimatum given to the Germans and soon afterwards the declaration of war issued by France: 'It is inexpressibly tragic and at the same time indescribably inspiring to see the entire nation sacrifice all what's most dear to them in order not to defend themselves, their land or homes, but in order to help another nation in a fight against lawlessness and violence, and in order to fight for the principles which constitute the foundation of their lives. 2 September 1939 is a meaningful date in the history of France: This date marks the death of egoism. How long will this last? Months or years? This depends on the length of the war.'[48]

The Allied forces continued their flyer drops. *Social-Demokraten* posited that the British were likely expecting the revival of anti-Hitler opposition in Germany and that they did not want to put the German nation off.[49] In spite of the fact that they were continuously describing the on-going preparations for the offensive in the West, they also agreed that by the time it took place it would already be too late to save Poland.[50] The western front was still quiet on the following day.[51] According to *Göteborg Handels- och Sjöfarts-Tidning* this was the calm before the storm: 'It has already been repeated several times that Germany would note great successes during the first 6–8 weeks of the

---

[46] S. Bergelin, 'Västmakternas understöd', *Göteborg Handels- och Sjöfarts-Tidning*, 8 IX 1939.
[47] 'Utan krigsförklaring', *Svenska Dagbladet*, 5 IX 1939.
[48] G. Cederschiöld, '2 augusti 1914–2 september 1939', *Göteborg Handels- och Sjöfarts-Tidning*, 14 IX 1939.
[49] 'Det stora luftkrigets premiär', *Social-Demokraten*, 14 IX 1939.
[50] H. S., 'Polska fälthären skingrad', *Nya Dagligt Allehanda*, 19 IX 1939.
[51] 'Fortsatt lugn på västfronten', *Svenska Dagbladet*, 20 IX 1939.

war. They have started the war using all their reserves. The Western Allies need time to mobilize their armies. When they reach full readiness, the Germans will start to retreat.'[52]

German announcements confirmed Swedish public opinion that the Allies had no interest in opening the western front and that they were incapable of relieving Poland by attacking Germany from the air.[53] French announcements from the western front, stating that operations were progressing normally, were considered humourous. The Swedish Attaché Juhlin-Dannfelt explained to his superiors on the seventh day of the war that nothing was going on in the west, because 'the French army was prepared for a defensive battle along the Maginot Line but had no intention of crossing it.'[54]

Almost nobody doubted that the Germans, using all their motorized military force, would break through the Polish defence, which would then move from borderline territories to the line of the Vistula and Bug rivers. According to Colonel Bergelin it was obvious that the aggressor's superiority over the line of the Polish defence, which was disadvantaged and excessively stretched out along the borders, was not only in numbers and technology but also strategy. The commentator also stressed the significance of air forces which were destroying ground targets and resorting to acts of terror.[55] Hitler's former colleague Otto Strasser, who was his opponent at the time, predicted in *Göteborgs Handels- och Sjöfarts-Tidning*, that the Polish army was doomed to withdraw. He maintained that it was paradoxical to expect that the quicker the Poles withdrew to the main line of defence on the Vistula River, the greater the chance would be of an effective counter-attack. He also claimed that long-lasting defensive combat could thwart the chances of victory over the Germans. The Western Allies should at least launch an air offensive against Germany, in order to support Poland.[56] *Sydsvenska Dagbladet Snällposten* daily also underlined the fact that 'the strategic location of the young Polish state was difficult from the very beginning and the situation had become even worse over the last two years.' Additionally, the mobilization was not carried out completely, and mild weather favoured the quick relocation of motorized German army. At the same time, it was pointed out that

---

[52] 'Fortsättning följer', *Göteborg Handels- och Sjöfarts-Tidning*, 20 IX 1939.
[53] NA, FO 419/33, letter by the Envoy of Great Britain to Stockholm, E. Monson, to the Minister of Foreign Affairs Halifax, Stockholm, 11 IX 1939.
[54] RA, UD 1920 års dossiersystem, HP 1, vol. 717, memorandum by Swedish Military Attaché to Berlin Colonel Juhlin-Dannfelt on the reports up to 7 September, Berlin, 7 IX 1939.
[55] S. Bergelin, 'Krigsöppnandet', *Göteborgs Handels- och Sjöfarts-Tidning*, 4 IX 1939.
[56] O. Strasser, 'Uppmarschen vid fronterna', *Göteborgs Handels- och Sjöfarts-Tidning*, 5 IX 1939.

the Soviet offensive of 1920 was stopped on the outskirts of Warsaw. A rhetorical question was asked whether 'the "Miracle on the Vistula" can be repeated now when Poland has such a terrifying opponent, and its allies are unable to provide it with direct support?'[57] In the eyes of the Swedish commentator the high-quality of the varied weapons as well as the overwhelming superiority in the air benefitted the Germans. Journalists for *Sydsvenska Dagbladet Snällposten* excused the Poles in some way writing that during the first week of the war it was impossible for the Poles to conduct a counter-attack due to intense German air raids, which made it difficult to gather reserves.[58] Most of the analyses were based on experiences from the First World War, and attempts were made to find similarities and point out the differences between the two conflicts. On the fourth day of the war *Stockholms-Tidningen* noted that the Germans were implementing a scenario from 1914, but this time their purpose was to conduct a 'lightning war' in the east, and then to attack France. On this occasion a fundamental question was asked about whether it was possible for the Polish army to stop the Germans, just like the French had done during the Battle of the Marne in 1914, and so, a Polish counter-offensive was expected.[59] The head of Swedish military intelligence, Colonel Carlos Adlercreutz, was sceptical, though he would not deny, as the press commentators did, that there would be 'another battle of the Marne', as the Vistula and Bug rivers were considered to be a natural line of defence.[60] The military campaign would begin then, but based on reports coming from the front at first doubts as to the feasibility of such defence were voiced as early as 8 September. News was breaking that entire Polish divisions were downing weapons and ammunition surprised by unusually quick moving armoured forces equipped with heavy machine guns.[61] The retreat, therefore, looked like a chaotic escape and the first announcements of the defeat of Poland were received. On 9 September *Dagens Nyheter* published news about a catastrophe near Warsaw, namely the threat of cutting off the withdrawing Polish armies from the main forces.[62] These predictions were supported by statistics showing that many Polish soldiers were taken prisoner by

---

[57] 'Den polska krigsskadeplatsen', *Sydsvenska Dagbladet Snällposten*, 6 IX 1939.
[58] 'Tysk-polska fronten', *Sydsvenska Dagbladet Snällposten*, 8 IX 1939.
[59] 'Vad sker i Polen?', *Stockholms-Tidningen*, 7 IX 1939.
[60] E. Norberg, 'Det militära hotet. Försvarsattachéernas syn på krigsutbrottet 1939' [in:] *Stormvarning...*, pp. 76, 78.
[61] 'Tysk-polska fronten', *Sydsvenska Dagbladet Snällposten*, 8 IX 1939.
[62] 'Katastrofen vid Warszawa', *Dagens Nyheter*, 9 IX 1939.

the Germans.[63] Other dailies reported that a siege of Warsaw had begun.[64] On 9 September Colonel Sune Bergelin described the position of the Polish army as dramatic: 'One glance at the situation plan is enough for us to see that catastrophe may await the Polish armed forces to the west and north-west of the capital.' The withdrawal was hindered seriously by continuous bombardment of Polish units. What was striking for Bergelin was the complete lack of initiative on the Polish side, as a result of which the open flanks of the quickly charging German army were left alone.[65] Quite different was the opinion of the situation presented by *Social-Demokraten*. Here it was stated that according to official announcements the Polish army was retreating, but that this was done in complete order, while retaining high morale and a brave attitude. It was pointed out that even though the Polish Commander-in-Chief Marshall Edward Śmigły-Rydz had once before, in 1920, been forced to retreat from Kiev to near Warsaw, a victory over Bolshevik Russia was eventually secured by the Poles. Journalists predicted that the autumn would slow down the German army and that there was a chance that the fate of the war would change.[66] Part of the Polish army in Pomerania and the province of Poznań was cut off from the rest of the country. A commentator for *Social-Demokraten* wrote: 'The impression is nonetheless that the Poles have not suffered a conclusive defeat but that they have been trying to limit the number of casualties and reach the internal line of defence on the other side of the Bug-Vistula-San rivers, where the chances for a more effecttive and dense resistance are greater.'[67]

On 11 September, commentators for *Göteborgs Handels- och Sjöfarts-Tidning* analysed the Soviet Union policy. The conclusion of the campaign in Poland was all but accepted and an increasing amount of speculation appeared on the subject of a possible intervention by Stalin: 'Why is Russia mobilizing its forces? Perhaps due to the situation in the Far East. [...] Perhaps Moscow actually wants to protect its interests in Europe and also tries to prevent the incorporation of the part of Poland which belonged to Russia until 1914 [...]. This may result in another partition of Poland along the border from 1914 or make Poland play the role of a buffer state between Russia and Germany. In the first case the current mobilization would conclude with Russia entering Poland from the east and dividing its winnings

---

[63] '25 000 fångar tagna', *Sydsvenska Dagbladet Snällposten*, 8 IX 1939.
[64] 'Än är Polen ej förlorat', *Svenska Dagbladet*, 9 IX 1939.
[65] S. Bergelin, 'Krigssituationen i Polen', *Göteborgs Handels- och Sjöfarts-Tidning*, 9 IX 1939.
[66] 'Polackerna betrakta läget med optimism', *Social-Demokraten*, 9 IX 1939.
[67] 'Krigsläget', *Social-Demokraten*, 9 IX 1939.

with Germany. In the second case it would be all about pressures from Russia to stop the German march to the east. If a hypothesis that the mobilization of Russia is caused by the situation in Poland turns out to be true, it would bring serious consequences for the small Baltic States which in 1914 belonged to Tsarist Russia.'[68] *Aftonbladet* argued: 'It would seem that the ill-fated history of Poland will be repeated, in spite of the fact that *polsk riksdag* [Swedish expression for a chaos or mess or disorder, but directly translates to Polish Parliament] is now a matter for the past.' But it was highlighted: 'Overestimating one's own importance is a dangerous deficiency;' and also stated: 'Valour must go hand in hand with reason, insight and caution.' It is worth focusing on the last statement of this article, where the author suddenly changes the subject and claims that under the German–Soviet contract 'Russia would sooner send its soldiers than goods.'[69] On 12 September the syndicalist daily *Arbetaren* (The Worker) drew attention to the discussions on the position of Stalin who 'is dreaming of territorial expansion disguised in a revolutionary mask.' *Arbetaren*'s commentator suggested this issue be examined from a nationalist point of view, because the aggression of Russia against Poland would most importantly lead to the enlargement of Stalin's empire. The people of Poland – a half-totalitarian country – would find themselves in a fully totalitarian country. Restricted freedom would become lack of freedom, and the Polish nation would be jumping out of the frying pan into the fire. The journalist in *Arbetaren* made optimistic predictions that the labourers of Europe would not allow themselves to be deceived and that they would recognize Fascism, 'even if it dresses up in a red mask.'[70] Another opinion journalist for the same newspaper wondered why Stalin had stationed such large armed forces so close to the Polish border and whether he was preparing for an invasion. Added to which news began to appear in the German press of Ukrainians' standing against Poles, which could constitute a prelude to a revolutionary movement proclaiming the incorporation of Poland into the Soviet Union.[71]

Svenska Dagbladet, in an article from 12 September entitled 'Prior to the conclusion' predicted the course of events for the very near future. It was not hard to guess the anticipated conclusion, as it was noted that Germany continued its attack and the two Polish allies did little to minimize the pressure.[72]

---

[68] 'Osäkerhet', *Göteborgs Handels- och Sjöfarts-Tidning*, 11 IX 1939.
[69] 'Observatör, Hur vållades den polska tragedien?', *Aftonbladet*, 11 IX 1939.
[70] 'Stalin och Polen', *Arbetaren*, 12 IX 1939.
[71] 'Skymtas Sovjet i bakgrunden?', *Arbetaren*, 12 IX 1939.
[72] 'Inför avgörande', *Svenska Dagbladet*, 12 IX 1939.

Meanwhile, Colonel Karl-Axel Bratt in his article for *Dagens Nyheter* awaited news of the defence of Warsaw. He noted that keeping the capital in Polish hands was morally significant. He also predicted that the Germans would decrease the pace of their attack because 'even mechanised units get tired.' But he added that the Germans were entitled to feel tired after such 'a fantastic achievement.'[73] Swedish newspapers were full of announcements detailing the steady progress of the German army and the total collapse of the Polish defence. *Dagens Nyheter*, on 14 September, though constantly highlighting the bravery of the Polish army, heralded its utter defeat in the ongoing great battle near Warsaw.[74] One day later, *Stockholms-Tidningen* stated that the resistance by the Polish army was pointless because its sacrifice would delay the German achievements by only a week. This was still an incommensurately short period of time as compared to the losses incurred by the Poles, which most probably would prevent them from launching a counter-offensive. Slowly everyone arrived at the conclusion that the Polish army should have organized its defence along the line of the Vistula river from the start.[75] Experts on the subject pointed out the crucial role of panzer divisions in breaking the line of the Polish defence and confirmed the opinion of German soldiers that warfare was turning into the slaughter of Polish infantry and that valour helped nothing in that case.[76] An expert for *Sydsvenska Dagbladet Snällposten* issued a reminder on 16 September about the expected defence of the Bug-Vistula-San line. The rapid movement of the German army and their crossing of the Bug and San rivers rendered such deliberations pointless and the Polish army ended up surrounded. The resistance of Poland was from then on no longer described by him as valiant but as desperate and hopeless.[77]

The picture of total war

Between 12 and 15 September, Colonel Juhlin-Dannfelt together with other military attachés travelled from Berlin to the Polish–German front. The planned German expedition to the vicinity of Częstochowa, Kielce and to the north of Warsaw had to be limited to north of Warsaw only as roads were blocked by Polish snipers. Consequently, the foreign observers eventually

---

[73] K. A. Bratt, 'Över de polska slag fälten', *Dagens Nyheter*, 12 IX 1939.
[74] K. A. Bratt, 'Förintelse slaget kring Warszawa', *Dagens Nyheter*, 14 IX 1939.
[75] 'Situationen i Polen', *Stockholms-Tidningen*, 15 IX 1939.
[76] 'Pansardivisionernas roll', *Dagens Nyheter*, 16 IX 1939.
[77] 'Dubbel omfattning i andra omgången', *Sydsvenska Dagbladet Snällposten*, 16 IX 1939.

travelled to Pułtusk, Mława, Wyszków and several other towns and villages located near the Polish capital. According to a Swedish officer, the quick movement of the German army was the result of its exceptionally high level of mechanization as well as the frequent use of the air force, which paralysed the movement of the Polish army and, most importantly, dampened its morale. Juhlin-Dannfelt had no doubt that the technical superiority of the Germans that he observed characterized other sections on the front. He also maintained that both sides had suffered immense losses in the ever continuing combat. According to the Swedish Attaché, due to the Germans' plans to occupy the territories of Poland, they were not striving to destroy the conquered towns and villages, and, as a matter of fact, this activity neither slowed down the pace of military operations nor increased the losses. Only due to the fact that 'the Polish units were taking pleasure in putting up resistance in locations of which many were fortified, there are voices among the Germans that it was necessary to subject many towns and villages to artillery shelling in order to carry out the bombardments of the Polish army. They also claim that civilians and soldiers from defeated units often acted as snipers, shooting at the German soldiers who were marching through the towns. This often led to acts of retaliation, such as setting fire to individual buildings or to entire neighbourhoods.'[78] This was how the Germans were able to justify the complete destruction of Wyszków, Mława, Pułtusk and many other locations, which were examined by the foreign visitors. Juhlin-Dannfelt predicted that over the forthcoming week Poland would be defeated and entirely occupied by the Germans. Rumours spread among the circle of attachés about the impending Soviet attack: 'This would seal the loss of independence for the Polish state.'

Reports by Swedish daily newspapers about ordeals endured by civilians were to a large extent truthful, yet their coverage of the bombardments of the Polish cities was restrained. In contrast, the newspapers had written about the bombardment of Gdańsk by the Polish air force.[79] In the first days of the war, to quote the PAT, the press published only the official announcements to the public from the president and political parties.[80] On 4 September, however, *Göteborgs Handels- och Sjöfarts-Tidning* quoted the United Press and the PAT correspondent, Edmund Allen, who stated that several hundred

---

[78] RA, UD 1920 års dossiersystem, HP 2, vol. 717, report by Swedish Military Attaché to Berlin Colonel Juhlin-Dannfelt, Berlin, 16 IX 1939.
[79] Observatör, 'Tyska flyget blott sparsamt med i Polen', *Aftonbladet*, 2 IX 1939.
[80] 'Patriotisk appell till Polens bönder', *Jönköpings-Posten*, 2 IX 1939; 'Polens president manar till kamp mot arvfienden', *Stockholms-Tidningen*, 3 IX 1939.

civilians had died as a consequence of the bombardments of the Polish cities by the Germans.[81] This news was confirmed by the first group of Swedish refugees from Poland who arrived at Stockholm on 7 September. At the same time *Aftonbladet*, citing the German press reports, argued that the Germans were not engaged in bombarding churches.[82] This pro-German daily admitted that 'the air battle began on 1 September with the bombardment of numerous localities all over Poland.' However, it was also added: 'It seems that the German fighter-bombers have attacked only military targets and bridges, and not civilians.'[83] On 11 September, the Germans announced themselves that they were bombing Warsaw, and that in requital for civilians' resistance and active fights with the German army, involving shooting at German soldiers from windows and attacking German tanks, their actual fate was beyond the Germans' concern.[84] Photographs of a bombarded Warsaw were published at the same time together with the announcement of the PAT that attacks by German panzer divisions on the capital had been repulsed.[85] An analyst for *Svenska Dagbladet* confirmed on 12 September that roads, bridges and railways were under constant bombardment, as well as units of the Polish army. His conclusion was nevertheless reassuring: 'The air *blitzkrieg*, which terrified many who thought that it would be an unexpected attack on settlements and civilians, turned out to be a violent but short strike aimed only at Polish military bases.'[86] Even *Aftonbladet*, on 18 September, quoting the English press, came with news about repeated air raids by German fighter-bombers on defenceless refugees.[87] The heroic picture of Warsaw subjected to relentless German bombardments was also presented by an anonymous opinion journalist in the syndicalist daily *Arbetaren*. The article, entitled 'Warsaw, a city in fire and blood' was concluded with the military-announcement-style statement: 'Warsaw is still defending itself.'[88] The correspondent for *Dagens Nyheter*, Vladimir Semitjov, submitted continuously his reports from the Polish capital. He focused mostly on describing the misery of civilians who would likely suffer repeated German bombardments. He also reported that the citizens of Warsaw were persistently retaining their

---

[81] 'Tyskarna intensifiera luftkriget', *Göteborgs Handels- och Sjöfarts-Tidning*, 4 IX 1939; '27 plan bombarderade Bydgoszcz', *Göteborgs Handels- och Sjöfarts-Tidning*, 4 IX 1939.
[82] 'Tyskarna i Warszawa', *Aftonbladet*, 7 IX 1939.
[83] 'Luftkriget – en sammanfattning', *Aftonbladet*, 7 IX 1939.
[84] 'Repressalie-bombardemang av Warszawa?', *Svenska Dagbladet*, 11 IX 1939.
[85] 'Fortsatt strid i Warszawas yttre områden', *Svenska Dagbladet*, 11 IX 1939.
[86] 'Luftkriget i Polen', *Svenska Dagbladet*, 12 IX 1939.
[87] 'Polska flyktingarna beskjutas av flygare', *Aftonbladet*, 18 IX 1939.
[88] 'Warszawa, en stad i eld och blod', *Arbetaren*, 14 IX 1939.

discipline and bravery.[89] Contrary views were also published. A commentator for *Göteborgs Handels- och Sjöfarts-Tidning* opened his report with a statement that the current events differed substantially from those of the First World War, but that, as far as he was concerned, predictions from previous years, that the next war would be dreadful, had hitherto failed to come true: 'Havoc-wreaking poisonous gas bombardments of civilians, destruction of entire cities and provinces by air raids and other acts of violence connected with the declaration of war or even prior to the so-called blitzkrieg, no such things have happened. The fact that attacks were also targeted at unfortified locations is undeniable, but it would be difficult to juxtapose these events with the so-called terrorizing of civilians, who, as it in fact turns out, were fighting beside a regular army.'[90]

Few precise descriptions of the consequences of the German bombardment of civil targets were published in the newspapers. This changed at the close of September, when another, larger group of Swedish refugees from Poland reached their homeland and were encouraged by the dailies to provide an account of their war experiences in Poland. At the time it transpired that the most important public utility buildings in Warsaw, including the National Museum and the Polytechnic had been reduced to rubble, with substantial number of civilian casualties. *Göteborgs Handels- och Sjöfarts-Tidning* announced on 26 September that the bombardments brought a moderate death toll of 5 thousand civilian inhabitants of Warsaw.[91] On 27 September the newspaper published a heart-breaking picture of children observing the Warsaw sky in expectation of an air strike.[92] In spite of this fact the opinion journalist for *Sydsvenska Dagbladet Snällposten*, Gösta Torelius, described German pilots as energetic heroes of the sky. And in general he claimed: 'The people of the German aviation are one big family'.[93]

The ruthlessness of the German army was also addressed, though rarely, by diplomats. During a visit to Poland, 9–12 October 1939, the assistant of attaché Juhlin-Dannfelt, Lieutenant Göran Hedin noted that the German

---

[89] W. Semitjov, 'Gråtande kvinnoskaror kring bombernas offer', *Dagens Nyheter*, 5 IX 1939. Following his return to Sweden: 'Många tyska agenter. Vägledande signaler' *Dagens Nyheter*, 25 IX 1939.
[90] 'Erfarenheter från världskriget' *Göteborgs Handels- och Sjöfarts-Tidning*, 19 IX 1939.
[91] Likewise, the news that was pouring in from the Eastern Borderlands was not describing the atrocities performed by the Soviet soldiers but about the process of breaking up landed estates controlled by the new authorities. See 'Den ryska ordningen införes omedelbart i östra Polen', *Göteborgs Handels- och Sjöfarts-Tidning*, 26 IX 1939.
[92] 'I väntan på bombanfall' *Göteborgs Handels- och Sjöfarts-Tidning*, 27 IX 1939.
[93] G. Torelius, 'Luftens käcka kavaljerer', *Sydsvenska Dagbladet Snällposten*, 15 X 1939.

methods of conducting war were tough even following the defeat of Warsaw, and, when it comes to civilians, were comparatively merciless.[94]

At the beginning of October, *Sydsvenska Dagbladet Snällposten* published a three-part report by Carl Herslow concerning the fate of a Swedish colony in Warsaw. Throughout the entire siege the Swedes had remained in the building of the Swedish legation and their evacuation took place just before the capitulation with the Germans' approval – firstly to Königsberg, and from there via Riga to Stockholm.[95] Soon after the conclusion of the campaign the newspapers also started publishing reports from Eastern Poland,[96] including the account by Semitjov, who was travelling towards the Romanian border through Brest and Kowel.[97] A series of his reports became the basis for a book published at the close of 1939 entitled *Ett land försvann. Ödesveckor i Polen* (*A State Has Dissappeared. Crucial Weeks for Poland*). The text was filled with sympathy for civilians who were traumatized with bombardments. Semitjov quoted vulnerable victims of air strikes: 'This is not war, this is slaughter.' He was at that time also making ironic comments about Polish military propaganda which kept trying to persuade the public that the defence proved effective although poverty, starvation, epidemics and first signs of anarchy were clearly evident. No less favourably he evaluated the bravery of Polish soldiers who were doing everything they could in that hopeless situation. Everyone was in high spirits. Refugees were also helping one another. Semitjov was surprised by the apparent lack of theft: 'This was a sign of Polish solidarity, unwavering in its suffering, as long as there was something that could be shared with others.'[98] The propaganda machine orchestrated by Goebbels was effective and the Swedes were convinced that it was the Poles who were the repressors of a German minority. Archbishop Erling Eidem influenced by accounts from Germany even asked the Swedish Ministry of Foreign Affairs to intervene in the case of German ministers, with Polish

---

[94] RA, UD 1920 års dossiersystem, HP 2, vol. 717, report by Lieutenant G. Hedin, Berlin, 23 X 1939. The cruelty of Wehrmacht, its paranoid fear against 'Polish partisans' are described by Jochen Böhler: 'Auftakt zum Vernichtungskreig. Die Wehrmacht in Polen 1939', Frankfurt am Main 2006; 'Deutschlands Krieg gegen Polen', Frankfurt am Main 2009.

[95] C. Herslow, 'Septemberdagar i Warszawa', *Sydsvenska Dagbladet Snällposten*, 2 X 1939; idem, 'Hela våningen borta på en natt'. 'Några intryck från septemberdagarna i Warszawa', *Sydsvenska Dagbladet Snällposten*, 6 X 1939; idem, 'Tysklands luftvapen från början överlägset', *Sydsvenska Dagbladet Snällposten*, 9 X 1939.

[96] E. P. Andersson, 'Ryssen kommer!', *Arbetaren*, 3 X 1939, 4 X 1939.

[97] W. Semitjov, 'Alla tåg vände: ryssarna komma', *Dagens Nyheter*, 5 X 1939.

[98] W. Semitjov, *Ett land försvann. Ödesveckor i Polen*, Stockholm 1939, pp. 31, 86, 117, 134, 174.

citizenship, who the Poles allegedly evacuated to the East following the outbreak of the war and probably murdered. Following the conclusion of the campaign, the emissary of the B Division of the Swedish Ministry of Foreign Affairs tasked with the duty of protecting Polish citizens in Germany, Major Carl Petersen, confirmed that one protestant priest was dead, and another was still missing. Archbishop Eidem expressed his gratitude for the information on the fate of these priests 'in former Poland.'[99]

The attack from the East

Active propagandist preparations for the Soviet invasion of Poland were launched by announcements from the Russian News Agency TASS, on 13 September, about several violations of Soviet airspace by Polish aircraft. On this basis an opinion journalist for *Göteborgs Handels- och Sjöfarts-Tidning* claimed on 14 September that 'the position of Russia in this conflict is still a mystery.'[100] One day later *Aftonbladet* announced the intensification of the anti-Polish campaign, conducted by the Soviet information services, which was described as 'a declaration of war on the entire minority and cultural policy of Poland.' The Moscow newspaper *Pravda* criticised Poland for oppressing Ukrainians and Belarusians. The paper compared the policy of the Polish authorities to the terror of the Tsarist period.[101] The analysis of the defeat presented by *Ny Dag* was simple: 'If Poland had a worker-peasant government, which would motivate all the forces of the nation to defend the sovereignty of the country, it would have been different.'[102] In the same issue of *Ny Dag* a journalist criticized Poland, providing an extensive quotation from *Pravda*, where it was explained that the reason of Poland's defeat lay in its persecution of minorities: 'That is why it is hard to call up a united force, filled with the will to put up resistance to the invader.' Polish fighter-bombers were accused of violating Soviet airspace on 12 and 13 of September.[103]

---

[99] RA, UD avdelningar och byråarkiv 1864–1952, Andra B-avdelningen, vol. 297, letter by Archbishop E. Eidem to Deputy Minister of Foreign Affairs E. Boheman (including attachment), Uppsala, 22 IX 1941; letter by C. Petersen to UD, Berlin, 17 X 1939; letter by Archbishop E. Eidem to J. Beck-Friis, Uppsala, 21 X 1939.
[100] 'Nya tyska terrängvinster i östra Polen', *Göteborgs Handels- och Sjöfarts-Tidning*, 14 IX 1939; cf. 'Ryska anklagelser: polska flygarna kränka gränsen', *Svenska Dagbladet*, 14 IX 1939.
[101] 'Ryssland och Polen', *Aftonbladet*, 15 IX 1939.
[102] G. J., 'Fjorton dagars krig', *Ny Dag*, 15 IX 1939.
[103] 'Förtrycket mot de nationella minoriteterna hämnar sig', *Ny Dag*, 15 IX 1939; 'Polska flygare kränker Sovjet-unionens gränser', *Ny Dag*, 15 IX 1939.

2. AGGRESSION OF GERMANY AND THE SOVIET UNION

On 16 September, *Sydsvenska Dagbladet Snällposten* broke the news about specific territorial claims that were raised against Poland by the USSR during the talks in Berlin with the representatives of the Third Reich.[104] The correspondent Sven Tillge-Rasmussen reported from London that nobody doubted any longer that Russia was supporting the other side and that the only question that remained unclear was 'is Russia going to engage militarily in order to help the Germans?'[105] On 15 September, *Stockholms-Tidningen* received a letter from one of its reporters in Berlin, Christer Jäderlund, who quoted the opinions of the highest government officials in Germany stating that the fourth partition of Poland was already a fact and that talks on the question of the future Polish–Soviet border were finally coming to an end.[106] The editors of *Social-Demokraten* wrote on 16 September that they had no illusions that Stalin was in the middle of preparations to enter Poland. This was evident not only because of the high concentration of troops near the border but also by the propaganda campaign which attacked the minority policy of the Polish government. Somewhat puzzling was the position of the Western Allies, which in the light of their obligations towards Poland, should have declared war on the Soviet Union.[107] According to a commentator for *Social-Demokraten*, the active side in this war was the USSR, which would probably launch a military offensive towards the Turkish straits, and possibly an attack in the territory of Central Asia. One of the experts writing for *Sydsvenska Dagbladet Snällposten* was also certain that the Soviet Union, which mobilized 4 million soldiers, was only waiting for the right moment to enter Poland.[108] *Göteborgs Handels- och Sjöfarts-Tidning* reported news from the BBC that an agreement between Hitler and Stalin would turn Poland into a small buffer state.[109]

Speculation in the press was confirmed by the Swedish Envoy to Moscow, Wilhelm Winther, who reported on 13 September that the Soviet authorities had ordered wide-ranging military mobilization. About half a million men were recruited and joined the existing army of one million soldiers.[110]

---

[104] 'Ryssland anmäler anspråk i Polen', *Sydsvenska Dagbladet Snällposten*, 16 IX 1939.
[105] S. Tillge-Rasmussen, 'Tysk-ryska samtalen hade pågått länge', *Sydsvenska Dagbladet Snällposten*, 16 IX 1939.
[106] Ch. Jäderlund, 'Hur tyskarna tänka sig Polens fjärde delning', *Stockholms-Tidningen*, 16 IX 1939.
[107] 'Sovjet och Polen', *Social-Demokraten*, 16 IX 1939.
[108] 'Dubbel omfattning i andra omgången', *Sydsvenska Dagbladet Snällposten*, 16 IX 1939.
[109] 'Stalin vill ej sända ryska armén in i Polen', *Göteborgs Handels- och Sjöfarts-Tidning*, 16 IX 1939.
[110] RA, UD 1920 års dossiersystem, HP 1, vol. 516, letter by Swedish Envoy to Moscow W. Winther to Minister of Foreign Affairs R. Sandler, Moscow, 13 IX 1939.

According to Winther, who was carefully following the tone of the Soviet press, by 10 September comments had already appeared on the need to secure the borders because of the Polish–German war. At the same time, the Soviet Deputy of People's Commissioner for Foreign Affairs Vladimir Potemkin gave assurances that the USSR had no plans concerning the Baltic States. Deputy of People's Commissioner Solomon Lozovsky, however, convinced Winther that the Soviet authorities had no intention to interject into the internal affairs of Poland and were not concerned with protests by Ukrainian civilians in eastern Galicia, about whom the Soviet press wrote. As far as the 'rumours spread by the Swedish press on Russian plans to enter Poland were concerned – he described them as pure fantasy.' During their talks, Winther and the diplomats representing the Baltic States and Poland arrived at a joint conclusion that Stalin would not risk involvement in a military conflict with the Western Allies, which would happen in the event of Soviet aggression against any of the European neighbours of the USSR. However, in a report to his headquarters the Swedish envoy pointed out: 'This certainly does not mean that the position of the Soviet Union regarding this matter may not be changed.' Soviet representatives in Brussels declared that the Russian nation was far from supporting territorial changes in Europe, and constantly described the Germans as the worst enemy of the USSR.[111] Quite different was the message of Swedish Envoy Richert's report from his meeting with Ambassador of the USSR to Berlin, Aleksander Shkwarcew, appointed to the office on 3 September. When asked about the meaning of the Ribbentrop-Molotov Pact, the Soviet diplomat said that the arrangement was preparing the foundations for the future friendly relations between Germany and the Soviet Union and for the development of their political, economic and cultural ties. When it came to other matters he talked evasively and practically failed to take a stand on both specific commercial and credit agreements and Soviet plans regarding Poland.[112]

All speculation ceased with news about the Soviet aggression of 17 September. All daily newspapers announced that the Soviets had crossed the entire line of the Polish border. In this situation the resistance of the Poles was deemed pointless.[113] The *Nya Dagligt Allehanda* newspaper explained:

---

[111] RA, UD 1920 års dossiersystem, HP 39, vol. 1538, letter by Swedish Envoy to Brussels G. von Dardel to Minister of Foreign Affairs R. Sandler, Brussels, 13 IX 1939.
[112] RA, UD 1920 års dossiersystem, HP 39, vol. 1538, letter by Swedish Envoy to Berlin A. Richert to S. Söderblom, Berlin, 15 IX 1939.
[113] 'Rysk inmarsch i Polen', *Nya Dagligt Allehanda*, 17 IX 1939.

We know sufficiently much to understand that the crossing of the borders took place in agreement with Germany. It is also evident that the Russians have learned new methods to justify their invasion of Poland with a public ordering action aimed at seeing to the "Russian interests" in Poland and protecting Belarusian and Ukrainian minorities in Eastern Poland, "otherwise the government's escape would create a serious threat of chaos".

The author of the article admitted that the minority policy of the subsequent Polish governments was not always appropriate and that the Polish state was being weakened by the continuous ethnic conflicts. At the same time, he asked a rhetorical question about the situation of Belarusian and Ukrainian residents in the USSR, 'Is it really so certain that they are enjoying free will out there? Would the ethnic minorities residing in Poland like to swap places with the subjects of Stalin in the red Soviet state?'[114] An opinion journalist for *Svenska Dagbladet* wondered about the consequences of the Soviet intervention in Poland for the remaining part of Europe: 'It seems that we are the only ones who notice that Russia is again casting its grim shadow over Europe.'[115] More extensive reports and commentaries regarding the Soviet aggression started to appear in the press from 18 September.[116] *Social-Demokraten* published a statement by a leading activist and social democratic opinion journalist Zeth Höglund: 'What gradually starts to show is the true character of the German–Russian pact thanks to which, according to *Ny Dag*, Stalin has saved European peace and forced Hitler to retreat.' His comments on the justification of the Soviet intervention were cutting: 'We have found a partner in sophistry. Stalin is actually a student of Machiavelli, not of Marx, of Hitler – not Lenin.' Höglund made an optimistic prediction that when it comes to the defeated Poland the last word would be left to its Western allies, but at the same time he noted that if the Soviet Union joined the war on the German side the clash would be terrible.[117] An opinion journalist for *Sydsvenska Dagbladet Snällposten*, having compared Stalin, just like Höglund, to Machiavelli, made an emotional comment about the aggression of 17 September: 'The sphinx has now revealed his true intentions! The Russian army enters the arena to take part in the fourth partition of Poland, which, as everything

---

[114] 'Polens fjärde delning som krigsmål', *Stockholms-Tidningen*, 17 IX 1939.
[115] 'Rysslands skugga', *Svenska Dagbladet*, 17 IX 1939.
[116] 'Röda armen har anfallit Polen', *Social-Demokraten*, 18 IX 1939; 'Ryssarna attackera ort under tysk bombraid', *Social-Demokraten*, 18 IX 1939; 'Den ryska noten till diplomaterna', *Sydsvenska Dagbladet Snällposten*, 18 IX 1939; 'Polen bemöter Sovjets motiv', *Sydsvenska Dagbladet Snällposten*, 18 IX 1939; 'Sovjet måste värna egna intressen', *Göteborgs Handels- och Sjöfarts-Tidning*, 18 IX 1939.
[117] Z. Höglund, 'Sovjet vill dela bytet', *Social-Demokraten*, 18 IX 1939.

seems to indicate, was arranged, or at least prepared before the German army went to battle. This came as a surprise to all those who have forgotten that Russia also presents revisionist claims! [...] Russia prefers to play the role of jackal and snatch its prey after Polish resistance has been broken.'[118]

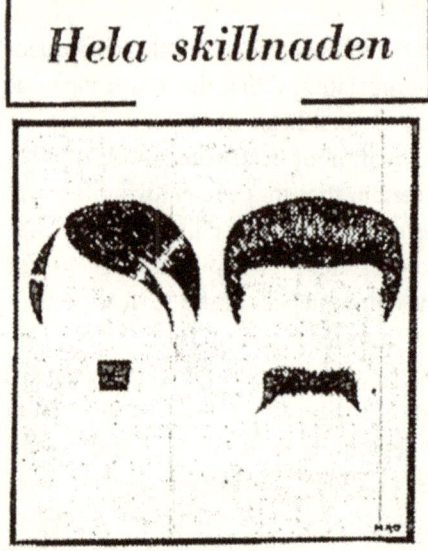

Illustration 3: 'Hela skillnaden' ['The only difference'], by Marianne, *Nya Dagligt Allehanda*, 20 September 1939.

A characteristic drawing equating Stalin with Hitler was published in *Nya Dagligt Allehanda*.[119] Likewise, *Social-Demokraten* compared the National Bolshevik Party to the Nazi Party.[120] Whereas, the communist *Ny Dag* contented itself with publishing, for several days in a row, quotations from the official Soviet notes on the collapse of Polish resistance and overwhelming chaos. Based on these quotations, the paper formulated serious accusations against Poland, considering it to be a fascist country oppressing ethnic minorities and above all a country that had, owing to the support from Great Britain and France, robbed Soviet Russia of Belarus and Ukraine in 1920.[121] The paper also stated that Winther, the Swedish Envoy to Moscow, received an assurance from the Soviet government that the neutrality of Sweden would

---

[118] 'Sfinxen röjer sig', *Sydsvenska Dagbladet Snällposten*, 18 IX 1939.
[119] 'Hela skillnaden', *Nya Dagligt Allehanda*, 20 IX 1939.
[120] 'Kombination', *Social-Demokraten*, 27 IX 1939.
[121] 'Röda armen skyddar Västukraina efter polska regeringens flykt', *Ny Dag*, 18 IX 1939; 'Polska regeringens bankrutt nödvändiggör Sovjets aktion', *Ny Dag*, 18 IX 1939; 'Röda arméns aktion', *Ny Dag*, 19 IX 1939; 'Röda arméns inmarsch', *Ny Dag*, 19 IX 1939; 'Rövartåget mot Sovjetunionen för 19 år sedan', *Ny Dag*, 20 IX 1939.

be respected, just as the neutrality of the other states of Scandinavia, the Baltic States and Romania.[122]

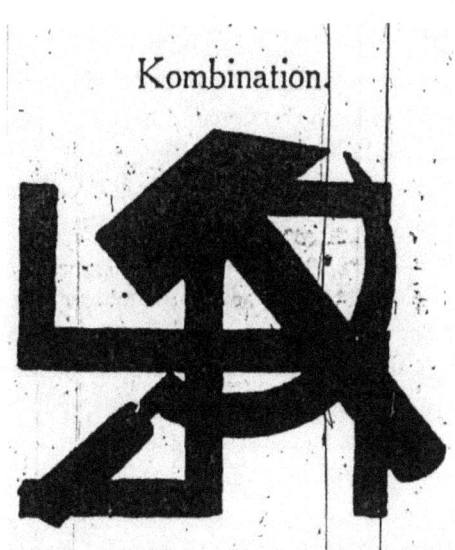

Illustration 4: 'Kombination' ['Combination'], *Social-Demokraten*, 27 IX 1939. The caption reads: 'Proposal for a new party logo for the Nazi-Communists'.

According to the commentator for *Göteborgs Handels- och Sjöfarts-Tidning*, the real situation was rather different. He thought that the involvement of the Soviet Union in the war complicated the situation of the neutral states and predicted that northern Europe could end up 'under a terrible pressure of turbulences,' both war-related and political, in connection with the rivalry of powers for the influences in the Baltic Sea region.[123] A lead article by another journalist published on the same day opened with the conclusion: 'Russian question mark has straightened up. It has turned into an exclamation mark.' However, it is surprising to read in further passages of the article that Stalin thwarted Hitler's plans to seize Ukraine and that the German dictator was forced to put a brave face on the matter. Equally surprising is the view that the Soviet army, in full combat readiness, was protecting the Baltic States against the German aggression. The opinion journalist of the journal which was well-known for its anti-fascist attitude clearly disregarded the threat

---

[122] 'Sovjet neutralt gentemot Sverige', *Ny Dag*, 18 IX 1939. For more information on this issue, see: 'Den ryska noten', *Nya Dagligt Allehanda*, 18 IX 1939.
[123] 'Rysslands inblandning försvårar de neutrala staternas läge', *Göteborgs Handels- och Sjöfarts-Tidning*, 18 IX 1939.

from the Soviet Union.¹²⁴ Meanwhile, a commentator of *Nya Dagligt Allehanda* stated: 'Most probably the partners have determined the demarcation line much earlier. It is not at all excluded that we shall now become the witnesses of fraternization between the Russian and German soldiers, which has already taken place in Poland during the First World War when the Bolsheviks surrendered Russia.'¹²⁵ A few days after the Soviet aggression against Poland, Swedish diplomat Gunnar Hägglöf noted that he considered that what had happened was horrendous because the cooperation between two so far deadly enemies, Nazi Germany and the Soviet Union, was as gloomy as it was ominous.¹²⁶

Colonel Karl-Axel Bratt, an expert for *Dagens Nyheter* on military affairs, asked his readers on 18 September whether following the Soviet attack there was any point in examining the strategic position of the Polish and German armies. He considered the campaign to be concluded in a strategic sense. As a matter of fact, according to his views, what happened on the front could be only described as tragedy not strategy, and this tragedy was only extended and speeded up by the Soviet invasion.¹²⁷ On the next day he announced the already outdated news that the Polish government was still residing in Kuty, near the Romanian border, which was nonetheless considered by him as a sign of Poland's defeat. As for the Soviet invasion, he added that even without this 'Russian shot to the head' the position of Poland was hopeless, but Stalin's intervention shortened the Poles' fight.¹²⁸ *Nya Dagligt Allehanda* in a short situational review entitled 'The Dying Poland' stated that 'in given circumstances we will not have to wait long for the collapse of Warsaw.'¹²⁹ Two days later the same analyst claimed that it was hard to predict how much longer the battles in Poland would continue.¹³⁰ Whereas, *Stockholms-Tidningen* reported: 'Perhaps it is too soon for us to announce that "everything has been lost besides soldierly honour",' but it followed from the description of the situation that the defeat of Poland was obvious.¹³¹ *Svenska Dagbladet* wrote: 'The closing act of the drama may not last long.'¹³² The resistance continued, but the Polish army kept fighting only in a small number of isolated

---

[124] 'Mellankommandepart', *Göteborgs Handels- och Sjöfarts-Tidning*, 18 IX 1939.
[125] H. S., 'Polska fälthären skingrad', *Nya Dagligt Allehanda*, 19 IX 1939.
[126] G. Hägglöf, *Möte med...*, p. 197.
[127] K. A. B[ratt], 'Den ryska invasionen', *Dagens Nyheter*, 18 IX 1939.
[128] K. A. B[ratt], 'Den polska arméns dödskamp', *Dagens Nyheter*, 19 IX 1939.
[129] H. S., 'Det döende Polen', *Nya Dagligt Allehanda*, 18 IX 1939.
[130] 'Ryska invasionen', *Nya Dagligt Allehanda*, 20 IX 1939.
[131] 'Polackernas kamp', *Stockholms-Tidningen*, 19 IX 1939.
[132] 'Slutakten', *Svenska Dagbladet*, 19 IX 1939.

locations.'[133] On 21 September Karl-Axel Bratt stated in *Dagens Nyheter*: 'the disintegration process is fully-fledged, but the Polish bravery is still erecting its memorial.' According to him this was due to be celebrated with at least a minute of silence. Although, he was critical about the government and Polish command, who had abandoned both the country and the remaining fighting soldiers.[134] For *Svenska Morgonbladet*, it was certain that Poland was losing its independence: 'The cry: the end of Poland – *Finis Poloniae*! which resounded more than once throughout Europe, is heard once again. All neutral countries are sad to hear this. A free nation is like a healthy part of the human body, an enslaved nation is withering and only half-alive.'[135] A commentator for *Svenska Dagbladet* turned his thoughts towards the August pact between Germany and Russia and wondered what else could have been arranged at the time between the two dictators: 'Could the Germans say no to the Moscow protectorate over the Baltic States and Finland, thereby putting a halt to the summer negotiations with the Western Allies?'[136] Meanwhile, a military expert highlighted the significance of the Soviet invasion which thwarted the hopes for continuing the resistance against the Germans and receiving support from the West.[137] The position of the Soviet Union was described most bluntly by the social-democratic and syndicalistic dailies. *Arbetaren* claimed that:

> Stalin's intention [...] was to perform the same imperialist expansion as the one that lies at the root of the German aggression. [...] This was easy to anticipate. Firstly, Stalin made it possible for Hitler to carry out the invasion. Then he weakened the Polish defence by concentrating the Russian army near the Russian–Polish border, engaging a substantial part of Polish military forces, thereby making it easy for Hitler to conduct his attack. Eventually, when Poland was fighting a life-and-death battle which brought it closer to death – not life – the noble, wonderful and brilliant Stalin chose the right moment to plunge a dagger into Poland's back. The remarkably talented leader of the world proletariat spoke and acted like a regular gangster who wielded political power. Stalin's official intention was to "protect" Belarusians and Ukrainians. He acted like Hitler, who placed the Czechs under his "protection" and later

---

[133] 'Ryssarna rycka fram i ilmarscher', *Svenska Dagbladet*, 20 IX 1939.
[134] K. A. Bratt, 'Det polska hjältemodet', *Dagens Nyheter*, 21 IX 1939.
[135] 'Finis Poloniæ-for denna gång', *Svenska Morgonbladet*, 18 IX 1939.
[136] 'Finis Poloniæ', *Svenska Dagbladet*, 18 IX 1939.
[137] 'Nådastöten', *Svenska Dagbladet*, 18 IX 1939.

deported and forced hundreds of thousands of them to slavish labour in Germany.[138]

In the commentaries of syndicalist journalists, Stalin was depicted as being no different to Hitler. They also highlighted only slight differences between the two totalitarian regimes: 'The fascist and the Bolshevik national totalitarianism are in all cases twins and both these regimes are the enemies of the socialist working class. It is only a matter of time before the workers understand this.'[139]

The communist daily newspaper *Ny Dag* claimed that the war between Germany and the Allies was an imperialist war and because of that it was necessary to avoid it.[140] The Soviet Union not only wanted to protect Belarusian and Ukrainian people, but also bring peace to the Polish people. John Garter (a pseudonym for Per Meurling) rejected Zeth Höglund's earlier claims, arguing in *Ny Dag* that 'the oppression of people by the landed gentry of Volhynia finally ended.'[141] *Ny Dag* attacked the social-democratic press on 25 September, accusing it of being engaged in British propaganda, which heralded the outbreak of war between democratic and fascist countries. This vision meant an attack on the Soviet Union, but, after all:

> We kept reading that people from the territories annexed by the Red Army were welcoming their liberators. We were reading that the units of the workers' guard were formed, that peasants were appointed as commissioners, that estates were divided and given away, that workers were taking control over the factories, that landowners, manufacturers and fascist officials were fleeing like crazy, fearing the wrath of the people, and that a red banner was raised before the fascist terror broke out.[142]

According to *Ny Dag*, Poland broke down because its people were not willing to defend their homeland that was controlled by the fascist government. In particular, ethnic minorities were considered to have no interest in doing so. It was stated: 'In the Soviet Union there are no ethnic minorities, only free

---

[138] 'Stalin avslöjar sig', *Arbetaren*, 18 IX 1939.
[139] Ibidem.
[140] N. Holmberg, 'Vår ställning till kriget', *Ny Dag*, 18 IX 1939.
[141] J. Garter, 'Den röda armén marscherar', *Ny Dag*, 22 IX 1939.
[142] H. H., 'Slå tillbaka splittrarna', *Ny Dag*, 25 IX 1939.

people.'[143] This version was consequently presented in successive publications devoted to the defeat of Poland.[144]

The final phase of the campaign

As early as on 19 September the first reviews of the campaign hit the newspapers. All analyses pointed to the same causes of the defeat of the Polish army: the speed of the German attack, the high mobility of the Germans owing to motorized units, the very poor strategic situation of Polish units which were excessively stretched out along the open borders, the lack of panzer divisions in the Polish army, the lack of support from France and Britain, and eventually the Soviet invasion. What was the subject of most severe criticism was that the Poles had trusted in receiving support from the Allies, overestimated their chances of success, showed excessive optimism and were poorly commanded. At the same time journalists highlighted that the Polish troops were known for their bravery and dedication.[145] Experts drew attention to the breakthrough achievements of the Germans in the sphere of warfare. They were the first to use, on an unprecedented scale, armoured and motorized panzer divisions, supported by numerous squadrons of fighter-bombers. The assumption that this type of weaponry would not perform well when confronted with the poor-quality roads of Poland proved spurious. Gösta Torelius, who had been a war correspondent during the time of the First World War, summed up the military campaign in Poland with the following words:

> The defeat of Poland somehow proves that in this century it is the machine that starts to dominate over the human being. Even so, it may not be left unmentioned that it was not only the inferiority of the Polish military equipment that contributed to the lightning victory of the Germans. [...] One valiant army has been defeated by an equally valiant counterpart – a better armed and more skilfully managed machine of war.'[146]

---

[143] 'Polska folkets väg till friheten', *Ny Dag*, 27 IX 1939.
[144] E. Karlsson, 'Den polska katastrofen', *Ny Dag*, 26 X 1939; J. Garter, 'Polsk rapsodi', *Ny Dag*, 8 I 1940.
[145] A. Gyllenkrok, 'Det tyska blixtkriget och Polens fjärde delning', *Aftonbladet*, 28 IX 1939; G. Torelius, 'Det polska blixtkriget', *Sydsvenska Dagbladet Snällposten*, 3 X 1939; 'Erfarenheter från kriget i Polen', *Sydsvenska Dagbladet Snällposten*, 25 X 1939.
[146] G. Torelius, 'Det polska blixtkriget', *Sydsvenska Dagbladet Snällposten*, 4 X 1939. The attitude that was generally dominant was admiration for the German war machine, and at times even its glorification. See for example the evaluation of commentaries by Colonel Axel

The Swedish consul, Carl Herslow, who was very sympathetic towards the Poles, sought the reasons for the Polish army's quick defeat, which took place despite a third of the national income having been allocated to its support for over a decade and despite it boasting very good soldiers, in the highly disadvantageous strategic location of Poland, German superiority in the size and number of panzer units and fighter-bomber squadrons, as well as in the Soviet invasion.[147] According to other journalists the Polish defence would have been successful with immediate support from Great Britain and France. In such a case, the Poles would not have found it difficult to hold off the German army, of which a considerable part would have to be relocated to the western front.[148] Nonetheless, the clear majority of commentators considered the very fact that the Polish had been expecting such support to be a mistake. Could the Polish experiences during the campaign be of any use to the Swedes? The commentators highlighted the crucial importance of using modern weaponry on the battlefield and demanded the mechanization of the Swedish army and the advancement of military aviation.[149]

Aftonbladet claimed that the conclusion of the campaign was the German–Soviet victory parade in the city of Brest on 22 September. The paper regarded the town to be a historically symbolic location and recalled that it was there that Suvorov had defeated the Poles before the Third Partition and where peace was reached between the Central Powers and Soviet Russia in 1918.[150] A military analyst for *Svenska Dagbladet* claimed that from the cultural, economic and ethnological perspectives the placement of the border along the line of the Narev-Vistula-San rivers had been a detestable act, but also that these particular factors were attributed little importance in Europe at the time.[151] Meanwhile, Berlin correspondents for *Dagens Nyheter* and *Svenska Dagbladet* reported about the previously determined border that ran along the Vistula River, as well as about the German plan to form a tiny 'Polish buffer state.'[152]

Gyllenkrok published in the *Dagens Nyheter* J. Torbacke, *Dagens Nyheter och demokratins kris 1937–1946. Genom stormar till seger*, Stockholm 1972, p. 82.
[147] C. Herslow, 'Tysklands luftvapen från början överlägset', *Sydsvenska Dagbladet Snällposten*, 9 X 1939.
[148] 'Erfarenheter från kriget i Polen', *Sydsvenska Dagbladet Snällposten*, 25 X 1939.
[149] Ibidem; S. Bergelin, 'Krigserfarenheter', *Göteborgs Handels- och Sjöfarts-Tidning*, 29 IX 1939.
[150] A. Gyllenkrok, 'Det tyska blixtkriget och Polens fjärde delning', *Aftonbladet*, 28 IX 1939.
[151] 'Polsk epilog', *Svenska Dagbladet*, 23 IX 1939.
[152] 'Provisoriska gränsen går genom Warszawa', *Svenska Dagbladet*, 23 IX 1939; 'Tysk-ryska gränsen dras genom Warszawa', *Dagens Nyheter*, 23 IX 1939.

2. AGGRESSION OF GERMANY AND THE SOVIET UNION

An opinion journalist for *Social-Demokraten* claimed that the Russian invasion added to the tragedy of the Polish nation, though he did not make any prejudgements about the future fate of the inhabitants of the territories which were included in the Soviet empire: 'They have already experienced that living under the shadow of Soviet bayonets is not something one could envy. One can only hope that their fate would not be equally difficult as that of the Poles and the Jews who are staying on the territories occupied by the Germans.'[153] What was certain, however, was that these people were subjected to severe indoctrination. *Dagens Nyheter* broke the news about the transports of half a million portraits of Marx, Engels, Stalin and Lenin, 1.4 million books and brochures in Ukrainian, 10 thousand gramophone records and Soviet films which were shown immediately in cinemas.[154]

Stockholms-Tidningen speculated about the next possible move by Stalin, who for the first time managed to push the borders of his state further to the west: 'It is understandable that the Baltic States and Romania are uneasy. Russia again showed its ambition to come into possession of a year-round port on the Baltic Sea and Moscow never accepted the incorporation of Bessarabia into Romania.' Also, the idea of creating a pan-Slavic empire and to exercise hegemony over the Balkans was reintroduced. The war, at least in the immediate future, would progress, 'The Germans against the Western Allies, the USSR against [...] its weaker neighbours.'[155] According to a journalist for *Svenska Dagbladet*, the Soviet invasion made a greater impression on international public opinion than the catastrophe which was brought to the Polish nation. Stalin established the border with Slovakia and Hungary. The concentration of Soviet military forces near the Estonian border heralded the conclusion of 'the remarkably successful Baltic status quo that Sweden and Finland made use of for two idyllic decades.'[156]

Dagens Nyheter, expressing anxiety and uncertainty, commented on the increasing military mobilization in the USSR: 'What for? After all the Soviet Union is completely unthreatened by Romania or the Baltic States.' There was speculation that perhaps the cooperation with Germany would soon come to an end. The worst scenario of the Soviet expansion in the Baltic Sea region was obviously ignored.[157] Commentators in *Social-Demokraten* seemed convinced that the division of Poland had been introduced as early

---

[153] 'Minoriteterna i Polen', *Social-Demokraten*, 23 IX 1939.
[154] 'En miljon Marxbilder till Ukraina', *Dagens Nyheter*, 24 IX 1939.
[155] 'Bolsjevismens marsch västerut', *Stockholms-Tidningen*, 24 IX 1939.
[156] 'Sovjet flyttar västerut', *Svenska Dagbladet*, 24 IX 1939.
[157] 'Ryssland i förgrunden', *Dagens Nyheter*, 26 IX 1939.

as in August 1939 and that Stalin had only pretended that the agreement with the Western Allies was important to him.[158] A question was asked whether the Soviet–German cooperation would continue, and if so in what form.

On 22 September Attaché Juhlin-Dannfelt, referring to information obtained from Colonel Mellenthin, head of the group of Swedish military attachés to Berlin, passed the news to his headquarters that the Narev-Vistula-San river line had been agreed between the German and Soviet authorities some time earlier, but the final decision regarding the course of the border had not yet been made. He also learned that at that moment the issue of the possible restoration of the Polish state, even in the form of a rump state, had not yet been examined, summing up, 'such question is not yet on the agenda.'[159]

On 24 September, *Dagens Nyheter* published an article covering foreign and internal policy of Poland during the reign of Piłsudski. The article, illustrated by two photographs of Piłsudski and one of Hitler standing in one of the Kielce churches in front of a monumental plaque commemorating Piłsudski, sounded like the obituary of the Second Polish Republic.[160]

The end of September passed by with announcements concerning the poor defence of Warsaw and expectation of surrender.[161] The brutality of German attacks in the closing phase of the fight for the capital was justified with the intention of conducting the fastest possible occupation of the city before the arrival of the Soviets. According to Colonel Bratt, it was impossible to explain such conduct to the public.[162] The capitulation of Warsaw was unanimously considered by the military commentators to be the symbolic conclusion of the campaign, even though on 2 October the fall of the last Polish bastion was noted in the Hel Peninsula.[163]

The Swedish dailies almost immediately speculated on the possible course of the German–Soviet border. Based on the reports from the front, news broke about the line along Białystok-Brest-Lviv.[164] Rumours poured in from Berlin that the Germans were attempting to take over oil fields near Drohobych and that areas around Warsaw and Łódź were to be placed under

---

[158] 'Omkastningen i Östeuropa', *Social-Demokraten*, 28 IX 1939.
[159] RA, UD 1920 års dossiersystem, HP 2, vol. 717, letter by the Swedish Military Attaché to Berlin Colonel C. Juhlin-Dannfelt to the head of intelligence, Berlin, 22 IX 1939. [The original manuscript is erroneously dated to November]
[160] H. M., 'Marskalk Pilsudskis Polen', *Dagens Nyheter*, 24 IX 1939.
[161] 'Budet om kapitulation stoppade ej striderna', *Stockholms-Tidningen*, 29 IX 1939; A. Kronika, 'Det brinnande Warszawa ett ohyggligt skådespel', *Sydsvenska Dagbladet Snällposten*, 29 IX 1939.
[162] K. A. Bratt, 'Warszawas vita flagga', *Dagens Nyheter*, 28 IX 1939.
[163] 'Halvön Hela kapitulerar', *Stockholms-Tidningen*, 2 X 1939.
[164] 'Polens fjärde delning', *Svenska Dagbladet*, 20 IX 1939.

the joint German–Soviet protectorate.[165] News that Stalin wanted to scoop up more than the Germans expected also rolled in and that the new border was to be similar to that of 1914.[166] The latest reports from the territories being annexed by the Soviet army revealed details about, among others things, barricades in the streets of Vilnius and the mass plundering of Polish property. The effectiveness of the Soviet propaganda was reflected in the descriptions of the interactions between Soviet troops and locals. This vision of the initial phase of Soviet occupation presented by *Ny Dag* is not surprising: 'Both adults and children embraced and kissed the soldiers of the Red Army and their officers',[167] 'young ladies were giving them flowers' and peasants were crying: 'Long live comrade Stalin!'[168]

Remarkable, however, were the reports – to a large extent similar, but at the same time lacking the enthusiasm which was characteristic of the Communist Party of Sweden – published in other dailies, for instance in *Dagens Nyheter*: 'After a short time the main streets of the city [Vilnius] filled with tanks, armoured cars and military units. The infantry and cavalry arrived after a few hours. Polish soldiers were disarmed and released. They were soon back in the streets unarmed and without their shoulder straps and cockades. At street corners there appeared Russian military posts and one could notice women chatting with the soldiers and laughing. The windows of many houses were adorned with peculiar red flags. People were cutting red and white Polish flags in two, and displaying only the red halves.[169]

Göteborgs Handels- och Sjöfarts-Tidning on 27 September stated: 'Moscow has just become the hub of European diplomacy.'[170] This was to be confirmed by a simultaneous visit to the capital of the USSR by the Estonian Minister of Foreign Affairs Kaarel Selter, head of the Turkish diplomacy Sükrü Saradjoglu and Joachim von Ribbentrop. According to Swedish observers, these talks indicated that Stalin was planning to launch an expansion to the Baltic Sea region and the Balkans. On the following day the same newspaper published the opinion that 'Hitler and his comrades are fully dependant on the good will of Moscow' and that it was Stalin who became the main beneficiary of the agreement of 23 August, because the Germans had lost their hegemony over the Baltic Sea region and their access to the deposits of oil in South-

---

[165] 'Polenkonferens Tyskland-Sovjet inledd i Moskva', *Dagens Nyheter*, 21 IX 1939.
[166] B. Svahnström, 'Vad blir Polens öde? Ryssarna får mer i Polen än man väntat i Berlin', *Svenska Dagbladet*, 22 IX 1939.
[167] 'Rödarmisterna hälsas med leverop för sovjetmakten', *Ny Dag*, 21 IX 1939.
[168] 'När Väst-Ukraina led under polskt förtryck', *Ny Dag*, 22 IX 1939.
[169] 'Stadens fängelser öppnades, polska förråden plundrades', *Dagens Nyheter*, 20 IX 1939.
[170] 'Situationen', *Göteborgs Handels- och Sjöfarts-Tidning*, 27 IX 1939.

Eastern Poland. What is more, the commentator for the paper claimed that Germany had to reckon with the Communists' considerable influence.[171] Similar was the role of Moscow perceived by a commentator for *Svenska Dagbladet*, who noticed:

> [Stalin], in striving to meet his political goals, does a great job of imitating the methods – which were earlier adopted by Hitler – based on evoking paralysing fear and whose violence could be compared to a clap of thunder. Unfortunately, as one may expect, this strategy would be now turned against the Baltic States. What had become impossible to realize during the coup d'état on 1 December 1924 [...] may be now achieved by means of more effective methods. [...] The moment of the opening of the tragedy of all the states bordering with the Baltic Sea becomes increasingly evident and this tragedy may be entitled: *Stalin ante portas!*[172]

The Berlin correspondent for *Svenska Dagbladet*, Bertil Svahnström, wrote the article 'Are Russia and Germany dividing the Baltic States into pieces?' He reported that Estonia and Latvia were to be incorporated in to the Soviet Union, and Lithuania in to Germany.[173] The Swedish journalist most probably learned of the details of the secret protocol of the arrangement of 23 August. In turn, *Göteborgs Handels- och Sjöfarts-Tidning* predicted that [Europe] would have to count not only on changes within the Baltic Sea region, but also in the Balkans.[174] An entry in *Arbetaren* lay forth the love between Russia and Germany and concluded: 'Stalin supports Fascism – and this is a fact.'[175] *Svenska Morgonbladet*'s predictions for Soviet territorial acquisitions were the most far-fetched. It claimed that Stalin would annex all the Baltic States, Bessarabia and take control of all the Turkish straits: 'The table cloth has already been laid, the only thing left is to serve the meal. We can only hope that the Nordic States would not be subjected to any gruesome secret agreements.'[176] *Arbetaren* wrote: 'The pact between Stalin and Hitler is not an ordinary pact of non-aggression. It represents the striking of a bargain between the twin regimes of two totalitarian states and sealing their friendship directed against liberal-capitalist democracies.' The journalists also lamented the following fact: 'the clear majority of workers from Western

---

[171] 'Idag', *Göteborgs Handels- och Sjöfarts-Tidning*, 28 IX 1939.
[172] 'Stalin ante portas', *Svenska Dagbladet*, 28 IX 1939.
[173] B. Svahnström, 'Ryssland och Tyskland dela Baltikum?', *Svenska Dagbladet*, 30 IX 1939.
[174] 'Situationen', *Göteborgs Handels- och Sjöfarts-Tidning*, 30 IX 1939.
[175] 'Rysk-tysk kärlek', *Arbetaren*, 3 X 1939.
[176] 'Polens delning och dess följder', *Svenska Morgonbladet*, 30 IX 1939.

Europe have no idea that the revolutionary Soviet system is nothing more than dictatorship of the Bolsheviks.[177]

Meanwhile, Soviet propaganda was working well. On 27 September, in *Folkets hus* in Stockholm, a public debate was held about the Soviet policy, organized by communist and social-democratic youth organisations. The representative of the Communists, newspaper editor Sven Landin argued that the Soviet army had liberated Eastern Poland. He called the authorities of the Western Allies, together with the government of Poland, the perpetrators of war in Europe. And as for Hitler, he never mentioned his name. These views were contested by editor Torsten Nilsson, who represented the Social Democrats.[178] But *Ny Dag* continued to report that ethnic conflicts in the territories controlled by the Soviet army were solved based on the principle of self-determination, 'at least fifteen million people have been freed from the burden of Fascism' and 'the Soviet authorities, as usual, act in the name of peace.' According to the editors of *Ny Dag*, in connection with constant pressures from Germany and the Western Allies, the best solution for Sweden was to conclude the peace agreement and to accept the liquidation of Poland.[179]

The fate of Swedish diplomats in Warsaw

Swedish diplomats in Warsaw did not send much information to Sweden about the situation in Poland during the campaign. Although, several reports by Envoy Joen Lagerberg are known about. Initially, on the basis of these reports the conclusion was drawn that 'the mood is rather grim but so far there are no signs of panic.'[180] On 1 September, Lagerberg paid a visit to Deputy Minister Jan Szembek and proposed that he would organize a system allowing for constant telegraphic communication between Poland and other countries via Stockholm.[181] The diplomats also discussed the evacuation of Polish diplomatic and consular employees from Germany, which on the request of Poland was to be taken care of by Sweden. An agreement to this

---

[177] 'Den bruna, svarta och röda fascismen', *Arbetaren*, 3 X 1939.
[178] 'Röda arméns krig i Polen debatteras', *Social-Demokraten*, 28 IX 1939.
[179] G. J., 'Fred i öster', *Ny Dag*, 30 IX 1939.
[180] RA, UD 1920 års dossiersystem, HP 39, vol. 1538, note from 9 IX 1939.
[181] The aforementioned telegraphic connection was indeed established on the first day of the war. The Polish ambassador to London wrote in his journal that the Polish Embassy in London contacted Warsaw via telephone in the morning of 1 September. See: E. Raczynski, *W sojuszniczym Londynie. Dziennik ambasadora Edwarda Raczyńskiego 1939–1945*, 3rd edition, London 1997, pp. 37–38.

effect was signed in the last days of August.[182] The Germans requested a similar protection of German citizens in Poland from the Dutch.

In the evening of 4 September, a decision was made that the Polish Ministry of Foreign Affairs, which had been operating as normal, would be quickly evacuated on the following day, 5 September, to Nałęczów and Kazimierz on the Vistula.[183] The prospect of an evacuation had been conceived of several months prior to the outbreak of war and some preparations were already in place to make it easier. The actual process, though, was largely improvised. Most importantly, there was no contact between the individual units of the ministry, and the diplomatic corps was isolated from the government and Minister Beck. According to Sven Grafström's report, when Lagerberg was to make an independent decision whether or not to evacuate, his feelings of confusion were obvious: 'Having received the telegram [...] that he was to make the decision on his own, poor Lagerberg broke down and I felt very sorry for him.'[184] Eventually he proceeded with the evacuation. The diplomatic mission in Warsaw remained under Grafström's supervision.

As early as 6 September it was decided that, in the face of unfavourable developments at the front, the ministry staff and foreign diplomats would be relocated further away to Volhynia, and then to Kremenets [Polish name: Krzemieniec], where the evacuees arrived on 8 September.[185] Minister Beck, who together with the entire government was staying in Brest, had joined them by the night of 10 September. The following day the town was bombarded by the Germans. Part of the diplomatic corps, fearing for their safety, demanded they be evacuated to Romania. Lagerberg was not particularly visible. He neither initiated further evacuations nor did he support protests by other diplomats about neglecting anti-raid procedures. There is no confirmation either that he took a stand on the eventually criticised plan of a joint protest at the German attacks on civilian targets. Another stage of the evacuation of the Polish Ministry of Foreign Affairs towards the Romanian border, to Zalishchyky, was ordered on 14 September. Next, Beck directed the diplomatic corps to Kosovo and the staff to Kuty. Following the arrival in Kosovo, it transpired that the quarters were already occupied by the Ministry of Military Affairs. Part of the corps decided to remain in Kuty, whereas a larger group,

---

[182] J. Szembek, *Diariusz wrzesień–grudzień 1939*, compiled by B. Grzeloński, Warszawa 1989, p. 20.
[183] *Historia dyplomacji polskiej*, vol. 5: 1939–1945, ed. B. Grzeloński, Warszawa 1999, p. 10.
[184] S. Grafström, *Anteckningar 1938–1944*, p. 79.
[185] Z. Nagórski, *Wojna w Londynie*, Paris 1966, p. 19. The author reminded that in Nałęczów, which was one of the places where the evacuees stopped on their way, Lagerberg stayed at his mother's house.

after the bombardment of Zalishchyky, crossed the border in to Romania on 15 September.[186] Lagerberg was part of this group, and he stopped in Chernivtsi. Straight after his arrival in to Bucharest, Lagerberg set off by train to Berlin. From Grafström's report we know that Lagerberg was shocked by the air-raids inflicted by the Germans on the defenceless civilians.[187]

Lagerberg, in his letters to Staffan Söderblom, Head of Political department of the Swedish Ministry of Foreign Affairs, described how he organized the work of the legation in the extreme conditions during the bombardments of the city in the first days of the war. He often compared the dramatic events he witnessed to his experiences in France from the First World War, when he was also a passive observer. Based on these experiences Lagerberg distanced himself from the military announcements, especially those from Germany. Nonetheless, on 10 September he became aware of the defeat of the Polish army and, despite the immense scale of the defeat, admired the remarkably high level of discipline and order among the Polish soldiers. Lagerberg, whilst cut off from reliable sources of information, noted down views he heard in conversations with other diplomats. In the first days of the war he was in high spirits. Over time though, as the living conditions gradually worsened during the hasty evacuation, depression and sarcasm replaced his optimism.[188]

Following his departure from the capital of Poland, Grafström, together with the greater part of the Swedish colony and diplomatic corps, reached Berlin on 21 September, right before the German army's final storm. The only ones left in the Swedish legation were the staff members of the Swedish–Polish Chamber of Commerce, Hilding Molander with his wife, the long-standing typist, Margit Vingquist, and Per Olof Silfverskiöld from *Svenska Kullagerfabriken AB* (Swedish Ball Bearing Factory AB or *SKF*). At first they put a lot of effort into convincing the Poles to stop converting the building of the Swedish mission into a hospital, and then in to dissuading the Germans from turning it in to a military quarters. Eventually, on 2 October, they received confirmation that the building would not be occupied by the army or by the police.[189] Diplomatic accounts contained no mention of the participation of the Swedes

---

[186] *Historia dyplomacji polskiej*, vol. 5, p. 13.
[187] S. Grafström, *Anteckningar 1938–1944*, p. 134. See also: Z. Nagórski, *Wojna...*, p. 23. The author recalled meeting Lagerberg in Chernivtsi on 17 September: 'What struck me was a change in his behaviour: he seemed cold and indifferent – no sign whatsoever of the kindness he showed before. Times have changed'.
[188] P. Jaworski, *"Rapporter" från det svenska sändebudet i Warszawa Joen Lagerberg i september 1939*, 'Acta Sueco-Polonica', nr 12/13 (2003–2005), Uppsala 2006, pp. 217–234.
[189] RA, UD 1920 års dossiersystem, R 20, vol. 565, copy of report by H. Molander for the Swedish Envoy to Berlin A. Richert, Warsaw, 2 X 1939.

in the warfare of September 1939. Hence the article by Anders Jobs, published in *Sydsvenska Dagbladet Snällposten* and presenting the story of a young Swede who was surprised by the war in Gdynia, was considered a sensation. The twenty-year-old seaman from Blekinge did not manage to flee from Poland on 1 September and, as he said: 'The only thing I could do was to enlist, more or less "voluntarily", to the auxiliary units which were being mobilized.' Having done so, he encountered no linguistic barrier, because he found himself surrounded by marines who had previously served on Swedish ships. The situation with arms and uniforms was worse. The army had an insufficient stock of equipment and he had to manage without it. The young man witnessed the annexation of Gdynia by German soldiers, whom he remembered rather fondly. This could not be said of his encounters with the police and the Gestapo. He mentioned hearing the salvos of firing squads executing the defenders of Gdynia.[190] Unfortunately there are no further sources to confirm that this press material was anything other than a hoax.

Representation of Polish interests by Sweden in Germany

Representation of interests of a country in a state of war by a neutral country is common. Sweden played such role as early as in the 19th century (its first mission involved the defence of Italian interests in Austria in the 1860s), and during the First World War, on fifteen occasions. At the time, particularly for this purpose, the Ministry of Foreign Affairs established the B Division (*B-avdelningen*) with around a hundred employees.[191] The appointment procedures and the powers of the welfare state were not defined precisely, but the foundations for such activities during the Second World War were laid by the Geneva Convention of 1929 which introduced many regulations in this respect. In general, it had been established that the representatives of a country-guardian were to remain officials of their homeland and carry out a mission of good services. They were also to act as intermediaries in the transmission of news, documents and financial assets, as well as to supervise the treatment of prisoners of war.[192] The mission was paid by the government, by whom it was requested.

---

[190] A. Jobs, '*Svensktalande* kompanier sattes upp i Gdynia!', *Sydsvenska Dagbladet Snällposten*, 20 IX 1939.
[191] B. Åkerrén, 'Schweden als Schutzmacht' [in:] *Schwedische und Schweizerische Neutralität im Zweiten Weltkrieg*, ed. R. L. von Bindschedler, H. R. Kurz, W. M. Carlgren, S. Carlsson, Basel 1985, pp. 112–144.
[192] See: M. Flemming, *Jeńcy wojenni: studium prawno-historyczne*, Warszawa 2000, pp. 186–190.

2. AGGRESSION OF GERMANY AND THE SOVIET UNION

When the Second World War broke out, the B Division was re-established in Stockholm. Before the war, Poland had already requested that the Swedish government represent its interests in Germany and Italy in the event of the outbreak of war. Talks regarding this matter were initiated relatively late – in the last days of August. The final approval was granted to the Polish Ministry of Foreign Affairs on 29 August 1939. Did this act have a political dimension? Choosing Sweden was certainly dictated by hope for its friendly attitude and consistent defence of Polish interests. What is more, a country with whom Poland would engage in military conflict was to be banned from asking Sweden for a similar service. Regardless, by 3 September, the Germans had done just that, asking Sweden to represent their interests in France and their colonies, namely one of Poland's allies.[193] Several days later the Swedes agreed to represent Germany in Egypt and South Africa in Germany.[194] A balance in treatment by the Swedish diplomacy could be said to be evident from then on. As the war spread to other countries, Sweden was asked on many occasions to represent the interests of both sides. Requests were made in the spring of 1941, when the Third Reich threatened the Balkans. The Swedish government then agreed to protect the interests of Germany in Greece, the interests of the Netherlands in Hungary and the interests of Hungary in Great Britain (from 9 April 1941 onwards). Later on, with every subsequent act of aggression, the number of countries asking for assistance grew. Protocols from the sessions of the Swedish government show that Sweden was asked as many as seventy-eight times.[195] As number of European countries left untouched by German, Italian or Soviet aggression became smaller, so too did the chances of finding a neutral representative. Sweden was still available to fill this role, however. From 1941 onwards, it had already become evident that the Swedes sometimes assumed the role of intermediaries between the

---

[193] RA, Kabinettet/UD Huvudarkivet, Statsrådsprotokoll, serie A3A, vol. 106, Protokoll över utrikesdepartementsärenden, Stockholm, 3 IX 1939.
[194] Ibidem, Protokoll över utrikesdepartementsärenden, Stockholm, 6 IX 1939.
[195] RA, Kabinettet/UD Huvudarkivet, Statsrådsprotokoll, serie A3A, vol. 110, Protokoll över utrikesdepartementsärenden, Stockholm, 9 IV, 25 VI, 28 VI, 31 VII, 30 VIII, 19 IX, 10 X, 21 XI, 12 XII, 19 XII 1941 r.; vol. 112, Protokoll över utrikesdepartementsärenden, 16 I, 6 II, 27 II, 6 III, 27 III, 17 IV, 30 IV, 8 V, 22 V, 29 V, 13 XI 1942 r.; vol. 114, Protokoll över utrikesdepartementsärenden, 29 I, 19 XI, 3 XII 1943 r.; vol. 116, Protokoll över utrikesdepartementsärenden, 28 I, 4 II, 11 II, 2 VI, 30 VI, 15 VII, 12 VIII, 14 IX, 30 IX, 6 X, 17 XI, 24 XI 1944 r.; vol. 118, Protokoll över utrikesdepartementsärenden, 19 I, 23 III, 4 V, 25 V, 8 VI, 31 VIII 1945 r. One of Swedish authors calculated that, in total, in the period between the 19th century and 1985 Sweden defended the interests of 28 foreign countries 114 times. As he noted, Great Britain and USA had never been included in this group, see: B. Åkerrén, 'Schweden als Schutzmacht' [in:] *Schwedische und Schweizerische Neutralität im Zweiten Weltkrieg*, red. R.L. von Bindschedler, H. R. Kurz, W. M. Carlgren, S. Carlsson, Basel 1985, p. 116.

fighting sides, for example, representing the interests of the USSR in Slovakia (from 25 June 1941) as well as of Denmark and Finland (from 28 June 1941) in the USSR. Similar cases include acting as representative between Finland and Germany (from 14 September 1944), Argentina and Bulgaria, Romania and Hungary (government decisions of 4 and 11 February and 2 June 1944), Finland and Hungary (from 30 September 1944), Finland and Japan (from 30 September 1944), Japan and Romania (17 November 1944), Japan and Bulgaria (24 November 1944), Japan and Denmark (25 May and 8 June 1945) and Japan and the USSR (31 August 1945). The B Division's activity was extended to include continents outside of Europe. By the third year of the war, it was insignificant whether countries had requested such representation in advance. Towards the end of the war, the decision by the government to represent both sides could be made during more than one session. Several countries submitted requests after their military opponent, yet they were accepted. This proves that representation of interests in 1939 was quite different in the following years when the opportunities for a country-guardian's successful actions diminished. These were virtually restricted to maintaining contact between enemy countries through neutral Sweden.

The Poles were counting primarily on the safe evacuation of embassy and consulate staff, as well as on securing both national and private property. The outbreak of the war meant the liquidation of the Polish Embassy in Berlin and the liquidation of 16 Consulates scattered across Germany. The evacuation of Embassy staff began as late as 3 September, following the news that staff at the German Embassy in Warsaw had left Poland. According to the agreement of August 1939, the Swedish diplomacy took over the representation of interests of Polish citizens in Germany. Józef Lipski entrusted the care of embassy buildings and all the consulates to the Swedish Legation in Berlin.

Consulate staff located in northern and central Germany were interned in Hamburg, and staff in southern Germany were detained in Vienna. When the news broke that the German consular corps had evacuated itself from Poland, on 13–14 September the staff who were interned in Hamburg moved to Denmark, and those in Vienna fled to Hungary. Jerzy Warchałowski, Consul General to Königsberg was held in Germany for a year. His colleagues, Deputy Consul General to Królewiec Witold Winiarski and Consul to Allenstein (Olsztyn) Bogdan Jałowiecki were murdered. The entire staff of the Consulate General of the Republic of Poland in the Free City of Gdańsk were arrested. Only after several days of physical and mental harassment, were they freed and by 6 September had reached Kaunas.

Initially, the role of head of the reactivated B Division was passed on to Johan Beck-Friis, whereas Carl Petersen was assigned to the Swedish Legation in Berlin as B Division's representative for the protection of Polish citizens. Regarding this activity the institution employed officials from Polish consulates, which were in the process of liquidation.[196] On 15 September the division was moved to the building of the Consulate General of the Republic of Poland in Berlin.

Among the interventions carried out by the Swedish diplomacy, one in particular deserves special attention, namely the efforts of Arvid Richert in the release of Poles interned in Królewiec and the Free City of Gdańsk. The latter case was also involved property confiscated by the Germans. Through the Swedish Consul to Gdańsk, those Poles in the direst financial situations received, secretly and unofficially, three thousand German marks a month.[197] Buildings that were left for use by Polish consular representatives in the territory of Germany were either rented out or their lease agreements were terminated. Anything that could be moved as well as archives were taken over by the Swedish Legation in Berlin or by Swedish consulates.[198]

The Germans had apprehended nearly 1200 Poles in total, but within a week only about one hundred remained under arrest. Petersen also reported that some Polish citizens sent to regular concentration camps where German citizens were detained for similar offences. He did not see any possibility for Sweden to intervene in these cases.[199] Towards the end of October Petersen was permitted to inspect a prisoner-of-war camp nearby Kielce. The Swede claimed that the day-to-day life in the camp was virtually the same as that in military barracks, that prisoner morale was high, and that the release of prisoners, due to the demand for manpower in agriculture, was probably about to happen.[200] Tolerable conditions were also present in other camps that observers were granted access to by the Germans.

Beck-Friis claimed that despite Sweden's lack of a legal basis to devote attention to the Poles who remained in the Soviet-occupied territories, it nonetheless needed to be concerned with their fate for humanitarian reasons, as they

---

[196] PISM, A 11, E/430, report by Polish Envoy to Stockholm G. Potworowski to the Ministry of Foreign Affairs, Stockholm, 20 XII 1939.
[197] Ibidem, letter by Polish Envoy to Stockholm G. Potworowski to the Ministry of Foreign Affairs, Stockholm, 22 XI 1939.
[198] Ibidem.
[199] RA, UD avdelningar och byråarkiv 1864–1952, Andra B-avdelningen, vol. 297, letter by C. Petersen to UD, Berlin, 14 X 1939.
[200] RA, UD avdelningar och byråarkiv 1864–1952, Andra B-avdelningen, vol. 278, letter by C. Petersen to UD, Berlin, 27 X 1939.

were protected by no one.[201] Nevertheless, the authorities in Moscow refused to cooperate on the subject, justifying their position with procedural constraints. Requests concerning people were directed to Soviet diplomatic missions abroad.[202] Enquiries about Polish prisoners were met with ominous silence. Sometimes attempts to obtain information about civilian refugees through German diplomats brought positive results. This was not the case when it came to information about soldiers who had been taken prisoner in 1939.[203]

In the beginning of November, the Poles sent two letters proposing to cede the task of protecting Polish interests in Germany and in the occupied territories to the Swedish Legation in Bern.[204] This issue was communicated by Swedish Envoy to Bern Hans Beck-Friis in his letter from 16 November. First, he requested more details and instructions concerning the case, which was unusual for the Swedes and, for this reason, difficult. Normally, the commonly adopted regulations concerning the issue of representing the government of one of the fighting sides were applied. In this case Germany did not acknowledge the Polish government. The German's reaction to the Swedish diplomacy came possibly because of the reference to the Polish government. According to Beck-Friis, when the mission of protecting Polish interests continued, the duty should lie with the Swedish Legation in Berlin and all instructions should come directly from the B Division in Stockholm. He could not understand why the Polish side was so concerned with including the mission in Bern in this system. Perhaps the reason was a matter of communication – a better connection between France and Berlin via Bern than via Stockholm.[205] The Polish Ministry of Foreign Affairs was planning to develop their humanitarian activity based on the mission which was entrusted to the Swedish diplomacy. On 16 November 1939, Secretary-General at the Ministry of Foreign Affairs Jan Ciechanowski instructed Franciszek Maleszka, who was staying in the Swedish Legation in Berlin: 'The Polish government still intends to keep all the establishments of Polish consular institutions in Germany – including those which were formally vacated – and

---

[201] RA, UD avdelningar och byråarkiv 1864–1952, Andra B-avdelningen, vol. 417, letter by J. Beck-Friis to Swedish Envoy to Moscow W. Winther Stockholm, 6 XI 1939.

[202] Ibidem, letter by Swedish Envoy to Moscow W. Winther to J. Beck-Friis, Moscow, 16 XI 1939.; copy of letter by J. Beck-Friis to the Consulate General in Pretoria, Stockholm, 16 XII 1939.

[203] RA, UD avdelningar och byråarkiv 1864–1952, Andra B-avdelningen, vol. 278, letter by Swedish Envoy to Moscow V. Assarsson to B. Johansson, Moscow, 5 V 1941.

[204] RA, UD 1920 års dossiersystem, HP 39, vol. 1586, letter by Head of Political department of the Swedish Ministry of Foreign Affairs (UD) S. Söderblom to Swedish Envoy to Bern H. Beck-Friis, Stockholm, 6 XI 1939.

[205] Ibidem, letter by Swedish Envoy to Bern H. Beck-Friis to S. Söderblom, Bern, 16 XI 1939.

pay rent from consular funds deposited in German marks in the Swedish Legation in Berlin.' Besides, Ciechanowski informed: 'Having confirmed oral instructions passed to you by Consul General Sir Korsak regarding the issue of exercising protection over the Polish citizens in Germany, the Ministry emphasizes that it attaches great significance to continuing this protection in the widest possible extent and expects detailed reports regarding this particular issue.'[206] The widest possible extent meant not only the form of future representation but also the territory it was to include. On the same day, when Ciechanowski sent a letter to Berlin, Envoy Potworowski sent a telegram to the Ministry of Foreign Affairs, where he explained: 'The Swedes have already protested several times against accepting the duty of exercising protection over our citizens in other countries except Germany. If we make a statement, we will be surely risking unquestionable refusal.'[207] Potworowski did not intend to worsen relations with the Swedes. According to him the Swedes treated the issue of representation and care 'very conscientiously and they are trying to do everything they can to defend our interests.' At the same time, he noted that: 'they are facing great difficulties from the Germans, which they do not always want or can successfully fight.' According to Potworowski, their opinion was that the issue of representation of interests is 'admittedly often a heavy duty, but still a duty of a neutral state',[208] however it should not be treated by the Polish diplomatic circles as a signal to charge the Swedes with additional tasks.

The plans for further development of Polish–Swedish cooperation, in exercising protection over Polish citizens, were rendered pointless when on 20 November 1939 the German authorities submitted a note to the Swedish representatives. In this note, they were informed that the German offices were taking over Polish interests: 'The *Auswärtiges Amt* [Foreign Office of Germany or AA] has an honour to inform the Royal Legation of Sweden, in connection with the note of 1 September of the current year, regarding the issue of protection over Polish interests in the German Reich exercised by the Government of the Kingdom of Sweden, that the reasons on the basis of which this protection was initiated, according to the government of the German Reich, had ceased to exist and that the duty of exercising protection

---

[206] PISM, A 11, E/430, letter by Secretary of State of Foreign Affairs J. Ciechanowski to F. Maleszka, Paris, 16 XI 1939.
[207] Ibidem, telegram by Polish Envoy to Stockholm G. Potworowski to the Ministry of Foreign Affairs, 16 XI 1939.
[208] Ibidem, telegram by Polish Envoy to Stockholm G. Potworowski to the Ministry of Foreign Affairs, 22 XI 1939.

fulfilled by the Legation of the Kingdom of Sweden should therefore no longer be considered valid. The Auswärtiges Amt asks the Royal Legation of Sweden to recognize the fact that the protection over the matters and items, which have been so far exercised by the legation, is from now on ceded to the relevant German offices.'[209]

An eminent Polish historian and a specialist in history of diplomacy, Henryk Batowski, who conducted a detailed analysis of the note, highlighted the fact that the Germans did not write openly that the Polish state ceased to exist to avoid discussion in the area of international law.[210] The Swedes could only ask at best what development of events the Germans had in mind, but the discussion was not initiated. Potworowski informed the Ministry of Foreign Affairs, which was already in exile in France: 'The Swedes are clearly shocked and claim that this is contrary to all international customs, but they are nevertheless powerless, for it is impossible to introduce any protection without the consent of a relevant government.' The envoy highlighted 'a highly critical attitude towards the German decision' of the Swedish Ministry of Foreign Affairs.[211] Richert, on the same day, in the Division of German Protocol under the Ministry of Foreign Affairs expressed surprise at German demands. Most of all, he criticized the fact that they were not announced earlier, which put the Swedes in a somewhat embarrassing situation. He suggested that the Germans agreed to the transitory period in the process of revoking the duties of the B Division on Polish matters.[212] On 22 November, Richert was informed by the head of the Political department of the AA, Ernst Woermann, that such a transitory period, revoking the duty of the Swedish diplomacy in representing the interests of Poland, should end no later than 1 December. The Germans permitted, however, a possible cooperation with Petersen after 1 December on consular issues connected with searching for missing persons, as well as matters concerning prisoners of war and the management of Polish property.[213]

---

[209] RA, UD avdelningar och byråarkiv 1864–1952, Andra B-avdelningen, vol. 183, copy of verbal note by the AA to the Swedish Legation in Berlin, Berlin, 20 XI 1939. On that very same day Swedish Envoy A. Richert sent the letter to Stockholm, asking for specific instructions. See also: H. Batowski, *Walka dyplomacji niemieckiej przeciw Polsce 1939–1945*, Kraków–Wrocław 1984, p. 57 (Polish translation), p. 169 (original note quoted in full).
[210] H. Batowski, *Walka...*, pp. 57–59
[211] PISM, A 11, E/430, telegram by Polish Envoy to Stockholm, G. Potworowski, to the Ministry of Foreign Affairs, 22 XI 1939.
[212] RA, UD avdelningar och byråarkiv 1864–1952, Andra B-avdelningen, vol. 183, letter by Swedish Envoy to Berlin A. Richert to J. Beck-Friis, Berlin, 20 XI 1939.
[213] Ibidem, note from a telephone conversation with Counsellor of the Swedish Legation in Berlin E. von Post, Stockholm, 23 XI 1939.

2. AGGRESSION OF GERMANY AND THE SOVIET UNION

Following consultations on 29 November with the headquarters of the Ministry of Foreign Affairs, Richert submitted a letter to the AA, where he stated that the Swedish government acknowledged the German note and accepted the fact that it was no longer possible for it to fulfil its duties towards the Polish government.[214] This decision was also announced to the press.[215] At the same time, the demand 'to terminate the activity of the section for the protection of Polish citizens operating under the legation in Berlin until 1 December' was accepted.[216] In this situation Minister Zaleski considered the issue of interest representation to be closed and asked Potworowski to clarify the question of returning or safeguarding the private property left by the officials of Polish diplomatic missions in Germany. The inventories of this property remained in Swedish hands.[217] Both the Embassy of the Republic of Poland in Paris and Potworowski in Stockholm demanded that the Swedes safeguard the private property of Polish diplomatic and consular officials. A high priority was assigned to the property of Ambassador Lipski, who had built up a valuable collection of items and accumulated a lot of wealth.[218] On 27 November, the headquarters of the Ministry of Foreign Affairs instructed Richert that the Germans must not be granted access to any funds deposited in Berlin by Ambassador Lipski. According to the Polish Legation in Berlin's archive, it was said that the archive should be moved to the seat of the Swedish Legation and sealed. Furniture and other items, everything except private property, were to be returned to the Germans after being catalogued. The Swedes also took it upon themselves to take care of four Polish officials working for the B Division, to whom the Germans did not grant permission to leave Berlin. The search for missing persons was to be ended, even open

---

[214] Ibidem, copy of verbal note by Swedish Envoy to Berlin A. Richert to Auswärtiges Amt, Berlin, 29 XI 1939.
[215] 'Polens intressen i Tyskland. Svenska regeringens bevakning av Polens intressen upphör', *Svenska Dagbladet*, 30 XI 1939.
[216] PISM, A 11, E/430, telegram by Polish Envoy to Stockholm G. Potworowski to the Ministry of Foreign Affairs, Stockholm., 25 XI 1939.
[217] Ibidem, telegram by Minister of Foreign Affairs A. Zaleski to Polish Envoy to Stockholm, G. Potworowski, 21 XII 1939.
[218] RA, UD avdelningar och byråarkiv 1864–1952, Ander B-avdelningen, vol. 221, ibidem, letter by R. Gyllenram to UD, B-avdelningen, Paris, 8 I 1940 r.; ibidem, letter by J. Beck-Friis to the Swedish Legation in Berlin, 12 I 1940; letter by J. Lagerberg to E. von Post from the Swedish Legation in Berlin, Stockholm, 5 III 1940.

cases were to be concluded with relevant reports, although Potworowski persisted in telling Beck-Friis that proceeding with this sort of activity without Swedish assistance would be impossible.[219]

When considering the events connected with revoking the duty of representing Polish interests in Germany by the Swedish diplomacy, one needs to highlight that Sweden, like every neutral country, continued to acknowledge the existence of the Polish government and did not accept the official German stance in this matter. One could agree, however with Batowski that Hitler's diplomats achieved success at a very low cost.[220] It is worth noting that, according to Swedish Minister of Justice Karl Gustaf Westman, the answer of Minister of Foreign Affairs Sandler to German demands was cutting, despite the head of the Swedish diplomacy being in favour of Berlin's request not to make it public.[221] One should also recognise that a natural consequence of this course of events should be termination the B Division's operations at the Swedish Legation in Berlin regarding Polish interests. This was not the case. Instead, one of the major agents of this section became the former Military Attaché to Warsaw, Colonel Erik de Laval. For obvious reasons nobody was willing to draw too much attention to this. It is also difficult for us to estimate the actual scale of this activity. Nevertheless, drawn from what little information there is on the subject, a consequence was undoubtedly that Polish issues were present.

Petersen reviewed the humanitarian action conducted in the General Government initiated by the American Red Cross and the organisation of American Quakers. He then proposed that due to Swedish diplomatic activity being prevented by the Germans such duties were to be taken over by the Swedish Red Cross.[222] The issue was discussed in Stockholm at the beginning of December, following the Soviet aggression towards Finland.

Both the management of the Swedish Red Cross and *Utrikesdepartementet* (Ministry of Foreign Affairs), despite this, believed the current developments prevented any wide-ranging humanitarian activity in Poland.[223]

---

[219] RA, UD avdelningar och byråarkiv 1864–1952, Andra B-avdelningen, vol. 183, letter by J. Beck-Friis to the Swedish Legation in Berlin, Stockholm, 27 XI 1939.; letter by J. Beck-Friis to Swedish Envoy to Berlin A. Richert, Stockholm, 29 XI 1939.
[220] H. Batowski, *Walka dyplomacji niemieckiej przeciw Polsce 1939–1945*, Kraków–Wrocław 1984, p. 59.
[221] K. G. Westman, *Politiska anteckningar september 1939–mars 1943*, Stockholm 1981, pp. 59–60.
[222] RA, UD avdelningar och byråarkiv 1864–1952, Andra B-avdelningen, vol. 417, copy of letter by C. Petersen to the Swedish Legation in Berlin, Berlin, 29 XI 1939.
[223] Ibidem, copy of letter by J. Beck-Friis to C. Petersen, Stockholm, 6 XII 1939.

When in December 1939 Potworowski held a meeting with Beck-Friis, he heard that the B Division at the Swedish Legation in Berlin had officially concluded its activity on 1 December. The process of its liquidation, though, was still in progress and Petersen would visit Stockholm and submit a liquidation report no earlier than 22 December. Formally, the task of exercising protection over Polish citizens was ceded by the Swedes to the new office created by the Germans and to the German Red Cross. Any property that could not be moved was given to the Germans. Ambassador Lipski's private property and the large sum of money that he had left at the disposal of the Swedish Legation were secured. According to the information obtained from the German authorities, four Polish officials who had been working for the Swedes for a short while intended to remain in Germany, and two of them even expressed a willingness to work for the Germans. Richert was to intervene once more in the releasing of Polish consuls. Potworowski revealed: 'Richert, I have been told, did everything he could in this matter, intervening several times and with all his force, but unfortunately he achieved nothing specific, and the resistance came not as much from the Auswärtiges Amt as from internal authorities. Giving very little hope for releasing the interned abroad, the Germans would be rather ready to release them into occupied Poland. Richert, however, reserved the right to return to this issue at a later time and his intention is to continue his interventions, viewing them already from the perspective of his personal prestige.'[224]

At the time the Swedish press published information about the suspending of the mission's activity and eventual liquidation of the B Division at the Swedish Legation in Berlin on 16 December in connection with the establishment of the General Government and civil administration in the occupied territories.

It was only on 19 December that the Germans together with the Swedes wrote a protocol concerning the issue of 'handing the authority of former Polish missions in the Third Reich over to the Foreign Office in Berlin.' A copy of this protocol was submitted by Petersen to Potworowski following his arrival in Stockholm. In the document it was recorded that both movable and immovable property had been transferred, but not confiscated. That which could be moved was placed in a special warehouse. Cash was entrusted to the legal counsellor of the Swedish Legation, German lawyer Dix, and it

---

[224] PISM, A 11, E/430, report by Polish Envoy to Stockholm G. Potworowski to the Ministry of Foreign Affairs, Stockholm, 20 XII 1939.

was to him that one turned to on the issue of storage payments. As Potworowski discovered: 'Otherwise these movables would be in danger of being sold at auction.' The Swedes rescued the funds transferred by Ambassador Lipski, concealing their existence from the Germans. Potworowski added: 'What is more, these funds have increased by nearly 44 thousand marks recovered from individual consulates, and following the payment of all expenses incurred from protection over Polish interests and its termination, they currently amount to over 200 thousand marks.' On Petersen's request, the Poles were to refrain from using these funds, at least for some time, as, according to the Swedes, 'revealing, in any way, the existence of […] sums allocated for Poland-related purposes, would risk them being swept up by the German authorities, not to mention the trouble this could cause for the Swedish Envoy to Berlin.'[225] The Swedes suggested that the funds be transferred abroad or to the occupied territories, but a transfer to Warsaw was considered impossible at that moment.[226] Potworowski informed his headquarters: 'when the current vigilance of the Germans and the apprehension of the Swedes die down, I will try to get back to the issue of making use of this sum in one way or another.' For the time being the funds were to be used to cover the storage costs of the Polish property, since all bank accounts belonging to the Poles were blocked by the German authorities. Next, Potworowski began negotiations to transfer the sum in Swedish crowns to the Poles in Stockholm.

Petersen confirmed that the cases involving the search of missing civilians in Germany and occupied Poland were taken over by the German Red Cross. He also confirmed that the Polish officials who remained in Germany had done so of their own will: Maleszka and Waligórski remained in Berlin, Berent moved to Hamburg, and Tworowski to Katowice. The honorary consul of Sweden to Königsberg continued his efforts to release the interned employees of the Polish consulate.[227] Potworowski intervened constantly with Envoy Richert during each of his visits to Stockholm. Richert took a personal interest in the issue, telling Potworowski: 'I am not in favour of leaving the issue unsolved on revoking the duty of Swedish protection.' Most importantly, the Polish envoy asked for an intervention in the case of Consul Warchałowski, in

---

[225] Ibidem, report by Polish Envoy to Stockholm G. Potworowski to the Ministry of Foreign Affairs, Stockholm, 20 I 1940.
[226] AAN, HI/I/245, telegram by Polish Envoy to Stockholm G. Potworowski to the Ministry of Foreign Affairs, Stockholm, 28 XII 1939.
[227] PISM, A 11, E/430, report by Polish Envoy to Stockholm G. Potworowski to the Ministry of Foreign Affairs, Stockholm, 20 I 1940.

the still unclear case, for the Polish authorities, of Maleszka and other Polish officials, as well as for sending financial aid to Lithuania for Madam Jałowiecka. By the spring of 1940 Potworowski informed the Polish Ministry of Foreign Affairs (in exile after September 1939, by summer 1940 in France, later in London) that the matter of the transfer of funds gathered by Ambassador Lipski was on the right track, but the fulfilment by the Swedes of their obligations regarding the protection of Polish interests he evaluated unequivocally: 'My overall impression from the conversation with Richert, as I have already noted many times during conversations on this subject in the local Ministry of Foreign Affairs, is that the Swedes are helpless in dealings with the German authorities and have no authority that would allow them to oppose effectively their lawless orders, as a matter of fact they don't want to fall out of favour with the Germans by supporting our cause. Nevertheless, they would genuinely like to help us, with their modest abilities and means, all the more so as what is at stake is their prestige, about which they are very sensitive.'[228]

In May 1940 Minister Zaleski continued to ask Potworowski why Warchałowski was still being detained by the Germans in the *Pawiak* (this was a common name for the Warsaw prison on Pawia street). According to the announcement of the AA, Warchałowski had been given to return home.[229]

The issue of Polish property was addressed again in 1941, when the property was sequestrated and other items were put up for auction by the Germans. Richert directed an entreaty to the Germans to call off the sequestration. He wrote to the incumbent head of the B Division, Birger Johansson: 'I am deeply saddened by the fact that I failed to salvage the private property of my former Polish colleagues, which has been confiscated today by the German state. Unfortunately, there is no possibility to undertake another action in this matter.'[230]

From the report prepared by Potworowski in October 1941 it is evident that the issue of Swedish protection over the interests of Poland did not conclude with the auctioning of property left in Germany by the staff of the Polish Legation in Berlin and the consulates: 'Following the official liquidation (at the outset of December 1939) of the Swedish protection over our

---

[228] Ibidem, report by Polish Envoy to Stockholm G. Potworowski to the Ministry of Foreign Affairs, Stockholm, 26 III 1940.
[229] AAN, HI/I/256, telegram by Minister of Foreign Affairs A. Zaleski to Polish Envoy to Stockholm G. Potworowski, 9 V 1940.
[230] RA, UD avdelningar och byråarkiv 1864–1952, Andra B-avdelningen, vol. 221, letter by the B Division of Utrikesdepartementet to the Polish Legation in Stockholm, 8 V 1941; IPMS, A 11, E/430, translation of letter by Swedish Envoy to Berlin, A. Richert to B. Johansson, Berlin, 2 V 1941.

interests in Germany, we have managed to maintain contacts both within the local Ministry of Foreign Affairs, as well as with the Swedish Legation in Berlin in the sphere of assistance and care regarding several cases mentioned below. This protection is unofficial and based on rules of politeness, and so far, the Swedes have managed to respond to our demands in a courteous manner.'[231]

First, through the Swedes, information about the imprisoned Polish consular officials continued to be collected. It was also possible, on a regular basis, to make use of the funds deposited by Lipski. In Stockholm Potworowski received a payment of 50 thousand crowns from these funds, calculated at the official conversion rate.[232] Someone perhaps came to the conclusion that leaving at least part of the money half way between neutral Sweden and the General Government would be more beneficial than submitting it to London. Potworowski described the allocation of the money in a very general way: 'These funds are used by the Swedish Legation in Berlin to cover the expenses connected with settling our matters.'[233] Part of this amount was allocated to the purchase of some of the more precious items of the Polish property that were auctioned off by the Germans. The Swedes on the consent of the Polish Ministry of Foreign Affairs bought the items at two auctions (28 May and 11 June 1941) for over 18 thousand marks. From the German authorities they demanded, also for fundamental reasons, that the payments for the storage of the property were returned, but they received no answer.

What is especially puzzling about this relationship is the information about 'settling our matters' through the legation and by means of funds that were deposited there. In connection with what little news there was about the courier activity, organized partially by the Union of Armed Struggle (Związek Walki Zbrojnej, from 1942 Armia Krajowa) in occupied Poland and partially by the VI Division of the Staff of the Commander-in-Chief in London, the issue of point of contact in the Swedish Legation becomes more understandable. The group of individuals acquainted with the subject had to be limited, but Envoy Richert knew that Potworowski had been depositing additional, non-inventoried, large sums of dollars at the Swedish mission in Berlin.[234] It

---

[231] PISM, A 11, E/430, report by Polish Envoy to Stockholm G. Potworowski to the Ministry for Foreign Affairs, Stockholm, 10 X 1941.
[232] AAN, HI/I/246, telegram by Polish Envoy to Stockholm G. Potworowski to the Ministry of Foreign Affairs, Stockholm, 15 VII 1940.
[233] PISM, A 11, E/430, report by Polish Envoy to Stockholm G. Potworowski to the Ministry of Foreign Affairs, Stockholm, 10 X 1941.
[234] RA, UD avdelningar och byråarkiv 1864–1952, Andra B-avdelningen, vol. 127, letter by Swedish Envoy to Berlin A. Richert to the Swedish Ministry of Foreign Affairs, Berlin, 8 II

2. AGGRESSION OF GERMANY AND THE SOVIET UNION

is not a secret that in the Swedish Legation there existed the so-called Polish fund (*den polska kassan*), which was used to cover the storage costs of Polish items. In November 1941 de Laval passed on information that after the transport costs of some Polish items to Sweden had been met, 7 thousand marks were left for the auctions, announcing though that the fund would need to be replenished.[235] In July 1941 Potworowski asked Richert to submit to three female former officials of the Polish Ministry for Foreign Affairs (Ms Gradowska, Ms Halina Jałowiecka, Ms Winiarska) 1500 marks each from the funds of Ambassador Lipski.[236] Richert was not officially allowed to do so. He informed Johansson that he would try to make a payment through the agency of Carl Herslow or Hilding Molander, who directed the Swedish Chamber of Commerce in Warsaw. It was precisely from the Polish fund that de Laval took the money he handed in to the female officials mentioned by Potworowski.[237] In 1943 about 17 thousand marks were kept in the Polish account at the Swedish Legation in Berlin, and in 1945 there was more than 15 thousand marks. Money deposited by other officials from the embassy and Polish consulates in Germany was taken to Stockholm in two lots by Adolf von Rosen in November 1942.[238]

When in the second half of 1944 the Polish government in exile gradually started to prepare itself for a nationwide protest, the of representation of Polish interests by Sweden was again examined. It would establish whether Poland had suffered financial loss, and if it had, how much the Swedes should pay to cover it. In the Ministry of Foreign Affairs, a draft of the protest letter was prepared, in which it was pointed out that the Swedish Legation in Berlin had fulfilled its task in an improper way and that the Swedish government should bear the material responsibility for its negligence. Polish lawyers argued, firstly that: 'The Swedish government became the Polish government's mandate holder for this matter and as a consequence is subject to legal obligations which bound each mandate-holder, and as such responsibility for exercising protection.' And secondly they argued that: 'The Swedish government so far did not waive its duty towards the Polish Government to exercise

---

1941. The reference is made here to the amount of 2500 dollars, which was not included by Carl Petersen in his financial reports from December 1939.
[235] Ibidem, copy of letter by E. de Laval to B. Johansson, Berlin, 30 X 1941.
[236] Ibidem, letter by Polish Envoy to Stockholm G. Potworowski to B. Johansson, Stockholm, 15 VII 1941.
[237] RA, UD avdelningar och byråarkiv 1864–1952, Andra B-avdelningen, vol. 362, confidential letter by E. de Laval to B. Johansson, Berlin, 21 X 1941.
[238] RA, UD avdelningar och byråarkiv 1864–1952, Andra B-avdelningen, vol. 127, letter by A. de Rosen to the B Division of UD (together with attachment), Berlin, 10 XI 1942.

protection over the Polish citizens in Germany, which is also confirmed by the fact that it did not prepare any reports concerning the funds received for this purpose, this also includes the losses and damage suffered as a consequence of transferring the Polish property to the Germans.'[239]

In this draft it was highlighted that, so far, the Polish government did not bring up this issue so as not to further complicate the situation of the Swedish government. The draft concluded emphatically: 'Without a doubt the Swedish government realizes that it acted improperly by yielding to the German pressure and avoiding tensions, even though this was a clear violation of international customs and it made the government a partner in a crime against Poland. Drawing attention to this issue once again now may make it easier for Sweden to redeem itself in the eyes of Poland, it may prove helpful in negotiations with the Germans on other issues, and for this very reason the Ministry of Foreign Affairs considers this to be a suitable moment to raise this issue. Not mentioning our demands towards the Swedish government could be considered by the latter as silent consent of the Polish government to the accomplished settlement of this matter by the German government.'[240]

The tone of the drafted *démarche* was the result of opinions expressed by the employees of the Ministry of Foreign Affairs. Legal expert Stefan Lubomirski pointed out in his analysis: 'The Swedish government, with a tremendous amount of effort and good will, set about the task of carrying out the accepted mandate of protection', and 'the submittal of the buildings of consular offices and the property of Polish officials to the representatives of the Swedish authorities in Germany was performed, in most of the cases, in a satisfactory way.' Nevertheless, on 19 December 1939 the Swedes transferred the Polish property to the Germans. Lubomirski stated: 'When the Swedish government came across obstacles from the Germans that made it difficult for it to continue the maintenance of the pledged protection, it had two options to choose from:

- to waive the mandate of protection in relation to the Polish government and to demand the instruction as to whom this matter needed to be ceded to;
- to state formally before the Polish and German government that the German authorities made it impossible for Sweden, being a neutral

---

[239] PISM, A 11, E/430, draft of letter to the Polish Legation in Stockholm, [November 1944]. Probably prepared by A. Lisiewicz; not accepted.
[240] Ibidem.

country, to exercise the protection – according to the rules of international law – over the interests of the country in a state of war, and return to the Polish government the keys to all the buildings that had been placed under its supervision.

The Swedish government took another path, which was in fact very original. Namely, it tried to settle this matter opportunistically.'[241]

What is more, Lubomirski pointed out that the Germans had violated the protocol of property transfer by offering it all for auction. The Germans' answer to the Swedish protests was that the Polish country did not exist, which was clearly against the rules of international law. The lack of reaction from the Swedes gave rise to considerable concern from Poland. Especially that, according to Lubomirski, right after the outbreak of the war the Swedes had exercised their protection in a way that was 'demonstrative or even ostentatious according to the Germans.' Later, the character of this protection became private. The Swedish side had never accounted for the 200 thousand marks that were left after Ambassador Lipski and was responsible for all the losses incurred by Poland. Lubomirski claimed: 'the Swedes' case should be still considered open, as we have not yet discharged the Swedish government from exercising the protection and, furthermore, the settlements with the Swedes concerning protection have not yet been taken care of.'[242]

The legal counsellor at the Ministry of Foreign Affairs, Włodzimierz Adamkiewicz, having scrutinised the issue, pointed out that the Swedes had demonstrated a lack of caution. This was so since they managed Polish property without consulting the Poles on the matter: 'It is important that it was impossible for the Swedish government to refer to any clear or even silent consent of the Polish government for the transfer of management of Polish property to the German government.'[243]

The Ministry of Foreign Affairs sought justification for submitting material claims to Sweden at all costs. A more balanced analysis was given by an anonymous member of staff of the Ministry of Foreign Affairs, Jan Ciechanowski is the most likely author, who, in fact, agreed that the arguments of Lubomirski and Adamkiewicz were logical and legally well justified, but who at the same pointed out: 'their presumption that the Swedish government did not inform the Polish government about the German demand to withdraw the Swedish management of the property, commissioned by the Polish

---

[241] Ibidem, a note by S. Lubomirski to Minister of Foreign Affairs T. Romer, 20 X 1944.
[242] Ibidem.
[243] Ibidem, a legal opinion of the counsellor W. Adamkiewicz, 28 X 1944.

government, and ignored the Polish interests is highly improbable.'[244] The author of the note considered such a hypothesis to be very unlikely and suspected that the records regarding this matter had been destroyed during the evacuation of Angers (France) in 1940.[245] His proposal was to examine whether the Swedish government had turned to the Polish authorities on this matter in any form and what was the reaction of the Polish authorities. He was the only one to draw attention to the political aspect of the entire issue: 'But even if the legal status was fully explained in accordance with the assumptions of Lubomirski and Adamkiewicz, there still remains a question of whether the Swedish government should be called to account. For throughout the entire war the Swedish government acted *extremely* [the word was crossed out] kindly towards Poland and Poles (internment of ships, tolerance of the refugees, assistance for the country, action of the Red Cross etc.) [anonymous note on the margin: not always, not always – author's note] and its assistance is still necessary, and – in the future – also other tokens of this kindness may be needed. Therefore, accusing the government of being an accomplice in the violation of international law may be a very severe accusation for the Swedes, even more so that Sweden is making consistent efforts to gain a positive reputation in the world in this respect.[246]

The best method for referring to this case was to be the submission of an *aide-mémoire* to the Swedish Ministry of Foreign Affairs by Envoy Henryk Sokolnicki with a reminder that the Polish government would demand satisfaction from Germany for the violation of the rules of international law. It would also be possible for the Swedish government to raise this issue in Berlin at that point. The beneficial consequence of the possible entry of the Allies in to the territory of Germany would be the renewal of the Swedish mandate to exercise protection over the buildings of former Polish consular posts to save the archives and furnishings from damage.

Following on from that, Sokolnicki also requested the Swedish Professor of Law, Håkan Nial, provide his evaluation. Nial confirmed that: 'according to the Swedish perception of international law, the confiscation of Polish property in Germany must be considered contrary to the rules of international law because it constitutes a discrimination of Poland based on the false

---

[244] Ibidem, a note, London, 16 XI 1944.
[245] The former Polish Envoy to Stockholm, G. Potworowski, confirmed that the Polish government did not protest the statement issued by the Swedish government regarding the German government preventing it from seeing to the Polish interests in Germany. See PISM, A 11, E/430, note by J. Ciechanowski from 28 XI 1944 on the note from 16 XI 1944.
[246] PISM, A 11, E/430, note, London, 16 XI 1944.

premise that Poland as a country does not exist. Regardless, the confiscation of Polish private property in Germany must be considered illegal within a broader concept of private property protection by the international law.'[247]

The value of the property was estimated by Poland to be 5.1 million francs in gold, 2 million of which was owned by the Polish state and the remainder by the diplomatic and consular personnel. Sokolnicki admitted that Nial's evaluation added nothing new to the issue, though it brought clarification and facilitated further interventions.[248] Based on this evaluation on 19 March 1945 Sokolnicki submitted a note to *Utrikesdepartementet*. At the same time, Lipski sent a private letter to Eric von Post, and the counsellor of the Polish Legation in Stockholm, Tadeusz Pilch, spoke to Grafström. Sokolnicki wrote: 'this conversation, besides confirming the best will of the Swedish Ministry of Foreign Affairs, did not bring any particular results.' Nevertheless, the Poles used various ways to communicate their postulates to the Swedish diplomats. Post asked about the actual demands of Poland. Plans to seize the German property in the territory of Sweden were formulated, and the matter was discussed by the Poles with the British authorities.

In response to Nial's evaluation, counsellor Adamkiewicz highlighted the responsibility of the Swedish government for the fate of the property that was placed under its supervision: 'The issue of special treatment, resulting from the fact of assuming, at a certain point, the care by the Swedish government, which was entirely omitted in the disquisitions of Professor Nial, should be used as an argument to make this government *prioritize* [underlined in the original text] the aforementioned demands.'[249]

The Minister of Foreign Affairs, Adam Tarnowski, asked Envoy Sokolnicki to consider the opinion of counsellor Adamkiewicz and to settle the matter as quickly as possible: 'The Ministry is asking You, Sir, to take all possible measures to obtain the decision of the government on this matter of specific nature, in the quickest time possible. Haste is all the more so justified that our demands were not included as part of the global demands raised in the territory of Sweden by the Allies towards Germany.'[250]

---

[247] PISM, A 11, E/188, Håkan Nial: Memorandum regarding the issue of Polish property sequestrated and confiscated in Germany, Stockholm, 7 V 1945. (translated from Swedish).
[248] Ibidem, letter by Polish Envoy to Stockholm H. Sokolnicki to the Ministry of Foreign Affairs, Stockholm, 19 V 1945.
[249] Ibidem, opinion from legal counsellor W. Adamkiewicz regarding a memorandum by H. Nial devoted to the issue of the Polish property sequestrated and confiscated in Germany, 4 VI 1945.
[250] Ibidem, letter by Minister of Foreign Affairs A. Tarnowski to Polish Envoy to Stockholm H. Sokolnicki, London, 8 VI 1945.

The withdrawal of the Swedish authorities' recognition to the Polish government in exile on 6 July 1945 and simultaneously granting recognition to the Provisional Government of National Unity in Warsaw shattered the efforts of the Polish Legation to settle this matter.

3. In the Face of Consequences of the Ribbentrop-Molotov Pact

Following the defeat of Poland

When the military campaign in Poland ended, the fate of the Second Polish Republic ceased to be a popular theme for current affairs news services and commentaries of opinion journalists. There were a few voices, but these mostly expressed indifference. The editors of *Social-Demokraten* conveyed their optimism about the future: 'This situation may not continue much longer. One may not fail to appreciate the unprecedented force of Polish desire for independence. The history of Poland reflects the indomitable spirit of freedom this nation has. On the western front, the war has not yet started. In 1918 all of Poland was occupied by the German army, and when the occupation concluded in the West, the young Polish state ascended like a phoenix from the ashes.'[1] According to a commentator for *Arbetaren*, the end of the campaign in Poland did not put an end to the problems with the Poles who, in his opinion, constituted an 'open wound' for Germany and the Soviet Union.[2]

Initially, the Polish matter was evaluated quite differently in *Göteborgs Handels- och Sjöfarts-Tidning*, where the significance of the September Campaign had been disregarded entirely. According to an anonymous opinion journalist: 'The events that are taking place in Poland are horrifying, and the heroic attempt of the Polish nation to repel the aggressor deserves admiration. Nonetheless, the reality is that the fate of Poland is of minor importance for the result of the entire war, which as a matter of fact, has not yet started. For this reason, it is of even less importance to us.'[3]

Relations with the Polish government in exile were not a high priority for the Swedish diplomacy, though the rebirth of the Polish army in France was observed with interest. The Swedish Envoy to Paris, Einar Hennings, watched with curiosity the actions of the Polish authorities, who initiated the organizational activity in France. At the same time, he commented with embarrassment on the severe evaluations of foreign policy conducted by Józef Beck, who was strongly criticised for each diplomatic step and deemed responsible

---

[1] 'Avgörande i Öster?', *Social-Demokraten*, 15 IX 1939.
[2] 'Hitler hotar', *Arbetaren*, 23 IX 1939.
[3] 'Erfarenheter från världskriget', *Göteborgs Handels- och Sjöfarts-Tidning*, 19 IX 1939.

for the defeat in September 1939: 'Over and over again voices repeat that the so-called Polish policy of perching between the powers was such an immense mistake that everyone could predict where, sooner or later, this would lead. The tragedy of Poland is a result of a lack of reason and insight shown by those who assumed the responsibility for the fate of this country.'

Nevertheless, Hennings, on summing up the discussions in Paris on the subject of Polish foreign policy prior to the outbreak of war, stated: 'the fact that must raise absolute admiration is simply the energy and dedication which here, within the Polish circles in the present critical situation, drive the search for possibilities to serve the national cause, which, is nevertheless not yet treated as lost.'[4]

Meanwhile, Envoy Torsten Undén reported from Budapest about the fate of Marshal Śmigły-Rydz based on information obtained from the Romanian head of diplomatic protocol, Georges Crutzesco. The Romanian expressed a very unfavourable opinion about the Marshal. He accused him of behaving improperly at the border, as the Marshall did not accede to the request of Romanian authorities nor did he take off his uniform. However, much more interesting for the Swedish diplomat were the remarks of the representative of the Romanian Ministry of Foreign Affairs that the Soviet Union would not decide to declare war on Finland and Romania, but chose to reach its political goals by adopting the Hitlerian method of terror and intimidation.[5]

Following the annexation of entire territory of the Second Polish Republic by the German and Soviet armies, the Swedish authorities, first of all, attempted to find out what was going on in the territory of Poland and become familiar with the plans of the Polish government. Swedish Envoy to London Björn Prytz in his letter from 26 September gave an account of his meeting with Ambassador Edward Raczyński. The Polish diplomat informed him that the Soviet authorities had launched the process of a systematic slaughter of landowners.[6]

In the Swedish Legation in Berlin a memorandum was prepared on 27 September about the planned course of the German–Soviet border. It was written there that the demarcation line, initially provisional, was to become a border between the two countries. At that point Hitler was to ponder over

---

[4] RA, UD 1920 års dossiersystem, HP 1, vol. 485, letter by Swedish Envoy to Paris E. Hennings to the Minister of Foreign Affairs R. Sandler, Paris, 30 X 1939.
[5] Ibidem, letter by Swedish Envoy to Budapest T. Unden to the head of the Political department of UD, S. Söderblom, Budapest, 6 XI 1939.
[6] RA, UD 1920 års dossiersystem, HP 39, vol. 1539, letter by Swedish Envoy to London B. Prytz to the head of the Political department of UD S. Söderblom, London, 26 IX 1939.

3. CONSEQUENCES OF THE RIBBENTROP-MOLOTOV PACT

the future of the Polish territories which were not part of Germany in 1914. Rumours started to spread about creating a substitute for the Polish state which would be completely subordinate to the Germans. Richert predicted that a peace conference could be held in such a situation, which would settle all disputes between the powers, as well as disarmament issues, commercial issues, colonial issues and the Jewish issue. Göring warned that since peace had not been concluded in Europe quickly enough, the Soviet Union would easily scoop up Estonia and Latvia, though he failed to mention that Finland was also at risk.[7]

On 30 September, Envoy Potworowski informed Minister Sandler that the Polish nation would never accept the decisions of the German–Soviet arrangement of 28 September 1939 regarding the division of Poland. At the same time he stressed the existence of a legal Polish government, whose intention was to fight until victory in a just war for the liberation of its country.[8] On the next day he sent another letter about the appointment of the new president of the Second Polish Republic, Władysław Raczkiewicz, and about the formation of a new Polish government in Paris headed by General Władysław Sikorski.[9] Two days later Staffan Söderblom replied that the Swedish government acknowledged the note,[10] whereas Minister Sandler confirmed personally that Envoy Lagerberg remained accredited at the Polish government.[11] At the same time Potworowski managed to appoint Major Feliks Brzeskwiński as military attaché.

At the beginning of October 1939, Hitler offered a peace deal to the Western Allies. These negotiations were observed in Stockholm with interest.[12] According to the Swedish government, reaching agreement between the sides was beneficial. Although the authorities officially distanced themselves from the engineer Birger Dahlerus, whose mission was to act as intermediary between the Swedish government and Hermann Göring, Stockholm

---

[7] RA, UD 1920 års dossiersystem, HP 39, vol. 1538, memorandum of A. Richert, Berlin, 27 IX 1939.
[8] RA, UD 1920 års dossiersystem, HP 1, vol. 485, letter by Polish Envoy to Stockholm G. Potworowski to the Swedish Minister of Foreign Affairs R. Sandler, Stockholm, 30 IX 1939.
[9] Ibidem, letter by Polish Envoy to Stockholm G. Potworowski to the Swedish Minister of Foreign Affairs R. Sandler, Stockholm, 1 X 1939.
[10] Ibidem, letter by the head of the Political department of UD, S. Söderblom, to Polish Envoy to Stockholm G Potworowski, Stockholm, 3 X 1939.
[11] *Polskie dokumenty dyplomatyczne 1939 wrzesień–grudzień*, doc. 135, telegram by Polish Envoy to Stockholm G. Potworowski to the Ministry of Foreign Affairs, Stockholm, 3 X 1939, p. 131.
[12] AAN, HI/I/245, telegram by Polish Envoy to Oslo W. Neuman to the Ministry of Foreign Affairs, 17 X 1939.

permitted the possibility of concluding peace at the expense of Poland and adjusting to the new deal in Central Europe. Similar contacts to those of Dahlerus had a famous Swedish traveller, Sven Hedin, who was received in Berlin by Hitler.[13] Both Swedes heard from the Führer that the Polish country would be restored, but only with the co-participation of Germany and the Soviet Union.[14] In spite of the outbreak of the war, Dahlerus continued his efforts to conclude the European conflict by reaching a compromise. On the seventh day of the war he continued to convince British politicians that Göring was 'the only person that could save the peace' and rebuild 'autonomous Poland.' According to a British expert on the subject, throughout the first three months of the war no other negotiator was held in such a high esteem by the Nazi high command or received by them on as many occasions as Dahlerus.[15]

Deliberations on the subject of the powers' peace agreement at the expense of Poland were taking place, until December end 1939, mostly for fear of what would happen next in the Baltic Sea region. From the two-year perspective, one of the Polish opinion journalists overemphasized: 'Following the conclusion of the Polish campaign, the Swedish public opinion was that this was the end of the storm in a teacup. They intoxicated themselves with the hashish of peace up until the attack on Norway on 9 April 1940.'[16] This attitude also dominated among the members of the political elites, in spite of the fact that they were aware of the brutal actions of the Germans towards the Poles.

On 16 November, Swedish Consul to Gdańsk Knud Lundberg informed his superiors in Stockholm about the situation in the city following the entry of the German troops on 14 September. He quoted an appeal of the local head of the NSDAP, Albert Forster, who announced that the Germans would finally demonstrate to the Poles who was the master. He also wrote: 'With brutality which may be equalled with that of the [Soviet] GPU, actions were taken against the local population.' The arrested were placed in confined spaces and forced to remain in an upright position for a long time without

---

[13] W. M. Carlgren, *Svensk utrikespolitik 1939–1945*, Stockholm 1973, p. 48, 127.

[14] This is mentioned by Cz. Madajczyk, *Polityka III Rzeszy w okupowanej Polsce*, vol. 1, Warszawa 1970, p. 86. Hitler, in the conversation that took place on 16 October in the presence of S. Hedin was to express a willingness to create a separate Polish national entity, because he wanted to 'keep this mob outside his territorial limits'.

[15] Detailed information on the subject based on British documents: P.W. Ludlow, 'Scandinavia between the Great Powers. Attempts at Mediation in the First Year of the Second World War', *Historisk tidskrift* 1974, iss. 1, pp. 7–9.

[16] J. Townacki [sic!; T. Nowacki?], 'Ewolucja polityczna Szwecji (1939–1942)', *Wiadomości Polskie*, 4 X 1942.

food or water. Mass displacements of Poles were ordered. They were forced to leave their homes in only a couple of hours, taking only things they were able to carry. The Poles were robbed of their cash and valuables, taken to a railway station and loaded onto freight trains. According to Consul Lundberg, Gdynia was forced in to economic stagnation.[17] The displacement of 36 thousand Poles was suspended by the end of October. Lundberg justified this action as being due to insufficient manpower. This was because the German authorities announced the obligation of work for those aged 16–65. Thanks to this, nearly 50 thousand Poles were able to remain in Gdynia.[18]

Staffan Söderblom passed on the news of the displacements to the International Red Cross and asked permission to send his representative to personally witness the inhumane treatment of the Polish people. However, Max Huber, the secretary general of the organisation, refused. Following this Söderblom informed Envoy Richert that: 'it is difficult for us for the time being to think about any interventions for our part in this matter.'[19]

In turn, Military Attaché Colonel Juhlin-Dannfelt, in his notes from the visit to occupied Poznań at the end of October 1939, wrote: 'the feelings of German officers towards the Poles seem to be to a large extent the same as their feelings towards the Jews, and they even speak about them in the same way.'[20] He also took note of the curfew that was imposed on the Poles. He noticed that the head of the Province of Posen (Poznań) was Arthur Greiser, from whom the Poles could not expect anything good. He, first of all, drew attention to the economic drain of Polish people, from whom almost all cash was confiscated. Poles were prohibited from pursuing many professions: that of doctor of medicine, lawyer etc. Clerical workers were forced to take up manual labour. Each Polish house or apartment, confiscated by the Germans, needed to be vacated within two hours. The Swedish officer reported that the SS and the Gestapo launched raids on settlements, arrested the Poles they found suspicious and executed them by firing squad without trial. What was striking for the Swedish attaché were the overcrowded churches, where the

---

[17] RA, UD 1920 års dossiersystem, HP 1, vol. 485, letter by Swedish Consul to Danzig K. Lundberg to the head of the Political department of UD S. Söderblom, Danzig, 16 XI 1939.
[18] RA, UD avdelningar och byråarkiv 1864–1952, Andra B-avdelningen, vol. 417, copy of letter by the counsellor to the Swedish Legation in Berlin, E. von Post, to the head of the Political department of UD, S. Söderblom, Berlin, 31 X 1939.
[19] RA, UD 1920 års dossiersystem, HP 1, vol. 485, letter by the head of the Political department of UD, S. Söderblom, to Swedish Envoy to Berlin A. Richert, Stockholm, 16 XI 1939.
[20] RA, UD 1920 års dossiersystem, HP 2, vol. 717, report by Swedish Military Attaché to Berlin Colonel C. Juhlin-Dannfelt to the General Staff, Berlin, 31 X 1939.

Poles were seeking comfort in this hopeless situation. Those who remained, suffered from the lack of food supplies and stove coal. On summing up his report, the Swede, however, justified the actions of the Germans: 'My strongest impression from this journey was that the restoration of the former good condition of the roads and bringing order to many areas of life is taking place in Posen thanks to German energy and diligence. At the same time, German administration is carried out using brutal measures, as pay back for the Poles' previous cruelties towards the *Volksdeutsche*.'

Juhlin-Dannfelt's assistant, Lieutenant Göran Hedin reported that on 17 November an institution of forced labour was introduced in Poznań and acts of terror against the Poles were taking place: 'The harshness of conduct towards the Polish people seems unbelievable.'[21] In Kraków though food shortages started to affect the population. All over Poland road and railway maintenance works started, which employed many Poles. When it came to the mood of the Poles, he claimed: 'The attitude of the people is uncertain but tamed.' He also noted: 'Hatred seems common and immense.'

Little information came from the territories that were occupied by the Soviet Union. By the end of October, Envoy Winther reported from Moscow: 'Just like in other formerly despotic countries, so it happens now in the Soviet Union that the current regime refers to the manifestations of "the will of the people", creating the impression that this regime is founded on the majority of the population and realizes its aspirations.'[22] This was how Winther justified the need to organize a performance whose main actors would be the parliaments of western Ukraine and western Belarus, who were then to decide on the matter of their own incorporation in to the USSR. The Swedish diplomat was under no illusion that elections to these assemblies had anything to do with commonly understood free elections. Following the entry of Soviet troops, the process of power takeover by the working class and the peasants was sparked. Landowners were chased away, and their estates were divided. The confiscation of land, as well as the nationalisation of banks and industry was approved by special decrees. As Winther confirmed: 'These declarations abounded in lyrical reflections about ideal relations within the Soviet Union and they were concluded with cheers in honour of both the state and the Communist Party.'

Virtually all Nordic States, Finland especially, whose relations with the Soviet Union were tense, were interested in ending the conflict between

---

[21] Ibidem, memorandum by Colonel G. Hedin, Berlin, 1 X 1939.
[22] RA, UD 1920 års dossiersystem, HP 1, vol. 516, letter by Swedish Envoy to Moscow W. Winther to Minister of Foreign Affairs R. Sandler, Moscow, 31 X 1939.

Germany and the Western Allies. The Finnish Minister of Foreign Affairs, Elias Erkko, in a conversation with the Swedish Envoy to Helsinki, Stig Sahlin, even expressed a wish that Minister Sandler on behalf of the entire Nordic nation submit a proposal to begin mediation with the Germans.[23] According to Wilhelm M. Carlgren, Sandler thought that it would not be well received if Sweden engaged in peace mediation, considering the protection of Polish interests in Germany. However, he did not question the idea of a peaceful settlement based on creating 'a smaller Polish state located between the former German border and the new Russian border, and real autonomy for Bohemia and Moravia.'[24] A different evaluation of Sandler's attitude was provided by British historian Peter Ludlow, who claims that it was Sandler who wanted Sweden to become engaged in peace mediation. He was nevertheless faced with opposition from other ministers who, not without reason, considered every initiative of this sort – while the opinion of the British government was that the negotiations could start right after the change of regime in Germany – to be a token of friendship towards Hitler.[25]

The heads of the Nordic States held a meeting 18–19 October in Stockholm to discuss the current situation. This was the second such conference. The first, attended by prime ministers and foreign ministers, took place 18–19 September in Copenhagen, after the Soviet army had entered Poland. The consultations were modelled on the meeting of three Scandinavian monarchists in Malmö, 1914. These meetings were a manifestation of Nordic unity and their will to preserve neutrality during the on-going war. At the same time, as Gunnar Hägglöf pointed out, they were also evidence of these countries' helplessness and their lack of influence on the events in the Baltic Sea region. Sweden looked on during the conquest of Poland by Hitler and Stalin, as well as the process of imposing political-military arrangements on Estonia (28 September), Latvia (October) and Lithuania (10 October) by the Soviet Union. The invitation, submitted on 5 October by Moscow, for the Finnish government to discuss specific political questions, did not bode well either.

---

[23] UD Handarkiv, series 3, Rickard Sandler, vol. 2, Report by S. Sahlin do Swedish Ministry of Foreign Policy (Conversation with Finnish Foreign Minister Erkko, 4 October 1939), Helsinki, 4 X 1939.
[24] W. M. Carlgren, *Svensk utrikespolitik.*, Stockholm 1973, pp. 38. Cf. H. Batowski, *Agonia.*, pp. 400–401.
[25] P. W. Ludlow, *Scandinavia...*, pp 33–34. It is worth noting that the eventual peace mediation of the Scandinavian states was opposed by the French. See: *Polskie dokumenty dyplomatyczne 1939 wrzesień...*, p. 203, Envoy Potworowski informed the headquarters on 16 X 1939: 'the local French Envoy announced at the Ministry of Foreign Affairs that their peace proposals were unwelcome.'

The initiative to hold a meeting in Stockholm came from Sandler, who expected that this would help him reinforce the Finnish position in the negotiations. One hundred thousand people demonstrated in support of Finland on 18 October at the royal castle in Stockholm, but the statements of support for president Kallio stimulated only the Swedish public opinion and had no influence on the development of events on the diplomatic scene.[26]

From early October, Minister Sandler pursued an active policy that was to support the Finns in their diplomatic game with the Soviet Union. He claimed that this would scare Stalin off and prevent aggression. Hansson was not willing to take the risk, however. His motto was 'in politics one should never act prematurely'. The prime minister believed waiting until the end of the Finnish–Soviet negotiations would suffice, and that the related tensions in his government would naturally fade away.[27] When it came to foreign policy, his goal was to avoid complications. That is why, following the outbreak of the Winter War, on 30 November, Sandler was forced to resign. As a consequence, the general reconstruction of the government took place.[28] The government programme, adopted on 5 December 1939, following negotiations between the four major government coalition parties, highlighted that the policy of neutrality required the maintenance of relations with both sides and avoiding complications, as well as vigilance of one's own sovereignty. The Swedish government pledged to help Finland,[29] but – to protect its own interests – following a few weeks of negotiations, it concluded commercial agreements with Great Britain (7 December 1939) and Germany (22 December 1939).[30] These agreements formed the basis for trade that proved satisfactory for Sweden until the German attack on Denmark and Norway on 9 April 1940. At the time, the Polish government in Angers hoped that orders for missiles for the destroyers *Grom* and *Błyskawica* would be completed in Sweden, but attempts to initiate discussions on this subject proved fruitless.[31]

---

[26] Y. Möller, *Rickard Sandler. Folkbildare. Utrikesminister*, Stockholm 1990, pp. 376–377.
[27] More information about the policy of Sandler towards Finland, see: A. W. Johansson, *Per Albin...*, pp. 63–80.
[28] Of certain importance could also be the campaign launched in the Hitlerian newspaper the *Völkischer Beobachter*, which was directed against Sweden and Sandler who was perceived as 'an enemy of Germany' and 'a servant of England'. See: Y. Möller, *Rickard...*, p. 386.
[29] ARAB, SAP arkiv, Protokoll, partistyrelsen (a microfilm) 1931–1939, vol. A2C 005, protocol from the meeting of the party leadership with the parliamentary group; attachment: memorandum devoted to the core lines of the coalition government's programme adopted following the negotiations between the representatives of the four main parties, 5 XII 1939.
[30] W. M. Carlgren, *Svensk utrikespolitik...*, pp. 29–35.
[31] *Polska Marynarka Wojenna 1939–1947. Wybór dokumentów*, vol. 1, selected and compiled by Z. Wojciechowski, Gdynia 1999, p. 57.

3. CONSEQUENCES OF THE RIBBENTROP-MOLOTOV PACT

By 10 October 1939 the Polish government in exile adopted guidelines for directors of foreign diplomatic missions. Here it was highlighted that the task of Polish propaganda was to consolidate the truth about the bravery of the Polish army and civilians during the September Campaign.[32] On Swedish ground this task was not easy. Members of the Swedish–Polish association maintained moderation when voicing their positive opinions about Poland. Baron Georg Stiernstedt reminded the public of Poland's indecent acts towards Czechoslovakia in 1938. He justified his statement on the subject to Envoy Potworowski with the need to maintain a neutral attitude towards the conflict between Poland and the other country, as 'the sympathies of some of the members of the association *can* [underlined in the original] be not on the side of Poland.'[33]

It is hard to establish whether this view was determined by the mixed feelings towards the foreign policy of Poland, strong influences of Germany or the struggle for the utopia of absolute neutrality. However, generally, the greatest competition for deliberations on the fate of Poland was the Finnish–Soviet war, a conflict which was closer to the Swedes both geographically and emotionally. Nevertheless, in 1939, several papers discussing the conflicts in Poland were still being published in Sweden.

Zeth Höglund, in his foreword to a collection of articles he published with the suggestive title *Alliansen Hitler-Stalin (Hitler–Stalin Alliance)*, wrote: 'Bolshevism, which in its entire history, and still in August, wanted to be perceived as the leading defender of peace, the strongest opponent of all imperialist aspirations, a defender of the right of nations to self-determination and a sworn enemy of Fascism, in a month took the following form:

- vanquisher of peace as an aggressor against Poland,

- oppressor of free nations (starting with Poland and Estonia),

- supporter of imperialist policy, striving to extend its power in all possible directions (Poland, the Baltic States, the Balkans and Asia),

---

[32] *Protokoły posiedzeń Rady Ministrów Rzeczypospolitej Polskiej*, vol. 1: *październik 1939–czerwiec 1940*, scholarly editing by M. Zgórniak, compiled by W. Rojek in cooperation with L. Neuger, Kraków 1994, p. 16.

[33] A polemic on this subject: AAN, the Polish Legation in Stockholm, 65, letter by the Press Attaché of the Polish Legation in Stockholm, A. de Pomian, to General G. Stiernstedt, Stockholm, 28 XI 1939, pp. 4–6; ibidem, letter by General G. Stiernstedt to the Press Attaché of the Polish Legation in Stockholm, A. de Pomian, Stockholm, 29 XI 1939, pp. 10–11.

- agreement and alliance with the German Nazis, executioners of the working class and democracy.

[...] Nazism and communism became intertwined in a loving embrace. Their offspring is called war and bondage.'[34]

Höglund unmasked the true character of the two totalitarianisms in order to resist both German and Soviet propaganda and treat them as *nazikommunistiska propaganda* (translation: Nazi-Communist propaganda). The opinion journalist predicted that this propaganda marked the beginning of the road to enslavement for Sweden, and decided to give testimony regarding the crime of both regimes against Europe.[35]

The collective work *Polen fjärde delningen* (Poland. The Fourth partition), which constituted the first volume of the chronicle of the Second World War, was laced with compassion and sympathy for the noble and brave Poles, who, despite their greatest efforts, sacrifice and heroism were no match for the German war machine. The opinion journalist Karl Olof Hedström prepared the first four chapters of the book, where he presented the overview of the history of Poland starting from the pre-partition period, through the pro-independence activity of Józef Piłsudski and Roman Dmowski, the regaining of independence in 1918, up until the internal situation and foreign policy of the Second Polish Republic. The author described the achievements of Poles with recognition and respect, including Gdynia and the Central Industrial District, which he visited just prior to the outbreak of the war. He noted that the September defeat resembled the events of the 18th century, when Prussia and Russia partitioned the Polish–Lithuanian Commonwealth. This proved that the Polish state could develop in peace while its two neighbouring powers were at odds. The correspondent for *Stockholms-Tidningen*, Gösta Persson, described the Polish–German conflict from the perspective of the fate of the Free City of Gdańsk majority of population was German, but which could develop successfully under the aegis of the League of Nations and Poland. In turn, the lieutenant of hussars, Stig Facht, examined the campaign from a military point of view. He admitted that due the lack of precision and many distortions in Polish military announcements, he had to base his analysis on the reports of the German command. A reporter for

---

[34] Z. Höglund, *Alliansen Hitler–Stalin*, Stockholm 1939, pp. 3–4.
[35] The first article was published on 23 August 1939, but Z. Höglund already in May that year predicted that the German-Soviet alliance was quite real. See: T. Erlander, *1901–1939*, pp. 262–263.

3. CONSEQUENCES OF THE RIBBENTROP-MOLOTOV PACT

Dagens Nyheter, Vladimir Semitjov, reiterated his impressions, given previously as articles, of the exodus of people fleeing from the Germans during the military campaign in Poland. In the conclusion, Hedström emphasized that the Swedes reacted with grief to the news about the defeat of the great nation, with whom 'our country maintained remarkably friendly relations', as well as that the Polish government continued to exist, although it temporarily had no control over its territory.[36]

Analyses of the September Campaign were also published as part of a series entitled *Kriget* (The War) and in the military magazine *Ny militär tidskrift* (New Military Journal). Their overall tone was favourable towards Poland, and their assessment of the course of combat and the causes of defeat was realistic.[37]

Shortly afterwards collections of diplomatic documents were published in Sweden under the auspices of each side engaged in the war whose intention was to present its opponent as the initiator of the conflict. The Germans published the White Paper at the Bonniers publishing house that made them an object of scorn in the eyes of supporters of the Western Allies: 'This very same publishing house was described by Goebbels as one of the worst Jewish octopuses.'[38] The British published the British War Blue Book at the Bonniers publishing house and in the *Kooperativa Förbundets Förlag* publishing house. Their reviewers highlighted that it was of great importance that readers take their own stand in relation to the content of both publications. Only on a few occasions did they pointed out that the diplomatic conflict had in fact already reached its climax and the avoidance of confrontation was impossible.[39]

Göteborgs Handels- och Sjöfarts-Tidning informed its readers that Polish patriots were pouring in to France to continue fighting the Germans. It was believed possible to recruit as many as 200 thousand soldiers from Polish expatriates in France.[40] Albert Ehrensvärd, in the same daily newspaper, stated that the new Polish government had finished with its non-democratic past. He predicted the rebirth of not only Poland, but all other countries that had been conquered by Hitler: 'There is no reason to doubt in the resurrection of Poland and Czechoslovakia, though perhaps in a new form and within the new borders. In the times we live in, cultured and developing

---

[36] *Polen fjärde delningen*, Stockholm 1939, pp. 8, 102, 197–199, 209.
[37] M. Cygański, 'Publicystyka państw skandynawskich wobec agresji...', *Przegląd Zachodniopomorski* 1983, iss. 1–2, p. 95.
[38] '*Oförsynt judetilltag*', Trots Allt!, 21 X 1939.
[39] '*Dokumenten*', Östgöta Correspondenten, 24 X 1939.
[40] '*Situationen*', Göteborgs Handels- och Sjöfarts-Tidning, 28 IX 1939.

nations cannot be held in captivity [...]. The sooner their liberation takes place, the quicker order and stability will be restored in Europe.'[41]

One year later, Jacob de Geer called for remembrance of Poland and the Poles: 'We are speaking about the rebuilding of Denmark, Norway, France, but is there any one speaking about Poland? Each defeat reveals mistakes and weaknesses. The gloomy notions of *polsk riksdag*, *Polnische Wirtschaft* as well as of quarrelsome and incautious Poles have returned. People are saying that they have suffered a defeat because of their customary defiance. Nevertheless, throughout the last year the Polish nation has turned out to be the only one, except for the British, to shed its blood in defence of its homeland. In many aspects it should serve as an example for other nations.'[42]

Further, he noted that Poland did not face up to the German war machine, but when defeat had been experienced by France, it was then France that was pointed to as an example of a power that proved incapable of resisting the Germans. According to de Geer, another argument for remembering Poland, and the need for its resurrection, was that no traitor like the president of Czechoslovakia Emil Hácha or Norwegian Vidkun Quisling operated there. What should be noted is that the liberal daily newspaper *Göteborgs Handels- och Sjöfarts-Tidning* was included in the circle of leading Swedish newspapers that openly opposed the new German order in Europe. The editor-in-chief, Torgny Segerstedt, had warned his readers already about Hitler's possessiveness before the outbreak of war. Despite the constant threat of confiscation, he continued his uncompromising attacks on the totalitarian rules of Germany on the continent, as well as on the Swedish government, who was trying to prevent the invasion by means of a policy of concessions. For Segerstedt, the fight with Hitler was tantamount to the fight for freedom, law and democracy.[43]

From the end of 1939, it was difficult to make reference to Polish affairs, both due to the lack of interest and freedom of press limitations. On 20

---

[41] A. Ehrensvärd, 'Polen i landsflykt', *Göteborgs Handels- och Sjöfarts-Tidning*, 22 XII 1939.
[42] J. de Geer, 'Efter tjugu års mellanakt', *Göteborgs Handels- och Sjöfarts-Tidning*, 13 XII 1940.
[43] See T. Nybom, *Motstånd - anpassning - uppslutning. Linjer i svensk debatt om utrikespolitik och internationell politik 1940–1943*, Stockholm 1978, pp. 47–49, 70. Worthy of note is the difference in the attitude towards the German and the Soviet totalitarianism. The opinion journalists for *Göteborgs Handels- och Sjöfarts-Tidning* consequently stated that the Soviet Union was not expansive and aggressive by nature. Also the social-democratic daily *Arbetet* propagated the view that the communist dictatorship in Russia, as opposed to Fascism, was not striving for external expansion. Segerstedt, even following Stalin's aggression against Finland in 1939, perceived Germany as the main threat. These views are reflected in the commentaries on the subject of Polish–Soviet relations in 1943 and later.

3. CONSEQUENCES OF THE RIBBENTROP-MOLOTOV PACT

December 1939 laws changed resulting in restrictions on civil liberties, including freedom of speech and publication. On 20 January 1940, during a public debate on these restrictions, the most-right leaning member of parliament, Ivar Anderson, said: 'Swedish society must adapt to the new era.'[44] In practice this meant avoiding voicing opinions which could provoke a reaction from the countries involved in the war.

From 1940 only a few articles were published that pointed out the policy mistakes of the pre-war Polish authorities which led to the defeat in September 1939. It was highlighted that the government formed after the lost campaign was composed of 'brave and wise people, who can offer a new future to the Polish nation.'[45] Following the defeat of France in July 1940, Polish military efforts in autumn 1939 began to be assessed differently: 'France had to defend itself against the attack of 80 million Germans and 40 million Italians while being supported by well-prepared fortifications, natural barriers and Great Britain. Poland was defeated by 80 million Germans and 170 million Russians while not being supported by any fortifications whatsoever.'[46] German successes on the western front made the Swedish press revise their opinion of Polish army's weakness in 1939. Opinions were even voiced that the Poles had done a better job than their powerful allies.[47]

In 1940, the brochure *How it Happened! From Versailles Until Today* was published, in which an anonymous author explained the genesis and course of the Polish–German conflict in the interwar period. The author mostly focused on the situation of the German minority in Poland and the Polish minority in

---

[44] A. W. Johansson, *Per Albin.*, pp. 99–103. Also during this debate a renowned historian and opinion journalist, Herbert Tingsten, drew attention to the absurdity of the situation: 'The only ones who may not be criticised are the governments of the countries who are attacking our government'. The influence of restriction on freedom of speech in Sweden during the war on the general presence of Polish theme was described by A. N. Uggla, *Den svenska Polenbilden...*

[45] Tasp., '*Politisk tvekamp i armén vållade Polens katastrof*', *Dagens Nyheter*, 11 I 1940.

[46] '*Orsakerna till Polens nederlag*', *Arbetaren*, 25 VII 1940.

[47] See the quotation from the *Social-Demokraten* daily reprinted in the Polish newspapers published in the USA: A. K. Kunert, *Rzeczpospolita Walcząca. Styczeń–grudzień 1940. Kalendarium*, Warszawa 1997, p. 306. Paradoxically, these opinions were more likely to be made public by the closely observed and systematically criticised by the Germans – due to, according to Berlin, excessive virulence – Swedish press rather than by an allied broadcasting station. Minister of Information and Documentation S. Stroński addressed this issue during the government session on 8 January 1941: 'At times we had problems with the BBC in relation to the preoccupation of the British with avoiding putting the French off. This was the reason for the BBC's unwillingness to repeat the opinion of the Swedish press, who considered our army better than that of the French'. See: *Protokoły posiedzeń Rady Ministrów Rzeczypospolitej Polskiej*, vol. 2: *czerwiec 1940 – czerwiec 1941*, scholarly editing by M. Zgórniak, compiled by W. Rojek in cooperation with A. Suchcitz, Kraków 1995, p. 259.

Germany, and polemicized with the propaganda of Goebbels and described the position of the German minority as much better.[48] In turn, lawyer Stanisław Adamek, who came to Sweden with refugees from Poland and started to cooperate with the *Trots Allt!* magazine, argued that Poland needed peace more than any other country in Europe, that it did not want war and that it was not prepared for it. Adamek also exposed the brutal conduct of the Germans towards civilians during the campaign and later on.[49] It is worth noting that *Trots Allt!*, which was published by Ture Nerman, was famed from its conception for its crusade against totalitarianism and defeatism, which spread increasingly among Swedish society following Hitler's victories.[50]

As well as some favourable studies in the Swedish publishing market, there appeared an anti-Polish work devoted to the defeat of the Second Polish Republic. Torun Hedlund-Nyström (a Secretary of the Editorial Board for the journal *Sverige-Tyskland*), in the beginning of her book *Polens fjärde delning. Dess förhistoria och fullbordan* (The Fourth Partition of Poland. Its Genesis and Execution) presented the argument that the Polish nation, like no other of similar size, was never able to maintain a strong national culture, and the epithets *polsk riksdag* and *Polnische Wirtschaft*, therefore, were the result. Absurd decisions concerning the location of borders, approved by the Treaty of Versailles, as well as Polish chauvinism, fuelled by the activity of ultra nationalist associations, were responsible for the Poland–Germany conflict, which centred on Gdańsk.[51] Hedlund-Nyström did not explicitly blame any of the sides, but remarked that the Germans were neither the exclusive nor the main perpetrators and that part of the responsibility rested on the shoulders of Great Britain. On a map depicting the concentration of armies of both sides before 1 September 1939, the author drew arrows that allegedly showed the planned attacks of the Polish armies. She did not deny the bravery of Polish soldiers, but quoting General Edmund Ironside she accused the higher command of a lack of sufficient organisational skills.

---

[48] Justus, *Hur det skedde! Från Versailles till i dag*, Stockholm 1940.
[49] ESWU [Stanisław Adamek], *Folkens frihetskamp. Det nya världkriget*, Stockholm 1940, pp. 14, 16, 21–22, 82.
[50] For more information about the circles centred around the *Trots Allt!*, see: L. Drangel, *Den kämpande demokratin. En studie i antinazistisk opinionsrörelse 1935–1945*, Stockholm 1976, pp. 34–73.
[51] T. Hedlund-Nyström, *Polens fjärde delning. Dess förhistoria och fullbordan*, Malmö 1940, pp. 11, 95, 109, 135, 139, 159.

3. CONSEQUENCES OF THE RIBBENTROP-MOLOTOV PACT

During the Winter War

In the face of growing tensions in Finnish-Soviet relations, which by Stalin's order, on 30 November 1939, evolved into the so-called Winter War, the Finnish issue became the number one story both in the press and during the sessions of the Swedish government. Insofar as during the September Campaign opinions as to the genesis of the war were divided. The Swedish public opinion clearly condemned the Soviet aggression, using such blunt terms as cynicism, brutality and aversion to describe the overt injustice inflicted upon a peaceful nation. The attack on Finland was received almost like an attack on Sweden itself. Supporters of an active military engagement by Sweden in defence of Finland repeated the slogan *'Finlands sak är vår'* (Finland's business is ours). People also started to wonder how Hitler and Stalin actually divided up Europe and in which of the two spheres of influence Sweden found itself.[52] The Polish matter was pushed into the background, and therefore appeared only in the margins of political debate.[53]

In connection with the growing interest in the Soviet expansion – following the aggression against Finland and later annexations in the territories of the Baltic States – publications describing the situation in the Polish Eastern Borderlands began to be put out. In the preface to the brochure *Rysslands nya imperialism: de små nationernas drama i diktaturstaten* (The New Russian Imperialism. The Tragedy of Small Nations in a Dictatorial Country) by Paul Olberg (a former activist of the Mensheviks, editor of *Social-Demokraten*, and Swedish citizen) a well-known social-democratic activist Zeth Höglund argued that Stalin's aggressions were a continuation of Russian imperialism, the only difference being that the Bolshevik imperialism used methods which were far more clever, sophisticated, and brutal, under the veil of social liberation. Olberg concluded that the Soviet policy conducted in the Polish territories led to the spread of disorganisation and anarchy, lawlessness and poverty. These views of opinion journalists who moved in social democratic circles were echoed by the Swedish journalist Letta Rudnicka-Jaroszynska in *Mitt möte med Röda armén* (My Meeting with the Soviet Army) published in 1943, where she described her life under Soviet occupation. The reign of the Bolsheviks in Poland was, according to her, tantamount to the reign of terror

---

[52] J. Torbacke, *Dagens Nyheter och demokratins kris 1937–1946. Genom stormar till seger*, Stockholm 1972, pp. 103–104.
[53] When in the beginning of December 1939 S. Grafström returned to Berlin from occupied Warsaw, he found that the only matter that was discussed in the Swedish Legation was the Finnish-Soviet war. Same was the case in the capital of Sweden. See: S. Grafström, *Anteckningar 1938–1944*, p. 200, 203.

and lawlessness, propaganda brainwashing, poverty and hunger, deportations and atheisation of social life.[54]

According to Envoy Potworowski, over the following several months the Swedish press became increasingly neutral, and, to escape exposure to any charges, hard-hitting commentaries were avoided. News from the General Government, introduced by the Germans in the occupied territories of Poland, was mostly neglected.[55] In spite of this, Potworowski, based on his experience from working in Stockholm for several years, stressed that the press was showing a lot of good will by periodically reporting on the activity of the Polish government in exile, the development of Polish Armed Forces in the West or about the tragic situation in the territories occupied by the Germans and the Soviets.[56] Moreover, attacks on Poland in the press were rare or pointless. This was also how Potworowski evaluated screenings of *Blitzkrieg*, which portrayed the 1939 campaign in Poland. According to the Polish envoy, the film was weak, and therefore harmless. Most reviewers of the film agreed with his opinion.[57] This was one of the reasons why, in March 1941, the Polish diplomat asserted that the attitude of the Swedish press on

---

[54] L. Rudnicka-Jaroszynska, *Mitt möte med Röda armén, Malmö 1943*, pp. 55–56, 62, 86, 101–102, 109–110, 113, 181.

[55] During the initial months of the war, the British propaganda services in Sweden were concentrating particularly on the dissemination of descriptions of brutal actions of the German occupying forces in Poland. See: Ch. Cruickshank, *SOE in Scandinavia*, Oxford–New York 1986, p. 49.

[56] See: discussion on these articles in the Polish newspapers in London: 'W Szwecji o Polsce. Nie ma Quislingów wśród Polaków', *Dziennik Polski*, 26 XI 1940; 'Szwed o rujnującej gospodarce niemieckiej w Polsce', *Dziennik Polski*, 15 I 1941; *Tak jest w Warszawie*, 'Dziennik Polski', 18 VII 1941; 'Szwedzki dziennikarz, który był w Polsce', *Dziennik Polski*, 1 XI 1941; 'Szwecja nie tai prawdy o Polsce', *Dziennik Polski*, 19 XI 1941; 'W Szwecji o Armii Polskiej', *Dziennik Żołnierza*, 3 VI 1942; 'Szwedzi o cierpieniach Polski', *Dziennik Polski*, 27 VIII 1942; 'Prasa szwedzka o nas', *Dziennik Polski*, 17 XI 1942; 'Co widział obserwator szwedzki w Polsce? Smutne życie w zburzonej Warszawie', *Dziennik Polski*, 16 I 1943; 'Dziennik szwedzki o życiu w Warszawie', *Wieści Polskie*, 12 III 1943; 'Dziennik szwedzki o życiu w Warszawie', *Orzeł Biały*, 4 IV 1943. It is worth noting that the Polish press in London quoted Swedish articles about Poland very rarely, as it perceived them as a valuable intermediary in the process of acquiring information on the situation in the occupied territories and it was not reasonable to attract the German attention to these sources.

[57] This most probably refers to the documentary film by F. Hippler *Feldzug in Polen* (*Campaign in Poland*), screened in Germany from 6 February 1940. Or possibly another documentary film devoted to the same subject – H. Bertram's *Feuertaufe* (*Baptism of Fire*), which was presented for the first time in Oslo on 5 April 1940 and one day later in Berlin. See: A. K. Kunert, *Rzeczpospolita Walcząca. Styczeń–grudzień 1940*, p. 156. Polish newspapers published in London highlighted that the film did not arouse much enthusiasm in Stockholm, see: 'Film, który się nie podoba Szwedom', *Dziennik Polski*, 5 V 1941. British press attaché Peter Tennant mentions Swedish screenings of the film *Feuertaufe*, see: P. Tennant, *Vid sidan av kriget. Diplomat i Sverige 1939–1945*, Stockholm 1989, p. 115.

3. CONSEQUENCES OF THE RIBBENTROP-MOLOTOV PACT

the Polish matter was 'more than appropriate, as it was friendly and full of understanding and sympathy for our situation.'[58] Throughout the entire war the *Svio-Polonica* annual was published by the Polish–Swedish Academic Association of the Stockholm University College (*Svensk-polska studiesällskapet vid Stockholms högskola*). Those who deserve the most credit for safeguarding Polish–Swedish academic relations during the war were the Polish language teachers at the higher education institutions in Stockholm, Uppsala and Lund – Zbigniew Folejewski, Jerzy Trypućko and Zygmunt Łakociński.

In 1942 Otto Sjögren, the author of a university handbook in geography, devoted a chapter to Poland. Based on pre-war sightseeing descriptions, he presented a picture of Warsaw before the bombings – a city, not enchanting at first sight, but which improved on closer inspection, and Gdynia – the best Polish interwar investment. The author predicted that 'history may once more allow us to see Poland reborn.'[60]

Gunnar Lundberg, in 1940, published his evaluation of the foreign and domestic policy of the Second Polish Republic. He described Poland as a country with a meaningful Russian minority and quite severe social oppression. In his view, its victorious opponents were worse still. The Soviet Union, in exchange for its will of cooperation with the Third Reich, received a payment in the form of half of Poland and the Baltic States.[61]

A negative picture of Poland and the Poles re-emerged in contemporary Swedish diary literature. In his memoirs, published 1942–43, Swedish diplomat Einar af Wirsén, and official of the Swedish Legation in Warsaw in 1921, emphasized the capital city's dirt, 18th-century mentality of Polish politicians, their ignorance, recklessness, quarrelsomeness and ruthlessness.[62] Other books of this genre were also published. In 1942 *Det har inte stått i tidningen. En svensk utlandsjournalists minnen från två krigsår* (This Was Not in the Newspaper. A Swedish Foreign Correspondent's Memoirs of Two Years of War) was published. It was written by Gunnar Müllern, a Berlin correspondent for *Aftonbladet*, who travelled to the General Government twice – at the beginning of 1940 and again in mid-1941. Müllern recalled the 'bloody Sunday' in Bydgoszcz as an example of repression used by the Poles on the Germans.

---

[58] AAN, HI/I/199, press report by Polish Envoy to Stockholm G. Potworowski for the Ministry of Foreign Affairs, Stockholm, 12 III 1941.
[60] O. Sjögren, *Geografisk läsebok*, vol. 2: *Europa utom Norden*, Stockholm 1942, pp. 765–777.
[61] G. Lundberg, *Missnöjets missionärer. En vidräkning med de kommunistiska sabotörerna*, Stockholm 1940, p. 6.
[62] E. af Wirsén, *Minnen från krig och fred*, Stockholm 1942; idem, *Från Balkan till Berlin*, Stockholm 1943. See: B. Skarżyński, *Motywy polskie w piśmiennictwie szwedzkim w czasie wojny (ciąg dalszy)*, 'Nowa Polska' 1946, iss. 1, pp. 62–64.

When addressing the German policy during the occupation, he did not encounter any anomalies, describing it instead as 'iron discipline.' Polish people complained about increase in prices, but – according to Müllern – the Germans made sure that factory employees and their families were offered cheap meals by field kitchens. The German Governor Hans Frank also assured him that he was planning to rebuild Poland. An indicator of situation in the Kraków Ghetto was the availability of coffee and other goods, although at inflated prices. In general, the views of Müllern were infused with anti-Semitism. His account does not mention acts of terror and massacres committed by the Germans. Instead it focuses on the filth and stench, for which he blamed the Jews.[63]

Memories of Poland can be found in *Hakkorsets tidevarv* (The Era of the Swastika), a book published only in 1944 by a Berlin correspondent for *Svenska Dagbladet* and *Stockholms-Tidningen*, Bertil Svahnström. This publication covers Svahnström's work in Germany. It contains few Polish threads, but Svahnström describes the damage incurred by Poland in September 1939. The visit to occupied Warsaw was a particularly meaningful experience for him: 'It was shocking to see the first city that was reduced to rubble during the Second World War. Over the first five years of the war we gradually became less sensitive [...], but what we saw during these memorable days of September have been our most striking experience.'[64] Although at the outset of the war his attitude was pro-German, he expressed disbelief at the Soviet bestiality presented to the foreign press correspondents by the Germans in the Lviv prisons occupied in the summer of 1941. He also mentions the process of Germanisation and the misery of Poles from Poznań province, which had been incorporated in the Third Reich.

The decline in the public interest in Sweden as to the fate of the Second Polish Republic harmonized with the passivity of the Swedish government, which was at the beginning of 1939 and 1940 preoccupied with issues that were marginal in the sphere of Polish–Swedish relations. On 19 January 1940, for instance, Swedish authorities examined the case of a butler at the Swedish Legation in Warsaw, Józef Szymański, who died during the bombing of the city on 24 September 1939 when he was at working in the building of the legation. The minister's request was that the Swedes cover all the costs of his

---

[63] G. Müllern, *Det har inte stått i tidningen. En svensk utlandsjournalists minnen från två krigsår*, Stockholm 1942, pp. 52–57, 179–184.

[64] PISM, A 21, 8/26, the study devoted to the book by B. Svahnström entitled *Hakkorsets tidenarv* (*The Era of Swastika*).

3. CONSEQUENCES OF THE RIBBENTROP-MOLOTOV PACT

funeral, 663.14 crowns, from the additional expenses fund.[65] In the Swedish diplomatic correspondence it is difficult to find the echoes of Polish efforts to launch protests against the harsh occupational policy in Poland.[66] Sweden behaved the same as other neutral countries, which for fear of reprisals from Berlin and Moscow 'had to pretend that the Polish matter did not exist.'[67]

At the outset of November 1939, the Polish Ministry of Foreign Affairs ordered Potworowski to enquire in to proposing the novel *Sól ziemi* (*The Salt of the Land*) by Józef Wittlin for the Nobel Prize in Literature.[68] There was speculation that Wittlin had a chance of winning, which would be of great significance, in terms of propaganda, for the Polish matter. The Winter War, however, diverted attention away from the subject of Poland even in this instance. The prize was awarded to the Finnish writer Frans Eemil Sillanpää.

Joen Lagerberg was not delegated to London to continue the mission as Swedish envoy at the Polish government. The Nordic States also agreed not to delegate their diplomatic representatives to Paris. Administrative changes introduced by the Germans and Soviets were accepted, and further developments were anticipated. In January 1940 Lagerberg, who had remained in Stockholm and been given little to do, was made director of the B Division, charged with the protection of interests for countries at war. Lagerberg reassured Potworowski that his accreditation to the Polish government was intact, maintaining that was the reason Lagerberg had been assigned a task in his homeland and not delegated abroad.[69] As well as the Swedish wait-and-see attitude, there are several examples of closer relations between Polish and Swedish diplomats at various posts. According to Polish Ambassador to Ankara Michał Sokolnicki, to give one example, the attitude of Swedish Envoy Einar Modig towards Poland was friendly. In 1942, after Envoy Potworowski had been expelled from Sweden, Modig visited Sokolnicki to explain this decision citing

---

[65] RA, Kabinettet/UD Huvudarkivet, Statsrådsprotokoll, series A3A, vol. 107, 'Protokoll över Utrikesdepartementets ärende', Stockholm, 19 I 1940.
[66] The Polish government kept calling for such protests to the neutral states, especially to the USA and Vatican, referring to speeches delivered by Americans in reaction to the Soviet Union's pressures on Finland. See: *Protokoły posiedzeń Rady Ministrów Rzeczypospolitej Polskiej*, vol. 1, p. 88 (the statement of the Undersecretary of State at the Presidency of the Council of Ministers during the sessions of the Government on 23 November 1939).
[67] Report by Deputy Minister of Foreign Affairs Z. Graliński at a December meeting of the League of Nations, 9 I 1940 [in:] *Sprawa polska w czasie drugiej wojny światowej na arenie międzynarodowej. Zbiór dokumentów*, ed. S. Stanisławska, Warszawa 1965, p. 132.
[68] AAN, HI/I/245, telegram by Minister of Foreign Affairs A. Zaleski to the Swedish Legation in Stockholm, 2 XI 1939.
[69] AAN, HI/I/256, telegram by Polish Envoy to Stockholm G. Potworowski to the Ministry of Foreign Affairs, 11 I 1940.

pressures from Germany.[70] In turn, the presiding attaché to Bern, Stanisław Edward Nahlik, mentioned many years later that he had close relations with Swedish Envoy Zenon Przybyszewski-Westrup.[71] Incidental meetings with the Swedes were also acknowledged by ambassador Raczyński (though he omitted meeting with Prytz on September, 26, 1939).[72] From the second half of 1941, Swedish envoy to Moscow Vilhelm Assarsson discussed the situation and policy of the Soviet Union with the Polish ambassador professor Stanisław Kot. From the beginning of 1942 the Polish diplomat was fearful of Stalin's attitude to the Polish issues. He predicted that the Soviet Union would adopt an imperialist policy similar to that of tsarist Russia.[73]

Mutual relations between diplomats mostly involved contacts between the Swedish Ministry of Foreign Affairs and the staff of the Polish Legation in Stockholm. Yet, the Swedes were very cautious and situations determined precisely the limits of their mission. In March 1940 they demanded that the Polish Legation stop their radio station broadcasts. Potworowski explained that using operating a radio station was in line with international legislation and customs, but he did not manage to convince his interlocutor and the Poles eventually had to capitulate.[74] Envoy Potworowski drew the attention of the Polish Ministry of Foreign Affairs to the inappropriate content of articles published by the official press bulletin of the Ministry of Information and Communications *Głos Polski* (*The Voice of Poland*), which 'systematically attacks Sweden in connection with the Finnish matter by means of offensive expressions and arguments.' Potworowski maintained that this was politically harmful and could make the operation of the Polish diplomatic mission in Stockholm even more difficult. For the Germans it provided an opportunity to launch anti-Polish propaganda.[75]

Polish diplomatic circles attributed even greater significance to relations with Sweden. Jan Ciechanowski, the newly appointed Secretary of State at the Ministry of Foreign Affairs in Angers, the right hand of Zaleski, proposed that the operation of the ministry in exile be organized along the traditional

---

[70] M. Sokolnicki, *Dziennik ankarski 1939–1943*, pp. 420–421; idem, *Ankarski dziennik 1943–1946*, London 1974, pp. 265, 293. These social meetings have been recorded in the book.
[71] S. E. Nahlik, *Przesiane przez pamięć*, vol. 2, Kraków 2002, p. 277.
[72] E. Raczyński, *W sojuszniczym...*, p. 152.
[73] V. Assarsson, *I skuggan av Stalin*, Stockholm 1963, pp. 104–105.
[74] AAN, HI/I/256, telegram by Polish Envoy to Stockholm G. Potworowski to the Ministry of Foreign Affairs, 13 III 1940.
[75] Ibidem, telegram by Polish Envoy to Stockholm G. Potworowski to the Ministry of Foreign Affairs, Stockholm, 21 III 1940.

divisions: allied, hostile and neutral states.⁷⁶ The new division was not introduced, but Minister Zaleski, during the session of the National Council on 28 March 1940, highlighted that even though priority would be given to the relations with France and Great Britain, actions in other directions should entertained. He discussed separately the relations with the neutral states, mentioning firstly the Holy See and the USA. He regretted the fact that many states with which the Polish government maintained diplomatic relations decided not to delegate their representatives to France because of pressures from Germany. In fact, he did not mention Sweden, but it could be included in the group of countries, to which Zaleski thanked for 'not refusing to grant temporary asylum to numerous Polish refugees and who helped them to survive these difficult times.' Gratitude was extended both to the authorities and to associations and private persons.⁷⁷ Minister of Labour and Social Welfare Jan Stańczyk distinguished Sweden among the countries who took part in the humanitarian action for occupied Poland. He stated that around 20 thousand Swedish crowns together with clothes were donated by Sweden.⁷⁸

Despite these facts, the outbreak of the Winter War was equivalent to the opening of a new chapter in Polish–Swedish relations. In December 1939, when the fighting on the Finnish–Soviet front was already in progress, Boheman admitted, during a conversation with counsellor of the British Legation William Montagu-Pollock, that the Swedish government was groping in the dark, as it was unfamiliar with the exact intentions of either the Germans or the Soviets. According to Envoy Richert, the Germans were to attack Sweden instantly if Sweden supported Finland against the Soviet Union. At the same time, Göring encouraged them to help the Finns. According to the Briton's view, Swedish military circles and public opinion were in favour of launching a specific aid operation for Finland, whereas the government considered such support to be suicide.⁷⁹ The Swedes were convinced that what needed to be prevented was the merging of two European military conflicts where the Germans and the Soviet Union would join forces against Great Britain and France. That is why Stockholm firmly opposed the plans of launching an intervention of the Western Allies in Scandinavia.

---

[76] S. Zabiełło, *Na posterunku we Francji*, Warszawa 1967, p. 58.
[77] E. Duraczyński, R. Turkowski, *O Polsce na uchodźstwie. Rada Narodowa Rzeczypospolitej Polskiej 1939–1945*, Warszawa 1997, pp. 38, 256–262.
[78] RA, UD avdelningar och byråarkiv 1864–1952, Andra B-avdelningen, vol. 417, bulletin of the agency Pol-Radio, no. 132, Stockholm, 2 IV 1940.
[79] NA, FO, 371/23709, memorandum by W. Montagu-Pollock, 19 XII 1939.

The decision to grant military support to Finland was made by the Allies on 19 December 1939. They hoped that this would also solve the issue of suspending deliveries of Swedish iron ore to Germany.[80] On 27 December, the Swedish government was acquainted with the plan to transit the English and French armies from Norway, through Sweden, to Finland. The main advocate of this plan was the incumbent First Lord of the Admiralty, Winston Churchill.[81] Several days later, the Swedes submitted their reply, where they refused to participate in the operation. They explained that this would lead to a countermove by the Germans and Soviet Union, and that it was in the Allies' interest that Sweden maintained its neutrality.[82] The fear of the Germans also prevented the Swedes from launching their individual campaign in Finland, because Hansson was convinced that Hitler would interpret such an engagement as consent for an intervention by the Allies.[83] The proposal to grant special warranties of security by London were accepted by the Swedes with reserve. They pointed to the example of Poland, where British warranties were of no use. Sweden did not support the resolution on excluding the Soviet Union from the League of Nations, abstaining from voting together with Denmark and Norway.[84] The Swedish delegation left the session room during voting.[85] On 4 January 1940, the Swedes expressed their willingness to facilitate the action of the Allies, but not so as to be accused of violating the principles of neutrality.

At the same time, the Finns initiated talks about possible support from the West through the port in Petsamo. A specific proposal was introduced that the operation be performed with the backing of Polish Navy vessels in the event that the British wanted to avoid fighting with the Soviets. General Sikorski maintained that this benefit the Polish matter, but disapproved of the French and the British barring Polish officers from participating in the

---

[80] A. Suchcitz, 'Polska a wojna fińsko-sowiecka 1939–1940', *Niepodległość 1988*, pp. 167–168.
[81] See: W. S. Churchill, *The Second World War*, vol. 1: *The Gathering Storm*, London 1985, pp. 490–493; P. R. Osborne, *Operation Pike: Britain Versus the Soviet Union, 1939 –1941*, Westport, CT, USA, 2000.
[82] A. W. Johansson, *Per Albin och kriget*, Stockholm 1984, p. 115. Before the Allies officially turned to Stockholm in the matter of transit of their army, Hansson, at a meeting of the leadership of the social-democratic party, explained that the Swedish government needed to think carefully before accepting any support from the Western Allies, as it was necessary for considering the fate of their smaller allies.
[83] *Ibidem*, p. 122.
[84] J. Nevakivi, *The appeal that was never made. The Allies, Scandinavia and the Finnish winter war 1939–1940*, London 1976, p. 60.
[85] B. Piotrowski, *Wojna radziecko-fińska (zimowa) 1939–1940. Legendy, niedomówienia, realia*, Poznań 1997, pp. 103–104; J. Szymański, *Skandynawia–Polska...*, pp. 204–205.

3. CONSEQUENCES OF THE RIBBENTROP-MOLOTOV PACT

staff discussions. Meanwhile, the Allies' plans included the landing in Northern Finland of an alpine rifle brigade, two battalions of foreign legions, four (or two) Polish battalions and one British brigade – in total approximately 17 thousand troops.[86]

The Polish government proposed that the first troops to be transported through Stockholm to Finland would be those of the Polish divisions, interned in the Baltic States and in the Balkans (Polish pilots, soldiers of the Border Protection Corps (*Korpus Ochrony Pogranicza*) and other units), reinforced by French troops. The Poles expected Sweden to transfer military equipment, the purchase of which was being negotiated between the Allies and Stockholm.[87] The armament company Bofors, which prior to the war supplied equipment and licenses, had obligations towards Poland. The talks were to be held in Helsinki and Stockholm and Lieutenant Colonel Tadeusz Rudnicki was to participate in them. Sikorski hoped that Rudnicki would convince the Swedes to take Polish volunteers in, and even to equip them with arms and military attire. He considered a more probable scenario would be the setting up of aviation divisions in Sweden, and relocating the Border Protection Corps to the Åland.[88]

According to Marshal Carl Gustaf von Mannerheim, the plan failed due to opposition from Sweden, but Polish documentation reveals Finland was also reluctant towards the negotiations between the Polish and Finnish governments in Helsinki.[89] Nevertheless, Lieutenant Colonel Rudnicki, who talked to the Finns with authorisation from the Polish government, agreed with General Rudolf Walden that the main obstacle to bringing the Poles from Latvia to Finland was the refusal of the Swedish government to their transit.[90]

The new Swedish Minister of Foreign Affairs, Christian Günther, on 9 January 1940, assured the German Envoy, Prince Victor of Wied, that Sweden would not provide military support to Finland, at the behest of the League of Nations, as this would be against the policy of neutrality. He added

---

[86] J. Nevakivi, *The appeal...*, pp. 50, 65, 70–73, 87–89, 105.
[87] *Protokoły posiedzeń Rady Ministrów Rzeczypospolitej Polskiej*, vol. 1, p. 133.
[88] AAN, HI/I/246, telegram by Prime Minister and the Commander-in-Chief General W. Sikorski do Lieutenant Colonel T. Rudnicki, 4 II 1940.
[89] We may certainly speak of ambiguous attitude of the Finns towards the plans of their support from the Allies, because they did not regulate their political-diplomatic relations with Poland following the September Campaign and avoided direct negotiations at high level. The question also arises of whether the plan to transfer circa 10 thousand Polish troops and officers from the Baltic States to the Finnish front was at all feasible. See: A. Suchcitz, Polska., p. 177; K. Tarka, 'Z Litwy do Finlandii? Polacy w wojnie sowiecko-fińskiej', *Zeszyty Historyczne* 1996, iss. 115, p. 222.
[90] J. Nevakivi, *The appeal...*, pp. 179–183.

that he would oppose every attempt of setting up an Ally military base in his country, and even the attempt to transfer the British or French forces through its territory.⁹¹ In turn, towards the end of February, in a conversation with a Member of the British House of Commons, Harold Macmillan, Minister Günther highlighted that his government's principal aim was to prevent Sweden from engaging in a worldwide military conflict. That is why he considered a swift conclusion to the Finnish–Soviet peace agreement to be the best solution.⁹²

At the outset of February 1940, Secretary General Boheman met with Gustaw Potworowski. During their conversation he repeated arguments presented by the Swedish diplomats to the representatives of the powers. He stated that Sweden would not join the war, as victory would be impossible in the clash with the Germans, and Great Britain would not be able to help. He argued: 'In such situation no country would desire to spread the war to its own territory. The war with us would not be easy for the Germans either, and is without doubt undesirable, but they would not hesitate to start it, if we gave them even the smallest reason to do so. That is why we must be very careful not to fall into the trap.'⁹³ According to Potworowski, Boheman's statement reflected the mood of the majority of the political elite and the Swedish public. The Swedes were, however, in favour of the idea of offering military support to Finland, which was fighting with the Soviet Union, for, as claimed the deputy minister: 'Each Swede understands today that the military defeat of Finland would pose a direct threat to the borders of Sweden.'⁹⁴ On the other hand he appealed: 'under no circumstances may we grant this support, directly or indirectly, for this would involve Sweden in "the great war."' The challenge of reconciling the attitude of neutrality towards the powers with the increase in support for Finland was difficult.⁹⁵ The Swedes endeavoured to bring an end to the Winter War by

---

⁹¹ W. Wilhelmus, 'Det tyska anfallet mot Skandinavien' [in:] *Urladdning. 1940 – blixtkrigens år*, ed. B. Hugemark, Luleå 2002, pp. 64–65. On the Swedish-German talks on the subject of the fate of Finland in the autumn of 1939, see: S. Dębski, *Między Berlinem a Moskwą. Stosunki niemiecko-sowieckie 1939–1941*, Warszawa 2003, pp. 271–273.
⁹² H. Macmillan, *The Blast of War 1939–1945*, London 1967, pp. 47–48.
⁹³ PISM, A 12, 3/2, vol. 2, letter by Envoy G. Potworowski to the Ministry of Foreign Affairs, Stockholm, 8 II 1940, p. 528.
⁹⁴ Ibidem.
⁹⁵ Ibidem. At around the same time S. Grafström, on commenting in the daily on the current policy of Sweden, stated perversely: 'Neutrality is indeed an art of balancing on a rope, but when one is balancing and dancing at the same time, one risks falling off.' See: S. Grafström, *Anteckningar 1938–1944*, p. 208–209. See: A. W. Johansson, 'I skuggan av operation Barbarosa. Attityder och stämningar 1940/1941' [in:] *I orkanens öga. 1941 – osäker neutralitet*, ed. B. Hugemark, Luleå 2002, pp. 84–85.

means of an amicable settlement. They attempted to prevent, where feasible, preparations for the British–French military intervention with the co-participation of Poland, as well as work out a peaceful solution for Finland and the Soviet Union.[96] Sweden, for which peace was vitally important, put pressure on the Finns to achieve this, and Stalin considered such a mediator to be ideal. Subsequent pressure from the Allies regarding the transit resulted in the peace negotiations evolving into a race, in which Sweden, due to its promise of support, had to save Finland from military collapse and at the same time convince it to accept the conditions of peace as soon as possible, prior to the intervention of the Western Allies.[97]

Sweden's engagement on the side of the Allies was therefore limited. It is accepted that the Swedes secretly conveyed all their information about the Soviet army to the military and naval attaché of Great Britain. This example served British Envoy Victor Mallet as an explanation of the characteristic features of the Swedish style of action. Officially, the Swedes forwarded worthless information in writing. Conversely, in unofficial conversations, they were extremely helpful and willing to answer all questions, provided they related to the Soviets. Simultaneously, they were very cautious in their comments about Germany.[98] Mallet even put a special emphasis on the fact that officials of *Utrikesdepartementet* were disciplined and extremely cautious when talking with foreigners and – in contrast – officials of the Foreign Office were much more indiscreet.[99] The Swedes in their conversations with Mallet pointed out that a total defeat of Germany was not in their interest, as it would shatter the political balance in the Baltic Sea region.[100] The relations between Sweden and Germany were not good, especially in the initial months of the war, when the dissatisfaction with unfavourable press articles pub-

---

[96] W. M. Carlgren, *Svensk utrikespolitik...*, p. 81. The Swedes clearly communicated to British Envoy V. Mallet that they would never agree to the transit of Allied forces, as this would result in termination of deliveries of iron ore to Germany, which would be never accepted by Hitler and make him launch an invasion of Sweden. See: E. Boheman, *På vakt. Kabinettssekreterare...*, pp. 103–104.
[97] A. W. Johansson, *Per Albin...*, pp. 131–132.
[98] E. Boheman, *På vakt. Kabinettssekreterare...*, p. 8. The author explains that in the initial years of the war it was never certain whether a sudden German attack would not make the archives of the Swedish Ministry of Foreign Affairs end up in the hands of the Gestapo, just like it happened in the case of the countries that had been conquered by Hitler. That is why not all issues of foreign policy were documented.
[99] NA, FO, 371/29684, letter by British Envoy to Stockholm V. Mallet to L. Collier, 8 III 1940.
[100] W. M. Carlgren, *Svensk utrikespolitik...*, p. 116.

lished in the Swedish liberal and leftist daily newspapers was expressed openly in Berlin. Also, Minister Sandler was not particularly liked in Berlin.[101] His successor, Christian Günther, was better regarded by the Germans, who described him as the man with whom one may talk openly even about the most sensitive of subjects. As a professional diplomat, the Swedish Envoy to Oslo, and with no association with any political party (according to Carlgren he joined a social democratic party following his appointment as minister[102]), Günther was to make pragmatic decisions, bordering on cynicism.

At the outset of March 1940, Envoy Potworowski sent his first press report to Angers, in which he discussed the second half of February.[103] His general observation that the Polish affairs were pushed into the background due to the outbreak of the Winter War is not at all surprising. Nevertheless, Potworowski highlighted that the Swedish dailies were publishing – though only occasionally – more important news about Poland thanks to the foreign press correspondents for Swedish dailies and a correspondent for the Polish Telegraphic Agency (PAT), Jan Otmar-Berson. It was thanks to Otmar-Berson that the bulletin *Pol-Radio* (the aforementioned *zielonek*) was submitted every second day to leading opinion journalists and other individuals connected with Swedish media. It also served the British, who published their own bulletin *Nyheter från Storbritannien* (News from Great Britain). The envoy admitted that the news provided by the Polish Legation was much less popularized by the Swedish media than others, because of the general tendency to avoid irritating German diplomacy.[104] It was at that moment that the Swedish government gained an essential tool of press control in the shape of statutory authorisations, which allowed for a substantial (though not formal) censorship of newspapers. According to Potworowski, the propaganda activity pursued by the legation was not pointless. For, as envoy explained: 'propaganda, by means of regularly submitted bulletins, sinks into the minds of people and shapes real views, which is reflected both in private conversations and articles either specially devoted to Polish matters or addressing

---

[101] Grafström noted in his journal on 21 December 1939 that Sandler's resignation from his position was perceived by Sweden as a concession towards Germany. See: S. Grafström, *Anteckningar 1938–1944*, p. 204.

[102] W. M. Carlgren, *Svensk utrikespolitik...*, pp. 75, 127.

[103] PISM, A 10, 5/11, a press report for the period of 15–29 February 1940 by Polish Envoy to Stockholm G. Potworowski, Stockholm, 6 III 1940.

[104] Even S. Grafström, who was famous for his anti-Nazi views, agreed with the timid statement of Swedish Envoy to Berlin A. Richert in December 1939: 'Sweden is currently too small and not sufficiently armed to have the luxury to view the current developments from an outdated perspective of seeking justice – just like the press, who does it in the name of humanitarian ideas'. See: S. Grafström, *Anteckningar 1938–1944*, p. 200.

the subjects from the area of European relations and the policy of the countries engaged in the war.'[105]

Nevertheless, Swedish society was much more intent on switching the economy and living conditions to military mode, and the government was preoccupied with clever manoeuvring within the diplomatic labyrinth created by the continually expanding European conflict. The Winter War left the Swedish government unscathed. Prime Minister Hansson, in his speech on 9 February at his party's parliamentary club, explained: 'The government, like no one else, wants to help Finland, and although we all sympathize strongly with Finland, we most importantly have to think about Sweden.'[106] When on 12 March 1940 a Finnish–Soviet truce was signed, relief was felt in Stockholm.[107]

---

[105] PISM, A 10, 5/11, a press report for the period of 15–29 February 1940. Polish Envoy to Stockholm G. Potworowski, Stockholm, 6 III 1940.

[106] A. W. Johansson, *Per Albin...*, p. 127. H. Batowski, *Rok 1940...*, p. 249, positively evaluated the activity of Swedish diplomacy during the Winter War, as 'it showed much artistry in avoiding extremes in both directions'.

[107] Churchill Archives Centre, Sir Victor Mallet, Memoir, p. 69, reminds that from 1941 onwards the Swedes, while highlighting their behaviour during the Finnish-Soviet war, claimed that it was actually thanks to them that Great Britain did not end up in a state of war with its later ally. In turn A. Kollontai, *Diplomaticeskie...*, pp. 482–489, 505–506, 512–517, provides details of the Swedish intermediation (in particular of Minister Günther) in the Finnish-Soviet talks.

4. Consolidation of German Hegemony in Europe – Polish Strategy of Maintaining Relations and Swedish Dodging

A freeze in relations following Hitler's invasion of Scandinavia

From 9 April, following attacks on Denmark and Norway by Germany, Sweden found itself close to military operations on the front. It quickly transpired that Hitler did not have his sights on Sweden, but would demand political and economic concessions. When Halvdan Koht, Minister of Foreign Affairs of Norway, asked if the Swedish government would agree to King Haakon VII paying a short visit to Stockholm with his son and their entourage, he was told that the Swedes could not provide the Norwegians with any guarantees that personal freedoms would be respected in Sweden. Minister Günther invoked the conduct of the Romanians, who several months earlier had interned Polish authorities under pressure from Germany.[1] The Swedes sought to prove that they would do everything to preserve their neutrality, steering clear of engagement in the war and avoiding being accused of not adhering to the principles of neutrality.[2] Nevertheless, in practice they were increasingly succumbing to the influence of victorious Germany.[3]

---

[1] W. M. Carlgren, *Svensk utrikespolitik...*, p. 153.
[2] In Stockholm there were fears that the conflict would spread further and that Germany would enter the territory of Sweden. Henryk Batowski pointed out that certain role in holding off eventual plans of launching an attack on Sweden was played by the Soviet diplomacy. On 13 April 1940 Molotov informed German Envoy to Moscow Schulenburg that the neutrality of Sweden should be respected. See: H. Batowski, *Rok 1940...*, pp. 81–190.
[3] W. M. Carlgren, *Svensk utrikespolitik...*, pp. 162–163. See T. Nybom, *Motstånd...*, p. 34. The dilemmas of ordinary Swedish citizens following the German aggression against Denmark and Norway are mentioned by A. Bogusławski, *Pod Gwiazdą Polarną. Polacy w Finlandii 1939-1941*, Warsaw–Paris 1997, pp. 10–11: 'You see – they said [Swedish volunteers who wanted to defend Norway] – what is the trouble: as a member of Scandinavian union we should stand in defence of Norway, as a neutral country – we should not do so. As a brother country we should at least send volunteers, as a neutral country – which is additionally surrounded by the German armies – we should refrain from doing this as this would make us risk being accused of not adhering to the rules of neutrality. And, consequently, become attacked just like other countries. We could not give them any pretext for such attack'.

At the time, communication between Stockholm and London was all but broken. Correspondence between Stockholm and France was occasional. Attaché Brzeskwiński reported on 24 May 1940 that frequent talks with Latvia and Sweden about purchasing Polish aircraft – which following the September Campaign ended up in Latvia – were not concluded successfully. Brzeskwiński assessment was: 'both the first ones and the second ones are tied up: the former by the Soviets, and the latter – by the Germans.' It was obvious to him that this was due to the fear of the totalitarian neighbours and that the refusal was grounded politically, not factually.[4] An expert in Swedish foreign policy during the Second World War, Wilhelm M. Carlgren, confirmed the opinion of the Polish attaché: 'A small peripheral European country, in the last week of May 1940, on considering its own policy, could not disregard the magnificent German victories in the West and prospects for German victory overall.[5] The Swedes started to balance between the policy of neutrality and policy of opportunistic adaptation to the German hegemony in the region. The Swedish government eventually agreed to the German claims, repeated during the campaign in Norway, concerning the transit of wounded *Wehrmacht* (German army) soldiers from Narvik through Sweden and of medical personnel together with dressings and medicines in the opposite direction. Following the defeat of France, Swedish authorities made further concessions. At the outset of July, in a public speech delivered in the city of Ludvika, Prime Minister Hansson argued that Sweden 'takes in to account the development of events in line with which seven European countries are entirely or partially occupied, and France has called a truce.'[6] In addition, the neutrality of Sweden was scrutinized as a result of the Swedish government's consent to establish a minefield in the Øresund strait, which complemented the blockade introduced by the Germans.[7] The agreement on the transit of the German army, concluded on 8 July 1940, became a symbol of humiliating submissiveness of Sweden during the Second World War.[8] Every day a train passed through Sweden, carrying German troops from Germany to Trelleborg and further to the border with Norway, and once a week – from Trelleborg to Narvik and back. German dominance was virtually accepted.

---

[4] PISM, Lot, A V, 1/43, letter by Polish Military Attaché to Stockholm Major F. Brzeskwiński to the Polish Ministry of Military Affairs, Stockholm, 24 V 1940.
[5] W. M. Carlgren, *Svensk utrikespolitik*..., p. 175.
[6] A. W. Johansson, *Per Albin*..., p. 210.
[7] W. M. Carlgren, *Svensk utrikespolitik*..., p. 176.
[8] A. W. Johansson, *Per Albin*..., p. 172.

The press even suggested that the best solution for Europe would be to conclude a compromise peace, and appeals were made in this matter to Great Britain.[9]

The concessions also involved the conclusion of annual commercial arrangements, which guaranteed that the Germans would receive deliveries of raw materials (iron ore, timber) and machines in exchange for coal and coke. Another consequence of the opportunistic attitude towards Germany were further restrictions on freedom of speech, introduced to bring down the criticism pointed at the Hitlerian regime. Control over the press was exercised by the *Statens Informationsstyrelse* (SIS, translation: Sweden's Board of Information), established on 1 February 1940.[10] Interventions concerned mostly anti-German opinions. Politicians of the coalition government concluded that the only alternative to the concessions was suicidal confrontation with the Germans.[11] That is why the Swedish government chose the strategy of adaptation to the international situation that emerged as a consequence of German conquests. The tightening of policy towards the press was considered by Minister Günther to be one of the instruments of foreign policy. Confiscation of newspaper issues or introducing a ban on distribution of individual titles was to prove to the foreign states that the Swedish government reacted to their diplomatic protests.[12] At the same time the programme of accelerated armament was launched.[13] Sympathies of the Swedish public were divided, as were those of the members of the highest government and diplomatic circles. It was commonly known that the attitude of Gustaf V and Commander-in-

---

[9] T. Höjer, *Svenska Dagbladet och det andra världskriget september 1939-maj 1945*, Stockholm 1969, pp. 26-27; Today it is estimated that the total number of 2.1 million German troops passed through Sweden during the three-year period of the war. See: Dahlberg, *I Sverige...*, p. 294.

[10] G. Andolf, *De grå lapparna. Regeringen och pressen under andra världskriget* [in:] *Nya fronter? 1943 - spänd väntan*, ed. B. Hugemark, Stockholm 1994, pp. 304-349.

[11] K. Molin, *Försvaret, folkhemmet och demokratin. Socialdemokratisk riksdagspolitik 1939-1945*, Stockholm 1974, p. 256. E. Boheman, *På vakt. Kabinettssekreterare...*, pp. 13-16. The author argues that concessions to Germany were unavoidable because of military weakness of Sweden.

[12] K. Zetterberg, 1942 - 'Storkriget vänder, Sveriges utsatta läge bestar' [in:] *Vindkantring. 1942 - politisk kursändring*, ed. B. Hugemark, Luleå 2002, p. 87; H. Dahlberg, *I Sverige...*, p. 226. Official letters on green paper contained orders as to what information was to be published, and letters on grey paper - what news should not be distributed. About the realities of functioning of Swedish press from the British point of view, see: P. Tennant, *Vid sidan...*, pp. 78-84.

[13] K. Zetterberg, 'Neutralitet till varje pris? Till frågan om den svenska säkerhetspolitiken 1940-42 och eftergifterna till Tyskland' [in:] *I orkanens...*, pp. 17-20, 23.

Chief General Olof Thörnell was pro-German,[14] and that of social democrats and liberals – pro-Ally. Still, all jointly supported one line of politics of neutrality and preparations to eventual aggression.[15]

In July 1940, Potworowski judged that the Swedes were faced with actual German hegemony and the necessity to use their support in case of further Soviet expansion on Finland and Scandinavia. In the circle of government the sense of almost complete military and economic dependence on Germany started to dominate and that is why the Polish envoy expected 'that Sweden would continue to gradually slide under the German influence.'[16] One week later, in his subsequent report that he delivered by chance, he summarized events from preceding weeks.[17] In his opinion, the majority of government members, together with Prime Minister and the minister of foreign affairs, supported the Allies but wanted to avoid any accusations of abandoning neutrality in order to save Sweden from engagement in the war. Yet, under increasing pressure from Germany, Sweden embarked on a road of – as Potworowski put it – gradual and small concessions. From the point of view of the Polish envoy, restrictions on the freedom of press were most important, as they greatly reduced the opportunities to promote the Polish matter at a public forum.

The Polish envoy maintained that in April and May of 1940, the Swedes had been determined to defend their homeland. According to him, a royal address of 23 June, where King Gustaf V called for drawing conclusions from the termination of military operations in Norway and introducing changes in policy towards Germany, was a breakthrough moment. The statement was

---

[14] See: L. Björkman, *Sverige inför Operation Barbarossa. Svensk neutralitetspolitik 1940–1941*, Stockholm 1971, p. 177; K. Zetterberg, 'Storkriget går mot sitt slut – Sveriges läge förbättras' [in:] *Vårstormar. 1944 – krigsslutet skönjes*, ed. B. Huldt, K.-R. Böhme, Stockholm 1995, p. 31; W. Agrell, *Fred och fruktan. Sveriges säkerhetspolitiska historia 1918–2000*, Lund 2000, p. 68.
[15] K. Zetterberg, 1942 – 'Storkriget vänder, Sveriges utsatta läge bestar' [in:] *Vindkantring...*, p. 99.
[16] AAN, HI/I/246, telegram by Polish Envoy to Stockholm G. Potworowski to the Ministry of Foreign Affairs, Stockholm, 15 VII 1940.
[17] PISM, A 12, 3/2, part 2, letter by Polish Envoy to Stockholm G. Potworowski to the Ministry of Foreign Affairs, Stockholm, 22 VII 1940, p. 533. During the evacuation of the Polish government of Angers, communication with its members was strongly hindered, for instance the Polish Embassy in Ancara had no contact with the headquarters of the Ministry of Foreign Affairs from 22 June to 5 July 1940 (see: M. Sokolnicki, *Dziennik ankarski 1939–1943*, London p. 113). The mission in Stockholm was in an even worse position, when one considers the effects of the conquest of Denmark and Norway by Germany and the political offensive of Stalin in the Baltic States.

mostly interpreted as consent of the German transit to Norway. It was also perceived as a general sign of the Swedish authorities' capitulation.[18]

Boheman informed Potworowski that the Germans expressed their expectations resolutely, though without threat. For Swedish public opinion, it meant the acceptance of German hegemony in Europe. Fear of the Soviet Union was of immense significance. The Swedes hoped that the Germans would act as a solid counterweight for the Soviet pressure on Finland. Cooperation in the economy was developed both with Germany and the Soviet Union. At the same time relations with Great Britain were deteriorating. Loss of prestige by the British proved crucial here, but also the sense of resentment due to the ineffectiveness of the Allies' during the spring campaign as well as the detaining of two destroyers – whilst on their way to Sweden from their point of purchase in Italy – on the coast of Scotland. The warships were released eventually, but the issue left a bad after-taste in Stockholm. In his report Potworowski underlined that the growing dependence of Sweden on Germany, did not in any way signify its intention to yield to Hitler. The envoy quoted the Swedish right-wing daily *Svenska Dagbladet*: 'The Swedish nation would not pay for its life by losing its freedom.'[19] Nonetheless, following the defeat of the Allies in France, the Swedish policy of maintaining balance in the relations between Great Britain and Germany became outmoded. Potworowski aptly considered the arrangement of 8 July, concerning the transit of military equipment and German troops on military leave, to be an adjustment to reality in a situation when there were not enough premises to repulse the German pressure.[20]

In spite of such a radical change in the international situation Potworowski maintained that the attitude of the Swedes towards Poland in mid-1940 was positive. Even the growth of respect and recognition for its uncompromising political stance was visible. This tendency however was not reflected in the newspapers, which became the target of the ever-growing control of SIS. The envoy emphasized in his report though that anti-Polish incidents occurred rarely and were inspired by the Germans. While considering the general trend that was prevalent in the press commentaries devoted to the current policy, Polish affairs were virtually left unmentioned. Almost nothing was written about Poland. The envoy highlighted, however, that the attitude of the Swedish authorities to the Polish Legation was impeccable: 'On settling

---

[18] See: K. Åmark, *Att bo granne med ondskan...*, pp. 101–105.
[19] PISM, A 12, 3/2, part 2, letter by Polish Envoy G. Potworowski to the Ministry of Foreign Affairs, Stockholm, 22 VII 1940, p. 536.
[20] W. M. Carlgren, *Svensk utrikespolitik...*, p. 189.

various matters of the local mission, the Ministry of Foreign Affairs always shows a lot of good will and understanding for our position, as well as caution resulting both from a fear of falling in to disfavour with the Germans and possibly, too, with the Soviets, and from the currently prevalent general suspicion towards foreigners.'[21]

Potworowski was aware of the German pressures regarding the issue of liquidation of the Polish Legation. At that time, the Swedes were forced to close their diplomatic missions in Oslo, Hague and Brussels. The envoy also discovered that the Germans considered the possible accreditation of a new Swedish envoy at the Polish government as proof of a hostile attitude. The treatment of interned Polish seamen (submariners had reached the Swedish coast in September 1939) was described by Potworowski as correct, though the Swedes towed away the Polish submarines to Lake Mälaren as a precaution. This all but prevented the seamen from escaping, but the decision was not evaluated by the envoy as negative: 'The crews enjoy much freedom of action and there are no signs of misconduct in the attitude of military authorities towards them, perhaps except for some minor incidents, which are as a matter of fact settled directly by interventions of our naval attaché.'[22]

The attack of the German diplomacy concerned the Polish consulate in Malmö. German consul to this city on 19 July 1940 informed the Auswärtiges Amt and the German Legation in Stockholm that the Polish diplomatic mission, which had been closed for some time, had resumed its propaganda activity. The Envoy of the Third Reich to Stockholm, Wied, filed a protest with Utrikesdepartementet, but never received an answer.[23]

On 30 July 1940, during the session of the Polish Political Committee of Ministers (then already in London), principal theses of foreign policy were adopted. Sweden was named in paragraph 6, together with other neutral countries conquered by the Third Reich: Belgium, the Netherlands, Norway and Denmark. It was stated that the growing economic influence of these countries would be an important condition for balance in Europe, which may

---

[21] PISM, A 12, 3/2, part 2, letter by Polish Envoy to Stockholm G. Potworowski to the Ministry of Foreign Affairs, Stockholm, 22 VII 1940, p. 537. Cf. information on the German pressures regarding censorship: W. M. Carlgren, *Svensk utrikespolitik*, p. 216. The scale of restriction on freedom of speech is reflected by an incident that took place in one of Stockholm's higher education institutions when a rector reprimanded his employee – Bolesław Skarżyński who was a Pole – for mentioning during his lecture the fate of Polish professors who were sent by the Germans to a concentration camp, because politics and propaganda were unacceptable. See: A. N. Uggla, *I nordlig hamn.*, pp. 144–145.
[22] PISM, A 12, 3/2, part 2, letter by Polish Envoy to Stockholm G. Potworowski to the Ministry of Foreign Affairs, Stockholm, 22 VII 1940, p. 538–539.
[23] H. Batowski, *Walka.*, pp. 108–109.

4. CONSOLIDATION OF GERMAN HEGEMONY

support Polish political strategy. That is why 'Poland will strive to develop as intimate political relations as possible with the governments of these countries.'[24] In the case of Sweden, such an aim, at least at that moment, was unrealistic. This, not only due to the pressure exerted by Berlin, but also to the political offensive of the Soviet Union in the Baltic States. News was also coming in from London on the will of the British to conclude peace with Hitler.[25] Göring persisted to push the opinion on to Dahlerus that Gustaf V should be the mediator in a peace deal with Great Britain. The reaction to the idea of mediation met with the understanding of Stockholm, since a relaxation of tensions with the West would impede Soviet aspirations in the Baltic Sea region. Both Hitler and King George VI eventually rejected the idea of peace talks, condemning Poland to the position of a satellite state of Germany with borders determined by the Molotov-Ribbentrop Pact.[26]

The most prevalent political interpretation published in the Swedish press was that this was a conflict between the powers, similar to the First World War, and one Sweden should steer clear of. Slogans of the British propaganda about the clash between democracy and totalitarianism were rejected. The Germans were absolved from their policy of expansion, for the origin of the conflict was thought to lie in the Treaty of Versailles. The church circles accentuated a collective blame for the outbreak of the war. Opinions on Germany were positive, as a consequence of the fear of communism and due to a lack of knowledge about Hitler's plans. The difference between the Third Reich and the German state, with which Sweden had previously maintained long-term close and friendly relations, was not always realized. The editor of the daily *Arbetet* and, at the same time, Allan Vougt, one of the leading members of the Social Democratic Party (and Minister of Defence 1945–51), expressed a view on 27 July 1940 that despite the prospect of Germany's victory potentially being a cause for concern, nobody had the right to doubt the honesty of German aspirations for shaping a better Europe.[27] Not long after, the Swedish Trade Union Confederation (LO) called for the lifting of a boycott of German commodities, which had been declared following the aggression against Denmark and Norway.[28]

---

[24] *Armia Krajowa w dokumentach 1939–1945*, vol. 6: *Uzupełnienia*, ed. T. Pełczyński, Wrocław 1991, doc. 1614, p. 70.
[25] W. M. Carlgren, *Svensk utrikespolitik...*, pp. 186, 193.
[26] Ibidem, pp. 196–198. Gustaf V's diplomatic démarches are mentioned by W. S. Churchill, The *Second World War*, vol. 2: Their finest hour, London 1985, pp. 229–232.
[27] A. Vougt, *Ur svensk synvinkel. Inlägg i den utrikespolitiska debatten*, Malmö 1943, p. 98.
[28] G. Richardson, *Beundran och fruktan. Sverige inför Tyskland 1940–1942*, Stockholm 1996, pp. 201.

During a public address delivered in March 1941, Swedish Minister of Defence Per Edvin Sköld stated that the victory of neither side was in the interests of Sweden. He highlighted: 'Victory and defeat deepen the hatred and lead to new conflicts and wars.' The Swedish Minister also argued: 'Great nations cannot be exterminated and their areas of settlement cannot be changed. Reaching a partial agreement without the humiliation of either side is, therefore, in our interests.' That is why the best solution would be a compromise between the fighting sides, and 'nothing weighs in favour of Sweden benefitting as a result of engagement in this conflict.'[29] Such views were dominant within Swedish political circles. Gunnar Hägglöf recorded in August 1940 that in parliament there could be noted 'a tendency to present a critical evaluation of both of the blocs of powers and describe them as being equal to one another.' The actions towards the government and the king of Norway during the campaign of 1940 were certainly a manifestation of this particular way of thinking.[30]

It is not surprising that in such an atmosphere the supporters of a close cooperation with Nazi Germany proposed extreme scenarios of development of mutual relations with Poland and excluded the possibility of their continuation. In the autumn of 1940, Erik Arrhén, a historian and right-wing member of parliament, visited Germany and occupied territories twice, and following that prepared extensive reports for Swedish intelligence. Based on racist theories he described with disgust the 'filth, pathology and degradation' of the Polish proletariat. His views concerning the Jews were similar. He claimed that the Star of David attached to their clothes may be treated as an emblem of a future Jewish state, provided that the Germans carried out their plan to gather all the Jews in one territory, for instance in Madagascar. In the reports Arrhén presented his vision of a new European deal based on the power of Hitler, and in line with which Poland was to disappear from the map of the continent once and for all.[31] The attitude of the Swedish government was not as extreme, but the adaptation to the situation created by the conquests of Hitler was, naturally, connected with a gradual weakening of diplomatic activity in the area of relations with the Polish government.

---

[29] AAN, HI/I/10, letter by Polish Envoy to Stockholm G. Potworowski to the Ministry of Foreign Affairs, Stockholm, 12 V 1941.
[30] G. Richardson, *Beundran...*, pp. 197–199, 205, 212, 216–217.
[31] Ibidem, pp. 104–113. Arrhén published his impressions from a visit in Poland in *Nya Dagligt Allehanda*. He mostly emphasized the low level of material culture. See: 'Szwed o rujnującej gospodarce niemieckiej w Polsce', *Dziennik Polski*, 15 I 1941.

On 13 September 1940, the Swedes officially dismissed their military attaché Colonel Carl Axel Torén, who had been accredited at the Polish government from 1937. According to Envoy Potworowski: 'this dismissal needs to be considered as resulting from the normal course of Colonel Torén's service and of no political significance whatsoever.' He nonetheless highlighted that the form of the dismissal aroused much doubt, as it initially took the form of a private letter from Colonel Torén to Military Attaché Major Brzeskwiński, which was sent by the Swedish Ministry of Foreign Affairs to Potworowski. However, the Polish government in London received no direct information about it. That is why Envoy Potworowski intervened with Envoy Lagerberg, who was accredited at the Polish government. Langberg, in turn, promised to take care of the matter, but it was not returned to. Potworowski considered his reservations insufficient, and did not want to provoke further discussion about the matter, which he thought trivial.[32] In April 1941 Lagerberg was appointed as Swedish envoy to Madrid. The Swedish Ministry of Foreign Affairs stated at the time that his accreditation at the Polish government would be still valid, but it was hard to agree that in such a situation this type of mission could be carried out.[33]

In the autumn of 1940 the Germans officially announced that they would make a declaration to the governments of the neutral states that 'further recognition of Polish legations would be considered acts of hostility towards the Reich.' Potworowski anxiously followed developments, since both Minister Günther and Secretary-General Boheman informed him that 'although relations with Germany are not strained, they are nonetheless dissatisfied with the stance of Sweden, which does not understand the necessity to adapt to their demands and submit to "the new deal" in Europe.'[34] As early as 6 November he sent a reassuring letter to his headquarters of the Polish Ministry of Foreign Affairs where he stated that as far as he knew the Germans had not submitted any démarches to the Swedish authorities regarding the liquidation of the Polish legation. The Swedes in turn reassured him as follows: 'If, after all, they [Germans] demanded the liquidation, the Swedes intend to refuse it, relying upon courtesy.' Taking into consideration the information from a source in the Swedish legation in Berlin, Potworowski

---

[32] AAN, HI/I/57, letter by Polish Envoy to Stockholm G. Potworowski to the Ministry of Foreign Affairs, Stockholm, 16 X 1940.
[33] PISM A 12, E/430, telegram by Polish Envoy to Stockholm G. Potworowski to the Ministry of Foreign Affairs, Stockholm, 22 I 1941, p. 22.
[34] PISM, A 12, 53/37J, telegram by Polish Envoy to Stockholm G. Potworowski to the Ministry of Foreign Affairs, Stockholm, 27 X 1940, p. 10.

excluded Sweden from the circle of states to whom this demand was to be directed as the Germans were interested only in the states which were 'not engaged in the war and friendly', such as Spain.[35]

Diplomats from the Polish Legation in Stockholm were very understanding when evaluating the stance of Swedish government in 1940.[36] Following the Norway campaign relations with Germany became more relaxed, but as claimed the Polish envoy: 'Nonetheless, traditional distrust towards Russia, mysteriousness of the Soviet policy, and especially its constant pressures on Finland and the simultaneous sense of Sweden's powerlessness against Germany, resulted in a defeatist attitude of Swedish public opinion, who was ready to passively accept the German "care" for fear of an invasion from the East.'[37] According to Attaché Brzeskwiński, in October 1940 it was difficult to talk about maintaining 'strict neutrality', but the issue was nonetheless ambiguous. For one thing, the Germans accused the Swedes of an unwillingness to accept the changes which had taken place in Europe following Hitler's and Stalin's conquests. They had expected Sweden to become part of great Germany, even though such a proposition to join the alliance of the Axis Powers was never made.[38] For another, the highest-ranking commanders of the Swedish army –

---

[35] Ibidem, telegram by Polish Envoy to Stockholm G. Potworowski to the Ministry of Foreign Affairs, Stockholm, 6 XI 1940, p. 12.

[36] What is distinctive against this background is the critical evaluation of the Swedish foreign policy that was performed in the Polish newspapers in exile, where up until 1943 the Swedes were continuously called on to join the Allies. See: 'Neutralni', *Polska Walcząca*, 29 XI 1939 ('Not "neutrality", but only the fall of Hitler can save the independence of European countries'); 'Pół tuzina neutralnych', *Dziennik Żołnierza*, 30 VI 1941 ('Sweden serves Germany not only with its territory but also industry and natural resources [...] All this falls within the scope of the so-called "neutrality"'); 'Neutralność z wyłomami', *Dziennik Żołnierza*, 17 IX 1941 ('In fact, Sweden – seemingly neutral and independent – is now totally dependent on the Third Reich'); Z. Racięski, 'Neutralni', *Orzeł Biały*, 22 XI 1942 ('Nobody has the right today, when we have been going through the most tragic but also the most significant period of our history, to satisfy oneself with the role of observer. In such situation, when each nerve and each muscle, each heart and each mind may be of precious value in the joint effort of the entire nation, nobody is permitted to escape into a safe retreat, and – taking advantage of others' engagement in the fight for the common good, focus even more effectively on their private interests').

[37] AAN, HI/I/10, letter by Polish Envoy to Stockholm G. Potworowski to the Ministry of Foreign Affairs, Stockholm, 19 II 1941. Potworowski, already in December 1939, following the dismissal of minister Sandler, announced that Sweden would be 'more submissive' and 'more pliable' towards Germany. See: *Polskie dokumenty dyplomatyczne 1939 wrzesień.*, doc. 399, telegram by Polish Envoy to Stockholm G. Potworowski to the Ministry of Foreign Affairs, Stockholm, 7 X 1939, doc. 430, telegram by Polish Envoy to Stockholm G. Potworowski to the Ministry of Foreign Affairs, Stockholm, 14 XII 1939.

[38] W. M. Carlgren, *Svensk utrikespolitik...*, pp. 219–220.

4. CONSOLIDATION OF GERMAN HEGEMONY

General Olof Thörnell and Admiral Marc Giron – paid courtesy visits to Germany. Thörnell accepted a German military decoration. The Swedes agreed to grant the German army access to the new communication route via Karlskrona to Norway. Rumours spread that a secret agreement was reached between Swedish and German military commanders on military cooperation against the USSR.[39] Nonetheless, at the same time Attaché Brzeskwiński drew attention to the issue of the Swedish–Soviet economic arrangement that concluded on 7 September, in which a special credit was to be granted to the Soviets. Sweden was to deliver railway equipment, machines, steel and ball bearings worth 100 million Swedish crowns (compared with exports in 1938 totalling 12 million crowns). In exchange the Soviet Union was to send oil, iron ore, grain, furs etc.

Despite the apparent submissiveness of Stockholm, the leading politician of the Polish Socialist Party (PPS) Adam Ciołkosz (then in exile in London), evaluated the policy of Swedish Social Democrats with optimism. He informed the PPS leadership in occupied Warsaw: 'The [socialist] Movement is strong in Sweden: it obtained absolute majority in parliamentary elections, but it is trying to maintain neutrality, and its liking of Poland.' Such an evaluation was intended to cheer up comrades back in Poland, but the positive picture mostly came as a result of reports by the PPS representative in Stockholm, Maurycy Karniol, who preserved good relations with SAP leaders, especially the head of the party's information office – Gunnar Lundberg.[40] To promote the activity of the PPS abroad, Karniol, from his first days of his exile in Stockholm (March 1940), prepared and distributed a modest press bulletin in English, the factual basis of which was the socialist journal *Robotnik Polski we Francji* [Polish Worker in France], published in Paris. The bulletin was sent to the editorial boards of social democratic newspapers and to the information office of the Social Democratic party.

Karniol's circle of Swedish acquaintances expanded gradually. Lundberg put him in touch with other leading Social Democrats in Sweden including Member of Parliament and chief editor of *Ny Tid*, Rickard Lindström, and editor of *Arbetet*, Allan Vougt. Those who Karniol became acquainted with arranged appointments for him with other activists from various organisations connected with the Social Democrats. He developed good relations both with

---

[39] PISM, A XII, 4/175, report by Polish Military Attaché to Stockholm Major F. Brzeskwiński from October 1940, Stockholm, 3 XI 1940.

[40] '*My tu żyjemy jak w obozie warownym*'. *Listy PPS-WRN Warszawa–Londyn 1940–1945*, London 1992, p. 15. On the activity of Karniol in Sweden in during of the Second World War and soon after its conclusion, see: P. Jaworski, 'Maurycy Karniol – przedstawiciel Polskiej Partii Socjalistycznej w Szwecji w latach 1940–1946' [in:] *Od Napoleona do Stalina. Studia z dziejów XIX i XX wieku*, ed. T. Kulak, Toruń 2007, pp. 182–214.

August Lindberg, the chair of the Swedish Trade Union Confederation (LO), and Ragnar Casparsson, head of LO's press department. Equally, good relations were established by the PPS with Adolf Stenbom, editor of *Metallarbetaren* and Karniol's relationship with Albin Lind, a trade union's activist, was a precious one. Karniol also met Paul Olberg, who remembered his prewar connections with Poland – visits and personal meetings with socialists Mieczysław Niedziałkowski and Kazimierz Czapiński. In turn, it was thanks to Olberg that Karniol met the distinguished social democratic activist Zeth Höglund.[41] He developed contacts with Finnish social democratic activists Alexei Altonen and Eero Vuori, as well as with Norwegian socialist Martin Tranmæl. Thanks to Karniol's activities the *Robotnik Polski w Wielkiej Brytanii* [Polish Worker in Great Britain] received his interviews with various individuals from Scandinavian political life, and started publishing articles about the PPS and Polish affairs in the Swedish local press.[42]

Karniol, encouraged by Lundberg, then concentrated his efforts on participating as an observer in the 16th congress of the Social Democratic Party at the beginning of June 1940. Lundberg promised that the question of Poland would be addressed. Nevertheless, Torsten Nilsson, who was responsible for organising the congress, reacted to the matter with reserve. It was Nilsson who informed Karniol of the party's resolution, in line with which only representatives of social democratic parties from the Nordic States were invited to the congress. However, a possible resolution regarding Poland was to be accepted by the government, making the situation even more complicated.[43] The efforts to obtain the consent from Gustav Möller, Minister of Social Affairs, ended in a fiasco. No official commentaries about Poland were issued, which related to the successes of the German army on the western front. However, thanks to the grant of 200 crowns from Envoy Potworowski, Karniol was able to prepare the distribution – particularly with the SAP's

---

[41] PISM, col. 133, vol. 160, letter by M. Karniol to A. Ciołkosz, Stockholm, 5 IV 1940.
[42] Karniol made favourable comments about the internal and foreign policy of Sweden, highlighting especially the positive role of Swedish social democrats. All of the following articles were published in the *Robotnik Polski w Wielkiej Brytanii*: 'Szwecja jest socjalistyczna', 29 IX 1940; 'W Szwecji o Polsce', 29 IX 1940; 'Szwecja w czasie wojny', 1 XII 1940; 'Sprawy polskie w Szwecji'. 'Hołd towarzyszy szwedzkich pamięci Hermana Liebermana', 1 XII 1941; 'Pogotowie obronne Szwecji', 1 IV 1942; 'Socjaliści u władzy w Szwecji', 1 VI 1942; 'Działalność PPS na kraje skandynawskie', 1 VI 1943; 'Współpraca socjalistów polskich i szwedzkich', 1 VII 1943; 'Szwecja w czasie wojny', 15 IX 1943; 'Szwedzka młodzież socjalistyczna', 1 X 1943; 'Jak Szwecja troszczy się o swych żołnierzy', 1 XI 1943; 'Coraz mniej strajków w Szwecji', 15 XII 1943. See also the article: 'Pozdrowienia z Szwecji', *Przedświt*, 1 V 1941.
[43] PISM, col. 133, vol. 160, letter by M. Karniol to A. Ciołkosz, Stockholm, 5 IV 1940.

congress in mind – of the brochure *Hälsning från Polska socialdemokratiska partiet (PPS) till Svenska Socialdemokratiska Partiets kongress 1940* (Greetings from the Polish Social Democratic Party to the Congress of the Swedish Social Democratic Party 1940), which contained the party's resolutions, speeches from Herman Lieberman and from the representative of the PPS at the Polish government in exile – Minister of Labour and Social Welfare Jan Stańczyk – from 1 May 1940, as well as a passage about Poland from the book *Rysslands nya imperialism* (New Russian Imperialism) by P. Olberg, and a selection of articles about Poland from Swedish newspapers and comments about Poland made by Swedish, Finnish and Norwegian social democrats. When in August 1940 the 9th congress of the Swedish social democratic youth was opened, Karniol prepared another brochure *Socialismen kommer att uppbygga det nya Polen* (Socialism Will Rebuild New Poland) and sent a letter with his regards. He soon received a polite answer with thanks.[44] The propagandist success of the brochures inspired Karniol to continue this method of popularising the PPS activity. In 1941 he published another brochure *Polska Socialistiska Partiets (PPS) andel i uppbyggandet av den polska staten* (Participation of the Polish Socialist Party in the Building of Polish State).

In the last weeks of 1940, the heads of the Swedish diplomacy were overwhelmed with pessimism. Erik Boheman gave Great Britain only a 20 percent chance of winning the war. Grafström, who was Chief of the Press Office at the Swedish Ministry of Foreign Affairs at the time, made some unfavourable comments in his diaries about his superior's statements. He wrote that he was disappointed with him because of his opportunistic attitude, which may signify a severe depression within the pro-Ally circles.[45] Defeatism was fuelled by German propaganda supported by part of the Swedish academic circle,

---

[44] ARAB, SAP arkiv, Brevsamling, E1, vol. 19, copy of letter to M. Karniol, 2 XII 1940. On the occasion of the social democratic youth congress the leadership of the PPS party sent another telegram with their regards, where they reminded the misery of the Polish nation and the activity of its underground resistance movement. Karniol, in his letters to the *Robotnik Polski w Wielkiej Brytanii* highlighted: 'This telegram received a great applause of the delegates'. See: M. K[arniol], 'W Szwecji o Polsce', *Robotnik Polski w Wielkiej Brytanii*, 29 IX 1940, p. 9.
[45] S. Grafström, *Anteckningar 1938–1944*, pp. 281, 290. The stance of Boheman was evaluated quite differently by the British Envoy Mallet. He claimed that as a person with an anti-Nazi attitude, in the moments of war which were worst for the British, he maintained good relations with the Allied diplomats, to whom he also paid private visits (Churchill Archives Centre, V. Mallet, Memoir, pp. 93–94).

Lund University in particular.[46] Karl Olivecrona, a professor of law there, published the brochure *England eller Tyskland?* (England or Germany?), in which he argued in support of Germany in its efforts to establish hegemony over Europe. The argument for the support was Germany's traditional close cultural and political relations with Sweden, and since German was the first foreign language taught in Swedish schools. Academic literature collections at Swedish universities included mostly German works. Germany was also the most frequent destination for study trips by Swedish students. Close contacts between the two countries were also evident in religion, and especially organisational ties between the Protestant church in Germany and Sweden. The merits of the Germans were highlighted in the brochure *Tysk väsen och svensk lösen* (The Essence of German Character and the Motto of Swedish Character) by a specialist in literature, Fredrik Böök, who argued that 'no other nation has contributed more to European culture.' These comments echoed those made about the Germans by the traveller Sven Hedin, mentioned previously, who glorified the policy of Hitler.[47] These views surely influenced Swedish society, though, according to Potworowski, grandees from the circle of Swedish intelligentsia and economic spheres, who officially supported the new Hitlerian deal, were incidental.[48] However, it is undeniable that the disillusionment with the Germans was sparked only by the reports about their occupational policy in Norway and Denmark. Terror and economic depletion resulted in the Swedes starting to negate the idea of joining the new European deal orchestrated by Hitler.

A small dose of moderate optimism was brought about by a partial raising of the economic blockade. At the end of November, the Swedes were granted permission from Great Britain for four merchant ships to travel from and to the harbour in Gothenburg, Sweden, for a month (mainly from South America). The Germans accepted this alternative on 7 February 1941. Over the next two months, and then from summer until the end of 1942 the Swedes were in touch with territories outside those controlled by the Germans. It was about more than just the goods, mostly from South America, that were delivered along this route. *Göteborgstrafiken* or *lejdtrafiken*, that is Gothenburg's transport or transport with the so-called safe conduct pass, gained a great psychological meaning. Swedish society was felt they were less isolated

---

[46] See more, S. Oredsson, *Lunds universitet under andra världskriget. Motsättningar, debatter och hjälpinsatser*, Lund, 1996.
[47] G. Richardson, *Beundran...*, pp. 222–227.
[48] AAN, HI/I/10, letter by Polish Envoy to Stockholm G. Potworowski to the Ministry of Foreign Affairs, Stockholm, 19 II 1941.

from the world and less dependent on Germany.⁴⁹ In spite of this fact, the decline in living standards bit hard. The limitations on obtaining fuel and food rationing were considered minor by the head of the Polish diplomatic mission and he did not qualify them as signs of poverty or even privation.⁵⁰ Nevertheless, opinions on the future were pessimistic as the prospect of victory of any side would be catastrophic. Within the highest circles of Swedish military command, just like those of politics, by 1941, it was maintained that 'neither the defeat of England nor of Germany is in the interest of Sweden, because the first would entail Nazi hegemony, and the second communization of Europe.'⁵¹

Potworowski quoted the counsellor of the Swedish Ministry of Foreign Affairs, Östen Undén, who, in one of his speeches, highlighted: 'we do not want to be an object of egoistical policy of other countries and we shall stick to our national ideas.' Per Edvin Sköld, Minister of Defence and a socialist, admitted: 'Our purpose is to buy time that would allow us to decide on our own what is acceptable for us and what needs to be rejected. [...] On the other hand, we may not make exaggerated evaluations of what is going on and not confuse submissiveness with natural adaptation to foreign countries [...]. All great powers have their supporters in our country, and these supporters easily confuse the notion of Sweden's interests with their personal sympathies. It is nonsense to imagine that any country could place the interests of Sweden before its own. We are living in times when we, the Swedes, have to place our interests above everything else. That is why resolute and honest neutrality is at present the only basis of the policy of Sweden.'⁵²

At the turn of 1940 Sweden decided to maintain its neutrality at all costs and extended its defensive capabilities further. The rise in armament expenditures was possible thanks to an increase in taxes and internal loans. The Swedish National Home Guard (*Hemvärnet*) was established and could be joined by men who were not subject to military service (17–20-year olds and 45). Brzeskwiński informed the headquarters of the Ministry of Foreign Affairs about the large number of candidates for the Home Guard. Many applications were declined as a result. The effective mobilization of Swedish

---

⁴⁹ E. Boheman, *På vakt. Kabinettssekreterare...*, pp. 138–139.
⁵⁰ AAN, HI/I/10, letter by Polish Envoy to Stockholm G. Potworowski to the Ministry of Foreign Affairs, Stockholm, 19 II 1941.
⁵¹ AAN, HI/I/10, copy of telegram by Military Attaché to Stockholm Major F. Brzeskwiński sent by the head of the II Division of the Staff of Commander-in-Chief Colonel L. Mitkiewicz to the Ministry of Foreign Affairs, London, 7 II 1941.
⁵² AAN, HI/I/10, letter by Polish Envoy to Stockholm G. Potworowski to the Ministry of Foreign Affairs, Stockholm, 19 II 1941.

society was motivated by the government's growing propaganda activity promoting the country's defence. From mid-1939 until mid-1942 army expenditures totalled 5 billion crowns. The Swedish ground forces and navy were extended by 50 percent and the air force by 100 percent. The number of soldiers, depending on the risk of invasion, fluctuated between 160 thousand and around 260 thousand. Until the end of 1943, the Swedish navy consisted of 7 battleships, 2 cruisers, 12 destroyers, 12 small destroyers for coastal defence, 21 torpedo boats, 26 submarines, 44 patrol cutters, 2 minelayers and 42 minesweepers. When war broke out Sweden had 57 bombers and 33 fighter planes. Despite the capacity of the air force being doubled, it was still the weakest link of Swedish defence. Modern aircraft were introduced only when the war was coming to an end, when SAAB equipped the Swedish air force with B17 and B18 bombers and J21 and J22 fighter planes.[53]

This gradual change was also evident in the tone of the press commentaries. German journalists taking part in a visit to Sweden, on the invitation of the Ministry of Foreign Affairs, expressed their 'disappointment and dissatisfaction', at strong attachment of local public opinion to "the conservative democratic attitude" and the extent "of the English propaganda".' Karl Megerle from the *Berliner Börsenzeitung* had already previously described the Swedes as 'a retired nation.' Following the visit, he promised Grafström that he would write that the Swedes were 'a nation on a holiday leave', as they were continuously reluctant to join Hitler in his efforts to introduce a new European order.[54]

In early 1941, the Swedish Telegraphic Agency (TT) re-established cooperation with the PAT. It started to receive broadcasts from the *Polagence* information service, which was an exception among the agencies of the occupied countries.[55] According to Potworowski, despite the Swedes succumbing to German pressure in many cases, this did not have much impact on their attitude towards the Poles. Potworowski stated in his report from February 1941: 'The attitude of local official bodies towards the legation and our matters was always very correct and, as a matter of fact, virtually never gave ground to any serious objections. Rumours and commotion which

---

[53] K. Zetterberg, 1942 – Storkriget vänder, Sveriges utsatta läge består [in:] Vindkantring..., pp. 118–121, 126.
[54] In his reply, Grafström stated that if in this case the word 'leave' meant a leave from war, what Sweden considered normal was the state of peace, maintained from 150 years. S. Grafström, *Anteckningar 1938–1944*, pp. 305–307.
[55] AAN, HI/I/270, telegram by Polish Envoy to Stockholm G. Potworowski to the Ministry of Foreign Affairs, Stockholm, 10 I 1941.

spread here in the autumn about the fate of the occupied countries' diplomatic missions – which was, anyway, never officially confirmed – have died away of late. The interned submarine crews, thanks to the compassionate and comprehensive cooperation of local military personnel, are now staying together with our naval attaché in conditions which are, without a doubt, much better than in any other neutral country. Civil refugees (about 300 people) are in most cases free to move and choose their place of settlement, and are all granted decent support thanks to the attention of social welfare institutions (Polish Aid Committee, Jewish community), whereas the Polish Committee is subsidised by Swedish social and governmental institutions. In the second half of the past year quite irritating became the close police surveillance caused by general suspicion towards foreigners and numerous espionage-related issues, whereas the local bodies, which were first and foremost trying to defend themselves against the German "fifth column", "in order to maintain balance" were forced to closely follow all signs of pro-Ally information activity.'[56]

It was evident that the Swedes, by tracking foreign agents, attempted to affect both sides of the conflict. When a Nazi organisation was discovered in Gothenburg, and its members arrested, similar punitive measures were taken against Polish citizens accused of espionage, a sentence of several months in prison. In March 1941, Boheman informed Potworowski that, according to police reports several employees of the Polish Legation, headed by Wacław Gilewicz and Tadeusz Rudnicki, were conducting intelligence activities. He did not want to request officially their expulsion from Sweden so instead he made a discreet appeal, suggesting that consideration be given to the difficult situation of the Swedish government, which was systematically pressurized in the matter of the liquidation of the Polish diplomatic mission. Boheman, as usual, stressed that he would carry on resisting the pressure, but made it clear that the distinctively undiplomatic activity of the legation was to the detriment of both Poles and Swedes.[57] Potworowski was satisfied with this form of unmasking Polish espionage. Moreover, he informed the headquarters of the Ministry of Foreign Affairs: 'The efforts of the German propaganda, the aim of which is to disparage everything that is Polish in the eyes of local public, are mostly unsuccessful here', and 'occasionally published articles of this sort are received coldly and with disbelief.' What is significant

---

[56] AAN, HI/I/10, letter by Polish Envoy to Stockholm G. Potworowski to the Ministry of Foreign Affairs, Stockholm, 19 II 1941.
[57] AAN, HI/I/270, telegram by Polish Envoy to Stockholm G. Potworowski to the Ministry of Foreign Affairs, Stockholm, 14 III 1941.

is that the Swedish Ministry of Foreign Affairs always supported Polish interventions regarding the anti-Polish press articles. At the same time, opportunities to publish pro-Polish articles were restricted: 'every message concerning our matters needs to be stripped from all anti-German accents.' As a result, the press continued to be all but silent about Polish affairs.

From the beginning of 1941 there was further proof that the Swedes were changing their attitude towards the Allies. There were also attempts to balance the opinion regarding the two warring sides. According to Potworowski, the volume of New Year wishes was relatively large, and the Swedish–Polish Association, the activity of which had been suspended effectively in autumn 1939, resumed operation. On 28 April 1941, the Stockholm section of the Social Democratic Party organized the commemoration of Mieczysław Niedziałkowski, who was murdered by the Germans. During the event, speeches were delivered by Senator Georg Branting, Editor-in-Chief *Social-Demokraten* Rickard Lindström and Maurycy Karniol. The attendees included Envoy Potworowski, the representative of the Czechoslovak emigration government and former Envoy of the Czechoslovak Republic to Stockholm, Vladimír Kučera, as well as almost 150 Polish, Czech and Swedish guests. Potworowski requested the headquarters of the Ministry of Foreign Affairs not to make information about the celebrations public due to the possibility of German protests.[58] The envoy was realistic and knew that everything was dependent on the situation on the front: 'These are only the first harbingers, and knowing the slow and lumbering thinking of the Swedes, I am convinced that as far as the war continuing in the direction that is favourable for us, our situation here will slowly but constantly improve, and the working conditions, those involving informational-propaganda tasks in particular, will become gradually easier.'[59]

In March 1941 the Swedes said no to the increase of German transits to Norway and ordered a partial mobilization of the army in the southern part of their country.[60] By mid-March the Swedish government promptly doubled

---

[58] AAN, HI/I/57, telegram by Polish Envoy to Stockholm G. Potworowski to the Ministry of Foreign Affairs, Stockholm, 30 IV 1941; RA-Arninge, Sapo arkiv, P 201 Polish Legation, löp no. 8, copy of invitation to the memorial service following the death of M. Niedziałkowski. The London *Dziennik Polski* daily published only the information about articles that were found in the Swedish newspapers on the subject of martyr's death of Maciej Rataj – the former speaker of the parliament of Poland – and Mieczysław Niedziałkowski: 'Prasa szwedzka o Rataju i Niedziałkowskim', *Dziennik Polski*, 13 II 1941.

[59] AAN, HI/I/10, letter by Polish Envoy to Stockholm G. Potworowski to the Ministry of Foreign Affairs, Stockholm, 19 II 1941.

[60] AAN, HI/I/10, telegram by Polish Envoy to Stockholm G. Potworowski to the Ministry of Foreign Affairs, Stockholm, 20 III 1941.

150 thousand troops by calling on reservists. According to Envoy Potworowski, these orders were undoubtedly 'a riposte to the German pressures concerning the transit of armies, and especially military equipment, to Norway.'[61] Potworowski sensed that there was tension in German–Swedish relations, which was built on Sweden meeting Hitler's demands to permit the transit of *armed* German troops, which would be a breach of their present agreement.

The worsening of German–Soviet relations became of particular interest to the Swedes. If there were to be a military conflict, Finland, it was predicted, would be dragged into the war by Germany for fear of Soviet aggression. From September 1940 Swedish–Finnish discussions took place regarding a common political union between the two countries. For Sweden this would be a good way to prevent Finland from being infiltrated by the Germans and to dissuade the Finns from supporting Hitler's plans for launching an attack on the Soviet Union.[62] When the idea was abandoned, Hansson and Günther agreed that passivity was the best strategy and that the situation also called for a wait-and-see attitude.[63] Despite the official deterioration in the mutual attitude towards the unilateral relations[64] Boheman held regular meetings with Potworowski and consulted with him on a number of various political questions. In May of 1941 Boheman discussed Finland's plans with the Polish envoy. Boheman was convinced that the Finns were not willing to go to war, but that the maintenance of neutrality was not only a matter for Finland, it could easily become the subject of the policy of the powers.[65] What Potworowski considered to be reliable evidence of Sweden's strategy were the words of Minister Günther, who in a speech delivered on the radio on 3 May 1941, confirmed that the purpose of Sweden's foreign policy was 'to preserve its independence, internal and external freedom and keep away from the war between the powers.' The Swedes were therefore willing to provide support to its neighbour to the east, but only to the extent that would not involve itself in the war.[66] Troops totalling 250 thousand were maintained throughout March, and new military investments were constantly undertaken, for instance, the building of fortifications along the border with Norway.

---

[61] AAN, HI/I/10, letter by Polish Envoy to Stockholm G. Potworowski to the Ministry of Foreign Affairs, Stockholm, 9 V 1941.
[62] A. W. Johansson, *Per Albin...*, pp. 225–235.
[63] Ibidem, pp. 241, 249.
[64] It was so described by H. Batowski, *Z dziejów dyplomacji polskiej na obczyźnie (wrzesień 1939 – lipiec 1941)*, Kraków 1984, pp. 222–223.
[65] AAN, HI/I/10, letter by Polish Envoy to Stockholm G. Potworowski to the Ministry of Foreign Affairs, Stockholm, 9 V 1941.
[66] Ibidem.

However, King Gustaf V had no doubt that if the Swedish army came face-to-face with German aggression it would last two weeks at the most.[67] According to Attaché Brzeskwiński, the feelings of Swedish society were growing increasingly negative towards the Germans, tradition hostility remained towards the Soviet Union, and towards Poland and other occupied countries – they were favourable out of courtesy.[68] Envoy Potworowski confirmed: 'Fear against the Germans or rather the feeling of tremulous unawareness of their plans for the near future is the dominant feature of these feelings.' He also added that the anti-German mood was growing in all sections of society.[69] According to Potworowski, these were not the few supporters of Germany who posed a real threat to Sweden but rather the opportunists who were susceptible to the Nazi propaganda.[70] He claimed the Swedes would react to the victory of Great Britain with joy, yet, the threat from Germany was indeed real and close. As early as 1941 they feared that the setbacks of the closing phase of the war could force their country to participate in the beating of Germany.[71]

The Swedes were consequently directing the policy of avoiding war as much as possible by yielding to the side with the advantage. In the second half of April, a Polish source in Helsinki broke the news that the Swedes were about to yield to German pressures and agree to the transit of the Nazi armies to Finland. The Germans had such plans, and their actions brought moderate success, as both General Thörnell and Minister Günther were unwilling to do anything that would cause annoyance in Berlin.[72] The same source also announced that the Germans were planning to declare war on the Soviet Union, but because of the on-going campaign in the Balkans they postponed the date of their attack by two or three months.[73]

In the context of the possible German aggression against the Soviet Union, pursuing the policy of balance was growing increasingly difficult for Sweden, although Boheman, whom Potworowski considered intelligent, sober, devoid

---

[67] AAN, HI/I/10, letter by Polish Envoy to Stockholm G. Potworowski to the Ministry of Foreign Affairs, Stockholm, 14 V 1941.
[68] AAN, HI/I/10, letter by the head of the II Division the Staff of Commander-in-Chief Lieutenant-Colonel I. Banach to the Ministry of Foreign Affairs A. Zaleski, London, 6 V 1941.
[69] AAN, HI/I/10, classified letter by Polish Envoy to Stockholm G. Potworowski to the Ministry of Foreign Affairs, Stockholm, 12 V 1941.
[70] Ibidem.
[71] AAN, HI/I/10, letter by Polish Envoy to Stockholm G. Potworowski to the Ministry of Foreign Affairs, Stockholm, 9 V 1941.
[72] L. Björkman, *Sverige...*, pp. 195, 328.
[73] IPMS, A 12, 3/3, copy of the note for General K. Sosnkowski, 21 IV 1941.

of filo-German attitude and well informed, argued during the conversation with the envoy that in spite of many political and economic reasons, the German–Soviet war would not happen.[74] Potworowski became familiar with the views of the Soviet diplomatic representative Aleksandra Kollontai, who frequently made unfavourable comments about the Germans. Nonetheless, the Polish envoy underestimated her statements, as he thought that Kollontai was 'both shrewd and insincere, and that she is perfect at both manoeuvring in the local difficult conditions and in relation to the competent authorities in Moscow.'[75] This picture was disrupted by news that was coming in from Moscow about the fear of the war and plans to evacuate the diplomatic corps in the face of the looming German attack.[76] Based on the information obtained from 'one of the colleagues who [...] came back from Moscow', Press Attaché Wiesław Patek informed the Ministry of Foreign affairs: 'The members of the diplomatic corps in Moscow currently estimate the chance of war breaking out between Germany and the Soviet Union to be 50 percent, with a tendency similar to one announced by the English press following ambassador Cripps' arrival in London, that is, that the conflict would once again fall into imbalance.'[77] Patek reported some other rumours from Moscow. Most of all he highlighted: 'Stalin's attitude is evaluated as being very inclined to make concessions to Germany. The limit of these concessions is incredibly hard to determine, the German claims towards Ukraine and Caucasian oil are being announced in Moscow – currently based on press articles, and earlier on other sources.' The reports of the Poles who managed to escape Lithuania and enter Sweden confirmed that the Soviets were preparing for war by the rebuilding of airports and fortifications and the increasing food stocks. The clear tension in German–Soviet relations had no influence, according to Patek, on the mood in Sweden, which did not predict becoming engaged in the military conflict.[78] In reality, these preparations triggered great anxiety within the Swedish authorities.[79] It was obvious that

---

[74] AAN, HI/I/10, classified letter by Polish Envoy to Stockholm G. Potworowski to the Ministry of Foreign Affairs, Stockholm, 12 V 1941.
[75] AAN, HI/I/10, letter by Polish Envoy to Stockholm G. Potworowski to the Ministry of Foreign Affairs, Stockholm, 14 V 1941.
[76] Ibidem.
[77] AAN, HI/I/10, copy of the report by Press Attaché of the Polish Legation in Stockholm W. Patek for the Ministry of Foreign Affairs, Stockholm, 19 VI 1941.
[78] Ibidem.
[79] PISM, A 12, 53/37J, telegram by Polish Envoy to Stockholm G. Potworowski to the Ministry of Foreign Affairs, Stockholm, 17 VI 1941, p. 25.

German pressures on Sweden were again gaining on force, especially in connection with the transit of troops to the Finnish front.

Meanwhile, Boheman, whose attitude was pessimistic from autumn 1940, in conversation with Potworowski in mid-May, stated that a long war would take place between Germany and the USA, leading Europe into ruin. Potworowski had difficulties in obtaining a binding opinion about the attitude of the Swedish politicians towards the situation of Poland, but it is worth mentioning his conversation with Minister Günther at the beginning of June 1941. The head of the Swedish diplomacy expressed a fuzzy conviction that the Germans would abandon the policy of extermination, as the methods they were using were 'so very much against their own interests, that they simply could not last long and one needs to hope that there would take place changes for the better', and, besides, '90 percent of them [Germans] would prefer to live peacefully.' According to the Swedish minister, Poland had to be treated as an exception saying: 'Hitler decided that the territory of Poland would be populated by the Germans.' And in general he claimed: 'People want to live in freedom and peace – and so do the Germans.'[80]

The most important issue for Sweden was to keep foreign trade as developed as possible. Envoy Henryk Sokolnicki, when considering the matter from an almost three-year perspective commented: 'Maintenance of an independent trade policy was possible in Sweden thanks to slick juggling between concessions of not only an economic but also a political nature. This brought such a result that the policy of Swedish concessions in relation to Germany was more flexible than the policy of Switzerland, which mostly applied trade-related concessions, thereby leading to the considerable economic dependence of Switzerland on Germany.'[81]

What was most important for the Poles, however, was the issue of possible attempts to liquidate their diplomatic mission. On 12 May 1941, the AA once again instructed the German Legation in Stockholm to force the Swedes to close down the Polish Legation and the Polish consulate in Malmö.[82] As a result, on 23 May, the German Envoy to Stockholm submitted a memorandum to the Swedish Ministry of Foreign Affairs, where he protested against the employment of an increasing number of staff at the Polish Legation in

---

[80] AAN, HI/I/10, letter by Polish Envoy to Stockholm G. Potworowski to the Ministry of Foreign Affairs, Stockholm, 5 VI 1941.
[81] AAN, HI/I/51, report by Polish Envoy to Stockholm H. Sokolnicki to the Ministry of Foreign Affairs, Stockholm, 28 III 1944.
[82] H. Batowski, *Walka...*, p. 187, entire document quoted here.

4. CONSOLIDATION OF GERMAN HEGEMONY

Stockholm, the re-launching the Polish consulate in Malmö and the spreading Polish propaganda in Sweden. The Swedes responded on 31 May with a memorandum, where they argued that none of the accusations were just. They stated that they were convinced for some time that the number of staff should not be increased and that they were not only keeping their eye on the matter but had even dismissed several staff members for misconduct. The Polish consulate in Malmö could not be 're-launched' either as it had only moved to a smaller office but never closed. At the time, the Swedish authorities did not agree to establish new consulates. They also rejected the claim concerning showing excessive tolerance for the Polish propaganda. It was explained that as a consequence of appeals from the Swedish authorities, these actions by the Poles were virtually eliminated. Swedish police were in complete control of the operation and, in cases when the principles of diplomatic activity were violated, intervened immediately demanding the dismissal of disgraced officials. There was a common belief that the Poles were dealing exclusively with humanitarian aid and taking care of a relatively large group of refugees from their own country, who arrived to Sweden following the outbreak of the war mostly from territories occupied by the Soviet Union. This is why the Swedes disagreed with the opinion that relations with the Poles had intensified. Quite the opposite, these relations were to a large extent limited, or even broken.[83]

Yet, on 31 May, Boheman summoned Potworowski to his office and informed him of the German demand that the Polish mission, which they considered to be the centre of intelligence, be liquidated. The Secretary-General pointed out that the Swedes refused to do so. The Germans were told that it was necessary to postpone the examination of this case until the conclusion of the war. Boheman assured Potworowski that the Swedish government would not reverse its decision, but, nonetheless, a moment later he added diplomatically: 'unless there were exceptional and unforeseeable circumstances.'[84] He also asked the Poles not to give the Germans even the smallest pretext to make similar demands in the future and 'not to make it difficult for Boheman to maintain a fundamental viewpoint of the Swedish government.' He also advised that the legation should refrain from assuming patronage over the press bulletin *Pol-Radio*, which seemed quite strange, because the mission never flaunted its relations with this source. In general, however, Potworowski's impressions of the conversation with Boheman were

---

[83] RA, UD 1920 års dossiersystem, HP 12, vol. 890, P. M., Stockholm, 31 V 1941.
[84] AAN, HI/I/57, letter by Polish Envoy to Stockholm G. Potworowski to the Ministry of Foreign Affairs, Stockholm, 6 VI 1941.

positive. Polish envoy regarded Boheman's attitude towards the entire issue as friendly.[85]

Potworowski thought that 'it is better to voluntarily and temporarily limit or even suspend some tasks', than to risk the closing down of the mission. In connection with this he proposed the dismissal of all Polish officials who compromised themselves in the eyes of the authorities, and ban them from pursuing their activities until they left Sweden and introduce a temporary ban on the arrival of intelligence agents. Potworowski cared most about the moving of the branch of the II Division of the Polish intelligence to the headquarters of the British Legation, which would benefit from the protection of Envoy Victor Mallet. The officers of the VI Division of the Staff of Commander-in-Chief, who were responsible for contact with occupied Poland, were still to operate in the Polish Legation. The envoy highlighted: 'the foundations of this work are already present [...] and they are intact' and 'in the current conditions Sweden is virtually the only channel of communication with the country.' The letters contain several warnings from the envoy against excessively rash, ill-considered, hasty actions, which could thwart the end result.[86] At the end of May, he informed the headquarters of the Ministry of Foreign Affairs that he was able to launch a radio station in the legation, but the attempts to bring operators from London could risk it being uncovered, and the consequences of such exposure would be disastrous for the envoy. That is why he advised that London send people with passports other than Polish or to continue using a Norwegian transmitter.[87] What highlighted the importance of the fate of the Polish diplomatic mission in Stockholm were special greetings sent by the President of Poland in exile, Władysław Raczkiewicz, to King Gustaf V on the National Day of Sweden, 6 June 1941.

Operation Barbarossa and the apparent improvement in Polish–Swedish relations

Polish–Swedish diplomatic contacts were revived following the German aggression against the USSR. It was Poland who took the initiative. Potworowski met with Boheman to relay to him General Sikorski's statement on

---

[85] Ibidem.
[86] Ibidem.
[87] PISM, A 9, E/14, letter by Polish Envoy to Stockholm G. Potworowski to the Ministry of Foreign Affairs, Stockholm, 31 V 1941.

4. CONSOLIDATION OF GERMAN HEGEMONY

Poland's attitude towards the German-Soviet conflict.[88] Boheman emphasized 'the understanding for the complex situation of Poland.' He understood that taking any position was an extremely sensitive issue, and described it neatly in French as *sagesse même* meaning 'pure wisdom'. He also knew that the Germans needed to retain their leading position, especially in their occupation of the entire territory of Poland. He denied that the Germans had resumed applying pressure regarding the liquidation of the Polish Legation.[89] The Swedes decided that none of the representatives of the occupied countries could be added to the mission's staff. From that moment on, it was only possible to exchange serving diplomats.[90] According to the telegram from Brzeskwiński, the signing of the Polish-Soviet arrangement generated much interest in the press, as well as in political and diplomatic circles in Sweden, and generally – just like in the case of Boheman – met with an understanding for the position of the Polish government.[91] The Swedes, Potworowski claimed, were very much aware that a conflict between two enemies of Poland put the country in a favourable situation, although, according to Boheman, the position became complicated at the time.[92] London feared that the anti-Soviet oriented public opinion in Sweden would deteriorate further with the restoration of normal Polish-Soviet relations. According to Potworowski, these fears were not realised because of the Swede's realism and certain parallels between Sweden and Poland, of which the most important was the attitude towards Russia and Germany. Any agreement between these two powers would constitute a threat to the independence of both Sweden and Poland.[93] Swedish press recounted the talks between the Poles and the Soviets

---

[88] The content of General Sikorski's speech from 23 June 1941 to his country, see: *Protokoły posiedzeń Rady Ministrów Rzeczypospolitej Polskiej*, vol. 3: *czerwiec 1941 – grudzień 1941*, scholarly editing by M. Zgórniak, compiled by W. Rojek in cooperation with. A. Suchcitz, Kraków 1996, pp. 5–13. Sikorski highlighted that the outbreak of the German-Soviet war was beneficial for the Polish matter, as it would considerably weaken Germany and make the agreement of the Polish government with the Soviet Union much easier.
[89] PISM, A 12, 53/37J, telegram by Polish Envoy to Stockholm G. Potworowski to the Ministry of Foreign Affairs, Stockholm, 30 VI 1941, p. 27. *Notes by Polish envoy to Stockholm G. Potworowski 1939-1942*, entry from 27 VI 1941.
[90] NA, FO, 371/37082, letter by the Legation of Great Britain in Stockholm to the Northern Department of the FO, Stockholm, 17 X 1943, p. 249.
[91] AAN, HI/I/10, letter by the head of the II Division of the Staff of Commander-in-Chief Colonel L. Mitkiewicz to the Ministry of Foreign Affairs, London, 14 VIII 1941.
[92] PISM, A 11, 49/sow/1c, letter by Polish Envoy to Stockholm G. Potworowski to the Ministry of Foreign Affairs, Stockholm, 10 VII 1941.
[93] This was at least the attitude of the members of Polish government and diplomatic circles. See: memorandum submitted to A. Eden by Minister of Foreign Affairs A. Zaleski from 8 July 1941. It was stated there that the fall of the Soviet government as a result of the war with Germany would bring 'a great relief to both indirect and direct neighbours of Russia, from

in London precisely and objectively, in most of the cases, but without comment.[94] As we know, the negotiations were concluded with the signing of the Sikorski–Mayski Agreement (Mayski was the Soviet ambassador to London) on 30 July 1941. Diplomatic relations were resumed, Polish citizens were to be freed from prisons and Soviet labour camps, and the Polish army was to be formed in the USSR. However, the issue of the Polish–Soviet border was left unmentioned.

Meanwhile, the Germans used the aggression against the Soviet Union to make Sweden more dependent on Germany. According to the commercial counsellor at the Polish legation, Tadeusz Pilch, the Swedes were dependent on coal supplies, which was their Achilles heel. The Germans wanted to take over railway track construction materials, lathes and various installations – all intended for the Soviet market – in exchange for an increase in coal supplies. In connection with this, Pilch, at the outset of July 1941 reported: 'So far, based on a vast number of premises, it may be concluded that everything here is done with the intention of pleasing the Germans.'[95] The orientation of most of the newspapers which provided reports from the front was pro-German, and as Pilch put it: 'they were merely a megaphone for the German propaganda.' That is why he was pessimistic about the chances of maintaining the operation of the Polish diplomatic mission. In the first days following the aggression against the USSR, Germany forced Sweden to consent to the transit of the 163th Infantry Division, 'Engelbrecht', from Norway to Finland. In an official statement, Prime Minister Hansson admitted that the decision was met with public opposition, which was evident, for example, in press articles that accused the government of self-limitation of sovereignty. Nevertheless, the government announced that the decision was taken with Nordic solidarity in mind and the need to support Finland, which was under threat from the USSR. The concession to Germany was, then, in line with the strategic objective of the Swedish government, that is, resisting being dragged in to war. That explains why most of the press comments were still in favour

---

Sweden and Hungary to Turkey and Iran'. *Documents on Polish-Soviet relations 1939–1945*, vol. I: *1939–April 1943, London–Melbourne–Toronto 1961*, p. 124.

[94] The members of the Swedish diplomatic circles maintained that the Soviet-German conflict would contribute to restoring the balance of power in the Baltic Sea region, upset in favour of the Soviet Union following the annexation of Lithuania, Latvia and Estonia, and that at the same time it would weaken Germany. For more information, see: L. Björkman, *Sverige...*, pp. 314–320, 430–431.

[95] AAN, HI/I/10, excerpts from letter by the counsellor to the Polish Legation in Stockholm, T. Pilch, Stockholm, 30 VI 1941.

4. CONSOLIDATION OF GERMAN HEGEMONY

of the government.[96] Minister Günther, following the parliamentary resolution on this matter, passed on the news to Great Britain, the USA and the USSR. He also agreed to take care of Soviet citizens in Germany. For the Germans it was important that the Allies condemned Sweden for its flexible approach towards neutrality. Given the situation, Hitler hoped that the Swedish government would establish a closer cooperation with Germany. The Swedes, however, despite their submissiveness, pointed out that this was only a one time concession[97] and volunteers were less willing to enlist in into the Finnish army as during the Winter War.[98] So as not to worsen relations with the Germans any further, a compromise was proposed – maritime transport across Swedish waters with a Swedish escort.[99] Military claims were accepted, but the political fallout from this decision was rejected, which was highlighted by Günther when Sweden was denied entry in to the Tripartite Pact.[100] Instead of ending relations with the Soviet Union, Sweden concluded a new commercial agreement with the USSR on 4 November.

In July 1941, Envoy Potworowski met with the head of the Political department of the Swedish Ministry of Foreign Affairs, Staffan Söderblom, to settle a number of matters. He asked Söderblom about Swedish views on the situation on the eastern front. Swedish experts had no doubt that the German army, by defeating elite Soviet units, had achieved immense military success. Nevertheless, Söderblom expressed the following view: 'even if the Germans achieved the ultimate military victory, they will eventually face tremendous organisational problems, and it is impossible to predict how this entire party ends.'[101] Consequently, the military engagement of Germany in the USSR was perceived by the Swedes as a chance for diminishing German pressures on Scandinavia. For Potworowski this was only an official expression of optimism by the Swedish Ministry of Foreign Affairs as Söderblom was known for his servile attitude towards Germany.

---

[96] PISM, A 9, VI 21/1, report by head of the II Division of the Staff of Commander-in-Chief Lieutenant-Colonel T. Tokarz for the Minister of Internal Affairs, S. Kot, 13 VIII 1941.
[97] For more information see: L. Björkman, *Sverige...*, p. 374.
[98] AAN, HI/I/10, letter by Polish Envoy to Stockholm G. Potworowski to the Ministry of Foreign Affairs, Stockholm, 10 VII 1941.
[99] L. Björkman, *Sverige...*, pp. 148–149.
[100] A. W. Johansson, *Per Albin...*, pp. 270, 273. The decision of the Swedish government regarding the transit of the 163th Infantry Division 'Engelbrecht' seems to be somewhat paradoxical for the author, and this is because Sweden simultaneously lost and regained the status of a neutral state.
[101] AAN, HI/I/10, letter by Polish Envoy to Stockholm G. Potworowski to the Ministry of Foreign Affairs, Stockholm, 17 VII 1941.

To develop a specific strategy towards Polish affairs, the Swedes monitored the relations of other neutral countries with representatives of the Polish government in exile. The Swedish Envoy to Bern, Zenon Przybyszewski-Westrup, on 11 July 1941 recounted the course of a funeral mass in commemoration of the death of the eminent Polish politician and pianist Ignacy Paderewski. He recounted that the mass was attended by representatives of the Swiss authorities, neutral states and Western Allies, which presented an opportunity to learn of their opinion on the Polish matter.[102] Westrup learned that the Germans had never directed the Swiss government to close down the Polish Legation, but instead made numerous cutting remarks on this issue. They expressed their astonishment that the representatives of the Baltic States were removed from the list of diplomats by the Swiss, and that the Poles, who according to the Germans were not more privileged, were treated as they had been prior to the September Campaign. Moreover, according to Westrup, the Poles caused many problems for the Swiss authorities. Firstly, they denied for a long time that the legation possessed a radio station, despite its discovery by local technicians. Secondly, the Polish consul general to Geneva made it easy for interned Polish soldiers to flee abroad, and the new Polish representative used the title of envoy, arriving in Bern with accreditation letters in hand, whilst only having been granted the title of chargé d'affaires by Switzerland.[103]

Several days later the Germans once again attempted to pressurize the Swedes regarding the matter of liquidation of the Polish Legation. The counsellor of the German Legation in Stockholm, Carl von Below, met with Söderblom on 15 July to inform him that the Polish Legation acted as an interface between 'the so-called Polish government' in London and 'former Poland.' According to German intelligence, this activity was directed by 'a certain major R.' What is more, the Germans accused the Swedes of allowing the new official to join the Polish mission, which clashed with the declaration contained in the memorandum of 31 May. In connection with this, von Below expressed his hope that the Swedish government would gradually complete the liquidation of the Polish Legation.[104] The Swedes did not yield even on that occasion, and

---

[102] Mourning ceremonies in Sweden were much more modest. They took place within the Polish community in Malmö. See: 'O Paderewskim w Turcji i w Szwecji', *Dziennik Polski*, 14 VII 1941; A. N. Uggla, *Polacy na południu Szwecji*, Stockholm 1993, p. 26.

[103] RA, UD 1920 års dossiersystem, HP 12, vol. 890, letter by Swedish Envoy to Bern Z. Westrup-Przybyszewski to the head of the Political department of the Swedish Ministry of Foreign Affairs S. Söderblom, Bern, 11 VII 1941.

[104] RA, UD 1920 års dossiersystem, HP 12, vol. 890, memorandum by the head of the Political department of the Swedish Ministry of Foreign Affairs, S. Söderblom, Stockholm, 17 VII 1941.

the position of the mission was reinforced by the ostentatious support of the Soviet diplomats. Thanks to the services of the British Chargé d'affaires, Montagu-Pollock, on 6 August Potworowski met with the Soviet Envoy to Stockholm, Aleksandra Kollontai.[105] Later on, this meeting bore fruit through a series of subsequent visits. Potworowski, in his reports to the headquarters of the Ministry of Foreign Affairs, recapped that up until 17 September 1939 Kollontai had sympathised with Poland and shown distrust towards Germany. He also quoted her views, which were in line with his, on the Swedes' susceptibility to pressures from Germany. Like Potworowski and the envoys of Great Britain (Mallet) and the USA (Johnson), Kollontai showed moderation in her views as well as consideration for the Swedish policy of concessions, which was for the most part divergent from the conclusions drawn in London, Washington and Moscow.[106]

Nevertheless, the Poles were under no illusion. In August 1941, Attaché Brzeskwiński stated that renewed pressures on Sweden from Germany should be expected.[107] Envoy Potworowski followed attentively articles in the Swedish newspapers. His intention was to track the current mood. A text he considered particularly important was published on 12 August by *Dagens Nyheter*. Potworowski claimed: 'it gives an objective and mostly accurate, although [...] cautious picture of currents that are penetrating Swedish society and of changes taking place as events unfold.'[108] It was stated there that during the Winter War Sweden had managed to provide considerable support to Finland. By April 1940 the threat from Germany was considered too great for Sweden to deal with alone. Consequently, any initiative of further engagement in support for Denmark and Norway was abandoned. An opinion journalist from a liberal daily emphasized: 'What was especially striking was the unfolding of events in Norway and what happened there still feeling like a festering wound.' When Hitler launched Operation Barbarossa, Finland chose to join the alliance with the Germans, and Norway, an ally of Great Britain, allied with the Soviet Union. In Sweden, where 'the instinctive disgust of Soviet governing methods' had always reigned, the British-Soviet

---

[105] IPMS, A 11, 49/sow/1c, letter by Polish Envoy to Stockholm G. Potworowski to the Ministry of Foreign Affairs, Stockholm, 22 VIII 1941.

[106] K. Zetterberg, 'Neutralitet till varje pris? Tillfrågan om den svenska säkerhetspolitiken 1940–42 och eftergifterna till Tyskland' [in:] *I orkanens...*, p. 28; idem, '1942 – Storkriget vänder, Sveriges utsätta läge består' [in:] *Vindkantring...*, p. 134.

[107] AAN, HI/I/10, letter by the head of the II Division of the Staff of Commander-in-Chief Colonel L. Mitkiewicz to the Ministry of Foreign Affairs, London, 14 VIII 1941.

[108] AAN, HI/I/10, letter by Polish Envoy to Stockholm G. Potworowski to the Ministry of Foreign Affairs, Stockholm, 21 VIII 1941.

agreement was hard for some to understand. The same opinion journalist warned: 'They are forgetting that the priority of the great powers taking part in the war is the strategic situation and not ideologies.' This was the justification for Sweden's foreign policy: 'One needs to keep an eye not on the changing moods, but on the permanent interests of Sweden. [...] it is also in the interest of Sweden not to take the side of any of the opponents, simultaneously preserving its independence and honour. [...] A casual and relaxed attitude at the moment of the conclusion of the war is what we, the Swedes, are expecting and striving for.'[109]

One attempt to counteract foreign propaganda was a public address by Prime Minister Hansson on 17 August 1941 in Östersund, and a protest rally organized in the Auditorium Hall in Stockholm on 21 August, where two thousand people gathered who were connected with the Social Democratic Party. The speech delivered by Hansson a retrospective and an assertion of the party's programme. It was a sign of a will to reduce concessions to Germany, but without a doubt it also justified the flexibility of the Swedish policy towards the claims of Hitler. Hansson stated emphatically: 'The policy of Sweden follows *the Swedish* [underlined in the original text] course, and the Swedish nation rejects all possible attempts that could be made in order for it to abandon this course. Our position has been made by us not as a result of some accidental decision, but solely on the understanding of the true interests of our country. [...] Neutrality is a difficult policy. When war had broken out, and we were proclaiming our neutrality, our assumption was that it would be possible for us to maintain good relations with all powers. Our aim was to adhere to this policy. Both sides assured us that our neutrality would be respected [...]. However, soon even we felt the effects of the war. [...] The policy of neutrality of Sweden could neither be conducted exactly as we intended nor according to our expectations.'[110]

The staff of the Polish Legation recognized the true intentions behind this rally: 'In practice, the purpose was naturally to protest the German propaganda, which roamed Sweden with impunity while restricting freedom of speech and writing when it comes to the facts or commentaries which Germans considered unpleasant.'[111] During the rally the floor was taken by Minister of Defence Per Edvin Sköld, representative of the liberals Sam Larsson and representative of the right wing Folke Kyling. Larsson stated that

---

[109] 'Svenska stämningar och intressen', *Dagens Nyheter*, 12 VIII 1941.
[110] AAN, HI/I/10, letter by Polish Envoy to Stockholm G. Potworowski to the Ministry of Foreign Affairs (together with attachments), Stockholm, 29 VIII 1941.
[111] Ibidem.

4. CONSOLIDATION OF GERMAN HEGEMONY

Sweden should not, as the defeatists were advising, take the side of the stronger opponent, but note that the war was not over. He also added: 'They keep saying that democracy is doomed to failure. But what does the system of countries, who abolished democracy, look like? In these countries there is no place for civil liberties, no freedom to gather, no freedom of speech, religion or even of thought. We are asking now, is it worth living when everything that is dear to us, is to be taken away from us?'[112]

Characteristic is the difference in the attitude towards the situation of Polish diplomats who resided permanently in Stockholm and reacted with understanding to the opportunistic attitude towards Germany and of observers to whom Sweden was a new and unknown territory. It is hard to see the influence of their critical views on the Polish expatriate community in Great Britain, but worth noting that various divergent views on the Swedish policy towards Germany were reaching London.

In April 1941, in connection with the plans to activate the Swedish messenger route, Professor Olgierd Górka, the historian, publicist and political activist visited Stockholm. During the war Górka worked for the Polish government in exile as an expert on national and ethnic issues. In a report to the Minister of Foreign Affairs he presented his impressions, stating that he found himself in the territory of free and unhindered German propaganda, where around 700 people were dedicated to the German Legation. According to Górka, despite the Swedes' fundamental pro-democratic attitude, they lacked widespread faith in a British victory. The German propaganda offensive was much more effective than the actions of the British. In connection with this Professor Górka witnessed 'the picture of unsteadiness of opinion and, from day to day, the succumbing to the influence of current news.' According to Górka, the Swedish nation had divided sympathies, although the pro-German inclinations were balanced only with the reluctance of the democrats towards totalitarianism. Górka predicted that if a German–Soviet conflict broke out the Swedes would show their absolute support to the Germans in the face of pervasive animosity towards the Soviets. According to the Polish analyst, the British propaganda had no chance of success, because the Swedes anticipated pressures from the Germans. And as far as the Polish matter was concerned: 'there were sympathies, yet strictly platonic, and therefore with no trace of courage that would allow anti-German manifestations.' It was possible from time to time for the Poles to smuggle in their views, whereas the Germans were unfettered. Berson, the correspondent for

---

[112] Ibidem.

The Polish Telegraphic Agency (PAT), even asked London not to disclose the source of information that was published by the Polish press in Great Britain, unless it was him, as this could cause difficulties with the Swedes.[113]

In turn, in mid-August, an anonymous employee, most probably Norbert Żaba, of the Polish Ministry of Information and Documentation from Helsinki, who was 'currently staying in Stockholm' submitted his first impressions: 'Based on my observations of other missions, I must say that contrary to some opinions *German influences are growing here at an alarming rate* [underlined in the original] and against continuously internal appearances this country can no more be considered entirely neutral from a political point of view. [...] In some areas (police) collaboration with the Germans has already taken place.'[114]

One may suspect that the Swedish pro-Ally circles, which intended to counteract the one-sided picture of their own country that was transmitted abroad, accentuated the will to maintain balance between the sides of the conflict even more. Such example was certainly the 12th Swedish Trade Union Confederation (LO) Congress held on 7 September 1941. Opened by Prime Minister Hansson, the congress was attended by delegates from Great Britain (represented by George Gibson), Finland (Eero Vuori), Denmark (Laurits Hansen) and Norway (Martin Tranmæl, living in exile in Sweden). During the sessions a telegram from a representative of the Polish Socialist

---

[113] PISM, A 9, VI 7/1, letter by O. Górka to the Minister of Foreign Affairs, Stockholm, 19 IV 1941. It needs to be noted that, for an observer who witnessed military actions, occupation or even everyday life in an ally country involved in the war, arrival in Sweden always meant a relocation to a somewhat unreal world. Jan Nowak-Jeziorański (after the war the head of the Radio Free Europe Polish Section in Munich) found himself in Sweden in April 1943 as a courier of the Polish Home Army: 'If it was not for the radio, press and rationing of some imported articles, the residents of the town of Slite [on Gotland] would not be aware there was a war raging in the world. [...] I am already tired of the lovely Stockholm, the true Venice of the north, with its famous Skansen museum, cinemas screening long-unseen Western films, elegant cafés and restaurants. In comparison to exhausted and impoverished occupied Europe, the capital of Sweden was a true oasis of peace, well-being and safety' (J. Nowak, *Kurier z Warszawy*, Kraków 1989, pp. 110, 124). Even a correspondent of one of the Swiss weeklies was surprised by the visit in Sweden: 'I enter an impeccably clean, airport coffee shop dressed with flowers. Here, one may have as much milk as one only wants, and strong coffee [...] To my surprise a completely full sugar-bowl is placed right in front of me! The waiter has no idea, how unusual this is to me. Food looks appetizing, fresh and colourfully cheerful. It would be great to be able to stay here longer.' The correspondence was reprinted in a Polish daily published in Hungary: 'Samolotem do Stockholmu', *Wieści Polskie*, 15 X 1943 and in 'Dziennik Armii Polskiej na Wschodzie', 23 XI 1943. See also: J. Ray[kowski], 'List ze Szwecji', *Wieści Polskie*, 11 IX 1942.

[114] AAN, HI/I/10, note by Minister of Information and Documentation S. Stroński, London, 28 VIII 1941.

Party, Maurycy Karniol, was read out: 'On behalf of the working people of Poland, I am greeting your congress. The Polish nation is in bondage. It is being exploited by an alien force. The Polish nation is suffering from hunger and cold. It is forced to work like slaves. But the Polish people have not broken down, they keep fighting and believe in the victory a of new, better, democratic world.' In addition to the everyday heroism of Poles living under occupation, Karniol accentuated the presence of socialists in the Polish government in exile and then concluded courteously: 'You, the Swedish labourers, now remain the only free, democratic, class-divided worker's movement in Europe. That is why we are following your efforts and your work with sympathy. We wish you victory, we hope that your mighty Swedish trade unions will continue to develop, and that your democracy will survive in your beautiful country.'[115] The telegram was received with enthusiastic applause. Moreover, the participants of the congress adopted a declaration condemning the Germans for murdering two activists of the Norwegian workers' movement – Viggo Hansteen and Rolf Wickstrøm. Following the intervention of the authorities, information about this protest was submitted to the press in a much-softened version.[116]

A misunderstanding in the Polish–Swedish diplomatic relations became an issue for the bulletin *Pol-Radio*. In the beginning of September 1941, the head of the Political department of *Utrikesdepartementet*, Staffan Söderblom, summoned Potworowski and informed him about the German interventions. He implied that the best solution would be to suspend publication of the journal. In spite of the bulletin being sent anonymously, its connections with the Polish Legation were, according to the Swede, well known. Potworowski claimed that 'widespread censorship' meant the bulletin was the only source of information about Polish affairs. Initially, Söderblom sought a compromise, for example, announcing that the author of the bulletin was a Swedish citizen.[117] However, after preparing another issue, Söderblom's assistant, Ragnar Kumlin, requested that distribution be suspended. He argued that: 'the Germans are perhaps attaching too much importance to this issue, and as far as the Polish affairs are concerned, its distribution cannot possibly be of key importance.' Having distributed yet another issue, having witnessed

---

[115] AAN, HI/I/10, letter by Polish Envoy to Stockholm G. Potworowski to the Ministry of Foreign Affairs, Stockholm, 18 IX 1941.
[116] AAN, HI/I/10, letter by Polish Envoy to Stockholm G. Potworowski to the Ministry of Foreign Affairs, Stockholm, 3 XI 1941.
[117] AAN, the Polish Legation in Stockholm, 62, letter by Polish Envoy to Stockholm G. Potworowski to the Ministry of Foreign Affairs, Stockholm, 5 II 1941. p. 8.

further German protests and having seen that the Swedes' negative position remained, by November Potworowski had decided to halt publication. Instead, texts devoted to Polish affairs were published in British periodicals and distributed all over Sweden in various languages.[118] In December 1941, Potworowski informed the headquarters of the Ministry of Foreign Affairs in London that Sweden had become prone to peaceful propaganda, 'publishing various notes, articles, etc. concerning the activity of our Government and our army, propagating certain political concepts etc.' The envoy wanted to make use of the situation,[119] but he never returned to the idea of publishing the bulletin.

Polish diplomats did their best to make their presence felt within the circle of Stockholm diplomatic corps. On 18 September 1941, Envoy Potworowski shared his condolences during visits to the Swedish minister of defence and the commander of the Swedish navy in response to the sinking of three Swedish destroyers, caused by an explosion the day before. Attaché Brzeskwiński paid a condolence visit to the head of the cabinet of the naval minister of defence.[120]

On 18 September 1941, Envoy Potworowski also met with Minister Günther to notify him about Polish–Soviet relations and the change in position of the Polish minister of foreign affairs (Minister August Zaleski, whose attitude to the Polish–Soviet agreement was critical, was replaced by the Polish ambassador to London Edward Raczyński). Envoy Potworowski presented the Swedish minister with the notes that had been exchanged between the Polish and Soviet governments, and the text of the arrangement of 30 July

---

[118] Ibidem, letter by Polish Envoy to Stockholm G. Potworowski to the Ministry of Foreign Affairs, Stockholm, 20 XI 1941. pp. 9–10.

[119] Ibidem, letter by Polish Envoy to Stockholm G. Potworowski to the Ministry of Foreign Affairs, Stockholm, 12 XII 1941. pp. 11–12.

[120] PISM, A 11, E 25, letter by Director of the State Protocol of the Ministry of Foreign Affairs, A. Jażdżewski to Head of the Polish Navy Command (KMW) Rear-Admiral J. Świrski, 9 X 1941. Grafström mentions in his diary that in December 1941 he informed the police about a conversation he heard in the Stockholm Opera House between Schreiber from the German Legation and Captain Olof Carl Arboren. According to Grafström, the interlocutors discussed possible options of performing a sabotage in Sweden and they considered the procedure of filling oilers with sand to be the best one. Arboren was also to promise to submit to the German information on the head of the Swedish intelligence, Colonel Carlos Adlercreutz, and his entire team. Special attention of Grafström was drawn to the mention of the Swedish officer that the attack on the Swedish navy base in September 1941 was definitely performed by the Poles. Grafström filed a report on the conversation with the police, as a result of which Arboren was subjected to surveillance. See S. Grafström, *Anteckningar 1938–1944*, pp. 377–379. For the police report in this matter, see: RA-Arninge, SÄPO arkiv, P 201, memorandum by G. Persson, Sztokholm, 18 XII 1941.

(so-called Sikorski–Mayski agreement), and discussed it point by point. According to Minister Günther, the German–Soviet war was the so-called ray of light for Poland, but he made the value of the concluded arrangement conditional on the result of the war with the Germans. He believed that the Germans had overestimated their chances and if they were unable to conclude the campaign within six weeks and move on to a winter campaign, predicting the result of the war would be impossible. Günther pointed out: 'We are observing the course of events with astonishment, since it is incomprehensible to us what the Germans' reasons were for starting the war with the Soviets'. In his letter to the headquarters of the Polish Ministry of Foreign Affairs, Potworowski explained that the views of the minister were characteristic of the political elite of Sweden and a reflection of changes over several months when the attitude towards Germany became more critical. This was even more so worth highlighting because it concerned the interlocutor who was 'cautious in words, very "neutrally" oriented in his policy and who was generally accused of, in my view not rightly so, pro-German sympathies.'[121] Günther's counsellor, Östen Unden, in a conversation with an anonymous source of the Polish Legation, confirmed that Sweden had decided to engage in the war if there came an ultimatum from Germany. Nevertheless, he did not believe that Hitler take such a decision because, as he said, the Germans 'are too clever to commit such a blunder in relation to the Swedes.' What he anticipated was a gradual increase in pressure from Berlin.[122] According to Carlgren, a post-war researcher of Swedish foreign policy, Hitler had no reason to attack Sweden because it granted all his wishes. Swedish–German relations remained stable following Hitler's aggression on the USSR. Sweden, however, did not live up to everyone's expectations. On matters of lesser importance, the Swedes took every opportunity not to, or at best partially, carry out what was being asked of them. The transit of German troops, however, progressed without disruption, German ships used Swedish shipping routes with the protection of the Swedish navy and German courier aircraft passed through Swedish airspace. Regular trade also took place, and as a result Germany had a supply of strategic resources and products, mainly iron ore and ball bearings.[123] Only Allied success could improve Sweden's situation in relation to Germany. This 'strategy of balance' was easier at the turn of

---

[121] PISM, A 11, 49/sow/1c, letter by Polish Envoy to Stockholm G. Potworowski to the Ministry of Foreign Affairs, Stockholm, 19 IX 1941.
[122] PISM, col. 183/55, letter by N. Żaba to the Ministry of Information and Documentation, 28 IX 1941.
[123] W. M. Carlgren, *Svensk utrikespolitik...*, p. 336.

1941 and 1942 than in the Autumn of 1941. Yet, at the beginning of 1942 the gravest reports since the outbreak of war were heard, as it was understood that Germans were preparing to attack Sweden.[124]

Nevertheless, the Swedes maintained good relations with the Germans by remaining cautious in their diplomatic contacts with the Polish side. Following the conclusion of the mission of Naval Attaché Commander Tadeusz Morgenstern on 24 September 1941, Potworowski tried to convince Boheman to appoint a successor. The Swedish government rejected the possibility in line with the rule on not permitting personnel changes in diplomatic missions of occupied countries in Stockholm. Potworowski explained an expert on naval affairs was necessary due to the Polish submarines detained in Sweden. He proposed a compromise involving the appointment of a naval officer in the legation who would act as an appraiser, which was eventually approved by Minister Günther.[125] Commander Eugeniusz Pławski, a former commander of the *Piorun* destroyer, was brought to Stockholm and appointed in December 1941.

In the autumn of 1941 a parliamentary debate was held on the foreign policy of Sweden. On 27 October, the government conducted a closed information session of both houses, and two days later a public debate ensued.[126] Perhaps the most critical view, in relation to the position of the government, which defended a flexible policy of neutrality, was that of Fredrik Ström, who remarked on Sweden's support of Finland, its permitting of the transit of the German forces to the eastern front, and its nonchalance towards the situation of Norway. Eventually, all speakers agreed as to the correctness of the policy. They only expressed the need to oppose the far-fetched demands of foreign powers, as doing anything else would risk Swedish sovereignty. According to Potworowski, 'the vast majority of society favoured victory of the democratic countries', but at the same time 'they are not brave enough to take up arms and stand beside any of the opponents.' This resulted in the flexible policy of the government to avoid engagement in the war.[127] Minister Günther speech in the parliament is an example of skilful manoeuvring between the expectations of putting a stop to German claims and joining Hitler's vision of New Europe. He stated emphatically that Sweden 'categorically rejects anything

---

[124] Ibidem, pp. 338–341, 346–347, 365, 393. E. Boheman, *På vakt. Kabinettssekreterare...*, p. 294.
[125] AAN, HI/I/360, letter by Polish Envoy to Stockholm G. Potworowski to the Ministry of Foreign Affairs, Stockholm, 7 X 1941.
[126] AAN, HI/I/10, letter by Polish Envoy to Stockholm G. Potworowski to the Ministry of Foreign Affairs, Stockholm, 3 XI 1941.
[127] Ibidem.

that could mean participation in a military or economic action, as well as in any other action pursued by any of the fighting sides against its opponent.'[128] The speech was very well received by the German press as some fragments did not rule out that Sweden would be willing to adapt to the situation created by the development of military operations.[129] The speech was also a pleasant surprise for one of the pro-Ally members of the parliamentary commission for foreign affairs, as it addressed the issue of the enslavement of Denmark and Norway.[130] Envoy Potworowski drew attention to the practical side of the policy, 'Such a guideline – in the current geopolitical situation of Sweden – is impossible to follow without concessions to Germany, on which Sweden is dependent politically, economically and militarily to a much greater extent than it is Great Britain and America.'[131]

In November 1941, in a conversation with Envoy Potworowski, Boheman stressed that the Germans were displeased with Sweden. He was, therefore, ready for further offences to be committed by the neighbour to the south. Fundamental for Potworowski at the time were his good relations with the Swedish authorities.[132] As usual, Boheman reassured Potworowski that the issue of the possible liquidation of the Polish Legation was not the subject of the German–Swedish talks.[133] He was most interested in hearing from the Poles about the situation on the Eastern front. He feared stagnation or the break-up of the Soviet Union, because he predicted that in such situation the Germans would 'get rid of the snag in the shape of a democratic and independent Sweden.'[134] However, he was hoping that the Germans would not attack Sweden, because – as the Swedish correspondent in Berlin convinced attaché Norbert Żaba, who came from Helsinki and became officially appointed in the British Legation – 'they are aware that the Swedes are ready to resist.'[135]

---

[128] AAN, HI/I/10, report by N. Żaba entitled 'Szwecja w cieniu swastyki', attachment to letter by Polish Envoy to Stockholm G. Potworowski to the Ministry of Foreign Affairs, Stockholm, 3 XI 1941.
[129] Ibidem, letter by Polish Envoy to Stockholm G. Potworowski to the Ministry of Foreign Affairs, Stockholm, 3 XI 1941.
[130] Ibidem, letter by Polish Envoy to Stockholm G. Potworowski to the Ministry of Foreign Affairs, Stockholm, 8 XI 1941.
[131] Ibidem.
[132] NA, FO, 371/29704, confidential letter by A. Baliński to F.K. Roberts, 7 XI 1941.
[133] AAN, HI/I/10, letter by Polish Envoy to Stockholm G. Potworowski to the Ministry of Foreign Affairs, Stockholm, 8 XI 1941.
[134] Ibidem.
[135] AAN, HI/I/10, report by Press Attaché N. Żaba to the Minister of Information and Documentation, S. Stroński, Stockholm, 8 XI 1941.

Potworowski was appeased continuously by Boheman and did not predict any surprises from the Swedish policy. Similar was the tone of the reports of Attaché Brzeskwiński. Based on the analysis of the discussion in parliament, Brzeskwiński summarized the fundamental assumptions of this policy, 'a constant aim to stay out of the conflict, an armed defence of this position if need be and a willingness to maintain good relations with other countries [...] [especially Denmark and Norway], and eventually, if possible, showing economic support to Finland [...]. In the field – the continuation of constructive preparation of armed forces to defend the political stance of the government.'[136]

Towards the end of 1941, whilst struggling to defy German pressure, the Swedes did not intend to support the Allies, mostly owing to their fear of the Soviet Union. Yet, they wished the Finns military success and a beneficial border arrangement.[137] According to the Polish envoy, Sweden was to reach an agreement with the government in Helsinki to, on its behalf, prevent Great Britain from declaring war on Finland. In exchange, the Finnish government was to prevent German aggression against Sweden.[138] As noted by the London correspondent for *Svenska Dagbladet*, Knud Bolander, following a visit to Sweden, it was beyond any doubt that the mood of Swedish society was more pro-Ally oriented than expected. The journalist was convinced that public opinion, despite strong sympathies for the Finns, supported the British. The only exceptions were young doctors and engineers educated in Germany.[139]

In December 1941, Envoy Potworowski informed the Ministry of Foreign Affairs that attacks by the German and Italian press 'are currently affecting the Swedish public to a much smaller degree than a few months ago.' He also noted 'The stiffening of the Swedes' attitude towards the threats and demands of the Germans [...] is constantly gaining strength.[140] During his talks with the Swedes, Potworowski heard with increasing frequency that 'the Germans cannot possibly win this war.' This mostly related to the representatives of economic spheres travelling to Germany and Poland. These changes also had an impact on the attitude towards the Polish circles focused around the Polish

---

[136] PISM, A V, 31/11, report by Polish Military Attaché to Stockholm Major F. Brzeskwiński for October 1941, 5 XI 1941.
[137] AAN, HI/I/10, letter by Polish Envoy to Stockholm G. Potworowski to the Ministry of Foreign Affairs, Stockholm, 5 XII 1941.
[138] Ibidem.
[139] NA, FO, 371/29666, note by O. Lancaster from a conversation with K. Bolander, a London correspondent for *Svenska Dagbladet*, 17 XII 1941.
[140] AAN, HI/I/10, letter by Polish Envoy to Stockholm G. Potworowski to the Ministry of Foreign Affairs, Stockholm, 5 XII 1941.

Legation in Stockholm. In connection with this, the envoy wrote to the Ministry of Foreign Affairs, 'On the legation's horizon (for instance on Polish Independence Day, 11 November, during the session of the Polish–Swedish Chamber of Commerce or the so far modest resumption of activity by the Swedish–Polish Association etc.) persons have started to appear who often hold serious offices and who, so far, preferred not to display the interest they had in Poland from September 1939.[141]

As usual, the officials of the Swedish Ministry of Foreign Affairs were cautious in voicing their opinions, but even they admitted that the breakdown of the military offensive along the Eastern front undermined the position of the Third Reich. For Sweden this meant the consolidation of its position. On 27 November, during the session of the Swedish Association of Military Defence, Minister Günther justified the consolidation of the system of national defence as to 'maintain the freedom of conducting the policy of neutrality without making concessions to any of the fighting sides which would be either humiliating for the country or put its independence in jeopardy.' The actions of the Swedish politicians were to be governed by national egoism.[142] Even the Swedish press was taken aback by the tone of the minister's statement, which was, as for him, 'determined and marked with patriotic temperament.'[143]

Attaché Brzeskwiński confirmed Envoy Potworowski's views. At the outset of December 1941, he conveyed to the headquarters of the Ministry of Foreign Affairs in Poland, 'the position of Sweden in relation to German pressure seems to be reinforced.' The Swedish government yielded to the Germans only on matters of secondary importance, whereas on fundamental issues it continued to resist. This meant the Germans were not granted a loan of 100 thousand crowns or permission to transport two divisions, and the Swedish twice announced information about the Polish army and General Sikorski's journey to the USSR, which as Brzeskwiński stated, 'would have been out of the question several months earlier.'[144]

In the run up to Christmas, following the Japanese attacks in the Pacific Ocean and Southeast Asia, the belief that the war would continue a lot longer became widespread across Sweden. Losses in the American and British navies weakened the Allies and fortified the position of Germany in Europe. In

---

[141] Ibidem.
[142] AAN, HI/I/10, 'Reakcja prasy osi na mowy Günthera', attachment to classified letter by Envoy G. Potworowski to the Ministry of Foreign Affairs, Stockholm, 5 XII 1941.
[143] Ibidem.
[144] PISM, A V, 31/11, report by Polish Military Attaché to Stockholm Major F. Brzeskwiński from November 1941, Stockholm, 5 XII 1941.

December 1941, rumours proliferated within the diplomatic circles in Stockholm that the Germans had initiated peace talks with Stalin. Such were the first reactions to the news of the Japanese attack on Pearl Harbour. According to Norbert Żaba, the rumour was the sign of 'somewhat concern and confusion that temporarily broke out in Swedish political circles in connection with Japanese aggression and success in the first days of the war. Tension intensified here even yesterday due to Hitler's criticism of Sweden.'[145] On the whole though, Swedish opinion was in no doubt that Japan's attack was 'an act of desperation [...] in the face of the tremendous resources of America.' Stockholm reckoned with becoming more isolated from the Western world, while considering not only the conflict in Asia, but also the declaration of war on Finland by Great Britain on 6 December, 1941. That is why the reserved attitude of Poland was very well received.[146]

In his report for December 1941, Naval Attaché Commander Eugeniusz Pławski underlined that the USA entering the war, the failures of the Germans on the eastern front together with successes of the British in Northern Africa 'are a powerful driver for the further hardening of the Swedes' political backbone in relation to the Germans.' German military exercises over the Baltic Sea, which could have indicated the possibility of German attack on Sweden raised concern. The Swedes were convinced, however, that they could rally against the 18 German divisions concentrated in Northern Europe.[147]

Did the military situation in Europe and Asia influence on the attitude towards Polish affairs? Attaché Pławski wrote: 'The attitude of the press seems to be increasingly bold and independent. There are pronouncements about the Polish army and the visit of the Commander-in-Chief in Moscow.' Besides this, the Polish pilots who had been interned after an emergency landing in November 1941 were released and awaited evacuation to Great Britain. Attaché Pławski relayed: 'The Swedes are perfectly aware that the crew is Polish.' What was also addressed was the possible release of some of the interned seamen. Envoy Potworowski discussed this matter with Ragnar Kumlin, the vice head of the Political department of the Ministry of Foreign Affairs. Attaché Pławski also announced with a degree of happiness that he visited the internment camps unhindered, whereas other attachés (from

---

[145] AAN, Norbert Żaba's collection, letter by Press Attaché N. Żaba to the Ministry of Information and documentation, Stockholm, 12 XII 1941.
[146] PISM, A 12, 53/37J, copy of telegram by Polish Envoy to Stockholm G. Potworowski [?] to the Ministry of Foreign Affairs from Stockholm, 19 XII 1941, p. 26.
[147] PISM, MAR, A V 9/2, report by Polish Naval Attaché to Stockholm Captain E. Pławski to the deputy of the head of the Polish Navy Commander T. Morgenstern, 7 I 1942.

4. CONSOLIDATION OF GERMAN HEGEMONY

Norway and the USSR) faced obstacles on the same occasion. He highlighted: 'on the contrary, I am encountering good will on the part of the military authorities on this issue,' and summed up, 'even these small facts prove that a certain amount of relaxation took place in the attitude of the Swedish authorities towards us. Indeed, not long ago a Polish citizen who travelled from Gdańsk to Sweden without a ticket was handed over to the Germans, but this was an isolated incident which occurred most probably as a result of pressure from the Germans, as just before Christmas the Swedish authorities did not send back four Polish refugees to the Germans but delivered them to the Polish legation. Lately, there has also been no pressure on the activities of some of our divisions (Branch O. II, O. VI Of the Staff etc.), or the observation of the attaché's office.'[148]

The change in attitude could also have been caused by the course of the visit of General Sikorski in Moscow (December 1941). In his report from the visit to the Soviet Union, the Prime Minister and Commander-in-Chief highlighted the importance of Stalin's declaration about the Soviet Union refraining from engagement in the internal affairs of other countries – which was received joyfully by the Swedish Envoy to Moscow Vilhelm Assarsson as well as diplomats from other states that 'are living under the threat of Soviet imperialism.'[149] This thought was developed by Sikorski in his letter to British Minister of Foreign Affairs Anthony Eden from 10 March 1942. He warned him against the Soviet possessiveness, which was ignored, according to the Polish Prime Minister, by Great Britain and the USA. Sikorski acted as a defender of not only the interests of Poland but also the interests of all neutral states.[150]

Maurycy Karniol, in his report to the leadership of the PPS in London, quoted the newspaper *Stockholms Extrablad*, where on discussing the article from the British *Weekly Review* it was highlighted: 'Currently […] under the impact of recent events – correct views on the key significance of Poland for the conclusion of the peace issue seems to penetrate into the minds of international management circles.'[151] However, *Göteborgs Handels- och Sjöfarts-Tidning*, on 27 December 1941, published the complete and full of pathos correspondence of Ilya Ehrenburg about the Polish army that was being formed in the USSR. The author of the letters focused on overcoming

---

[148] Ibidem.
[149] *Protokoły posiedzeń Rady Ministrów Rzeczypospolitej Polskiej*, vol. 4: *grudzień 1941 – sierpień 1942*, scholarly editing M. Zgórniak, compiled by W. Rojek in cooperation with L. Neuger, Kraków 1998, p. 93 See a relevant passage of letter by Sikorski to Churchill from 17 December 1941: *Documents…*, vol. 1, p. 256.
[150] Ibidem, p. 175.
[151] PISM, A 9, III 4/14, report by M. Karniol 'Szwedzka prasa o Polsce', Stockholm, 22 I 1942.

national antagonisms between the Poles, Ukrainians and Jews within the units, and he also planned to target Polish–Russian antagonisms, as 'the Poles were speaking of Russian generals with much admiration.'[152]

At the outset of 1942, Potworowski informed the Ministry of Foreign Affairs: 'from the moment of our conclusion of an arrangement with the Soviet Union, Madam Kollontai emphasizes most insistently and manifests her friendly feelings and good relations with myself and with the rest of the members of the Legation.' This attitude was characteristic of all the personnel of the Soviet Legation. Potworowski feared the representative of Moscow would treat good relations with the Poles instrumentally. He stated: 'This strategy is perfectly understandable in the current environment, where, dependent on the usually negative and at least full of reserve attitude of the Swedes towards Soviet Russia, manifesting friendly relations with us in particular is an ideal propagandist factor as well as promotion of Soviet policy.'[153] At the same time this was a good occasion for strengthening Russia's position in relation to the Swedes. The Polish envoy recounted that as early as autumn 1941 Kollontai had invited him and his wife to dinner, and following a return visit, he was again asked on 6 January 1942 to another dinner, with Minister Günther in attendance.

During a conversation with the head of Swedish diplomacy, Potworowski was asked about General Sikorski's journey to the USA and the news from Warsaw. Günther revealed that he was receiving information about the situation in occupied Poland through Consul Carl Herslow.[154] Other Swedish businessmen were also informing their diplomats on the German policy in the General Government. It is in this circle where one ought to seek the sources of information that were arriving in Stockholm, both directly or through the Swedish Legation in Berlin. In May 1941, Eric von Post reported from the Berlin mission that he had obtained information about the situation in the General Government from a reliable source. He stressed that: 'over the last fourteen days an increase in the prices of various essential items has taken place in the market. [...] People cannot afford to buy food. Many are starving. [...] People are becoming apathetic because of the difficulties in buying goods.

---

[152] I. Ehrenburg, 'Polska armén i Ryssland sättes snart in i striden. Målet som hägrar är – Warszawa', *Göteborgs Handels- och Sjöfarts-Tidning*, 27 XII 1941.
[153] AAN, HI/I/19, letter by Polish Envoy to Stockholm G. Potworowski to the Ministry of Foreign Affairs, Stockholm, 8 I 1942.
[154] Herslow's visit to UD headquarters in December 1941 is mentioned by S. Grafström, *Anteckningar 1938–1944*, p. 380: 'He informed that the situation of the people in Poland is terrible, that they are on the verge of starvation, all this topped by disease and atrocities of the occupants.'

4. CONSOLIDATION OF GERMAN HEGEMONY

Often, instead of going to work, they are staying at home because they are too tired, hungry and indifferent to do their job.' According to von Post, the behaviour of German soldiers was flawless, which cannot be said about the SS and SA.[155] Envoy Richert, on supplementing the information from von Post, added in June that the prices in the free market of Warsaw increased further still, bringing tragic social consequences. Richert also stated: 'One may say that the capital is suffering from famine and there are cases of people collapsing in the street, because they are suffering from emaciation. It is estimated that 60 to 100 people die of starvation every day in the ghetto.'[156] In his opinion, the lack of food in the General Government was a consequence of the concentration of the German army near the border with the Soviet Union.[157]

Richert clearly closed his mind to the fact that the occupied territories of Poland were the subject of an intentional policy of economic disorganization, and that terror, murders and robbery were occurring on a daily basis. The news from the General Government was covered up. One of the most extreme examples was the treatment of the report by the Swedish consul to Szczecin, Karl Yngve Vendel, who in August 1942 obtained information from the German officers not only about everyday life under occupation but also about the mass murder of the Jews.[158] On summing up the question of provisions, he stated that 'people will have to die from starvation.' He mentioned the questions of illegal trade and inflated prices. Primarily, however, he described the German intention to slaughter all the Jews: 'The ones who are most under threat by extermination are the Jews over 50 years of age and children below 10 years of age. The rest have been left alive in order to fill the place of the missing manpower; they will be liquidated when they are no longer needed. Their property is being confiscated, it mostly falls into the hands of the SS men. In towns, the Jewish population is gathered in one place after being officially informed that they would be "deloused". As they enter the building, they are told to take off their clothes, which are sent to the "centre for yarn materials"; whereas delousing means gassing, after which all the bodies are buried in the previously prepared mass graves.' In the Swedish Legation in Berlin all similar news was consistently taken too lightly due to a

---

[155] RA, UD 1920 års dossiersystem, HP 1, vol. 485, letter by E. von Post to S. Söderblom, Berlin, 26 V 1941.
[156] Ibidem, letter by Swedish Envoy to Berlin A. Richert to S. Söderblom, Berlin, 10 VI 1941.
[157] Also S. Grafström was rather regularly meeting Sigge Häggberg and Sven Norrman, who were visiting Warsaw on a steady basis. See: S. Grafström, *Anteckningar 1938–1944*, s. 296, 382, 366, 409–410.
[158] A commentary on the document: J. Lewandowski, 'Raport Vendla. Próba mikro- i makroanalizy', *Biuletyn Żydowskiego Instytutu Historycznego* 1992, iss. 4, pp. 33–46.

commonly held belief that they were unbelievable. Many Swedish diplomats, including Richert and Söderblom for the most part at the headquarters, were convinced that Sweden should refrain from any action that might worsen relations with the Germans. They judged the overcoming of the information blockade, imposed on the occupied territories by the Germans, to be risky.

During a conversation on 8 January 1942, Potworowski did not conceal the fact that he was in contact with several Swedes who were travelling to the General Government and who, despite difficult conditions, were trying to survive and sustain local Swedish companies. Günther mentioned the strengthening pre-war Polish–Swedish relations, and expressed his hope for future developments, adding, 'Nobody knows what the course of events will be, but one thing is clear, and this is that when the war ends, everything would change diametrically in comparison with the current situation, which, what is more, cannot even serve as a foundation for the future development of relations.'[159]

Perhaps this unclearly formulated statement already expressed a vision of Soviet dominance over East-Central Europe. At the same time the Swedish Ministry of Foreign Affairs was forced to analyse forecasts for the future, when on 3 February 1942 Boheman asked Potworowski about Soviet claims on the Polish Eastern Borderlands.[160] This was, however, interpreted by Potworowski as the sign of the Swedes' continuous conviction that the threat from Germany was more dangerous than that from the Soviet Union. Primarily they believed that the latest developments on the front, both in Russia and the area of the Japanese offensive in Asia and the Pacific, indicated the conclusion of the war was long in the future. Everyone hoped that an attack on Sweden would not bring any benefits to the Germans, although the policy of the Third Reich was followed with apprehension: 'They are, nonetheless, prepared here for all surprises which could result from an "irrational" character of Hitlerian policy, for which even reasons of an emotional nature may come into play, for instance a desire to eliminate one of the last countries in Europe that refuses to be subject to "the new European order" for the sake of the very order itself.'[161]

Nevertheless, Potworowski accepted the words of Minister of Social Affairs Gustav Möller, who said that a German assault on Sweden would lead them in to battle. To raise morale and the will to oppose the Germans, the

---

[159] AAN, HI/I/19, attachment to the letter by Polish Envoy to Stockholm G. Potworowski to the Ministry of Foreign Affairs, Stockholm, 8 I 1942.
[160] *Notes by Polish envoy to Stockholm G. Potworowski 1939–1942*, entry from 3 II 1942.
[161] AAN, HI/I/19, letter by Polish Envoy to Stockholm G. Potworowski to the Ministry of Foreign Affairs, Stockholm, 16 II 1942.

Swedish authorities permitted dissemination, to a limited extent, of information about the German terror in Norway.

In January 1942, following talks with the commanding officer of the army, the chief of staff, the director of the cabinet of the minister of defence and the head of the intelligence, Attaché Brzeskwiński relayed the views of the highest military circles in Sweden about the situation in Europe to the headquarters of the Polish Ministry of Foreign Affairs. These insights are interesting, distinctive and worth close attention. 'It is in the interest of the Swedish reason of state that Great Britain and its allies claimed victory, however it is not in the interest of Sweden and most probably of the entire civilized world that Germany was defeated by the USSR, as this would mean Bolshevik hegemony all over Europe, and at least in countries that neighbour the USSR, among which is Sweden. From the Swedish point of view, an ideal conclusion to the war would be a situation where both sides (the USSR and Germany) are left as weak as possible. According to Swedish perception, evil is not Russia or Germany, but evil which needs to be annihilated is a) Bolshevism and b) Nazism. If both these regimes manage to secure a complete victory over each other, Europe would find itself on the brink of catastrophe – very serious in the first case, and less serious in the second. [...] The Germans proposed Sweden to take part in "a pan-European battle" against communism. This is out of question considering the Swedish policy, because in such case it would place itself automatically on the side of the block fighting against Great Britain and its allies, to which the Swedish government cannot agree. The possible all-out victory of the USSR would threaten the political and economic independence of its neighbours (Finland, Sweden, Romania and Hungary), and if Poland regains independence thanks to this particular victory, it won't be for long. That is why, according to the Swedes, victory for the USSR is not in the interest of Poland. All these conditions put Sweden in an extremely delicate situation, which in the future could drag the country into the turmoil of war.'[162]

The views of the Swedish interlocutors of Brzeskwiński were convergent with the Polish analyses of the development of the situation in Europe and with expectations that the situation from the closing months of the First World War – the defeat of Russia in the battle with the Germans and the defeat of the Germans on the western front – would be repeated. Nevertheless, neither Sweden nor Poland had much influence on what was happening.

---

[162] Ibidem, extract of the report by Polish Military Attaché to Stockholm Major F. Brzeskwiński for January 1942.

The former acted only as a passive observer, the latter was at war, but despite its efforts it did not play a decisive role in the struggle nor did it have much impact on strategic and political decisions of the powers.

In mid-February 1942 the Polish Staff of the Commander-in-Chief informed Brzeskwiński about German preparations to attack Sweden. The reports on this matter were sent to London from occupied Poland, where detailed maps of Sweden were printed for the units of the Wehrmacht. The Attaché immediately communicated this fact to the Swedish military authorities and Envoy Potworowski met with Boheman on 19 February to discuss it. The Swede, however, undervalued the news. On many occasions previous, it seemed the Germans were preparing to launch an attack, yet the real purpose was usually to warn the British of a possible attack on Scandinavia. Anyway, Boheman assured Potworowski that in the event of attack, Sweden would take up arms and 'expressed his gratitude for the passing on of valuable information to the Swedish staff by our military attaché.'[163] For Sweden the so-called February crisis was a breakthrough in relations with the Germans; from then on relations eased somewhat.[164] Nobody ruled out that Hitler could decide to launch an attack but the danger was said to be much smaller and dependent on the action of the Allies in Norway. A disinformation campaign took place until July 1944, the purpose of which was to convince the Germans that a second front would be opened in Scandinavia and not in France.

Polish and Swedish federalist concepts for post-war Europe

In line with the instructions of the minister of foreign affairs from 17 March 1942, on 27 March Envoy Potworowski attended a meeting with Minister Günther and acquainted him with the current state of Polish–Soviet relations. The head of Swedish diplomacy was clearly interested with the General Sikorski's eastern policy. Potworowski assured him that Poland, following the conclusion the arrangement of 30 July 1941, had not abandoned the plan to guarantee independence and safety for itself and its northern and southern neighbours. Any tensions in bilateral relations were the fault of Stalin, who was eager to make the USA and Great Britain recognize borders agreed before

---

[163] AAN, HI/I/19, a PS to letter by Polish Envoy to Stockholm G. Potworowski to the Ministry of Foreign Affairs, Stockholm, 20 II 1942. The author of the monograph devoted to the February crisis does not make a single mention about the Polish sources of information. This is however done by E. Boheman in his memoirs. See: Å. Uhlin, *Februari-krisen 1942. Svensk säkerhetspolitik och militärplanering 1941–1942*, Stockholm 1972; E. Boheman, *På vakt. Kabinettssekreterare...*, p. 294.

[164] A. W. Johansson, *Per Albin...*, p. 294.

22 June 1941. Potworowski explained to Günther, 'the Polish government claims that all allies should grant the Soviet Union as much help as possible, especially in the shape of materials, and that, after all, all concessions which have been made to the Soviet territorial claims would have a weakening impact on the military effort by undermining the occupied nations' fate in the rightness of the common cause and in the basis which, in line with the content of the Atlantic Charter, is to serve as a foundation of the victory. [...] While considering the overcoming of German possessiveness to be the first and most important aim of the war, we cannot at the same time give our consent to the Soviet possessiveness, driven both by Russian imperialism and revolutionary doctrine.'[165]

Potworowski wanted to draw his interlocutor's attention to the fact that Poland and Sweden shared common interests. In connection with this, he highlighted that the position of the Polish government was in conformity with the interests of other countries with whom Poland wanted to 'develop close cooperation in order to create a powerful block of countries which would be able not only to oppose German greediness, but also Russian aspirations to achieve hegemony over Central Europe.' According to the Polish envoy, the Baltic and Scandinavian States were part of a group of countries, to which 'the German problem and the Russian problem constitute the key conditions of their independence and national integrity.' Potworowski felt that the conversation was promising and prepared ground for continuing the discussion in the future. Günther listened to the envoy with a clear interest and understanding, but saw no reason for alarm even if the territorial integrity of Poland was not yet established. Potworowski was too optimistic about Günther's position perhaps. While asking questions about various details, Günther would only confirm his views regarding certain issues and wanted to become acquainted with the Polish government's tactics towards the Soviet Union.[166] Three days later, having agreed the course of the visit with the director of the diplomatic protocol, Potworowski submitted a courtesy note to King Gustaf V with president Raczkiewicz's message of congratulations on the occasion of the monarch's return to good health.[167]

At the outset of May, Potworowski spoke with Boheman, repeating what he had earlier passed on to Minister Günther. The Secretary-General of

---

[165] AAN, HI/I/63, letter by Polish Envoy to Stockholm G. Potworowski to the Ministry of Foreign Affairs, Stockholm, 30 III 1942.
[166] Ibidem.
[167] PISM, A 11, E/25, letter by Polish Envoy to Stockholm G. Potworowski to the Civil Chancellery of Polish President W. Raczkiewicz, Stockholm, 15 IV 1942.

Foreign Affairs was not surprised by the attempts by Stalin to settle the issue of the Polish border based on the situation from 1941 adding, 'this issue is very interesting for Sweden due to its location in relation to Russia and especially because of the situation on the Baltic Sea coast.' Both diplomats also mentioned the German problem. Boheman feared that following the defeat of Hitler, the hatred of the beaten nations would make it difficult to establish peace. He also became interested in the fate of the Polish middle class. In February 1942 Potworowski informed the headquarters of the Polish Ministry of Foreign Affairs with resignation, 'The idea of Baltic–Scandinavian federation was not addressed by the local Ministry of Foreign Affairs in any way', and that Boheman 'sees no possibility of its execution.'[168] Potworowski returned to the subject and the need to create a map of post-war Europe. He acquainted his interlocutor with the idea of Polish–Czechoslovak federation, and his desire for Poland to play a central role in a strong and large block of countries between Germany and Russia. He also referred to the concept of the Nordic federation, which had been discussed recently in the Swedish press. According to Potworowski, Boheman picked up this subject and supported the idea of a common defensive policy for the Nordic States. Moreover, he pointed out that by maintaining its neutral position (which Boheman described as almost impossible) Sweden 'would play a wonderful international role of being nearly the only country in Europe with an intact political and social organisation.'[169] Potworowski's argument was an expression of his strategy of convincing the Swedish authorities that, as was the case in Poland, the most pressing problem for the international policy of Sweden is the attitude towards Germany and the Soviet Union.[170]

At the same time a public debate had sparked in Sweden regarding the future of Scandinavia. The debate was triggered by *Nordensförenta stater* (The United States of the North), a brochure published in 1942 by Karl Petander, an activist of the *folk* universities (adult education institutions) and famous for his harsh criticism of the Nazi philosophy, Colonel Willi Kleen and Anders Örne, a social democratic politician who was also head of the Swedish postal service management board.[171] The authors underlined the

---

[168] AAN, HI/I/285, telegram by Polish Envoy to Stockholm G. Potworowski to the Ministry of Foreign Affairs, Stockholm, 6 II 1942.
[169] AAN, HI/I/19, letter by Polish Envoy to Stockholm G. Potworowski to the Ministry of Foreign Affairs, Stockholm, 8 V 1942.
[170] *Notes by Polish envoy to Stockholm G. Potworowski 1939–1942*, entry from 19 II 1942.
[171] AAN, HI/I/19, attachment no. 1 (Nordic project of united states) to letter by Polish Envoy to Stockholm G. Potworowski to the Ministry of Foreign Affairs from 10 VIII 1942, Stockholm, 17 VI 1942.

need for creating a common Nordic defence staff and common military units. They supported the idea of forming one government for conducting integral foreign and parliamentary policy. They also proposed that a Nordic national association should be established, which would be free from the powers' influence and tied by strong economic bonds and a military alliance. They even suggested that the royal seat of Drottningholm should become the capital of the future union. The project was in line with the British concept of building a federation of countries in post-war Europe. Envoy Potworowski followed these discussions closely. He stressed their significance also from the Polish point of view, 'Political guidelines for the Nordic States' block, founded on the basis of a common defence of freedom and independence for its members, would be therefore undoubtedly be in keeping with, or at least parallel to the purposes of a federation of Central European countries with Poland at its centre. This block, located between Russia to the east and Germany to the south, would naturally extend the Central European federation to the north, and its role in the north would be that of a barrier to the German expansion and a barrier separating Germany from Russia.[172]

Potworowski admitted that Sweden would be of crucial importance in such a Nordic association, for which it was not prepared, and that the discussion on the presidency of the association 'would be academic.' According to the Polish envoy in Sweden, there were 'many people who are thinking of the bigger picture, who understand the role which may and should be played by Sweden in post-war Europe, foremost for the sake of the consolidation and unification of the Nordic States.' Among such people he mentioned Sandler, the former minister of foreign affairs, and 'a group of young and intelligent officials who had a strong interest in these matters.' In fact, Potworowski admitted that "reliable" authorities were very cautious in their enunciations stressing that, 'setting out our position on this subject in the present moment would be premature and unrealistic due to the inability to foresee the shape of post-war relations.' Potworowski discussed this subject several times with Boheman. He always heard reserved remarks regarding the idea of future cooperation between the Nordic States, which were characteristic of the broadly-understood government circles, 'By describing the ideas of the authors of the aforementioned [...] brochure about a close union between the Nordic States as "dreams", he was bringing to my attention dif-

---

[172] Ibidem, letter by Polish Envoy to Stockholm G. Potworowski to the Ministry of Foreign Affairs, Stockholm, 10 VIII 1942.

ficulties in realizing closer cooperation and also pointed out that arrangements to this cooperation were even less advanced on the side of the remaining Nordic States than in Sweden.'

Besides, Boheman argued that the policy of neutrality did not collapse in April 1940. He claimed that the reason for Norway's defeat was not due to this particular policy, but to negligence in the organisation of the country's defence and the betrayal by many high-ranking military men. In connection with this, the Swedes were convinced that 'the best policy for the Nordic States is one of defence without alliances.' Boheman excluded the alliance between Sweden and any of the powers as too dangerous, although he assured Potworowski that this did not mean isolation from the Western Allies. Potworowski was aware that the Swedes were reluctant to develop closer relations between the countries, and, despite everything, he did not expect them to change their position. He informed the headquarters: 'In my conversations on similar subjects I always try to emphasize the interest with and the understanding of the concept of Nordic rapprochement, and point to parallel political interests as well as to the lack of opposing interests between the united North, Poland and the block of countries, whose centre Poland would become; I'm naturally doing this with caution, which is necessary due to the Swedes' suspicion connected with the possibility of being dragged into the conflicts between the powers in Central Europe; a suspicion I have witnessed from the moment of my arrival in Sweden, and it has naturally grown considerably from the moment of the outbreak of war.'[173]

Potworowski summed up in the report he had prepared previously, 'much work still needs to be done to let this idea [of integration] dim the remarkably deeply rooted particularistic spirit of the Scandinavian nations.'[174] This was first indicated by a Norwegian protest. The government periodical *Norsk Tidend*, published in London, was heavily critical of the concept of a Nordic federation. An alliance with Great Britain and the USA, however, garnered support. Also characteristic were the commentaries of the Swedish press, which, despite the views expressed, agreed that the matter was closed for the time being. The arguments progressed along familiar lines, 'Nobody knows how Europe will be organized after the war and who would introduce this new deal.'[175] According to Potworowski: 'The discussion [...] contributed to

---

[173] Ibidem.
[174] AAN, HI/I/19, attachment no. 1 (Nordic project of united states) to letter by Polish Envoy to Stockholm G. Potworowski to the Ministry of Foreign Affairs from 10 VIII 1942, Stockholm, 17 VI 1942.
[175] Ibidem.

the explanation of the view present in Scandinavia, which by no means determines the issues of defensive post-war Nordic cooperation, leaving it in suspension at the present moment, and making its form dependent on the shape of the post-war relations.' The initiative of the talks on the post-war federation in Central Europe was of a unilateral character. The Swedes were becoming acquainted with the Polish position, but approached the plans with reserve. The press commented rarely on the situation, and what was both most striking and crude were the statements found in pro-Nazi-oriented newspapers. In June 1942, the author of an article in *Dagsposten* contemptuously described the plan of establishing Polish-Czechoslovak federation. He wrote about the member countries' very low level of development, that the relations in Central Europe could be determined only by the Germans, who would lead the Slavs. Moreover, the opinion journalist argued that Sweden was geographically isolated and that no social democratic dreams about a European federation would change this situation.[176]

Nevertheless, the idea of an association of Nordic States was supported by leading Swedish politicians. In an article published in the social democratic *Ny Tid* daily, on 31st of December 1942, former Swedish minister of foreign affairs, Rickard Sandler, called for the establishment of a Nordic federation after the war.[177] In March 1943, the concept of a Scandinavian defence union was introduced by Minister Sköld. In the same year, on the initiative of Prime Minister Hansson, the Committee of Foreign Affairs of Sweden's Social Democratic Workers' Party prepared a memorandum regarding the issue of a future Nordic federation, which was to be a point of departure for international cooperation. Nevertheless, the Swedish press was dominated by negative views about the plan to establish a Nordic federation. One may even risk saying that the purpose of the initiators was to polemicize with the Norwegian plan to establish a so-called Atlantic policy, namely, connecting the political fate of post-war Norway with that of the Anglo-Saxon countries.[178] Östen Undén, a leading social democratic party activist, diplomat and lawyer, took the floor in a discussion about the draft of the federation. He warned against the consequences of establishing associations of this sort without approval from the powers. The lack of such consent could, according to him,

---

[176] J. Hultström, 'Östeuropeiska problem', *Dagsposten*, 5 VI 1942.
[177] 'Enade vi stå, söndrade vi fala', *Ny Tid*, 31 XII 1942. See Y. Möller, *Rickard Sandler...*, pp. 442–443.
[178] On the Norwegian–British polemics on the subject of post war future of Scandinavia, see W. M. Carlgren, 'Norsk-brittisk-svenska meningsutbyten 1942 om Norden efter kriget' [in:] *Vindkantring...*, pp. 305–320. The author of the article proves that in Sweden there was not much support for the federalist concept.

lead to isolation and failure in regional cooperation. That is why Undén proposed a close Nordic cooperation, based on common labour market and customs union, but placed within a larger union modelled after the League of Nations, despite the imperfections of this organisation, which were known from the interwar period.[179] These concepts had been developed for the most part in social democratic circles, which were founded on traditional cooperation between related parties from the Nordic States.[180] It is beyond any doubt that the federalist concepts within the Nordic region were developed without connection to similar concepts related with Central Europe. The conversations of Potworowski and Boheman only confirm this. Studies advanced by the Polish government apparently ignored these circumstances,[181] much like the deliberations of opinion journalists. Ignacy Matuszewski, a famous opinion journalist for a pre-war Polish pro-government-oriented newspaper, convinced the readers of a newspaper for Polish expatriates in the USA that Poland's fate determined the fate of the Baltic and Scandinavian States, and therefore Poland's freedom and independence determined the future of the entire Baltic region.[182] This view was not popular in Northern Europe.

In November 1942, the Command of the Polish Navy submitted a letter to the Commander-in-Chief where it was opined that the real threat was the establishment of hegemony of the Soviet Union over the region. This could be counteracted by, among other things, cooperation with countries that were against such dominance. Commander Karol Korytowski counted mainly on support from the USA and Great Britain, but saw a potential ally in Sweden. He stated, 'The dominance of the Soviets over the Baltic Sea is neither in the interest of Sweden nor of Poland. Poland especially should be wary. And, bearing this in mind, we later need to establish contact with Sweden.'[183] This aspect was reflected in an article by Julian Ginsbert, a famous maritime journalist, in the *Polska na morzach* monthly in London. Ginsbert

---

[179] Y. Möller, *Östen Unden. En biografi*, Stockholm 1986, pp. 219–222.
[180] On Swedish discussions on the subject of integration of Scandinavia during the Second World War, see: B. Piotrowski, *Tradycje jedności Skandynawii. Od mitu wikińskiego do idei nordyckiej*, Poznań 2006, pp. 175–185.
[181] At this point it is worth to cite the words of the Polish Ambassador to London E. Raczyński, otherwise a devoted supporter of a Polish-Czechoslovak federation, who years later recalled: 'Poles always fantasized: while being in exile, they developed visions of alliances, for instance with Scandinavian countries, and these countries were not even aware that we made them do what we wanted'. See: E. Berberyusz, *Anders spieszony*, London 1992, p. 75.
[182] I. Matuszewski, *Wybór pism. Kulisy historii Polski (1941–1946)*, Rzeszów 1991, pp. 75–76, 269.
[183] *Polska Marynarka Wojenna*, pp. 40–41.

explained that the Baltic Sea was a northern supplementation of the Mediterranean Sea and what was happening there was as important for European peace as what was happening behind the Pillars of Hercules. He suggested that Great Britain, Sweden and Poland cultivate a cooperation to stabilize the situation in the Baltic Sea region. In Ginsbert's view, these waters could neither be controlled by a country as weak as Denmark nor by an international institution. He proposed extending the territory of Denmark and returning to the concept of John III Sobieski, who, many centuries earlier, considered marking out a Polish–Danish border to the west of Szczecin. Ginsbert argued that the Soviet Union should not feel threatened, but purposefully did not mention either the Åland Islands or access to the Gulf of Finland. The Swedish Legation reacted to the text with confusion, and then described it as a curiosity. In response to the Swedes' démarche regarding this matter, the Polish Embassy in London stated that the article was not inspired by the Polish authorities but merely the private views of its author.[184]

Nevertheless, the article was generally in line with the content of studies devoted to Polish war aims connected with the Baltic Sea region. In September 1942 Jan Starzewski, a former Polish Envoy to Copenhagen, prepared the monograph *Rękojmie wolności Bałtyku (Ogólne uwagi w sprawie przyszłego uregulowania zagadnienia bałtyckiego)* [Warranties of Freedom

---

[184] RA, UD 1920 års dossiersystem, HP 1, vol. 485, letter by the Swedish Legation in London to R. Kumlin, London, 18 XI 1943. On the need for cooperation between Poland, the Baltic States and Scandinavian States see the writings of a former Polish ambassador in Paris, Juliusz Łukasiewicz: J. Łukasiewicz, 'O sprawach bałtyckich', *Wiadomości Polskie*, 15 III 1942. He reminded the achievements of J. Beck's foreign policy. These achievements were treated by him as a point of departure to establishing future relations. Nevertheless, Sweden (Scandinavia) was rarely mentioned in Polish press commentaries devoted to the idea of the federation. There are several examples of important publications where this region of Europe was not mentioned: T. Piszczkowski, 'Federacja... ale jaka?', *Myśl Polska*, 20 I 1942; Junius, 'Europa Środkowa – ośrodkiem pokoju', *Myśl Polska*, 20 V 1942; T. Piszczkowski, 'Polska a Europa Środkowa', *Myśl Polska*, 1 VII 1942; H. Strasburger, 'Bałtyk a bezpieczeństwo Europy', *Nowa Polska* 1942, iss. 7; A. Pragier, 'Rejon środkowo-europejski', *Nowa Polska* 1942, iss. 8; J. Stańczyk, 'Federacja krajów środkowo-wschodniej Europy – podstawą trwałego pokoju i dobrobytu w Europie i świecie', *Nowa Polska* 1943, iss. 3; N. V. Tilea, 'Stany Zjednoczone Europy Środkowej', *Nowa Polska* 1943, p. 4; Arp, 'Bałtyk czy Dunaj', *Orzeł Biały*, 15 VIII 1943; P. Janecki, 'Strefa środkowa', *Myśl Polska*", 1 XII 1943; A. Pragier, 'Federacja środkowo-wschodnia. Sprawy polityczne', *Wiadomości Polskie*, 6 II 1944. A similar lack of interest could be observed in Sweden. An isolated (and pointless) view was presented by Tadeusz Nowacki, who noted in November 1944: 'In Sweden we may observe an increasing understanding of growing chances for the formation of potential community of political fate with the countries of Central Europe in the nearest future, and primarily with Poland. This is a trend in political evolution, which may be also taken up by other Scandinavian countries following their liberation from the German occupation.' T. Norwid[-Nowacki], 'Ewolucja polityczna Szwecji', *Dziennik Polski i Dziennik Żołnierza*, 25 XI 1944.

for the Baltic Sea (General Remarks Regarding the Future Settlement of the Baltic Sea Issue)]. A crucial postulate appeared here, which according to the author was the condition of Poland's recognition following the conclusion of the war – the capacity to establish a federation as the only measure that would guarantee the survival of smaller countries. Starzewski stated, 'The ability to create federal countries would be a test of political maturity for the nations populating the Baltic Sea region, particularly as this issue is a matter of their existence or non-existence.'[185]

The envoy noted that due to geographical conditions it was possible to distinguish two groups of countries – Poland, Lithuania, Latvia and Estonia would form a southern federation and Finland, Sweden, Norway and Denmark a northern federation. Cooperation between these two federations, including military cooperation, seemed natural. The members of the government circles were aware of the awkwardness of plans of this sort for the current policy. When Starzewski wanted to deliver a lecture as part of the so-called Allied Circle[186] and present his reflections, both the Ministry of Foreign Affairs and the Ministry of Congress Work consulted with each other regarding amendments to the content of the lecture, so as not to cause rifts in relations with other countries. Starzewski was to refrain from mentioning several countries in a specific context. He could not associate Norway with the concept of federation as 'the Norwegians are against, as we know, the Nordic federation.' So as not to irritate the Soviets, under no circumstance should he mention that the future federation was to include Estonia and Latvia. Neither could he call for the return of the northern bank of the Kiel Canal to Denmark, 'because Denmark may be against it.'[187] Sweden was not even mentioned.

Sweden's role started to be gradually reduced by both experts in the field of economy and military affairs. In February 1943, Andrzej Cienciała presented the issue of future maritime policy of East-Central Europe in a confidential study. He rejected the option of a closer cooperation with Sweden claiming, 'Cooperation with Scandinavian countries is not desirable for us since the economic potential of Scandinavian countries is not enough to allow them to employ their own navy in its entirety. They would therefore exploit the economic potential of East-Central Europe, giving no equivalent

---

[185] PISM, col. 30/V/2, Jan Starzewski, *Rękojmie wolności Bałtyku (Ogólne uwagi w sprawie przyszłego uregulowania zagadnienia bałtyckiego)*, p. 34.
[186] PISM, PRM-K-63, letter by A. Romer to the Ministry of Congress Work, London, 9 IX 1942, iss. 423.
[187] Ibidem, letter by the Ministry of Foreign Affairs to the Ministry of Congress Work, London, 22 IX 1942, iss. 441.

in return. [...] Locating the Swedish navy on long-distance routes leading from our ports would be particularly dangerous.'[188]

Barely comprehensible was the study's explanation of the fear of the Swedish navy, more so that Scandinavian countries were named alongside Great Britain, the USA and the Netherlands, as the countries of origin of the ship owners, with whom Poland was to cooperate on the handling of foreign trade by mapping out their route to the eastern coast of South America.

In the autumn of 1943, the Command of the Polish Navy submitted Commander Karol Korytowski's confidential memorandum *Assurance of Freedom for the Baltic Sea Following the War* to the Command of the Polish Armed Forces. This was a summary devoted to the issue and repeated the theses of the author's previous papers, which were entirely approved by Rear-Admiral Jerzy Świrski, commander of the Polish Navy.[189] Sweden was not included in the list of Polish alliances. As Korytowski stressed, 'Its small population and geographical location, away from the centre of Europe, doubtless does not predestine it to this role.' The views of the Command of the Polish Navy were pompous: 'Poland, owing to its geographical location, demonstrably positive marine conditions regarding both organisation and our vessels' sea operation during the war, could be a factor in counterbalancing the Russian hegemony.'

This issue was perceived slightly differently by the Staff of the Commander-in-Chief, since it emphasized the need to improve the security of Poland 'within the union of countries of East-Central Europe, within the economic community including Scandinavian countries and Turkey', and also in close cooperation with Great Britain.[190] According to the author of the study, Poland had to ensure that it maritime links with Sweden would be maintained in the event of war. This lay at the foundation of a basic demand: 'Control over the southern part of the Baltic Sea together with Great Britain and Scandinavian countries is therefore a marine demand of Poland.' What was mostly emphasized was the necessity to cooperate with Sweden and Norway on exercising

---

[188] PISM, B 3124, A. Cienciała, *Zarys przyszłej polityki morskiej Europy Środkowo-Wschodniej*, London, February 1943, p. 40.
[189] PISM, B 1127, letter by the head of the Polish Navy Command (KMW), Rear-Admiral J. Świrski, to the head of the Administration of Armed Forces, General M. Norwid-Neugebauer, London, 24 IX 1943.
[190] PISM, A 21, 2/16, postulates of the Staff of the Commander-in-Chief regarding naval war aims, attachment to letter by the head of the Staff of the Commander-in-Chief, General S. Kopański, from 17 XI 1943.

control over the Danish straits – Skagerrak and Kattegat. However, the establishment of military bases for aircraft protecting sea lines across the Baltic Sea required cooperation with Sweden and the Baltic States.

On 21 December 1943 the government eventually adopted a document entitled *A Draft of Points Regarding the Naval War Aims of Poland*.[191] The Ministry of Congress Work, the Ministry of Defence and the Ministry of Industry, Trade and Shipping jointly endorsed the draft, the priority of which was to ensure a free use of marine routes from Poland to Sweden and to the North Sea as well as creating a Gdynia–Gdańsk port complex. Germany was to be practically eliminated, both politically and economically from the Baltic Sea area. The importance of the strategic–political situation in the Baltic Sea area for all of Europe was recognized, and the presence of Great Britain in the Baltic Sea region was acknowledged as indispensable for the freedom of marine transport and the security of Western Europe. An opinion was also expressed that the Baltic Sea region was not of great significance for Soviet interests, and Denmark would not be able to control the Baltic Sea straits on its own.[192] To assist with this task, it was necessary to extend Polish access to the Baltic Sea by the annexation of East Prussia, Gdańsk and the Baltic Sea coast as far as Szczecin. Another demand was that the Baltic States should be granted independence, Germany should be deprived of the Kiel Canal and the islands in the North Sea, any Soviet military bases should be moved far away from Polish ports, and British military forces should be allowed into the Baltic Sea area. A strong navy was to become an instrument of Polish Baltic Sea policy. It was believed that in connection with the ambitions of the Soviet Union, it was necessary to introduce a division of spheres of influence in the Baltic Sea area, and in the case of Poland the foundation for this division was to be an alliance with Great Britain and Sweden.[193] That is why it was crucial to encourage construction of numerous naval bases on the Polish coast and to increase the number and improve the quality of Polish warships. Discussions between the ministries continued until October 1944 when the Polish government adopted the plan *Points Regarding the Naval War Aims*

---

[191] J. K. Sawicki, 'Polskie cele wojny w dziedzinie morskiej w koncepcjach rządu RP w Londynie (1940–1944)' [in:] *Polityka morska państwa w 40-leciu PRL*, Gdańsk 1986, pp. 19–21.
[192] W. Wrzesiński, 'Polska a problem bałtycki. Ze studiów nad stanowiskiem polskim wobec Bałtyku w okresie drugiej wojny światowej', *Przegląd Zachodni* 1990, iss. 5–6, pp. 108–109.
[193] B. Zalewski, *Polska morska myśl wojskowa 1918–1989*, Toruń 2001, pp. 211–212.

of Poland.[194] Consultations with Swedish authorities, about the principal provisions laid out in the plan, were never conducted.

Overcoming stagnation in bilateral relations following Hitler's defeat in Moscow

By mid-1942 the belief that the Allies would be victorious became increasingly widespread across Sweden. This converged with a growing interest in the Polish matter, which, as claimed Envoy Potworowski in his report, even received a semi-official sanction. It was possible for the Polish Legation to develop its propagandist activity and make the Swedes aware of the realities of the German occupation, the military effort of the Polish Armed Forces in the West and the politics of the Polish government in exile. On 17 April, the Swedish–Polish Academic Association organized an annual meeting during which Carl Palmstierna delivered a speech devoted to the Polish–Swedish ties in the 18th century. Of particularly solemn character was the commemoration of the 3rd May National Holiday, which was modelled after a pre-war habit of organising celebrations for around 300 people. A group of several dozen Swedish guests included Sven Grafström, a unique event as Grafström admitted in his diary, because the Swedish Ministry of Foreign Affairs officials preferred not to show their support in public for occupied countries.[195] A large Swedish audience also gathered at a concert of the Polish and English pianists Roman Maciejewski and Martin Penny, organized under the aegis of the Polish and British, in the Stockholm Concert Hall on 8 May 1942. Around 700 people attended an exhibition of artwork created by refugees and interned seamen held in the Polish club *Ognisko* on 5 June 1942. On summing up the achievements of the legation in the field of propagandist activity, Potworowski drew attention to the need of exercising special caution and adapting to the general political situation in the context of current procrastination tactics of the Swedes.[196] What he probably had in mind were, among others, the events that had taken place three months earlier, when

---

[194] *Protokoły posiedzeń Rady Ministrów Rzeczypospolitej Polskiej*, vol. 7: *maj 1944– listopad 1944*, scholarly editing M. Zgórniak, compiled by W. Rojek in cooperation with A. Suchcitz, Kraków 2006, pp. 525–536.
[195] Grafström's sympathy for Poland is unquestionable. Most probably for this reason a correspondent of the Polish Telegraphic Agency (PAT), Jan Berson, considered him to be the best candidate for Swedish envoy to Warsaw following the conclusion of the war. See: S. Grafström, *Anteckningar 1938–1944*, p. 414.
[196] AAN, HI/I/63, letter by Polish Envoy to Stockholm G. Potworowski to the Ministry of Foreign Affairs, Stockholm, 16 VI 1942.

several Swedish newspapers published witness testimonies detailing torture by the Germans in Norwegian prisons. In connection with this, Minister of Justice Westman, issued a directive on 11 March 1942 regarding the simultaneous confiscation of these journals, which caused an outcry. In April 1942, a major parliamentary debate took place, during which the government was accused of abandoning the principle of freedom of reporting information from Norway.[197] Westman, as usual, referred to a paragraph of the constitution that allowed the confiscation, without a court order, of newspapers publishing materials that could cause a conflict with another country. All activity directed against the German policy towards the occupied territories had been prosecuted for a long time, but less interest was shown for reports about Soviet atrocities and attacks by pro-German dailies on Great Britain and the USA. Accusers in this debate were former ministers of foreign affairs Sandler and Undén (also Günther's counsellor), who both blamed Westman for his officiousness and acting as editor-in-chief for Swedish newspapers. However, the government coalition emerged unscathed from the debate. Nevertheless, in his report to London Potworowski highlighted 'the very fact of addressing questions and freely expressing opinions by leading politicians criticising the system which represses both freedom of the press and humanitarian impulses of healthy sections of the nation, proves that there is a reaction to the news about the German atrocities inflicted upon the occupied countries every time these news items reach wider audience.'[198] The representatives of the Swedish government preferred to take the precaution of not irritating the Germans. On 9 April 1942, therefore, they did not attend a solemn mass in commemoration of the Norwegians who fought for the freedom of their homeland, which was observed in Stockholm.

No wonder then that the ban on the publication of reports about the atrocities that were taking place in other occupied countries, including Poland, was persistently maintained. In the beginning of 1942, the *Black Book of the Government of Poland* by the Polish Ministry of Information and Documentation, published by Ture Nerman's *Trots Allt!*, was confiscated as well as one of the issues of the communist *Ny Dag* magazine, in which it had been commented on.[199] Readers of the *Black Book*, which was an abridged booklet version of the English edition, could learn about the deportations, the ruthless

---

[197] AAN, HI/I/19, letter by Polish Envoy to Stockholm G. Potworowski to the Ministry of Foreign Affairs, Stockholm, 8 IV 1942.
[198] Ibidem.
[199] AAN, HI/I/19, classified letter by Polish Envoy to Stockholm G. Potworowski to the Ministry of Foreign Affairs, Stockholm, 16 II 1942.

economic exploitation and extermination of the Poles. The authors of the Swedish edition highlighted that the German repressions, which were known to the Swedes thanks to Norway, were much greater in Poland. At the end of the booklet, it was noted that the Swedes could not do much to help the victims. In fact, they could only think over the information they received and take their personal stand on what was going on in Poland. In the conclusion there stood the following: 'Poland's fate was never unimportant for humankind, and it never will be, and the heroism of the Polish nation touches us all.'[200] According to research of Klas Åmark, the *Black Book* was confiscated after only a few weeks of distribution. One week after it had been published, the German legation in Stockholm protested 'the attack on the German nation, army and police'. It took some time before the booklet was banned.[201]

The Polish Legation, undaunted by this failure, intensified its propagandist activity. In the autumn of 1942, Norbert Żaba expressed the following: 'The German difficulties on the front bring positive results in Sweden as far as our interests are concerned.'[202] Whereas, on 6 November he reported that pro-Ally moods had been gaining strength over the past several weeks.[203] In connection with this, another attempt was made to spread the news about German terror in occupied Poland. In November 1942 the book *Polens martyrium* (translation: The Martyrdom of Poland), appeared under the imprint of *Trots Allt!*.[204] The prospect of confiscation was taken into account (the book was soon forbidden as an example of propaganda of cruelty (*grymhetspropaganda*)),[205] as it was decided that the publication would be mostly available in pre-sale. Materials for the book were selected by Consul Alf de Pomian-Hajdukiewicz from the official *Black Book of the Government of Poland* and supplemented by Norbert Żaba with news taken from the German press. What was presented were the events which took place in the Polish territories under German control between 1939 and June 1941. The intention of the authors was not simply to issue complaints or accusations, but to give a testimony of Polish resistance. Although the tragic fate of Poland was generally recognised, the purpose was to present a detailed picture of German policy in relation to the Poles: bombings of defenceless civilians, mass executions,

---

[200] *En polsk svart bok om den tyska „nyordningen" i Polen*, Stockholm 1942, p. 14.
[201] K. Åmark, *Att bo granne med ondskan...*, p. 241–242.
[202] AAN, Norbert Żaba's collection, letter by N. Żaba to M. Thugutt (Ministry of Internal Affairs), 16 X 1942.
[203] Ibidem, letter by N. Żaba to M. Thugutt (Ministry of Internal Affairs), Stockholm, 6 XI 1942.
[204] *Polens martyrium. Forhållanden under tyska ockupationen belysta av Polska informationsministeriet*, Stockholm 1942.
[205] K. Åmark, *Att bo granne med ondskan...*, p. 243.

and the torture of arrested patriots. At the end of the book, which contained photographs from execution sites, the publishers argued that the facts presented were not fragments of an overheated imagination. Quite the opposite, they were 'only partially exposing the hell, into which Poland was transformed by the German invaders.' According to Żaba, 'the content of the book has made a deep impression on Sweden.' Whereas based on his own observations he stated, 'The grim content of the book is nevertheless so hard to bear for the Swedes, who did not suffer the atrocities of war, that many of them are unable to finish reading it.'[206] According to diplomatic reports of the Polish Legation almost an entire edition, 2983 copies, was sold out quickly in pre-sale, before the police managed to react. Only 19 copies of the book were confiscated. Żaba wrote with satisfaction, 'The police may now step in. It's all over.'[207] The case was similar with the second edition of the book, which appeared in February 1943. Two thousand copies were sold, of which only 2 were confiscated by police.[208] In his report to London, Żaba emphasized that many daily newspapers had reviewed the publication. Moreover, in May 1943 Erland Björklid protested the confiscations of 10 November 1942 and 3 March 1943, in an open letter on behalf of the editorial board of *Trots Allt!*, and demanded the Swedish government repeal the ban on the book's distribution. However, this intervention had no effect.[209] The book was never available in libraries and as a result probably reached only a small circle of readers. In mid-1942 British Envoy Mallet, in his report to London, highlighted that the Swedes, although accepting of various forms of cultural propaganda, continued to avoid reporting news about the brutal conduct of the occupants in newspapers and on film.[210] This trend continued for a long time. According to news published in *Trots Allt!* in September 1943 the third edition of *Polens martyrium* was also confiscated.[211] The fiasco of another attempt at the legal distribution of information about the terrors of occupation proved that the Swedes continued to believe that controlling publications was necessary, at least as far as this particular thematic scope was

---

[206] AAN, Norbert Żaba's collection, letter by N. Żaba to the Ministry of Information and Documentation, Stockholm, 8 XI 1943.
[207] Ibidem, letter by N. Żaba to M. Thugutt (Ministry of Internal Affairs), Stockholm, 6 XI 1942.
[208] Ibidem, copy of letter by N. Żaba to the Ministry of Information and Documentation, Stockholm, 8 VI 1943. See: L. Drangel, *Den kampande.*, pp. 109–110.
[209] 'Tysk massgravsgreuel fri. Varför beslag på Polens martyrium?', *Trots Allt!*, 7 V 1943.
[210] NA, FO, 371/33055, telegram of Envoy of Great Britain to Stockholm V. Mallet to FO, 5 VII 1942.
[211] AAN, Norbert Żaba's collection, copy of report by N. Żaba to the Ministry of Information and Documentation, Stockholm, 15 XI 1943.

concerned. The distribution of the book started to go on without obstacles as late as 1944. Until that time, as Åmark underlined, the Swedish authorities actively tried to stop important accounts of the German terror in Poland, including information about Holocaust.[212]

A different fate awaited *Det kämpande Polen* (translation: Fighting Poland), a book published in 1942, which was an anthology of articles, studies and excerpts from Polish books prepared by Norbert Żaba and Margit Hansson. The publication, crowned with the Swedish translation of the poem by Władysław Broniewski '*Co mi tam troski*' ('I Leave My Worries Behind') was to present the Polish struggle with the Germans from September 1939, through the campaign on the western front and the underground resistance in the occupied country. The Polish version of the poem was included in the volume *Bagnet na broń* (Fix Bayonettes), published in 1943. The book also presented the works of Polish authors, including poet Kazimierz Wierzyński, writer Maria Kuncewiczowa, reporter Ksawery Pruszyński. Despite humorous stories, the readers could also acquaint themselves with descriptions of heroic events. The publication immediately aroused the interest of Swedish press and garnered very good reviews. In his write-up published in *Upsala Nya Tidning* on 18 November 1942, Gunnar Gunnarsson stressed that the publication 'in terms of its value may be compared to that of a diary and thanks to its restrained reserved style and interesting content may earn a great popularity' and that it proved that Poland 'has grown up to the status of a military power, where both minors and adults, labourers and elites are united in one soldierly comradeship, all sharing one aspiration: striving for freedom and saving the centuries-old Christian and humanist world view.'[213] Some reviews announced that the Poles were struggling not only with the aggressor but also with internal problems, which could lead to a fight for the change of the social system. The communist *Ny Dag* also published an extremely favourable assessment, emphasizing Polish heroism, and added, 'if it was not for the naive politics of the Polish upper classes towards the Soviet Union [...], the Polish soldier would surely leave much more severe marks on the skin of the German fist, other than those he was allowed to inflict upon it thanks to his own bravery.'[214] The discussion of the book in the syndicalist *Arbetaren* daily contains a note that Poland was fighting not only with a foreign invasion, but also with a class of owners, who 'always lived off the

---

[212] K. Åmark, *Att bo granne med ondskan...*, p. 244, 274.
[213] G. Gunnarsson, 'Det kämpande Polen', *Upsala Nya Tidning*, 18 XI 1942.
[214] S. Olsson, 'Hos kämpande polacker', *Ny Dag*, 2 I 1943.

sweat and blood of the people.'²¹⁵ However, in general the reviewers highlighted that the book abandoned the image of Poland as a country, which was only suffering. This time, Poland was also presented as a fighter for freedom and independence.²¹⁶

Another example of a propagandist campaign was the exhibition of art by Polish and Norwegian refugees shown in Stockholm in November 1942, where sixteen Poles and eighteen Norwegians supported by art historian and painter Wacław Reybekiel, who was associated with the Royal Swedish Academy of Arts in Stockholm, presented as many as 169 artworks of their own making.²¹⁷

In a letter to the Polish Ministry of Foreign Affairs from 12 June Potworowski highlighted that, 'the local moods are dominated by even more general and consolidating conviction that the Axis Powers would not manage to win the war and that its conclusion in Europe is a question of relatively short time.'²¹⁸ News of the impending end of the Third Reich was mostly popularized by the Swedes who had just returned from Germany. This only made the Polish Ministry of Foreign Affairs suspect that the rumours could have come from the Germans themselves. Whereas the Swedes interpreted this propagandist move as a method to raise anti-Soviet moods and to demonstrate the threat that would be posed on Sweden in the event of a sudden Soviet victory. According to Potworowski, this propaganda had missed its target because, 'the only things gaining in strength was the pro-Ally mood and self-confidence founded on the belief that it would be increasingly difficult for the weakened Germany to risk an attack on the already well prepared, both militarily and morally, Sweden.' Rumours broke out again about the distinct German–Soviet peace, but Potworowski, following the talks with his Swedish sources, did not take them seriously, as they were not confirmed.

---

²¹⁵ V. B., 'Det kämpande Polen', *Arbetaren*, 30 I 1943.
²¹⁶ Other reviews: M. H., 'Polens kamp', *Nya Dagligt Allehanda*, 13 XII 1942; A. von Arbin, 'Det kämpande Polen', *Östgöta Correspondenten*, 12 XII 1942; Viator, 'Slöjan lyftes', *Arbetet*, 18 XII 1942; A. Rods, 'Polen kämpar vidare', *Stockholms-Tidningen*, 28 XII 1942; R. I., 'Hur Polens lidande folk ser på kriget', *Morgon-Tidningen*, 16 I 1943; Jc., 'Martyrfolken', *Göteborgs Handels- och Sjöfarts-Tidning*, 9 XII 1942; W. S[emitjo]v, 'Det väpnade Polen', *Dagens Nyheter*, 14 XII 1942.
²¹⁷ The pieces included paintings, sculptures, dolls, a model guitar made of matches, a miniature of the church of Mariefred, a model submarine ORP Orzeł. See: 'Malarze polscy w Szwecji', *Wiadomości Polskie*, 28 II 1943. For more information see: J. Raykowski, 'Polsko-norweska wystawa prac uchodźców w Sztokholmie', *Wieści Polskie*, 16 XII 1942. The exhibition was organized with co-participation of painter and pedagogue Tadeusz Potworowski, whose work was presented in July 1941 at the Gripsholm Castle.
²¹⁸ AAN, HI/I/19, letter by Polish Envoy to Stockholm G. Potworowski to the Ministry of Foreign Affairs, Stockholm, 12 VI 1942.

The turning point of the war was close but according to Żaba, London was not preparing itself for it. The Attaché thought that the Polish government circle did not appreciate the role of the neutral states or the systematic propagandist activity on their territory. In his reports he formulated the following arguments: 'Our government in London needs to devote growing attention to the neutral countries when it comes to the future situation of Poland and the matter of borders etc. These matters are already starting to make an impact on the press. It should not be forgotten that many momentary "allies" from the circle of opinion journalists would be our enemies tomorrow. I am referring here to the people who desire a strong and democratic Germany and a powerful Russia, or even that both these things should occur in tandem with greater Czechoslovakia. For there also exist people who do desire this. And all these people will want to harm us.'[219]

Żaba thought that it would be enough to organize regular meetings for the press to convince its representatives to support the Polish cause.[220] A similar method was used in London, where minister Stroński threw a breakfast for Swedish journalists, including local correspondents. Among the guests were head of the SIS Sven Tunberg, social democratic politician and opinion journalist Ivan Pauli, correspondent for *Svenska Dagbladet* Knud Bolander and correspondent for *Dagens Nyheter* Daniel Viklund. The extraordinary rank of the meeting was confirmed by the presence of General Sikorski, ministers Mikołajczyk and Raczyński as well as many officials from the Ministry of Foreign Affairs and Ministry of Information and Documentation. It is not known whether these talks bore fruit in any specific agreement. Even the Polish offices, which were very interested in the Polish matter, received only a laconic and typically diplomatic information that the atmosphere was very warm.[221]

Żaba asked that the propagandist materials of the government should be sent immediately and regularly to Stockholm and that the Swedish journalists in London were inspired. He argued, 'I would like to point out that the neutrals will play a more significant role at the peace congress than it was initially expected and this is particularly because the influential American

---

[219] AAN, Norbert Żaba's collection, letter by N. Żaba to M. Thugutt (Ministry of Internal Affairs), Stockholm, 15 XII 1942.
[220] Ibidem.
[221] AAN, Norbert Żaba's collection, telegram by N. Żaba, 14 VIII 1943.

circles, and even, allegedly, their English counterparts are willing to consider the views of those neutral ones "not blinded by hatred".'²²²

Nevertheless, in mid-1943 Żaba complained continuously about delays caused by the Ministry of Information and Documentation, which sent materials to the Swedish press much too slowly. He explained the needs of the diplomatic mission in Stockholm in a dramatic tone: 'It would be inappropriate for me to reprimand the Ministry of Information for the fact that the department of propaganda has been operating very slowly or at times not at all. Despite having received the telegram from the legation, sent three weeks ago, we have not yet received the résumé and photography of [a new Prime Minister] Mikołajczyk. [...] Whereas yesterday we received, after over a month, a bundle of photographs from the funeral of General Sikorski. Some cretins in the photographs' shipping department and our department of propaganda believe that Poland is the axis of the world, around [which] everything revolves, and they are forgetting that the entire world, at this very moment, is being shaken to its foundations, that dramatic events are taking place every day, obscuring the view of things that happened three days before. Two-week-old photographs may still be published in periodicals, but for God's sake, not six-week-old.'²²³

The Ministry of Internal Affairs in London agreed with the opinion of Żaba, much to his satisfaction in the context of the development of propaganda in the neutral states that was being brushed off by the Polish Ministry of Foreign Affairs: "Popularizing the news all over the world by means of the neutrals and referring to "the objective", neutral opinion is well used and an old propaganda trick.' According to Żaba, however, Polish diplomatic mission in Sweden was by now completely neglected by the government in exile.'²²⁴

Swedish politicians and diplomats constantly mentioned the caution expressed in most cases relating to the attitude to Polish activity in Sweden. German pressures could pose an immediate threat to the operation of the Polish Legation in Stockholm. Following the crisis in the spring of 1941 another crisis took place in July 1942 when the Germans arrested seven Swedish employees of the Polish Match Monopoly and the L. M. Ericsson telephone company, who were visiting Warsaw for business purposes. Those

---

²²² Ibidem, letter by N. Żaba to M. Thugutt (Ministry of Internal Affairs), Stockholm, 9 IV 1943.
²²³ Ibidem, copy of note by N. Żaba for J. Kwapiński [no date].
²²⁴ AAN, HI/I/191, letter by Minister of Information and Documentation S. Stroński to the Ministry of Foreign Affairs, 28 IX 1942.

arrested were accused of cooperation with the Polish resistance movement.[225] The Gestapo also arrested several dozen Poles. However, Sven Norrman and Gösta Gustafsson, two leading couriers of the underground movement, as well as Harald Axell evaded capture as they were visiting Sweden at the time. Most of the mail of the Government Delegation for Poland and the Polish Home Army was passed on to London through Norrman and Gustafsson. Norrman, head of ASEA's daughter company (Polish Electrical Association), smuggled all 'Home Situational Dispatches' that were produced until the moment of the arrests. Gustafsson, working in the same company, transported the greater part of the Home Army Headquarters' dispatches. Staff members of the Swedish Legation in Berlin were also known to be engaged in courier activity for the Swedish industrialists. Envoy Richert had no knowledge of any of this. In the correspondence with the Ministry of Foreign Affairs there is an abundance of information about transfers of funds and letters from Envoy Potworowski, containing delivery location guidelines. Evidence points to funds being sent most often to Berlin through the diplomatic channel so as not to attract the attention of the intelligence services in Stockholm. Next, Colonel de Laval handed the letters to the couriers. In the summer of 1941 Staffan Söderblom prepared a manual to put an end to this activity, to which de Laval willingly gave consent, afraid that continuation could lead to dire consequences for him personally if the Germans were to learn of it. Nevertheless, Svante Hellstedt from the B Division maintained that the ban on transferring private letters could not include financial support for the Poles living in severe poverty, adding that the issue had already been examined. He also assessed the potential risk that could arise from the intermediation prior to the launch of the entire action, advocating that the parcels be transferred as long as the head of the mission considered further activity in this area impossible. De Laval explained that Richert was all but unaware of the issue and the Swedish authorities knew nothing about it officially. De Laval was the only person responsible for the execution of a consequence agreement between Lagerberg and Potworowski, which was concluded in 1940. He was afraid that the Poles would be indiscreet and draw the attention of the German authorities. An example he gave was a conversation with engineer Berglind, who was aware that the cash he had taken from the

---

[225] Relatively quickly, on 4 August the London periodical *Dziennik Polski* informed about the arrests. The author of the note 'Szwedzi aresztowani w Warszawie. Niemcy usuwają świadków zbrodni' ['Swedes arrested in Warsaw. Germans are getting rid of the witnesses of the crime'] aptly stated that the Germans were using every opportunity to remove from Poland all the observers from neutral countries.

legation was intended for the Polish underground organisation in Warsaw and not for philanthropic purposes. At least for a moment, Berglind's carelessness prevented further postage as Birger Johansson, the current head of the B Division, supported de Laval's view. On 15 September 1941, Potworowski learned that the dispatch had stopped.[226] Nevertheless, the confidential courier activity continued.

Based on the news communicated to Potworowski in the Swedish Ministry of Foreign Affairs, it was assumed that the arrests were intended to break the last ties between the General Government and the neutral states.[227] Minister Günther did not wait for the German intervention in Stockholm. On 13 August Günther summoned Potworowski, telling him that he had irrefutable evidence that the Polish Legation maintained contact with secret organisations under German occupation and used the intermediation of Swedish citizens to send money and post. The evidence was coded telegrams deciphered by Swedish cryptologists. The Polish envoy failed to keep his promise from the spring of 1941, when Sweden expelled Captain Gilewicz for espionage, that the diplomatic mission would keep away from illegal activity. That is why the Swedish government decided to consider Potworowski a persona non grata. They also asked the Polish government to appoint a chargé d'affaires who would become the new head of the mission. In a telegram to the Polish Ministry of Foreign Affairs, Potworowski noted that the above fact did not mean breaking relations or closing down the Polish Legation. The Swedes also demanded that the Polish diplomat leave Sweden immediately.[228] Potworowski acted honourably, admitting that he knew about the activity of his staff. When asked about the cipher texts, he did not reveal that the name 'Adam' contained therein was the name of the Swedish couriers' contact Mieczysław Thugutt. He explained that the name referred to one of the organisational units of the mission.

On 18 August a meeting took place in Copenhagen between an officer of Swedish intelligence and the representative of the Abwehr concerning the arrested Swedes. Against the expectations of the Swedes the representative of

---

[226] RA, avdelningar och byråarkiv 1864–1952, Andra B-avdelningen, vol. 417, letter by E. de Laval to S. Hellstedt, Berlin, 22 VIII 1941; copy of letter by S. Hellstedt to E. de Laval, Stockholm, 26 VIII 1941; letter by E. de Laval to S. Hellstedt, Berlin, 29 VIII 1941; letter by B. Johansson to E. de Laval, Stockholm, 12 IX 1941; letter by E. de Laval to B. Johansson, Berlin, 15 IX 1941.

[227] AAN, HI/I/285, telegram by Polish Envoy to Stockholm G. Potworowski to the Ministry of Foreign Affairs, Stockholm, 3 VIII 1942.

[228] Ibidem, telegram by Polish Envoy to Stockholm G. Potworowski to the Ministry of Foreign Affairs, Stockholm, 13 VIII 1942.

the Abwehr did not raise the issue of closing down the Polish Legation. He nevertheless expected that the Swedish authorities would take action in order to break up the Polish spy organisation and prevent the Poles from maintaining contact with the General Government. The Germans demanded access to the materials of investigation on this matter, yet did not intend to harass of companies the detainees worked for. Instead, they demanded that people cooperating with the Polish resistance movement be no longer sent to the occupied territories (at that point one name was mentioned – Sven Norrman).[229] On 10 September a meeting took place in the Swedish Ministry of Foreign Affairs, during which the demands of the Germans regarding the detention of Swedish the citizens were discussed. Boheman proposed that the Germans be granted access to the documentation on various matters from 1940–41. According to him, the choice to expel Envoy Potworowski was the right one. A decision was made during the discussion that the deciphered telegrams, which incriminated the Polish diplomatic mission, would not be revealed to the Germans. In case the Germans were dissatisfied with the information, they were given an opportunity to see materials concerning nine Polish citizens arrested in Stockholm during the Gestapo operation against the Swedes in Berlin and Warsaw. Further talks were to be conducted between the heads of intelligence of both countries.[230]

The Poles never managed to re-establish the connection via Stockholm. In December 1942 Rowecki sent the following telegram to London: 'There is no contact with Anna [base in Stockholm]. From the moment of launching the arrests of the Swedes in Warsaw, Anna is only in the phase of designing connectivity with us.'[231] According to the British sources, General Sikorski was furious about the entire matter, and the career of the minister of internal affairs, Mikołajczyk, who was responsible for communication with Poland, was hanging by a thread due to a criminal negligence.[232] Envoy Potworowski predicted that the exposure of Mieczysław Thugutt was only a matter of time, so he asked London to remove him from the mission. The Swedes however

---

[229] MUST arkiv, Försvarsstaben, Säkerhetsavdelningen, F VIII e, Underrättelsetjänst och sabotage, Polsk underrättelsetjänst, vol. 27, copy of a note: A conversation on 18 August in Copenhagen with a representative of the Abwehr, concerning Swedish citizens arrested in Poland for espionage, pp. 408–409.

[230] MUST arkiv, Försvarsstaben, Säkerhetsavdelningen, F VIII e, Underrättelsetjänst och sabotage, Polsk underrättelsetjänst, vol. 26, copy of the protocol of a meeting at UD, 10 IX 1942 at 16:00, pp. 99–100.

[231] *Armia Krajowa w dokumentach 1939–1945*, vol. 2: *Czerwiec 1941 – kwiecień 1943*, edited by T. Pełczyński, Wrocław 1990, doc. 359 (General Rowecki's report no. 169], 3 XII 1942), p. 373.

[232] NA, HS, 4/135, letter by P.A. Wilkinson to E.O. Coote, 20 VIII 1942.

proved to be quicker.²³³ On 31 August and 1 September 1942 they arrested eight Polish citizens, including Thugutt, who was about to fly back to London. Several days later the captives were released, but only two were given permission to stay in Sweden, these were Maurycy Karniol, who, as a delegate of the Polish Socialist Party, had good connections with the SAP, and Przemysław Kowalewski, who represented the Polish Red Cross. This was how the Swedish authorities showed the Germans that they were responding to illegal activity on their territory and to the transfer of money and post between Great Britain and the General Government.²³⁴ Potworowski was clearly disgusted with the decision of Swedish authorities. It transpired that the Swedes were willing to tolerate the undiplomatic activity of the legation until it posed a real threat to their relations with the Germans. The Polish envoy understood the motivation behind the actions of the Swedish diplomacy, but at the same time stated, 'the way I was faced with the issue was extremely brutal, and I never expected this to happen following my six-year stay here and best possible relations with the Swedish authorities that I always maintained.' Potworowski resented suffering personal consequences. This was highlighted by counsellor Pilch, who was appointed temporary head of the mission, in a conversation with Ragnar Kumlin. The envoy was considered 'a man of balance, familiar with the current situation of Sweden, and a man who on numerous occasions, to mutual satisfaction, settled more than one difficult problem.'²³⁵ Günther declared acceptance of a successor, but at a lower rank. Several months later Henryk Sokolnicki became the new representative of Poland. On a personal basis Sokolnicki enjoyed a title of special envoy and minister plenipotentiary, but officially acted as chargé d'affaires

---

²³³ PISM, A 9, III 4/14, telegram no. 98 by Polish Envoy to Stockholm G. Potworowski, Stockholm, copy from 19 VIII 1942.
²³⁴ The case of Thugutt was described by Lief Björkman in his book about the Swedish secret police actions against foreign intelligence activity. L. Björkman, *Säkerhetstjänstens egen berättelse om spionjakten krigsåren 1939–1942. Så gick det till när säkerhetstjänsten skapades*, Stockholm 2007, pp. 148–150.
²³⁵ AAN, HI/I/100, letters by Polish Envoy to Stockholm G. Potworowski to the Ministry of Foreign Affairs, Stockholm, 13 VIII, 21 VIII 1942; report by counsellor to the Polish Legation in Stockholm T. Pilch from his conversation with vice head of the Political department of the Swedish Ministry of Foreign Affairs R. Kumlin from 18 VIII 1942, Stockholm. Nevertheless, in a conversation with President W. Raczkiewicz which took place on 27 August 1942 in London, Potworowski stressed: 'In general the attitude of the Swedes towards Poland is very warm, and their conviction that the Germans would lose the war is almost widespread'. See *Dzienniki czynności Prezydenta RP Władysława Raczkiewicza 1939–1947*, vol. 1, compiled by J. Piotrowski, Wrocław 2004, p. 590.

en pied.²³⁶ To appease the Germans, he was accredited by the Swedish government and not King Gustaf V, which was the tradition. On 23 January 1943, Sokolnicki, submitted letters of credence to Minister Günther, and on 4 February he visited Grafström. Sokolnicki was surprised that no conditions were specified for the operation of the legation. He maintained that this was 'undoubtedly a result of a change in the general political situation and of favourable moods that were currently felt as far as the attitude towards us of both the local Ministry of Foreign Affairs and various Swedish circles is concerned.'

Minister of Foreign Affairs Edward Raczyński, on 10 October 1942, sent information to all the diplomatic missions to resolve any doubts of Polish diplomats as to the reasons for Potworowski's dismissal and its consequences: 'In the face of inaccurate commentaries in the press I would like to let it be known that Envoy Potworowski has been moved to the headquarters of the Ministry of Foreign Affairs as a result of German pressure on Stockholm following the arrest of the Swedish industrialists. The Polish Legation in Stockholm shall continue operating.'²³⁷

He was wrong about the German pressure, however, as in the end there was none. The Swedes removed Potworowski as part of a preventive measure and as part of the argument against the liquidation of the legation. Nevertheless, the matter quickly ceased to be important for the Germans. What happened to the arrested Swedes? Two of the accused were cleared of charges (but kept in prison), one was sentenced to life imprisonment, and four received capital punishment. On 16 August 1943, Hitler commuted their death sentences to imprisonment. The Germans were striving expressly to maintain good relations with Stockholm and at the end of 1944 released all the prisoners.²³⁸

---

[236] H. Batowski, *Walka*..., p. 142. Henryk Sokolnicki (1891–1981) started his diplomatic career as a secretary of the Polish Legation in Brussels (1919–21), then he spent three years (until 1924) in Christiania (now Oslo) in the rank of chargé d'affaires. Following his return to Warsaw, he worked in the Political-Economic Department under the Ministry of Foreign Affairs. In the years 1934–36 he was counsellor at the Polish Embassy in Moscow. In the years 1936–41 he was Polish Envoy to Helsinki. In the years 1941–42 he was counsellor to the Polish Embassy in Kuybyshev. Following the war he remained in exile in Sweden and Finland.

[237] AAN, HI/I/63, telegram of Minister of Foreign Affairs E. Raczyński to diplomatic missions, 10 X 1942.

[238] The so-called Swedish case has already been described in detail. Most of all see: J. Lewandowski, *Swedish*...; the most recent works: idem, *Knutpunkt Stockholm*...; L. Kliszewicz, *Placówki wojskowej łączności kraju z centralą w Londynie podczas II wojny światowej*, vol. 5: *Baza w Sztokholmie*, Warsaw–London 2000; P. Jaworski, 'Brev kring det ockuperade Warszawa' (1942), *Acta Sueco-Polonica* 2003–2005, iss. 12–13, pp. 287–293; S. Thorsell, *Warszawasvenskarna. De som lät världen veta*, Stockholm 2014; about a lot of the Swedes after

Counsellor Pilch informed the Ministry of Foreign Affairs in December of 1942 that the Swedes considered that the result of the war would be detrimental for Germany and were increasingly open in expressing their liking for the Poles. He also noted, 'The anti-Nazi orientation of the Swedish press is increasingly visible and the way various events are presented is now much less like the traditional restraint we were used to until quite recently.' Despite this, the circles of government fragrantly emphasized their neutral position. Pilch argued that apprehension about Soviet successes, however, and the possibly crucial role of Stalin in the introduction of the new European deal was discernible. The staff of the Polish Legation informed the Swedes about the situation in the Soviet Union. The Swedes continued asking questions about General Sikorski's journey to the USA.[239]

During a reception organized by Maurycy Karniol at the outset of November, counsellor Pilch held a longer conversation with Minister of Social Affairs Möller. According to Pilch, the Swedish minister talked to him 'openly, without a doubt.' Möller confirmed that the Germans had refrained from making claims about Sweden for a long time, but he did not dismiss that pressure could increase in the future 'in the name of defending what the Germans called *Die Festung Europa* [Fortress Europe].' Möller considered military resistance in the occupied countries to be premature and he did not believe in the possibility of softening the German terror, which could have been interpreted as the sign of weakness when the hatred of the conquered nations towards the Germans reached its climax.[240] The Swedish minister assured him that the Swedish army was developed extensively and its equipment was modern. Its weakness was the officer corps, which was lacking intelligence and professional skills. Möller was aware that the on-going war transformed the role of diplomatic missions, becoming the basis for the operation of intelligence services. He also shared his opinion as a head of the Swedish counter-intelligence that 'the Allied intelligence is much less careful while performing its operations in the territory of Sweden than its German counterpart',[241] which clearly suggested that the Swedish authorities were well acquainted with the activity of Polish intelligence.

---

imprisonment: G. Engblom, *Himmlers fred. Tyska fredstrevare genom Sverige under andra världskriget*, Lund 2008, pp. 11–18.

[239] AAN, HI/I/19, letter by chargé d'affaires of the Polish Legation in Stockholm T. Pilch to the Ministry of Foreign Affairs, Stockholm, 14 XII 1942.

[240] Ibidem, letter by chargé d'affaires of the Polish Legation in Stockholm T. Pilch to the Ministry of Foreign Affairs, Stockholm, 10 XI 1942.

[241] Ibidem.

5. Revival of Bilateral Relations Following the Battle of Stalingrad

Polish diplomatic activity in the period of the Wehrmacht's failures

Signs of a breakthrough in the relations with the Allies were visible by mid-1942. At the time the British started to push Sweden to abandon the politics of concessions to Germany. In March 1942 the analysts of the Foreign Office advised that applying political and economic pressure was an adequate solution. They pointed out that 'in this war there is no such thing as a neutral country; there are only the countries who are fighting and those who are not, and the latter change their course depending on the force of wind coming from their fighting counterparts.'[1] The Germans on the other hand abandoned their tough policy towards Sweden and from the outset of 1943 replaced their claims with postulates and their threats with persuasive arguments of discussion.[2] There was no doubt that the Germans would lose the war. Only the date and the circumstances were unknown. The unfolding of events in Europe dictated the change in course of Swedish foreign policy. Sweden became a country that supported the Allies, yet one that avoided participating in the war.

In January 1943 counsellor Pilch directed a question to the Swedish Ministry of Foreign Affairs on the Swedish political objectives for the end of the war. The response came that the Swedish government had yet to tackle this problem since it assumed that everything would be decided by the Great Powers. An occasion to raise this issue was the memorandum of Norwegian socialists on war objectives, which was passed on to the representatives of Swedish social democrats. For Pilch, it was important that a declaration was made on this matter. Opinion was drawn up on the subject of the document, issued by the Norwegians, due to its specific content. The document defined the treatment of both victorious and defeated countries, the reintroduction of borders from 1938, the need to develop cooperation between the powers of the anti-Fascist coalition following the war, the possibilities of creating regional connections and the necessity to commence cooperation with the

---

[1] W. M. Carlgren, *Svensk utrikespolitik...*, p. 356.
[2] Ibidem, pp. 401–402.

Soviet Union. Pilch's anonymous interlocutor avoided giving an explicit answer. He suggested that Sweden become subordinate to the winners. Nevertheless, on commenting on the vision of introducing regional connections, he considered cooperation between the Nordic States to be improbable.[3] The key to understanding later actions of the Swedish government, in foreign policy, may be an opinion shared by Höjer, a leading journalist for *Svenska Dagbladet*, in the presence of American journalists visiting Sweden in spring 1943. He stated that the Swedes were extremely afraid of the Soviet Union, but counting on its expansion bypassing Scandinavia.[4]

In October 1943 Kumlin wrote a memorandum, where he analysed the unfolding of events in the Nordic region in the face of Germany's defeat in Europe. He highlighted that the Soviet Union's position regarding this matter needed to be taken into account, because Stalin was without doubt interested in the events on the other side of his north-western borders. Kumlin expressed his hope that the maintenance of neutrality by the Nordic States should correspond with the interests of Moscow, but did not exclude the division of the region into spheres of influence, whereas to Sweden he attributed the role of neutral territory.[5]

The views of the Swedes are contained in the records of talks with diplomats from other countries. British Envoy Mallet shared a dinner with Minister Günther on 4 January 1943, during which he discussed the situation in the context of recent military successes of the Soviet Union. Günther was convinced that the Germans would not win the war. The way the head of the Swedish diplomacy spoke about the situation made Mallet formulate an opinion that described his attitude as pro-German as unjust. This was indicated by the Swede saying, 'If the Germans somehow managed to win the war, this would naturally mean our end.' It is worth noting Mallet's conclusion following his conversation with Günther. He claimed that the Swedes hoped that the Soviet Union would be weakened to the extent that it would be impossible for it to enjoy military preponderance in Eastern Europe.[6] When at the outset of 1944 Mallet prepared an annual review of events that took place in Sweden, he repeated the same thought: 'It is commonly, though reluctantly, admitted that following the defeat of Germany the Soviet Union

---

[3] AAN, HI/I/130, letter by Chargé d'affaires of the Polish Legation in Stockholm T. Pilch to the Ministry of Foreign Affairs (together with attachment), Stockholm, 22 I 1943.
[4] T. Höjer, *Svenska...*, p. 53.
[5] R. Kumlin, 'Småstatsdiplomati i stormaktskrig. Promemorior från krigsåren', *Historisk tidskrift* 1977, iss. 4, pp. 447–448.
[6] NA, FO, 371/37077, report by British Envoy to Stockholm V. Mallet to the Minister of Foreign Affairs A. Eden, 5 I 1943.

would annex the Baltic States, part of Poland and Bessarabia. A slight trend of protesting this possibility is noticeable at least in the official circles, although the majority of the Swedes would prefer this never came true.[7]

A sense of ease in everyday life was evident following the turning point in the war. The fashion was typically English ladies' suits and hairstyles.[8] The Stockholm National Museum organized an exhibition of modern American architecture 'Amerika bygger' (America Builds).[9] It was probably no coincidence that in 1944 the Nobel Prize in six categories was awarded to an American. The Nobel Prize in literature went to a Danish writer, Johannes V. Jensen, however, which was in line with the policy of Nordic solidarity and the arrangement of relations between the Nordic neighbours in the post-war period. At the outset of 1943 there was a breakthrough in the way events in Europe were communicated to the public. News from the occupied countries was increasingly published in the press, more often announced on the radio, and mostly related to Norway, Finland and Denmark.

The Poles recognised the first signs of the return to strict neutrality for the Swedes. Grafström again appeared at a reception held in the Polish Legation on 31 October 1942. On 15 January 1943 he held a meeting with Press Attaché Norbert Żaba and Chargé d'affaires Tadeusz Pilch, who told him of the mass murders of the Jews.[10] The next visit in the legation was by Grafström on 18 June. Together with Head of Political department of UD Söderblom, high-ranking officers of the Swedish army and navy as well as representatives of the diplomatic corps, Grafström then attended a mournful mass at the St Eugene Catholic Church in Stockholm on 15 July 1943 following the Gibraltar B-24 crash in which general Sikorski died.[11] Minister Günther limited himself, sending only a letter of condolence to Envoy Sokolnicki.[12]

---

[7] NA, FO, 371/43 501, report by British Envoy to Stockholm V. Mallet to the Minister of Foreign Affairs A. Eden, 11 II 1944, pp. 26–27.
[8] H. Dahlberg, *I Sverige...*, p. 47.
[9] Ibidem, p. 184.
[10] S. Grafström, *Anteckningar 1938–1944*, pp. 435, 465.
[11] PISM, col. 1/3, letter by Polish Envoy to Stockholm H. Sokolnicki to the Ministry of Foreign Affairs, Stockholm, 23 VII 1943 (photographs from the ceremony were attached to the letter).
[12] PISM, col. 1/3, copy of letter by the Minister of Foreign Affairs of Sweden Ch. Günther to Polish Envoy to Stockholm H. Sokolnicki, Stockholm, 6 VII 1943 r. The death of General W. Sikorski roused a considerable interest of the Swedish press. It published articles, where it was stressed that the tragedy complicated both the internal relations within the Polish political circles in London and the position of the Polish government on the international arena. See: K. Andersson, 'Sikorskis död ökar Polens svårigheter', *Morgon-Tidningen*, 6 VII 1943; Griggs, 'Sikorskis död upprullar många delikata problem', *Svenska Dagbladet*, 6 VII 1943;

Good moods did not mean the end of close surveillance. When Henryk Sokolnicki arrived in Stockholm in January 1943, the Swedish Security Service (*Säkerhetspolisen* or SÄPO) pointed out that the wife of the new representative of Poland was Finnish and anti-Swedish. In one of the reports the point was raised that her father, a former shipbuilding businessman, several years earlier had participated in an anti-Swedish campaign in Finland.[13] The opinions of the security services, however, held no particular sway over the quality of the mutual diplomatic contacts. Sokolnicki declared in his memoirs that he maintained very good relations both with Prime Minister Hansson, with whom he shared regular night-long bridge sessions, as well as Minister Günther.[14]

On 14 October 1943, the Swedish Ministry of Foreign Affairs forwarded a note of consent for the appointment of Commander Marian Wolbek as Polish naval attaché. Wolbek had already replaced Commander Eugeniusz Pławski in the post of expert on naval affairs in February. The Ministry also granted permission for the nomination of Norbert Żaba to the post of deputy press attaché.[15] Expanding the number of the legation's staff was unprecedented by diplomatic missions of other occupied countries, because previously dismissed officials had been replaced by new ones. According to Żaba: 'The positive decision of the Swedish Ministry of Foreign Affairs reflects the changes that have taken place in Swedish Foreign Policy and is also evidence of the positive attitude towards Polish affairs.'[16] The elimination of the Polish propagandist activity became less persistent, and the activity itself focused on reporting the news of life under occupation and presented principal assumptions of Polish foreign policy.

In January 1944 the new head of the bureau of the Polish intelligence service, Colonel Witold Szymaniak, arrived in Stockholm. In his memoirs he emphasized that the Swedes were very easy going. They gave their permission to establishing radio communication between the Polish Legation and London. They offered help in the preparations for the escape of Poles from labour camps in Norway and the transfer of Polish captives imprisoned by

—

'Svårt att hitta efterträdare till general Sikorski', *Morgon-Tidningen*, 7 VII 1943; M. Karniol, 'Wladyslaw Sikorski – soldat och politiker', *Morgon-Tidningen*, 15 VII 1943.

[13] RA-Arninge, SÄPO arkiv, P 201 Polish Legation, löp 9, memorandum by N. Fahlander, Stockholm, 19 XI 1942 r, k. 740.

[14] H. Sokolnicki, *In the service...*, p. 291.

[15] NA, FO, 371/37082, letter by the Legation of Great Britain in Stockholm to the Northern Department of the FO, 17 X 1943, p. 249.

[16] AAN, Norbert Żaba's collection, copy of letter by N. Żaba to the Ministry of Information and Documentation, Stockholm, 23 X 1943.

the Finnish army as Soviet soldiers called to the Soviet army as Soviet citizens and became prisoners-of-war in the Soviet–Finnish front.[17]

Making use of the favourable situation, Sokolnicki raised the issue of elevating his rank formally to that of envoy. This case was examined for the first time by the Polish Ministry of Foreign Affairs in May 1943 when the Swedes sent their diplomatic representative to act as envoy to the Norwegian government in exile. Potworowski, who at the time served in the headquarters of the Ministry of Foreign Affairs, believed that the best option for the Poles would be a wait-and-see attitude. The former envoy to Stockholm was convinced that rapprochement between Sweden and the Allies, particularly Poland, would be in its interest, as following the war it would risk isolation. The beginning of talks about the participation of Sweden in the rebuilding of Poland was the earliest evidence of this.[18] Envoy Sokolnicki shared a similar opinion to Potworowski, his predecessor in the Swedish post. He explained in his report to London that 'the case is still in its infancy.'[19]

When at the close of 1943 Sokolnicki raised the question of envoy's rank, he referred to the Norwegian and Dutch envoys who were considered rightful envoys. Nevertheless, Minister of Foreign Affairs Tadeusz Romer advised that this had not occurred during the complicated Polish–Soviet crisis.[20] The conversation between counsellor Pilch and Ragnar Kumlin was crucial. Although Kumlin did not say anything specific, he nonetheless pointed out that envoy nominations in relation to other countries set a beneficial precedent for Poland.[21] Sokolnicki and Kumlin's next conversation was entirely different as the Swede explained that his government considered the situation in Eastern Europe as still taking shape and, moreover, persisted in asking questions about Poles supporting the communist movement, namely gen. Zygmunt Berling (the commander-in-chief of the Polish Army in the Soviet Union) and activist Wanda Wasilewska. Sokolnicki was sure he would fail to attain specific commitments from the Swedish government about the future. Nevertheless, he refused to accept the unequal treatment of individual representatives of the occupied countries, this time to the detriment of Poland,

---

[17] PISM, B 3035, report by Colonel W. Szymaniak entitled 'Polskie sprawy przed 30 laty w Szwecji' (Polish affairs in Sweden 30 years ago), Stockholm, June 1974.
[18] AAN, HI/I/30, note by G. Potworowski, n.d, n.p. [May–June 1943].
[19] Ibidem, letter by Polish Envoy to Stockholm H. Sokolnicki to the Ministry of Foreign Affairs, Stockholm, 5 VI 1943.
[20] AAN, HI/I/323, telegram by Minister of Foreign Affairs T. Romer to Polish Envoy to Stockholm H. Sokolnicki, 18 I 1944.
[21] AAN, HI/I/30, letter by counsellor to the Polish Legation in Stockholm T. Pilch to the Ministry of Foreign Affairs, Stockholm, 17 XII 1943.

which in his view was considered a second-rate country. The Swedes it would seem were afraid of the anti-Soviet overtone of such a decision.[22] Sokolnicki's views, based on the earlier reports, confirmed that Prime Minister Hansson and his ministers were opportunists, carefully weighing each word. According to Sokolnicki, even Boheman, despite showing sympathy, did not turn out to be a time tested friend, and as an opportunist he 'occupied himself with navigating across the still dangerous Swedish waters.' He also considered Minister Günther to be a particularly pliant and cautious person.[23]

In a conversation with Boheman on 13 April 1944, Sokolnicki raised the issue of delegating a Swedish envoy of the Polish government in exile to London. While speaking to Minister Günther in an earlier conversation, he referred to the candidacy of Gunnar Hägglöf, who oversaw economic negotiations with Great Britain and the USA in London, and who, allegedly, was to represent Sweden in the governments of the occupied countries.[24] Sokolnicki convinced Boheman that common economic interests should be a starting point for broader cooperation and developing one's own concept of the development of this part of Europe based on the idea of the Atlantic Charter. It is enough to recap an ironic remark from Boheman regarding the name of the charter indicating the area of its application as well as the formal summary of the discussion that he would present to his government.[25] Sweden was engaged in challenging truce negotiations between Finland and the Soviet Union, and therefore avoided actions that could unsettle Stalin.[26] Sweden preferred not to expose itself to the pressure from the powers on the issue of joining the war against the Germans. Kumlin assured Pilch that attacks by the press on the Polish government were not in the interest of Sweden.[27] Despite hearing promises on this matter, efforts by the authorities to hush down critique of Poles in the Swedish dailies were barely noticeable, leaving them free to repeat accusations of the Soviet propaganda.

---

[22] AAN, HI/I/80, letters by Polish Envoy to Stockholm H. Sokolnicki to the Minister of Foreign Affairs T. Romer, Stockholm, 30 XII 1943, 25 II 1944.

[23] AAN, HI/I/206, letter by Polish Envoy to Stockholm H. Sokolnicki to the Minister of Foreign Affairs T. Romer, Stockholm, 28 III 1943.

[24] PISM, A 9, VI 21/1, note by N. Żaba, Stockholm, 11 XII 1943.

[25] AAN, HI/I/80, letter by Polish Envoy to Stockholm H. Sokolnicki to the Ministry of Foreign Affairs, Stockholm, 13 III 1944.

[26] AAN, HI/I/71, letter by Polish Envoy to Stockholm H. Sokolnicki to the Ministry of Foreign Affairs, Stockholm, 29 III 1944.

[27] AAN, HI/I/71, letter by Polish Envoy to Stockholm H. Sokolnicki to the Ministry of Foreign Affairs, Stockholm, 3 III 1944.

Swedish public opinion on the situation in occupied Poland and Polish–Soviet relations

A slow retreat from the cooperation with the Germans and rapprochement with the Allies brought about the gradual breakdown of the wall of silence about Polish affairs.[28] Previously, the Swedes had been pragmatic when justifying their actions in this area. There were doubts as regards informing the public about the crimes or protesting without guaranteed results.[29] Andrzej Nils Uggla suggests there were additional circumstances: isolation from reality and an unwillingness to admit that all ethical norms were being violated with each and every subsequent act of German aggression. That is why commentators, independent of recommendations expressed by the authorities, did not believe the reports about mass murders and occupational terror in Poland.[30]

Individual accounts from occupied Poland were published increasingly often. They were not treated by officials controlling publications as uncompromisingly as books, because they presented the news on the realities of life under occupation in a moderated form. On presenting a description of slavish labour performed by Poles and Jews, *Svenska Dagbladet*, on 19 January 1942, reported: 'They [the Jews] do not receive sick pay, have the option to take a

---

[28] For many months either no publications appeared about Poland or they presented the country in a negative light. One of such examples was the book written by Boguslav Kuczynski (original spelling) *Panik i Polen* (Panic in Poland), translated from German in 1941. It told a fictional story of a group of Polish refugees who were heading from Warsaw to the Romanian border. Opinion journalist Eric Arrhén, who was famous for his pro-Nazi sympathies discussed the book underlining its positive aspects and especially the fact that it showed how 'a primitive nation yields to its opponent whose methods of warfare and technical skills are very advanced'. See: E. Arrhén, 'Det polska sorgespelet i närbild', *Svenska Dagbladet*, 30 III 1941. Duchess Virgilia Sapieha in her memoirs published towards the end of 1941 entitled *Mitt liv i Polen* (*My Life in Poland*) showed no signs of sympathy for the homeland of her husband. See Grafström's opinion in vol. 1 of his diary (p. 376). He considered the harsh assessment of achievements of Poles and Poland following the interwar period to be highly unjust. In 1944 a Germany-inspired book was published by Adolf Vysocki *Ett polskt livsöde* (*The Polish Fate*), which presented the situation of Poles under the Soviet occupation.

[29] During one of the closed-door debates a discussion took place on the subject of possible necessity for the Swedish government to react to the acts of unlawfulness inflicted by the Germans upon the occupied countries. Prime Minister Hansson argued that the protests, unless they had influence on the change of the situation, were completely pointless. Nevertheless, in a reply, liberal politician Bertil Ohlin presented his support for the protests and called for warning the German side against the consequences of the repressive policy conducted in Norway for the Swedish-German relations. It needs to be highlighted that polemics took place in December 1943. See: *Protokoll...*, p. 247.

[30] A. N. Uggla, *Den svenska Polenbilden...*, pp. 30–31.

leave of absence or receive pay for working on public holidays. A Jewish labourer is paid only for the work he does. [...] Unemployment benefit is limited to the mandatory minimum. [...] Pensions make up part of general insurance.'[31] The following day, special penalties for the Poles were mentioned, which involved sending them to strict camps. On 21 January 1942, an opinion journalist for *Social-Demokraten* wrote that the ghettos were being isolated to protect the country from an epidemic of typhus.[32]

What may be considered to be a reliable assessment of the state of awareness of the Swedish public, when it comes to the occupational policy of Germany, is Envoy Potworowski's opinion of June 1942: 'The current atmosphere prevents us from directly and more thoroughly informing the Swedish public about the relations present in Poland under German occupation, which are nevertheless quite well known thanks to the Swedish correspondents in London and Berlin. The competent authorities, however, which moreover possess their own information, are well aware, which I managed to confirm several times, of the current relations present in Poland.'[33]

The society was unaware of the murderous practices taking place in Polish territories, and suggestion from the Swedish politicians that they not surrender to foreign propaganda was certainly understood as a distancing from the facts announced by the Allies. However, even the official declarations of the German authorities were enough to imagine the occupational terror on an unprecedented scale. The communist German newspaper *Die Welt*, which was published in Stockholm, referring to this stated, 'These declarations reveal only the hint of the mystery behind what happened in Poland, but over two years of occupation the occupants announced [...] how the Poles were executed, how villages were razed to the ground as if hit by an earthquake, how Polish property was annexed, how joint responsibility was introduced and how the mass relocations of Polish citizens of western provinces were ordered.' The authors of the article estimated that from the beginning of the occupation the Germans executed as many as 82 thousand Poles, which they considered to be a gruesome figure. The purpose the German policy was obvious, namely the gradual eradication of both the Poles and the Jews.[34] They also claimed that the battle with German propaganda was connected

---

[31] PISM, A 9, III 4/14, study by M. Karniol 'Szwedzka prasa o Polsce' (Swedish press on Poland), Stockholm, 22 I 1942.
[32] Ibidem.
[33] AAN, HI/I/63, by Polish Envoy to Stockholm G. Potworowski to the Ministry of Foreign Affairs, Stockholm, 16 VI 1942.
[34] PISM, A 9, III 4/14, study of M. Karniol 'Szwedzki organ komunistyczny o Polsce' (Swedish communist periodical on Poland), 22 I 1942 r.

5. REVIVAL OF BILATERAL RELATIONS

with popularization of slogans from the Soviet propaganda at the time, writing, 'Large masses of class-conscious Polish labourers and revolutionary-oriented small peasantry have long had a great appreciation for the neighbouring socialist countries, and these masses trust in the strength of the Red Army and strongly believe in the victory of freedom.'[35]

The Polish Legation had much to do in the area of propaganda such as delivery of documentation and completed texts to the editorial sections of newspapers and organising lectures by Swedish public figures. The generously illustrated exhibition *They burnt our villages down* that included photographs, statistical schemes and information boards about the situation in the occupied countries was very popular. It was organized by the Swedish social democratic youth and exhibited over a three-week period in Stockholm.[36]

On 14 September 1942 *Sydsvenska Dagbladet* broke the news about special controlling and penal orders for Polish farmers. The intention was to force the farmers to supply grain quotas determined by the German authorities. A correspondent for a Berlin newspaper revealed that only 20 percent of the grain was not subject to quota demands. One day later *Arbetaren* reported on the dreadful health conditions affecting Polish society and an epidemic of typhus. At times the news was of murder of the Poles committed under guise of the joint-responsibility rule. Based on a telegram from London, *Aftontidningen* reported that 150 Poles were hung along the railway line near Kraków as part punishment for the derailment of a train.[37] In October 1942 *Göteborgs Handels- och Sjöfarts-Tidning* published the article 'Extermination of the Jews' written by Hugo Valentin, in response to articles on this topic in British newspapers a month before.[38] *Arbetaren* then published an article based on Valentin's report and information from the Polish Legation on 23 October 1942, recounting the extermination of 700 thousand Jews in total.[39] On 19 December 1942, however, *Arbetaren* reported on the occupation of Poland based on materials from the Polish Legation, following a debate in the House of Commons, entitled 'One Million Jews Have Been Killed.' In the

---

[35] Ibidem.
[36] AAN, HI/I/63, letter by Polish Envoy to Stockholm G. Potworowski to the Ministry of Foreign Affairs, Stockholm, 16 VI 1942.
[37] AAN, HI/I/97, press report by Chargé d'affaires T. Pilch to the Ministry of Foreign Affairs, Stockholm, 10 XI 1942.
[38] H. Valentin, 'Utrotningskriget mot Judarna', *Göteborgs Handels- och Sjöfarts-Tidning*, 13 X 1942. The authors of a book on Swedish attitude to Holocaust underlined the meaning of the publication: I. Svanberg & M. Tydén, Sverige och Förintelsen. Debatt och dokument om Europas judar 1933–1945, Stockholm 2005, pp. 242–246.
[39] Ibidem.

commentary it was declared that remaining indifferent to such crime would be impossible, as one would have to bear the burden of the tragedy. Therefore 'it is our duty to speak of it, and staying silent is tantamount to participating in the crime.'[40] Over time the descriptions of German crimes appeared more and more frequently, but it was not until 1944 that Mia Leche Löfgren, one of the organizers of humanitarian aid campaign for occupied Poland, admitted with sorrow: 'it has been silent for too long about this country, which was the first country to experience war, which received the least help of all the countries in need, and whose martyrdom is greater than the misfortunes of all other nations.'[41] Poland became the centre of attention when journalists could write openly about the occupied countries. Poland was presented as one of the victims and at the same time a stand was taken towards the German attempts to include Sweden in the system of the new European deal.[42]

On 15 January 1943, *Svenska Dagbladet* published an excerpt from a speech of Minister Mikołajczyk about the relations within the Lublin district (*Lubelszczyzna*), the omnipresent terror and the Polish peasants' attempt to put up resistance against the enemy.[43] Similar notes were published by *Arbetaren* and *Aftontidningen*.[44] A speech by Clement Atlee, leader of the Labour Party, highlighting the German terror in Poland was also published. On 13 February, a telegram from the Reuters Agency describing the shooting of seventy people in Warsaw was given priority the newspapers. According to Żaba, this information was the first in a long time about Poland and it was even displayed even on advertisement posters in the street.[45] On 2 February, *Ny Tid* published an account of a Swede in Warsaw, who described everyday life, including the high prices as well as German attempts at Germanisation, the most conspicuous examples of which were the German street names.[46] At the outset of February 1943 *Arbetaren* printed photographs from the Warsaw ghetto that were submitted by Maurycy Karniol.[47] On 12 April the *Nerikes*

---

[40] 'En miljon judar dödade', *Arbetaren*, 19 XII 1942.
[41] M. Leche, 'För Polen', *Göteborgs Handels- och Sjöfarts-Tidning*, 26 VI 1944.
[42] 'Ny ordningen i praktiken', *Arbetaren*, 17 II 1943.
[43] 'Polska böndernas självförsvar', *Svenska Dagbladet*, 15 I 1943.
[44] 'Polacker bränna hellre byar än de överlämnas', *Aftontidningen*, 16 I 1943; 'Bönderna brände nedfjorton byar. Motståndet hårdnar i Polen', *Arbetaren*, 18 I 1943.
[45] AAN, Norbert Żaba's collection, copy of report by N. Żaba to the Ministry of Information and Documentation, Stockholm, 6 III 1943.
[46] '500 kronor för en middag i Warszawa', *Ny Tid*, 2 II 1943.
[47] 'Från Polen', *Arbetaren*, 8 II 1943 (the photographs present the ghetto wall and Jewish children cleaning the street; instead of a commentary a quotation from General W. Sikorski's speech is provided about the German murders of Polish Jews); 'Judeförföljerserna i Polen',

Allehanda circulated an article on the extermination of Polish Jews. At the same time, it was pointed out that only a miracle could save the few who still remained alive.[48] On 2 March 1943, *Arbetaren* published what was, according to Żaba, one of the best articles by a Jewish refugee from the General Government about occupied Poland, which had been published in Stockholm up until that point. The author mentioned neither Poland nor Germany to avoid interference by the inspectors of publications. Readers, nevertheless, guessed the inference to occupied Poland. The terror of everyday life under the rule of Germany was presented in the article in a literary form. The title character, described as 'indifferently neutral', had a dream in which his own country was at risk of occupation. 'It seemed like the scales have fallen from his eyes, and from this night on he was no longer indifferent towards injustice, oppression and barbarity.'[49] It is worth noting that the reports about manhunts in the centre of Warsaw, execution of hostages and razing entire villages to the ground were treated like sensational news events by the Swedes. *Nya Dagligt Allehanda* promoted its 8 March 1943 issue containing an article on this subject using garish leaflets.[50]

It is not known when Karniol started to produce and distribute (most probably at irregular intervals) the press bulletin *Från de ockuperade områdena* (From the Occupied Territories) that was directed mainly at editorial teams of dailies and periodicals. In September 1943, the 79th issue of this bulletin reached socialist Adam Ciołkosz.[51] Later, Karniol changed its title to *Polska Nyheter* (Polish News). Every quarter, nearly 30 issues were sent out to all workers' newspapers in Sweden, to socialist members of parliament and senators, to trade unions as well as to international correspondents.

Over time an increasing amount of information about the Polish resistance movement poured in. What is more, the minister of information issued an order regarding the distribution of reports about the armed efforts of the Polish underground. Żaba held a meeting with the famous Swedish opinion journalist Gunnar Thorstenson Pihl to hand him documentation for an

---

Arbetaren, 9 II 1943 (the photographs present Jews wearing armbands and a sign warning of typhus placed at the entrance to the ghetto).
[48] 'Polens judar troligen räddningslöst förlorade', *Nerikes Allehanda*, 12 IV 1943. In the autumn the press informed that only 300 thousand Jews had been left alive in Poland. See: AAN, Norbert Żaba's collection, copy of report by N. Żaba to the Ministry of Information and Documentation, Stockholm, 15 XI 1943.
[49] J. S-a., 'Den likgiltigt neutrale', *Arbetaren*, 2 III 1943.
[50] AAN, Norbert Żaba's collection, copy of report by N. Żaba to the Ministry of Information and Documentation, Stockholm, 22 III 1943.
[51] PISM, col. 133, vol. 295, Bulletin *Från de ockuperade områdena*, iss. 79, received on 27 IX 1943.

article in *Sydsvenska Dagbladet Snällposten*.[52] Żaba described the article that was published as perfect. Its author focused on brutal German repressions, Germanisation, displacements, manhunts, transportation of workers to the Reich, as well as development of the Polish underground press and gradual preparations for the rising.[53]

German propaganda made efforts to convince the Swedes that the occupied nations were not suffering under German rule. On 18 January 1943, *Dagsposten* published an interview with Swedish engineer, Jörgen N. Guldbrandsen, who returned from Lida, Baranowicze and Nowogródek, where he had worked. From his observations during his travels there emerged a picture of economic development and satisfied locals.[54] On the whole, he praised the Germans for food rationing, which allegedly allowed for the holding of considerable stocks of basic provisions.

In 1943 the motif of Polish resistance fighter became the subject of literary interpretation. In the novel *Attentat i Paris* (Attack in Paris) Marika Stiernstedt created a character of a Pole, a painter and officer named Szczyt, who symbolized Polish bravery and the battle against the Germans from September 1939.[55] Another example promoting Poland in Sweden was the novel *Spelet kring en drottning* (translation: Intrigue Around a Queen) by Py Sörmann, which was published in 1943. The novel told the story of the Queen of Sweden, Catherine Jagiellon, who brought Polish culture to Sweden centuries ago.[56]

The Swedish journals also became interested in the development of Polish--Soviet relations, which were in turn followed closely by political–diplomatic circles. In private conversations, Polish diplomats were advised to adopt a compromised attitude.[57] Żaba claimed that as far as this matter was concerned, the Polish propagandist activity in Sweden was conducted with extreme

---

[52] [G.] Th-son [Pihl], 'Polska motståndrörelsen har blivit en hemlig armé, *Sydsvenska Dagbladet Snällposten*, 23 XI 1943.
[53] AAN, Norbert Żaba's collection, copy of report by N. Żaba to the Ministry of Information and Documentation, Stockholm, 25 XI 1943.
[54] 'Puck, Svensk ingenjör i Östland: Halvsvältande befolkning får äntligen äta sig mätt. Beundransvärt återuppbyggnadsarbete i de besatta områdena', *Dagsposten*, 18 I 1943.
[55] See: B. Skarżyński, 'Motywy polskie w piśmiennictwie szwedzkim w czasie wojny', *Nowa Polska*, 1945, iss. 3, pp. 185–188.
[56] B. Skarżyński, 'Motywy polskie w piśmiennictwie szwedzkim w czasie wojny' (continuation), *Nowa Polska* 1946, iss. 1, pp. 62-64: 'The book contains numerous passages where Poland and the Poles are presented as a country of the civilized West in contrast to the primordial life in Scandinavia and where the royal family of Jagiellons is presented as particularly standing out from the Swedish House of Vasa, showing almost parvenu features.'
[57] AAN, HI/I/30, letter by Chargé d'affaires of the Polish Legation in Stockholm T. Pilch to the Ministry of Foreign Affairs, Stockholm, 25 I 1943.

caution. For him, the extremely aggressive Polish opinion journalists posed a greater threat than the disapproving Swedish commentators. He also noted:

> Apart from a few small exceptions the discussion is reported in a way which – as far as I am concerned – is convenient for us. What becomes evident is the deviousness of Moscow, which is only to our advantage. Nevertheless, our society needs to be controlled as far as this matter is concerned, including reactionary military men, everywhere, even in Stockholm, together with the disgruntled as well as with those opinion journalists who are too candid. They are more harmful than the foreign journalists, [...] since I am afraid that people who are suffering from the anti-Soviet complex will campaign against the Russians, and this will only put wind in the sails of most diverse factors.[58]

Żaba claimed that making threats with communism as penance was unnecessary as this fear was deeply rooted already in the minds of the Swedes. Besides, this position harmonized with Goebbels' propaganda, which the Swedes were very critical, especially until they realized Germany would lose. Żaba defined another problem that came to light saying, 'some circles of trade unionists, socialists and radical-liberal intelligentsia believe that Russia has legitimate ethnographic claims towards our eastern territories. At the same time, we are denied our right to East Prussia, because, according to them, this is against the Atlantic Charter.' A portion of the radical circles surrendered to the charm of the Soviets. Nonetheless, the social-democratic leadership 'fears Moscow as if it was the devil.' In connection with this, Żaba was convinced that the Swedish government would insist the press stifle 'everything which could provoke the Soviets (eastern borders of Poland), and, on the other hand, for fear of Bolshevism it strives to save Germany so that a strong democratic Reich is created, which would become a counterweight for the Soviets.' Karniol complained to Żaba that in the face of such an attitude of the colleagues from the Swedish social-democratic party, he had great difficulty in gaining acceptance for the position of the Polish government. Żaba strove to intensify high level contacts between the PPS and the SAP, to promote the Polish point of view more effectively. In his report to London, he

---

[58] AAN, Norbert Żaba's collection, letter by N. Żaba to M. Thugutt (Ministry of Internal Affairs), Stockholm, 26 II 1943.

proposed that an eminent Polish socialist politician should visit Stockholm and deliver a speech to win over the Swedish government circles.[59]

Illustration 5: '*Stygg gosse*' ['Naughty boy'] meaning Poland as represented by the boy in the sailor uniform (*Aftontidningen*, 3 March 1943).

Deputy director of the Political department of the Swedish Ministry of Foreign Affairs Ragnar Kumlin revealed to counsellor Pilch on 25 February, that the discussion in the press on the Polish–Soviet conflict is needless,

---

[59] Ibidem.

5. REVIVAL OF BILATERAL RELATIONS

because Swedish opinion, as far as Polish–Soviet relations were concerned, was usually in favour of Poland.[60] However, an argument came to light in the press discussion that the territories of eastern Poland were mostly inhabited by non-Polish people, who were treated poorly by the Polish government in the pre-war period. The Poles were also blamed for selling the bear's skin before the hunt, when they put forward a claim for taking over East Prussia. Besides which, the Polish opposition press in London was considered chauvinist and imperialist.

The commentaries of Swedish press appeared following the deterioration of relations between Sikorski's government and Moscow. This was in connection with Minister Edward Raczyński radio speech that laid out Polish war aims. The Minister stated that the Polish government fought to restore the free, sovereign Polish state with the pre-war course of eastern borders and the favourable course of western borders. The speech caused a sensation in Sweden and reflected badly on Poland. The first news about the Polish–Soviet conflict, announced on 22 February 1943 in the Swedish press, was submitted by London correspondents and presented the British point of view, which was hostile towards Poland. Much of what was criticised were Polish territorial aspirations, in particular the proposal to establish a new border with Germany. The conservative, pro-Ally newspaper *Nya Dagligt Allehanda* presented a review of opinions from the Polish press and the Moscow newspaper *Pravda*. It considered the ambitions of the Polish government to establish post-war deal in Europe as excessive. Polish dailies published in London were accused of promoting fantasies in discussions about peace and re-arranging the map of Europe from the Baltic Sea to the Black Sea.'[61] The opinion journalist of the social-democratic afternoon newspaper *Aftontidningen* expressed his concern with the relations among the Allies. He supported the British view that 'nothing should hinder the cooperation between Great Britain, the Soviets and the USA, which determines not only the military victory, but also the issue of winning peace.' On the question of future relations in East-Central Europe, he took an ambiguous stand. He questioned the rightness of maintaining the current Polish–Soviet border. Yet, he did not believe that Stalin would be content with territorial acquisitions and refrain from taking over control of Poland: 'Russia has the right to demand security of its borders. Nevertheless, its neighbours also have the right to demand that their borders be respected. It is all right that Russia does not desire conquests,

---

[60] Ibidem.
[61] B. H., 'Tilltagande irritation Sovjet-Polen', *Nya Dagligt Allehanda*, 22 II 1943.

but its only intention is to provide security to those territories that belong to it. This may nonetheless be bought for the price of freedom of the countries that lie close to it. Strategic borders are justified when they may be aligned with national borders, but when they are introduced at will, they defeat their own purpose and undermine security rather than increasing it. Evidence of the best possible security that may be provided for both large and small countries is the satisfaction of its surrounding neighbours.'[62]

In the end however, as Żaba wrote in his letter to Thugutt: 'a view became widespread here that we have made territorial claims not only towards Germany, but even towards Russia, and that these claims are to be the fruit of Polish imperialism and conceited romanticism, as they write.'[63] In March 1943, Envoy Sokolnicki assured the headquarters that the Swedish press had taken a pro-Polish stand in the conflict with the USSR, in spite of the fact that Swedish correspondents in London yielded to the Soviet propaganda and as a consequence relayed that 'the Poles are demanding Ukraine as far as Kiev', accusing the Poles of imperialism and a lack of tolerance for national minorities.[64] Much more dangerous, according to Żaba, were the so-called good Germans (the German expatriate community), whose access to the Swedish press was, in his view, much easier than that of the Soviet agents. This positive attitude towards Germany in the moment of its defeat was predicted much earlier by Gustaw Potworowski. In February 1942, he communicated this to Ministry of Foreign Affairs,

> Our attitude towards Germany is so clear and understandable, and arguments we may use are so strong that political justification of our points presents no doubt whatsoever. What needs to be considered in the future, nonetheless, is that the point about "the good Germans" would nowhere else in the world cause as strong of a reaction as in Sweden, where the mentality of the entire society always is to defend the weak, the defeated and therefore the alleged "disadvantaged" party. This is to a large extent the reason of the negative attitude of the Swedes towards the Treaty of Versailles, and therefore counteracting this type of attitude would be here a difficult task during the future negotiations.[65]

---

[62] 'Gränsstaternas ställning', *Aftontidningen*, 28 II 1943.
[63] AAN, Norbert Żaba's collection, letter by N. Żaba to M. Thugutt (Ministry of Internal Affairs), Stockholm, 13 III 1943.
[64] PISM, A 12, 53/38Z, copy of telegram by Envoy H. Sokolnicki [?] to the Ministry of Foreign Affairs [no information about the date of sending], London, 5 III 1943 r. [the date of issuing a copy in London].
[65] *Notes by Polish envoy to Stockholm G. Potworowski 1939–1942*, entry from 19 II 1942.

5. REVIVAL OF BILATERAL RELATIONS

As time went by the motto of kind treatment of Germans after the war gained on importance.[66]

The majority of provincial newspapers claimed that Poland sparked the argument with the Soviet Union and was responsible for the worsening of relations between the Allies.[67] Characteristic was the statement that both the Poles and the Soviets were mocking at the Atlantic Charter, as the Poles aimed to enlarge their territory at the expense of Germany, and Russia aimed to do the same, but at the expense of Poland. The Soviet claims, based on ethnographic grounds, were not always described as imperialist, and the border determined by the Peace of Riga was considered unfair in this respect.[68] Poland, with its Jagiellonian tradition, was considered to be unrealistic when compared to the strong Soviet Union.[69]

Influenced by the Germans, the dailies opposed the idea of depriving the Reich of East Prussia,[70] and announced with satisfaction that Great Britain 'in spite of the warranties it granted to Poland at a certain time in the past, wanted to leave it to the mercy of the Bolsheviks.'[71] The most pro-Polish article was by Knut Hagberg that was published in *Nya Dagligt Allehanda*. Hagberg argued that if Poland lost independence, Sweden's existence would

---

[66] PISM, A 21, 8/26, letter by L. Plater-Ankarhall to the Ministry of Congress Work, Stockholm, 12 V 1944. The activity of German emigration in Sweden is proven by a note in the memoirs of the then employee of the German Section of the Ministry of Congress Work, Józef Winiewicz, see: J. Winiewicz, *Co pamiętam z długiej drogi życia*, Poznań 1985, p. 308: 'The closer we are to the conclusion of the war, the sharper is the opposition of the rest of the German expatriates against any concessions to Poland. The London *Sozialistische Mitteilungen* among others published the results of a survey conducted among the Germans in Sweden. Most of the answers were unfavourable to us. One of the arguments mentioned was that Germany should not be weakened, and even that the issue of "the corridor" should be settled in favour of Germany. Should the Poland's access to the sea be cut off in these conditions?' More information about the battle between Polish diplomacy and the German propaganda in the years 1939–1945, see: *Historia dyplomacji...*, vol. 5, chpt. IX by T. Dubicki and A. Suchcitz. Polish newspapers made efforts to expose the attempts to establish contact with the Allies by the false German opponents of Hitler. They pointed out that this was Führer's trick. See: '»Dobrzy Niemcy« grasują w Szwecji. Baron von Cramm – tenisista gestapo', *Dziennik Żołnierza*, 19 XI 1943; 'Tajemnicza wizyta księcia Bismarcka w Szwecji', *Dziennik Żołnierza*, 23 XI 1943; 'Sztokholm – barometr wojny', *Dziennik Żołnierza APW*, 10 XII 1943.
[67] AAN, Norbert Żaba's collection, copy of report by N. Żaba to the Ministry of Information and Documentation, Stockholm, 2 IV 1943.
[68] E. B., 'Polens affärer', *Karlshamns Allehanda*, 1 III 1943; 'Moskvasplaner och polackerna', *Sydsvenska Dagbladet Snällposten*, 3 III 1943.
[69] AAN, Norbert Żaba's collection, copy of report by N. Żaba to the Ministry of Information and Documentation, Stockholm, 2 IV 1943.
[70] 'Illusioner', *Aftonbladet*, 27 II 1943.
[71] 'England ger Ryssland halva Polen', *Folkets Dagblad*, 27 II 1943.

be in jeopardy.[72] In turn, on 6 March, *Aftontidningen* published (after Soviet *Pravda*) an opinion that Ukrainians wanted to be part of the Soviet Union following many difficult years of suffering under Polish anti-minority policy and being discriminated against by the authorities.[73]

According to Żaba, the most harmful opinion journalist was the Hungarian Stefan Szende, who had communist sympathies and had resided in Stockholm since the pre-war period. Szende explained to Karniol that the territorial ambitions of the Soviet Union needed to be satisfied to prevent it from taking control of Europe. In response to articles written by Szende in *Aftonbladet*,[74] Karniol, on 5 April, published his polemics in that very same daily.[75] He argued that the government of General Sikorski was widely supported in Poland, remained in contact with it, and that for these reasons it would be hard to deprive it of the mandate. He also attempted to demonstrate that the Eastern Borderlands' affiliation with Poland was a question of international justice and that ethnic minorities would be granted all liberties in post-war Poland.

The current critics of Swedish submissiveness towards Germany, with Torgny Segerstedt and Ture Nerman at their centre, did not give credence to Stalin's plans of expansion. They considered him first and foremost Europe's saviour. Following 22 June 1941, a noticeable feature of their commentaries was tolerance for communism and in 1944 even acceptance of communists becoming the members of the Swedish government. Such an attitude was also adopted by the leading opinion journalist for *Dagens Nyheter* Johannes Wickman, chair of the influential association *Kämpande demokrati* (Fighting Democracy) Karin Schulz and writer Marika Stiernstedt, who was famous for her sympathies towards Poland and Polish roots.[76] The criticism of Stalin's dictatorship seemed psychologically unacceptable. The Soviet Union was perceived as having suffered the greatest human and material losses in the fight with Nazi Germany. People deluded themselves by thinking that following the war democracy would be established in the Soviet Union. Not without significance were the growing communist influences in Sweden, as the German–Soviet front moved westwards, intensified by the worsening economic situation of the civilian population.[77] What hit the Swedes hardest was

---

[72] K. Hagberg, 'Sverige och Polen', *Nya Dagligt Allehanda*, 28 II 1943.
[73] 'Polackerna i minoritet i omstridda Östpolen', *Aftontidningen*, 6 III 1943.
[74] S. Szende, 'Allierade statsmän om Europas framtid', *Aftontidningen*, 11 XII 1942; idem, 'Polackerna i minoritet i omstridda Östpolen', *Aftontidningen*, 6 III 1943.
[75] 'Polen och dess framtida gränser', *Aftontidningen*, 5 IV 1943.
[76] L. Drangel, *Den kämpande...*, pp. 117, 161.
[77] Ibidem, pp. 170–171.

the lack of fuel and food. From 1942 onwards virtually all goods were rationed and many were unavailable. Maintenance costs increased by 40 percent whilst wages dropped by 10–12 percent. In order to calm radical feelings, the social democratic party presented, prior to the upcoming parliament elections in 1944, a new social and economic programme (the so-called 27 points), which would ensure the improvement of the civilian population's living conditions after the war by means of full employment, the fair division of gross national income and the democratization of economic life.[78] The communists were successful in the elections and also gained stronger influence within the trade unions, especially within the union of metalworkers. In the spring of 1945, though, the popularity of the communists started to fall. On 5 February 1945, they announced a strike by the metal-working industry and began demanding higher wages. The Swedish Trade Union Confederation (LO), dominated by social democrats, did not support the strike. LO was satisfied with the higher wages proposed by the government. The protest did not bring the communists the intended propagandist result, since the agreement they concluded with the government on 6 July 1945 was the same as the agreement concluded with LO six months earlier. Difficulties in the industry, caused by prolonging the opposition, further undermined their authority.[79]

Żaba noticed that in terms of attitude it was possible to distinguish four groups of commentaries devoted to Polish matters published in the Swedish press at the outset of 1943: the reports from London, which were critical of Poland, then (between 28 February and 1 March) the articles in provincial newspapers which were mostly in support of Poland's position, later the telegrams from Great Britain and the USA without any commentaries, and finally, between 6 and 10 March, the favourable statements of dailies from Stockolm. Nevertheless, Żaba summed up:

> The ones who have spoken were the opinion journalists who were reluctant to accept our position on eastern affairs for both fundamental and ideological reasons, such as an aversion to our pre-war political system, Polish nationalism, the attitude of the Poles towards minorities, social inequality, contesting the right of Poland to retain the land inhabited by the non-Polish population or yielding to the suggestion of the Soviet power etc. Eventually, not without a certain influence, was the, on this occasion, accidentally anti-Polish attitude of

---

[78] For more information see: S. Hadenius, B. Molin, H. Wieslader, *Sverige efter 1900. En modernpolitisk historia*, Stockholm 1988, pp. 170–172; H. Dahlberg, *I Sverige...*, pp. 120–121.
[79] H. Dahlberg, *I Sverige...*, pp. 143–144.

as many as three sources of propaganda: Soviet agents, Nazi agents and German expatriates, that is of the elements favouring "the good Germans".[80]

It was only in mid-March that the Swedish press began to publish commentaries that were favourable towards Poland, which was associated by Żaba with the interventions of the Polish legation both in the Press department of the Swedish Ministry of Foreign Affairs and directly in the editorial sections of the principal dailies. The Polish diplomatic mission was forced to deal with a relatively delicate issue. Żaba explained: 'Our inspirational action is hampered to the extent that we may not oppose the Soviets as actively as we would like to, because this would only consolidate the erroneous opinion of the pro-Ally circles of Stockholm that Poland is responsible for inflaming the relations, all the more so that the Soviet legation [...] behaved quite properly in this matter.'[81]

Some understanding towards the Polish government, however, was shown by the Swedish government circles, conservatives and trade union leadership. Whereas the pro-Ally liberal circles supported the watchwords of Soviet propaganda, which was noticeable in *Dagens Nyheter*, *Trots Allt!* and *Göteborgs Handels- och Sjöfarts-Tidning*. Karniol, during his talks with social democrats, learned that they were against Polish postulates regarding the course of the borders, not only in the east but also the west. The idea to incorporate East Prussia in to Poland was openly described by them as a manifestation of imperialism. They could not understand the reasons for Polish persistence and explained that losing part of one's territory was not a tragedy. They highlighted that Sweden had also been great in the past, but that those days were over, and this 'did not harm its internal happiness.' They accepted the desire of Poland to retain Lviv within its territory, as this area had never been part of Russia, though they were less inclined to accept the arguments of Poland to do so in the Vilnius Region.[82] The pre-war borders of Germany were defended by many circles. The opinion journalists of *Dagens Nyheter*, headed by Wickman, were convinced that the errors of the Treaty of Versailles should not be repeated by building foundations for the new German revanchism.[83] One of the journalists

---

[80] AAN, Norbert Żaba's collection, copy of N. Żaba's report to the Ministry of Information and Documentation, Stockholm, 20 III 1943.
[81] Ibidem.
[82] Ibidem.
[83] Norbert Żaba sent his protests to the editorial section of the *Dagens Nyheter* several times in connection with Wickman's articles devoted to Poland. According to the Polish attaché, the Swedish opinion journalist was lacking comprehension of the politics of the Polish government

5. REVIVAL OF BILATERAL RELATIONS

for *Göteborgs Handels- och Sjöfarts-Tidning* stated bluntly, 'the Polish matter has been hindering the peaceful development of Europe for 400 hundred years now.' He considered Poland's claims towards the course of the borders both in the east and west to be preposterous arguing that, 'It is not due to its territorial size but due to social justice and uniformity that Poland may fulfil its historical mission to the benefit of both the Polish nation and the world.'[84] In turn, a commentator of *Gefle Dagblad* presented the border issue in terms of the so-called *realpolitik*. He wrote candidly, 'Futile are the Polish hopes that the victorious Soviet Russia would be inclined to renounce things it has won with the help of Germany.'[85]

The new Polish minister of information and documentation, Professor Stanisław Kot, presented the manual of 'counteracting the Soviet propaganda directed against Poland' during the government session of 31 March 1943.[86] The document called for the emphasizing of the fact that the elections conducted by the Soviet authorities in the occupied territories in 1939 were unlawful, highlighting that the relative majority of the population of the nationally mixed eastern territories was Polish, proving that the Soviet Union was fulfilling a policy of national identity deprivation. Informing the public about plans for internal reforms, especially agricultural, in Poland following the war was considered appropriate. These arguments appeared earlier in numerous propagandist publications produced on the initiative of the Polish Legation in Stockholm.[87]

The Polish Legation carried out a propagandist campaign the intention of which was to convince Swedish readers of the arguments broadcasted by the Polish government in exile. The young Swedish opinion journalist and Polonophile John Walterson, who cooperated with the legation, published 'The Future of Poland' in *Reformatorn*, a magazine by prohibitionist organisations. He argued, 'The discussion about Poland's future is an important matter to all of us' because 'it considers principally the right and chance of small

---

in exile. Part of the newspaper's managers believed that the only way to rescue Finland would be concessions to Stalin in other spheres. See J. Torbacke, *Dagens...*, pp. 339, 344.

[84] L. S., 'Vis pacem - eller den polska frågan', *Göteborgs Handels- och Sjöfarts-Tidning*, 6 V 1943.

[85] I. M. S., 'Konflikten Polen-Sovjet', *Gefle Dagblad*, 8 III 1943.

[86] For the full text of the manual, see: *Protokoły posiedzeń Rady Ministrów Rzeczypospolitej Polskiej*, vol. 5: *wrzesień 1942 – lipiec 1943*, scholarly editing by M. Zgórniak, compiled by W. Rojek in cooperation with A. Suchcitz, Kraków 2001, pp. 328–343.

[87] It is worth to emphasize that the actions undertaken by the Polish diplomatic mission were noticed and appreciated by the Press Attaché of Great Britain, Peter Tennant. He was one of the few diplomats in Stockholm who actually took note of the Polish activity in Sweden. In his memoirs he mentioned N. Żaba: 'this courageous Pole, who was full of wit, battled with words with utter chivalry, characteristic for his nation.' See P. Tennant, *Vid sidan...*, p. 75.

nations' existence as independent nations.'[88] Walterson made a positive statement about the Polish government's plans to establish a federation, and appealed to the Western Allies for economic support that would be necessary to rebuild Poland and redevelop it economically. On 20 February, he published an article about Poland in the periodical *Svensk underbefälstidning*, which was intended for non-commissioned officers in the Swedish army.[89] The text indicated that the Poles were striving to achieve peace, but were facing hostile Soviet policy. On 12 March, Walterson published another article about Polish war objectives in the *Nu* periodical with intellectual ambitions. He aimed to convince the reader both of the idea of a federation and of the Polish arguments regarding returning the eastern border to where it was at the beginning of the war.[90]

To counter this, Karniol, Żaba and Pomian began to visit and conduct frank conversations with chief editors of Swedish newspapers. During Żaba's meeting with the editor of the conservative *Svenska Dagbladet* newspaper, Otto Järte, who favoured Poland, it emerged that Järte was convinced that the Poles were to blame for the current conflict with the Soviet Union. He also criticised the pre-war policy of Poland in relation to its national minorities.[91] His position was in fact decisive for the political orientation of the daily, as it was he who prepared the majority of its editorials.[92]

The news that received broad coverage in those days in the entire Swedish press was the shooting of two socialist activists in the Soviet Union who were members of the Bund, Henryk Ehrlich and Victor Alter. This event was commented on in the context of Polish–Soviet relations; it also gained a strong response from the social democratic periodicals. According to Żaba, 'this issue has to a large extent contributed to putting an end to some illusions that continued to exist within various circles as far as the attitude of Moscow towards socialism is concerned.'[93] The author of the Poles-inspired article

---

[88] J. Walterson, 'Polens framtid', *Reformatom*, 14 II 1943.
[89] J. Walterson, 'Polen och Ryssland', *Svensk underbefälstidning*, 20 II 1943.
[90] J. W[alterson], 'De polska krigsmålen. Hur polackerna tänker sig sin framtid', *Nu*, 12 III 1943. The publication of Walterson ('an outstanding opinion journalist, a great friend of Poland') drew the attention of the Polish press in London already in January 1941: 'W Szwecji o wielkości Polski', *Dziennik Polski*, 22 I 1941; and soon after: 'W Szwecji o jedności i przyszłości Polski', *Dziennik Polski*, 10 XII 1941.
[91] AAN, Norbert Żaba's collection, N. Żaba's letter to the Ministry of Information and Documentation, Stockholm, 9 XI 1943.
[92] T. Höjer, *Svenska...*, p. 9.
[93] AAN, Norbert Żaba's collection, copy of N. Żaba's letter to the Ministry of Information and Documentation, Stockholm, 3 IV 1943. See 'W Swecji [sic!] o rozstrzelaniu Ehrlicha i Altera', *Robotnik Polski w Wielkiej Brytanii*, 1 V 1943.

published in *Arbetaren* remembered the deportations of civilians from the Eastern Borderlands deep into the Soviet Union and wondered what the subversive activity of the two activists was that had led to their execution,

> Already the very fact that one does not share the views with those who hold the power is considered a sign of subversiveness. Sharing one's thoughts with other people is considered high treason, which may be punished in no other way than by execution. The Polish Jews most probably had a different understanding of socialism than the Bolsheviks, and in Russia this is already enough to end up strung from the gallows.

It was reiterated that it was Stalin who had made it easier for Hitler to start the war by concluding the pact of non-aggression in August 1939. 'This agreement somehow opened the door to war. It saved Hitler from battling on two fronts and made it possible for the Germans to eliminate Poland by means of a lightning attack in a joint effort with Russia and to rush at the Western Allies soon thereafter with all the military power.'[94] Equally strong words appeared in *Arbetet*, 'An atrocious illustration of ruthlessness which accompanies law enforcement in Russia, to treat the Poles in the Russian fashion, is the news that both of the Jewish worker leaders, Ehrlich and Alter, were executed. [...] While the occupied country is the place of martyrdom for the Polish nation, and especially for the Jewish nation, the Russians, by means of several rifle bullets, gave their answer to the trust these two men offered Russia when they were seeking refuge there from their unrelenting enemy.'[95]

The fate of the two Polish socialists most probably ruined the image of the Soviet Union as a country in the process of democratization, but in general it had no impact on the evaluation of the Polish–Soviet relations. The majority of Swedish opinion journalists proposed that the government in London follow the policy of concessions and repeat the declarations of Stalin in which he desired a strong and sovereign Poland. Similar was the behaviour of the members of the diplomatic circles. Only Grafström did not hesitate to reassure Żaba that the Swedish government supported Poland and that the press campaign in opposition to Poland, against the background of its dispute with the Soviet Union, harmed all small countries as well as the right of nations to self-determination. Nevertheless, it was hard to expect that his personal intervention in the editorial sections of Swedish periodicals would have the potential to change the commentaries. In general, Swedish opinion journalists

---

[94] 'Kriget i all sin härlighet', *Arbetaren*, 6 III 1943.
[95] A. V[ou]gt, 'Ehrlich och Alter', *Arbetet*, 6 III 1943.

considered East-Central Europe to be an area of complex and insoluble international disputes and left the decision about its future to the powers. In contrast, predictions for the unfolding of events in this area were at times merciless for the Poles. One of the commentaries published in *Nya Dagligt Allehanda* remarked,

> The speculation that the United States of America would risk a row with its two allies because of Poland – even though Polish demands were never more justified – seem to be, at least from the Swedish point of view, short-sighted, especially if the Poles' hopes are founded on the meeting of Sikorski with the bishop of New York [Francis] Spellman and the protests of American workers against the execution of two Polish worker leaders by the Russians.[96]

Pro-German *Stockholms-Tidningen* claimed that the reason for Stalin's actions was Moscow's desire for expansion in the west and the re-establishment of borders from the tsarist period.[97] In the face of these efforts, Poland ended up in a very unfavourable position, as in the event of the German victory it could not count on anything more than becoming a German vassal. In the event of Soviet victory, the Polish government would be forced to accept the loss of half of its territory and the transformation of Poland into a Soviet republic. Both the opinion journalists for *Stockholms-Tidningen* and *Aftonbladet* staunchly defended the position that the mistake of humiliating Germany, as the Allies had following the First World War, should not be repeated. And, Sweden should support only such peace plans that ensured the existence of a militarily strong and anti-communist Germany.[98] The Polish government was criticised for its pre-war cooperation with Germany on the partition of Czechoslovakia. Anti-Polish stereotypes were weaponised, the undemocratic governance and internal disputes were criticised, and eventually the issue of unwise behaviour in relation to the so-called Katyń issue was brought up: 'Polish blood is, as it would seem, slightly too hot. This hot blood often makes Poles act before they think, which leads to unpleasant complications.'[99]

---

[96] 'Polen och Sovjet', *Nya Dagligt Allehanda*, 1 IV 1943.
[97] 'Randstaternas dystra framtidsutsikter', *Stockholms-Tidningen*, 1 V 1943.
[98] T. Nybom, *Motstånd...*, pp. 344–346.
[99] Similar comment was published in the article 'Självmords politik', *Göteborgs Posten*, 28 IV 1943 and in the editorial 'Konflikten om Polen', *Sydsvenska Dagbladet Snällposten*, 30 IV 1943 ('The uncontrolled Polish nationalism was always more characteristic for its temperament rather than for its political prudence').

5. REVIVAL OF BILATERAL RELATIONS

From *Göteborgs Tidningen* readers learned that following the First World War, the Polish borders had been drawn to Poland's benefit owing to the support of France, and that Poland had no such ally at present.[100]

There were numerous unfavourable commentaries about Poland but there also appeared alternative views. An opinion journalist for *Kalmar Läns Tidning*, quoting *Ny Tid*, criticized harshly the opportunism of the Swedish press:

> Unfortunately, some Swedes who once openly condemned the German superpower policy are today more submissive towards the superpower policy of a different tinge. They are ready to consider any kind of "new deal" and they trade boldly in independence and territory of other countries. They better stop being so submissive when Swedish independence is at stakwe.[101]

According to an opinion journalist from Kalmar, the Swedes should have reacted to all signs of violence from all sides, as the future of all small countries whose fate was dependent on the will of the powers was at stake.

The most matter-of-fact articles were published by the intellectual periodical *Svensk Tidskrift*. Its cooperating journalist Stanisław Adamek criticised the politics of the British government, which complimented Moscow and failed to examine objectively the territorial and minority-related problems of Central Europe. In May 1943, Adamek convinced Swedish readers that only the communist government would accept the Polish–Soviet border along the Curzon Line (in a shape established by Ribbentrop–Molotov pact in 1939).[102] It is worth remembering that the Curzon line was the demarcation line proposed during the Polish–Soviet war in 1920 by the British Foreign Secretary Georg Curzon to serve as a basis for the future border agreement. Consequently, Adamek also defended the Polish government in London against Soviet accusations of reactionism and representing exclusively the interests of landowners.[103]

Generally, it was possible to discern a characteristic line of thinking in the press articles discussing Polish–Soviet relations. Firstly, that the martyrdom of the Polish nation aroused the pity and compassion of neutral observers was beyond doubt. And, secondly, that the Polish government was criticised

---

[100] 'Polska tvister', *Göteborgs Tidningen*, 1 V 1943.
[101] 'Småstaternas rätt', *Kalmar Läns Tidning*, 28 IV 1943.
[102] Curzon line is a term from the time of Polish–Soviet war of 1920. The British foreign minister earl Curzon proposed Bug river as a border between Poland and Soviet Russia, but the war was continued. The final shape of the border much east of "Curzon line" was confirmed by Polish-Soviet peace treaty in Riga in 1921.
[103] Dagens frågor: 'Det polska gränsproblemet', *Svensk Tidskrift*, 24 V 1943; Dagens frågor: S. Warta [S. Adamek], 'Ryssland-Polen', *Svensk Tidskrift*, 18 XII 1943.

for not being composed of wisest politicians. This was the tone of the article in *Mellersta Skåne*:

> Even if we feel compassion for the Polish nation, due to the fact that it never encountered peace and always had to bear the pressure of its neighbours, who desired conquests and were tearing the unfortunate country apart bit by bit to eventually put an end to its independence, we nonetheless cannot free ourselves from thinking that the Poles themselves are to a large extent to blame for their own misery.[104]

Swedish discussion on Katyń

News regarding Polish–Soviet relations were submitted directly to the Ministry of Foreign Affairs from its diplomatic mission in Moscow, which was directed by Envoy Vilhelm Assarson. He noted in his memoirs meetings with Polish ambassador Kot who was in the beginning of 1942 already fearful for the future of Polish–Soviet relations and 'felt deeply disgusted by all difficulties he experienced from the Russian side'.[106] Tadeusz Romer, Kot's successor in the post of the ambassador, tried to assure the Soviet authorities of the will to clear up all misunderstandings in mutual relations. However, as Assarsson noticed, the Soviet side was not open to such discussions.[107]

In March 1943 Assarsson's subordinate, Sverker Åström, wrote in a report from Kuybyshev that a certain consistency in Stalin's policy towards Poland could be detected. The Swedish diplomat repeated that after the Soviet Union had annexed half of Poland in September 1939, its Bolshevisation took place immediately. He also noted: 'At the time, the Polish political, economic and intellectual elite was exiled to the east and interned in labour camps and prisons. A vast number of these people died while imprisoned in Russia or was reported missing'[108] Although, as he highlighted, following the conclusion of Sikorski–Mayski Agreement, 30 July 1941, bilateral relations were normalized. As early as June 1942, the Soviet authorities accused representatives of the Polish authorities in the USSR of espionage and began to dismiss members of the Polish administration and soldiers. According to Åström, it seemed as if the Soviet government was planning to set up Polish divisions

---

[104] I. S., 'Polsk politik', *Mellersta Skåne*, 29 IV 1943.
[106] V. Assarsson, I skuggan av Stalin, Stockholm 1963, pp. 107.
[107] Ibidem, p. 133.
[108] RA, UD 1920 års dossiersystem, HP 1, vol. 485, report by S. Åström to Minister of Foreign Affairs Ch. Günther, Kuybyshev, 10 III 1943.

5. REVIVAL OF BILATERAL RELATIONS

under Russian command. The Swedish diplomat saw the genesis of the conflict in the dispute about the border, which in 1943 seemed exclusively theoretical, but to which 'a far-reaching political symptomatic significance was attributed', and the fact that the Western Allies postponed the opening of a second front in Europe depreciated Poland's position considerably, and Stalin increasingly often implied that he would like to get his way. Which is why, according to the Swede, the outset of 1943 brought a political attack in the shape of the decision of the Soviet authorities to grant USSR citizenship to all Poles residing in the territories which had been annexed after 17 September 1939. Åström explained that the talks of Polish ambassador Tadeusz Romer with Stalin brought no positive results and that they were conducted at a time when, in the Soviet press, there appeared commentaries accusing the Polish government in exile of being unrepresentative of Polish society. At the same time the Polish communists in Moscow started to publish the *Wolna Polska* (Free Poland) periodical. In this situation Åström described Polish–Soviet relations as tense, and chances of reaching compromise as slim.[109] According to the Swedish diplomat, there were clear signs of a nearing turning point in the Polish–Soviet relations. The German revelation of mass graves discovered near Smolensk near Katyń proved to be this turning point.

Sweden was not directly involved in the Katyń issue. The diplomats treated it with considerable suspicion.[110] When the Germans began to set up an international commission of experts to examine the Katyń graves, they proposed a Swedish doctor of medicine, Erik Karlmark, join it. However, following a consultation with Prime Minister Hansson, Karlmark communicated to the Germans that he was unable to make such decision without being authorized by the Swedish government. This issue was discussed on 27 April by Söderblom and Dankwort from the German Legation. The Swede ex-

---

[109] Ibidem.
[110] In 2003, upon the request of the Polish Congress in Sweden, the copies of documents connected with the Katyń issue – so far held in Swedish archives *Riksarkivet* and *Krigsarkivet* – were moved by the Swedish government to the Archives of Polish Emigration (*Polska Emigratinsarkivet i Sverige*). This collection was then passed on to the Institute of National Remembrance in Warsaw in the presence of Ambassador of Sweden Mats Staffansson. Contrary to press reports these were not specially declassified documents but diplomatic reports or private writings which had been available to researchers for many years.

plained that the application was sent to Geneva and that Sweden's engagement on this matter would be limited to the activities of the International Red Cross.[111] Thus, he considered this matter to be closed.

On the following day Swedish Envoy to London Björn Prytz forwarded a message he obtained from a credible source to UD. The message disclosed that the British and the Americans who mediated in the Polish–Soviet dispute were trying to persuade Stalin to satisfy himself with the Polish government's withdrawal of the motion for the examination of the Katyń issue by the International Red Cross. They encouraged Moscow to retract its request to reshuffle the Polish cabinet, as this would alarm the Soviet Union's neighbours and support German war propaganda, which called for a fight with the Red Army to the last soldier.[112]

At the outset of May, Envoy Assarsson sent his report to the Ministry of Foreign Affairs, which was a continuation of previous correspondence by Åström, discussing the circumstances of the break-up of the Polish–Soviet relations by the Soviets on 25 April 1943.[113] According to Assarsson, the progress of these relations needed to arouse interest for two reasons. Firstly, it related to the attitude of the Soviet authorities towards the Polish government and towards the Poles residing in the territory of the USSR. Secondly, a question was posed whether this break-up could be considered symptomatic for Soviet authorities and their aspirations towards the neighbouring smaller countries in the post-war period. According to the Swede, the Poles seemed shocked at the turn of events and expected relations would be established quickly. Assarsson was pessimistic:

> Although it is indeed noticeable that at this point the Russians are not yet closing the door on a possible reconciliation, it nevertheless seems obvious that in order to make it possible for Stalin to re-establish relations with the Polish government in London and acknowledge its authority over the Poles residing in Russia, it [this government] needs to be subjected to thorough reconstruction, and what also needs to undergo drastic changes is Polish policy, especially as far as the issue of the border is concerned.

From a wider perspective, the Swedish diplomat pointed out that the decision to break off relations with the Poles had been made despite doubts which

---

[111] RA, UD 1920 års dossiersystem, HP 1, vol. 485, letter by head of the Political department of UD S. Söderblom to Swedish Envoy to Berlin A. Richert, Stockholm, 28 IV 1943.
[112] Ibidem, telegram from Swedish Envoy to London B. Prytz to UD, London, 28 IV 1943.
[113] Ibidem, report by Swedish Envoy to Moscow V. Assarsson to Minister of Foreign Affairs Ch. Günther, Kuybyshew, 2 V 1943.

appeared because of the Allies. This was most probably a further confirmation of the intentions, often declared by the Soviets, using all possible measures to secure a solid border to the west following the war, meaning a return the boundary of 1940 as a minimum. According to Assarsson, Stalin's behaviour was to be interpreted as a clear signal that after the war the Soviet Union would not tolerate hostile governments in its neighbouring countries. The Swede predicted that:

> [Stalin's] intention is to become surrounded by formally independent countries, which would cooperate with the Soviet Union and never oppose such policy. Whether this purpose may require complete incorporation and, wouldn't it in fact turn out to be a temporary stage leading to this incorporation, it is currently too early to judge.[114]

The Swedish diplomacy viewed and examined the Katyń issue and its diplomatic repercussions in a broader European context, and not only in the context of Polish–Soviet relations. The Swedes were most interested in the consequences of the discord between the Polish government and Russia. Assarsson's commentary was certainly read in Stockholm not only as a prophecy for Poland, the Baltic States and the Balkans, but also for Finland, which continued to participate in the war on the side of Germany. From Assarsson's correspondence, it follows that the Swedes shared the opinion of the Allies about the Polish government policy, which according to them was 'unwise and unrealistic both towards the border issue as well as towards the mass murder issue [Katyń]', as it was in line with the Goebbels' propaganda. Assarsson conveyed from the diplomatic circles of Moscow the disbelief that Stalin would form a puppet government in Poland. At the same time nobody imagined that the Soviet dictator would allow Sikorski to return to Warsaw as head of the government either.[115] Turbulence around Katyń was meticulously analysed in Stockholm, which was reflected in the newspapers.[116]

First announcements, followed by articles, broke on 16 and 17 April, alluding to the killing of 10 thousand Polish officers. The news came not only from the German information services; the Swedish dailies were also awaiting the reports from their correspondents in London. From the note by Daniel

---
[114] Ibidem.
[115] RA, UD 1920 års dossiersystem, HP 1, vol. 485, telegram of Swedish Envoy to Moscow V. Assarsson to the Ministry of Foreign Affairs, Moscow, 3 V 1943.
[116] See the review of press announcements on the subject of the Katyń Massacre: A. N. Uggla, 'Den svenska bilden av Katyńmorden. Från uppdagande till historisk tillrättaläggelse', *Multi-ethnica* 2003, iss. 29, pp. 18–23; idem, 'Szwedzkie spojrzenie na zbrodnię w Katyniu', *Relacje* 2004, iss. 5, p. 22.

Viklund for *Dagens Nyheter*, based on an announcement by the Polish government, it followed that despite the Poles had distancing themselves from the German propaganda, they actually confirmed the accusations addressed to the Soviet authorities by revealing information about Polish captives reported missing in 1940.[117]

Almost all the dailies published the news about the simultaneous submission to Geneva of a German and Polish request to examine the issue of the mass graves in Katyń,[118] but only pro-Nazi and communist commentators considered this news to be a propagandist success.[119] *Svenska Dagbladet* published reports by the Finnish author Örnulf Tigerstedt.[120] He stated emphatically: 'one thing cannot be denied: that the Bolsheviks executed prisoners of war.' He added, 'in this case we may not speak of a crime of passion, as it was neither committed because of a momentary surge of vengeance nor by an undisciplined pack.' Christer Jäderlund wrote ironically in *Stockholms-Tidningen*, 'the Polish appeal to the International Red Cross is welcomed with contentment by Berlin.'[121] Even more blunt was the communist *Ny Dag*, where the slogans of the Soviet propaganda were repeated in the article 'Organized cooperation between Sikorski and Hitler exposed', which affirmed 'The statement of the London government proves that pro-Hitlerian elements have a decisive impact on the Polish government and they are employing new measures in order to worsen the relations between the Soviet Union and Poland.'[122]

An anti-German position was taken by the magazine *Nu*, where Westin Silverstolpe published a series of articles about Katyń, starting from issue 26 on 30 April. He argued that what raised doubts was the 10 thousand victims

---

[117] D. Viklund, 'Polens regering vill ha utredning om *massgraven*', *Dagens Nyheter*, 17 IV 1943; as well as: Griggs, '*Röda korset bör undersöka vid Smolensk*. Tyska uppgifter om massgravar oroapolackerna', *Svenska Dagbladet*, 17 IV 1943; 'Polen beggar Röda korsundersökning av påstådda ryssmord på krigsfångar', *Stockholms-Tidningen*, 17 IV 1943.

[118] 'Polsk och tysk hänvändelse till Röda korset', *Svenska Dagbladet*, 18 IV 1943; 'Röda korset dryftar Katyń', *Stockholms-Tidningen*, 20 IV 1943; 'Internationella Röda korset behandlar den polska anmälan', *Social-Demokraten*, 20 IV 1943.

[119] Head of the department of propaganda of the Third Reich Joseph Goebbels was disappointed with the reactions of the Swedish press. In his private writings he noted down on 18 April 1943 that 'The Swedish dailies were defending themselves from publishing the reports of their Berlin correspondents', which was, according to him, a proof for the fact that it was hard to call Sweden a neutral country. See J. Goebbels, Tagebücher 1924–1945, ed. R. G. von Reuth, vol. 5: 1943–1945, München-Zürich 2000, p. 1924.

[120] Ö. 'Tigerstedt, I dödsskogen vid Kotyn [sic!]', *Svenska Dagbladet*, 28 IV 1943.

[121] Ch. 'Jäderlund, Berlin välkomnar Polens appel till Int[ernationella] Röda Korset', *Stockholms-Tidningen*, 18 IV 1943.

[122] 'Organiserat samarbete mellan Sikorski och Hitler avslöjas', *Ny Dag*, 20 IV 1943.

(in contrast to the Polish government announcing the search for 8 300 officers) and the good condition of the uniforms found in the graves. Apart from this, the opinion journalist noted that the Germans in their propagandist campaign emphasized anti-Semitic threads, spreading news that four executioners of the Poles had been of Jewish origin, 'It may be unquestionably concluded that these four people are an invention. It is known that the German propaganda, whenever it sees any possibility to sanction its anti-Jewish stunts, completely loses its scruples.[123]

In another article, Silverstolpe derided the individuals who examined the bodies of those murdered, questioning their qualifications and the methods used for establishing the date of the massacre. He even suggested that Germany started to withdraw its accusations as it was impossible to prove that the crime was not its own. He remarked ironically:

> One indeed does not know what one should think about the Katyń issue. Following a careful analysis, all that has been so far presented as the so-called irrefutable evidence turned out to be totally insufficient. However, no new evidence has been submitted so far in this case. The German press has been silent about Katyń from the second week of May.[124]

Several weeks later, another article was published in response to the protest by Finnish historian Eirik Hornborg against two earlier texts supporting the Soviet position. Silverstolpe consistently defended his views. He gave examples of other fraud orchestrated by German propaganda and manipulation scenarios used by the Nazis.[125]

A different tone was adopted by the Nazi *Dagsposten*, referring to the testimony of the Finns who had visited Katyń. An interview was conducted with Professor Herman Gummerus, a representative of Finnish public opinion, which was deeply moved by the news from Katyń, highlighted that he could not understand the Swedish mentality of concealing information about what had happened. He could not understand those Swedes who tried to place blinkers over the eyes of the public. This, however, made it possible to present the Bolsheviks in a new light. Meanwhile, according to Gummerus, a view that Bolshevism had evolved somewhat, was an example of wishful thinking,

---

[123] G. W[estin] S[ilverstolpe], 'Massgravarna vid Katyń. Lag där 12000 polska officerare?', *Nu*, 30 IV 1943.
[124] G. W[estin] S[ilverstolpe], 'Mera om massgravarna vid Katyń. Vad de medicinska experterna sade', *Nu*, 2 VII 1943.
[125] G. Westin Silverstolpe, 'Gravarna vid Katyń än en gång. Inre och yttre sanningskriterier', *Nu*, 30 VII 1943.

contrary to all experiences in Europe: 'The mass murder in Smolensk is not any kind of propaganda, this is a true and tragic reality.'[126]

However, *Aftonbladet* explained, 'From the Soviet-Russian point of view, and marked with, which is alien to us, an Asian world view, the execution of the Polish officers has most probably turned out to be a necessary security measure. [...] It would be easy to find the reasons for this act, but this does not lessen its cruelty.'[127]

Pro-Ally *Göteborgs Handels- och Sjöfarts-Tidning* initially demanded cautiously in the title of an article published on 19 April that Russia needed to explain what had happened to the prisoners of war. Later in the text, another part of the Polish announcement from London was mentioned for balance: 'accusations towards others are not a defence of Germany.'[128] Nevertheless, only one day later the Polish government was openly attacked in the editorial. It was accused of stupidity and boorishness towards the Soviet Union, fighting for sovereignty of not only Poland but also other countries conquered by Hitler:

> It is understandable that the Germans are testing various methods. Their peace surveys have brought no positive results. A very clumsy attempt to break up the allied camp curiously has generated a response from the Poles. They have risen to the bait in the form of the mass grave of 10 thousand people resembling Polish officers. The Poles are generally charming individualists. They are hot blooded and bold. [...] A squabble with the Russians was the most ill-fated thing they could engage in. The sovereignty of Poland is totally dependent on the victory of the Russian army. Europe, in its entirety, becomes indebted to Russia for being rescued from the bondage which was placed upon it by Hitlerism. Poland would have no prospect of regaining independence if the Russians did not crush the backbone of the German military power. Russia did not do this out of non-reciprocated love for Europe. The Russians themselves do not say this, they are extreme realists, and neither do the others. Nonetheless, the facts remain unchanged. Now the conflict between the Poles and the Russians is devoid of the dimension that the German propaganda intends it to have. In reality it does not influence the course of events. [...] The Swedish government continues to make it easier for the Germans to fight against the nations who are

---

[126] 'De polska massgravarna i Smolensk ha i Finlandgjort oerhört intryck', *Dagsposten*, 19 IV 1943.
[127] 'Gravarna vid Smolensk', *Aftonbladet*, 19 IV 1943.
[128] 'Ryssland måste förklara var dess krigsfångar blivit av', *Göteborgs Handels- och Sjöfarts-Tidning*, 19 IV 1943.

battling for democracy, freedom of nations and individuals, as well as for the rules of law.'[129]

Attaché Brzeskwiński ascertained that the meaning of these publications was unflattering for Poland:

> What we need to state is that the Swedish press' position towards us in the conflict with the USSR was in most part negative. The tactics of the Polish Government was criticised, and the fact of its turning to Geneva was evaluated as an inappropriate action. The rumours on the possibility of the Polish government's resignation were endorsed and the Polish press in England was accused of contributing to the unleashing of the conflict and therefore being responsible for it. The Swedish correspondents from Berlin emphasized that the official German authorities were satisfied with the conflict.[130]

The Swedes did not evaluate the entire issue against the backdrop of the conflict, but in terms of the functioning of an anti-Fascist coalition focused on defeating Hitler. *Göteborgs Handels- och Sjöfarts-Tidning*, famous for its pro-Ally orientation and acting as a defender of democracy in Europe, criticised the Poles. This diminished the meaning of the earlier published article by de Geer, who demanded that the problem be solved quickly and that the second front be established in Europe. According to him, this would help to both temper the arrogant tone of the Soviets and successfully regulate the issue of the borders.

According to Norbert Żaba, towards the end of April 1943 'there took place a major turn in the way the Polish–Soviet issue was commented on' to the benefit of Poland. According to the Polish attaché, this change occurred under the influence of brutal and deceitful Soviet accusations, which 'have made an unpleasant impact here and partially opened even the eyes of the circles, which due to their anti-German orientation, surrendered too easily to wishful thinking as far as the policy of the Soviet Union is concerned.'[131]

Voices supporting the Polish government could be heard. Favourable articles were published by *Arbetaren*. On 24 and 27 April, Stalin was accused of imperialist policy, terror and deportations of civilians. In the 28 April issue, a Soviet announcement was quoted that pointed out the relations with

---

[129] 'I dag', *Göteborgs Handels- och Sjöfarts-Tidning*, 20 IV 1943.
[130] PISM, A XII, 3/41, monthly report for April 1943 by Polish Military Attaché to Stockholm Major F. Brzeskwiński to head of the Intelligence Department of the Staff of Commander-in-Chief, Stockholm, 6 V 1943.
[131] AAN, Norbert Żaba's collection, copy of report by N. Żaba to the Ministry of Information and Documentation, Stockholm, 13 V 1943.

Poland could have been re-established if 'the semi-Fascist clique of the Polish government resigned and was replaced by a new, more democratic government.' The commentary of the editors was concise: 'This small example proves to us what kind of independence is available for small and middle-sized nations who are living under the shadow of great states.'[132] In another article, the Polish government was praised for its extensive achievements in encouraging society to combat the Germans and creating a gallant regular army in Great Britain.[133]

Having consulted Żaba, Otto Järte published an article in *Svenska Dagbladet* on 1 May, accusing Stalin's policy of striving to subdue Poland. He was not surprised with the break-up of the Polish–Soviet relations, as he thought that this was the result of developments in relations between the two countries from September 1939 and of the extensive conflict, which together with the Katyń issue, had reached its climax.[134] It would seem that thanks to Żaba argument, Järte became an advocate for the Polish matter. He consequently opposed both Stalin's imperialist plans and the concessions made by the Western Allies in this area.[135]

Even Torgny Segerstedt attacked the Soviet diplomacy in one of his cyclical commentaries on current topics from 27 April. He compared the statements of Molotov to the tactics used by Ribbentrop: 'One does not answer an accusation, only puts forward a counter accusation.'[136] He maintained that Stalin broke up relations with the Polish government based on some minor pretext to have the liberty to conduct activity in the territories that were part of the Polish Republic in the moment of the war's outbreak. After all, one should note that in the context of the pro-Soviet commentaries, which were dominant in this daily, this statement was exceptional. That very same newspaper, on 10 July 1943, published an article by Jacob de Geer.[137] In this case Norbert Żaba pointed out that the text was 'characteristic of the pro-Polish Swedish circles' views.'[138] This circle was small though, and even de Geer had reservations about the Polish policy towards the Soviet Union, both

---

[132] 'Den diplomatiska fronten', *Arbetaren*, 28 IV 1943.
[133] 'Vad döljer sig bakom förlåten?', *Arbetaren*, 28 IV 1943.
[134] 'Kabal eller kris?', *Svenska Dagbladet*, 1 V 1943.
[135] T. Höjer, *Svenska...*, p. 78. Regular meetings of Järte and Żaba are mentioned by the biographer of the Swedish journalist: I. Andersson, *Otto Järte – en man för sig*, Stockholm 1965, s. 276.
[136] 'Situationen', *Göteborgs Handels- och Sjöfarts-Tidning*, 27 IV 1943.
[137] J. de Geer, 'Polen och Ryssland', *Göteborgs Handels- och Sjöfarts-Tidning*, 10 VI 1943.
[138] AAN, Norbert Żaba's collection, copy of report by N. Żaba to the Ministry of Information and Documentation, Stockholm, 18 VI 1943.

before the war and after July 1941. What he considered a mistake was moving the Anders Army, formed following the Sikorski–Mayski Agreement, from the Soviet Union to Iran and then to the Middle East in 1942. The conduct regarding the Katyń issue he described as 'great blunder'. Such an attitude within the Polish diplomatic circles was interpreted as the result of the influence of British propaganda. The publicists at *Göteborgs Handels- och Sjöfarts-Tidning* perceived the Soviet Union as a defender of liberal-democratic ideas. They optimistically predicted that Soviet communism, thanks to cooperation with the Anglo-Saxon countries, would start to evolve in the direction of democracy.[139] In turn, Johannes Wickman from *Dagens Nyheter* on 3 May called for the focusing of efforts on defeating Germany rather than sparking conflicts between the Allies. He accused the Polish government of conducting improper policy, as a result of which German propaganda could triumph. The Swedish opinion journalists suggested that these Poles wanted to establish the course of the border before the war was over, oblivious to Stalin's attempt to approve its change as quickly as possible. Żaba treated this type of commentary as offensive, since the dailies announcing such views often hired members of the Swedish–Polish Association.[140] In light of these press releases, Żaba's opinion that a breakthrough had taken place in commenting on the Katyń issue and Polish–Soviet relations by the Swedish opinion-forming circles should be considered an exaggeration.

It was only in the report about the opinion of the provincial press on Poland-related topics, in May 1943, that Żaba observed,

> contrary to what was happening in February and March, the provincial press showed consideration for the essence of the conflict and supported, in most cases, the Polish matter. Only several dailies continued to accuse Poland of having a lack of diplomatic far-sightedness, maintaining that it was in the interest of Poland and peace to reach a compromise agreement with victorious Russia, more so that the Polish eastern territories were not ethnographically part of Poland.

Żaba believed that the attitude of the press changed to the benefit of Poland. It was mostly understood that 'this was not only about certain revisions to the Polish–Soviet border, but the existence of nations neighbouring with the Soviets, and therefore a pan-European problem, which poses a danger to

---

[139] T. Nybom, *Motstånd...*, p. 340.
[140] AAN, Norbert Żaba's collection, copy of report by N. Żaba to the Ministry of Information and Documentation, Stockholm, 13 V 1943.

Sweden in the future.'[141] An anonymous opinion journalist for *Östgöta Correspondenten* explained that the issue was not about the graves in Katyń, but the fate of Poland, especially its independence and borders, and that the solution to this issue depended on the position of the Soviet Union in the group of Great Powers.[142] The majority of commentators agreed that the Allies that were bothered by conflicts inside the anti-Fascist coalition stood in opposition to the Poles. The Polish government insisted on regulating the issue of the border during the war, whereas the Polish–Soviet border from prior to 1 September was ethically questionable.[143] As highlighted, Russia's help was more important for England than that of Poland.[144] A commentator for *Sydsvenska Dagbladet Snällposten* admitted, 'from a purely human point of view one sympathizes with the Poles. This is the worst affected nation in this war. Both the Russians and the Germans inflicted great damage upon the country. General Government is a colony in the middle of Europe.' He also added that, 'one may find a grain of truth in the Katyń issue' and that the demand to re-establish the border from 1939 was 'in many respects sensible and understandable.' However, he eventually acknowledged, 'It is highly improbable that the Poles will benefit from their hasty and poorly conducted action,' and, 'they are completely dependent on England and its mighty friend – America.'[145]

Some commentators bore no illusions as to Stalin's intentions or the motifs behind his actions. *Arbetaren* accused the British of disloyalty towards its Polish Ally, laying blame on the Germans without examining the issue and accusing the Poles of disrupting the relations between the Allies:

> Here we have the modern art of diplomacy! [...] The Polish government asked for an examination of the issue. [...] In this situation the Poles faced charges from England and America. Naturally there are no similar charges directed at Russia, as Russia is strong, and at the moment its force is brutal and abides by no laws. It was Poland who insulted Russia by submitting a request for an impartial investigation regarding the issue of mass graves. One should not do so, not when one is so small and dependent on the powers. The powers of England and America need the power of Russia.'[146]

---

[141] AAN, Norbert Żaba's collection, copy of report by N. Żaba to the Ministry of Information and Documentation, Stockholm, 11 VI 1943.
[142] 'Misstänksamma vapenbröder', *Östgöta Correspondenten*, 28 IV 1943.
[143] 'Ryssland och Polen', *Upsala Nya Tidning*, 28 IV 1943.
[144] R. Essén, 'Det polska svaret', *Dagsposten*, 29 IV 1943.
[145] 'Konflikten om Polen', *Sydsvenska Dagbladet Snällposten*, 30 IV 1943.
[146] 'Statsmannakonst', *Arbetaren*, 7 V 1943.

On 10 may, in the article 'The Saviour of the Polish Nation', *Arbetaren* severely criticised the policy of the Soviet Union towards Poland. The article closed with, 'robbing the Poles of their Polish nationality and violently imposing on them the Soviet nationality is disgusting, anti-democratic and contrary to the principles propagated by the Allies as their war aims. What is more, it was noted, 'Soviet brutality is by no means different than German brutality.'[147]

During this time, attaché Brzeskwiński heard a pessimistic prognosis for the future in a conversation with General Henry Kellgren, head of the cabinet of the Minister of Defence. The general stated:

> Russia would like to be amply rewarded for its contributions to the war on the side of the Allies. It is probably counting on obtaining Finland and the Baltic States, over whose territories none of the Allies would most probably crush their swords during the upcoming peace conference. Russia, in turn, will demand for itself, and partially it already demands, the eastern provinces of Poland, the Balkans and India.[148]

General Henry Kellgren also noticed that compensation in the shape of East and West Prussia would by no means strengthen Poland, for it meant facing the minority issue once again, this time a German one and much more difficult than the pre-war Ukrainian issue. The Polish criticism of the Swedish press, which favoured the Soviet side as regards the Katyń-related conflict, sparked an interesting reaction from Kellgren. Brzeskwiński reported,

> the General's answer to this was that the Poles in the current worldwide turmoil may end up either on the side of the Allies or on the side of the Axis Powers, they should never end up alone in the middle, which may actually happen due to the current conflict. The Swedes want to see Poland take the side of the Allies. Hence the critical but kind stand of the Swedish press, which had to be taken, in the Polish–Soviet conflict.

The Swedes therefore instructed that, for their own good, the Poles should avoid ending up on the losing side. Kellgren's closing comments were that after the announcement about the breaking up of Polish–Soviet relations,

---

[147] 'Det polska folkets räddare!', *Arbetaren*, 10 V 1943.
[148] PISM, A XII, 3/41, monthly report for April 1943 by Polish Military Attaché to Stockholm Major F. Brzeskwiński to head of the Intelligence Department of the Commander-in-Chief, Stockholm, 6 V 1943.

suggestions emerged in the circle of military attachés of the Axis Powers that they would soon be joined by the attaché of Poland.[149]

In this vein, Arvid Richert reported from Berlin that the attitude of Great Britain and the USA was fuel for the German propaganda, as the Allies' governments left Poland to its own fate and, in the context of the Katyń tragedy, accepted the course of the future Polish–Soviet border established following the September Campaign of 1939.[150] The information conveyed by the German propaganda was confirmed by the Swedish Envoy to London – Prytz. To the Ministry of Foreign Affairs he wrote, 'the Polish government [is] very worried lately', as 'people are saying that Eden and Roosevelt have reached an agreement in Washington and are intending to offer Stalin the Curzon Line as the future Polish–Russian border.'[151] Prytz pointed out that the British press almost entirely omitted publishing information about Polish prisoners held in the Soviet Union, and that there was even less news about the murdered officers. He highlighted that, according to a person in Prime Minister Sikorski's closest circle, the Poles had irrefutable proof that the massacre had taken place and that they rejected the position of the Allies, who were trying to present the issue as if it were a crime committed by the Germans. At the same time the Swedish envoy noted that Sikorski could not officially engage in any controversy with his allies.

How can one evaluate the Swedish reaction to the Katyń issue? It seems that the representative of South Africa in Stockholm, Stephanus F. N. Gie (the first South African diplomat and a historian) came close to the truth. According to Gie, which was recorded by the Foreign Office, Swedish comments about the Polish–Soviet conflict were on the whole unfavourable towards Poland. The publication of the German brochure *Nackskottet. Dödskogen vid Katyń* (A Shot in the Neck. The Forest of Death in Katyń), presenting the accounts of people who had been invited to see the site of the massacre, did not generate the desired result. Gie's Swedish interviewees maintained that the British should have imposed a greater control over the official statements of the Polish government, since the Poles should not have been raising issues which could

---

[149] Kellgren described Brzeskwiński with sympathy in his memoirs as 'very cheerful companion', always with a smile. He gave a similar, positive opinion about Brzeskwiński's predecessor (until the outbreak of the war) colonel Andrzej Marecki. See H. Kellgren, *Sex krigsår i Skölds skugga*, Stockholm 1951, pp. 172–175.
[150] RA, UD 1920 års dossiersystem, HP 1, vol. 485, letter by Swedish Envoy to Berlin A. Richert to head of the Political department of UD S. Söderblom, Berlin, 28 IV 1943.
[151] Ibidem, letter by Swedish Envoy to London B. Prytz to Minister of Foreign Affairs Ch. Günther, London, 22 IV 1943.

5. REVIVAL OF BILATERAL RELATIONS

harm the anti-fascist coalition and which, as they believed, were currently impossible to explain anyway. Interestingly, none of them doubted that the Soviet NKVD had committed the crime, but at the same time everyone was aware of the Soviet Union's sacrifice in the fight with Germany. In general, a view prevailed that the Poles should arrange its relations with the Soviet Union even through force. The Katyń issue was treated by Swedish public opinion as an unpleasant discord in the relations among the allies. This was considered dangerous, not particularly due to the rift in the common front against Germany, but that it was an ominous sign for the worsening of relations between the victorious powers following the conclusion of the war.[152]

A representative opinion for Sweden's position on the Polish–Soviet conflict came from Sven Grafström, who in a conversation with Norbert Żaba explained, 'Given the geographical and political situation of Poland, it is impossible to conduct simultaneous anti-Soviet and anti-German policy in the face of which it would be more reasonable not to raise the border issue at the present moment and not to react to the Soviet action.' According to Żaba, such a view was relatively widespread within Swedish pro-Ally political circles. Their only option for Poland was to choose the lesser evil, namely to cooperate with the Soviet Union against Germany.

The Swedish diplomats avoided revealing openly their position to the Poles, though their contacts were again more intense than during the German hegemony in Europe. Maintaining these relations did not harm the external image of Sweden.[153] It is known that Prytz, Swedish Envoy to London, attended a reception at the Polish Embassy in London, although no surviving Polish documentation proves that these meetings were anything more than courtesy visits.[154] The Polish matters were discussed at times during meetings between the Swedes and representatives of other countries. In a conversation with British Envoy Mallet, in May 1943, Boheman stated that in his view the Poles were extremely unreasonable. He knew the territories of the Polish–Russian borderland from personal experience and claimed that the issue of the border between these two countries was of no importance for the rest of Europe. Mallet presented Boheman's views in the following way:

---

[152] NA, FO, 371/37077, telegram by the representative of South Africa in Stockholm, S. Gie, to the South Africa House in London, 30 IV 1943.
[153] Grafström even wondered in May 1943 whether Potworowski would be expelled from Stockholm if the arrest of 'the Warsaw Swedes' took place at the time. See: S. Grafström, *Anteckningar 1938–1944*, p. 490.
[154] PISM, A 12, 651/10, guestbook used during receptions at Polish embassy in London.

He claimed that except for a few great landowners whose estates are in the disputed province, most peasants' lives under Soviet occupation would be at least as good as under Polish rule. He judged that the situation in the villages located in the Polish part of these territories seemed even worse than in its Russian section. Besides, these people may not be ethnically Polish. Without a doubt [however] the way the Russians addressed this issue in the context of the current conflict is unjust.[155]

Boheman highlighted that the majority of Swedes thought the same as he did, but naturally except for 'the ordinary anti-Russian maniacs.' The Swedes pitied 'the poor, stupid Poles', but even though they were convinced that the murder of the Polish officers was committed by the Soviets, they believed that there was no justification for the conduct of the Germans, who exploited Katyń as if they had never committed similar acts in Poland. That is why the break-up in relations with the Poles by the Soviets was accepted with apparent calm in Stockholm. According to Boheman, the Swedish press and public opinion followed the entire Polish–Soviet dispute with objectivity.[156] It is certain that the Katyń issue caused a breakthrough in the Swedes' approach to the examination of various scenarios of political developments in Central Europe. The statement by a Soviet Foreign Minister's first deputy Oleksandr Korniyczuk was a clear guideline for analytical papers devoted to this area. He convinced Envoy Assarsson that Sikorski would never return to Warsaw, even though a 'certain liberal element in the Polish government in London' had a chance to do so.[157]

---

[155] NA, FO, 371/37078, letter by British Envoy to Stockholm V. Mallet to the Minister of Foreign Affairs A. Eden, 25 V 1943, pp. 13–14. The Swedes probably associated the break-up of the Polish-Soviet relations exclusively with the issue of the eastern border of Poland. See: S. Grafström, *Anteckningar 1938–1944*, p. 486.

[156] NA, FO, 371/37078, letter by British Envoy to Stockholm V. Mallet to the Minister of Foreign Affairs A. Eden, 25 V 1943, pp. 13–14.

[157] RA, UD, 1920 års dossiersystem, HP 1, vol. 519, letter by Swedish Envoy to Moscow V. Assarsson to the Ministry of Foreign Affairs, Kuybyshew, 6 VI 1943 r. What may be considered the crowning achievement of the Soviet military propaganda in Sweden regarding the issue of the mass murder of Polish officers, is the screening of the film entitled *Katyń*, which took place on 15 August 1944 in the Soviet Legation. The film presented the testimonies of the eye witnesses of the crime, who were to be forced by the Germans in 1943 with beatings and tortures to testify to the disadvantage of the Soviet authorities. See PISM, A XII, 3/41, Note of Colonel S. Gano 'Propaganda sowiecka' (Soviet propaganda), 14 IX 1944.

6. Sweden's Return to Strict Neutrality and the Normalisation of Relations with the Polish Government

The visit by the Minister of Industry, Trade and Shipping Jan Kwapiński to Stockholm

The most important political event for the Polish–Swedish bilateral relations of 1943 was the visit by Jan Kwapiński, Minister of Industry, Trade and Shipping to Stockholm. Maurycy Karniol prepared the ground for this visit in Sweden. He proposed to Torsten Nilsson, the leading activist of the SAP, that the Polish minister become one of the international guests of the celebrations of 1st May, organized by the Swedish social democrats Nilsson, who in mid-April 1943 paid a visit to London, invited Kwapiński officially.[1]

During his stay in Sweden, Kwapiński met the most important representatives of the Swedish Social Democratic Party: August Lindberg, Torsten Nilsson, Rickard Lindström, Prime Minister Hansson and Minister of Social Affairs Gustav Möller. On 29 April, Kwapiński participated in a conference with representatives of socialist parties from fourteen different countries. He also took part in a session of the Polish–Swedish Chamber of Commerce (4 May) as well as a reception held by the Stockholm authorities (30 April).

When Kwapiński's visit was agreed, Attaché Żaba would give this event a much broader appeal. Following the example of a Belgian politician, who visited Stockholm and acquainted the public with the politics of his government in exile, he convinced London that Kwapiński's visit, as far as propaganda was concerned, should be expanded beyond the party-related sphere. Żaba wrote to the Ministry of Internal Affairs, 'He would then have an opportunity to redress the view that our Government consists purely of reactionists, as well as explain the eastern issue during private conversations.'[2]

The programme for the visit was productive and Żaba's expectations were fulfilled to a large extent. Although, on issuing an entry permit, the Swedes made it clear that this would be an unofficial visit. The planned speeches were

---

[1] AAN, HI/I/305, telegram by Polish Envoy to Stockholm H. Sokolnicki to the Ministry of Foreign Affairs, Stockholm, 31 III 1943.

[2] AAN, Norbert Żaba's collection, copy of letter by N. Żaba to M. Thugutt (Ministry of Internal Affairs), Stockholm, 15 IV 1943.

to be treated as private.³ Kwapiński spoke not only as an activist of the PPS, but also as a representative of the Polish government in exile. He stressed this both in informal conversations as well as during public meetings. Even if the intentions of organizers, or Kwapiński himself, were different, the Katyń issue and the break-up of the Polish–Soviet relations created a unique atmosphere in Kwapiński's meetings.

The climax of the public activity of the Polish minister in Sweden, was his participation in an international convention on Labour Day, held 1 May in *Medborgarhuset* (The Civic Building) in Stockholm. Its rich musical and literary programme did not overshadow the political significance of the celebrations or, most importantly, the speeches of the representatives of various countries. This part of the meeting was opened by Walter Åman, the leading activist of SAP, trade union secretary and famous for countering communist tendencies in the party. He highlighted that the crucial moment of the war had passed and that peace and the restoration of law were dawning. Among the heroic victims of the battle with dark forces, he named Alter, Ehrlich and Niedziałkowski. Willy Brandt, who was secretary of the International Group of Democratic Socialists of Stockholm (the so-called Little International), focused on presenting the plan for developing, following the war's conclusion, a new deal founded on democracy. He opened his speech with the watchwords of the Atlantic Charter and talked about the need for integration of European countries and cooperation dependent on a resignation from war reparations and the division of vanquishers, neutrals and the vanquished. After Brandt spoke Martin Tranmæl from Norway, who supported of the idea of integration. In turn, Fritz Tarnow suggested that Germany be treated carefully and that all actions be guided by reason and not blind hatred to avoid killing off German democracy. The expectations of the German social democrats were accentuated further by Edgar Hahnewald, who claimed that Germans were the victims of terror and violence too. Jiří Jakerle from Czechoslovakia was among the speakers who most clearly marked their presence. He expressed his admiration for the heroic fight of the Russian nation and the Red Army as well as for the armies of other countries and soldiers of the underground resistance movement, including the Germans. Jakerle's words were in support of unity leading to victory, declaring, 'We welcome everything that strengthens this unity, we reject everything that hinders it.' In a tone very similar to that of Jakerle was the

---

³ AAN, HI/I/305, telegram by Polish Envoy to Stockholm H. Sokolnicki to the Ministry of Foreign Affairs, Stockholm, 22 III 1943.

speech of the Hungarian, Wilhelm Böhm, who also expressed his admiration for the brave fight of the Russian nation and proclaimed that 'the workers' movement is determined to oppose with all its might all that could be harmful to the security of the Soviet Union.'

The message of the speech delivered by Jan Kwapiński was different by comparison. He warned the participants against the threat of communism. He recounted the experiences of the interwar period, when the ranks of several workers' parties in Europe and France 'were burst from the inside' by the Comintern. That is why, according to Kwapiński, the workers' class 'was unable to defend itself with due force against the developing Fascist movement in Europe, which was born and grew up on the havoc wreaked by the communist party.' His pointing to the threat from the Soviet Union, whose army was about to reach the centre of Europe, was isolated and did not harmonize with the choir of activists, who expressed their admiration for the military effort of the USSR. Kwapiński simultaneously paid tribute to the hosts of the meeting and reminded prematurely: 'We were striving to create good living conditions for the working class, according to your example. We visited you often [...], to jointly confer on the building of a better future and working for it.' Most of all, however, the Polish socialist emphasized the question of current assistance, which had been provided by the Swedes to the Polish refugees. He also presented the programme of the Polish government which was to be implemented in the event of the Red Army's entrance in to the territory of the Second Polish Republic and the vision for the future close Polish–Swedish cooperation:

> Poland would rise to become an independent being, and we are sure that the democratic nations would offer us their helping hand and grant us their support. Poland does not feel alienated in its underground battle. We know that we have allies in free nations, that we have friends and allies here, in a country of democratic liberties and social progress. [...] Our country is divided from yours only by a small space – a rather narrow strip of sea. We have always lived in friendship, we maintained good political and economic relations. I may assure you and your government that as soon as Poland regains independence, it will establish a new, most friendly cooperation and coexistence with you. Our sister parties will be brought even closer together, because both our countries will have common purposes and common aspirations. We know that following the war, you shall be firmly defending, just like you are today, justice and rightness in international life and you shall not acknowledge acts of violence committed

during the war. Our friendship, cemented during the war, would last as long as I shall live and develop our nations.[4]

According to the source in the British Legation, the speech given by the Polish minister during the 1 May celebrations was received with offence rather than sympathy owing to its hostile attitude towards Russia. In the discussion part, Prime Minister Hansson related to it formally, not leaving any doubts about his disapproval. Minister of Social Affairs Möller was clearly irritated and practically told Kwapiński that he was not a good politician. As a matter of fact, during other meetings Kwapiński was also criticised for his anti-Russian attitude. The Swedes maintained that Poland and the Soviet Union should regulate their mutual relations in a friendly atmosphere, which is why speeches that accentuated animosities towards Moscow were perceived as unreasonable.[5] Eventually, the members of the workers' parties from fourteen countries adopted a resolution where they wished the Allies victory, and opted for the post-war renewal of democracy and integration of the workers' movement. They proposed that peace was based on democratic-socialist solutions and experiences of the interwar period.

Polish fears and expectations for future events were accentuated by Kwapiński on 4 May during an official dinner organized by the leadership of SAP and LO in the Grand Hotel in Stockholm. While expressing gratitude for the opportunity to spend several days in beautiful and happy Sweden, he highlighted, 'I am relaxing here mentally in an atmosphere where one senses neither the war nor its consequences.' He did not mention Germany, as he claimed that its defeat was certain. He focused on the threat from the east: 'We, the Poles, are after all situated between Russia and Germany. Bolshevik Russia would be a victorious power and we are doomed to its neighbourhood. [...] and this Russia is preparing itself to play a great role in post-war Europe.' He then recounted that it was the attack from the east that put an end to the fights in the first stage of the war:

> But this was not the worst thing. The worst thing was the communist propaganda, which tortured our nation, pulling apart its future, its establishments and its life. Each and every one of us has forgotten his personal detriment, but we have not forgotten and we may never forget our moral damages. For our internal order, with all its errors, faults, shortcomings and defects, was better

---

[4] PISM, col. 20, vol. 23, M. Karniol's report from J. Kwapiński's visit to Sweden, part 2, Stockholm, June 1943.
[5] NA, FO, 188/403, note by counsellor to the British Legation in Stockholm G. N. Lamming, 18 VI 1943.

than theirs. I am saying this on the basis of what I saw with my own eyes in Soviet Russia.

For one thing, Kwapiński mentioned collectivisation, forced labour and the terror reigning in Stalin's country. For another, he pointed out that Poland wanted to live with Russia in peace, but this was not permitted by the Soviet leader himself:

> We appreciated and are appreciating its current contribution in the fight against Hitler. As a nation with chivalrous traditions we admired the heroism of the Red Army, whose best expression is the legend of Stalingrad. But as an Allied country and at the same time a country which was the first to put up armed resistance to Hitler's attack, we could not agree to lose half of the territory of our country in the east in favour of Russia. We could not agree to a situation where our Jewish, Ukrainian and Belarusian citizens would be considered Russian citizens. On fighting for the support for these deported people we were facing Soviet countermeasures.[6]

Kwapiński patiently pointed to the absurdity of Soviet accusations emphasizing the idleness of Polish underground resistance. He explained that calling for an immediate battle at that moment 'would be tantamount to calling for the murder of the Polish nation, as the Germans are still in possession of sufficiently large military and police forces in Poland.' In conclusion, he brought up the Katyń issue: 'On the subject of graves discovered near Smolensk, the Soviets had told us that all our men had been released and that they were free. Only now do they tell us that these people were left somewhere nearby Smolensk. They were indeed left, but in graves.'

On summing up his speech the Polish Minister repeated that the Polish nation had not turned Quisling. Without commenting on this fact he stated, 'You understand this, because You feel who Quisling is for your fraternal Norwegian nation.' Prime Minister Hansson did not refer to Kwapiński's speech. He responded courteously:

> We, the Swedes, find ourselves in an undoubtedly better geographical situation. Nevertheless, the same problems that are encountered by Poland are also encountered by Sweden. Our security is dependent on the balance of forces in Europe, and most importantly in Central and Eastern Europe. In order to make

---

[6] PISM, col. 20, vol. 23, report by M. Karniol from J. Kwapiński's visit to Sweden, part II, Stockholm, June 1943.

this balance of forces really exist, there must exist free Poland. I unwaveringly believe that free Poland would again rise to life and develop successfully.[8]

During his visit, Kwapiński met with Minister of Commerce Herman Eriksson. Next, on 7 May, he sent him a letter presenting detailed plans concerning the development of Polish–Swedish economic relations following the war.[9] Telegrams of thanks sent from London by Kwapiński straight after his return (14 May) may prove that he also had other interlocutors not mentioned in the reports. Kwapiński expressed his gratitude to Prime Minister Hansson for his kind reception, to the head of LO, August Lindberg, for his hospitality and, surprisingly, to Ernst Paul, representing the German minority in Czechoslovakia, for his cooperation.[10] On reporting the course of Kwapiński's talks in Sweden, Żaba highlighted the significance of Prime Minister Hansson's statement: 'Sweden believes that an independent and strong Poland will come into existence and is willing to strengthen the exchange of economic and cultural goods with Poland to a much greater extent than before the war.'[11] However, it would be hard to view this speech as something more than just a courtesy to a colleague from an ideologically similar party. As was customary for Swedish politicians, the speech was not made public and therefore did not gain the dimension of a political declaration. Hansson promised Kwapiński that Poland would receive deliveries of food, which initiated the process of preparing such arrangements.[12] Procedural issues delayed considerably these actions and the support was granted no sooner than 1944.

Kwapiński also contacted the Swedish cooperative movement, with the intention of developing a future cooperation on the rebuilding of Poland. At least this was what counsellor Tadeusz Pilch communicated to the Ministry of Industry, Trade and Shipping in February 1944. Pilch was to make use of the favourable atmosphere that was created because of talks conducted by Kwapiński and tried to maintain these contacts. Their dimension was not only economic but also political, as the Swedish cooperative movement was

---

[8] M. K[arniol], 'Współpraca i przyjaźń socjalistów polskich i szwedzkich. Z pobytu tow. Kwapińskiego w Sztokholmie', *Robotnik Polski w Wielkiej Brytanii*, 1 VII 1943.
[9] NA, FO, 371/37126, letter by W.H. Montagu-Pollock to A. Eden, 5 VII 1943.
[10] PISM, col. 20, vol. 23, telegrams by J. Kwapiński to P. A. Hansson, A. Lindberg and E. Paul, London, 14 V 1943.
[11] AAN, Norbert Żaba's collection, copy of letter by N. Żaba to M. Thugutt (Ministry of Internal Affairs) [?], Stockholm, 30 IV 1943.
[12] AAN, HI/I/305, telegram by W. Babiński to Polish Envoy to Stockholm H. Sokolnicki, 18 IX 1943.

dominated by social democrats who constituted the strongest party in parliament and government, and the meaning of this party following the conclusion of the war, according to Pilch, was to gain further power.[13] The editor-in-chief of the periodical *Kooperatören*, Thorsten Ohde, and the entire management of *Kooperativa Förbundet* (*KF*, or the Swedish Co-operative Union) headed by Albin Johansson were introduced to Kwapiński during his stay in Stockholm. The union even threw a special breakfast in honour of the Polish minister. During the celebrations of the anniversary of Niedziałkowski and Thugutt's death, Ohde delivered a speech on the Polish cooperative movement and Stanisław Thugutt. Ohde assisted Leon Rappaport in his studies on the cooperative movement in Sweden and in general was interested in the rebuilding of this movement in Poland following the war.[14] Rappaport proposed setting up a special commission for the expansion of the cooperative movement in Poland according to the Swedish model. In May 1943, he also developed the theses for Minister Kwapiński's talks with the director of KF Albin Johansson. What was expressed there was the will to cooperate with the Swedish members of cooperatives on the organization of the cooperative movement in Poland. According to Rappaport: 'This co-operation could include export and import of natural resources and commodities, exchange of patents, professional and technical support, various types of agreements.'[15]

Kwapiński's visit received a wide coverage in the Swedish newspapers.[16] It should be mentioned that on 7 May a special press conference was held, during which the Polish minister answered the questions that were considered most sensitive. He adopted a defensive attitude; most of all in response to the attacks in Soviet propaganda, which depicted the Polish government as being gentry-oriented, undemocratic and out of touch with its country. The minister talked about the development of the Polish Underground State, its military and civilian section. In his summing up, he pointed out, 'The nation is listening to

---

[13] AAN, HI/I/51, letter by T. Pilch, counsellor to the Polish Legation in Stockholm, to the Ministry of Industry, Trade and Shipping, Stockholm, 11 II 1944.
[14] Ibidem, note by L. Rappaport regarding the relations with Kooperativa Förbundet, Stockholm, 11 II 1944.
[15] Ibidem, L. Rappaport: Wytyczne w sprawie wyzyskania spółdzielczości szwedzkiej dla sprawy odbudowy w Polsce [Guidelines regarding the Utilization of the Swedish Cooperative Movement for the Rebuilding Process in Poland], Stockholm, 10 V 1943.
[16] PISM, col. 20, vol. 23, report from J. Kwapiński's visit to Sweden from 25 IV 1943 to 12 V 1943, part. 3: 'Pokłosie prasowe' (Press comments), 2 VI 1943.

its government, moving blindly along the lines set by this government, and it shall be doing so both now and in the future.'[17]

The following day, this meeting was reported on by the main dailies. The account by *Svenska Dagbladet* polemicized with the Soviet propaganda and was meaningfully entitled 'The Polish Government is Democratic – the Visit of the Polish Minister from London.' The newspaper drew attention to the meaning of the visit for the future of the Polish–Swedish relations. It highlighted that the minister:

> [...] conducted preliminary talks with representatives from Swedish industry as regards Swedish post-war supplies connected with the planned rebuilding of Poland. These talks, relating first and foremost to the materials that Sweden was able to deliver quicker than other countries, including equipment for treating peat, residential homes and building materials, were crowned with concrete Swedish proposals, which are taken by the minister to London.[18]

Thanks to the information obtained from Karniol, Allan Vougt wrote the article 'Poland is Fighting', which was devoted to the 50th anniversary of the setting up of PPS. The article, published 9 May in *Social-Demokraten*, underlined the significance of developing relations between the parties for the future international relations.[19] In one of the issues of the socialist youth periodical *Frihet*, Torsten Nilsson, who was one of the leading activists of the Social Democratic Party, presented Kwapiński's profile. He also referred to the dispute about the Katyń issue and Soviet accusations in the following words: 'To say that the Polish government is accommodating Hitler, is definitely over the top.' He then pointed out that Kwapiński's visit to Stockholm, which was so important for the development of Polish–Swedish relations, took place during an exceptionally heated period in the relations between the Polish government in exile and the Soviet Union. He described Kwapiński with unconcealed appreciation:

> Born in 1885 in Warsaw, he is the same age as Per Albin Hansson. Like many Polish politicians, he had a very turbulent past. This has nevertheless left no mark on him. He is cheerful, his countenance looks almost Swedish and one might think that his origin is both Swedish and Polish. His soft and delicate hands do not show that this man was throwing bombs and his gentle glance

---

[17] Ibidem, M. Karniol's letter to the Central Executive Committee of the PPS party, Stockholm, 7 VI 1943.
[18] 'Polens regering är demokratisk. Polsk londonminister på besök', *Svenska Dagbladet*, 8 V 1943.
[19] A. Vougt, 'Polens kamp', *Social-Demokraten*, 9 V 1943.

shows that he is full of wit and joy of living. His outlook proves that Poles are aptly called the Frenchmen of Eastern Europe.[20]

On analysing the reaction of the press to Kwapiński's visit in Sweden, Karniol noted the provincial press continued to publish numerous editorials devoted to Poland for two weeks and, with few exceptions, they were pro-Polish and anti-Soviet.[21] Making use of the interest in the Polish subject, Karniol not only inspired, but also published his own articles in the Swedish press. On 13 May 1943, the social democratic *Aftontidningen* daily, published 'Poles and Ukrainians' (most probably written by Karniol), where the author polemicized with the Soviet propaganda and explained that nationality-related problems of Central-Eastern Europe were simple only for dictators using repression and deportation. The author of the article did not take sides in the dispute about the Eastern Borderlands of the Second Polish Republic, but he questioned the one-sided vision created by the Soviet Legation, which had started to dominate Swedish public opinion.[22] Karniol published a text in *Landsarbetaren* devoted to the subject of the Polish Association of Agricultural Workers, where he presented the profile of Jan Kwapiński. In the article, he also highlighted that the reborn Poland would be founded on the principles of democracy and social justice.[23] On 2 June, the article '50th Anniversary of the Polish Workers Movement' by Karniol was published in *Metallarbetaren* weekly. The publication of this text proved that Kwapiński's visit brought some propaganda-related results. The article was received by the newspaper's editorial office in November 1942 yet published over half a year later. In the article Karniol provided a detailed description of the origin of the Polish–Soviet conflict and explained the compromised character of the border established by the treaty of Riga in 1921.[24]

Following his return to London, in an interview for the Polish government newspaper *Dziennik Polski*, Kwapiński highlighted that he had visited Stockholm on the invitation of SAP as chair of the Foreign Committee of PPS to speak at the celebrations of 1st May. He pointed out that, 'Already, the very

---

[20] PISM, col. 20, vol. 23, M. Karniol's letter to the Central Executive Committee of the PPS party, Stockholm, 8 VI 1943.
[21] Ibidem, report from J. Kwapiński's visit to Sweden from 25 IV 1943 to 12 V 1943, part. 3: 'Pokłosie prasowe' (Press comments), 2 VI 1943.
[22] 'Polacker och ukrainare', *Aftontidningen*, 13 V 1943; IPMS, col. 23, vol. 23, M. Karniol's letter to the Central Executive Committee of the PPS party, Stockholm, 20 V 1943.
[23] PISM, col. 20, vol. 23, M. Karniol's letter to the Central Executive Committee of the PPS party, Stockholm, 20 V 1943.
[24] PISM, col. 20, vol. 23, M. Karniol's letter to the Central Executive Committee of the PPS party, Stockholm, 10 VI 1943.

fact of inviting a Polish socialist who is also a member of government to deliver a public address in the capital of neutral Sweden, is a telling sign. My taking the floor during this celebration prompted an ovation, which lasted almost three minutes.'[25] The minister evaluated his visit positively and expressed many courteous views about Swedish politicians, but the positive statements were probably dictated by the requirements of the war propaganda. Karniol's correspondence, prepared for the *Robotnik Polski w Wielkiej Brytanii*, was also enthusiastic. According to the representative of the PPS in Sweden, Kwapiński 'corrected his erroneous views on the reactionism of Polish government in London and Polish policy.'[26] The Polish press on the whole promoted a picture of success regarding the visit to Stockholm by the Polish minister. The contacts established they were to bear fruit in the immediate future. Following the war they led to the renewal of economic relations between Poland and Sweden.[27]

Stockholm buzzed with rumours of the real purpose for Kwapiński's visit to Sweden. A Finnish journalist told Żaba of speculation about the intermediation between Great Britain, Hungary and Bulgaria regarding peace. The Polish minister's main achievement at a special conference devoted to this issue allegedly was to be Stalin's agreement to the establishment of a federation of countries headed by Poland and Czechoslovakia. According to Żaba, this rumour was to confirm that 'the news promoted here by various rival subversive groups should be treated with reserve',[28] but one could not entirely exclude that secret talks were conducted by the Polish minister. It is a fact that Żaba maintained contacts with Hungarian diplomats with whom

---

[25] 'Wrażenia i uwagi po powrocie ze Szwecji. Wywiad z ministrem Janem Kwapińskim', *Dziennik Polski*, 18 V 1943.
[26] M. K[arniol], 'Współpraca i przyjaźń socjalistów polskich i szwedzkich. Z pobytu tow. Kwapińskiego w Sztokholmie', *Robotnik Polski w Wielkiej Brytanii*, 1 VII 1943.
[27] The Polish press, right before the minister's visit, provided a positive evaluation of the policy of engaging in the cooperation with Sweden, seeing it as a good basis for Kwapiński's plans. CH., 'Szwecja na progu 1943 r. Stosunki polsko-szwedzkie i sympatie narodu szwedzkiego', *Dziennik Polski*, 5 II 1943; 'Z pobytu min. Kwapińskiego w Szwecji', *Dziennik Polski*, 12 V 1943; 'Po zerwaniu stosunków dyplomatycznych', *Dziennik Polski*, 29 IV 1943 (There we find an explanation that London correspondents of the Swedish press were avoiding anti-Polish tons, but they were making it clear that the Poles had no chances whatsoever in the conflict with the Soviet Union). Following his return to London, Kwapiński held a meeting with President Raczkiewicz, but no detailed description of their conversation has survived. See: brief information about the meeting on 18 May 1943: *Dzienniki czynności...*, vol. 2, p. 71.
[28] AAN, Norbert Żaba's collection, copy N. Żaba's letter to the Ministry of Information and Documentation, Stockholm, 17 VI 1943. During a government meeting on 17 May 1943 Kwapiński submitted a report from his stay in Sweden, but the manuscript has never been found. See *Protokoły posiedzeń Rady Ministrów Rzeczypospolitej Polskiej*, vol. 5, p. 439.

he exchanged information on international developments. This was also the source of his information on the situation in the General Government. For many countries, Stockholm was a convenient venue to maintain casual contacts, also because of military actions it welcomed political refugees with ambitions to represent the nations of their origin, and most of all, to formulate original political programmes. By autumn of 1940 Polish diplomats in Stockholm were trying to launch talks with pro-Ally oriented Estonians.[29] No documentation, however, survived confirming the speculation surrounding a secret mission by Kwapiński.

Did Kwapiński's visit to Stockholm bring success or failure? According to Żaba, Kwapiński's visit was very important, as it allowed the Swedes to become familiar with the Polish point of view on current political issues, and especially the Soviet issue. According to counsellor Pilch, discussions on economic matters were also successful. For Żaba, it was also important to organize Kwapiński's meeting with the journalists, to challenge the view that the Polish government was reactionary. According to Żaba, this venture was successful: 'The interviews were published in the press, they are brilliant and highlight that the Polish government is democratic and in touch with the country.'[30]

Żaba considered the only tension to be a discussion on 1 May, during which Jakerle issued a manifesto where he condemned all actions harming the unity of the Allies (he meant the actions of the Poles) and during which he held the Czechs as a model for national unity. Were the kind and courteous welcoming statements a cover for the brutal political reality that prompted the Polish government in exile to descend gradually from the diplomatic stage? And, in the face of the passive attitude of the Western Allies, would the Swedish government respect only the views of the Soviet Union regarding the Polish matter? The Swedes decided to wait for the situation to develop. The talks with Kwapiński were surely an important stage in the thawing of mutual relations and taking up the discussion on the future of both countries following the conclusion of the war. They paved the way to bilateral negotiations mostly on the subject of economic cooperation, as well as, to some extent, political cooperation. At the same time, the cool reception of the Polish minister's remarks on the subject of the aggressive policy of the Soviet Union again proved that the best possible relations with the Soviet Union were more important for the Swedes than the revival of relations with the Polish

---

[29] This was mentioned during the parliamentary session on 19 November 1940 by Minister A. Zaleski. See *Protokoły posiedzeń Rady Ministrów Rzeczypospolitej Polskiej*, vol. 2, p. 180.

[30] AAN, Norbert Żaba's collection, N. Żaba's letter to M. Thugutt (Ministry of Internal Affairs) [?], Stockholm, 6 V 1943.

government in exile. The more the Polish–Swedish talks could harm these relations the slimmer the chance for their continuation.[31] Kwapiński thought that an affinity between PPS and SAP would improve the position of Poland in Sweden. Envoy Sokolnicki was right, however, when he treated this view sceptically and disagreed with Kwapiński's suggestion that he join PPS to facilitate contact with the Swedish government.[32]

Change in the policy of the Swedish government

A breakthrough year in the Swedish policy was 1943, as it marked the conclusion of concessions to Germany. Together with the weakening of commercial ties, a tendency appeared to intensify economic cooperation with the USA and Great Britain.[33] Part of the Swedish public opinion continued stubbornly to support the Germans. During the meeting of the German–Swedish Chamber of Commerce in September of 1943, Sven Hedin expressed his deep conviction that the Germans would win the war and 'save Europe from the Asian plague.'[34] Nevertheless, the Swedish government was striving for the return to strict neutrality and on 2 July 1943 cancelled the agreement of the German army's transit on the last day of that month.

The agreement was terminated on 29 July,[35] and by 9 August 1943 the transit had virtually stopped. This decision received a warm reaction from the press, although the pro-Ally dailies criticised the government for acting too late.[36] Prime Minister Hansson explained that the agreement concluded three years earlier did not mean the abandonment of the policy of neutrality and was not

---

[31] The fact that the visit was closely followed by the Soviet authorities was repeated by the ambassador to the Ally governments in London, Aleksandr Bogomolov, who during a conversation with the Swedish diplomat kept asking for the details of the meetings which were widely reported in many Polish newspapers. RA, UD 1920 års dossiersystem, HP 1, vol. 519, Swedish Legation in London to the head of the Political department of UD S. Söderblom, London, 6 VII 1943.
[32] H. Sokolnicki, *In the service...*, p. 292.
[33] AAN, HI/I/51, report by Polish Envoy to Stockholm H. Sokolnicki to the Ministry of Foreign Affairs, Stockholm, 28 III 1944.
[34] AAN, Norbert Żaba's collection, copy of N. Żaba's note, Stockholm, 1 X 1943.
[35] A. W. Johansson, *Per Albin...*, pp. 316–317.
[36] AAN, Norbert Żaba's collection, copy of report by Polish Envoy to Stockholm H. Sokolnicki to the Ministry of Foreign Affairs, Stockholm, 13 VIII 1943. The Polish newspaper in London as early as at the end of April 1943 predicted Sweden's abandonment of the policy of concessions to Germany: 'It then becomes completely clear that the era when the Swedish government maintained that it couldn't allow itself to resist the German claims, is now over. That now the direct German threat is no more the same absolute and undisputed bugaboo for Stockholm as it was only a year ago.' CEP, 'Postawa Sztokholmu wobec Berlina. Barometr szwedzki', *Dziennik Polski*, 29 IV 1943.

tantamount to taking a side. During a rally in Roslagen on 8 August 1943 Hansson highlighted, 'The neutrality we had proclaimed not only had a negative purpose of keeping us far away from the war but also a positive purpose of maintaining friendly relations with all fighting sides.' As early as 5 August, the Polish Legation sent a report to the Polish Ministry of Foreign Affairs, warning that the Swedes confidentially informed the counsellor about the forthcoming termination of the transit.[37] What was accurate was the later commentary regarding the termination of the transit, sent to London by Envoy Sokolnicki. He evaluated Swedish foreign policy from the beginning of the war:

> No matter the actual reasons for the conclusion of the transit agreement in 1940 (the threat of German invasion or economic pressure in connection with the collapse of France and victorious advance of Germany) and the reasons for the termination of the agreement (the dawning victory of the Allies – as some say – and the weakness of Germany, or the sense of military fitness of Sweden following the three years of feverish rearming, or, eventually, the intention to win the favour of the Allies) – it is certain that the Swedish government only strives to rescue its country from the disaster of war and to survive the period of tempest raging over Europe peacefully and safeguarding political independence and territorial integrity of Sweden. It is also certain that at the same time its intention was to avoid indisposing anyone for the future, which is proven by how shrewdly the transit agreement was done away with, without risking the prestige of Germany and at the same time preparing ground for better future neighbourly relations with Norway. The politics of Sweden, besides generous financial and material support for Finland in 1939 and 1940, during the current war has not been characterized by any heroic features, but has immediately set an example of caution and fitness in implementing hurried corrections to the pacifist ideology of the preceding years and realist, or let's say "flexible", policy, which probably saved and will continue to preserve Sweden's freedom and sovereignty from the disaster of war.[38]

From mid-1943, the process of breaking-up all Swedish dependencies on Germany was in progress, but the policy in this respect was extremely cautious.[39] It transpired that the transit of military materials nonetheless continued for some time, as Germany's arms and ammunition supplies were stored on Swedish territory. In official government announcements, there is no mention of German transports following 20 August. When the issue came to light it was severely criticised by the opposition press. What is more,

---

[37] AAN, Norbert Żaba's collection, classified report by N. Żaba, Stockholm, 5 VIII 1943.
[38] AAN, Norbert Żaba's collection, copy of report by Polish Envoy to Stockholm H. Sokolnicki to the Ministry of Foreign Affairs, Stockholm, 13 III 1943.
[39] A. W. Johansson, *Per Albin...*, p. 331.

thanks to a special agreement, the Germans were permitted to continue flights of their courier aircraft, which maintained contact between Norway and Finland over Sweden. Sweden also allowed the movement of two German postal carriages a day, from Norway to Germany. For Envoy Sokolnicki this was a sign of the government ignoring public opinion. In addition, in August the Germans moved the 25th Panzer Division from Norway to France, indicating that the threat of the attack on Sweden was over, even if more than 300 hundred thousand German soldiers remained in Norway.[40] The Swedish authorities, however, provided humanitarian aid for the Nordic countries occupied by the Germans. In October 1943, the Swedes challenged Berlin over the German policy towards Jews in Norway and Denmark. Subsequently, they would intervene following the arrest of professors and students of Norwegian higher education institutions on 1 December 1943.[41] In the second half of 1943, informal censorship ceased. Interference in the content of the articles published in the Swedish newspapers also ended and the freedom of speech put pressure on the Germans.[42] The German courier flights continued until April 1944, when customs officers discovered strategic maps of Sweden in one of the trains heading to Norway. This discovery was used as a pretext for the termination of the agreement permitting German postal flights over Sweden. Between August and October 1944 the movement of Swedish and German vessels between ports in both countries also gradually came to end.[43]

London maintained that the end of the German transits via Sweden was an appropriate moment to stimulate bilateral political relations. Minister Romer, on 21 August 1943, ordered Envoy Sokolnicki to start talks on postwar cooperation opening with economic issues. Romer did not propose that the discussion with the Swedes include the issue of complete normalisation of diplomatic relations, as he was convinced that 'this should happen somehow automatically as the talks progress.'[44]

New threats, in the shape of excessive submissiveness of the Swedes towards the Soviet Union, were emerging that would regulate mutual political relations. According to an anonymous analyst, 'This process is so careful

---

[40] AAN, Norbert Żaba's collection, copy of report by Polish Envoy to Stockholm H. Sokolnicki to the Ministry of Foreign Affairs, Stockholm, 27 III 1943. Johansson, *Per Albin...*, p. 328.
[41] PISM, A XII, 3/41, classified study *Polityka zagraniczna Szwecji*, Sztokholm, December 1943.
[42] A. W. Johansson, *Per Albin...*, p. 300.
[43] G. Hägglöf, *Svensk...*, p. 300.
[44] AAN, HI/I/305, telegram by Minister of Foreign Affairs T. Romer to Polish Envoy to Stockholm H. Sokolnicki, 21 VIII 1943.

that it is only possible to grasp it behind the scenes of Swedish politics.'[45] Sokolnicki thought opening talks with Sweden about economic issues first was a sound decision, and in a reply to Minister Romer pointed to the difficult situation of the legation as regards the break-up of Polish-Soviet relations. He wrote, 'The Swedish policy towards the USSR [...] is and will be focusing on, as long as possible, avoiding everything that could expose it to the danger of conflict with Russia.' The Swedish government was interested in Stalin's attitude towards Poland and society sympathised with the government in exile, but for the sake of the state, Sweden avoided such matters, as the powers were yet to define their political aims in this respect.[46] Grafström advised avoiding everything that could create an impression that the Polish policy and the moods of Polish society were becoming more anti-Soviet than anti-German under the influence of the approaching Soviet danger, as this could harm the Polish matter in the Swedish territory.[47] According to Polish diplomats, Grafström confirmed the speculation that the Swedes were starting to conduct the policy of concessions to the Soviet Union similar to those conducted towards Germany 1940–41. The Swedish press published numerous articles about the German crimes in the occupied countries. The Poles estimated a greater number than that published in the English press. Whereas, the anti-Soviet commentaries were avoided. Based on expert opinion on Swedish policy, an anonymous Polish analyst predicted that in the near future Sweden would adopt an opportunistic attitude towards the USSR, more so now that Soviet influences were particularly strong in the USA and Great Britain. In Sweden it was now not only the leftist circles that showed sympathies towards the USSR. The industrialists expected that the development of the exchange of goods would bring them economic benefits. The author of the report claimed, 'That is why these circles are inclined towards cooperation with the Soviet Union, and they are even ready to support compromises at the expense of Russia's neighbours.'[48] According to the Press Attaché of the legation of Great Britain, Peter Tennant, the Swedish policy towards the Soviet Union was becoming more submissive than required by the geographical location of Sweden. There were not many supporters of communism in Sweden, but the 'realism which characterises the

---

[45] PISM, A XII, 3/41, study *Polityka zagraniczna Szwecji* (Swedish Foreign Policy), Sztokholm, December 1943.
[46] AAN, HI/I/71, letter by Polish Envoy to Stockholm H. Sokolnicki to the Ministry of Foreign Affairs, Stockholm, 27 VIII 1943.
[47] PISM, A XII, 3/41, study *Polityka zagraniczna Szwecji*, Sztokholm, December 1943.
[48] Ibidem.

Swedish policy and the sense of Sweden's weakness force it – although its attitude towards the Soviet Union is reluctant – to improve its relations with Russia, independently from the changes that would be taking place in the Swedish government.'[49]

By June Żaba had informed Mieczysław Thugutt, 'During the talks with foreigners the Swedes show more and more understanding and sympathy for us, but are nevertheless afraid to raise the Soviet subject.'[50] In September Żaba predicted that Sweden would establish a new political stance towards the Soviet Union:

> The Soviet problem terrifies the Swedes and makes them look to the future with apprehension. In the current situation, they are showing us more understanding, which nevertheless will not result in – knowing the Swedes – them granting us adequately strong and open political support. They will most likely employ the same tactics towards the Soviets as they did towards the Germans at one time – namely that of avoiding everything that would needlessly aggravate relations.[51]

These forecasts were quickly confirmed by the news that following the conclusion of the war the Swedes were ready to grant the Soviet Union a trade loan of 125 million crowns. For Żaba, this was evidence that 'certain Swedish circles are full of illusions when it comes to commercial relations with Russia.'[52]

Sweden's position on the Polish matter (January–July 1944)

In the last days of 1943, Polish intelligence analysts note, 'In the Swedish industrialist circle economic philo-Sovietism took root, which was based on the expectation of a large wave of exports to Russia immediately after the war.'[53] Some Swedish enterprises, like ASEA, were about to start production with the intention of exporting to the USSR. According to Polish experts, Swedish industrialists were convinced that the Soviets would make up their main market as the Allies were not in need of Swedish products and because Europe, now in ruins and led by the Germans, would be insolvent. The new partner searched for in fear of the post-war crisis and unemployment. As well

---

[49] Ibidem.
[50] AAN, Norbert Żaba's collection, letter by N. Żaba to M. Thugutt, Stockholm, 3 XI 1943.
[51] Ibidem, note by N. Żaba, 9 IX 1943.
[52] Ibidem, note by N. Żaba, 22 X 1943.
[53] PISM, A XII, 3/41, note by Colonel S. Gano 'Filosowietyzm w Szwecji' (Sovietophiles in Sweden), 22 XII 1943.

as that, the industrialists managed to persuade the activists of the social democratic party to support the concept of expanding economic contacts with the USSR. Nobody doubted that the USSR would be a dominant force in Eastern Europe.[54] At the same time, Germanophobia was increasingly evident, the evidence for which was the popularity of the anti-German book *Behind the Steel Wall. A Swedish Journalist in Berlin 1941–43*[55] by Arvid Fredborg, where he listed German crimes, and first and foremost the slaughter of 2 million Jews and 1 million Poles.

The course of the October conference in Moscow was followed closely. The Soviet–Polish agreement was expected to be reached under English–American patronage. *Nya Dagligt Allehanda* reported that:

> The Russians have shown their readiness to establish relations with the Polish government in London, which, nonetheless, surely neither means that they have withdrawn their claims nor that they recognise the government of Mikołajczyk [successor of Sikorski] as the future Polish government, all the more so that the latter adamantly defends his position. In connection with the future moving of eastern military operations to the former territory of Poland, the Russians intend to create some kind of modus vivendi, which would save their armies from guerrilla activity at the rear.[57]

The editorial team for *Svenska Dagbladet* expressed their fears that Moscow could become a new Munich, with the only difference that the role of Chamberlain was taken over by Churchill and Roosevelt.[58]

While the conference of the 'Big Three' was taking place in Tehran, Stockholm awaited announcements about proceedings with apprehension. The official statements, however, were a disappointment for the Swedish

---

[54] 'Polens affärer', *Aftontidningen*, 15 XII 1943.
[55] A. Fredborg, *Bakom stålvallen. Som svensk korrespondent i Berlin 1941–43*, Stockholm 1943.
[57] 'Sovjet och Polen', *Nya Dagligt Allehanda*, 23 X 1943.
[58] See 'Lęk przed *Monachium*. Szwedzi o konferencji w Moskwie', *Dziennik Polski*, 16 XI 1943. The Swedes were worried about their future. There were rumours that some concessions have been introduced in the territory of Scandinavia to the benefit of the Soviet Union. For the Allies it was important that Sweden joined the war and they expected intensified pressures in this respect. Indeed, Molotov proposed that the Swedes were forced to give up their air bases to the Allies. The British were less resolute as far as this question was concerned. Churchill wanted Sweden to join the war, but not under compulsion. See L. Leifland, 'They must get in before the end'. 'Churchill och Sverige 1944 och 1945' [in:] *Utrikespolitik och historia. Studier tillagnade Wilhelm M. Carlgren den 6 maj 1987*, Stockholm 1987, pp. 113–143; Churchill Archives Centre, Sir Victor Mallet, *Memoir*, pp. 147A–147D.

press as they were too vague and allowed for much freedom of interpretation.[59] A concern was expressed that the unity of the powers was established at the expense of smaller countries of Eastern Europe, especially Finland.[60] Żaba was under the impression that the Swedish press, in the face of the impasse in Polish–Soviet relations, was waiting for all information from English, American and even Soviet sources, and paid little attention to the Polish news service.[61]

Based on the press announcements from the close of 1943, one may conclude that the Swedish dailies had no unambiguous views on the Polish matters. Periodicals published contradictory texts, and views alternated, in favour of the Polish government or the Soviets at any given time. The causes of the conflict were not completely recognized, but a belief grew that the stalemate would be only resolved by Stalin forcing his position.

At the outset of 1944, the Swedish press published consecutive commentaries due to the crossing of Poland's pre-war border by the Soviet armies. Attention was drawn to the need for the settling of the Polish–Soviet agreement before the Red Army's entrance in to the territory of Poland, because 'the only person that can benefit from and be glad of the exacerbation of the Russian–Soviet conflict is naturally Hitler.' It was known from the start that the Soviet side would dictate the conditions of the agreement.[62] The main commentator for *Dagens Nyheter*, Johannes Wickman, stated disapprovingly that from among the ally governments only the Polish was provoking conflict between its brothers in arms. He noted with clear condemnation that these were the Poles who were setting the conditions of the cooperation with the Soviet Union, which contributed to freeing them from the German oppression. He lacked understanding for the stubbornness of the Polish government in defending their right to the Borderlands, which were conquered by Poland when 'chaos was reigning in Eastern Europe, when Russia was in the midst of its greatest difficulties', and which were mostly inhabited by Ukrainian and Belarusian people who 'were not doing well under the rule of their Polish lords.' What is more, Wickman presented Poland as an aggressive country, traditionally causing problems for Europe, manifested by, according to his

---

[59] AAN, Norbert Żaba's collection, copy of report by N. Żaba to the Ministry of Information and Documentation, Stockholm, 6 III 1943.
[60] Commentaries in *Svenska Dagbladet* from 7 XII 1943.
[61] AAN, Norbert Żaba's collection, copy of report by N. Żaba to the Ministry of Information and Documentation, Stockholm, 16 XI 1943.
[62] PISM, col. 133, vol. 195, report by delegate of the Central Executive Committee of the PPS party M. Karniol, 'Prasa szwedzka o obecnej fazie stosunków polsko-rosyjskich', 14 I 1944. 'Polen än en gång', *Social-Demokraten*, 7 I 1944.

view, the annexations of Vilnius in 1920 and Zaolzie in 1938 as well as the participation in the propagandist Goebbels' game around the Katyń issue.[63] According to Żaba, Wickman's attack on the Polish government was conducted in a decidedly dishonest manner. Such an attitude was explained by Wickman having become a very 'intimate – as it has been reported – guest of the Soviet Legation, and admirer of the Russians as the saviours of Europe.' The Polish attaché nevertheless predicted that this was only the first wave of actions against Poland in Sweden: 'From conversations held during these days by the Press Attaché of the Legation – Pomian – with the heads of political newspapers and Swedish politicians it follows that the management circles are alarmed by the discontentment that has been shown in response to the Swedish policy in Moscow, and which turned out to be impossible to appease, even by the Soviet Envoy, Ms Kollontai. Official and journalist circles, supported by industrial-economic circles, were therefore striving to get back into the good graces of the masters of the Kremlin by acting as lackeys of their propaganda.'[64]

Other Ally diplomats also noticed that Sweden was becoming increasingly friendly towards the Soviet Union. While being satisfied with the defeat of Germany, it showed intolerance towards the Finns, who did not see the need to agree a separate peace with Stalin. The resigning envoy of South Africa, Stephanus Gie, confirmed these opinions, pointing to signs of the growing support of the Swedish political elites for the Allies, together with the upcoming defeat of Germany and ever-diminishing concerns over Soviet expansion. At the same time the new representative of the South Africa, Leif Egeland, following a one-week stay in Stockholm, claimed that Swedish opinion was more rigid than he thought. He generally did not, however, contradict the views of his predecessor over the growing submissiveness of the Swedes towards Stalin. His views were formed based on the talks with Boheman and Söderblom as well as on reading the leading dailies. Boheman, during their first telephone conversation, demonstrated a deep mistrust towards the intentions of the Soviet Union, especially those connected with Poland and Finland. The Swede did not believe in the possibility of establishing an amicable long-term cooperation between the British and the

---

[63] J. Wickman, 'Polens affärer', *Dagens Nyheter*, 9 I 1944; PISM, col. 133, vol. 195, report by the delegate of the Central Executive Committee of the PPS party, M. Karniol, 'Prasa szwedzka o obecnej fazie stosunków polsko-rosyjskich', 14 I 1944.

[64] AAN, Norbert Żaba's collection, copy of report by N. Żaba to the Ministry of Information and Documentation, Stockholm, 12 I 1944.

Americans and Stalin. Against this background, he held a dim view for the future of Germany and predicted that the country would plunge into chaos.⁶⁵

As the conclusion of the war was nearing, the Allies exerted increasing pressure on Sweden to break up the relations with the Germans. The emissaries of the governments of Great Britain and the USA concluded an agreement with SKF (Swedish ball bearing factory AB) 12 June 1944, under which the Swedes obliged themselves to reduce the export of ball bearings to Germany by 60 percent within the next four months.⁶⁶ The forced arrangement was nonetheless beneficial for the Swedish side, because four months later all commercial relations with Germany all but ceased. On a limited scale, the Swedes also started to engage in military cooperation. In the summer of 1944, debris from the V-2 missile that fell on Sweden was given to the British.⁶⁷ In a conversation with Norwegian Foreign Minister Trygve Lie, on 1 November 1944, Prime Minister Hansson permitted an American aircraft to land in Sweden and to the transportation of Norwegian police forces (formed by refugees) to northern Norway on board this aircraft.⁶⁸ The Allies expected that in the last stage of the war Sweden would, despite not wanting to, assist Norway against the large German contingent.⁶⁹ There is no doubt that the desire to maintain best possible relations with the Soviet Union would influence the attitude of the Swedes towards the Polish matter.

Meanwhile in February 1944, the Swedish Chargé d'affaires to Moscow, Ingemar Hägglöf, explained to his superiors in Stockholm that the Soviet Union, from the break-up of relations in April 1943, rejected 'the reactionary

---

⁶⁵ NA, FO, 371/43518, report by the representative of the Union of South Africa in Stockholm, L. Egeland, 23 II 1944.

⁶⁶ G. Hägglöf, *Svensk...*, p. 300.

⁶⁷ On this subject see for instance: H. Denham, *Inside...*, p. 157; R. V. Jones, Most Secret War, Chatham 1997, pp. 430–432; Churchill Archives Centre, Sir Victor Mallet, *Memoir*, pp. 156–158.

⁶⁸ A. W. Johansson, *Per Albin...*, p. 339; K. Åmark, *Att bo granne med ondskan...*, chpt. Svensk flyktingpolitik 1939–1945 (Norrmännen).

⁶⁹ It is worth noting that the Polish press in Great Britain, which until then consistently called neutral Sweden to fight in the camp of the Allies, starting from 1944 entirely changed its attitude towards this issue. What became its point of reference was the expansionism of the Soviet Union, which according to Polish opinion journalists threatened entire Europe, and especially areas neighbouring the Soviets – from Scandinavia in the north to the Balkans in the south. See L. T., 'Czy Szwecji grozi wojna?', *Dziennik Żołnierza APW*, 6 III 1944; T. S., 'Po drugiej stronie Bałtyku', *Dziennik Żołnierza APW*, 20 V 1944; 'Kolej na Szwecję', *Dziennik Żołnierza APW*, 15 III 1945; 'Skutki *torpedowania* Karty Atlantyckiej. Turcja i Szwecja wolą neutralność', *Dziennik Polski i Dziennik Żołnierza*, 30 III 1944. Already at the outset of 1943 Erik Boheman told Mallet, Envoy of Great Britain, that Sweden's policy would be driven exclusively by its own interest and that Sweden would never become engaged in the war. See H. Denham, *Inside.*, p. 56.

and anti-Soviet-oriented emigrant clique from London.'⁷⁰ The Polish matter was becoming increasingly relevant on the international arena due to operations carried out by the Soviet armies in the Polish Borderlands from the outset of 1944. The Polish side hoped that mediation by Western Allies in the dispute with Stalin would take place, but it was becoming increasingly obvious that the future of the neighbours of the Soviet Union would be internal business. Together with the diplomatic offensive, a propagandist campaign against the Polish government in exile took place. The Katyń issue returned, as the Soviet authorities appointed a committee to examine it following the German retreat from Smolensk. On 26 January the committee announced that the Germans were guilty of the crime. Nevertheless, Hägglöf heard from a foreign journalist, who was among those invited to Katyń by the Soviet authorities, that 'the committee presented circumstantial evidence, pointing to the fact that the soldiers whose bodies were examined died no earlier than the autumn of 1941, but no irrefutable evidence was presented to support this claim, instead, gaps in the argumentation were evident.' It was at that moment that Katyń became the symbol of subordination of Poland to the will of Stalin. According to Hägglöf, the Allies lost hope that they would satisfy Stalin by reconstructing the Polish government. The Envoy of Canada in the Soviet Union, Leolyn Dana Wilgress, in conversation with the Swedish diplomat claimed that the commission's report was not accepted by the Polish authorities and announced that Stalin would hold an election in Poland under his control and, following the appointment of parliament, he would set up a government that would be obedient to him. Hägglöf, having made his observations of the relations between the Allies from the perspective of Moscow, concurred with the opinion that despite their contradictory official political declarations, the neighbours of the Soviet Union were becoming part of its sphere of influence.⁷¹

This speculation was confirmed to a large extent by an employee of the usually well-informed Czechoslovak embassy. The representative of Czechoslovakia, most probably Zdeněk Fierlinger, in a conversation with Hägglöf emphasized that the Red Army had been given careful instructions regarding suitable (*korrekt*) conduct towards the Polish people, including respecting their religion and traditions. He also presented a plan for establishing a local administration consisting of Poles, and a temporary high-level administration controlled by the Soviet command, but with the co-participation of

---

⁷⁰ RA, UD 1920 års dossiersystem, HP 1, vol. 486, letter by Swedish Chargé d'affaires to Moscow I. Hägglöf to Minister of Foreign Affairs Ch. Günther, Moscow, 6 II 1944.
⁷¹ Ibidem.

Berling's army (the Polish First Army). Additionally, he claimed that a great propagandist significance was to be attributed to the plan of introducing a radical agricultural reform and division of land, which would grant both the electoral victory to the supporters of close cooperation with the Soviet Union and the appointment of a Moscow-friendly Polish government.[72]

In February 1944 a memorandum was prepared in UD, likely because of internal discussions over the future developments in East-Central Europe. In the summing up, it was highlighted that the Soviet Union would not back down from the well-defined position on the Polish matter. Neither would it permit the debate over the fate of the Baltic States. It was even expected that far-reaching demands would be addressed to Stockholm. Some room for manoeuvre was seen on the question of the future of Finland.[73] Nevertheless, there was optimism regarding Scandinavia surviving the offensive policy of Stalin in Europe unscathed. Such position was presented predominantly by the Swedish Envoy to Moscow, Assarsson.[74]

On 5 March Hägglöf discussed the Polish matter with the ambassador of an English-speaking country, who confirmed the Soviet conditions of establishing relations with the Polish government were the reconstruction of the government, the acceptance of the border along the Curzon Line and the Soviet interpretation of the Katyń Massacre. At the same time, it became obvious that the Poles had toughened their position and that Polish–Soviet relations had reached a critical point. It was probable that Stalin would create a subordinate Polish government in the territories annexed by the Soviet armies. However, the Anglo-Saxon diplomat excluded the possibility of the incorporation of Poland into the USSR.[75] Such a vision of Poland's future was increasingly regarded in Stockholm as the inevitable scenario. Reports from Moscow were intensified by the anti-Polish propagandist campaign conducted by the Soviet diplomatic services. The attacks targeted at the London government took the shape of an organized action. Żaba explained:

> Unexpectedly, there flared up a violent anti-Polish campaign in the part of the Swedish press that remained under the influence of Soviet propaganda on the subject of the Russian claims towards the eastern territories of Poland. The

---

[72] RA, UD 1920 års dossiersystem, HP 1, vol. 486, letter by Swedish chargé d'affaires to Moscow I. Hägglöf to S. Söderblom, Moscow, 15 III 1944.
[73] RA, UD 1920 års dossiersystem, HP 1, vol. 520, pro memoria, Stockholm, 25 II 1944 r.
[74] Ibidem, report by Swedish Envoy to Moscow V. Assarsson submitted to the Riksdag's Commission of Foreign Affairs on 29 II 1944.
[75] RA, UD 1920 års dossiersystem, HP 1, vol. 486, memorandum by Swedish Chargé d'affaires to Moscow I. Hägglöf, Moscow, 6 III 1944.

synchronisation and orchestration of these attacks prove that the Soviet Legation inspired the work of several opinion journalists who have been at its service for a long time [...].[76]

The campaign was consequently conducted by the communist *Ny Dag* daily, which published the virulent 'Panic among Polish Landowners' on 7 January 1944. It was alleged that the Polish government withdrew the Anders' Army [the Polish Armed Forces in the East] from the Soviet Union so as to avoid offering help to the Red Army.[77] The Home Army was accused of helping the Germans for a long time. Whereas on 18 January 1944 an accusation was cast that, 'the Poles of London, instead of fighting Hitler, are planning imperialist conquests at the expense of the greatest opponent of Hitlerism' while being famous only for withdrawing their armies from the front and from propagandist collaboration with the Germans.[78] On 8 January, an attack was launched by *Göteborgs Handels- och Sjöfarts-Tidning*, where the Polish government was criticised for, 'its awful obstinacy regarding the issue of the borders places obstacles on the Allies' way to victory and helps the Germans to break-up the coalition', and after all 'the lands to which Russia makes its claims, are Russian, the Poles have always been an alien element in these lands, they oppressed the indigenous people who awaited the Russians like one awaits one's saviour.' An opinion journalist of a newspaper famous for its anti-German attitude added, 'The blame for the break-up of the diplomatic relations between Russia and Poland lies on the side of Poland and the world cannot understand the madness that has overcome the Poles.'[79] One month later the same journalist predicted, 'the Polish–Soviet border dispute will become the subject of negotiations between the republics of Ukraine and Belarus on the one hand and Poland on the other, whereas Russia would play the role of mediator.'[80] These examples are typical of many Swedish statements about the Polish–Soviet dispute.

The representative of the Ukrainians, who were fighting for their own independent country, was against the Poles. In 1943 the head of the Ukrainian Information Bureau in Helsinki, Bohdan Kentrschynskyj, who was born in

---

[76] AAN, Norbert Żaba's collection, copy of report by Polish Envoy to Stockholm H. Sokolnicki to the Ministry of Information and Documentation, Stockholm, 12 I 1944, a similar report: AAN, HI/I/80, letter by Polish Envoy to Stockholm H. Sokolnicki to the Ministry of Foreign Affairs, Stockholm, 12 I 1944.
[77] 'Panik bland de polska godsägarna', *Ny Dag*, 7 I 1944.
[78] 'Polens affärer', *Ny Dag*, 18 I 1944.
[79] 'Situationen', *Göteborgs Handels- och Sjöfarts-Tidning*, 8 I 1944.
[80] 'Idag', *Göteborgs Handels- och Sjöfarts-Tidning*, 8 II 1944.

Równe in 1919 and was a member of the Organization of Ukrainian Nationalists (a faction supporting Andrij Melnyk), published the book *Sanningen om Ukraina* (The Truth about Ukraine) in Swedish, where he argued that Ukraine, which stands out against other countries thanks to its coal mining, as well as grain and sugar beet production, could be a politically and economically sovereign country. Kentrschynskyj accused mostly the Russians and the Poles of having oppressed the Ukrainian nation for a long time and preventing it from peaceful development. He wrote that Poland was a country dreaming of grandeur and colonies, although its internal relations were not regulated, its economy was disorganized (industry and commerce were mostly in foreign hands), it was lacking political unity, appropriate roads and railway lines, had an insufficient number of schools, was wrestling with the problem of high illiteracy rates and had only one port along more than fifty kilometres of coastline. He confirmed that the Ukrainians from eastern Galicia started to develop their cultural educational and economic life only after being incorporated by the Germans in to the General Government. In his view, although acting legally in the interest of independence was forbidden, the Ukrainians were closer to making their dreams come true than at any time before, as their main enemies, the Russians and the Poles, were weakened.[81] In October 1943, he was contacted by the representative of the Polish intelligence service in Stockholm. Kentschynskyj, in a conversation with the Polish agent, declared confidentially, 'the nationalists connected with Melnyk wish that Poland not return West Ukraine to the Soviets. Leaving these lands within the limits of Poland based on the concept of federation or very wide-ranging autonomy they consider to be the lesser evil.' He would also to add that the Poles were 'more liberal and weaker than the Muscovites.'[82] He proposed that exchanging insults should be stopped, although he warned that he 'will continue to repeat loudly that Poland and Russia are at odds not over their own lands but over the Ukrainian ones.'[83] He presented similar views towards the end of 1944 in a conversation with Żaba, when he criticised the Western Allies for their indifference towards the plans of Stalin to introduce a Soviet hegemony in Europe. According to Żaba, such stance could have been used for the purposes of the propaganda.

---

[81] B. Kentrschynskyj, *Sanningen om Ukraina*, Helsingfors 1943, pp. 133–134, 152, 205–206.
[82] Quoted after: Cz. Partacz, K. Łada, *Polska wobec ukraińskich dążeń niepodległościowych w czasie II wojny światowej*, Toruń 2004, pp. 162–163.
[83] PISM, A 11, 85/b/18, letter by Polish Envoy to Stockholm H. Sokolnicki to the Ministry of Foreign Affairs, Stockholm, 10 II 1944.

Nevertheless, no traces of such attempts have ever been found.[84] According to Envoy Sokolnicki, Kentrschynskyj was a second-rate individual, or even possibly a German instigator.[85] That is why the Polish Legation in Stockholm insisted that there was no Ukrainian representation in Sweden.[86] On the one hand, Kentrschynskyj denied the announcements of the Soviet propaganda that Ukrainians wanted to join the Soviet Union, and, on the other hand, openly refuted the announcements of the Polish propaganda that they would prefer to become citizens of the Second Polish Republic.

A typical polemic on the subject of Polish border claims, based mostly on the defence of the integrity of Second Polish Republic, was published in the pro-Ally *Trots Allt!*. Józefa Armfelt, a Swede with Polish roots, protested calling Vilnius the capital of Lithuania. She pointed out that Lithuanians made up a small minority of the residents of Vilnius. Her anonymous adversary argued that the Poles had performed an armed annexation of Vilnius in 1920, and although the inhabitants of the city were Polish speakers this did not mean that they were Poles. In another article Armfelt proved that General Żeligowski rather than enslaving Vilnius in 1920, was liberating it, and that the Poles claimed no rights whatsoever to 'the proper Lithuania.' The discussion was joined by Ludwika Plater-Ankarhall, pre-war resident of Vilnius and official of the Polish Legation in Stockholm. She accused the Lithuanians of extermination operations against Jews and Poles, whose aim was to make the Vilnius region Lithuanian by means of the Gestapo and the Waffen-SS methods.[87]

Of the numerous articles that were unfavourable towards Poland a few were published, the authors of which attempted to remain objective. In the Swedish language daily *Huvudstadsbladet* from Helsinki, it was stated that, 'the incorporation of eastern Poland into the Soviet Union in 1939 was a conquest.'[88] *Svenska Morgonbladet* daily claimed that the law was on the Polish side and that it was unacceptable to settle questions of borders with violence and so one-sidedly. From Poland's point of view, as well, an alliance which

---

[84] AAN, Norbert Żaba's collection, copy of letter by N. Żaba to the Ministry of Information and Documentation, Stockholm, 20 XII 1944.
[85] PISM, A 11, 85/b/18, letter by Polish Envoy to Stockholm H. Sokolnicki to the Ministry of Foreign Affairs, Stockholm, 10 II 1944.
[86] Ibidem, telegram by F. Frankowski to the Polish Legation in Washington, 18 I 1944 r.
[87] J. Armfelt, 'Var finns Wilnos litauer? En fråga till Signaturen – son', *Trots Allt!*, 18 VIII 1944; eadem, 'Polen–Litauen. En replik', *Trots Allt!*, 8 IX 1944; L. Plater-Ankarhall, 'Fakta om Polen–Litauen', *Trots Allt!*, 22 IX 1944.
[88] 'Det polska ägoskiftet', *Hufvudstadsbladet*, 12 I 1944.

allowed for the annexing of half of its territory by one of the allies seemed peculiar.[89] Journalists for *Svenska Dagbladet* were of a similar opinion.[90]

From the outset of 1944 the Polish matter became an important subject of debate in the intellectual periodical *Svensk Tidskrift*. It was noted that history did not decide which border between Poland and the Soviet Union would be fair. At the same time, looking at the matter from a realist point of view, it was predicted that future depended on the military situation. The obvious advantage of the Soviet Union and the continuation of 'the diplomacy' of Ivan the Terrible left no room for illusions. Only the Western Allies could apply political pressure and stop Stalin's expansion, while bandying about with the argument of cooperation in the rebuilding of the Soviet Union. At the close of June 1944, it was expected that Stalin would appoint the new Polish government, which would administer the territories annexed by the Soviet army. Hopes were continuously expressed that the Anglo-Saxon Allies would engage in the Polish matter and treat it as a European matter.[91]

The Poles persevered with their point of view. On 28 January, Karniol gave an interview to the social democratic *Morgon-Tidningen* daily, where he presented a conciliatory position towards the Soviet Union. At the same time, he emphasised that one should not blame those Poles who did not want to lose half of their territory. He explained that the Polish government had developed a programme of radical social and political reforms and anticipated the introduction of autonomy for national minorities.[92] Adam Ciołkosz, in his letter from London, praised the publication. He said the article was excellent, though he warned Karniol that, 'in no event may we even create the slightest impression that we have assumed nationalist or imperialist positions.' This was a fervent highlighting of the following view: 'We are defending democracy, self-determination and respect for international law – this is

---

[89] 'Ryssarna i Polen ett nytt allierat problem', *Svenska Morgonbladet*, 5 I 1944; 'Polen hoppas på sin frihet genom Sovjet', *Svenska Morgonbladet*, 7 I 1944; 'Ångvält i gång', *Svenska Morgonbladet*, 10 I 1944; 'Öster om Bug', *Svenska Morgonbladet*, 1 II 1944.

[90] 'Problemet Polen-Sovjet mycket svårt', *Svenska Dagbladet*, 7 I 1944; 'Ryssland på framryckning', *Svenska Dagbladet*, 9 I 1944; 'Polska exilregeringens enda chans, tror London', *Svenska Dagbladet*, 12 I 1944; 'Tyskt land i kompensation erbjuder Sovjet åt Polen', *Svenska Dagbladet*, 12 I 1944.

[91] Dagens frågor: 'Skuggor över Polen', *Svensk Tidskrift*, 27 I 1944; 'Ryssland, Polen och Atlantdeklarationen', *Svensk Tidskrift*, marzec 1944; 'Dagens frågor: S. W., Ryssland–Polen och Sosnkowski än en gång', *Svensk Tidskrift*, 7 VI 1944; 'Dagens frågor: S. W., Tillpolskryska frågan', *Svensk Tidskrift*, 28 X 1944.

[92] 'Hemligt parlament leder Polens öden', *Morgon-Tidningen*, 28 I 1944; PISM, col. 133, vol. 297, letter by M. Karniol no. 154, Stockholm, 19 II 1944.

our stand, in agreement with our tradition and deepest conviction.'[93] The position of the Polish government and the PPS was explicit and proved that 'the road to the agreement with Russia leads not only through Russia's resignation from the acquisitions it owes to the agreement with Hitler.'[94] *Svenska Dagbladet* and *Sydsvenska Dagbladet Snällposten* published an interview with Prime Minister Mikołajczyk on 10 February, which was prepared by Norbert Żaba for the Swedish press on the basis of the conversation they had during his stay in London on 27 January 1944. When speaking to Żaba, Mikołajczyk declared that the entire nation would fight for independence. He explained that the Polish government wanted Poland to be a democratic country and that it had the support of Polish citizens for its social and political programme. He also confirmed the willingness for an agreement with the Soviet Union.[95] Despite the energetic reaction, the Soviet propaganda put the Polish information services on the defensive. They were forced to straighten out opinions, also prevalent in Sweden, that the Polish government was reactionary, showed no will to reach an agreement, was hostile towards the Soviet Union and that the Poles were traditionally quarrelsome. The dominance of the pro-Soviet orientation in the Swedish media was becoming increasingly visible. The development of this trend was emphasized by the emigrant Lithuanian political activist and diplomat Ignaz Scheynius. In a conversation with one of the Poles, he stated that the phenomenon was a result of the Swedes' opportunism and their hope for establishing economic relations with the Soviet Union following the war. From the information he possessed, it followed that the Swedish dailies were pro-Soviet-oriented in principle. Whereas, articles, in the case of *Svenska Dagbladet* and *Nya Dagligt Allehanda*, which were not in line with this trend, were not published.[96]

Another issue that complicated Polish–Swedish relations appeared on the political horizon, namely a different perception of the course of the Polish–German border as well as of the German future. The issue, which had been recognised some time earlier, was even more prominent in informal discussions and public debate.

At the turn of 1943 and 1944, the staff of the Polish Legation in Stockholm was told of the visit of high-ranking German Catholic and Protestant priests

---

[93] PISM, col. 133, vol. 296, copy of letter by A. Ciołkosz to M. Karniol, London, 1 III 1944.
[94] Ibidem, copy of letter by A. Ciołkosz to M. Karniol, London, 14 III 1944.
[95] 'Polen i dag en enda underjordisk stat', *Svenska Dagbladet*, 10 II 1944; 'Polen redo att bekämpa attentat mot sin frihet', *Sydsvenska Dagbladet Snällposten*, 10 II 1944.
[96] AAN, Norbert Żaba's collection, copy of note by N. Żaba to the Continental Action, Stockholm, 9 X 1944.

and their talks with Minister Günther among others. According to Sokolnicki, 'The purpose of this visit was to re-examine the possibility to appoint a temporary government in Germany, following the collapse of Nazi regime, composed of the members of ecclesiastical institutions.'[97] According to the first secretary of the legation, Wiesław Patek, 'the flexible-neutral politics of Sweden [...] would be increasingly open in seeking to counter-balance the growing Soviet power manifested in the attempts to save the remains of the German forces from their complete break-up by the Anglo-Saxons.' Patek also added: 'The democratic Germany is a term to which the Swedish policy would return increasingly often due to the existing – despite all the Norwegian protests and resolutions of cultural associations – common origin of the German nation.'[98] Wiesław Patek's reports presented a clear picture of Swedish politicians who were anti-Hitlerian, but who cultivated pro-German traditions at the same time. The information concerning a secret meeting of clerics from various countries in a villa near Stockholm was characteristic. The Germans tried to insist that it was the Nazi regime only that was responsible for the outbreak and the course of the war, and that German society was innocent. The opinion of the representatives of other nations was different: 'The issue of the collective blame of the German nation was put forward by the Norwegians and the Danes, whereas the Swedes seemed to be compassionate towards the poor Germans, who had not only the allies but all of Europe against them. The Englishman's position was that of an objective observer.'[99] In addition, the rumours were repeated about setting up units of Hitler's opponents, the so-called good Germans, since – as the Polish Legation discovered – nearby Norrköping a course in ideology was launched for several dozen German deserters under Robert Myrdal's supervision.[100]

The opinions which were heard only in the behind-the-scenes' conversations of diplomats gradually started to filter into the press. On 18 March an article by Josef Hofbauer appeared in *Arbetet* that was 'a typical example of the anti-Polish attitude of the German expatriates who are already in the

---

[97] AAN, HI/I/40, letter by Polish Envoy to Stockholm H. Sokolnicki to the Ministry of Foreign Affairs (together with attachment), Stockholm, 29 I 1944.
[98] Ibidem, report by first secretary of the Polish Legation in Stockholm W. Patek to the Ministry of Foreign Affairs, Stockholm, 27 I 1944.
[99] Ibidem, report by first secretary of the Polish Legation in Stockholm W. Patek to the Ministry of Foreign Affairs, Stockholm, 24 III 1944.
[100] Ibidem, note by the Ministry of Foreign Affairs, Stockholm, 27 X 1944.

course developing an active campaign in the defence of the new Reich.'[101] Hofbauer rejected all arguments supporting the incorporation of East Prussia, Pomerania and Silesia into Poland. He also warned, 'Following such a solution of the German issue, millions of Germans, expelled from their homes, would flock to Germany and call for revenge, making it impossible for the German pacifists to work on the re-education of the German nation.' He also admitted, 'an immense injustice is inflicted upon the Poles but why are they doing the same to the Germans?' His protest at the relocation of the western border of Poland was unusually emotional:

> Are there other reasons that would justify these claims than the lust for power? The Russians are explaining that this is about the territories that once belonged to Poland and which were taken away from it and Germanised. So then, does Poland have the right to East Prussia, Pomerania and Silesia? Maybe it has such a right, just like Denmark to England, on account of the fact that 900 years ago it was reigned by Cnut the Great.[102]

In turn, another expatriate, Immanuel Birnbaum, argued in *Svensk Tidskrift* that dividing the German lands before the conclusion of the war intensified the resistance of the German armies and excluded the battle of democratic forces of the Third Reich against Hitler.[103]

In connection with such actions, efforts were made to inspire texts that would be beneficial for Poland. In April 1944 *Mellanfolkligt Samarbete* magazine published 'The Issue of East Prussia' by John Walterson. The author highlighted that putting the territory of East Prussia in Polish hands would not compensate for lost territories in the east. He had no illusions, however, that it would end up within the territory of Poland. He pointed to economic reasons and a natural Polish base for east-Prussian farming. Moreover, he stated that, 'The Masurians [...] should be considered Poles, just like Bavarians and Saxons are German.' He also noted, 'the results of the referendum on 11 June 1920, devoted mostly to the Polish people, were mostly to the benefit of the Germans, but one should remember that voting

---

[101] AAN, Norbert Żaba's collection, copy of report by N. Żaba to the Ministry of Information and Documentation, Stockholm, 31 V 1944.
[102] J. Hofbauer, 'Polen och den tyska Östern', *Arbetet*, 18 III 1944.
[103] I. Birnbaum, 'Om Ostpreussens öden', *Svensk Tidskrift*, December 1944. Birnbaum with satisfaction quoted the neutral Swedish historian Nils Ahnlund, who was famous for his restrained evaluations and who on 27 October 1944 in the article 'Kompensationspolitik i öster' ('Compensation Politics in the East') in the *Svenska Dagbladet* presented his opposition to the claim of incorporating East Prussia into Poland.

was conducted when Poland was at war with the Soviet Union and the circumstances were not favourable for expressing objective opinions.' Walterson also added, 'It is beyond any doubt that separating East Prussia from the Reich would create safer conditions for the existence of Poland.' He summed up, 'in the interest of the future peace it is necessary to solve international problems fairly and thoughtfully.'[104]

Attaché Żaba planned to expand the action of creating the most beneficial atmosphere possible around Poland. He was reaching for diverse propagandist methods, and not only press publications. In May 1944 in Gothenburg, a screening took place of short Polish films.[105] In June, Żaba had taken the initiative of organising a large exhibition in Stockholm presenting the history of Poland with a particular emphasis on the achievements that followed the regaining of independence.[106] He also maintained contacts with Swedish radio to promote musical pieces of Polish composers.[107]

In March 1944 Żaba informed London, 'A number of articles have been published lately in the Swedish press presenting the Polish–Soviet issue in a positive light'. He particularly favoured 'Russia, England and Poland' an article published in *Trots Allt!*. The author analysed the Polish–Soviet dispute from the point of view of Swedish interests,

> It is not particularly interesting for Sweden whether the Polish–Russian border be settled 100 kilometres farther or closer eastwards, but it is Churchill's motifs that are depressing. Firstly, he did not say a word about examining the views of people of the discussed lands, and by doing so he violated the provisions of the Atlantic Charter. [...] And secondly, his attitude towards strategic reasons is astounding. Against whom should Russia be protected in the west? Against a considerably weakened Poland, which has not attacked Russia for hundreds of years, and which numerous times fell victim to Russian attacks? Or maybe this is about protection against the Germans, who will be defeated and helpless, with

---

[104] J. Walterson, 'Problemet Ostpreussen', *Mellanfolkligt Samarbete* 1944, no. 2; AAN, HI/I/40, letter by Polish Envoy to Stockholm H. Sokolnicki to the Ministry of Foreign Affairs (together with attachment), Stockholm, 28 IV 1944.

[105] AAN, HI/I/215, letter by Press Attaché of the Polish Legation in Stockholm N. Żaba to the Ministry of Information and Documentation (together with attachment), 23 V 1944.

[106] AAN, HI/I/221, report by Press Attaché of the Polish Legation in Stockholm N. Żaba to the Ministry of Information and Documentation Stockholm, 30 VI 1944. The exhibition was probably never organized.

[107] AAN, HI/I/214, confidential report by Press Attaché N. Żaba to the Ministry of Information and Documentation, Stockholm, 17 III 1944.

ruined cities and destroyed industry, without the possibility of rebuilding for several generations?[108]

For the author of the article, the course of the Polish–Soviet dispute was evidence for the fact that, in the future, force would continue to mean more in Europe than the law. This should nevertheless be of interest to the citizens of Sweden:

> We consider Finland our entrenchment. Poland is a no less important entrenchment for Sweden. History has proven that Finland was attacked only when Poland was unable to defend itself. For this reason, Sweden, for its own safety, needs – to use the words of Churchill – a strong, integral and independent Poland.

According to Żaba, what contributed to the change in attitude of the Swedish commentators was the development of Finnish–Soviet relations. Many dailies, which had condemned the policy of the Polish government, now defended it. Counsellor Pilch, who scolded Söderblom, head of the Political department of the Swedish Ministry of Foreign Affairs, for the negative attitude of part of the press towards Poland, heard, 'it is not in the interest of Sweden to weaken Poland, and same goes for the Swedish press' negative comments on the subject of Polish problems.' Żaba did not believe that the local Ministry of Foreign Affairs, owing to a somewhat opportunist trend in Swedish foreign policy, had instructed the press to treat the Polish authorities in London kindly. Whereas, of great importance was that the representatives of the ministry did not apply any pressure to stop all actions 'with a certain anti-Soviet tinge.'[109] All the more so that the subject of Polish–Soviet relations did not disappear from the press.

On 8 March, *Göteborgs Handels- och Sjöfarts-Tidning* published a telegram from a London correspondent, who explained, 'the Russian government has lost hope for ending the conflict about the border with the current Polish government.' And, in addition, after the order for the Home Army's cooperation with the Red Army was issued, 'following the urgent examination of Sosnkowski's speech, all doubts were dispelled in Moscow as far as the true intentions of Poles were concerned.'[110] In April 1944, Marika Stiernstedt

---

[108] 'Ryssland, England och Polen', *Trots Allt!*, 3–9 III 1944.
[109] AAN, Norbert Żaba's collection, copy of letter by N. Żaba to the Ministry of Information and Documentation, Stockholm, 14 III 1944.
[110] 'Ingen polsk-rysk uppgörelse utan regeringsförändring', *Göteborgs Handels- och Sjöfarts-Tidning*, 8 III 1944.

published two feature articles in *Svenska Dagbladet* from memoirs of childhood in the Eastern Borderlands. She denied that all the Poles who lived in these territories were landowners or that the relations with Belarusian people were hostile and the clergy had an unfavourable influence on the people. She saw the chance for the agreement between the Poles and the Soviets, but pointed out, 'If these are the Soviets who really want to reach an agreement with Poland, it is they who should take the first step in this direction, which is the privilege of the stronger party.' She also underlined that Poland had no other choice than to live in agreement with its eastern neighbour.[111]

The recurring and perhaps the strongest arguments put forward by the Poles were the contributions of Polish soldiers in the fight with the Germans and the nation's suffering under the brutal occupation. On 29 February 1944, *Dagens Nyheter* made use of the *Polska Nyheter* bulletin, prepared by Karniol, and published a note that, the title of which highlighted the disappearance of 3 million Poles from the territory of the General Government, could shock the Swedish reader.[112] At the same time, accusations towards the Poles of cooperation with the Germans were denied owing to information about the successful assassination of the leader of the Warsaw SS and police, Franz Kutschera. Swedish newspapers published reports about this event, mostly in the form of sensational stories. On 13 May, *Morgon-Tidningen* published an article about the fate of Polish women in concentration camps, the hunger, disease and medical experiments.[113] Following the Soviet armies' entering into the territory of General Government, numerous reports poured in discussing the painful traces of German rule. In August 1944, *Ny Dag* published a long and shocking description of German crimes in the Lublin district. The account included gruesome descriptions of crematoria, gas chambers and warehouses with clothes and shoes of the murdered people.[114]

At the outset of June, reviews appeared for *The Last Jew from Poland* by Stefan Szende. Żaba reviewed the book positively, despite criticism of some passages. The author, a journalist sympathizing with communism, had a bad

---

[111] M. Siernstedt, 'Polsk-ryska minnen', *Svenska Dagbladet*, 8 IV 1944; eadem, 'Polen och Ryssland', *Svenska Dagbladet*, 13 IV 1944.
[112] 'Tre miljoner polacker försvann under kriget', *Dagens Nyheter*, 29 II 1944.
[113] 'Polska kvinnotragedier i koncentrationsläger', *Morgon-Tidningen*, 13 V 1944. On the next day, the newspaper, still pursuing the feminine subject, published an extensive panegyrical article about 'female writer, minister of foreign affairs and honourable colonel of the Red Army' Wanda Wasilewska, see: C.-H. af Klintberg, 'Wanda Wasilevska', *Morgon-Tidningen*, 14 V 1944.
[114] AAN, Norbert Żaba's collection, copy of report by N. Żaba to the Ministry of Information and Documentation, 22 IX 1944 (*Ny Dag*, 19 VIII 1944).

reputation in the Polish Legation. Szende described the occupation in Poland through the eyes of Adolf Folkman, an escapee from the Lviv ghetto. He focused on the persecution of the Jews by the Germans and Polish blackmailers. Alongside that, the author accused the pre-war authorities of mistreating national minorities, underestimating the Soviet Union and resorting to Hitler's foreign and internal policy.[115] The reviewer expressed the opinion that the nation which performed the crimes described by Szende was on the margin of culture.[116] At the same time, the book *Landet utan Quisling* (The Country without Quisling) was published by the author under the pseudonym Stefan Tadeusz Norwid. In fact, the publication was the result of cooperation between a refugee from occupied Poland, Stefan Trębicki, and Tadeusz Nowacki, who wrote down his account. Trębicki came to Sweden on 8 August 1943 hidden on a coal vessel. It was not until 1944 that he could speak in public as a witness of the events that had taken place in the General Government. It was difficult to convince the Swedish audience that the tragedy was real. It ought to have been enough to mention that even Attaché Brzeskwiński, and his wife, did not accept news of the mass murders of Jews perpetrated by Germans about which Trębicki spoke. Żaba commented:

> Should we be surprised that foreigners do not always believe in our words? Today people believe less in the written word than in the testimonies of an eye witness, about which propaganda needs to remember. We also need to offer the journalists an opportunity to speak with the people who have come from the country and take them to meetings and lectures.[117]

At the outset of July 1944, German refugee Ernst Pfleging published *Det Tyska Storrumet* (The German Grossraum), documenting the system of legislation in the occupied territories. Pfleging demonstrated calmly and precisely that the Germans were striving to exterminate the Poles, resorting to the death sentence on any pretext.[118]

---

[115] S. Szende, *Den siste juden från Polen*, Stockholm 1944, pp. 5–6, 135, 140–141. See reactions of attaché Żaba: AAN, Norbert Żaba's collection, copy of report by N. Żaba to the Ministry of Information and Documentation, Stockholm, 30 VI 1944.
[116] 'Situationen', *Göteborgs Handels- och Sjöfarts-Tidning*, 2 VI 1944.
[117] AAN, Norbert Żaba's collection, report by N. Żaba, Stockholm, 28 VIII 1943. As writes A. N. Uggla, *Den svenska Polenbilden...*, pp. 29–30, one of the reviewers even stated that: 'We cannot believe this. This is a lie, a lie of the English propaganda. If it was about Russia, the case would be different. But after all the Germans are an enlightened (*upplyst*) nation. They do not make such shameful deeds'.
[118] AAN, HI/I/226, letter by Polish Envoy to Stockholm H. Sokolnicki to the Ministry of Foreign Affairs, Stockholm, 9 VII 1944.

Gunnar Almstedt was, according to Norbert Żaba, one of the most intelligent Swedish journalists. For some time he was employed in the Press Department of the Legation of Great Britain. Almstedt, in agreement with Żaba, prepared a series of five articles '*Dagligt liv i Polen*' ('Everyday Life in Poland'). These were based on the materials obtained from Żaba or owing to the interviews he facilitated. On the basis of conversations with refugees from the General Government, the author described the German policy of extermination, the fights with Polish culture and education, the development of the Polish resistance movement, the round-ups, and system of imprisonment. Almstedt's interlocutors convinced him that the nation supported the Polish government in exile, and that Moscow controlled the communist movement.[119] From June 1944, the texts appeared simultaneously in nineteen provincial periodicals. Afterwards, Żaba would to publish them as a brochure. The articles came from the account of Henryk Pawliszyn ('Henryk Ostoja'), a refugee who fought in the resistance movement, and in March 1944 left Warsaw. On 21 June, in the article 'I Cannot Forget…' , Żaba quoted Polish women who had escaped forced labour sites in Norway and told him about the status of women in occupied Poland.[120] They told of the obligation to work, constant street round-ups, limitations in electricity consumption and travel, and about crimes which 'in the civilized world […] are encountered only in protocols concerning more severe sexual crimes, described at court hearings, but only those on camera.' In 'One Buys Their Own Life on the Black Market', the author highlighted that food rations 'are too small to keep one alive, and therefore a Pole either needs to resort to illegal trade or die.'[121] He quoted prices of basic products converted into Swedish crowns. The conclusion was simple, everything was remarkably expensive and that is why everyone was trading in order to increase their income, in spite of the fact that doing so could not only bring the confiscation of goods but also severe reprisals from the Germans. Pawliszyn, independently from the series published by Almstedt, also gave interviews to various Swedish dailies, which created the basis for subsequent publications about occupied Warsaw.[122]

---

[119] G. Almstedt, *Dagligt liv i Polen*, Ängleholm 1944. The review of Almstedt's articles was published in the London press: 'W Szwecji o Polsce Podziemnej. Cztery artykuły Gunnara Almstedta', *Dziennik Polski i Dziennik Żołnierza*, 13 VII 1944.
[120] AAN, HI/I/102, translation of the article by G. Almstedt.
[121] Ibidem, translation of the article by G. Almstedt, attachment to letter by Press Attaché N. Żaba to the Ministry of Information and Documentation, Stockholm, 1 IX 1944.
[122] Ibidem, letter by Press Attaché of the Polish Legation in Stockholm N. Żaba to the Ministry of Information and Documentation (together with attachment), Stockholm, 9 VIII 1944.

6. SWEDEN'S RETURN TO STRICT NEUTRALITY

On 6 July, *Göteborgs Handels- och Sjöfarts-Tidning* a former correspondent of Italian periodicals, Mario Vanni, published the accounts of three Poles who escaped to Sweden. The Swedish reader learned about the round-ups, strictly observed curfews, burning down villages, lack of medication and hunger. Vanni highlighted:

> This hellish life is everyday life. Apart from this, active fighters of the underground movement are living in constant danger. Each of them carries poison, as they would rather die than be tortured and humiliated in German prisons. The Poles, surrounded and tracked down for the last five years, constantly in danger, and suffering innumerable torments, have not failed. Deprived of everything, forced numerous times to live in indignity, they have never decided to "cooperate". Their patriotism is so great that no Quisling would be tolerated by them, even for a moment.[123]

The Polish propaganda exposed the merits of defeating Germany and proved that the government in London was democratic and constituted the only real representation of the nation. On 4 April, Karniol gave a lecture on the Polish underground movement in the Swedish Social Democratic Youth League (*SSU*), and on 5 and 11 May in other locations in Stockholm. On 15 June, invited by the Commission for Foreign Affairs, he spoke about the Polish matter in front of Swedish parliament, which was the first case in the history of a Pole taking the floor in the *Riksdag* (excluding a speech in the plenary chamber).[124] In June 1944, Karniol concluded an agreement with the social democratic magazine *Aftontidningen*, which started to publish the news broadcast by the secret radio station *Świt*. The station was in London, but pretended to operate in occupied Poland in defiance of the Germans. As a result, news about guerrilla fights in the Borderlands was announced on 22 June[125] and on 3 June news broke of the victories achieved by Polish partisans. At the same time, news was published that the Germans were transporting thousands of Hungarian Jews to Auschwitz for immediate execution.[126] News began to pour in about the evacuation of Vilnius by the Germans and the announcement of the city's annexation by the Soviet armies. The appeal of the representative of the Polish government in exile called for a peaceful and

---

[123] M. Vanni, 'Det dagliga livet i Polen', *Göteborgs Handels- och Sjöfarts-Tidning*, 6 VII 1944.
[124] PISM, col. 133, vol. 195, report by M. Karniol no. 174, Stockholm, 14 VII 1944.
[125] Ibidem, note by M. Karniol no. 177, Stockholm, 18 VII 1944.
[126] 'Switrapport om stor drabbning', *Aftontidningen*, 3 VII 1944; IPMS, col. 133, vol. 195, note by M. Karniol no. 179, Stockholm, 20 VII 1944; 'Massavrättningar dagligen i Polen av ungerska judar', *Aftontidningen*, 3 VII 1944; PISM, col. 133, vol. 195, note by M. Karniol no. 178, Stockholm, 18 VII 1944.

friendly attitude towards the approaching army and for the setting up of a local administration.[127] However, when Prime Minister Mikołajczyk described Vilnius as a Polish city, *Svenska Dagbladet* described his utterance as unfortunate as the chances of the Polish government reaching an agreement with Stalin were so slight.[128] Subsequent reports brought news of the intensification of the Polish sabotage campaign on the railway, attacks on prisons and Gestapo officers.[129] The magazine *Murarnas Fackblad* on 5 May 1944 published 'The Polish Nation is United.' In the article it was highlighted, 'The only basis of the agreement [with Stalin] is the treaty of Riga', and 'Russia needs to resign from the acquisitions it made with help from Hitler.' The text was produced based on the Swedish version of a bulletin by the PPS.[130] In another article Jacob de Geer rejected the frequent accusations of anti-Semitism directed at the Poles. He explained that the attitude of the Poles towards the Jews was far from the slogans of Nazi ideology. He highlighted that one may criticise the Polish government in London for its ineptitude, but one may not deny that it was a coalition of all the main political parties. He stated with sympathy, 'What we see here is a great, strong and courageous nation, which is treated by the vile soldiery like a defenceless animal.'[131]

On summing up the review of the Polish publications in the Swedish press in June 1944, Żaba stated optimistically, 'the balance of references to and articles about Poland [...] was extremely positive.'[132] In June, efforts to convey a positive message about the politics of the Polish government were continued. Karniol advances the information bulletin he had produced. Based on this bulletin, *Trots Allt!* published a note that polemicized with communist propaganda. Its author argued that the Polish government was preparing legal foundations to transform the agricultural structure, 'so that the material existence of the masses will be regulated.' In addition, a universal suffrage

---

[127] 'Vilnas tyska befolkning flyr i panik', *Aftontidningen*, 7 VII 1944; PISM, col. 133, vol. 195, note by M. Karniol no. 180, Stockholm, 20 VII 1944.
[128] 'Olyckligt polskt uttalande', *Svenska Dagbladet*, 18 VII 1944.
[129] 'Väpnad motstånd av polsk civilbefolkning', *Aftontidningen*, 19 VII 1944; PISM, col. 133, vol. 195, note by M. Karniol no.184, Stockholm, 21 VII 1944 r.; 'Polska partisaner stormade fängelser', *Aftontidningen*, 17 VII 1944; IPMS, col. 133, vol. 195, note by M. Karniol no. 182, Stockholm, 21 VII 1944 r.; '42 Gestapoagenter dödade i Polen', *Aftontidningen*, 21 VII 1944; IPMS, kol. 133, 195, note by M. Karniol no. 181, Stockholm, 21 VII 1944.
[130] IPMS, col. 133, vol. 195, note by M. Karniol no. 176, Stockholm, 18 VII 1944.
[131] J. de Geer, 'Polen i motvind', *Göteborgs Handels- och Sjöfarts-Tidning*, 4 VII 1944.
[132] AAN, Norbert Żaba's collection, copy of report by N. Żaba to the Ministry of Information and Documentation, Stockholm, 30 VI 1944.

was to be granted.¹³³ Żaba on the other hand, met with the editor-in-chief of *Sydsvenska Dagbladet Snällposten*, a right-wing politician and a professor of classical philology, Claes Lindskog, to explain the condition of Polish–Soviet relations. During the exchange, he underlined that 'the issue of Poland is the touchstone of Stalin's politics towards Europe.'¹³⁴ This meeting bore fruit in the article in which Lindskog argued, 'it is beyond any doubt that most of Polish society recognizes the government in London and agrees with it in all cases that concern the country's interest.' If a Polish–Soviet agreement is not reached, the reason would be excessive demands from Stalin.¹³⁵

At the outset of July 1944, the Naval Attaché of Poland, Commander Lieutenant Marian Wolbek announced that the Poles had a chance to intercede in the contact between the Swedish authorities and the Allies, 'The Swedes are aware that they are currently isolated. It is no longer profitable to be on the side of the Germans and it is impossible for them to establish closer relations on local ground.' Nevertheless, what remained at odds with this announcement was Wolbek's belief that the Swedes cared a lot about good relations with the Soviet Union, which automatically excluded an association with the Poles. A Swedish opinion journalist was told by Soviet diplomats in Stockholm that Stalin was attempting to create something similar to the Polish Kingdom that was established following the Congress of Vienna in 1815.¹³⁶ Worth noting were the visits by former members of the Polish–Swedish Association to the Polish Legation and the suspension, at least temporarily, of press attacks on the government in exile. Attaché Wolbek clearly overestimated, however, the role of the Polish diplomatic mission in the foreign policy of Sweden.¹³⁷ At the same time, Ingemar Hägglöf, who lived in Moscow, was sure that the Soviet authorities had started to support the State National Council (KRN), which was established by the communists in occupied Poland, as 'the basis for the currently set up Polish civil authorities and government, while constantly keeping

---

¹³³ PISM, col. 133, vol. 195, note by M. Karniol, the delegate of Central Executive Committee of the PPS party, Stockholm, 15 VII 1944.
¹³⁴ AAN, Norbert Żaba's collection, copy of letter by N. Żaba to the Ministry of Information and Documentation, Stockholm, 8 XII 1944.
¹³⁵ 'Polens öde', *Sydsvenska Dagbladet Snällposten*, 31 VII 1944.
¹³⁶ PISM, A 11, 49/b/sow/16, letter by Polish Envoy to Stockholm H. Sokolnicki to the Ministry of Foreign Affairs, Stockholm, 10 VI 1944.
¹³⁷ PISM, MAR, A V 9/2, report by Polish Naval Attaché to Stockholm Commander Lieutenant M. Wolbek to head of the Intelligence Department of the Staff of Commander-in-Chief, Stockholm, 3 VII 1944.

the door open for the eventual participation of the interested so-called progressive circles of Polish expatriates.'[138] In his view, the KRN, was to play the role of executive in the territories occupied by the Soviet armies, until the government's formation, because in its resolution it referred to the democratic constitution of 1921 and declared the formation of a Polish army under the command of General Michał Rola-Żymierski. It also accepted Soviet demands concerning the border along the Curzon Line. Its delegates, who arrived in Moscow, had already met with representatives of Great Britain and the USA. Hägglöf reported to UD:

> They personally made a good impression. Judging from the propaganda [...], their internal policy would most importantly pursue the agricultural reform, although with preserving the right to private land ownership, and further – to the nationalization of large-scale industry and great banks. Whereas small sized industry will remain private.[139]

Based on the press commentaries on Polish affairs at that time, it is possible to detect the atmosphere of expectation for a breakthrough and Polish–Soviet agreement. The majority predicted that the turning point would coincide with the visit of Mikołajczyk to Moscow at the beginning of August 1944. Stalin, meanwhile, showed his hand earlier and announced the setting up of the Polish Committee of National Liberation (or Lublin Committee).

Swedish reactions to the birth of the Lublin Committee

The setting up the Polish Committee of National Liberation (PKWN) in July 1944 was commented on extensively in Sweden. It was obviously an alternative to the Polish government in exile with executive power formed under the auspices of Stalin. Karniol informed the leadership of the PPS:

> All periodicals, irrespective of political orientation, are providing details of the members of the Committee and are occupying themselves with the stance of the Polish government on this matter. In most cases the Committee does not meet with the approval of the Swedish opinion. The periodicals are demonstrating their apprehension about the future of Poland despite assurances

---

[138] RA, UD 1920 års dossiersystem, HP 1, vol. 486, telegram by Swedish Chargé d'affaires to Moscow I. Hägglöf to the Ministry of Foreign Affairs, Moscow, 5 VII 1944.
[139] Ibidem.

from Russia that there will be no Sovietisation of Poland or Russian interference in the internal affairs of Poland.[140]

On its front page Pro-German *Stockholms-Tidningen* ran with 'Wasilewska's Government in Poland – Stalin eliminates Mikołajczyk – the Poles from Moscow ahead of the New Committee.' It was obvious to one opinion journalist for this daily that 'the Soviets by means of their unilateral act came a long way towards the establishment of Russian hegemony in Europe.' He also stated, 'The Polish government in London, in practical terms, was marginalized.' The Swedes' mode of thinking is characterized further in the note, 'Nobody knows with whom the Polish masses sympathize. It is probable that the KRN has better contact with its compatriots than the government in London.' It is hard to deny that the communist propaganda triumphed, independently of the awareness that 'the choice of the civil authorities to take over the administration in Poland will be made by the Russian army.' Other dailies' commentaries were less enthusiastic, but all presented basic information about the setting up of new administrative authorities in Poland backed by the Soviets.[141]

In answer, as it were, to the establishment of the PKWN, Karniol gave interviews to more than a dozen Swedish dailies. He explained that the Polish Underground State, which functioned under the occupation, recognized only the Polish government in London and enjoyed the support of 95 percent of society.[142] The titles of the articles that followed were explicit, 'London Poles Represent 95 Percent of the Nation', 'Poles Support a Legal Government' and 'Majority of Poles Recognise the Government in London.'[143]

Svenska Dagbladet published 'The Future of Poland', which presented its favourable attitude towards the Polish government in London. Some doubts as to whether the body of the PKWN would be independent from Russia were expressed simultaneously. In the commentary 'Polish Affairs', referring to the so-called *Realpolitik*, the social democratic newspaper *Morgon-Tidningen* stated, 'The victorious Red Army is surely an argument that means more in London and Washington than the stance of expatriates, and this refers both

---

[140] PISM, col. 133, vol. 195, note by M. Karniol no. 186, Stockholm, 27 VII 1944.
[141] AAN, HI/I/102, internal bulletin of the Polish Telegraphic Agency, 26 VII 1944.
[142] 'London-Polen representerar 95 procent av folket', *Stockholms-Tidningen*, 25 VII 1944; PISM, col. 133, vol. 195, note by M. Karniol no. 186, Stockholm, 27 VII 1944.
[143] 'Majoriteten av polacker gillar Londonregeringen. Intervju med för polska socialistiska partiet', *Sydsvenska Dagbladet Snällposten*, 27 VII 1944; PISM, col. 133, vol. 195, report by M. Karniol no. 208, Stockholm, 6 XII 1944.

to the Baltic States and Poland.' An opinion journalist for *Sydsvenska Dagbladet Snällposten* claimed that Stalin was ready to make decisions concerning Poland without the participation of the Polish government in London. He was nonetheless hoping that Mikołajczyk, who 'is a good democrat and good patriot, but who is at the same time free from strong anti-Russian orientation – characteristic of many Polish politicians' – would be able to lead them to an agreement. Stalin was aware that the PKWN had no authority in Polish society. In case a settlement could not be reached, Poland would share the fate of Norway and face the so-called Quisling government.[144]

Preparations for Mikołajczyk's visit to Moscow were followed with interest. Although, following the announcement of the declaration of the establishment of the Polish Committee of National Liberation, some commentators lost hope that an independent cabinet would rule Poland. The experiences of the Winter War were recalled, when the puppet Finnish government was formed under the patronage of Stalin and everyone expected the dawn of the age of the Polish Kuusinen.[145]

The course of the visit, from the turn of July and in to August, was followed closely by the Swedes. They believed that the results were to determine further the strategy towards the Polish government. The Swedish Legation in London unofficially asked for information about the Polish Prime Minister's journey to Moscow. A member of the Polish delegation provided a confidential and exhaustive account of the negotiations, during which Stalin insisted that the Curzon Line be the future Polish–Soviet border. According to the Swedish report from London, the Poles were most concerned about the Soviet leader's statements regarding his desire to defend the freedom of Poland and military alliance, which was interpreted as the attempt to establish a system of Soviet garrisons in the strategically most important Polish cities, including Szczecin, with whose future the Swedes were particularly interested. The Poles suspected that Szczecin could not be enough for Stalin and that he would like to take control of Bornholm, which should attract the attention of the Swedes.[146] In turn, according to the new Swedish Envoy to Moscow, Staffan Söderblom, who was completely under the influence of his Soviet hosts, Mikołajczyk's mission failed, as the Polish Prime Minister

---

[144] 'Polens öde', *Sydsvenska Dagbladet Snällposten*, 31 VII 1944.

[145] 'Polske konseljpresidenten rekommenderas resa till Stalin', *Nya Dagligt Allehanda*, 18 VII 1944; 'Politiska utbölingar säger London-polackerna', *Stockholms-Tidningen*, 25 VII 1944; 'Polsk pjäs på rysk affisch', *Hufvudstadsbladet*, 26 VII 1944; 'Överenskommelsen mellan Moskva och polska utskottet', *Göteborgs Handels- och Sjöfarts-Tidning*, 27 VII 1944.

[146] RA, UD 1920 års dossiersystem, HP 1, vol. 486, memorandum by L. [?], London, 18 VIII 1944.

considered the PKWN to be a puppet government from the beginning. According to the Swedish diplomat, the common perception was that the PKWN was to stand at the forefront of the Polish country anyway, regardless of whether Mikołajczyk or another Polish politician from London would join it, or not.[147]

Newspapers published accounts from Mikołajczyk's stay in Moscow. On commenting about the Polish Prime Minister's journey to hold talks with Stalin, a correspondent for *Göteborgs Handels- och Sjöfarts-Tidning* in London explained, 'Moscow was very courteous towards Poland and its demands were moderate and well-motivated, and most of all – realistic.'[148] An opinion journalist for *Nya Dagligt Allehanda* had no such illusions about the situation and predicted that there was no chance of a Polish–Soviet agreement:

> The Russians turned out to be far more astute diplomats than the Germans and they are only using the slogan of independent and democratic Poland. Their purpose is nevertheless the same as that of the Germans – to take control over Poland. For everything points to the fact that the Russians are intending to set up a government in Poland, which would be sufficiently obedient and would become a tool for creating a new system of alliances and forcing the Curzon Line through. In the face of the victorious march of the Soviet army, the Western Allies would not have much to say to Eastern Europe.[149]

Aftontidningen announced, 'It is beyond any doubt that the Polish Prime Minister is doing everything he can to conclude the agreement with Moscow, but if the news about the establishment of diplomatic relations between the Soviet Union and the Polish Committee of National Liberation is true, the chances of reaching even a compromise are very slim.'[150] Reports about negotiations in Moscow depicted two governments at loggerheads. Some Swedish commentaries again invoked the saying about the Polish parliament (*polsk riksdag*). Compromise was considered the only solution to the Polish–Soviet dispute.[151] Following his return from Moscow to London, Swedish opinion

---

[147] Ibidem, note by E. von Post, Stockholm, 23 VIII 1944. Söderblom in the telegram from 29 July 1944 stated: 'The committee is now the only actual administrative authority in the liberated Poland.'
[148] 'Moskvas krav på Polen anses vara måttliga', *Göteborgs Handels- och Sjöfarts-Tidning*, 1 VIII 1944.
[149] 'Polens affärer', *Nya Dagligt Allehanda*, 29 VII 1944.
[150] 'Mikolajczyk-Molotov i god kontakt. Dock små utsikter för kompromiss tror London', *Aftontidningen*, 3 VIII 1944.
[151] K. Andersson, 'Kompromiss London-Moskva löser nya polska krisen', *Morgon-Tidningen*, 27 VII 1944; 'Polens framtid', *Svenska Dagbladet*, 27 VII 1944; D. Viklund, 'Polackerna i London gör sista förlikningsförsök', *Dagens Nyheter*, 28 VII 1944; 'Moskva- och London-Polen

journalists perceived Mikołajczyk as a statesman who was able to accept the Curzon Line and the communists' entry into the government as the foundation for compromise with the Soviet Union.[152] It was accepted with contentment that the leaders of the Polish underground movement supported Mikołajczyk in his efforts to come to an agreement with Stalin.[153] It should be noted that Soviet propaganda transformed the Polish matter from a conflict between the Soviet Union and the Polish government in to an internal dispute between the London government and the PKWN. The picture was additionally obscured by disputes in 'Polish London' between the political parties over tactics towards the Soviet Union. The socialist daily *Ny Tid* proposed that 'the only solution to the problem is for Mikołajczyk to ignore both the government in London and the president and take control of the administration in Poland.'[154]

Activity of the Union of Polish Patriots (ZPP) in Sweden

Activities of the group of Polish communists headed by Jerzy Pański trace back to September 1939. When the war broke out, Swedish ports held eight Polish commercial vessels and seven fishing cutters. In the second half of September, prior the ships' departure to Great Britain some of the seamen decided to desert.[155] Most sought the support of the Soviet[156] or German[157] authorities and some decided to remain in neutral Sweden. Among these seamen was Jerzy Pański, the second officer of the general cargo ship *Chorzów*, which lay in Gothenburg, who explained in his memoirs that the cause of his

---

väntas bilda samregering', *Stockholms-Tidningen*, 31 VII 1944; 'Molotov negligerar polska regeringen i London', *Göteborgs Handels- och Sjöfarts-Tidning*, 4 VIII 1944; 'Mikolajczyk ej utan chanser', *Svenska Dagbladet*, 12 VIII 1944.

[152] 'Lösning av polska frågan möjlig. Mikolajczyk accepterade Curzonlinjen i princip', *Morgon-Tidningen*, 13 VIII 1944.

[153] 'Polens underjordiska ledare stöder Mikolajczyks förslag', *Stockholms-Tidningen*, 29 VIII 1944.

[154] K. J. O-n, 'Mötet i Moskva', *Ny Tid*, 23 X 1944.

[155] It is not exactly known how many sailors deserted. In the literature we either find the information that desertions were frequent or that there escaped over 40 seamen and 1 officer. See: J. K. Sawicki, *Pod flagą komodora*, Gdańsk 1992, pp. 72–73; idem, *Polska Marynarka Handlowa*, vol. 1: *1939–1945*, Gdynia 1991, pp. 35.

[156] J. K. Sawicki, *Pod flagą...*, p. 72: 'Referring to their affiliation to the communist movement and Ukrainian nationality they volunteered at the consular post of the USSR'. Among them was coalman from the ship 'Wilno' Aleksy Bandura, who later became an activist of the Union of Polish Patriots in Sweden.

[157] The volunteers who appeared at the German post were immediately sent to Gdynia. See: J. K. Sawicki, *Pod flagą*, p. 73.

desertion on 29 September 1939 was his negative attitude towards the Polish government in exile and communist views.[158] Following the conclusion of the Molotov–Ribbentrop Pact, communists across Europe lost the ideological support of Moscow in the political fight with the Nazis. For them, the war with Hitler was not a just war, although Pański hoped that this would change.

> The stance of the communist parties was considered by us to be transitory, tactical. It was hard to imagine a coexistence with Fascism. Sooner or later there must have come the moment of armed intervention, and then the liberation of Poland in alliance with the Soviet Union seemed inevitable […]. We trusted the policy of the workers' left and we believed that ultimately all that was beneficial for the International Labour Movement would be also beneficial for Poland.[159]

On 30 September the group of seamen headed by Pański turned themselves in to the police to obtain refugee status. Pański explained that he would not go to Great Britain nor could he return to Poland, for, as he argued, 'he was a member of an anti-Nazi organization.'[160] He expressed a wish to travel to the Soviet Union. Other seamen likely did not share this intention, as police reports confirmed that they wanted to remain under the supervision of Swedish social services.[161] Pański maintains in his memoirs that at the very beginning of his stay in Sweden he established contact with local communists. The police took note of his meetings with a Lithuanian woman, Raja Prottas, who was a Swedish citizen and suspected of illegal political activity, which in police jargon probably meant being a communist. When it transpired that Prottas was planning to hide Pański from the police, the Swedish authorities decided on 7 December to deport the Poles and refuse them the right to return to Sweden.[162] The execution of this order was suspended due to the on-going war and the occupation of Poland. The seamen were taken in to custody. In the spring of 1940, they were moved to a prison camp in Långmora, Dalarna province. During his stay in jail, Pański applied for a Soviet visa, which was granted to him. Nevertheless, he refused to accept it

---

[158] On the circumstances of J. Pański's escape from the vessel, see ibidem, pp. 79–80.
[159] J. Pański, *Wachta lewej burty*, Gdynia 1965, pp. 39–40.
[160] RA-Arninge, SÄPO arkiv, P 2406 Jerzy Pański, löp 2, memorandum concerning the Polish citizen and currently stateless navy officer, J. Pański.
[161] Ibidem.
[162] AAN, ZPPwSz, 434/3, excerpt from protocol of the Royal Board of Social Affairs (K. Socialstyrelsen) from 7 XII 1939, pp. 18–19. The people who were to be subjected to deportations included: Jan Hins, Augustyn Jeka, Austin Lorenc (so written in Swedish text), Jerzy Pański, Jan Papuga, Sergiusz Patejeruk.

due to family reasons, as he allegedly became engaged to a Swedish woman, Gunvor Linde.[163] In December 1940, Pański was released on the condition that he would work on a Swedish ship. He was required to register with the police on a regular basis. Initially he worked on a tanker running along routes in the northern Baltic Sea. According to his memoirs, the vessel was torpedoed. Later he decided to work as a lumberjack. In 1941 he became a farm worker and in 1942 he enrolled in several month-long training courses for workers, organized in Uppsala. After completing the courses, which were financed by the Swedish authorities, he was assigned to work as a turner in a furniture factory in Mariestad. In the autumn of 1943 he travelled to Stockholm to continue his education and there he renewed his acquaintance with the seamen he had once worked with, and acquainted himself with other Polish refugees. He made contact with the Soviet Legation to become learn of opportunities for evacuation to the Soviet Union.[164] Sweden started to receive news about the formation of the Union of Polish Patriots (ZPP) in Moscow. Pański aspired to form a group of Poles to support the communists acting under the patronage of Stalin. He wanted the group to possess a certain organisational form. Whereas the instructions from Moscow and the direct aegis of the USSR were to be its ideological foundation.[165]

In 1943, following the break-up of Polish–Soviet relations, and especially in 1944, when after the conference in Tehran the picture of Poland's future under Stalin's control started to become clearer, Pański became an important figure both for the staff of the Soviet Legation in Stockholm and for the Polish communists in Moscow. Based on his group it was possible to create a counterbalance of sorts, at least in terms of propaganda, to the diplomatic representation of the Polish government in exile.

According to Pański's report, the founding committee of the Union of Polish Patriots in Sweden was appointed in November 1943[166] and at the time the principal tasks of the organisation were included in its statute: conducting cultural and educational activity among the members in line with the spirit of patriotism and democracy, establishing contact and cooperation with similar organisations abroad as well as providing mutual help. Each Pole who

---

[163] RA-Arninge, SÄPO arkiv, P 2406 Jerzy Pański, löp no. 1, copy of report, Stockholm, 13 II 1940, p. 2–3.
[164] J. Pański, *Wachta...*, p. 136.
[165] In January 1945 A. Kollontai reminded the headquarters about the support that was granted to the Polish communists in Sweden: 'Upon the order of the NKID we set up a local branch of the Union of Polish Patriots in Stockholm.' Quoted after: W. Materski, *Dyplomacja Polski „lubelskiej". Lipiec 1944 – marzec 1947*, Warsaw 2007, p. 33.
[166] Ibidem, p. 141.

accepted the statute of the union could become a member of the organisation. A membership fee of 1 crown a month was mandatory.[167] In December of 1943, Pański was to contact the ZPP in Moscow, specifically Zygmunt Modzelewski, who was a political-educational officer of the Polish army in the USSR. It should be highlighted at this point though that although this information seems likely, in the surviving documentation there are neither traces adopting a form of organisation prior to August 1944 nor of Pański's contacts with Moscow prior to October 1944.[168] The statute provisions, which are recalled by Pański in his memoirs, are identical with those contained in the statute adopted in August 1944. There is no doubt that already in 1943 people from Pański's circle began campaigning within Polish circles in Sweden. In July 1943, they reached the Polish Home in Traneberg (on the outskirts of Stockholm) where groups of 30–50 Polish refugees remained under the care of the Polish Legation during the war. Due to the very poor facilities there and difficulties providing sufficient food for the refugees, the agitation of the ZPP brought positive results, which Envoy Henryk Sokolnicki underestimated. He wrote to Minister of Foreign Affairs Tadeusz Romer in September 1943, 'The news that communism is spreading there and that it is the object of the Soviet propaganda are greatly exaggerated.'[169] Nevertheless, it was the house in Traneberg that was considered by Pański to be an adequate place to conduct agitation. And although first attempts to win keen supporters were unsuccessful, he emphasized, 'my colleagues who visited the refugees' house in Traneberg assured me that our initiative was met with interest.'[170]

---

[167] AAN, ZPPwSz, 434/1, The Union of Polish Patriots in Sweden. Statute, p. 1.

[168] It seems that Pański was closest to the truth in 1946, when, during a questioning conducted by the Special Committee for Fraud and Economic Harmfulness Prevention in Warsaw, he said: 'As far as I remember, in July or in August 1944 I founded the Union of Polish Patriots in Sweden and through the Soviet Embassy in Stockholm I established contact with the Union of Polish Patriots in Moscow'. See: AMSZ, iss. 6, w. 78, vol. 1163, transcript of the testimony of the witness [Jerzy Pański] put down on 30 September 1946 in the Executive Office of the Special Commission in Warsaw, 5 X 1946 r., p. 4. Cf. S. Jędrychowski, *Przedstawicielstwo PKWN w Moskwie*, Warszawa 1987, pp. 178–180.

[169] A. N. Uggla, *I nordlig hamn...*, p. 149.

[170] J. Pański, *Wachta.*, pp. 136–137. Communist agitation in the Polish Home in Traneberg was conducted by Iwan Tremtiaczy(j), who earlier became acquainted with socialist Jan Masiak and found himself there thanks to the his recommendation. The police record of the account by Kajetan Łowczyński, director of the post, indicates that Tremtiaczy was a communist agent whose task was to win the Polish refugees' trust towards the Polish authorities in Moscow which were currently being formed. He became the leader of the Home's residents who were dissatisfied with their situation and sought every occasion to criticise the Polish Legation. At the same time he informed everybody about the opportunity to join the Polish army of General Berling. According to the police intelligence, Tremtiaczy had close

The propagandist offensive build up by the Soviet diplomacy in Sweden drew the attention of the Polish Legation and related officers of the Polish intelligence. By the outset of 1944, the Soviet propagandist apparatus had grown. A note from an anonymous author (probably an employee of the Polish Legation in Stockholm) from February 1944 highlighted, 'What becomes evident is the great advance of Soviet propaganda and the growth of Soviet influence both in the press and the Swedish publishing industry.'[171] Nevertheless, the presence of Pański's group and its cooperation with the Soviet Legation had gone unnoticed for a long time. The Polish intelligence instead turned its attention to Aleksy Bandura, who was described as the pillar of the Soviet intelligence.[172] At the time his ambition seemed to be becoming leader of Free Ukraine, just as Pański aspired to become head of the Poles in Sweden. In February 1944 agents of the Swedish Security Service (SÄPO) recorded Bandura's meeting with the agents of the Soviet intelligence. During this meeting Bandura was to show his support for the separatist Ukrainian state, return the money he received for his espionage and from that moment on await the conflict between the USSR and Great Britain. Bandura's actions were beyond the control of the Soviet Legation, and were

---

relations with the Soviet Legation and frequently met with the members of its personnel. Allegedly, on 8 April 1944, he was to hand over a fourteen-page paper on the subject of Polish intelligence agents hired in the Polish Legation. Following his dismissal from Traneberg he hired himself in Grand Hotel. During the police hearing he told an incredible story about his work on Swedish ships, his return to Gdynia during the occupation, his arrest in Kraków and brutal Gestapo interrogations, and eventually his escape and making his way by ship to Sweden at the outset of November 1943. Over the first few weeks he stayed in Traneberg, and at the end of December 1943 he hired himself as a kitchen porter in Grand Hotel, where he worked until 1 February 1944. After that for a month he became a commandant of the camp in Fiskeboda. Later he returned to Stockholm and his work as a kitchen porter, but this time in Carlton hotel. He denied that there existed a communist organisation among the Polish refugees, he refused to admit that he was engaging himself in the communist propaganda, although he did not hide that he was in favour of communism. In spite of all that in the spring of 1944 it was still too early to turn to the Swedish authorities with the idea of creating an organisation which was to represent the future Polish government elite while being subordinated to Stalin. See: MUST arkiv, Försvarsstaben, Säkerhetsavdelningen, F VIII e, vol. 31, police pro memorias concerning Polish citizen Iwan Tremtiaczy, 8 V 1944; police report, 8 V 1944.

[171] IPMS, A 9, VI 21/1, note 'Wzrost wpływów sowieckich w Szwecji' (Increasing Soviet influence in Sweden), 10 II 1944.

[172] On the suspicions of the Swedish police and recording facts connected with Bandura's spy activity in favour of the Soviet Union see: RA-Arninge, SÄPO arkiv, P 4701 Aleksy Bandura, letter by M. Lundqvist (SÄPO) to M. Rosenström (*Statens utlänningskommission*), 14 II 1945. The document contains a strictly confidential recommendation that Bandura was refused a permit to stay in Stockholm. According to the sources of SÄPO, Bandura took pictures of industrial and military sites as well as repeatedly met with the residents of the NKVD in Stockholm.

therefore limited. In August 1944, he would become a close partner of Pański and a co-founder of the ZPP. It is not known how he was convinced to continue the cooperation with the intelligence services. The Soviet propaganda, in which he started to engage himself from that moment on, appealed to the political realism of its audience. It was argued that the Red Army would soon annex half of Europe, including all of Poland. Next, free elections would take place and a government representative for the Polish society was to be appointed, as opposed to the government in exile. It was also argued that Great Britain and the USA would not stand on the side of the government in exile, as their priority was to avoid a conflict with the Soviet Union.[173]

Initially the ZPP was managed by Mihail Vetrov. From 16 July, preparations to present it to a wider audience were directed by Vladimir Semenov. The day before, Pański met with an employee of the Soviet Legation, Oleynikov, among others, to discuss the forming of a branch of the ZPP in Stockholm. The intention was to find Swedish citizens who could guarantee the new organisation to the Swedish authorities.[174]

The breakthrough came with the formation of the PKWN and the announcement of its programme manifesto in July 1944. From that moment Pański's group, which was focused around the Soviet Legation, became an international branch of the new political elites that were being formed in Poland. An important occurrence was pointed out by Maurycy Karniol. He noticed in October 1944 that together with the wave of refugees from Norway and Finland the social structure of the Polish community in Sweden was changing: 'The refugees in Sweden were for the most part not divided into supporters of the government and supporters of the Union of Patriots in Moscow. Usually very few of them were pro-democratic. The majority of the Polish refugees in Sweden were representatives of bureaucracy, landowners and the families of military men staying in England. [...] That explained why the character of the local Polish colony was reactionary, both socially and politically, and they usually did not differentiate between the terms socialism and communism, both of which were used to spread fear. Nevertheless, the situation changed with the illegal influx of Poles from Poland and Poles from Norway and Finland. These included peasants, workers, craftsmen, working intelligentsia, as well as a considerable number of youths. The members of the former reactionary colony either emigrated to England or soaked into the local

---

[173] PISM, A 11, 85/b/18, note by Colonel S. Gano 'Zamierzenia sowieckie' (Soviet plans), n.d., n.p. (supplement to the letter from 24 II 1944).
[174] PISM, A XII, 3/41, note by Colonel S. Gano 'Związek Patriotów Polskich w Szwecji' (Union of Polish Patriots in Sweden), 14 VIII 1944.

bureaucratic apparatus, and even though some of them retained their sphere of influence, their reduced numbers made them a minority.'[175] At the outset of August 1944, in a confidential letter to the Ministry of Foreign Affairs, Envoy Sokolnicki, referring to information from the intelligence, predicted that the Soviet Legation would found a branch of the PKWN. At the same time Sokolnicki asked for information regarding the status of Polish–Soviet relations, maintaining that this was necessary to conduct a propagandist counter-campaign. What he also considered indispensable in the current conditions was increasing the subsidies from the Ministry of Social Welfare to support the refugees, because it was obvious that 'the suspension of these payments would make the Soviets' work much easier.'[176] Several notes regarding this matter, written by the head of the Department of Information and Intelligence of the Staff of Commander-in-Chief, Colonel Stanisław Gano, prove that the development of the activity of the ZPP in Sweden enjoyed much interest from the Polish intelligence. Karniol, who criticised the method of surveillance, claimed that it would be advisable to conduct a cultural campaign among the refugees rather than to focus on recruiting snoopers.

The reconstruction of the details of the organisational-propagandist action of Jerzy Pański, which was conducted by means of the Soviet diplomatic services in Sweden is not an easy task, due to the disparity of information announced by various sources. What is clear is that we can agree with the conclusion of the report prepared by the Polish intelligence: 'In August 1944 the Soviet Legation in Stockholm set about forming a branch of the Union of Polish Patriots in Sweden.'[177] That moment was mentioned by Pański in February 1945 during one of his speeches to the public. He said that the ZPP had existed for six months, during which it had to overcome many obstacles, including that many considered it a communist organisation.[178] Based on intelligence reports from Stockholm on 5 August 1944 in the headquarters of the Swedish Trade Union Confederation (*LO*) a ceremony of the opening of the ZPP (Union of Polish Patriots) in Sweden was held.[179]

---

[175] PISM, col. 133, vol. 195, report by M. Karniol no. 205, Stockholm, 20 X 1944.
[176] PISM, A 9, VI 21/1, letter by Envoy H. Sokolnicki to the Ministry of Foreign Affairs (no. 85) received on 2 VIII 1944.
[177] PISM, A 9, E/26, report 'Działalność »patriotów polskich« w Szwecji' (Activity of 'Polish patriots' in Sweden), 9 II 1945. The ending is missing from the document. The Swedish police was of the same opinion, see RA-Arninge, SÄPO arkiv, P 2406 Jerzy Pański, löp 2, pro memorias concerning Polish citizen and currently stateless navy officer J. Pański.
[178] RA-Arninge, SÄPO arkiv, P 2406 Jerzy Pański, löp 2, pro memoria, Sztokholm, 27 II 1945, p. 75.
[179] In the last sentence of the report an important information was provided: 'if the Swedish trade union [...] had known that this was the Soviets' work – they would have never agreed to

The endeavour nevertheless turned out to be unsuccessful due to the poor attendance of Polish citizens. One of the SÄPO agents explained what was to be obtained by Pański from the Soviet diplomats prior to the meeting: 'Do not order spy work, but manage the work so that every member considers its duty to be watching everything that is being done by the others.'[180] As there was scarce interest from the refugees, the meeting was concluded quickly. The Soviets blamed Pański for the weak and ineffective propaganda. He was accused of exaggerating his influence among the Poles in Sweden. The previously prepared membership cards turned out to be unnecessary. The information-propagandist materials were identified by Polish intelligence as a translation of the Soviet bulletins published in Stockholm. The activists of the ZPP justified the absence of the refugees with the sudden reluctance of the Poles towards the Soviet Union in connection with the suspension of military operations on the front following the start of the rising in Warsaw.[181]

Following the meeting on 5 August, which was considered an embarrassment by the Soviet diplomats, questions regarding the future of the ZPP in Sweden were taken on by the first secretary of the legation, Vasiliy Razin. Georg Branting, a well-known leftist activist and lawyer and the son of Hjalmar Branting, a former eminent social democratic leader (until his death in 1925), and who remained in touch with the diplomats, advised the organisation to engage people who were known and admired by the Poles. Negotiations were conducted with Zbigniew Folejewski, among others, who was a Polish language teacher at Stockholm University. He was even mentioned as a member of the ZPP, although, as far as we know, he eventually refused to affiliate himself with the organisation. The Soviet Legation advised Pański to visit the Swedish Ministry of Foreign Affairs. Colonel Gano highlighted, 'According to information from a reliable source, Pański did not visit the Secretary-General Boheman or any other official of the Ministry of Foreign Affairs. Branting, a lawyer, had paid them a visit, however. He could have heard from Boheman that the Swedish government did not have its representative to the Polish government in London or at the Polish govern-

---

leave their room at their disposal'; PISM, A XII, 3/41, strictly confidential note by Colonel S. Gano 'Zebranie organizacyjne ZPP w Szwecji' (Organizational meeting of ZPP in Sweden), 13 IX 1944. M. Karniol in his report provides the date of 4 August, see PISM, col. 133, vol. 195, report by M. Karniol no. 205, Stockholm, 20 X 1944.

[180] RA-Arninge, SÄPO arkiv, P 2406 Jerzy Pański, löp 2, memorandum concerning Polish citizen and currently stateless navy officer J. Pański, n.p., n.d.

[181] PISM, A XII, 3/41, note by Colonel S. Gano 'Zebranie organizacyjne ZPP w Szwecji', 13 IX 1944.

ment in Lublin, and that the Swedish government would not oppose the formation of the ZPP in Sweden.[182] The Swedish authorities allowed organisations of this sort, but they were prohibited from political campaigning. Cultural campaigning was permitted though. It appears that the half-solution was decided by the increasingly conspicuous Soviet advantage over Central Europe. In practice the Union was able to continue its propagandist activity, and the diplomatic mission of the Polish government, which was still recognized by Sweden, did not seem under threat, as it could count on official support from the Swedish authorities.

In another note, Gano, channeling Razin, wrote, 'the issue of the Union of Polish Patriots is progressing with much difficulty and in fact nothing has been achieved so far.'[183] Nevertheless, on the same day a note was written that conveyed the content of the cynical Soviet instruction given to the ZPP in Sweden.[184] The establishment of the ZPP would lead to a split among the Poles in Sweden and to a withdrawal, at least for some of them, from the Polish Legation in Stockholm. The pro-Soviet attitude of the Poles was to be nurtured by instilling in them that 'it is Stalin who grants freedom to Poland, and not England or America.' The commitment of spying and informing on others was introduced. Contact with the Soviet Legation was reserved for a small circle of the management of the ZPP and it was advised that this privilege was not flaunted. It was considered advisable that the news-sheet be published regularly and information that 75 percent of Polish refugees belonged to the Union be promoted. The news-sheet advised, 'To try to convince people that the Polish government in London is a band of thieves invoking the false constitution together with the stupid Atlantic Charter.' At the end it was proposed, 'Make the members of the Union believe that the London government works with the Gestapo.'[185] On the next day commentary on the note said, 'the authenticity of the instruction [is] questionable', but the hints it contained were confirmed by the actions of the ZPP. What draws most attention is the endless slander of the Polish government in exile and the diplomatic mission in Stockholm.[186] It is also worth pointing out the consequent passing over of the question of close cooperation with the

---

[182] Ibidem. Cf. J. Pański, *Wachta…*, pp. 144–145; A. N. Uggla, *I nordlig hamn…*, p. 151.
[183] PISM, A XII, 3/41, note by Colonel S. Gano 'Komitet Wyzwolenia Narodowego', 14 IX 1944.
[184] Ibidem, note by Colonel S. Gano 'Instrukcja ramowa dla ZPP w Szwecji', 14 IX 1944.
[185] Ibidem.
[186] A. N. Uggla, *I nordlig hamn…*, p. 159.

Soviet Legation, which was particularly notable in J. Pański's memoirs,[187] as well as the simultaneous emphasizing of harassment directed at the members of the ZPP from Poles who were connected with the Polish Legation.[188] Pański followed Razin's instructions from November 1944, so as to avoid official contact with the Soviet Legation and so that he could meet with Razin in neutral locations. This was to drive back the accusations towards the ZPP that it was created by the Soviet authorities.[189]

Despite the failures in acquiring new members, Pański was not discouraged and consequently pursued his objectives. The intelligence service of the Polish Armed Forces in the West recorded the attempts to recruit people who could report on the situation in the Polish Legation and the talks with the refugees from the occupied territories. This could lead to the obtaining of information of military significance. On 18 August, the Union published the one-off newspaper *Polska Wyzwolona* (Poland Liberated), which contained the most important legal acts of the KRN and discussed the PKWN's activities. Whereas every week, from 25 September the modestly edited *Informator Związku Patriotów Polskich w Szwecji* (The Guide of the Union of Polish Patriots in Sweden) was to be published. According to Pański's the print runs were issue 1, 100 copies; issue 2, 200 copies and issue 3, 250 copies.

The meeting of the management of the ZPP, which consisted of seven individuals, took place on 25 August. During the meeting both the statute and the organisation's authorities were approved. Jerzy Pański became chair, Aleksy Bandura, vice-chair, Norbert Kopeć (replaced by Feliks Spała), secretary, Tadeusz Borśniowski, treasurer and the members of the board were Leon Mandel and Hanna Mohr. The participants agreed the details of the subsequent meeting for the refugees, which was to take place on 31 August. On this occasion, the organizers presented themselves as the supporters of the PKWN. The meeting, which was attended approximately a dozen people,[190] was interrupted by Franciszek Górniak, who called it illegal, as the Polish Legation was not

---

[187] Apart from the aforementioned contact with the Legation when it comes to the issue of eventual evacuation to the Polish army which was being formed in the USSR, Pański mentioned in his memoirs the support of the cultural department of the Soviet diplomatic mission at the organisation of the screening of the newsreel service devoted to the Polish affairs (p. 146) and the fact that he became acquainted with the Soviet representative in Stockholm A. Kollontai (p. 151).

[188] J. Pański, *Wachta.*, pp. 145, 148. The agents of Polish intelligence were to beat up two activists of the Union of Polish Patriots in Sweden: Tremtiaczy and Sawczuk.

[189] IPMS, A XII, 3/41, note by Colonel S. Gano 'ZPP w Szwecji', 13 XI 1944.

[190] AAN, HI/I/79, letter by Polish Envoy to Stockholm H. Sokolnicki to the Ministry of Foreign Affairs, 9 IX 1944. The document contains the information that 24 people took part in the meeting.

involved. As a result 'the Polish refugees exited with cries of "Down with the Committee."'[191] According to Polish intelligence, Semenov, afraid of another embarrassment, sent a message to Moscow that the meeting had been attended by a hundred people and that those who had caused a disruption had been removed.[192] On 2 September, in *Aftontidningen* the article 'Poles in Sweden are Granting Their Support to the Lublin Government' was published. Subsequent meetings of a small group of activists of the ZPP took place in the headquarters of the Soviet Legation. Here newsreels and documentaries devoted to Poland were also shown.[193] At the same time, the Soviet Legation started to collect information about those who showed without reserve their aversion towards the ZPP, together with the addresses of their families in Poland.[194] On 15 September Pański appeared at the Press department of the Swedish Ministry of Foreign Affairs and requested registration as a correspondent of the Polpress agency. He was told that nobody had heard of such an agency and that the only agency known to them was the Polish Telegraphic Agency (PAT), the correspondent for which already resided in Sweden.[195] With support from the Soviet Legation, however, Pański was accredited at the Press department of Utrikesdepartementet as a correspondent of the Polpress agency on 18 September. The agency had been established in Moscow by the ZPP and the central press organisation of the ZPP in Moscow, the *Wolna Polska* (Free Poland).[196] At the time Pański considered changing the name of the organisation to the Division of the Union of National Liberation, which could be treated as a first step to the official representation of the PKWN.[197] Walter Taub of the Czech News Agency

---

[191] Ibidem. Eleven people 'protested and, manifesting their support for the Government and the fighting Warsaw, ostentatiously left the room'. In the room remained 'board members (5), our agents (2) and four Jews – communists [...] and two women citizens of Danzig – communists.'

[192] IPMS, A 9, E/26, report 'Działalność »patriotów polskich« w Szwecji', 9 II 1945. The ending is missing from the document.

[193] According to the Pański's account: 'Hundreds of people were coming to the cinema to watch the screenings, the small room was usually full', see: J. Pański, *Wachta.*, p. 146.

[194] AAN, HI/I/79, letter by Polish Envoy to Stockholm H. Sokolnicki to the Ministry of Foreign Affairs, Stockholm, 9 IX 1944.

[195] PISM, A XII, 3/41, note by Colonel S. Gano 'ZPP w Szwecji', 10 X 1944.

[196] It is worth to note that the current editor-in-chief of *Wolna Polska* was a namesake of the head of the Union of Polish Patriots in Sweden, Jerzy Pański (1900–1979) – a literary critic, a translator, an opinion journalist and a political activist. The first editor-in-chief of the weekly was Jerzy Borejsza (as of 1 March 1943). Pański took over this post on 20 July 1944 and held it until 1 March 1945, when he was replaced by Roman Juryś.

[197] PISM, A XII, 3/41, strictly confidential note by Colonel S. Gano 'ZPP w Szwecji – zmiana nazwy', 13 [?] IX 1944.

(*Československá tísková kancelář*, or *ČTK*) played an important role in familiarizing Pański with the circle of international correspondents. He acquainted Pański with people who were later persuaded to use the Polpress news service as well as information from the Polish–London journalists.[198] The service provided by Pański discredited the Polish government in exile and the Polish Armed Forces in the West. In official speeches Pański described Commander-in-Chief General Sosnkowski as a self-appointed commander, a fascist and an enemy of the people. In his view, 'The Polish army, which stays in England, is not actually fighting.' He also maintained, 'Officers sit back, do nothing and collect their inflated wages for the simple reason that they hold an officer rank.'[199] Another crucial role was played by Stanisław Milczarek, an employee of the Czechoslovak diplomatic mission in Stockholm, who was a Polish citizen before the war. He recorded information about the Polish Legation staff for future purposes as he claimed, 'to make their stay in Europe difficult' in the event they remained abroad as expatriates.[200]

It was only on 8 September 1944 that Pański sent a telegram to Lublin, where he informed the PKWN that, 'the Union of Polish Patriots has been established in Stockholm and is operating on the same basis as the Polish Committee of National Liberation', and asked to be contacted.[201] In October 1944, the management of the ZPP asked the PKWN for its official recognition and patronage.[202] On 12 October a report was sent to the PKWN with a description of the situation of the Poles in exile, consisting of various professions – researchers, students and seamen – and numbering about one thousand.[203] The authors of the report discredited the role of the Polish Legation. They argued that the Polish diplomats, supporters and people trusted by the Nazis were extremely unpopular among the refugees due to their laziness and organisational ineptitude. The weak position of the Polish government's diplomatic mission was, according to them, the consequence of 'the constantly emerging acts of corruption, negligence and sympathy for Fascism', and the only ways to influence the refugees was to threaten them with deprivation of

---

[198] PISM, A XII, 3/41, note by Colonel S. Gano 'ZPP w Szwecji', 3 XI 1944.
[199] Ibidem.
[200] PISM, A XII, 3/41, note by Colonel S. Gano 'ZPP w Szwecji', 15 IX 1944.
[201] RA-Arninge, SÄPO arkiv, P 2406 Jerzy Pański, copy of telegram by J. Pański to the PKWN, Stockholm, 8 IX 1944. The document was translated into Swedish from Russian.
[202] AAN, ZPP w ZSRR, 216/29, report by the Union of Polish Patriots in Sweden no. 2, 30 X 1944, p. 13–14a. The authors highlight in the report that: 'The attempts to reach an agreement, both written and telegraphic, have so far been insufficient'.
[203] This number was in accordance with the data announced in September 1944 by the Swedish authorities, see: A. N. Uggla, *I nordlig hamn...*, p. 41.

help or bribe them with donations. Pański unfolded his vision, not so much of breaking up Polish circles in Sweden but of moving into the political vacuum. Referring to the opinion of the Soviet diplomatic mission, the management of the ZPP suggested a need to create an official representation of the PKWN in Sweden. The report revealed that the ZPP's leader, Jerzy Pański, had great ambitions, 'The Union of Polish Patriots in Sweden has sufficient orientation, organisational skills and qualified manpower to engage in the preparatory work in this direction.'[204] At the same time he added to the contrary, 'Our own chances are small at the moment. We have neither the instructions that would help us conduct our work nor the access to your documents and literature, and no sufficient material resources whatsoever.' He pointed to the benefit resulting from the establishment of political and economic relations with Sweden, which was ready to grant loans.[205] According to the report, the moment of the formation of the ZPP in Sweden was thought to be the meeting of 25 August 1944, which confirms speculation that Pański was formerly the leader of an informal (and, it seems, a nameless) small group, which remained in touch with the Soviet Legation.[206] The report stated that the ZPP in Sweden consisted of 82 members, which seems to be an exaggeration. It was added that there was a constant rotation of the members due to travel to Great Britain and the influx of new people. In the correspondence of the ZPP, the Polish Legation in Sweden was presented as sufficiently disgraced and of no threat to activities undertaken in the name of the communist movement and the PKWN. All the more so that the Swedish government, despite continuous recognition of the Polish government in London, had not yet adopted any position regarding internal Polish affairs. According to the already quoted report, the Polish Legation in Stockholm tried to counteract the expansion of the group's influence through acts of violence towards the communist activists. There were reports of assaults, break-ins, brawls during meetings, the removal of benefits from Poles who

---

[204] AAN, ZPP w ZSRR, 216/29, report by the Union of Polish Patriots in Sweden, 12 X 1944, p. 6–12.
[205] Ibidem.
[206] The management of the Union of Polish Patriots in Sweden passed the meeting of 5 August in silence. It seems that it was not the idea of the Polish intelligence. Pański could not consider it a success, therefore he said nothing about it. Similar was the case with the meeting of 31 August. It would be also hard to imagine that the statute was adopted and the board was chosen only after the Swedish authorities had given their permission for the activity of the organisation. Rather, these organisational measures were confirmed only then. Cf. IPMS, A XII, 3/41, strictly confidential note by Colonel S. Gano 'Zebranie organizacyjne ZPP w Szwecji', 13 IX 1944; AAN, ZPPwSz, 434/4, excerpt from the protocol of the Union of Polish Patriots in Sweden produced on 5 X 1944, p. 16.

enrolled in the ZPP and informing on the supporters of the organisation to the Swedish authorities for being dangerous elements.[207] Pański reported a burglary to the Swedish police and a theft that was to take place in his apartment on 29 September 1944.[208] It is hard to escape the fact that this event coincided with the propagandist campaign in the press, which popularized the information about the assassinations of the supporters of the PKWN by soldiers of the Home Army.[209] According to the police report, no traces of burglary and no fingerprints were found in Pański's apartment.[210] According to the ZPP management, gaining the support of all Poles was very easy – namely, by granting them financial support which was so far provided only by the Polish Legation. Following the failure of the action, conducted with the help of the Soviet Legation, it has been concluded, 'The recognition of our union by the PKWN would have a decisive impact on the further development of the Union of Polish Patriots. It was also highlighted, 'This would give us extra room for manoeuvre within the Polish colony in relation to the Swedish authorities.' In the conclusion it was stressed, 'This would increase the number of members, and most importantly, attract a greater number of representatives of the Polish intelligentsia than before.' In response, the head of the PKWN Edward Osóbka-Morawski sent an invitation telegram to Pański, which he treated as the first written evidence that the PKWN recognized the organization. The activists of the ZPP, encouraged by the telegram, drew up another report discussing the current situation of the Polish refugees, the activity of the Polish Legation and the possibilities of entering commercial negotiations with Sweden and obtaining humanitarian aid from the Swedes as well as making Stockholm an opinion forming centre for other countries. The management of the ZPP in Sweden argued, 'Sweden as a neutral country has gained special meaning in Europe. It is Europe's window to the world, a forum for exchanging international views, and at the very least a source of information for Europe, as well as one of the few countries which preserved their production and export facilities.' That is why, 'the existence of the representation of Democratic Poland – the PKWN – becomes necessary in the Swedish territory.' Another request emerged that directives and

---

[207] 'Polska striden ger eko i Stockholm?', *Sydsvenska Dagbladet Snällposten*, 3 X 1944. Cf. A. N. Uggla, *I nordlig hamn...*, pp. 155–156.
[208] PISM, A XII, 3/41, note by Colonel S. Gano 'ZPP w Szwecji', 3 XI 1944.
[209] 'Moskva och Lublin varna för polskt inbördeskrig', *Göteborgs Handels- och Sjöfarts-Tidning*, 16 IX 1944.
[210] RA-Arninge, SÄPO arkiv, P 2406 Jerzy Pański, copy of pro memoria, Stockholm, 29 IX 1944, p. 62.

instructions were sent to the ZPP, and that in turn, it proposed that all Polish citizens staying in Sweden be registered.[211]

Suspicion arises that the attempts to establish close contacts with the PKWN resulted from Pański's declining position among the staff of the Soviet Legation. Towards the close of October 1944, Razin was dissatisfied with Pański's activities, as they did not bring the desired results contrary to initial announcements of the leader of the ZPP in Sweden.[212]

In the reply telegram sent from Moscow on 13 November 1944, the representative of the PKWN Stefan Jędrychowski assured Pański that he would be granted a fixed fee as a correspondent for the Polpress press agency and that the ZPP in Sweden would be given substantial funds to help the refugees. At the same time, he advised that the Poles who were staying in Sweden be registered, which would be helpful in preparation for repatriation. Personal details were to be sent to Moscow on an continuous basis. Jędrychowski was interested primarily in the military specialists and activists of democratic parties who could be transported to Poland immediately. In addition, the ZPP was asked to provide information about all the cases of Poles being persecuted by London agents so the PKWN to prepare an appropriate demarche to the Swedish Envoy to Moscow. The ZPP was also to collect evidence implicating agents of the London mission in a cooperation with the Nazi spy network.[213] Starting from autumn 1944, therefore, the ZPP in Sweden began to play the role of an unofficial representative of PKWN. The group of related activists included mostly the fugitives from Finland, Norway and Germany, who were unwilling to leave and join the Polish army in Great Britain: Kazimierz Kozłowski, Franciszek Pierkiel and Henryk Świętochowski (who fled from the Todt Organisation in Norway), Józef Bick (a refugee of Jewish origin who came to Sweden from Finland), Ludwik Prigonikier (an escapee from a prisoner camp in Germany) and Andrzej Gołuchowski.[214]

---

[211] AAN, ZPPwZSRR, 216/29, report by the Union of Polish Patriots in Sweden no. 2, 30 X 1944, p. 13–14a.
[212] PISM, A XII, 3/41, note by Colonel S. Gano 'ZPP w Szwecji', 13 XI 1944.
[213] AAN, ZPPwSz, 434/4, telegram by representative of the PKWN in Moscow, S. Jędrychowski, to J. Pański from 12 XI 1944, p. 15. The telegram was written in Russian.
[214] PISM, A 11, VI 21/590, letter by Envoy H. Sokolnicki to the Ministry of Foreign Affairs, 26 III 1945.

7. The Double Game of Swedish Diplomacy (from the *De-Facto* Recognition of the Lublin Committee Poland to the Establishment of *De Jure* Relations)

The rising in Warsaw from a Swedish perspective

The establishment of organisational structures by the Polish communists in Sweden coincided with the outbreak of the rising in Warsaw. *Aftontidningen* was likely the first newspaper to announce this fact on 3 August.[1] The rising was started by the Home Army (*Armia Krajowa* or *AK*) led by gen. Tadeusz Bór-Komorowski. The purpose of the rising was to seize the city before Soviet troops reached it to demonstrate that the Polish resistance movement answered to the Polish government in London, which was the true host of the country. The underground army was, however, insufficiently armed and quickly suffered heavy losses. The rising lasted for 63 days until 2 October when gen. Bór-Komorowski capitulated. About 16 thousand insurgents died and 20 thousand were wounded. The Germans responded with cruel repercussions against the civil population and killed 150–200 thousand inhabitants of Warsaw. Over 600 thousand were forced to leave the city.

Every day, both the Swedish press and the radio transmitted the latest news about the situation in Warsaw. Most opinions were pro-Polish. However, as highlighted Żaba, 'The only friction in the harmonious and favourable chorus in the Swedish press were the distasteful reports by *Göteborgs Handels- och Sjöfarts-Tidning* from London, as well as, naturally, those of the communist *Ny Dag*.'[2]

Żaba reported that the editorial section of the Gothenburg daily did not share the views of its correspondent, which was supported in a favourable article. The Press Attaché inspired numerous articles in many dailies, every day the telegrams of the PAT were sent out, as well as a special bulletin every three days.

In turn, the head of the base of communication with Poland, counsellor Józef Przybyszewski, reported that the Swedish press was avoiding publishing

---

[1] 'Öppen revolt i Warszawa', *Aftontidningen*, 3 VIII 1944; PISM, col. 133, vol. 195, note by M. Karniol no. 189, Stockholm, 27 IX 1944.
[2] AAN, Norbert Żaba's collection, copy of report by N. Żaba to the Ministry of Information and Documentation, Stockholm, 20 IX 1944.

views that could offend the British and the Americans, who the Poles criticized for not supporting the rising and not exerting pressure on the Soviet authorities to mount a military campaign around Warsaw. What was also noticeable was the self-restraint towards the Soviet Union. Although, the report's author highlighted, 'there are clear voices that Russia's negative attitude towards the issue of supporting the fighting Warsaw is intentional and its purpose is to force Poland to adopt the conditions of the agreement dictated by Russia.' Nevertheless, the report mostly highlighted the interest devoted to the developments in Warsaw:

> All in all, insofar as the indifference of Swedish society towards political issues that are not directly related to them is commonly known, when it comes to this issue the interest of the widest social spheres, who clearly sympathize with Poland, is immense. This is for instance proven by the fact that the entire press, including the provincial press, aside from other current events (France, Romania, Bulgaria), publishes detailed information on the course of the battles in Warsaw.'[3]

According to Przybyszewski, the Swedes received news of the rising in Warsaw with understanding. As he said, 'they are well-oriented in the entire situation, showing us great sympathy and providing accurate assessments of Russia's moves.'

Göteborgs Handels- och Sjöfarts-Tidning, which Żaba was critical of, published 'The Mystery of the Warsaw Battle Commander' on 9 August that was written by its London resident. The author wondered who had decided to initiate the rising, because 'the Russian army cannot adapt its offensive to the disposal of the Polish resistance movement, especially in the situation when it is managed by the London circles who are not in touch with the Russian commander.'[4] On 10 August a report was published mentioning the words of General Sosnkowski, who demanded that the allies grant support to the embattled Warsaw.[5] The Commander-in-Chief of the Polish army informed the public in Great Britain that the Germans were murdering the citizens of Warsaw indiscriminately. Nevertheless, the British passed their responsibility to the Polish government in exile, which – according to the

---

[3] PUMST, Sk. 8.26, letter by 'Gryf' [Józef Przybyszewski] to the head of the Special Division of Commander-in-Chief, 29 VIII 1944.
[4] 'Mystik kring ledaren av striderna i Warszawa', *Göteborgs Handels- och Sjöfarts-Tidning*, 9 VIII 1944.
[5] 'Brittisk omsvängning gentemot polska regeringen. Intriger kring tragedin i Warszawa framkalla olust', *Göteborgs Handels- och Sjöfarts-Tidning*, 10 VIII 1944.

British authorities – gave the order to start the rising without consulting the British and Soviet leadership.

Nya Dagligt Allehanda published the article 'The Blow of the Underground' by John Walterson that emphasized the loneliness of the insurgents. The author argued that the activity of the Poles had made the task of the Soviet army much easier and that it could initiate the attack on the Germans, but, nevertheless, failed to do so for political reasons. The activity of the Polish resistance movement, at least from 1941, and fierce battles in the streets of Warsaw had proven most importantly that, as Walterson concluded, the Resistance Movement of the Underground Polish State 'was not a product of propaganda, but an important element, which will have to be respected by everybody both now and in the future.'[6]

By 12 August the press published the Reuters' telegrams announcing the conclusion of the struggle in Warsaw. In the following days, however, other news reported that despite the advantage of the Germans and their cruelty towards the civilians, as well as considerable losses amongst the insurgent troops, the fight continued. On the same day, Gunnar Almstedt published an article in *Ystad Allehanda*. He wrote that the rising in Warsaw constituted only a part of the military effort of the Polish army, which from the very first day had ceaselessly fought on land, sea and in the air.[7] *Göteborgs Handels- och Sjöfarts-Tidning* also published a text that highlighted the heroism of the Polish underground movement during the several year-long struggle.[8]

On 24 August, *Stockholms-Tidningen* published an unusually suggestive article with a map of Warsaw on which were marked the most important sites in the city, including for the most part those which were currently in the hands of the Poles. What was nonetheless most noticeable about the map was the red line depicting the German–Soviet front, which exposed the intentional inaction of the Red Army. The authors highlighted that the tragedy of Warsaw being witnessed by Europe was the third that the city had encountered during the Second World War, following the German aggression in September 1939 and the ghetto uprising in April 1943. When the Soviet army reached the outskirts of the Polish capital, and when on 31 July the Soviet radio *Kościuszko* called the Poles to battle, it seemed as if the Germans faced defeat. The author of the article stated, 'That is why General Bór issued the

---

[6] J. Waltersson [sic!], 'Anfall från underjorden. Polska partisaner strida i Warszawa', *Nya Dagligt Allehanda*, 11 VIII 1944.

[7] G. Almstedt, 'Armén, som aldrig kapitulerat', *Ystads Allehanda*, 12 VIII 1944.

[8] M. Vanni, 'Storm. Den underjordiska kampen i Polen', *Göteborgs Handels- och Sjöfarts-Tidning*, 12 VIII 1944.

decision of the outbreak of the rising. Nevertheless, instead of receiving help, the Poles endured attacks from Soviet propaganda, which accused them of an armed attack without an agreement with Moscow.'[9]

Reports describing fights in the capital poured in throughout the following weeks.[10] 'Tragedy' appeared in these reports with increasing frequency.[11] The journalist for *Göteborgs Handels- och Sjöfarts-Tidning* changed his tone and reported that in London there were noises that the Soviet offensive was intentionally suspended and that the insurgents were left to mercy of the Germans.[12] On 5 September, Stalin was accused by the same newspaper of deliberate inaction on the outskirts of Warsaw:

> The Russians withheld their offensive several kilometres outside the city without any serious attempt to grant their support, and the gallant Warsaw heroes have been left to their own devices. [...] As long as the strategic reasons that held back the help remain unexplained, the world will not abandon its efforts to inquire into this mystery with feelings of reluctance.[13]

According to Żaba, the enthusiastic article by Torgny Segerstedt was sufficient evidence for *Göteborgs Handels- och Sjöfarts-Tidning* to evaluate the events in Warsaw in a different way. The Segerstedt article was published on the day of the anniversary of the war's outbreak and it praised the Poles for fighting for the freedom of Europe in 1939. Segerstedt highlighted towards the end, 'Poland, paying a great price, acquired the right to become reborn as a significant power in the European system of countries.'[14] In an editorial from 6 September, *Arbetaren* pointed out that the rising had broken out in response to the appeal from the Allies, including the calls from Moscow. In the first instance, the responsibility was placed on Stalin.

---

[9] 'Hemsk tragedi väntar Warszawas patrioter. Ryssarna vägrade hjälpa, kapitulation efter blodbad', *Stockholms-Tidningen*, 24 VIII 1944. See: PUMST, Sk. 8.26. Translation of the article quoted above.

[10] PISM, col. 133, vol. 195, notes by M. Karniol nos. 191–196, Stockholm, 27 IX 1944; 'Fasansfulla förhållanden i Warszawa', *Aftontidningen*, 28 IX 1944; IPMS, col. 133, vol. 195, note by M. Karniol no. 197, Stockholm, 29 IX 1944; 'Socialister hjälpa Warszawakämparna', *Morgon-Tidningen*, 31 VIII 1944; IPMS, col. 133, vol. 195, note by M. Karniol no. 198, Stockholm, 30 VII 1944.

[11] 'Warszawas hjältekamp för frihet världshistoriens största tragedi', *Morgon-Tidningen*, 20 VIII 1944; 'Den polska tragedin', *Svenska Dagbladet*, 21 VIII 1944; E. Lindquist, 'Tragedin i Warszawa', *Morgon-Tidningen*, 22 VIII 1944; 'Tragedin Warszawa hotar allierade enigheten', *Morgon-Tidningen*, 30 VIII 1944; Thorburn, 'Vatikanen komplicerar tragedin för Warszawa', *Sydsvenska Dagbladet Snällposten*, 4 IX 1944.

[12] 'Situationen', *Göteborgs Handels- och Sjöfarts-Tidning*, 25 VIII 1944.

[13] 'Idag', *Göteborgs Handels- och Sjöfarts-Tidning*, 5 IX 1944.

[14] [T. Segerstedt], 'Polens dag', *Göteborgs Handels- och Sjöfarts-Tidning*, 31 VIII 1944.

7. THE DOUBLE GAME OF SWEDISH DIPLOMACY

Within weeks, some Swedish public figures were successfully motivated to submit an appeal for aid for Warsaw. On 9 August, *Göteborgs Posten* circulated a fiery appeal entitled 'Hjälp Polen' (Help Poland) by Jeanna Oterdahl. She argued that no other country had suffered as much as Poland and that the 'innate humanitarianism of the Swedes makes it difficult for them to imagine the infernal measures that are used by the occupants in Poland, which are a brutal reality.'[15] On 31 August 1944, the Swedish Social Democrats, together with the refugees of twelve nationalities, organized a meeting in Stockholm where the situation in Warsaw was discussed. During the meeting, following the speech by Maurycy Karniol, a resolution was passed containing messages of kindness for the insurgents and an appeal to the Allies to provide support for the Home Army.[16]

The organisation *Hjälp Polens Barn*, headed by Marika Stiernstedt, initiated Polish Week, which started on 15 September. Honourable patronage over this event was assumed by Prince Eugen, brother of Gustaf V. The programme included concerts, theatre, ballet and film, which were coupled with charity collections for the citizens of Warsaw. In Stockholm, almost 100 thousand crowns was donated, but collections were also conducted in the farthest reaches of Sweden.[17] As part of Polish Week[18] an appeal was made to the Swedish society for the donation of books and teaching aids.

On 28 September, Bonniers, the largest of the Swedish publishing houses, launched the 44-page booklet *Warszawa!* (Warsaw) of which 5 thousand copies were printed. The booklet was co-authored by journalist Gunnar Almstedt and one of the most popular Swedish writers Eyvind Johnson. It was sold together with a 14-page supplement ('Famous Swedes on Poland') containing short statements by 20 Swedish personages – intellectuals and social activists of different political views – about Poland.[19] The branch office of the Ministry of Information and Documentation bought 3 thousand copies, which were immediately sent to public libraries, schools, parliament,

---

[15] 'J. Oterdahl, Hjälp Polen!', *Göteborgs Posten*, 9 VIII 1944.
[16] PISM, col. 133, vol. 195, report by M. Karniol no. 219, Stockholm, 25 I 1945.
[17] AAN, HI/I/80, letter by Polish Envoy to Stockholm H. Sokolnicki to the Ministry of Foreign Affairs, Stockholm, 7 X 1944.
[18] 'Hjälp Polen!', *Upsala Nya Tidning*, 19 IX 1944; 'Gripande Polen-soaré på KFUM i går', *Upsala Nya Tidning*, 20 IX 1944.
[19] G. Almstedt, E. Johnson, *Warszawa!*, Stockholm 1944; *Kända svenskar om Polen*, Stockholm 1944 (the supplement sold with the booklet *Warszawa!*). Cf: PUMST, Sk. 37.1, letter by Press Attaché of the Polish Legation in Stockholm N. Żaba to the Ministry of Information and Documentation together with two attachments, 5 X 1944.

various organisations and private individuals.[20] In the first editorial, 'The Rising' (dated 14 September), Almstedt pointed out, 'The bewildering pace of the attack of the Western Allies turned the attention of the public opinion away from the tragedy of Poland.' He also noted, 'due to the political conflicts between the powers it is so far advisable not to speak about the fighting Poles too openly', and 'even in Sweden there are many voices accusing the Poles of using the rising as a measure that would lead to the liberation of their country.' Almstedt repeated with sorrow that one could mostly read about reactionism connected with the Poles' 'pointless incident of taking up an armless battle':

> Whereas, the Warsaw Rising has nothing in common with the issue of reactionism or non-reactionism. It is only the expression of ardent yearning of the indomitable and freedom-loving nation to personally contribute to its own liberation, and in the seizing of arms on 1 August 1944, which was undertaken to shake off the yoke of bondage, there was equally little Polish "reactionism" as in the decision to use armed resistance against the Nazi aggression of 1 September 1939. At least in such a neutral country as Sweden one should avoid formulating such kind of accusations. It would be best for Sweden not to address any accusations towards the Poles that they are not being polite while being hanged!

Following an emotional introduction, Almstedt carefully clarified the genesis and the course of the rising and explained the political conflict, which took place around the fights in Warsaw at the behest of Stalin. The author concluded his text with an equally strong tone. He underlined that if the cannonade that was heard by the insurgents in the Praga quarter was not a sign of the upcoming liberation, then the war had become pointless.

The second text, 'Warszawa', written by Eyvind Johnson, was to convince the Swedish reader that they should not be indifferent towards the fate of Poland. The writer opened it with a phrase often repeated in Sweden: '*Vad angår oss polska affärer?*' ('Why should we care about Polish affairs?'),[21] and further, 'What do we care about the attempt to liberate Warsaw by General Bór and his soldiers? Do we have a reason to engage in this – embarrassing for most of us – conflict between the Polish government in London and the

---

[20] AAN, HI/I/227, letter by Press Attaché of the Polish Legation in Stockholm N. Żaba to the Ministry of Information and Documentation, Stockholm, 28 XI 1944.

[21] This is a reference to the words of the popular 18th-century Swedish poet Carl Michael Bellman, who commented on the fact that his friend got battered for playing Polish tunes: 'Why the hell do you get yourself into Polish affairs? [...] Avoid playing Polish tunes! Remember, from now on keep your mouth shut' (Fredman's epistle no. 45)

7. THE DOUBLE GAME OF SWEDISH DIPLOMACY

Soviet Union, or in the conflict between the Polish circles in the East and Polish circles in the West? Or within the Polish circles?' Johnson claimed that under the influence of the propaganda the average Swede was unable to take any position, had doubts, and that is why a neutral attitude was preferable, which allowed him or her to refrain from taking a stand on the Polish issue. This was so that these issues were so different from the Swedish needs, wishes and the currently on-going parliamentary campaign. Meanwhile, Johnson thought it should have been completely different, as Poland was the first country to resist Hitler, to live through the terrible occupation and to engage its troops on many fronts as well as underground. According to the eminent writer, all that was known about Nazism was mostly the result of Poland's sacrifice. Johnson did not answer the question that was posed at the outset of the text. As a matter of fact, he concluded it with, 'Will the appeal to the world for at least moral support, which is day after day sent out by the secret Polish radio station from the besieged Warsaw, remain unheard also in this free and enlightened country?'

The supplement 'Famous Swedes on Poland' opened with a statement by the executive director of the American Bank in Warsaw in the pre-war period, Harald Axell, who had stayed in occupied Poland for some time. He argued, 'We, the Swedes, who have so much in common with the Polish nation, were unable to help it in liberating its country, but it is exactly for this reason that we should not delay in providing as much of our help as possible to the rebuilding.' The activist of the Polish Aid Committee of Malmö, Sigma Blanck, pointed to the heroism of September 1939 and the fights in the ghetto in 1943. Warsaw was again making a sacrifice at the altar of freedom. Blanck summed up, 'May the world finally understand its debt towards You and hurry to pay it off, as this is a great debt.' Vicar Daniel Cederberg repeated the words of the late archbishop Nathan Söderblom, who towards the end of the First World War was 'one of the many who were greedily expecting positive aspects', and he found one such aspect in the resurrection of Poland. Cederberg stated, 'The tragedy of Poland and its uncertain future is for many of us the darkest point in the gloominess of this war', although 'Poland deserved the right to live more than any other country in the world.' Remembering the Swedish sympathies for the Polish fights for independence in the 19th century, he argued:

> this is not only about some romantic sense of humanitarianism in our national character. This understanding has its source in the awareness that our own existence is to a large extent dependant on the very same political factors that have decided on the fate of Poland. That very same awareness lives in us

also today, as a matter of fact not only in our own nation but generally in all small, freedom-loving nations around the entire world. For this awareness it is difficult to find a better motto than that which accompanied the *Polenhjälpen* ['Help for Poland', humanitarian aid organisation] on launching its charity collection: "The matter of Poland is the matter of mankind".

Editor-in-chief of the *Östgöten* daily, Rolf Edberg, asked rhetorically 'On 1 September we were convinced that the matter of Poland is the matter of the entire world. Is it still so?' Professor of Slavonic studies at the University of Uppsala Gunnar Gunnarsson pointed out that it was not only about the fate of Warsaw, but all of Poland, which the Soviet Union wished to enslave by seizing half of its territory. An opinion journalist for *Nya Dagligt Allehanda* Knut Hagberg, on the other hand, called for a strong and wealthy Poland. Writer Harry Martinson, in turn, expressed an idealist view saying, 'the world's conscience may set Poland free, may influence the statesmen's decisions at conferences and influence them in the name of justice.' An appeal for aid for Warsaw was submitted, although, as noted by professor Axel L. Romdahl at the Gothenburg University:

> Here in Sweden we are in the fortunate position that we are not forced to take a stand regarding what is going on in the wider world. And after all, as human beings, we must feel deeply outraged and moved by the suffering that has been encountered by the Polish nation, and most importantly its capital Warsaw, and by the fight they are now pursuing.

The director of the Swedish National Museum in Stockholm, Erik Wettergren, invoking the stereotypical picture of Poland, appealed to the logically thinking Swedes for specific help:

> We are now too used to the fact that the Poles are managing their internal and external disagreements on their own. However, this time we need to support them in their march to freedom. Those that are to create new Poland, need to have weapons and bombers, water and medicines, houses to live in and food to eat; their children – starving, naked and wandering about without supervision – must be given clothes, food and something that would resemble their family homes and parental care. With the help of our civilized world the heart of this country needs to start beating again. Warsaw must be rebuilt.'

These views were shared by: social activist Kerstin Hesselgren, professor at Lund University and editor-in-chief of *Sydsvenska Dagbladet Snällposten*

7. THE DOUBLE GAME OF SWEDISH DIPLOMACY

Claes Lindskog; leading activist of the Social Democratic Party and editor-in-chief of *Morgon-Tidningen* Rickard Lindström; authorizing officer of the Gothenburg museum and head of the National Tourism Office in Stockholm Gustaf Munthe; famous social activist Alva Myrdal; editor-in-chief of the *Trots Allt!* magazine Ture Nerman; director of the ASEA company and courier for the Polish underground movement Sven Norrman; women writers Marika Stiernstedt and Jeanna Oterdahl, editor-in-chief of *Göteborgs Handels- och Sjöfarts-Tidning* Torgny Segerstedt; writer Axel Strindberg and actress Naima Wifstrand. All their statements abounded in agitation, compassion and hope that the fate of Poland would change, as if it happened otherwise it would mean the failure of the ideals of freedom across Europe. An understanding started to dawn that the rising had fallen victim to international policy.[22]

Following the collapse of the rising, Elna Gistedt-Kiltynowicz travelled to Sweden and gave an interview to *Svenska Dagbladet*. In her statement she emphasized that despite the defeat 'the Polish spirit is not broken, the nation is alive and will live on.'[23] She then attended a meeting with the representative of the Polish Legation in Stockholm, to whom she told her story. On 7 September she was driven out of Warsaw by the Germans to Pruszków, where she spent three days, from 8 to 12 September, in appalling conditions. She told the legation's staff member about public sentiments before the rising and while it lasted.[24] She remembered that the rumours about the preparations before the rising were circulating for months, but everybody imagined that the riot against the Germans would last only about three days, after which help would arrive and the insurgents would somehow manage. Elna Gistedt, who was the owner of a coffee house on Nowy Świat street, became acquainted with most diverse gossip. On 31 July she learned about the insurgent alert but there again on 1 August news spread that the order was revoked. Later, at noon, one of the German customers told her not to leave home until 4 p.m. According to Gistedt, the Poles could not count on surprise, 'The Germans who had many spies at their disposal, were unfortunately informed

---

[22] 'Ropet från Warszawa', *Sydsvenska Dagbladet Snällposten*, 6 IX 1944.
[23] Attis., 'Warszawa finns inte mera, inte en polack kvar i ruinstaden', *Svenska Dagbladet*, 15 XI 1944.
[24] PISM, PRM 161, copy of the interview with Elna Gistedt, Sztokholm, 18 XII 1944 r., pp. 2–9. E. Gistedt-Kiltynowicz wrote the following memoirs: *Från operett till tragedi*, Stockholm 1946; Polish edition: *Od operetki do tragedii. Ze wspomnień szwedzkiej gwiazdy operetki warszawskiej*, translated by M. Olszańska, Warsaw 1982.

in detail about the planned outbreak of the rising. Betrayal was omnipresent, and the Germans had their men in almost all tenements.

Illustration 6: '*Ropet från Warszawa*' ['The Call from Warsaw']. The caption reads 'The mournful music is spoiling the mood'.

On presenting the commonly known picture of the technical superiority of the Germans and their cruelty, especially of the Kalmyk people and other soldiers from Soviet republics at the service of the Germans, Gistedt emphasized:

> At the beginning of the rising the Germans […] were in a very difficult situation and had Warsaw received sufficient support, the rising would have ended differently. […] The mood was however not entirely optimistic, people wanted to continue to believe in victory. Initially, each metre of the conquered

land was welcomed with enjoyment, because this land was "free". The enthusiasm which ruled in Warsaw at the outset of the rising cannot simply be described [...].

Elna Gistedt claimed that there were in fact some individuals who maintained that the fight in the barricades was folly and unreasonable. She then identified with the combatants: 'I nevertheless told them that although I am Swedish, I understand them, this moment is ours, and this piece of land is ours!'

The bitterness connected with the defeat turned most of all against the Soviets. According to the Swede, there also appeared disappointment with the position of the British. Żaba maintained that the intelligence had great propagandist value. He claimed, 'it breathes inexhaustible hope in the future of the nation, which can show such resistance, and it describes the moods in Poland – even following such horrible shocks, as being full of hope in victory.'[25]

The interest with the rising continued after its downfall. In *Arbetaren*, on 4 October, the article 'Warszawa' appeared, marked with a black cross. The attitude of the allies towards the insurgents was commented on briefly: 'They have been cold-bloodedly submitted to extermination.' The author named the reasons for the defeat with clear outrage: 'The insurgents gave up, because they did not receive help from the Allies, and they were not granted ammunition, because they were not granted weapons. That is why Warsaw will be 'a bloody stain in the register of deeds committed by the Allies, a wound, from which blood will always stream, an ever-lasting accusation, which would never be abated.' The author of the article quoted the accusations against the insurgents very emotionally. He was clearly on their side and proclaimed the following manifesto in their defence:

> Is it possible to find freedom fighters, which were as ridiculed as they were? Why did they start the rising? Why didn't they wait? Why didn't they establish cooperation with the Russian army? Why didn't they wait for the advice from the Allies? Why all the hurry? Such excuses are flung in their face by the antagonists who should have helped them like brothers and companions-in-arms. Why are people sometimes so defiant that they try to shake off the yoke of bondage? To free oneself from tyrants, to overcome the system of terror,

---

[25] AAN, Norbert Żaba's collection, copy of report by N. Żaba to the Ministry of Information and Documentation, Stockholm, 16 III 1944.

which took delight in their torment? Why do people love freedom so madly? Even the seven sages cannot answer these questions.[26]

In response, the communists launched a propagandist attack against the command of the Home Army and the Polish government in London. After the press announcement of the news from Osóbka-Morawski and Żymierski, there were claims voiced that Bór-Komorowski, who staged the rising, was not even in town, and the responsibility that was placed on him for what had happened, made him a traitor of the nation.[27] The role of the Soviet propaganda mouthpiece was continuously played in Sweden by *Ny Dag*. Following the failure of the rising in Warsaw, the newspaper lay blame for the defeat on the Home Army command, which gave the order to attack the Germans, as 'General Bór and his group were unfortunately controlled by political reasons, which had nothing to do with the interests of the Polish nation.' What was presented was the account of an anonymous Home Army soldier, who made his way to the other side of the Vistula River and accused Bór-Komorowski of conducting a private, harmful policy without considering the opinion of other officers of the Home Army. Only the PKWN rose to the occasion, as its members, though they 'considered the rising to be premature and criticised those who were responsible for it', 'at the same time all did their best to rescue the situation and to conquer the Germans.'[28] In this vein a series of articles devoted to the rising was created. The articles were to show 'how great the gap was between the Polish nation and these masters who, in pursuit of power, become involved in affairs, for which the nation has to pay.'[29] Despite the aggressive propaganda, after the collapse of the rising, probably nobody in Sweden had any doubts that Stalin sabotaged all attempts of help.[30] This did not change the predictions that after the Germans' withdrawal from the Polish capital, the PKWN would proclaim itself a legitimate government.[31]

The landscape after the battle was presented by *Göteborgs Handels- och Sjöfarts-Tidning*. The defeat of the rising, on 4 October, was named the most

---

[26] 'Warszawa', *Arbetaren*, 4 X 1944. Cf.: IPMS, col. 133, vol. 195, report by M. Karniol no. 220, Stockholm, 25 I 1945; AAN, Norbert Żaba's collection, copy of the Legation's press report for October 1944 ('Obrona Warszawy w prasie szwedzkiej').
[27] H. Shapiro, 'Warszawa-generalen hotas av befrielseutskottet', *Nya Dagligt Allehanda*, 1 X 1944; 'General Bor ansvarig for Warszawa tragedin', *Arbetet*, 2 X 1944.
[28] *Varför slutade upproret i Warszawa med nederlag?*, *Ny Dag*, 22 XI 1944.
[29] 'I Berlin ska Warszawa hämnas', *Ny Dag*, 24 XI 1944. 'Warszawas befolkning förde den utsiktslösa kampen med stort mod', *Ny Dag*, 23 XI 1944.
[30] 'Warszawa', *Vestmanlands Läns Tidning*, 4 X 1944.
[31] 'En europeisk fråga', *Dagens Nyheter*, 4 X 1944.

tragic event of the war.³² On the next day, the author of the series of articles on the current situation stated that it was possible to avoid the tragedy that took place in Warsaw, and he asked a rhetorical question about whether Warsaw fell victim of the cruel, cold Moscow imperialism. He also added: 'The fire of Warsaw illuminates not only the tragedy, but also sheds light on the intentions of Russia, which may be indeed fake, but which are noticed by the world not without anxiety.'³³

The series of articles on the city's capitulation was published in *Dagens Nyheter* by its Berlin correspondent Ivar Vesterlund.³⁴ The author highlighted that he was the only Swedish journalist who had an opportunity to visit the ruins of Warsaw:

> After about three hours the walk comes to an end. The most extraordinary and the most macabre walk, I have ever taken in my whole life. I walked through a completely deserted city. Not a single store, nor a sign of any life whatsoever. [...] The only people I met were either single German soldiers or groups of these soldiers on their way to the first line of the front or back.³⁵

Vesterlund presented a picture of ruined buildings. Stopping at the ruins of sites that were the symbols of the Polish capital, he told stories of the insurgents, about the defence of the barricades, about marching through sewers, about the extreme conditions in hospitals. The correspondent described the structure of the Home Army and the fate of the city's people following the fall of the rising. He passed over in silence the ordeal of the Poles who were chased off to the camp in Pruszków, and in general he was very understanding towards the German occupational policy. In his last report from 14 November he wrote about German efforts to persuade the Poles to fight with the Soviet army.³⁶

There is no doubt that the rising in Warsaw encouraged the Swedish media to write more favourably about Poland. In mid-September, Żaba reported to the Ministry of Information and Documentation that in the past weeks the Swedish press, in most cases, adopted a positive attitude towards Poland:

---

³² 'Krigets mest tragiska kapitel – Warszawa', *Göteborgs Handels- och Sjöfarts-Tidning*, 4 X 1944.
³³ Jc., 'Situationen', *Göteborgs Handels- och Sjöfarts-Tidning*, 5 X 1944.
³⁴ The first article: I. Vesterlund, 'Chopins hjärta räddad ur lagorna', *Dagens Nyheter*, 3 XI 1944.
³⁵ I. Vesterlund, 'Warszawas överleva boende i arbetsläger', *Dagens Nyheter*, 8 XI 1944.
³⁶ Polish government in exile daily in London *Dziennik Polski i Dziennik Żołnierza* (9, 11, 12, 13, 14 XII 1944) published a series of Vesterlund's articles.

Both under the influence of the developments in Finland and to the attitude of the Soviets towards us, the voices that are critical of Moscow are gaining in strength. If it wasn't for the cynical letters of the collaborator of the London *Göteborgs Handels- och Sjöfarts-Tidning*, as well as the naturally hostile articles of the communist press (*Ny Dag*) and, possibly, the somewhat cold attitude towards the socialist government presented by such newspapers as the social democratic *Aftontidningen*, the syndicalist *Arbetaren* and several provincial periodicals dependant on the aforementioned orientations, we would be dealing with almost uniform, sympathetic, Swedish opinion. What particularly stands out in terms of positive attitude is the provincial press.'[37]

Żaba emphasized the positive overtones particularly in the reports of Kurt Andersson from London for *Morgon-Tidningen*, Thorburn from London for *Sydsvenska Dagbladet Snällposten* and Per Persson from New York for *Svenska Dagbladet*.

The political circumstances, which were closer to the Swedes and which were presented by Żaba, had their meaning. As noted the Attaché, 'It was only the tragedy in Warsaw that has tilted the balance to our side.' He also pointed out: 'The lonely battle of Warsaw has undoubtedly stunned Swedish public opinion.' The provincial press 'pointed out Russia's behaviour towards Poland, holding it responsible for what has happened in Warsaw.' Żaba named several anti-Polish-oriented opinion journalists as exceptions. It is nonetheless worth noting that they were popular figures and their voice in the political debate was important. Two such examples were Johannes Wickman, opinion journalist for *Dagens Nyheter*, or Nils Lindh, a former counsellor of the Swedish Legation in Moscow and a consul of the Åland Islands – at the time a consultant for Soviet affairs by the Ministry of Foreign Affairs – who wrote articles for the social democratic *Morgon-Tidningen* newspaper.[38] The latter argued on 19 September, 'It would be difficult to assume that the Provisional Government, already functioning in Poland,

---

[37] AAN, Norbert Żaba's collection, copy of report by Żaba to the Ministry of Information and Documentation, Stockholm, 14 IX 1944.

[38] AAN, Norbert Żaba's collection, copy of report by N. Żaba to the Ministry of Information and Documentation, Stockholm, 25 X 1944. There is an interesting description of Lindh's work as a press expert, press attaché and finally chancellor of the Swedish legation in Moscow in the years 1924–1938 by Wilhelm Carlgren: Nils Lindh. Pressombudsman, pressattaché och legationsråd i Moskva, [in:] Människan i historien och samtiden. Festskrift till Alf W. Johansson, Stockholm 2000, pp. 82–91. According to Carlgren: "He was a cold and careful observer and thought that he was well informed". He built a network of contacts and used it to prepare long and detailed reports, but "the attitude of the Swedish Foreign Office to the Soviet Union was more critical and negative than the Lindh's one" (pp. 90–91).

which, what is more, obtained authorization from the [State] National Council would agree to hand over its power to the government in London and satisfy itself with a small representation in the new government.' In the next article, published on 21 September, he presented his doubts about the social support of the government in exile among its compatriots in Poland, which was invoked in the official speeches of Prime Minister Mikołajczyk. He considered the only possible solution to be a split in the government and seeking agreement with the PKWN through the representatives of the moderate circles.[39]

In the press report from the end of October, Żaba emphasized, 'the favourable situation continues.' Swedish public opinion was clearly interested in Stalin's behaviour towards his neighbours, as it was worried about the fate of Finland, whose capitulation coincided with the closing phase of the rising. According to Żaba, the Swedish government reacted too late to the spontaneous opinions, which reflected the critics of the ruthless Soviet policy:

> The opportunist attitude towards the Soviet Union of some the Swedish official circles, like for instance the Ministry of Foreign Affairs or some socialist groupings or financial circles, so far did not manage to exert any influence on the Swedish press, all the more so that some other, no less influential Swedish bodies are either granting their silent support to our propaganda or at least tolerate it. Therefore, despite only few exceptions, the Swedish press is not hiding their sympathy towards the Polish matter and expresses anxiety about the future fate of smaller European countries, while admitting that the Polish cause has become a cardinal issue of our continent.[40]

Independently of these political connotations, the feelings that were predominant in Swedish society following Warsaw's tragedy were reflected in the empathy-filled poem 'To Poland' ('Do Polski') by Jeanna Oterdahl, translated by Stanisław Baliński and published in the *Dziennik Polski* and the *Dziennik Żołnierza* on 30 October 1944.[41] The poetic appeal brought propagandist results, but also considerable material gifts for the people of Warsaw from the ordinary citizens of Sweden. Moreover, the popularity of

---

[39] R. I. [Nils Lindh], 'Polacker i öster och i väster', *Morgon-Tidningen*, 19 IX, 21 IX 1944; PISM, col. 133, vol. 195, report by M. Karniol no. 219, Stockholm, 25 I 1945.
[40] AAN, Norbert Żaba's collection, copy of report by N. Żaba to the Ministry of Information and Documentation, Stockholm, 25 X 1944.
[41] The Swedish first edition of the poem has not been found. The piece was not included in the writer's collected works.

the rising undoubtedly contributed to the decision by the Swedish government to organize a significant humanitarian campaign in the occupied territories of Poland.

The propagandist campaign for the recognition of Poland's right to sovereignty and territorial integrity

The Polish propagandist services made every effort to make the voice of the Polish government heard. They submitted reference materials to the editorial sections of the Swedish dailies and at times they inspired the publication of books. This led to several publications that attempted to familiarize the Swedish reader with the genesis, course and possible solutions to the conflict between the Polish authorities in London and Stalin. Of the least persuasive character was the publication by the famous journalist and historian Åke Thulstrup, who, in the brochure *Den polsk-ryska konflikten* (The Polish–Russian Conflict) dated 27 June 1944, discussed the ethnic relations in the Eastern Borderlands, the history of conflicts between the Poles and Russians throughout the 19th and 20th century, the minority-related issues of the Second Polish Republic as well as the difficult relations during the Second World War. The author tried not to take any position and only presented the facts. The closing excerpts, however, proved that, given Stalin's determination in setting the border along the Bug River, it would be difficult to imagine another solution. What needs to be treated as a postscript, which questioned the possibility of the London government's return to Poland, are the two closing paragraphs devoted to the PKWN. These were most probably added by Thulstrup after the publication had gone to press.[42]

Inspired by the Polish press attaché's office, other publications also appeared, presenting the fundamental controversial issues in the relations with the Soviet Union from the point of view of the Polish government in exile. These publications include *Öster om Bug. Fakta kring de östpolska problemen* (To the East of the Bug River. The Facts Around the Issue of Eastern Poland) by John Walterson and *Polens öde. Ett europeiskt cardinalproblem* (The Fate of Poland. The Fundamental Problem of Europe) by Paul Olberg.

Olberg opened with an outline of the history of Poland, primarily focusing on the post-partition chapter. He highlighted Poland's contribution to world culture, the work of Chopin, Słowacki, Mickiewicz, as well as the achievements in the field of education. He presented the history of Poland following

---

[42] Å. Thulstrup, *Den polsk-ryska konflikten*, Stockholm 1944.

the return to independence, its relations with Germany and the Soviet Union, crowned with the triumph of imperialism of both these countries in the shape of 'the fourth partition'. Then, Olberg discussed the brutal, contrary to international laws, everyday life of both occupations, including deportations, confiscations of property, economic drain and the extermination of people. An important excerpt from the book was devoted to the fate of the government and the Polish soldiers following the September defeat, as well as to the activity of the underground movement in Poland. Olberg argued that both political parties in exile and their representatives in occupied Poland were striving to rebuild their homeland not only as a sovereign country, but also a democratic one. The author acknowledged the difficult task of integrating parts of the country that were previously controlled by the partitioning powers. With respect and admiration, he named the examples of bravery among the soldiers of the Polish army during the defence of Poland against the German aggression and on other fronts later during the war. He perceived the Polish–Soviet dispute to be another manifestation of the imperialism of Stalin, whose successes in the war with Hitler encouraged him to launch a diplomatic offensive with the purpose of conducting the Sovietisation of Eastern Europe, and Poland in particular. Based on the arguments that were announced publicly by Adam Pragier, the famous activist of the PPS, Olberg rejected situating the border along the Curzon Line, which lacked historical foundation and was only a less awkward alternative to the demarcation line established by Stalin with Hitler in 1939. Olberg admitted that the Polish authorities treated national minorities unfairly before war broke out. He nevertheless added that the reign of the Soviet dictatorship was tantamount to the complete lack of national rights for Ukrainians and Belarusians. He compared the Polish Committee of National Liberation (PKWN) to the government of Kuusinen, an entity which was completely dependent on the thirst for territorial expansion by Stalin. Naming subsequent actions of the Home Army, he polemicized with the Soviet propaganda, which announced that the Polish resistance movement was inactive Galicia with Lviv were inseparably connected with the Polish state. He underlined that the Curzon Line had never constituted a Polish–Soviet border, and never before had either the Polish side or the Soviet side introduced a proposal to establish a common border on this basis. Making use of official statistics, popularized by the Polish Ministry of Information and Documentation, he presented a picture contrary to reality, that Polish group of nationalists existed in greater numbers than all other groups, although he emphasized that the Soviet deportations and policy of extermination which was conducted by the

Germans undoubtedly contributed to the decrease in the number of Poles in these areas. He also argued that there existed a friendly atmosphere that facilitated the development of the cultural-educational life of the Ukrainians, the Belarusians and the Lithuanians in the Second Polish Republic, and he provided information about grants for schools teaching Ukrainian language, financial support of the Polish government for the Ukrainian Scientific Institute in Warsaw and the unhampered activity of the national minorities' cooperative associations. Based on witness accounts, the situation in the Eastern Borderlands under the Soviet occupation was described by Walterson as 'the period of lawlessness, terror and fear.' He estimated, excessively, the number of deported Poles to be 2 million people. He summed up that, 'for the neutral Swedish observer it would be absurd if Poland was forced to give up 55 percent of its territory and one third of its population to the benefit of one of the Allies.'[43]

Both publications were well received, although accounts and reviews continuously highlighted the pro-Polish attitude of Olberg and Walterson.[44] The only exception was the review by Nils Lindh, who on 20 November 1944 in *Morgon-Tidningen* harshly criticized the publications inspired by the Polish diplomatic mission. According to Karniol, this was 'the first unfavourable review in a pro-Soviet environment.' In the opening sentence Lindh asked rhetorically, 'should we really make special efforts to arouse sympathy for Poland?' Personally, he maintained that despite some Swedes' belief that Polish affairs were none of their business, 'sympathy for Poland is so widespread and uniform in Sweden that convincing the Swedish public on Poland is excessive zealotry.' He claimed that the issue was exclusively about the Polish internal conflict between the government in London and the PKWN. He concluded, 'In this situation a Swede who sympathizes with Poland the most becomes helpless.' That is why the supporters of the London government decided to turn Swedish sympathies in their direction. Lindh concluded, 'The intention is to convince you that this Poland – with no state,

---

[43] J. Walterson, *Öster om Bug. Fakta kring de östpolskaproblemen*, Stockholm 1944, pp. 51–52, 71, 89, 94–95, 132–134, 150–153.

[44] See the review of eminent historian N. Ahnlund: 'Det polska problemet', *Svenska Dagbladet*, 11 IX 1944; others: 'En ny polsk september', *Östgöta Correspondenten*, 22 IX 1944; C. Br, 'Polens öde ett europeiskt kardinalproblem', *Norrbottens-Kuriren*, 9 X 1944; 'Den polska tragedien', *Aftonbladet*, 5 X 1944; 'Europeiska problem', *Norrköpings Tidningar*, 12 X 1944; S. S., 'En bok om Polen', *Upsala Nya Tidning*, 13 X 1944; 'Nya krigsböcker', *Barometern*, 14 X 1944; 'Polens öde', *Falu Kuriren*, 18 X 1944; F. Severin, 'Polens öde', *Aftontidningen*, 19 X 1944; Jc., 'Det polska problemet', *Göteborgs Handels- och Sjöfarts-Tidning*, 20 X 1944; E. Arrhén, 'Polen och Atlantachartan', *Göteborgs Morgonpost*, 8 II 1945.

with men, women, soldiers scattered across many countries and with its government in another nation – is right and the Soviet Union is wrong. When we understand this, we will start to feel a liking towards this Poland, and in connection with this, aversion and disgust towards the Soviet Union.' Lindh considered the aforementioned books about Poland to be biased, and the policy of the Polish government as 'simple speculation in the shape of contrasting the Western Allies with the Soviet Union.'[45]

The response by Soviet propaganda to the publications inspired by the Poles was the book *Om Västukraina och Västvitryssland* (On Western Ukraine and Western Belarus) written by Vladimir Pitjeta, first rector at Belarusian State University in Minsk. The author attacked the Second Polish Republic for persecuting national minorities and called the government in London fascist. In a perverse manner, he referred to the views of Polish historians, who considered the expansion of Poland to the east, in the period of the Nobles' Democracy, to be a mistake. Pitjeta described Walterson's discourse as biased, arguing that what needed to be remembered above all was the Polish imperialism, Polish conquests in the East and the policy of Polonisation. Whereas, it was hard to speak about the national pressure from the authorities in Moscow due to the Ukrainians' and Belarusians' consciousness, as well as their ethnic, linguistic and religious affiliation to the Russian nation. Pitjeta also refuted Walterson's thesis of the long-lasting (for centuries) hostility of the Russians towards the Poles, which was to be denied by the political actions of Tsar Paul and Tsar Alexander as well as the political writings of Decembrists, Alexandr Hercen and Russian revolutionists headed by Lenin. It was Poland which was to be responsible for the poor Polish-Soviet relations after the First World War, as almost all its governments, including the government in London, conducted aggressive eastern policy. According to Pitjeta, their thoughtless actions led to the downfall of the country in 1939. The Soviet scholar argued that Ukrainians constituted an ethnic majority in Eastern Galicia and in Volhynia. The entering of the Soviet army into the Polish Eastern Borderlands was considered by him to be the solution to the issue of Western Ukraine and Western Belarus. Pitjeta rejected the accusations of forceful incorporation of these territories into the Soviet Union. He also refused the Poles the right to evaluate the course of the plebiscite on this matter, for he considered them 'reactionists, who carried the tragedy of the Polish nation on their backs, who had clearly forgotten that

---

[45] R. I. [Nils Lindh], 'Polens sak', *Morgon-Tidningen*, 20 XI 1944; IPMS, col. 133, vol. 195, report by M. Karniol no. 219, Stockholm, 25 I 1945.

the nations of Western Ukraine and Western Belarus never voluntarily acknowledged the superiority of the Polish government, and these areas had been incorporated by force.' The issue was simple: 'Polish magnates and their satellites' should make no comments about 'the democratic character of the elections', thanks to which the rebuilding of Ukrainian and Belarusian economic and cultural life was initiated, the peasants were granted land and thousands of farm animals, and the Soviet government made a decision to fight illiteracy, which was widespread in the Polish era. He described the federation as a fantastical plan, where Poland played the central role. He explained, 'The entire plan is founded on the claims towards the alien territories and clearly reveals the plans of Polish fascists' expansion.' At the same time, he distinguished the Polish government in London from the Polish nation, which was capable of building a sovereign and strong country within ethnographic borders under the leadership of the Union of the Polish Patriots (ZPP) and the activists of the PKWN, who formed the Provisional Government in Warsaw. Surely the greatest calumny which appeared in the book was the accusation of the Polish government in exile of the plan of creating, together with the Germans, the Home Army (Pitjeta calls it a defensive army) to fight the Red Army. The command of these units was to be proposed to General Grot, who, after refusing to accept it, was instantly arrested.[46]

Following the breakdown of the rising, Karniol started to hold speeches on the subject of the current situation in Poland.[47] The principle purpose of Karniol's journalist activity, which was set by him in the spring of 1944 was to convince the Swedish public of the 'democratic spirit of the Polish Underground State.'[48] Karniol's writings on the Polish matters and interviews with

---

[46] V. Pitjeta, *Om Västukraina och Västvitryssland*, Stockholm 1945, pp. 39, 41, 47–56, 82–83, 98, 112–113, 136–137, 170–172, 174–176, 191–194, 209–210, 212–213, 219, 225. Gen. Stefan Grot-Rowecki was the first commander of the Home Army. After his arrest in 1943 the command was taken by gen. Bór-Komorowski. Grot was killed, probably just after the outbreak of the rising in Warsaw in August 1944.

[47] PISM, col. 133, vol. 195, telegram by M. Karniol no. 218, Stockholm, 12 XII 1944 r. The lecture on the subject of the defence of Warsaw was held on 12 October at the seat of the trade union of typographic workers, on 13 October that very same lecture was delivered for the union of the workers of the *Konsum* cooperative, on 1 November – in the seat of the trade union of urban property workers, on 21 November – in *Gustaf Vasa socialdemokratiska föreningen*, on 23 the lecture on the future of East-Central Europe was delivered in the council house *Alvik* on the invitation of the social democratic party unit of Bromma district. Karniol, on 11 and 27 November, met with the Poles from the refugee camp Rosöga nearby Strängnäs and in Traneberg on the anniversary of Poland's independence.

[48] PISM, col. 133, vol. 296, letter by M. Karniol to A. Ciołkosz, Stockholm, 10 IV 1944.

him were published in many Swedish dailies.[49] In September 1944 Karniol managed to publish an article in *Trots Allt!* by Adam Ciołkosz, a leading activist of the PPS residing in London. The name of its author was not disclosed by the newspaper. Ciołkosz did not disguise his feelings in the letter to Karniol: 'The omission of the name is surprising. The English never do such things...' Ciołkosz regularly provided Karniol with the issues of a written information service entitled *Kroniki Generalnej Guberni* (The Chronicles of General Government). Karniol's task was to translate the texts into Swedish and publish them in the Swedish press.[50] From 16 November 1944 onwards the newspaper of the Vasa quarter in Stockholm began publishing announcements about the fights in Warsaw, presented together in the bulletin published by Karniol.[51] Whereas, on 6 December *Morgon-Tidningen* published an interview with Karniol. The Polish socialist emphasized that the PPS was counting on the support of the international worker's movement in connection with the Polish matter.[52] According to him, the presence of Socialists in the government guaranteed social reforms in liberated Poland.[53]

Despite numerous acquaintances, Karniol did not always manage to convince the editors of the periodicals to publish the texts he suggested. In October 1944, Karniol wrote to Ciołkosz that the editorial section of *Social-Demokraten* halted his article about Tomasz Arciszewski. He commented, 'Perhaps this is a coincidence or perhaps it is not. Lately I have been noticing, even in the political party press, a somewhat adaptation to Russia, like the adaptation to Germany, just like in the years 1940–1941.'[54]

Karniol even mentioned to Allan Vougt, 'the authorities of the parties in Sweden often describe the government, where our party sits, to be reactionary, and they often paint an excessively rosy picture of Lublin, thereby going hand in hand with the communists.'[55] He managed to convince Vougt of the

---

[49] 'Expressporträttet: Jan Kwapinski', *Expressen*, 26 XI 1944; 'Expressporträttet: Arciszewski', *Expressen*, 1 XII 1944; M. Karniol, Thomas Arciszewski, 'Polens vicepresident', *Morgon-Tidningen*, 14 X 1944; PISM, col. 133, vol. 195, note by M. Karniol no. 212, Stockholm, 9 XII 1944. P. Grant, 'Warszawa Polens Paris-kommun', *Örebro-Kuriren*, 13 X 1944 (this was a local daily, but issued by vice-president of parliament H. Åkerberg); PISM, col. 133, vol. 195, report by M. Karniol for the period XXII 1944, Stockholm, 31 I 1945.
[50] PISM, col. 133, vol. 296, copy of letter by A. Ciołkosz to M. Karniol, London, 20 IX 1944.
[51] PISM, col. 133, vol. 195, two issues of *Vasaröster*, the organ of the Gustaf Vasa Soc. Dem. Förening, n.p., n.d.
[52] 'Polska regeringsskiftet stärkte hemlandskontakt', *Morgon-Tidningen*, 6 XII 1944; PISM, col. 133, vol. 195, note by M. Karniol no. 214, Stockholm, 10 VII 1944.
[53] 'Londonpolackerna lovar stora sociala reformer', *Aftontidningen*, 3 XII 1944; PISM, col. 133, vol. 195, note by M. Karniol no. 216, Stockholm, 12 VII 1944.
[54] PISM, col. 133, vol. 297, letter by M. Karniol to A. Ciołkosz, Stockholm, 13 IV 1944.
[55] Ibidem.

idea of summoning (on 30 October, during the session of the parliament) a special conference of the representatives of the party and its press organs. Karniol was to present the position of the Polish government towards the issues of international policy and situation in Poland. It is hard to evaluate the propagandist results of this event, as we do not have any sources on this subject. Nevertheless, what was characteristic was the content of Karniol's report to Adam Ciołkosz from December 1944, 'Political work needs to be conducted very carefully and discreetly in this period, for there are tendencies in the Swedish worker's movement to maintain a somewhat detachment as far as Polish matters are concerned.'[56]

In September 1944, Karniol appointed a citizen's committee, gathering mostly individuals who had recently come to Sweden from Poland, and on 13 September he held a special meeting where a resolution was passed in the honour of the Warsaw insurgents together with the declaration of loyalty towards the Polish government in London.[57] The founding committee included attorney Stanisław Adamek, teacher Zbigniew Folejewski, refugee Michał Lisiński, Associate Professor Bolesław Skarżyński, as well as Stefan Trębicki, co-author of the famous book *Country without Quisling*, which was translated into various languages.[58] Karniol intended to express the support of the Polish refugees for the Polish government in London, in response to the earlier meetings of the Union of Polish Patriots (ZPP) in Stockholm, which were attended by small groups of Poles who were dissatisfied with their fate. The meeting, prepared and led by Karniol, was attended by more than three hundred people. In a heartfelt speech, Rickard Lindström stated, 'if the freedom of Poland will be violated, then all what is noble and what humanity is fighting for will be violated.' On the next day, reports from the meeting were published in the main newspapers. In light of the Karniol's reports, the management of the Polish Legation considered it important to initiate an awareness campaign in the form of talks and lectures for the public.[59]

Meanwhile, Karniol tiresomely continued his propagandist activity. On 8 November, he organized a reception for Polish and Swedish guests on the anniversary of the formation of the first Polish socialist government in Lublin (1918). His intention was to point out that as a representative of the PPS he

---

[56] PISM, col. 133, vol. 296, letter by M. Karniol to A. Ciołkosz, Stockholm, 30 XII 1944.
[57] AAN, HI/I/79, letter by Polish Envoy to Stockholm H. Sokolnicki to the Ministry of Foreign Affairs, Stockholm, 9 IX 1944.
[58] PISM, col. 133, vol. 195, invitation to the meeting, 13 IX 1944.
[59] PISM, col. 133, vol. 195, report by representative of the Central Executive Committee of the PPS party M. Karniol. The first page is missing from the document.

was politically independent, and to gauge whether 'the current political situation and propaganda of the [Polish] Committee of National Liberation [PKWN], which made its presence felt in Stockholm, had an impact on the position of the Swedish leftist spheres.' A day after the celebrations of the anniversary of the October Revolution in the Soviet Legation, Karniol decided to organize his own meeting. It transpired that celebrations would continue until 8 November. In a note submitted to London, Karniol highlighted that despite this about seventy people attended the reception, including twenty Poles headed by Envoy Sokolnicki. The Swedish guests included vice president of the Riksdag Harald Åkerberg, president of Stockholm Carl Albert Andersson, president of the Association of Cooperatives Albin Johansson, Allan Vougt and editors-in-chief of six main dailies. The reception was also attended by the socialists, who were representing the groups of refugees from various countries. Karniol considered the reception a success. Although, some of his good friends, for example, Torsten Nilsson, August Lindberg, Ragnar Casparsson and several other leading social democratic activists, did not appear. He suspected that they preferred to attend a reception in the Soviet diplomatic mission instead. As a consolation, he quoted those members of parliament who had confirmed choosing his over the Russian invitation.[60]

In the first half of November 1944, articles about Poland were published less, which Press Attaché Żaba explained was due to, 'on the one hand the Polish–Soviet issue had come to a standstill, and on the other perhaps also pressure from the Soviets.' According to Żaba press opinions were mostly favourable towards Poland, 'The correspondents of the Swedish press in London reported the course of the Polish–Soviet relations objectively for the most part, maintaining that Prime Minister Mikołajczyk was making honest efforts to come to an agreement with Russia, and his moderate policy earned him more and more supporters. Attention was drawn to the fact that the Polish government could not accept the Curzon Line without being guaranteed the course of its western borders and the independence of the new Polish state.[61]

By the end of November, the Polish issues again gained in popularity. Two novels devoted to the Polish cause were published, *Indiansommar 39* (Indian Summer of 39) by Marika Stiernstedt and *Så lång vi leva* (As Long as We Are Alive) by Helen MacInnes. Stiernstedt's book focused on the events of

---

[60] PISM, col. 133, vol. 195, note by M. Karniol: The meeting on the anniversary of the formation of the first people's government of the Polish Republic, Stockholm, 10 XII 1944.
[61] AAN, Norbert Żaba's collection, copy of report by N. Żaba to the Ministry of Information and Documentation, Stockholm, 25 XI 1944.

September 1939 and MacInnes' presented everyday life under German occupation and paid tribute to the Home Army soldiers.⁶² Stiernstedt described the fate of villagers in the eastern Subcarpathia region until the outbreak of the war and tragic events of September 1939. According to a Polish reviewer, the author 'wanted to present how the peaceful, conservative, religious Polish countryside became transformed into a defensive fortress and opposed the invader, and how an industrious peasant who was cut off from the world and a researcher who was also a man of Europe [protagonists of the novel] turned into fearless fighters.'⁶³

In early December 1944, a Swedish radio programme, part of the series *Dokument och ögonvittnen* (Documents and Eyewitnesses), presented the stories of different occupied countries.⁶⁴ An episode devoted to Poland featured Slavicist Gunnar Gunnarsson, who talked about the Soviet occupation, industrialist Sven Norrman, who shared the reports about German occupation, Marika Stierntedt, who read excerpts from *Indiansommar 39*.⁶⁵ At the end of the programme, the Polish national anthem was played. At the same time, *Röster i radio* weekly published extensive material about the participation of the Poles in the Second World War.⁶⁶

Did the Polish propagandist activity bring notable results? Considering the evaluations expressed by attaché Żaba in his press reports, they were surely doomed to fail from the very start. In December 1944, Żaba noted the growth in the critical attitude of the Swedish press towards Polish government policy saying, 'Although the majority of Swedish society and Swedish opinion is essentially unfavourable towards Russia, and favourable towards us, the Swedish "realism" or "opportunism" force us to count on the *fait accompli* and with the currently mighty power.'⁶⁷

---

⁶² AAN, HI/I/226, letter by Press Attaché of the Polish Legation in Stockholm N. Żaba to the Ministry of Information and Documentation, Stockholm, 16 XI 1944.
⁶³ B. Skarżyński, 'Motywy polskie w piśmiennictwie szwedzkim w czasie wojny' (continuation), *Nowa Polska* 1946, iss. 1, p. 6264.
⁶⁴ K. Lindal, *Självcensur...*, p. 172. In May 1945 the recordings of 11 programmes were published in a book: *Detta hände i Europa. Härtagna länder 1938–1941*, Stockholm 1945.
⁶⁵ According to the opinion of the book's reviewer, who worked for *Göteborgs-Tidningen* (1 XI 1944) the novel by M. Stiernstedt was 'a noble product, which glows and warms'.
⁶⁶ 'Audycja w radiu szwedzkim o Polsce. Polska walczy na wszystkich frontach o najwyższe wartości moralne', *Dziennik Polski i Dziennik Żołnierza*, 7 XII 1944.
⁶⁷ AAN, Norbert Żaba's collection, copy of report by N. Żaba do the Ministry of Information and Documentation, Stockholm, 12 I 1945. The survey of the Swedish press' response to the establishment of T. Arciszewski's government was published in the London press: 'Prasa szwedzka o sytuacji Polski', *Dziennik Polski i Dziennik Żołnierza*, 9 XII 1944. It needs to be highlighted that the Polish press commentaries softened the negative evaluation of the Swedish opportunism. See T. Norwid[-Nowacki], 'Gospodarczo-wojenna polityka Szwecji',

7. THE DOUBLE GAME OF SWEDISH DIPLOMACY

The conservative press was favourable towards the Polish government, whereas the liberal dailies and a great many of the leftist press started to prefer telegrams from Moscow and Lublin instead of the Polish reports from London. The journalists for the *Ny Tid* daily were surprised that Moscow continuously considered the Polish government to be reactionary, since it was dominated by the socialists, 'The Poles of London may be accused of everything, but not of collaboration with the Germans. Neither can Arciszewski and Kwapiński be counted among the reactionaries.'[68] The commentators of the communist *Ny Dag* daily had another opinion, 'The composition of the new Polish government is, as it seems, even more reactionary than that of the former one. Just like the German Nazi leaders, it counts on turning England and America against Russia.'[69] Even Marika Stiernstedt, an advocate of the Polish matter and famous for many earlier publications in a slightly different vein, referred unquestioningly in *Ny Dag* to the economic and social achievements of the Soviet Union and was delighted when Stalin, to whom it was necessary to show gratitude for freeing Europe from Hitler, did not want to force kolkhozes on Poland, but to hand over the land to the peasants.[70]

The social democratic local *Skaraborgaren* daily explained the purpose of the Soviet attack on the Polish government. When new (from November 1944) Prime Minister Tomasz Arciszewski, a socialist who fought against tsarism and for the resistance movement after 1939, was hailed a reactionary in Moscow, it became obvious that the Soviet Union would only acknowledge a government that it had appointed.[71] This conviction turned out to be accurate, as in the first half of December Swedish dailies announced that the PKWN was to proclaim itself Provisional Government, and they reported news of the first transports of Polish repatriates, leaving the Eastern Borderlands and heading towards Central Poland. The communist *Ny Dag* daily commented that the government in London 'has been exposed as a reactionary junta of expatriates with no chance of playing a role, and whom

---

Dziennik Polski i Dziennik Żołnierza, 27 XI 1944: 'Both the certain growth of both the pro-Nazi trends in 1940 and pro-communist trends in 1944 do not deviate from the characteristics of a phenomenon occurring a result of current favourable circumstances, with no practical meaning whatsoever. The internal political structure of Sweden gives all the warranties that this country is unable to yield to totalitarian trends.'
[68] 'Polackernas nya regering', *Ny Tid*, 4 XII 1944.
[69] 'Reaktionens förhoppningar', *Ny Dag*, 1 XII 1944.
[70] M. Stiernstedt, 'Sverige och Sovjetunionen', *Ny Dag*, XII 1944.
[71] A. Jn, 'Polens affärer', *Skaraborgaren*, 6 XII 1944.

nobody can make see reason.'[72] The social democratic *Aftontidningen*, however, repeated in line with Moscow gossip about the collaboration between the Poles and the Germans.[73] For Żaba the significance of these commentaries pointed to the fact that Sweden wanted to continue its traditional foreign policy:

> What needs to be stated in general is that the position of the British press had a great influence on Swedish opinion, which, moreover – while intending to avoid all international complications in the future and re-acquire the lost sales markets – always sides with the mightiest power. Desiring to maintain peace in Europe and avoiding the outbreak of the third war at all costs, the attitude of the Swedish press towards the question of the division of Germany and us being granted East Prussia is normally negative, as it perceives such a solution of the Polish–German issue to be a hotbed of the third world war.[74]

Żaba highlighted that as far as the Polish government was concerned, the Swedish press' attitude was like that towards Finland, 'it wishes to save the independence of the nation and therefore it urges the introduction of concessions to Russia.'

On the issue of forming the new Polish cabinet in London, *Stockholms-Tidningen* daily commented bluntly that the Polish matter had no chance of being solved in a situation where the position of Arciszewski's government was uncompromising. It was suggested that the underground movement might have a different opinion to that of the politicians in London.[75] *Göteborgs Handels- och Sjöfarts-Tidning* presented the opinion of its London correspondent, who was hostile towards the Polish government, 'It is a hopeless thing to support the nation, which owes its doom to itself.'[76] *Svenska Dagbladet* daily regularly quoted the British press, which attacked the Polish government for its persistent adherence to the sanctity of the eastern border, although eventually it was suggested that the Western Allies' departure from Poland was improper.[77]

Opinions of the pro-Hitlerian press began to overlap those of the Soviet propaganda. In November 1944 the famous opinion journalist Rütger Essén,

---

[72] 'Polska frågan löses?', *Ny Dag*, 16 XII 1944.
[73] 'Regeringen i Lublin skapad av folkviljan', *Aftontidningen*, 10 I 1945.
[74] AAN, Norbert Żaba's collection, copy of report by N. Żaba to the Ministry of Information and Documentation, Stockholm, 12 I 1945.
[75] 'Den olösliga polska frågan', *Stockholms-Tidningen*, 5 XII 1944.
[76] 'Hopplöst söka hjälpa folk, som arbetar på egen undergång' *Göteborgs Handels och Sjöfarts-Tidning*, 1 XII 1944.
[77] 'London och Lublin' *Svenska Dagbladet*, 2 XII 1944.

for *Dagsposten*, stated, 'the role of the governments-in-exile residing in London was never more significant', and 'their moral authority in the countries they represent, was also small, as these countries, fairly or unfairly, had a sense of disappointment.' What is more, he sneered, 'When a government in exile is only a brief episode, this is still acceptable, but when it lasts years, the situation is becoming tragicomic.'[78] Gunnar Müllern from *Aftonbladet* could not comprehend the persistence of the Poles. He maintained, 'It is foreseeable that regardless of the circumstances Russia would include the area of West Belarus and West Ukraine in its territory.' A consequence of this was to be the promise of granting Poland compensation in the form of western territories. In the eyes of the pro-Hitlerian opinion journalist the fact that the Polish government was far from accepting this gift was evidence of political intelligence. Müllern explained:

> The Germans will get back on their feet after this war despite their terrible losses and material damage. And even a democratic and thoroughly rebuilt Germany would never accept the fact that its vast territories inhabited by a German population are to remain under Polish rule. To maintain their existence, the Poles will be then condemned exclusively to the help of Russian bayonets. The sovereignty of Poland will be a fiction.[79]

It was not only the commentators of the pro-Hitlerian dailies that re-submitted their doubts as to the merits of awarding Poland with German territories. The atmosphere was heated with the statements of the PKWN. Osóbka-Morawski and General Żymierski at a press conference held at the close of August 1944 announced that Poland should be awarded with East Prussia and the territory reaching to the Neisse (Nysa) and Oder (Odra) rivers, whereas the German population should be displaced.[80] The opinion journalist for *Svenska Morgonbladet*, who on 5 September called for joining the Warsaw insurgents in their suffering, soon afterwards asked how it was possible that a nation so touched by the fate and so freedom-loving intended to, against the professed values, oppress the entire, guilty and not guilty population of East Prussia.[81]

---

[78] R. Essén, 'Exilregeringas sorgliga lott', *Dagsposten*, 24 XI 1944.
[79] G. Müllem, 'Stormaktsdiktat i polska frågan', *Aftonbladet*, 1 XII 1944.
[80] 'Polen kräver Oder som gräns men ingen tysk minoritet', *Göteborgs Handels- och Sjöfarts-Tidning*, 29 VIII 1944; '*Vi önska ingen tysk minoritet*. Polskt uttalande om Östpreussen', *Hufvudstadsbladet*, 30 VIII 1944.
[81] EN., 'Också en förhoppning', *Svenska Morgonbladet*, 5 IX 1944.

The anxiety about the incorporation of substantial German territories into Poland, together with a great number of native people, was expressed by *Sydsvenska Dagbladet Snällposten*, 'It would be interesting to know what outline of this border will be established by the dictators.' The journalists also wondered if the Poles would be exporting coal to Sweden through Gdynia or through Szczecin.[82] Already at the outset of February 1945, information appeared in the press about the upcoming takeover of power by the Polish administration in Silesia.[83]

Falu-Kuriren newspaper continued to convince the Poles in London to make concessions regarding the issue of the eastern border, but at the same time expressed doubts when it came to the issue of compensation in the west:

> It is about time that men capable of taking over the management of Polish affairs finally emerged from the lowest classes of the Polish people, unburdened with the pre-war problems. Another issue is whether the territorial compensation on a larger scale – certain revisions of the borders must take place regardless – would be justified... The lands granted to Poland in this way need to be somehow cleansed off the German element.'[84]

Similar reservations were presented by *Göteborgs Handels- och Sjöfarts-Tidning*, 'expelling the Germans from East Prussia, the population of which is more or less of the same size as that of Sweden, is not an easy enterprise, for it is not known whether the Germans would be capable of absorbing such mass of people. Besides, in the future such a solution could become a hotbed of new political complications.'[85] The *Dagens Nyheter* daily noted in wonderment that the government of Arciszewski would like to keep the former border in the east and, what is more, move the Western border in a way that would be beneficial for Poland: 'It is hard to resist the impression that the Poles in London believe in the possibility of creating such great Poland, which – in the east, in the north and in the west – would be rounded off with Russian and German lands.'[86] *Skånska Socialdemokraten* suggested: 'The Polish–Russian issue needs to be of course regulated based on the principle of ethnicity.' This was to mean that, 'Part of the easternmost Polish lands are nothing more than Belarusian territories that were stolen by Poland, and the returning of which to Russia would not be, by any means, a sacrilege towards

---

[82] Pabang, 'Om gränsen blir vid Oder...', *Sydsvenska Dagbladet Snällposten*, 2 II 1945.
[83] 'Lublin och Moskva på väg att dela Östpreussen', *Upsala Nya Tidning*, 6 II 1945.
[84] G. A., 'Den polska regeringskrisen', *Falu-Kuriren*, 12 XII 1944.
[85] Jc [Emil Jacobsson], 'Situationen', *Göteborgs Handels- och Sjöfarts-Tidning*, 16 XII 1943.
[86] 'Polens öde', *Dagens Nyheter*, 17 XII 1944.

the Polish nation', and 'the Belarusians, who suffered at the hands of the Poles, would gladly return to the Soviet Union.' Naturally, the incorporation of East Prussia into Poland would be a true disaster and a reason for another world war.[87]

Diplomatic chess

For Swedish opinion journalists, the fundamental issue that stood in the way of solving the Polish issue was the impossible division into two political camps. It was imagined that the PKWN was a potential partner for the government in exile in sharing political power over Poland. *Göteborgs Tidningen* explained, 'The dispute between Bór and the Committee of National Liberation presents a very disheartening impression of an internal rift.'[88] At times the journalists demonstrated their helplessness, as it was impossible to establish the true reasons of the conflict around Poland. Commentary published in *Sydsvenska Dagbladet Snällposten* was extremely pessimistic, 'To the neutral observer the problem of Poland is so complex that it seems to be impossible to find its solution.' It was nonetheless obvious to everyone that there was hostility between the Polish government in London and Stalin, the main source of which was seen to be the dispute over the border.[89]

Meanwhile in Stockholm, Envoy Sokolnicki attempted to use Karniol's contacts to intervene with the Swedish authorities to appoint a Swedish envoy at the Polish government in London. Karniol threw a dinner and invited, among others, Allan Vougt, head of the parliamentary club of social democrats. Vought promised to show his support for the Polish efforts to Minister Günther.[90] Eventually, the only developments that took place were that the Swedish government approved Ragnar Victor Wengelin as Polish consul to Gothenburg and Folke Edgren as Polish vice-consul to Kalmar on 24 November 1944.[91]

With the onset of the autumn of 1944, the diplomatic deception accelerated in connection with another visit to Moscow by Prime Minister Stanisław Mikołajczyk. Following the August talks between him and Stalin, the counsellor of the Polish Legation in Stockholm, Tadeusz Pilch, explained to

---

[87] 'Polen allvarlig krigsfråga', *Skånska Socialdemokraten*, 18 XII 1944.
[88] 'Polens tragedi', *Göteborgs Tidningen*, 3 X 1944.
[89] 'Polens tragedi', *Sydsvenska Dagbladet Snällposten*, 12 X 1944.
[90] PISM, col. 133, vol. 195, telegram by M. Karniol no. 174, Stockholm, 14 VII 1944.
[91] RA, Kabinettet/UD Huvudarkivet, Statsrådsprotokoll, serie A3A, vol. 116, Protokoll över utrikesdepartementsärenden, Stockholm, 24 XI 1944.

Rolf Sohlman, head of the trade department of UD, that Mikołajczyk had suggested that the representatives of the PKWN be co-opted by the Polish government in London, and that the initiative regarding the border issue be handed over to Stalin. Mikołajczyk was to be offered, by the Soviet dictator, the Curzon Line in the east and the Oder river (excluding Stettin) in the west. In such a situation the Poles had to resign themselves to the loss of Vilnius, but they did not lose hope that they would keep both Lviv and the oil fields in Eastern Galicia. Whereas, all Upper Silesia was to become part of the territory of Poland.[92]

Pilch's assurances about the subjective treatment of the head of the Polish government in Moscow were most probably not treated seriously in the context of pessimistic information that poured in from other sources, as well as the anti-Polish campaign, inspired by the Soviet propagandist services.

The youth newspaper *Frihet* published the article containing the following statement, 'the Polish government is indeed not the same clique of reactionary generals and colonels as those who governed Poland in 1939 and whose policy led Poland to disaster, but old trends still have enough strength and influence in the new Polish army.' What was also mentioned were the anti-Jewish incidents in the Polish army.[93] The arguments about the anti-Semitism of Poles, which confirmed the lack of political tolerance, were used especially by the communists as a propagandist weapon.[94] Some opinion journalists were counting on conclusion of the Polish–Soviet agreement by means of further direct negotiations between Prime Minister Mikołajczyk and Stalin. These negotiations took place in October 1944.[95] In the press commentaries an optimistic approach towards the development of the Polish-Soviet relations would dominate, but at the same time concerns were raised as to

---

[92] RA, UD 1920 års dossiersystem, HP 1, vol. 486, memorandum regarding the statement of counsellor T. Pilch about Polish–Russian relations, Stockholm, 13 IX 1944.

[93] PISM, col. 133, vol. 195, M. Karniol's report 'Szwedzka prasa socjaldemokratyczna o Polsce. Czerwiec, lipiec, sierpień 1944', Stockholm, 26 X 1944; article in the issue no. 2 from 1944.

[94] PISM, A 11, 49/sow/16, letter by Polish Envoy to Stockholm H. Sokolnicki together with attachment (G. Brzeskwiński's report from the meeting of the international circle examining the problems of post-war Europe, which took place on 14 XI 1944 in *Ognisko*), Stockholm 1944.

[95] 'Till Moskva', *Ny Tid*, 28 VII 1944; 'Tre polska ministrar äro i Polen', *Ny Tid*, 29 VII 1944; 'Polens konseljpresident uppmanas besöka Stalin', *Arbetet*, 18 VII 1944; 'London-Polen söker kontakt med Moskva', *Morgon-Tidningen*, 27 VII 1944; 'Kompromiss London-Moskva löser nya polska krisen', *Morgon-Tidningen*, 27 VII 1944; PISM, col. 133, vol. 195, M. Karniol's report 'Szwedzka prasa socjaldemokratyczna o Polsce. Czerwiec, lipiec, sierpień 1944', Stockholm, 26 X 1944.

whether Mikołajczyk would manage to convince other politicians in London to make concessions to the communists.[96]

In October 1944, Söderblom, Swedish Envoy to Moscow, reported the results of the talks between Churchill and Eden (in the presence of Mikołajczyk) and Stalin. In his view, no results had been determined concerning the Polish matter.[97] He reported:

> Still in August, the Curzon Line was only a basis for setting the future border, and now the Russians have taken a firmer stance and are demanding that the Curzon Line be approved for definitive as the border. Mikołajczyk may still become Prime Minister of the new government, but he would have no influence over its formation. Such a government will be formed by the current Lublin Committee.'

Meanwhile the British were pressurizing Mikołajczyk to come to an agreement with the Polish communists, as Great Britain 'cannot risk serious complications in the relations with the Soviet Union due to the Polish government in London.' Similar was the tone of the telegram Envoy Prytz sent to Stockholm following his conversation with Polish Ambassador to London Raczyński after Prime Minister Mikołajczyk's return from Moscow. Raczyński confirmed that the quick agreement regarding the Polish matter was not to be counted on as the Polish authorities considered the proposal that they accepted the new border with the Soviet Union to be an imposed settlement and refused to approve it without a referendum in the territories annexed by Stalin in 1939.[98] In the subsequent confidential report, based on the conversation with a participant of Mikołajczyk's expedition to Moscow, the Swedish Legation in London presented the picture of a desperate and hopeless attempt to defend the position of the Polish government regarding the issue of the eastern border and the principles of the formation of the new cabinet including the representation of the PKWN. According to information obtained by the Swedes, the Poles had no illusions about the postulates of the British and pinned their hopes on the president of the USA.[99]

---

[96] 'Den polska bekymren', *Aftontidningen*, 7 IX 1944; 'Polacker i öster och i väster', *Morgon-Tidningen*, 19 IX, 21 IX 1944; 'Polens extremister driva ett farligt spel'. 'De allierade regeringarnas tålamod icke oändligt', *Göteborgs Handels- och Sjöfarts-Tidning*, 25 IX 1944.
[97] RA, UD 1920 års dossiersystem, HP 1, vol. 486, note by A. Croneborg, Stockholm, 23 X 1944.
[98] RA, UD 1920 års dossiersystem, HP 1, vol. 486, note by S. Grafström, Stockholm, 26 X 1944.
[99] RA, UD 1920 års dossiersystem, HP 1, vol. 486, memorandum on the subject of Polish-Soviet relations, concerning the meeting in Moscow 9–18 X 1944, London, 6 XI 1944.

By November 1944, the stance of the Swedish policy regarding the Polish matter was obvious. Söderblom took over the initiative. The diplomat, associated with the former concessions to Germany, was now, with a sense of mission, intending to provide Sweden with best possible relations with the Soviet Union.[100] On 6 November, he held a meeting with the representative of the PKWN in Moscow, Jędrychowski, and informed him of the quality of the relations between the Swedish government and Polish government in London. He explained that relations were practically not maintained for several years. The explanation resembled the justifications that were submitted to the German diplomats in the period of Third Reich's preponderance in Europe. Subsequently, the Polish envoy presented Jędrychowski with the list of Swedish companies operating in Poland and declared that the Swedes were willing to establish commercial cooperation with Poland, especially for the import of Polish coal. Jędrychowski took up this initiative and assured his interlocutor

---

[100] S. Grafström, *Anteckningar 1938–1944*, pp. 514, 622. The opinion which was devastating for Söderblom (son of the famous Protestant bishop Nathan Söderblom, who was a forerunner of ecumenism), noted down on 7 November (pp. 616–617): 'His reports about the Soviets are shocking. Servility and tail-wagging, which are presented to the people of the Kremlin, have only one equivalent – his own conduct at the time when the Germans were prevailing. He clearly does not notice this himself. He has simply forgotten the actions he performed in 1940 and 1941. I regret that I cannot quote here the report he submitted following his first visit at Molotov's'. On visiting Molotov on 22 July Söderblom highlighted that he was authorized by Gustaf V to deliver his personal greetings for Marshal Stalin and to express King's wish to maintain good and full of trust relations between Sweden and the Soviet Union. On passing on the greetings for the Prime Minister and the head of the Swedish diplomacy, he assured that 'the entire nation is unanimous in its will to develop and intensify the future good relations between our countries.' On discussing the subjects from the field of foreign policy, he assured Molotov that Sweden considered eo ipso the incorporation of the Baltic States into the Soviet Union. He highlighted that nobody in Sweden was thinking seriously about political-military integration of the Nordic States. He was forced to justify the submissive policy towards Germany. He announced that the Swedish-Soviet cooperation would be initiated, starting with commerce and ending on student and cultural exchange, 'as quickly as this would only be possible'. He convinced Molotov that the attack on the Soviet Union and its heroic defence made Sweden react with 'sympathy and interest to all signs of Russian intellectual life.' In his report from October 1944, on the basis of Moscow's example, he enthusiastically discussed the civilizational development of the Soviet Union in the period of several recent years: the increase in the number of cars, bridges, asphalt roads and residential buildings, the strengthening position of the Russian ruble in the financial markets. See: RA, UD 1920 års dossiersystem, HP 12, vol. 520, copy of report by Swedish Envoy to Moscow S. Söderblom to UD; telegram by Swedish Envoy to Moscow S. Söderblom to UD, Moscow, 27 VII 1944; vol. 521, strictly confidential report by Swedish Envoy to Moscow S. Söderblom to E. von Post, Moscow, 4 X 1944. On the role of Söderblom during the conversations with the representatives of the PKWN, and later the representatives of the Provisional Government, see: O. Österberg, 'Det problematiska erkännandet. Sverige och ett Centraleuropa i förändring' [in:] *Polen & Sverige 1919–1999*, H. Runblom & A. N. Uggla (ed.), Uppsala 2005, pp. 189–195.

7. THE DOUBLE GAME OF SWEDISH DIPLOMACY

that the entire Upper Silesia would be included in the territory of Poland, and that the wish of the authorities of 'new Poland' was the greatest possible trade with Sweden: 'Swedish experiences in the area of industry and its resources would be very useful at the rebuilding [the country].'[101] Jędrychowski also claimed that the Swedes were at that moment ready to send their humanitarian aid to Lublin via the Soviet Union. According to Söderblom, such gesture could have been of utmost propagandist importance. Jędrychowski also mentioned the formation of the Union of Polish Patriots in Sweden (ZPP), which was strongly fought against by the Polish Legation in Stockholm. Söderblom clearly accepted the Polish partners. In his reports he spoke well of Jędrychowski. He characterised him as 'an experienced and diligent person, surprisingly moderate in his opinions about the Germans.' Jędrychowski's co-worker, commercial attaché Wojciech Chabasiński, reminded him of 'the bright and intelligent student from Uppsala.'[102]

By the end of December, in a letter to Stockholm, Söderblom emphasised, 'Nurturing the best possible relations with Poland seems to me in line with the most important interests of Sweden, whereas when it comes to the territorial claims [of Stalin], one may think whatever one wants about them, but we, the Swedes, have no influence on them coming true.'[103] Count Folke Bernadotte, who managed Swedish humanitarian campaigns, most probably had taken these remarks to heart, as the visit to Lublin was included in the programme of his stay in Moscow at the outset of 1945, although the Swedish

---

[101] RA, UD 1920 års dossiersystem, HP 12, vol. 890, telegram by Swedish Envoy to Moscow S. Söderblom to the Ministry of Foreign Affairs, Moscow, 6 XI 1944. Jędrychowski in his correspondence to the Department of Foreign Affairs of the PKWN presented exactly the same course of the conversation. See: AMSZ, iss. 27, w. 2, vol. 15, report by representative of the PKWN in Moscow S. Jędrychowski to the Department of Foreign Affairs of the PKWN, Moscow, 8 XI 1944 r., p. 50; W. Materski, *Dyplomacja*..., pp. 31–32, see: facsimile of the report (p. 23). The author informs that Söderblom contacted Jędrychowski already in October. Similarly writes A. Kłonczyński, *Stosunki*..., p. 28. The conversation is mentioned by W.T. Kowalski, *Polityka zagraniczna RP 1944–1947*, Warszawa 1971, pp. 14–15. In Lublin, according to him, it was expected that Sweden would actively participate in the rebuilding of Poland. Stefan Jędrychowski provides in his memoirs the date of 5 November, when the meeting took place and quotes his full report from 8 November 1944. He also adds the description of the session of the PKWN from 22 November, when the floor was taken by head of the Department of Communication, Jan Rabanowski, who expressed his interest with the purchase of communications equipment from Sweden. Jędrychowski considered that coming into an agreement with Sweden was probable, as we may promise coal. See: S. Jędrychowski, *Przedstawicielstwo*..., pp. 158–160.

[102] RA, UD 1920 års dossiersystem, HP 39, vol. 1620, letter by Swedish Envoy to Moscow S. Söderblom to E. von Post, Moscow, 12 XII 1944.

[103] RA, UD 1920 års dossiersystem, HP 39, vol. 1620, report by Swedish Envoy to Moscow S. Söderblom to Minister of Foreign Affairs Ch. Günther, Moscow, 30 XII 1944.

government still refrained from establishing official relations with the Polish Provisional Government in Lublin.[104]

Towards the end of the year, Pilch, the counsellor of the Polish Legation, sent a summary of memoirs by Einar Ekstrand to London. Ekstrand participated in Swedish humanitarian actions following the First World War, including in Soviet Russia.[105] Pilch was planning common Polish–Swedish humanitarian undertakings in the territory of Poland. He maintained that making use of the Swedes' experience in countering the economic and health-related cataclysm that broke out in Poland several years after the occupation, was necessary. The Polish Legation, however, was no longer a partner for the Swedish government in such talks.

From the protocols of the PKWN, it follows that the circle of Polish communists started to attach considerable importance to relations with Stockholm by. This issue was the subject of the PKWN's session on 22 November 1944.[106] First to raise awareness was the community of Poles. Jędrychowski, on discussing this issue, stated, 'What we are facing is the issue of bringing these people back from Sweden to Poland.' Interest in Sweden was mainly due to its participation in the humanitarian campaign in the territories from where the German army was being driven out by Allied forces. The Committee wanted to make use of this support by forcing Swedish institutions to suspend talks regarding this matter with the Polish government in exile.[107]

On 21 December 1944, Pański was authorized by Jędrychowski's telegram to represent the interests of Poles in Sweden before the Swedish government and to register the future repatriates on behalf of the PKWN.[108] The financial resources Pański obtained from Moscow allowed him to conduct propagandist activity (the Polish intelligence suspected that Pański was in possession of considerable funds).[109] Pański also initiated the recruitment of the Polish army of General Berling, which was attached to the Soviet army. Not

---

[104] RA, UD 1920 års dossiersystem, HP 39, vol. 1620, memorandum by Count F. Bernadotte to Swedish Envoy to Moscow S. Söderblom, no date.
[105] AAN, HI/I/113, letter by the counsellor to the Polish Legation in Stockholm, T. Pilch, to the Ministry of Foreign Affairs (together with attachment), Stockholm, 19 XII 1944.
[106] AAN, PKWN, I/4, protocol from the PKWN's session that took place on 22 XI 1944, pp. 254–255.
[107] Ibidem. Cf: E.J. Pałyga, *Dyplomacja Polski Ludowej 1944–1984 (kierunki – treści – mechanizmy)*, Warszawa 1986, p. 35; P. Jaworski, 'Problemy stosunków polsko-szwedzkich w latach od 1944 do 1948', *Wrocławskie Studia z Polityki Zagranicznej* 2001, iss. 1, pp. 24–26.
[108] AAN, ZPPwSz, 434/4, telegram by Jędrychowski to J. Pański, n.p., 21 XII 1944, p. 17. The telegram was written in French.
[109] IPMS, PRM 163, secret note by director of the Security Department of the Ministry of Internal Affairs A. Ostrowski, London, 23 I 1945.

7. THE DOUBLE GAME OF SWEDISH DIPLOMACY

far from Huddinge, near Stockholm, a camp was set up to provide shelter for Poles who were ready to leave Sweden. Agents of the Polish intelligence declared, 'these are mostly people of low moral character.' They were granted financial aid in the amount of 60 crowns to cover the costs of their travel to the camp and minor daily expenses.[110] The Polish Legation attempted to counteract this campaign. Information was withheld about the group of 300 hundred refugees who allegedly declared their willingness to become relocated to the territories annexed by the Red Army.[111] In fact, according to the information of the Polish intelligence, no more than seven such people were registered until the end of 1944.[112] Pański was exposed as a deserter from the Polish merchant navy with no Polish passport.[113]

Meanwhile Pański continued his uncompromising political battle with the circles gathered around the Polish Legation. During the meetings held on 5 and 19 November, the items on the agenda were the attacks on Henryk Sokolnicki and other employees of the Polish diplomatic mission.[114] At the meeting of 10 December 1944, Iwan Tremtiaczy, who had 'his speech instructions written down on paper,' 'Instantly attacked [...] Minister Sokolnicki, called counsellor Pilch, Patek, Kowalewski and Karniol a pack of reactionaries, thieves and thugs. [...] He accused them of the lawless suspension of financial aid for those who refused to leave for England. [...] he then threw insults at the members of the [Polish] Aid Committee, and later, referring to them, told a joke which was allegedly famous all over Stockholm that "one makes a better living off the PPS than off any business".' The audience, and especially the board members, expressed their support for the speaker with repeated applause.[115] According to Karniol, Tremtiaczy, who introduced himself as a pre-war PPS councillor of the city of Gdynia, gained the trust of Jan Masiak, a socialist who had lived in Sweden for years. He nevertheless claimed, 'On

---

[110] PUMST, A.5.1.4.2, head of the Department of Information and Intelligence of the Staff of Commander-in-Chief Colonel S. Gano to the Special Division of the Staff of the Commander-in-Chief, n.p., 30 XI 1944 r., p. 144.

[111] In his memoirs, Pański mentioned that he managed to collect four hundred signatures of army volunteers. See: J. Pański, *Wachta*..., p. 158. The Polish Legation kept sending out disclaimers to the Swedish newspapers regarding the efficiency of the recruitment conducted by Pański. See: quotations from the Swedish press: 'Kompromitacja *delegata lubelskiego* w Szwecji', *Dziennik Polski i Dziennik Żołnierza*, 2 I 1945; 'Kompromitacja delegata Lublina w Sztokholmie', *Dziennik Polski i Dziennik Żołnierza*, 20 I 1945.

[112] IPMS, A XII, 3/41, note by Colonel S. Gano 'Polacy w Szwecji – wyjazd do Rosji', n.p., 30 XII 1944.

[113] A. N. Uggla, *Polacy w Szwecji*., pp. 170–172.

[114] IPMS, A XII, 3/41, note by Colonel S. Gano 'ZPP w Szwecji', n.p., 1 XII 1944; note by Colonel S. Gano 'ZPP w Szwecji', n.p., 19 XII 1944.

[115] PISM, A XII, 3/41, note by Colonel S. Gano 'ZPP w Szwecji', n.p., 30 XII 1944.

referring to us, he was nevertheless acting against us.'[116] The action of vilifying the employees of the Polish Legation was accelerating. On 27 December 1944, the Soviet Legation submitted a complaint to the Stockholm police regarding the alleged battering of the supporters of the Union of Polish Patriots. Notes on this subject were also submitted to the legations of Great Britain and the USA. For Razin it was important to spread the opinion that the Polish Legation occupied itself only with provocative activity. According to the information of the Polish intelligence, commissioner Lindberg from the Stockholm police department was aware that this was a political provocation of the Soviets and he considered staying away from it to be the best solution.[117] On 5 January, Pański was summoned to the headquarters of the criminal police force. There, he was advised to observe the ban on engaging in political and propagandist activity. The Swedish official pointed out that this recommendation 'is not caused by sympathy or antipathy towards this or other country or government, but its purpose is to maintain peace among the foreign refugees.'[118] As a result, the Soviet Legation advised Pański to suspend the Poles' registration so as not to irritate Swedish and Polish opinion in Stockholm. It certainly did not have the desired effect, and, from the Soviet point of view, it failed.[119]

Pański expanded his circle of acquaintances, for example, reaching out to Marika Stiernstedt, who was elected an honorary member of the ZPP.[120] Pański persuaded her (she was an activist of the Hjälp Polens Barn committee) to organize the sending of food and clothes to the territory of the Lublin Committee, Poland. For the Swedish authorities, this activity was to be the sign of good will in establishing relations with the new authorities in

---

[116] PISM, col. 133, vol. 195, report by M. Karniol no. 205, Stockholm, 20 X 1944.
[117] PISM, A XII, 3/41, note by Colonel S. Gano 'ZPP w Szwecji', n.p., 2 II 1945.
[118] PISM, A XII, 3/41, note by Colonel S. Gano 'ZPP w Szwecji', n.p., 26 I 1945.
[119] Ibidem.
[120] AAN, ZPPwZSRR, 216/29, report by the Union of Polish Patriots in Sweden no. 2, 30 X 1944, p. 14. Towards the end of the war Marika Stiernstedt, who was connected with Poland because of her Polish mother Maria Ciechanowiecka, accepted the new authorities in Poland, which were dominated by the communists. When at the end of July 1945, the building of the Polish Legation in Stockholm was taken over by the group who arrived from Warsaw, she wrote enthusiastically in her diary: 'Det nya Polen!' ('New Poland!'). Several months earlier she received a telegram with thanks from the Prime Minister of the Provisional Government, Edward Osóbka-Morawski, for her dedicated service at organising humanitarian aid for Polish children. In 1946, several months after her visit to Poland, she published the book *Polsk revolution* (Polish Revolution), where she shed a good light on the actions of Polish communists. See: Carolina Rediviva, 'Handskriftsavdelning, Marika Stiernstedts samling', *Dagboks-almanack 1944–1945*; telegram by E. Osóbka-Morawski from 3 IV 1945.

7. THE DOUBLE GAME OF SWEDISH DIPLOMACY

Poland.[121] Pański's aim was also to persuade the Union of Polish Jews in Sweden to grant humanitarian aid to Poland. In doing so he referred to the telegrams he received from Emil Sommerstein, the chair of the Central Committee of Jews in Poland, and asked for clothes, food and medication to be sent to the Jewish population residing in the territories annexed by the Soviet army. As a result, the Union of Polish Jews asked the Swedish Jewish organisations to grant financial support to the organisation Hjälp Polens Barn.[122] In March 1945, Marika Stiernstedt arranged a meeting in her apartment for the founders of the Polish–Swedish Association. According to an anonymous source, the meeting was attended by H. Axell, Professor Arne, Doctor Schück, merchant Dahn and Pański. It was Stiernstedt, who praised *Ny Dag* and everything relating to the Soviet Union. She was considered by the agent of the Swedish police, therefore, to be the most pro-communist oriented member of this group. Characteristic, nonetheless was that Pański explained that he did not want his companions to be communists.[123]

The Polish Committee of National Liberation (the PKWN and later the Provisional Government) expected Pański to prepare a repatriation campaign. First slogans calling for the return to homeland appeared in the New Year's proclamation of the ZPP, announced at the beginning of January 1945. The name of the Union of Polish Patriots in Sweden (ZPP) was also extended with the word 'Repatriation'. The proclamation contained the address of the ZPP (Fridhemsgatan 72/5, Stockholm), which was to welcome individuals willing to depart for Poland. It was announced that contact with Poland had been re-established. Catchy slogans were used to encourage people to return to their homeland, 'There is enough work for everyone. Farmers will be given land. Private property is being returned to its owners. All citizens, regardless of religion, social background and political views have an equal right to live in Liberated Poland.' At the same time it was emphasized, 'The borders of the Republic of Poland are closed only to traitors and agents of Fascism.'[124] This

---

[121] Pański was trying to make the plan of granting immediate aid to Poland a tool of propaganda, see: AMSZ, iss. 27, w. 3, vol. 45, series of Polpress reports entitled *Pomoc szwedzka dla Polski*, pp. 5–13.

[122] AMSZ, iss. 6, w. 79, vol. 1182, copy of memorandum for director G. Josephson, chair of the *Mosaisk Församlingen* in Stockholm, 12 I 1945.

[123] RA-Arninge, SÄPO arkiv, P 2406 Jerzy Pański, löp 2, pro memoria, Stockholm, 10 III 1945, p. 78.

[124] AAN, ZPPwSz, 434/1, copy of the appeal 'Polacy w Szwecji!', n.p., 8 I 1945, p. 3.

led to a campaign in Polish society, including information about the submarine crews who were interned in September 1939.[125] Efforts were made to distribute leaflets to all the Poles containing such content.[126] At the same time Pański sent an application, or rather a questionnaire, to the refugee camps that, according to its heading, consisted of formalities connected with departure to Poland. It was advised that the application be filled in immediately and sent back to the address of the Union of Polish Patriots in Sweden – Repatriation.[127] The declarations concerning a return to Poland were also declarations for joining the Union of Polish Patriots. Using these questionnaires, Pański collected about one hundred declarations, which he announced immediately in the press. Maurycy Karniol denied these assertions in *Aftontidningen*. He explained that the only reliable documents were the refusals to depart to Great Britain, of which there were only a few.[128]

On 27 December 1944, under the pretext of taking over care of the Poles in Sweden, Pański visited Sverker Åström, who was a high official of the Swedish Ministry of Foreign Affairs. Pański informed Åström that he had done so on the recommendation of secretary Razin from the Soviet Legation. Most of all, he presented the Swede with the telegram from Jędrychowski – the representative of the PKWN in Moscow – authorizing him to represent the Polish interests before the Swedish authorities. Pański stated that repatriation of Poles to their homeland via the territory of the Soviet Union had become a current issue. He knew of about two hundred people who allegedly wanted to return to their homes using this route. This was his reason for wanting to know whether the Swedish authorities would consider him the official representative of these Poles. Åström's defence was to argue that the Swedish government, just like American and British governments, did not recognize the PKWN, and therefore a delegate of the committee could not act as representative of Poland in Sweden. However, on the subject of refugees, Åström clarified that the Swedish authorities would not object to them returning to their homeland. He personally saw no obstacles to Pański helping his compatriots who asked him for a ticket or permission to travel to the Soviet Union as a private person. In case he would contact the National Migration Commission (*Statens utlänningskommission*), he would have the

---

[125] More about the sentiments of the seamen and marginal interest with the communist campaign, see: A. N. Uggla, *I nordlg hamn...*, pp. 156–158.
[126] PISM, A XII, 3/41, note by Colonel S. Gano 'ZPP w Szwecji', n.p., 30 XII 1944.
[127] RA-Arninge, SÄPO arkiv, P 2406 Jerzy Pański, notification by A. Lisiecki, p. 90.
[128] PISM, col. 133, vol. 195, report by M. Karniol for the period X–XII 1944, Stockholm, 31 I 1945.

right to represent only one Pole at a time with their permission and would not be able to act as an official representative for all his compatriots.[129] The caution expressed by the Swedish official did not hide the fact that the sphere of contacts between the Swedish Ministry of Foreign Affairs and the agendas of the Lublin Committee Poland gradually expanded. In the following months, pressure from the representatives of the PKWN, acting under the supervision of the Soviet authorities, towards granting recognition to the new Polish de facto authorities grew even more. The convenient means of exerting this pressure became the promises of a quick conclusion of the contracts for the supply of coal.[130]

Around Yalta

Towards the end of October 1944, in an analysis of the situation, the Swedish Staff of Defence claimed,

> Although the closing stage of the Second World War is most probably in progress – namely, the defeat of Germany – the development of situation is dependent on so many factors that each attempt of drawing a full picture of the military-political situation following the conclusion of the war must be burdened with considerable deficiencies.[131]

Following such a cautious introduction, the Swedish staff officers most probably considered that Germany would be defeated and temporarily occupied by the Allies. They also considered that the international policy would be substantially influenced by the existence of two global blocs – the Soviet Union and the USA and Great Britain – together with their voluntarily affiliates, whereas the neutral countries would encounter serious difficulties if they tried to conduct policy of complete independence. It was predicted that the course of the borders of Finland, unless the country became occupied, would remain the same as those set in the truce arrangement. In addition, the Soviet

---

[129] RA, UD 1920 års dossiersystem, HP 12, vol. 890, memorandum by S. Åström, Stockholm, 27 XII 1944. Full text of the document, see: RA-Arninge, SÄPO arkiv, P 2406 Jerzy Pański, löp 1, p. 69.
[130] W. Materski, *Dyplomacja...*, pp. 53–54, 60. As the author himself noted, similar strategy, encouraging to establish de facto relations with the authorities of Lublin Committee Poland, was used towards the governments of Belgium, Denmark, Finland, France, the Netherlands, Norway and Italy. Cf: K. Tarka, *Emigracyjna dyplomacja. Polityka zagraniczna rządu RP na uchodźstwie 1945–1990*, Warszawa 2003, pp. 13–47; K. Strzałka, *Między przyjaźnią a wrogością. Z dziejów stosunków polsko-włoskich (1939–1945)*, Kraków 2001, p. 495.
[131] RA, UD 1920 års dossiersystem, HP 1, vol. 40, Defence Staff Analysis: 'Military-political situation', 31 X 1944 r. General H. Jung's visiting card was attached to the document.

Union would be able to exert direct military-political pressure on the Finnish government. It was beyond any doubt that the Baltic States would be again annexed as Soviet republics, just like a considerable part of East Prussia, with Königsberg. In doing so, the Soviet Union was to guarantee itself a dominant role in the Baltic Sea region. The Polish–Soviet border was to be set along the Curzon Line and Bessarabia and Bukovina were to be definitively separated from Romania. The Swedish staff officers were cautiously predicting:

> One may establish that these territorial claims from Russia are final, but one may also think that they are only the first stage of its wide-ranging imperialism. There are also good reasons that support the first assumption – that Russia intends to provide security and shape the sphere of its influences in the western border through other means than direct territorial annexations.[132]

The examples of this were arrangements with Finland, Bulgaria and Romania. Attempts to reaching agreement with Marshal Tito and the formation of communist Polish government in Moscow proved that there were intentions to appoint ideologically similar authorities in the countries located within the intended sphere of influence. The support for General de Gaulle, and making use of the group of captive German generals, showed different ways of achieving objectives by the Soviet diplomacy. The Soviet zone was to include Poland, Czechoslovakia, Romania, Bulgaria, Yugoslavia, Eastern Germany, most probably Hungary and possibly Austria. Less certain were the predictions about the developments in other parts of Europe. The USSR gaining control over the Turkish straits was unlikely, and the situation in Italy was uncertain. It was stated that, 'strong communism in Western Europe could throw these countries into the arms of Russia.' Nevertheless, the support for the English and American liberators could also grant them income. The future of Denmark and Norway, all of which found themselves in the Soviet sphere of political interests was also unknown. What was considered seriously was the option of creating a Soviet enclave around Narvik. The dominance of Finnish language across the Norwegian and Swedish arctic regions could also become a crucial pretext for the territorial claims put forward by Moscow. It was beyond any doubt that the Soviet Union had strong military arguments, as with the support of the Allies it created an efficient military machine, which following the conclusion of the war was most probably to remain in combat readiness.

---

[132] Ibidem.

7. THE DOUBLE GAME OF SWEDISH DIPLOMACY

The Swedes believed that following the downfall of Germany, the victorious powers would likely continue their cooperation to maintain peace. The announcements of the foundation of the United Nations organization proved that things were heading in this direction, but even the best theoretical foundations could not grant an efficient and better – than that of the League of Nations' – operation of such an organisation. All was dependant on the possibility of further cooperation between the powers:

> That is why the fortunate development of the world requires the chief qualities of these countries' leaders to be utmost wisdom and moderation. The difficulties in the mutual understanding among the Allies when their common enemy is not yet defeated prove that there exist considerable differences and the overcoming of which would not become any easier even when this enemy is defeated.

In this situation, what was the best solution for Sweden? The answer:

> [...] our country has found itself in the borderline between two global blocs. That is why it is natural that the Swedish nation hopes for and, as far as it is possible, also strives to guarantee permanent peace. It would be however irresponsible not to consider the possibility of another conflict until the moment the new peace order is ready, working and meets all expectations.

The belief was now shared that Sweden risked being dragged into the war. The greatest risk was taking a position in the conflict between the USSR and Great Britain regarding the shape of the sphere of influences in Scandinavia. According to the Swedish staff officers, the Scandinavian Peninsula was no less exposed to a military attack following the conclusion of the war than during the war, since the territory of Sweden was an ideal location for launching operations of both the Soviet air force or the Royal Air Force. Following the victories over the German army, it was beyond any doubt that the Soviet army had no equal opponent in Europe, and aggression against the Swedish territory should be expected:

> The truth that we need to look straight in the eye is that in the event when – despite the peace-oriented actions – the new intense conflict cannot be avoided, the situation for our country will become highly critical. There is a risk that in case of conflict we may be exposed to pressures or direct intervention of the side that would attempt to gain a convenient starting position in the expected clash between the powers. The occupation of Sweden would bring the greatest strategic benefits directly to England and the USA. From the Russian point of view, the attack would be mostly motivated by preventive

objectives. The military weakness of Sweden would create a risky void that would encourage aggression.[133]

One consideration was the union of three neutral Scandinavian countries in defence of sovereignty. This excluded, however, that any of the powers would accept the idea. The only solution which was considered possible in the nearest future was further armaments with the intention to scare off an eventual opponent. It was stated that, 'the options for the Swedish government's actions in defending the freedom and peace of our nation in the uncertain and full of dangers future are increasing.'

On considering Sweden's limited room for manoeuvre in the sphere of foreign policy, a strategy of opportunism was chosen, focusing on preserving good relations with the victorious powers at the least cost. Support for the Polish government in exile was impossible in this situation; it would put Sweden at risk of international complications. In connection with this, Polish evaluations of the influence of the developments in Europe on the Swedish policy at the outset of 1945 had to be full of bitterness. Military Attaché Brzeskwiński reported cautiously, 'Swedish foreign policy has adopted a wait-and-see attitude, with a bias towards the USSR.'[134] At the same time, Envoy Sokolnicki informed the Ministry of Foreign Affairs more bluntly, 'Despite its neutrality, Sweden finds itself deeper and deeper in the sphere of Russian influence and is characterized by realism and opportunism.' In April he presented Sweden in his reports as a country entirely conquered by the Soviet propaganda, 'The military and political successes of the Soviet Union caused a change within Swedish society – especially in the circles of bourgeois intelligentsia, who were hitherto blindly devoted to the cult of Germany as a nation excellent in all fields of civilization – in the shape of a sudden wake of equally boundless adoration of the Soviet Union.'[135]

The Swedish press increasingly was publishing appeals calling for establishing closer relations with the Soviets, teaching Russian language and becoming more acquainted with Russian culture. The critics were in retreat:

> Very cautious voices, expressing doubts so as to the possibility of establishing closer relations with the society in Russia, were refuted either by the accusations of being blinded with the anti-Russian mania, or by assurances that

---

[133] Ibidem.
[134] PISM, PRM 163, secret note by deputy head of the Armed Forces Staff Colonel H. Piątkowski, n.p., 12 I 1945.
[135] AAN, Norbert Żaba's collection, copy of report by Polish Envoy to Stockholm H. Sokolnicki to the Ministry of Foreign Affairs, Stockholm, 19 IV 1945.

Russia has been in the course of transformation for dozens of years now, that Bolshevism is disappearing and that over time – and in fact in the nearest future – Russia will resemble western democracies.[136]

Such were the impressions of the head of Polish diplomatic mission in Stockholm in the spring of 1945.

The leaders of the Swedish diplomacy were convinced of the veracity of the policy of gestures of friendship towards the Soviet Union. Sven Grafström noted in his diary with distaste in January 1945 that former Envoy to Moscow, and at the time assistant of vice minister Vilhelm Assarsson, together with Rolf Sohlman claimed, 'we need to tread carefully with the Russians mostly because otherwise we will not sell anything to the Soviets. The consequence of this would be unemployment, increased dissatisfaction and the growth of communism in Sweden.'[137]

Opponents of the Polish government in London tried to disparage him in the eyes of the newspapers' readers. The adverse atmosphere around the London government was created by the repeated, starting from 1944, anti-Semitism accusations in the Polish army. The soldiers of Jewish descent were to desert due to the harassment they encountered from their Polish colleagues. These conflicts reportedly concerned even ministerial offices.[138] The other charge, which was aimed at disgracing the Polish government in exile, was the accusation of placing political opponents in special prisons in Scotland. *Göteborgs Handels- och Sjöfarts-Tidning* treated this charge as highly probable, 'If it is true what is being said about Polish prisons in Scotland and what is going on there, it needs to be said that English hospitality and patience are considerable.'[139] News was published about fights between the Poles – supporters of the government in exile – and the communists in refugee camps. That very same event, discussed several times over several weeks, gave the impression of constant politically motivated wrangles among the Poles, whereas the initiators of the rows were naturally the supporters of the London government.[140]

When the few reports from Poland were published, it transpired that Polish society had accepted the new state authorities. Ralph Parker wrote in

---

[136] Ibidem.
[137] S. Grafström, Anteckningar 1945–1954, ed. S. Ekman, Stockholm 1989, p. 629.
[138] For instance: 'Våldsam kris i det polska lägret. Militär antisemitism hotar spränga regeringen', *Göteborgs Handels- och Sjöfarts-Tidning*, 15 V 1944; 'Grov antisemitism frodas i londonpolackernas armé', *Ny Dag*, 12 IV 1945.
[139] Jc., 'Situationen', *Göteborgs Handels- och Sjöfarts-Tidning*, 13 VI 1945.
[140] 'Vilt politiskt gräl mellan två polacker', *Expressen*, 8 I 1945.

his article for *Svenska Dagbladet*, 'This is the only thing that explains the success of the grain harvest and relatively high abundance of food in towns, which caused a gradual drop in the free market prices, just like there is no other explanation for the success of army recruitment.' Parker in fact made it clear that he did not notice any enthusiasm towards the Lublin government, but 'time is on its side', and 'the division of land among the peasants has smoothed away the fear against collectivisation.' The key to success was also to be the unusual guardedness of the Soviet soldiers, whose behaviour was the example of excellent propriety.[141] *Aftontidningen* even published the content of a telegram from Moscow stating that the Provisional Government of Poland was the only lawful Polish government.[142] Generally speaking, on the issue of Polish–Soviet relations, the Swedish press used the easiest possible strategy by avoiding taking a position while reporting the course of events. When commentaries appeared, the government in London was accused of reconciling with the thought of ceding the Borderlands to the Soviet Union too late. At the same time Żaba wrote, regarding the western border, 'What is felt is the reluctance of Swedish opinion to grant us compensation at the expense of Germany, and this is for fear that it would become a hotbed of a new war.'[143]

The commentators of the pro-Nazi newspapers triumphed. Gunnar Müllern continued to argue in *Aftonbladet*:

> Versailles Poland was, in general, a structure which was impossible to maintain, which sooner or later had to fall apart by itself. The moment when Russia and Germany, weakened by the previous war, regained strength, the former territorial disputes have been settled. Now the Poles must feel bitterness. Although they were fighting more diligently than other allied nations and in spite of the fact that they did not create a Quisling, they are treated worse than the vassals of Germany.

This, according to Müllern, only proved that the powers should not be trusted.[144] Other commentators also maintained that the Polish London government was fighting a losing battle,[145] and the communist *Ny Dag* called the Swedish diplomacy to action, 'The quicker our ministry of foreign affairs

---

[141] R. Parker, 'Lublin regeringen vill skapa en stark polsk militärmakt', *Svenska Dagbladet*, 28 I 1945.
[142] 'Regeringen i London skapad av folkviljan', *Aftontidningen*, 10 I 1945.
[143] AAN, Norbert Żaba's collection, copy of report by N. Żaba to the Ministry of Information and Documentation, Stockholm, 9 II 1945.
[144] G. Müllern, 'Den polska frågan inför avgörandet', *Aftonbladet*, 13 I 1945.
[145] Y. Lg., 'Polskt fait accompli', *Aftontidningen*, 21 I 1945.

7. THE DOUBLE GAME OF SWEDISH DIPLOMACY

realizes that the government in London is not representing its country – the better.'[146] The Vistula river offensive of the Soviet armies, which began 12 January 1945, was to solve all issues of a diplomatic nature. Although, it was noted that the Polish army, which was fighting on several fronts, posed a certain problem.[147]

The Press department of the Polish Legation attempted to counter the Soviet propaganda. Nevertheless, modest bulletins, based on the news service of the Polish Telegraphic Agency (PAT) and translated into Swedish, could not match the political strength of materials sent out by the press services of the powers. Press Attaché Żaba noted, 'Unfortunately the news from Lublin, or inspired by Lublin, gain increasingly growing access to the Swedish press thanks to English and American agencies, which endorse these news items.'[148]

At times Polish disclaimers were taken into consideration. The editorial section of *Göteborgs Handels- och Sjöfarts-Tidning*, on 29 January 1945, quoted the explanations it obtained from the Polish Legation about the situation in the Polish territories and the rules of 'Russian–Polish Quislings' headed by Osóbka-Morawski. The following bitter conclusion was added at the time: 'Therefore there exists administration with dictatorial power, but it uses the support of foreign bayonets and it is only an instrument of foreign rule, contrary to the sovereignty of Poland. This explanation provides hopeless prospects for the future.'[149]

A famous social democratic activist and a close acquaintance of Karniol, Allan Vougt was right stating at the outset of February 1945 in *Arbetet*: 'The Lublin government enjoys actual popularity in Sweden, which is far greater than that of the London government.' He was seeking the explanation in the British–American and Soviet propaganda, which 'made most of the Swedes think that the Poles in London were a community of reactionary old fogeys (*perukstockar*), whereas their compatriots in Lublin were a true embodiment of the will of the Polish nation.' This attitude was not even changed by the actual target of the government in London, which was 'to create independent Poland, in the strict sense of this word.'[150]

According to Sokolnicki, the Swedes, towards the end of 1944, established de facto relations with the PKWN owing to a humanitarian action, which was

---

[146] 'Lublinregeringen', *Ny Dag*, 18 I 1945.
[147] 'Östoffensiven och östpolitiken', *Stockholms-Tidningen*, 22 I 1945.
[148] AAN, Norbert Żaba's collection, copy of report by Polish Envoy to Stockholm N. Żaba to the Ministry of Information and Documentation, Stockholm, 15 I 1945.
[149] Jc., 'Situationen', *Göteborgs Handels- och Sjöfarts-Tidning*, 29 I 1945.
[150] A. V[ou]gt, 'Kampen om Polen', *Arbetet*, 7 II 1945.

conducted in agreement with the new state authorities in Poland. The protests of the Polish government could, according to Sokolnicki, lead to the division of competences 'between ourselves and Lublin.' The Swedes at the time cared about the quick development of the humanitarian campaign and outclassing the United Nations Relief and Rehabilitation Administration (UNRRA), which would be of great propagandist benefit and contribute to diminishing political pressures from the Allies.[151] Sweden continued to convince the Western Allies that it did not need to join the military operations to support the rebuilding of the destroyed countries.[152] According to Sokolnicki, 'the attitude towards us essentially did not change.' Nevertheless, it was evident that the Swedes gradually started to develop relations with the Provisional Government in Lublin and with much attention observed the evolution of relations between the Western Allies and the Polish government in London. Prytz, Envoy of Sweden to London, passed on a confidential message to Stockholm. In the message it stood that Minister Eden informed Mikołajczyk on 11 January that although the British government continued to recognize the Polish government in exile, it would out of necessity establish relations with the Provisional Government in Lublin.[153]

At the same time, Pilch filed a protest at the Swedish Ministry of Foreign Affairs against the formation in Lublin of the Polish Provisional Government. He expressed his hope that in connection with the humanitarian aid sent to Poland, Count Folke Bernadotte would not travel to Lublin as this would give the action 'an official label', and Sweden did not recognize the Polish Provisional Government. According to his view, it would also seem odd if a representative of Sweden first discussed the subject of humanitarian aid for Poland with the representatives of the UNRRA and Poles in London, and then visited Moscow regarding this matter and contacted the local Polish community.[154]

Nevertheless, the Polish legation in Stockholm remained on the defensive. Swedish diplomats considered the most convenient moment to break off relations with the Polish government in exile. At the outset of January 1945 Polish Minister of foreign affairs Tarnowski, through the agency of Sokolnicki, requested Boheman take over custody of the Polish citizens residing

---

[151] PISM, A 11, E/1099, telegram by Polish Envoy to Stockholm H. Sokolnicki to the Ministry of Foreign Affairs, n.p., 6 I 1945.
[152] A. W. Johansson, *Per Albin...*, p. 314.
[153] RA, UD 1920 års dossiersystem, HP 12, vol. 890, pro memoria, n.p., 19 I 1945.
[154] RA, UD 1920 års dossiersystem, HP 12, vol. 890, pro memoria, Stockholm, 11 I 1945 r.

7. THE DOUBLE GAME OF SWEDISH DIPLOMACY

in Romania, which was annexed by the Russians.¹⁵⁵ The Poles had to face refusal, which was justified by the lack of contact with their legation in Bucharest.¹⁵⁶ In the Polish Legation in Stockholm methods were pondered for how to weaken the propagandist message of the action organized by the Swedes in support the people from the territories under the administration of the Lublin government. Minister Tarnowski wanted to force the Swedes not to make this action official and not to publicise it. For this reason, it was important for the Ministry of Foreign Affairs that the action's leader was not Folke Bernadotte.¹⁵⁷ Although, the stance could not be too insistently demonstrated, to avoid it being interpreted as a lack of consent of support for the Polish territories annexed by the Soviet army.

Nothing is known about meetings between Envoy Sokolnicki and Prime Minister Hansson which took place at the time. Only Karniol, the representative of the PPS, managed to meet with the head of the Swedish government and the Social Democratic Party. In a conversation on 3 February, Karniol lay bare the sacrifices of the Polish nation, 'These sacrifices have not managed hitherto to restore our freedom. The Russians treat our movement as hostile, they arrest our activists, bring the officers of the Home Army before the court and shoot many of them.'¹⁵⁸ Karniol convinced Hansson that Mikołajczyk showed the greatest possible submissiveness towards Stalin, which nevertheless brought no Polish–Soviet compromise, since the head of the government became the socialists, Arciszewski and Kwapiński. The measure of moderation and democratic approach was to be self-restraint towards the projects aiming at moving the western border of Poland closer to the Oder and Neisse rivers and incorporation of Wrocław (Breslau) and Szczecin (Stettin). The only Polish weapons were 'high moral values,' this included supporting the International Labour Movement and public opinion of democratic countries. Karniol maintained that it was the pressure from public opinion that could bring a favourable result. That is why he asked the Swedish government for support in not recognising the Provisional Government in

---

[155] AAN, HI/I/334, telegram by Minister of Foreign Affairs A. Tarnowski to Polish Envoy to Stockholm H. Sokolnicki, n.p., 5 I 1945.

[156] AAN, HI/I/334, copy of telegram by Polish Envoy to Stockholm H. Sokolnicki to the Ministry of Foreign Affairs, Stockholm, 5 III 1945; RA UD avdelningar och byråarkiv 1864–1952, Andra B-avdelningen, vol. 183, memorandum by S. Grafström, n.p., 11 I 1945 and a note from 17 I 1945. Grafström also added that Romanians would definitely not recognise the Swedish mandate to exercise such a custody.

[157] PISM, A 11, E/1099, telegram by Minister of Foreign Affairs A. Tarnowski to the Polish Legation in Stockholm, 9 I 1945.

[158] PISM, col. 133, vol. 195, copy of report by M. Karniol no. 223, Stockholm, 5 II 1945.

Warsaw. Hansson reassured, most of all, that his country was in a favourable position. The Germans no longer demanded anything from Sweden and that he was not expecting any complications even in the case of military operations in Denmark or Norway. As he noted, 'Currently there are no pressures on Sweden from any other side in any direction.' He added that after the war he would like to develop international cooperation founded on the sovereign decisions of individual countries. He also summed up, 'In this respect our efforts are overlapping with those of Poland.' He nevertheless did not hide that for the Swedes it was most important to cooperate with the Nordic countries. On the subject of the Provisional Government of Poland, he did not want to make any binding declarations, although he noted reassuringly, 'this matter is not current in Sweden, we are not interested in this matter and we are not intending to forward it ourselves.' He emphasized once again that there were no pressures regarding that matter. He moreover guaranteed, 'We are recognising Your Government and Your Legation in Sweden and we see no reason at the moment for this to change.' Somewhat contrary to these assurances was the policy of the Swedish government regarding the planning of humanitarian aid for Poland and attempts to establish economic relations with Poland. Hansson claimed, 'On these matters, we would naturally have to somehow consider the local de facto authorities. It is hard to determine at this point what form this would take. There are many possibilities in the entire spectrum between the de iure and de facto recognition.' Lastly, the Prime Minister offered support for the members of the PPS who wanted to make their way from Poland to the west of Europe.

Two days later, on 5 February, Karniol met with Gustav Möller, Minister of Social Affairs, who was also a high-ranking activist of the Social Democratic Party.[159] He addressed a similar request to the Prime Minister, asking the Swedish government to refrain from recognizing the Provisional Government of Poland. He used Swedish public opinion to support the Polish matter and made it easier for the PPS activists to escape from Poland. Möller was interested in the composition of political forces in Poland, whether the occupation had changed it and whether right-wing forces had started to dominate. He also raised the issue of national minorities. As Karniol reported, 'He always had an impression that Versailles Poland was excessively extended eastwards, had too many lands populated by a non-Polish majority and for this reason was unable to solve the nationality-related issue.' Karniol explained that the eastern border of Poland was a compromise and that the

---

[159] Ibidem.

Borderlands were an ethnically mixed region, whereas the lands Stalin wanted to incorporate into Poland in the west, were populated by not even one percent of a Polish population. According to Karniol, the position of the Polish government was not only in line with ethnography, devoid both of chauvinism and any traces of imperialism, but it was also a democratic approach to the issue of peace in future Europe. Möller accepted the plan of sneaking people out of Poland on Swedish ships and granting provisional passports to activists who wanted to leave Poland. He also confirmed the words of Prime Minister Hansson, that the Swedish government treated the issue of recognizing the Polish Provisional Government as no longer important. He nevertheless added that this situation could be changed by a relevant decision by Great Powers. He openly suggested that the Swedes adopt a wait-and-see attitude in the face of the opening of the Yalta conference. Möller gave an optimistic answer to Karniol's question on whether Stalin's creating dependent centres of power in Central and Eastern Europe against the people's will would not exert a negative influence on the development of the socialist movement, 'One beautiful day, the Russians, seeing the determined will of the people of occupied Europe in supporting democracy, would liquidate all these governments, and change the entire system.'

It would be hard to perceive Karniol's talks with the most important politicians of the Swedish government at the time as the Polish government's attempt to come out of international isolation, since the relations with Sweden had no impact on the position of Arciszewski's cabinet. Karniol was aware that the Swedes were traditionally guided by the international policy of the Great Powers and would never decide to undertake actions for the benefit of Poland which could considerably compromise their own position. It is worth underlining that Prime Minister Hansson talked with Karniol as if he was a regular representative of Arciszewski's government, which proved that the delegate of the PPS enjoyed a high status in the sphere of Swedish political elites. Nevertheless, the head of the Swedish government did not make any declarations and did not oblige himself to anything, which confirmed Karniol's opinion presented in the reports he sent to London about the Swedes' adaptation to the Soviet Union.[160]

At the outset of January 1945, the new Moscow ambassador of the Provisional Government of Poland sent a note to Söderblom, where he expressed his hope to establish relations with the representative of Sweden.[161] On 6

---

[160] PISM, col. 133, vol. 195, copy of report by M. Karniol no. 224, Stockholm, 5 II 1945.
[161] PISM, col. 133, vol. 296, letter by M. Karniol to A. Ciołkosz, Stockholm, 13 IV 1944.

February 1945 though, he paid him a visit. Modzelewski planned to find out whether the Swedish government discussed the issue of establishing official relations with the Polish Provisional Government and future commercial relations. Söderblom replied evasively that he possessed no thorough information on this subject. So far it was he who encouraged his government to take up more courageous actions in granting recognition to the new Polish authorities. He wrote to Stockholm:

> [...] for a long time now I have had the pleasure of maintaining the best possible relations with the representation of the Polish Provisional Government in Moscow regarding the discussion of the issues connected with the defence of Swedish economic interests in Poland and Swedish humanitarian aid. I am convinced that Sweden has already been devoting attention to the issue of developing the future Polish–Swedish commercial relations.'[162]

Modzelewski assured Söderblom that the Swedes could count on the supplies of Polish coal, because thanks to the rapid movement of the Soviet armies, the mines of Upper Silesia were saved from destruction. He announced that Poland would be mostly in need of agricultural machinery, rolling stock and diverse machinery. He mentioned that in connection with military operations, the gauge of the railway routes was adjusted to the Russian norms, but he assured that following the war Poland would re-introduce the European track gauge. Söderblom had a high opinion about Modzelewski, 'Ambassador Modzelewski impressed me as a kind-hearted person. In comparison to other representatives of new Poland he seems to be serious, determined and patriotically-oriented.'

Söderblom declared that the Poles' desire to establish good relations with Sweden seemed to be strong and true. He also claimed, 'Our country can count on lively sympathy from Poland.' On 8 February Modzelewski, sent a short telegram to the Ministry of Foreign Affairs:

> I met with the Swedes. I put the matter on a rational level. I think that it would be possible to start talks soon. They became interested in our possible orders of equipment and machines. Although they are making it clear that they possess coal supplies, they in fact do not, and this would put a pressure on them.[163]

---

[162] RA, UD 1920 års dossiersystem, HP 12, vol. 890, telegram by Swedish Envoy to Moscow S. Söderblom to the Ministry of Foreign Affairs, Moscow, 3 V 1945.
[163] RA, UD 1920 års dossiersystem, HP 1, vol. 486, letter by Swedish Envoy to Moscow S. Söderblom to Minister of Foreign Affairs Ch. Günther, Moscow, 15 II 1945.

7. THE DOUBLE GAME OF SWEDISH DIPLOMACY

As early as on 12 February, Söderblom paid a follow-up visit to Modzelewski and committed a minor indiscretion; he was not certain whether the conversation could be conducted in French. Meanwhile, it emerged that Modzelewski had studied in Paris in 1920s and had command of French. Söderblom was glad that he had another occasion to emphasize the Swedish interest in 'new Poland' before reaching arrangements at the conference in Yalta. The most important result of the meeting was the assurance made by Modzelewski that Poland could supply coal to Sweden. According to the ambassador, the coal mines were already exploited at the time, and from the moment of reaching Upper Silesia by the Soviet army 15 thousand carriages of coal were loaded and it was only the lack of rolling stock that slowed down output. Söderblom also discussed the details of donating 27.5 tons of food, clothes and shoes via *Hjälp Polens Barn*. He announced that the transport had already reached Turku and from there it would be taken to Leningrad by rail, where it should be delivered around 17 February 1945. In addition, 15 tons of crisp bread, oat flakes and medication, with an estimated worth of 40 thousand crowns, was being prepared for the Jewish population in Poland. Moreover, he promised that approximately 2 tons of clothes would soon be sent to Poland. There was also an expectation that the array of support resources would be expanded, as on 3 February a special academic committee was established in Sweden to collect scientific instruments, tools and literature for the universities in Poland.[164]

Mallet, British Envoy to Stockholm, informed London that some Swedish companies (Billners, Folke, Appelquist, Bratt) had already contacted the Soviet Legation to obtain information about the options of obtaining supplies from Polish mines.[165] On giving an account of his conversation with Boheman, Mallet informed London that Kindgren, director of the Committee of

---

[164] AMSZ, iss. 6, w. 78, vol. 1159, copy of message no. 144 by Z. Modzelewski to the Ministry of Foreign Affairs, Moscow, 8 II 1945, p 1.

[165] RA, UD 1920 års dossiersystem, HP 1, vol. 486, letter by Swedish Envoy to Moscow S. Söderblom to Minister of Foreign Affairs Ch. Günther, Moscow, 15 II 1945. The Swedes also cared about the property of their companies in the Polish territory. On 14 March 1945, Ingemar Häglöff, First Secretary of the Swedish Legation in Moscow, presented Commercial Attaché Wojciech Chabasiński with aide-mémoire regarding this issue. Chabasiński wrote: 'Having informed the Ministry about the above, I would like to draw attention to the fact that the memorandum was submitted at the request of the Minister of Foreign Affairs of Sweden, and not on the initiative of the Legation. The Swedish capital is undoubtedly seriously worried about the fate of the factories and the warehouses, which are its property and are located in the territory of Poland. The relevant pressure is exerted on the Ministry of Foreign Affairs. I would also like to mention that in the conversation, Häglöff showed a clear interest in the issue of possible safeguarding the rights of the Swedish companies in the

Swedish State Reserves, visited Moscow to discuss the issue of possible deliveries and prices of coal. Mallet predicted that Kindgren would most probably meet with the representatives of the Lublin government: 'The Swedes, as Boheman said, are naturally interested in the opportunity to obtain coal from the Polish coal mines, especially that the pace of the Russian march in the direction of Silesia allows one to assume that the coal mines will not be destroyed.' He justified the necessity of the existence of representation for the Polish Lublin administration, like that possessed by the French, who, despite continuously recognizing the government of London as the official government of Poland – sent what could be described as a commercial delegation to Lublin. Despite their commercial prospects, the Swedes had commercial interests in Poland, which required attention.[166]

Jerzy Pański presented offers of cooperation to the Swedes personally. He promised coal in exchange for machinery and prefabricated homes. Posing as the representative of 'new Poland' he accepted the offers of Swedish coal importers. The Swedish industrialists came directly to him to express their willingness to cooperate with the future authorities of Poland, whose harbinger was the PKWN.[167] Envoy Sokolnicki confirmed, 'Pański carried out diverse surveys in Swedish economic circles on the subject of future Swedish–Polish commercial relations.' However, he added, in a reassuring tone:

> 'these surveys are not serious, because Pański is not familiar with those issues and does not possess any reworked material. He initially tried to make some efforts with industrial and commercial companies, but when his interlocutors realised that he was not presenting any serious economic concepts, they broke contact with him. Therefore, he now limits himself to contacts with various minor companies, and especially with intermediaries, people who are considered irresponsible in this territory, and who are often placed on the index of the local Association of Exporters.[168]

---

territory of Poland.' See: AMSZ, iss. 6, w. 78, vol. 1164, report no. 2 by Commercial Attaché W. Chabasiński to the Ministry of Industry, Moscow, 7 IV 1945, p. 1.

[166] NA, FO, 371/48048, telegram by the Envoy of Great Britain to Stockholm V. Mallet to the FO, 1 II 1945.

[167] NA, FO, 371/48048, letter by Envoy of Great Britain to Stockholm V. Mallet to Ch. Lamming, 3 VI 1945.

[168] AMSZ, iss. 6, w. 78, vol. 1163, transcript of witness account [Jerzy Pański] put down on 30 September 1946 in the Executive Office of the Special Commission in Warsaw, 5 X 1946, p. 4–7. Pański, on mentioning his activity in Sweden in the years 1944 and 1945 – among the Swedish companies which addressed him with a request for information of a commercial nature – named the concern Axel Johnson (at first the owner handed to him 3 thousand crowns 'as a means of support for the Poles-democrats') and Svensk-Ryska AB (represented by Ruben Ljundberg, who promised his support in the propagandist activity in favour of the

7. THE DOUBLE GAME OF SWEDISH DIPLOMACY

Meanwhile, Pański informed Moscow in April 1945, 'commercial and industrial spheres in Sweden are showing interest in the opportunities of future relations with Poland', and 'Swedish companies divided themselves into "democratic" (namely believing in the permanence of the Provisional Government) and "London".'[169] There was a lot of truth in Pański's opinion, but his role in the initiation and development of bilateral relations was overestimated. What was crucial for the Swedes were direct conversations, conducted in Moscow with the representative of the Polish Provisional Government. It was there that the settlements of the issue of future mutual relations between Sweden and Poland were taking place. This nevertheless did not stop the Soviet political offensive in Sweden. Sokolnicki, whilst wanting to underestimate the possibility of establishing economic cooperation between Sweden and the Polish Provisional Government, also reported anxiously, in the summing up of his letter to London from March 1945, 'what is expected in the nearest future is the arrival to Stockholm of 15 new officials to the local Soviet Legation.' Among them was a specialist in Polish matters.[170] The Polish intelligence informed London in April 1945 about the special training in the Soviet Legation of Poles who were to be sent to their country as officials of different levels of administration. The group of trainees included Pański and other leading activists of the Union of Polish Patriots in Sweden.[171] According to the SÄPO files, Pański established an indefinite contact with British intelligence.[172]

On 3 February, Minister Günther met with Italian Envoy Giovanni Battista Guarnaschelli and explained to him that Pański had no official status and no steps had been taken to grant him such status. The issue of granting recognition to the government, about which Günther said 'it may be already

---

Lublin Committee Poland). Through Ljundberg's agency he met the representatives of the Union of Coal Importers.

[169] PISM, A 11, E/590, letter by Envoy H. Sokolnicki to the Ministry of Foreign Affairs, 26 III 1945. Sokolnicki gave one specific example of Pański's contactswith Ericsson's representative in Poland – Björklund. Also, in this case Sokolnicki consequently discredited Pański's activity: 'As a matter of fact Björklund also, on getting to know who Pański was, reported the meeting to the Legation and stated that he would not see Pański ever again.'

[170] AAN, ZPPwSz, 434/3, telegram by J. Pański to the Polish Embassy in Moscow, 3 IV 1945, p. 14. Last companies mentioned by Pański were the electrical concerns ASEA and SVEA Export, which allegedly financed the press campaign of the Polish Legation in Stockholm, whose purpose was to attack the Provisional Government.

[171] PISM, A 11, VI 21/590, letter by Envoy H. Sokolnicki to the Ministry of Foreign Affairs, Stockholm, 26 III 1945.

[172] PISM, A XII, 3/41, note by the head of the Department of Information and Intelligence of the Staff of the Commander-in-Chief, Colonel S. Gano, 'Szwecja – komuniści polscy', 19 IV 1945.

called Warsaw government', was not yet taken up by the Swedish government and it continued to recognise the Polish government in exile. Nevertheless, the Swedish minister of foreign affairs pointed out that what was at stake were the crucial economic interests of his country in the territory of Poland, which continued to remain under the control of the Provisional Government. This fact needed to be considered by the Swedish government. Günther provided an example of two French representations which existed in Stockholm during the war – that of Vichy and that of General de Gaulle – and announced that the Swedish government would wait for the situation to unfold and for an organic solution to this problem to present itself.[173]

Several days later, the Foreign Office (FO) advised the Swedes through Mallet to postpone the delegation of their representation to the Provisional Government in Lublin to the moment of the conclusion of the conference in Yalta.[174] When Mallet communicated this message to Boheman, the Secretary-General expressed his gratitude and replied that the Swedish government had already made such a decision.[175]

'The natural solution of the Polish matter' was to be delivered by the conference in Yalta. The Polish border was established along the Curzon line. Poland was to incorporate Eastern German territories. The future Polish government was to be formed by ministers of both the London government and the Provisional Government in Warsaw. Stalin promised to allowed free elections in Poland. During the first days following its conclusion, the Swedish press did not publish any information that would explain the development of the situation from the perspective of the Polish government in London. The only exception was the government's protest, which was published in all dailies. Żaba explained such a stance with the influence of the British press and fear of the Soviet Union, whose annoyance everyone wished to avoid.[176]

In general, the final settlements of the conference were received in Sweden with contentment. It was only on closer analysis of the resolutions that the initial enthusiasm on the part of the Swedish press, became more realistic

---

[173] RA-Arninge, SÄPO arkiv, P 2406 Jerzy Pański, note regarding J. Pański's meeting on 2 III 1945 with J. H. Walter, who remained in contact with the Naval Attaché of Great Britain, H. Denham.
[174] NA, FO, 188/492, telegram by Envoy of Italy to Rome G. B. Guarnaschelli to the Ministry of Foreign Affairs in Rome, 3 II 1945.
[175] NA, FO, 371/48048, telegram by FO to Envoy of Great Britain to Stockholm V. Mallet, 10 II 1945.
[176] NA, FO, 371/48048, telegram by Envoy of Great Britain to Stockholm V. Mallet to FO, n.p., 11 II 1945.

approach.[177] Żaba's remark referred to the conservative dailies (*Svenska Dagbladet*, *Sydsvenska Dagbladet Snällposten*) and the weeklies (*Svensk Tidskrift*, *Obs!*). The opinions of the press were divided. Positive commentaries in relation to the position of the Polish government were published by *Arbetet*, *Ny Tid* and *Arbetaren*. However, the leading opinion journalist for the liberal *Dagens Nyheter*, Johannes Wickman, traditionally believed that Polish politics is completely incomprehensible and Great Britain would end up in a conflict with the Soviet Union, in case it wanted to conduct such policy.[178] On 14 February, though, *Stockholms-Tidningen* commented on the results of the conference in Yalta with contentment and clear relief. It was stated, 'the Polish issue ceased to be a problem, owing to the most dangerous obstacle being removed.' The author confirmed that formally a compromise had been reached, but, 'the Russian point of view was acknowledged by both Anglo-Saxon powers.' This meant, 'The Western countries have saved their prestige, and the Soviet Union has won the case.'[179] A little anxiety was expressed due to the trimming of Poland in the east and extending of its borders in the west. The socialist *Ny Tid* considered that the faithful ally was aggrieved by the returning to the idea of the border established in the pact between Hitler and Stalin.[180] *Sydsvenska Dagbladet Snällposten* claimed that probably many Poles believed that they belonged to the losing camp in this war.[181] Other commentators for *Stockholms-Tidningen* daily, known for its pro-German sympathies earlier in the war, argued:

> We, the Swedes, are concerned about what is happening, not only when looking at it from the Polish perspective. Although we are also risking various accusations of joining the campaign of compassion for Germany, it ought to be stated that a similar case of relocating such a considerable portion of the population constitutes an unnecessary burden for those who are no more to blame for the deeds of Nazi Germany than other nations, and it would constitute a foundation for hatred, which may turn out to be dangerous in the future.'[182]

---

[177] RA, UD 1920 års dossiersystem, HP 1, vol. 486, letter by Swedish Envoy to London J. Beck-Friis to E. von Post, n.p., 19 II 1945.
[178] E. Boheman, *På vakt. Kabinettssekreterare...*, p. 304.
[179] AAN, Norbert Żaba's collection, copy of report by N. Żaba to the Ministry of Information and Documentation, Stockholm, 29 III 1945.
[180] What may be considered its expression is the characteristic graphic commentary: 'Hem med Curzonlinjen', *Sydsvenska Dagbladet Snällposten*, 16 II 1945.
[181] J. Wickman, 'Krimreflexer', *Dagens Nyheter*, 22 II 1945.
[182] 'Dokumentet från Krimkonferensen', *Stockholms-Tidningen*, 14 II 1945.

The most extreme commentaries mentioned the fifth partition of Poland.[183] Surely the Swedish diplomats were aware of the bitterness that prevailed in 'Polish London.' The Polish Envoy to the Norwegian government in exile, Władysław Günther-Schwarzburg, openly communicated to the Swedish Envoy to London, Johan Beck-Friis, that Churchill had sold Poland to the Soviets.[184] The Polish diplomat was pessimistic about the developments in Poland. He maintained that there was no chance for free elections and that the economy would undergo Bolshevisation. When he was asked by the Swede how Poles imagined the solution to such a complicated Polish issue, Günther-Schwarzburg replied, 'nobody is thinking about such a solution and in fact there exists no such solution.' Boheman most probably maintained that Sweden had no other option than to acknowledge the grim reality of the situation as the Western Allies were. In the first days of May, when defeat of Germany was being celebrated, he would nonetheless express his anxiety regarding the submissiveness of Great Britain and the USA towards Stalin, 'I am afraid, I said, that it would be either impossible or very difficult to force the Russians to leave the territories they now occupy.'[185]

After the Yalta agreements, the Swedes gradually prepared the diplomatic ground to establish international relations with the government in Warsaw. On 27 March, Söderblom talked to American ambassador Georg Kennan about the intention of sending a representative of the Swedish government to Warsaw.[186] He explained that Sweden was expecting the renewal of trade with Poland, including efforts to launch the deliveries of Polish coal. Nevertheless, the decision was not yet made, as the Swedes were unwilling to 'step over the line.' Added to which, there were fears that the representative chosen by the Swedes would not be accepted by the Soviets, which would make Stockholm risk an unpleasant refusal. Kennan explained informally that the chances of solving the Polish matter were few. British and American authorities, in his view, would have nothing against Sweden sending its representative to Poland, on the condition that such action would assume the character of a de facto recognition of the government in Warsaw and would be conducted without any excessive publicity. According to the American diplomat, the

---

[183] K. J. O-n, 'Polens affärer', *Ny Tid*, 15 II 1945.
[184] 'Polens sak', *Sydsvenska Dagbladet Snällposten*, 16 II 1945.
[185] 'Underhusdebatten om Polens framtid', *Stockholms-Tidningen*, 2 III 1945. E. Boheman, *På vakt. Kabinettssekreterare...*, p. 304.
[186] 'Polens femte delning genomförd av dess bundsförvanter. Rysk inblandning i Polens inrikespolitik legaliserades i Jalta', *Dagsposten*, 14 II 1945; 'Polsk lösning teknisk elegant', *Aftonbladet*, 13 II 1945.

7. THE DOUBLE GAME OF SWEDISH DIPLOMACY

Soviet authorities would construe such a move in a positive way, because it was important for them to stabilize the Warsaw government.

Meanwhile, on 3 April 1945, Modzelewski again asked in an official letter about the Swedes' plans concerning the establishment of relations with the government in Warsaw. The alleged reason became the Soviet army's arrival in Gdańsk and Gdynia. According to Modzelewski, the Swedish companies themselves started to report to the departments of Polish Provisional Government, but the ambassador emphasized that the Polish government preferred to negotiate with the Swedish government. He pledged that Poland was intending to export coal and zinc to Sweden, and that the only problem that needed to be solved were the transport difficulties, namely the lack of engines and trucks. Modzelewski stated that the agreement with Mikołajczyk was sealed and that Sweden was acting unwisely by suspending its decision to officially grant recognition to the Provisional Government of Poland. He expressed thanks for the aid, which had just arrived, and pursued questions about the deliveries of specialist equipment, which had already been discussed much earlier. Söderblom, as usual, could only assure his interlocutor that good relations with Poland were very important for Sweden and that he would hand a relevant report from the conversation to the appropriate party. Indeed, on concluding his account he emphasized:

> Personally, I have already suggested in August 1944 that a representative of Sweden be delegated to new Poland. I assume that it is now essential to find some form of answer to the Polish démarche that would be heading in a positive direction. If we had delegated our representative last autumn, we would have gained remarkably. When following the renewal of official relations with Czechoslovakia nothing was done or announced to Poland, I am afraid that the currently strong sympathies for Sweden will gradually pass and hinges in the doors will rust up when the contacts become established, which in any event must take place in the nearest future.[187]

Nevertheless, the government's instructions were different. The telegram from 7 April banned Söderblom from taking any initiative until negotiations between the powers concluded with an explanation of the fate of Poland. It is worth underlining that the officials of UD considered it appropriate to soften the message of its categorical instruction:

> We are naturally following the developments with utmost interest and it is important for us to establish traditionally friendly relations with Poland as soon

---

[187] RA, UD 1920 års dossiersystem, HP 1, vol. 486, pro memoria, Moscow, 27 III 1945.

as possible. At the same time, we are hoping that what becomes revived particularly quickly would be the booming trade, and we are ready – within the realms of our possibilities and obligations towards other countries – to support the rebuilding of Poland.'[188]

What is more, already on 14 April, the Swedish government ordered Söderblom to submit to Modzelewski a proposal to delegate a special representative to Poland – first secretary of Swedish Legation in Helsinki Brynolf Eng – to become acquainted with the options of trade between Poland and Sweden.[189] This decision could be somehow influenced by Mikołajczyk's decision to return to Poland and to accept the office of deputy Prime Minister in the Government in Warsaw. Besides, the coal mines and the ports were already occupied by the Soviet armies and, as the Polish interlocutors of the Swedes in Moscow maintained, the industrial infrastructure was not destroyed. The proposal was accepted by Poland on 22 April.[190] Meanwhile, in the Swedish Ministry of Foreign Affairs, Sokolnicki was reassured that Eng was not to travel as a diplomatic representative but only as a delegate of the government to accompany the members of the fuel commission. It was highlighted that the mission's character was exclusively economic and was by no means tantamount to granting recognition to the Warsaw government by Sweden.[191]

Ingemar Hägglöf based on the report of Elliot M. Shirk, the representative of the American Red Cross, on 10 April produced a report devoted to the humanitarian aid that was granted to Poland. From the turn of 1944 and 1945, Shirk spent five years in Poland and controlled the packages transported along the route that was like that used for the transports of the Swedish route – running through the Soviet territory, by air to Moscow, and then westwards by railway. The Americans, as opposed to the Swedes, demanded that the distribution of medication that were submitted to the Polish Red Cross be controlled. It was only after a couple of days in the second half of December that consent was given for Shirk to be transferred to Lublin together with the entire cargo. It turned out that the batch of medication that had been sent previously had never arrived. The authorities of the Polish Red

---

[188] RA, UD 1920 års dossiersystem, HP 12, vol. 890, telegram by Swedish Envoy to Moscow S. Söderblom to the Ministry of Foreign Affairs, Moscow, 2 IV 1945; vol. 890, memorandum concerning Polish-Swedish economic relations, Stockholm, 12 IV 1945.
[189] RA, UD 1920 års dossiersystem, HP 12, vol. 890, telegram by the government of Sweden to Swedish Envoy to Moscow S. Söderblom, 7 IV 1945.
[190] RA, UD 1920 års dossiersystem, HP 64, vol. 2736, telegram by Envoy of Sweden to Moscow S. Söderblom, Stockholm, 14 IV 1945.
[191] RA, UD 1920 års dossiersystem, HP 64, vol. 2736, telegram by Envoy of Sweden to Moscow S. Söderblom, Moscow, 23 IV 1945.

7. THE DOUBLE GAME OF SWEDISH DIPLOMACY

Cross had no idea about aid from Sweden. According to Shirk, the Polish Red Cross was the only organization which provided effective help for countless numbers of people in Poland, whereas the help from the Soviet Union was to be directed exclusively to the Warsaw Praga quarter. The orientation of the Poles was anti-Russian due to the numerous excesses of the Soviet troops towards the civilians, to the arrests of the members of the underground and to 'the fact that the Russians left General Bór at the mercy of events.' Sanitary conditions were in a critical state, and water supplies and sewers in large cities did not function. The American was already familiar with the popular Polish saying: 'since we have managed to survive five years of the German occupation, we will manage to survive a year of such freedom.'[192] Shirk's report, submitted to Stockholm through Hägglöf, painted a grim picture of the situation in Poland. Shirk viewed the Polish Provisional Government as a Soviet puppet government. Despite these alarming reports about the actual situation in the Polish territory, the Swedish government intended to continue its efforts to reach an agreement with the Polish authorities in Warsaw. Besides, according to the Swedish diplomacy, the Polish government in London found itself in the state of self-compromising internal disintegration. From the reports which were prepared by Envoy Prytz at the outset of April, it could be understood that 'the prestige of the Polish government in London, which was never too high, has recently plummeted.'[193] This was the result of four leading socialist activists dissociating themselves from the policy of the government directed by Arciszewski on 19 March. Later, on 22 March, the president dissolved the National Council, where a small number of politicians were considering an option of reaching a compromise with the Soviet Union and calling for the establishment of a democratic government in Poland based on the agreement with Moscow. For Prytz it was obvious that Prime Minister Arciszewski had no influence on the developments or decisions being made by the powers. The Swede drew attention to the announcement of the leaders of the underground movement, which accepted the invitation to hold talks with the Soviet authorities. On 27 and 28 March, fifteen Poles appeared on the spot where the meeting was to be held and from then on nothing was heard from them. It was discovered later that they had been

---

[192] AAN, HI/I/334, copy of telegram by Polish Envoy to Stockholm H. Sokolnicki to the Ministry of Foreign Affairs, Stockholm, 23 V 1945.
[193] RA, UD 1920 års dossiersystem, HP 39, vol. 1620, copy of secret memorandum by I. Hägglöf, Moscow, 10 IV 1945.

arrested.[194] The announcement communicated by Prytz contained an insinuation that they had been murdered. According to information he obtained, the Poles found themselves in Kiev and there they conducted the negotiations. These discussions were to, according to him, lead to the formation of the new government, announced at the conference of Yalta, which perhaps was to happen early enough to make its representatives take part in the conference in San Francisco. Prytz claimed that such a solution would put the British government in a delicate situation, since it could not refuse to grant recognition to such government.

At the outset of April, news was announced that several leaders of the Polish Underground State were missing. The issue was re-visited in May regarding Molotov revealing them to have been arrested by the Soviet authorities. Żaba wrote to London, 'It is beyond any doubt that the new cynical Soviet step has made a great impression here, and though the newspapers were filled with dramatic descriptions of Germany's agony, much space was devoted to the last event in the Polish–Soviet relations.'[195] Later, in June, the Soviet authorities held their show trial in Moscow.

A characteristic example of such press responses was the article by Gunnar Pihl in the *Sydsvenska Dagbladet Snällposten*. Pihl expressed serious fears about the political objectives of Stalin.[196] The dailies also provided the details of the Poles' arrests 'under large headlines and in a sensational form.' In mid-June, when the circumstances of the Poles' kidnapping to Moscow and the practices of Soviet authorities in the territory of Poland were already known, the tone of the articles changed slightly. *Göteborgs Handels- och Sjöfarts-Tidning* first published the comments about mixed feelings regarding the recent actions of the Soviet authorities towards the leaders of the Polish Underground State, and later more precise information about the mass arrests of Polish patriots and their deportations. The lack of knowledge on this subject was justified with the nearly complete isolation of Poland from the outside world.[197]

---

[194] RA, UD 1920 års dossiersystem, HP 1, vol. 486, letter by Swedish Envoy to London B. Prytz to Minister of Foreign Affairs Ch. Günther, London, 9 IV 1945.
[195] '15 framstående polacker försvunna', *Upsala Nya Tidning*, 7 IV 1945; 'Polska ledare försvann på väg till ryskt möte', *Dagens Nyheter*, 7 IV 1945; 'Polsk skuggregering borta. GPU uppges som kidnappare', *Stockholms-Tidningen*, 7 IV 1945.
[196] G. Pihl, 'Både demokrati och demokrati', *Sydsvenska Dagbladet Snällposten*, 7 IV 1945.
[197] 'Moskva löser polska frågan utan de västallierade. Det senaste schackdraget framkallar blandade känslor', *Göteborgs Handels- och Sjöfarts-Tidning*, 9 IV 1945; P-k, 'De bortförda polska patrioterna', *Göteborgs Handels- och Sjöfarts-Tidning*, 15 VI 1945.

7. THE DOUBLE GAME OF SWEDISH DIPLOMACY

The person who again commented on the Polish matter was Józefa Armfelt, who in an article for the liberal *Vestmanlands Läns Tidning* daily expressed her grief in dramatic words, 'The conscience of the world is not clear and neither is the conscience of Great Britain!'[198] It is worth underlining that voices critical of Stalin reflected a broader tendency which was particularly visible in the press.

In the first half of May, Press Attaché Żaba noted that the certain optimism regarding the settlement of the Polish matter by the Allies, which had been felt following the conference in Yalta, disappeared:

> What is noticeable is the clear concern with the turning of events around the Polish matter on the international arena, as well as with the frictions it causes in the Allied camp. Some evaluations of Russia's conduct are very bold, which deserves to be emphasized, especially because of the restraint or even timidity of the local press, which is very well known to us.[199]

Stockholms-Tidningen claimed that the greatest friends of Russia were not able to substantiate Stalin's conduct towards the leaders of the Polish underground movement.[200] Whereas, a commentator for *Svenska Dagbladet* maintained that Stalin's attitude towards the Polish matter proved that the dictator was not going to respect the agreements of Yalta, treated the future of Poland as the internal issue of the Soviet Union and could cause the greatest crisis from the time of the establishment of the anti-fascist coalition.[201] It was only at that moment when the voices were heard that the propaganda, which claimed that the Polish government of London was reactionary or that it only cared about the interests of upper classes of society, might have been false and failed to get to the root of the entire dispute over the Polish matter. *Falu-Kuriren* emphasized, 'We, the Swedes, naturally do not have any possibility to influence international developments, but we should focus our attention on the course of events in the country which will take control over a vast stretch of the Baltic Sea coast.'[202]

The reports about the repressions which had been used against the soldiers of the Home Army and the Polish Underground State did not stop the

---

[198] J. Armfelt, 'Polska röster om Polens sak, -och utländska', *Vestmanlands Läns Tidning*, 18 IV 1945.
[199] AAN, Norbert Żaba's collection, copy of report by N. Żaba to the Ministry of Information and Documentation, Stockholm, 24 V 1945.
[200] 'Stor bitterhet i London över ryska Polenkonflikten', *Stockholms-Tidningen*, 7 V 1945.
[201] T. G. W., 'Polska frågan prövosten för Jaltaandan', *Svenska Dagbladet*, 8 V 1945.
[202] 'Polens sak', *Falu-Kuriren*, 11 V 1945.

process of formalizing the contacts between Sweden and the Polish Provisional Government. On 11 May 1945, Eng received a phone call from Pański, who, under the pretext of the need to discuss some press-related issues, suggested a meeting. Eng defended himself by explaining that the press did not fall within his remit, nevertheless, Pański pressed him further and claimed that the information he was in possession of would spark the Swede's interest. The meeting took place a day later. Pański assured his interlocutor that despite acting as a representative of the Polpress agency, he was in fact authorized to act as intermediary in the contact between the Warsaw government and Sweden, as proof he had already presented relevant documents to *Utrikesdepartementet* (UD). Nevertheless, due to the lack of official relations between Stockholm and the Polish Provisional Government, he made it clear that his words should be treated as his private statements. Eventually, Pański, on behalf of the Polish representation in Moscow, stated that Eng was welcome to come to visit Poland with his secretary. Eng answered evasively that he had recently returned from Helsinki and lacked sufficient orientation on the issue of the Polish–Swedish relations. Nevertheless, Pański did not abandon his efforts to discover whether Sweden would recognize the Warsaw government. During the discussion, he expressed an opinion that the de facto recognition would be enough for the moment. He announced that Eng's visa would be prepared in the coming days, although he did not answer whether he had obtained confirmation from Moscow on this matter.[203]

The persistence of the representatives of 'new Poland' both in Moscow and in Stockholm was beneficial for the Swedish government as it wanted to establish relations with its Baltic neighbour as soon as possible, but at the same time was evasive towards London. In this instance, utilitarianism clashed with ethics. In Moscow on 18 May 1945, Söderblom discussed with Modzelewski, who had recently been appointed as deputy minister of foreign affairs of the Provisional Government of Poland, the future of Polish–Swedish relations. He considered the delivery of 1 million tons of coal during the coming summer to be possible in terms of production, but was not sure whether Poland was capable of its transport. Eng's arrival to Moscow was expected at any time. Prime Minister Osóbka-Morawski, on 3 May, publicly announced that the Polish Provisional Government had established cooperation with Sweden, but Modzelewski made no mention of the necessity to gain legal recognition of his government from the Swedish authorities. Still,

---

[203] RA, UD 1920 års dossiersystem, HP 12, vol. 890, memorandum by B. Eng, Stockholm, 12 V 1945. Economic issues raised by Pański on this meeting are discussed in Chapter 10.

7. THE DOUBLE GAME OF SWEDISH DIPLOMACY

Söderblom attempted to convince Stockholm that, 'sending a Swedish delegate to Poland would be highly beneficial for general policy-related reasons and would increase the chances of obtaining coal – otherwise this was excluded.'[204] The actions connected with sending a Swedish representative to participate in the talks on coal import, were treated by the European press as the first step by Sweden to recognising the Polish Provisional Government before the governments of the Western Allies.

The principal aim of the Swedish diplomacy was to secure Polish coal supplies while avoiding simultaneous legal recognition of the Polish authorities in Warsaw, which had been formed under Soviet control before the decision of the Western Allies. For the Polish side though, it was important that the commercial and political issues were connected. The following weeks brought cautious actions on both sides, who aimed to reach these two mutually exclusive objectives.[205]

In May 1945 the Swedes started to analyse the situation in Europe and its strategic position following the conclusion of the war. The tone of the report of Sweden's Defence Staff was pessimistic:

> The German armed forces have capitulated. Nevertheless, peace did not start to reign in Europe. The Allies completed *one* task together – so far the most important one – Germany has been militarily defeated. Other tasks were brushed

---

[204] RA, UD 1920 års dossiersystem, HP 12, vol. 890, memorandum regarding the establishment of relations with the Provisional Government of Poland, Stockholm, 22 V 1945.
[205] For Sweden it was undoubtedly important to rebuild economic relations with Poland, regardless of the shape of its new government, due to Sweden's own raw material needs. In turn, the new authorities, which were formed in the Polish territory under the Soviet supervision, were striving to become legitimized in the international arena. No less important was the economic motivation, namely seeking international partners at the rebuilding of the destroyed country. Cf. J. Dorniak, *Stosunki...*, pp. 46–48. It is also worth mentioning yet another aspect of the entire issue: for some communist activists the development of relations with Sweden was to constitute the evidence for the existence of some range of sovereign actions of the Provisional Government in Warsaw in the area of foreign policy. Leon Finkelstein during the session of the Central Committee of the Polish Workers' Party (e.g. communist party) on 20 and 21 May 1945 claimed with a clear exaggeration: 'The policy of Poland needs to be convergent with the foundations of the policy of the Soviet Union, but within this policy we have the opportunity to conduct the defence of our interests – there is much room for self-reliance [...] Relations between the Soviet Union and Sweden are frigid. In spite of this fact it is possible for us to maintain relations with Sweden.' See: Protokół obrad KC PPR w maju 1945 roku (The protocol of the session of the Central Committee of the Polish Workers' Party), compiled by A. Kochański, Warszawa 1992 (*Dokumenty do dziejów PRL*, iss. 1), p. 3. Cf. A Kłonczyński, *Stosunki...*

aside when fights were taking place, and new tasks appeared following Germany's downfall.[206]

Most of all, these tasks included relations between the countries and the establishment of borders as well as the countries' internal relations. The first issue concerned all Central Europe, the Balkans and Northern Europe (Bornholm, Finland and Norway), and the second Germany mainly, but also the Soviet Union. The analysts of the Swedish staff were aware that on many of these matters, the interests of Russia and the Western Allies were divergent:

> According to all probability both sides would like to solve their problems without starting an open conflict. The will of both sides is certainly reaching a successful solution (for each of the sides) or a good position for reaching these solutions during the next peace conference, in the situation when war-ravaged Europe may still be shaped and the powers themselves are in possession of the necessary military measures.'

Various scenarios of possible developments were appearing and from the Swedish perspective the need to remain cautious required considering any of the following options: 'In any case it would be unwise now, before it is possible to foresee the unfolding of events with much certainty, to take the steps which, in case the developments are unfavourable, could put our country in a risky situation.'

With regard to the landing of the British army in Denmark and Norway and the annexation of the entire eastern and southern coast of the Baltic Sea (including Bornholm) by the Soviet army, the Swedish staff officers proposed that the Swedish army remain in the highest operational readiness, and the counter-intelligence services were to play an exceptional role in the face of the expected revival of the activity of foreign intelligence services in the territory of Sweden in the nearest future. The clearly increasing concern with the Soviet infiltration was evident.

The propagandist activity of the Polish Legation in Stockholm started to bear fruit, although in April some commotion was caused by the fact that the Ministry of Labour and Social Welfare of the Polish government in exile authorized Maurycy Karniol as a delegate to Scandinavian countries. Pilch wrote with outrage to the Ministry of Foreign Affairs that according to Karniol the Ministry of Labour was not satisfied with the work of the Polish Legation as far as the preparation of Swedish humanitarian aid for Poland

---

[206] RA, UD 1920 års dossiersystem, HP 1, vol. 40, memorandum of the Defence Staff regarding the military-political situation of Sweden in the summer of 1945, 30 V 1945.

following the war was concerned: 'I must admit that the above statements of Mr. Karniol were particularly unpleasant to me, all the more so that according to the dictates of my conscience – they were unfair. For several months of the Legation's operation there has been not a single day that we would not devote our closest attention to this issue. In the current, very difficult for us, political situation when we are, unfortunately, no longer a valuable, irreproachable partner for the Swedes, we are using every moment and occasion not only to maintain all the necessary contacts with the Swedish relief authorities, but also to convince them to the rightness of our theses, to continue talks with us, to become interested with our projects etc.'[207]

Pilch was even more surprised with the opinions reported by Karniol that he formerly did not receive any negative signals whatsoever concerning his work in Stockholm, even during his latest visit to London. The counsellor openly asked his superiors whether he was to acquaint Karniol with the issue of the talks with the Swedes. He proposed that they were conducted exclusively by one person, if the stage of semi-official negotiations was over. He refused to provide Karniol with more detailed information concerning the negotiations, and at the same time he informed about the contacts of people connected with him with the activists of the Warsaw government.

What is more, on 16 April 1945 Żaba handed in his resignation from the office of head of the Delegation of the Ministry of Information regarding Karniol being granted the title of Polish envoy ad personam. In the letter to the ministry he pointed out that so far, he only came under the authority of Envoy Sokolnicki. In connection with that he explained:

> Making all my decisions dependent on the agreement of Doctor Karniol I must treat not only as my demotion from the currently occupied position but also as a so-far unheard of precedent of subordinating officials of other ministries, who are also diplomatic officials of the legation, to the trusted representative of the Party [PPS], equipped with more powerful authorizations from the Polish envoy himself, which is for me impossible to accept due to my perception of rightness and democracy.[208]

---

[207] AAN, HI/I/115, letter by the counsellor to the Polish Legation in Stockholm, T. Pilch, to the Ministry of Foreign Affairs, Stockholm, 18 IV 1945.

[208] AAN, Norbert Żaba's collection, copy of report by N. Żaba to the Ministry of Information and Documentation, 16 IV 1945. Simultaneously Żaba sent by the same mail the letter to the Ministry of Internal Affairs with a request to become appointed as an official of this Ministry at the Polish Legation in Stockholm, see: Ibidem, copy of report by N. Żaba to the Department of Continental Action of the Ministry of Internal Affairs, 16 IV 1945.

Together with Żaba, three of his clerks also resigned. The Attaché wanted to secure himself formally in the event of being subordinated by Karniol. He was hoping to continue his current duties in the very same team and place, but under a different title. Karniol's competences concerning the Delegature of the Ministry of Information and Documentation were quickly removed.

The conflict seems odd when one considers that both parties were aware that the mission of the Polish diplomatic post was coming to an end. In the current situation, the Ministry of Information and Documentation advised Żaba not to make any future commitments.[209] What was most important by the end of June was providing financial security for the post, which was to be liquidated, although the publishing activity was not suspended, and certain plans were still being pursued.[210]

The Polish military contribution to the defeat of Germany was still emphasized in the propaganda. The Swedish edition of the book *The Story of a Secret State* by Jan Karski, was published on 9 April 1945 by the prestigious publishing house Natur och Kultur.[211] Positive reviews for the book started to appear, which pointed out that emotions were held at bay and unbelievable things were presented in a matter-of-fact manner: German cruelty and the bold actions of the Polish nation.[212] Tadeusz Nowacki with Stefan Trębicki later wrote the book *Warszawa Rapsodin* (The Warsaw Rhapsody). This novel described the fate of the Warsaw Jews from September 1939 until the rising in the ghetto in 1943. Żaba convinced the editors of the Bonniers publishing house to publish the novel *En dam och sju excellence* (Seven Excellencies and One Lady) by Aleksander Piskor in 1945. Bo Enander's book *Så härskade herre-folket* (So Ruled the Nation of the Lords) rallied against the campaign of compassion for Germany. The wave of dislike towards Germany, however, was presented only in the reports about life in concentration camps following their liberation in the spring of 1945.[213] *Seger är inte nog*

---

[209] AAN, Norbert Żaba's collection, copy of letter by R. Przedpełski (European Department of the Ministry of Information and Documentation), London, 15 III 1945.

[210] Ibidem, copy of letter by N. Żaba to the Ministry of Information and Documentation, n.p., 27 VI 1945.

[211] J. Karski, 'Den hemliga staten', Stockholm 1945.

[212] Jc., 'En stat under jorden', *Göteborgs Handels- och Sjöfarts-Tidning*, 1 VI 1945; R., 'Korta recensioner', *Svenska Dagbladet*, 16 IV 1945; M. S-hl, 'Skräckinteriörer från de tyska likfabrikerna', *Karlstads-Tidningen*, 25 IV 1945; R., 'Hemlig stat', *Upsala Nya Tidning*, 27 IV 1945; Gvs., 'En stat under jorden', *Stockholms-Tidningen*, 30 IV 1945; G. Frösell, 'Polens strid efter nederlaget', *Aftonbladet*, 6 V 1945; Th:son, 'Över och under jorden', *Syd-svenska Dagbladet Snällposten*, 14 V 1945.

[213] AAN, Norbert Żaba's collection, copy of letter by N. Żaba to the Ministry of Information and Documentation, 9 VI 1945. See: H. Dahlberg, *I Sverige...*, p. 88.

(Victory is Not Enough), the book by the American journalist John Scott, translated into Swedish, was less favourable. The author's main source was Edmund Rappaport, supporter of the ZPP, who 'in exaggerated colours describes the pre-war anti-Semitism in Poland and claims that these were mostly the partisans of Eastern Poland who resisted the Germans.'[214]

In the press report Żaba highlighted, 'When it comes to Sweden, here it is followed nevertheless with great interest the development of the situation in the country which is one of the owners of the greatest stretch of the Baltic Sea coast.' Whereas, the attitude of Stalin towards Poland was to give an idea about the Soviet dictator's political plans towards his other neighbours.[215] On 9 May, in the liberal *Västernorrlands Allehanda* it was stated that, 'there is little hope of finding an agreed solution of the Polish matter.' According to the commentator of this local daily, the Western Allies had little to say at the time, and 'Russia, if it wants to, would throw up an iron curtain and close the door.'[216] The moderate daily *Karlshamns Allehanda* repeated on 12 May that it was Poland who suffered the most during the Second World War and that this happened also with assistance from of Stalin, who deported Polish people deep into the Soviet Union. The author concluded the article, 'no one should be so stupid as to think that what is normally called freedom in Sweden, could also develop in the territories that end up under Russian administration.'[217] Similar were the views of an opinion journalist for *Gotlänningen*, who on 22 May, referring to *The Economist*, claimed that Poland could undergo a quick Sovietisation. The author of the article believed that Poland found itself in a similar situation to Finland, as the Lublin government's policy had to consider the wishes of Moscow, but at the same time was free to manage internal policy. The Poles had to accept these limitations, as they had no other choice, even more so that Stalin was the only warrant of the new Polish-German border.[218] On 30 May, *Göteborgs Handels- och Sjöfarts-Tidning* published a protest by a group of Poles against unfriendly articles appearing in the same daily. They explained that such propaganda had already inflicted irreparable damage, and that they belonged to the group of unfortunates who would never again see their families residing in the part of Poland annexed by the Soviet Union where the population is never allowed to express their opinion.

---

[214] AAN, Norbert Żaba's collection, copy of report by N. Żaba to the Ministry of Information and Documentation, 27 IV 1945.
[215] Ibidem, copy of report by N. Żaba to the Ministry of Information and Documentation, Stockholm, 16 VI 1945.
[216] 'Den polska frågan', *Västernorrlands Allehanda*, 9 V 1945.
[217] E. B., 'Polen återigen', *Karlshamns Allehanda*, 12 V 1945.
[218] K. L., 'Polens affärer', *Gotlänningen*, 22 V 1945.

Finally, they called for their right to independence, equal to that of the Danes and Norwegians, be recognized. They appealed, 'Nobody paid for their freedom with more blood and suffering than we did.'[219] According to Żaba, 'The protest's tone is unfortunately too teary-eyed to make an impression.'[220] In fact, the editors appended the article with several opinions that were in favour of Poland, 'however with a reservation that [...] freedom and independence in publishing news would be a greater favour to the Polish matter than publishing the news that was in line with Poles' wishes.' In the final commentary, the Swedes claimed that they were carrying out their duty and not making any propagandist moves. Instead, they were trying to explain the complex issues concerning Poland to their local readership. Nevertheless, in mid-June an article prepared by the Polish consulate in Gothenburg was published on the mass deportations of Polish patriots, representatives of the intelligentsia and workers' leaders. It contained a detailed description of the arrest of the leaders of the Polish Underground State in Pruszków (March 1945), emphasizing that foreign observers were banned from visiting Poland.[221] Contrary to many Swedish press commentaries, the situation was evaluated soberly by Stanisław Adamek in *Svensk Tidskrift*. He had no doubt that Stalin was applying the policy of faits accomplis, the arrangements of the Yalta conference were not a compromise but a step towards the Sovietisation of Poland, and the trial of the sixteen leaders of the Polish Underground State he considered to be the ultimate proof for the enslavement of Poland.[222]

A different tone dominated in the communist press. The Polish government in London was attacked in the *Ny Dag* article 'The Carriers of the Nazi Poison' by Per Meurling, published on 22 June 1945. Meurling wrote, 'the bankrupt Kwapiński-Arciszewski clique keeps sending their smelly anti-Soviet bombs every day from Great Britain, which are reaching the press all over the world and destroying all reason.' Numerous crude accusations were made, using the famous language of the communist propaganda. The author argued, 'Last year the Polish reactionaries of London had started the Warsaw Rising too early, and subsequently they accused the Russians of deceiving the Polish patriots', and 'causing the English–German–Polish war against the country of socialism.' According to Meurling, the Trial of Sixteen in Moscow

---

[219] 'Polsk protest', *Göteborgs Handels- och Sjöfarts-Tidning*, 30 V 1945.
[220] AAN, Norbert Żaba's collection, copy of report by N. Żaba to the Ministry of Information and Documentation, Stockholm, 16 VI 1945.
[221] P-k, 'De bortförda polska patrioterna', *Göteborgs Handels- och Sjöfarts-Tidning*, 16 VI 1945.
[222] Dagens frågor: 'Polen under tyskt regemente', *Svensk Tidskrift*, 1 II 1945; Dagens frågor: S. W., 'Polen efter Jalta-konferensen', *Svensk Tidskrift*, 2 V 1945; Dagens frågor: S. W., 'Förlikningen i Polen', *Svensk Tidskrift*, 7 VII 1945.

had already proven that the Polish government was preparing an armed riot against the Red Army. Although the London expatriates remained in isolation, they continued to conduct a propagandist campaign against the government in Warsaw. A commentator of *Ny Dag*, with the Polish-Swedish economic negotiations in mind, explained, 'What is necessary is our fast and determined action, so as not to squander – due to the reactions and hostility towards the Soviets puppet government of Poland – the Swedish interests.' Responsibility for the daring campaign, and the worsening of relations between Sweden and the Soviet Union, he placed on 'the socialist renegade' Karniol (twice as hostile due to his contacts with the leadership of the LO and the SAP) and on 'the Nazi' Żaba. Both, according to the journalist, were spreading lies in the style of Goebbels.[223]

Sweden's break-up of diplomatic relations with the Polish government in exile

The Swedes attempted to maintain good relations both with the Western Allies and the Soviet Union. They expected that Stalin bore no bad intentions towards Sweden. The announcement of Aleksandra Kollontai's return to Stockholm, after a visit to Moscow, was interpreted as a continuation of Moscow's lenient policy towards Scandinavia. At the same time, during a closed session of the first chamber of the parliament, held on 27 April 1945, Fredrik Ström wondered why the Soviet authorities allowed for the brutal treatment of the staff of the Swedish Legation in Budapest: 'We must constitute a kind of bridge between the East and the West. It is odd that the Russian soldiers and officers, who behave impeccably in Norway and in other countries, as we hear, could behave in such a way towards Sweden.'[224]

On this subject, Günther replied that there was no reaction from the Swedes up to this point, but a protest and demands on the Soviets for compensation were planned.[225] On 19 April, the Stockholm press published extensive reports devoted to the fate of the Swedish diplomatic representation in Budapest.[226] It was known that the secretary of the legation, Raoul Wallenberg, disappeared without trace on 17 January, and fourteen members

---

[223] P. Meurling, 'Nazistiska giftspridare', *Ny Dag*, 22 VI 1945; AAN, Norbert Żaba's collection, copy of report by N. Żaba to the Ministry of Information and Documentation, Stockholm, 23 VI 1945.
[224] *Protokoll...*, p. 346.
[225] Ibidem, pp. 367–368.
[226] 'Budapestlegationen har bott i källare i Buda', *Svenska Dagbladet*, 19 IV 1945.

of staff were transported, first by bus and then by rail, to Bucharest. From there they were transported, via Odessa and Moscow to Turku in Finland. Some members of staff remained in Budapest.

Envoy Sokolnicki tried to prevent the forming of relations between the Swedish government and the Polish Provisional Government in Warsaw. In line with the instruction from Minister Tarnowski he emphasized that the Warsaw government would not be granted recognition by the Western Allies. Tarnowski explained, 'If Sweden agreed to delegate its observer, this fact would be undoubtedly exploited by the propaganda of the Lublin "government", which would certainly harm the Swedes in international eyes', and after all, 'in the face of the unstable situation and transport obstacles, such a step would not bring the currently anticipated economic benefits in the shape of coal supplies.'[227] Sokolnicki obtained an assurance from the Swedish Ministry of Foreign Affairs that 'there only existed the intention of sending a delegation with a limited purpose of examining the opportunities for coal supplies.'[228]

Having completed the visa procedure, Eng arrived in Moscow on 31 May. There is no doubt that this was the next stage in the consequent policy of the Swedish government towards the Polish matter.[229]

Following Eng's arrival to Moscow, the Poles wanted him to first sign a relevant commercial agreement with them in Moscow, and only then go on to Warsaw. For the Poles, it was clearly important that Sweden grant recognition to the Provisional Government of Poland on the international arena. Söderblom attempted to explain that the Swedish government had not been maintaining relations with the Polish government in London for many years by then and that the signing of a preliminary commercial agreement by the Swedish delegate with the representation of the Polish Provisional Government would be a sufficiently suggestive fact. He repeated the arguments to Stockholm and claimed that the possible coexistence of two Polish representations in Stockholm would be of no great significance, as proven by experiences with the French, who during the war were represented both by the Vichy government and by General de Gaulle. Besides, Söderblom made the effort to use the tense situation among the Poles in Sweden to his benefit.

---

[227] PISM, A 12, 53/40U, telegram by the Ministry of Foreign Affairs to Polish Envoy to Stockholm H. Sokolnicki, sent on 2 V 1945.

[228] PISM, A 12, 53/40U, telegram by Polish Envoy to Stockholm H. Sokolnicki to the Ministry of Foreign Affairs, received on 6 V 1945.

[229] NA, FO, 371/48057, telegram by the Ambassador of Great Britain to Moscow, A. Clerk-Kerr, to the FO, 17 IV 1945.

7. THE DOUBLE GAME OF SWEDISH DIPLOMACY

He maintained that the exacerbation of the confrontation between the supporters of the government in London and the government in Warsaw would be a setback. According to Söderblom, it was the gradual recognition of Osóbka-Morawski's government that would be more beneficial for Warsaw. In such a situation, Modzelewski only called for the Polish refugees who remained in Sweden. He emphasized that it was the will of the Polish government that these people return to their homeland. The Swedish envoy assured him that the will of the Swedish government was the same, but any obligation in this matter was naturally out of question.

Eventually, on 8 June, Eng, the first secretary of the Swedish Legation in Helsinki, was authorized by the government and the king following the signing of the commercial agreement with the Polish Provisional Government.[230] On 16 June Eng departed from Moscow on a flight to Warsaw. The Polish side proposed sending its representative to Stockholm. Söderblom could perform a satisfactory retrospective of his Moscow mission, which lasted until July 1944. He considered one of his principal targets to be the establishment of Polish–Swedish relations, 'most of all due to the Swedish demand for coal and coke, and later owing to general policy-related reasons.'[231] Söderblom revealed that he had been given no directives regarding this issue up until the close of 1944. The pretext for contact with the Poles in Moscow became the issue of passing on Swedish humanitarian aid, which as it turned out was the first gift from abroad for destroyed Poland.

With the formation in Warsaw of the Provisional Government of National Unity, on 28 June, which fulfilled the provisions of the conference in Yalta according to the Swedes, and with the expected recognition of this government by the USA, the USSR and Great Britain, the Swedish government made a decision one day later (on 29 June) to grant recognition to the new Polish government as soon as possible, in line with the powers listed in the resolution.[232] On that very same day information was published in the Swedish press about the government of Sweden granting recognition to the government in Warsaw, which was agreed with the Polish side.[233] At that point only the coal agreement was signed, although the Under-Secretary of State Jakub Berman

---

[230] RA, Kabinettet/UD Huvudarkivet, Statsrådsprotokoll, serie A3A, vol. 118, Protokoll över Utrikesdepartementets ärenden, 8 VI 1945.
[231] RA, UD 1920 års dossiersystem, HP 12, vol. 890, copy of report by Swedish Envoy to Moscow S. Söderblom to Minister of Foreign Affairs Ch. Günther, Moscow, 18 VI 1945.
[232] RA, Kabinettet/UD Huvudarkivet, Statsrådsprotokoll, serie A3A, vol. 118, Protokoll över Utrikesdepartementets ärenden, 29 VI 1945.
[233] RA, UD 1920 års dossiersystem, HP 39, vol. 1620, copy of letter by B. Eng to R. Sohlman, Warsaw, 29 VI 1945.

pressed the Swedes to grant legal recognition to the government in Warsaw earlier than Great Britain and the USA, which would be of great importance for the future development of the Polish–Swedish relations.[234] Simultaneously he proposed that the Swedes took part in the rebuilding of the ports of Gdańsk and Gdynia, which was accepted, as highlighted Berman, by the Soviet authorities.

According to the information obtained by Sokolnicki, in the conversation with Grafström, this was the same as granting recognition to the government in Warsaw. The granting of recognition was put off, as the Swedes were waiting for the decision of the Western Allies.[235] Similar information was passed ashamedly by Grafström to one of the staff members of the Legation of Great Britain.[236] Sokolnicki was prepared for the concluding his diplomatic mission. The Ministry of Foreign Affairs had earlier sent the text of the note which was to be submitted to the Swedes, following the withdrawal of recognition for the Polish government in exile.[237] On 2 July, Sokolnicki paid a visit to Minister Günther, and then to under-secretary Sohlman. Both confirmed what the Polish envoy heard from Grafström several days earlier.[238] The Swedish government granted recognition to the Polish Provisional Government of National Unity on 6 July 1945.[239] At the same time Eng was appointed temporary representative of Sweden in Poland in the rank of chargé d'affaires.[240] Günther and Grafström would inform Sokolnicki of this appointment. The Polish envoy, as Grafström noted in his journal, had tears in his eyes. According to the Swedish diplomat who was sympathetic towards Poland, this was 'one of those countries and unfortunate nations that were tormented by the recurring misfortunes and cursed.' On the one hand he noticed with disgust that the government, which fought with the Germans on all fronts, was sent away empty-handed, and on the other, as Grafström wrote, 'The Poles have many brilliant talents, but they are in fact crummy politicians.' He accused them being unable to make a timely prediction that

---

[234] Ibidem.
[235] PISM, A 11, E/1099, telegram by Polish Envoy to Stockholm H. Sokolnicki to the Ministry of Foreign Affairs, 30 VI 1945.
[236] NA, FO, 371/48057, telegram by the Legation of Great Britain in Stockholm to the FO, 30 VI 1945.
[237] PISM, A 11, E/1099, telegram by Minister of Foreign Affairs A. Tarnowski to Polish Envoy to Stockholm, 7 VI 1945.
[238] PISM, A 11, E/1099, telegram by Polish Envoy to Stockholm H. Sokolnicki to the Ministry of Foreign Affairs, 2 VII 1945.
[239] RA, UD 1920 års dossiersystem, HP 12, vol. 890, pro memoria, Stockholm, 8 VII 1945.
[240] RA, UD 1920 års dossiersystem, HP 12, vol. 890, telegram by S. Grafström to the Swedish Legation in Moscow, 6 VII 1945.

7. THE DOUBLE GAME OF SWEDISH DIPLOMACY

the support from the Anglo-Saxon powers would not be everlasting, especially regarding the possible aggravation of relations with 'the Russian bear.' On that occasion he compared the situation of Poland with that of Sweden and stated with relief that the Swedes, as opposed to the Poles, were not faced by Stalin with faits accomplis, to which he included the establishment of the border along the Curzon Line and the formation of 'the Polish counter-government under the aegis of the Soviets.'[241]

On 7 July 1945 in Moscow, Söderblom paid a visit to ambassador Modzelewski and announced Sweden's de jure recognition of the Provisional Government of National Unity.[242] He sent a letter to Stockholm on the same day, in which he reminded Stig Sahlin that it was a priority to transfer the detained submarines as quickly as possible to Poland and clear the advance payment for the purchase of the equipment ordered from the Bofors company by Polish authorities before the outbreak of the war. In addition, the buildings of the Polish Legation, located on Karlavägen in Stockholm, were to be handed over to the new authorities as soon as possible.[243]

---

[241] S. Grafström, *Anteckningar 1945–1954*, pp. 685–686.
[242] AMSZ, iss. 6, w. 78, vol. 1159, k. 2, The Polpress Information, Moscow, 7 VII 1945.
[243] RA, UD 1920 års dossiersystem, HP 12, vol. 890, letter by S. Söderblom to S. Sahlin, Moscow, 7 VII 1945.

PART 2
Economic Issues

8. Swedish Presence in Occupied Poland

During the war, the central economic aim for Sweden was acquire necessary supplies independently of the military developments in Europe. The Swedes wanted to avoid repeating the situation that occurred during the First World War, when a blockade was introduced and Swedish ships struggled to service the trade with other countries. The prime ministers and ministers of foreign affairs of the Nordic States met on 18-19 September in Copenhagen to affirm their will to preserve strict neutrality, and highlighted that it was important for them to maintain traditional commercial relations with all countries, including those which were currently engaged in the war.[1] Sandler warned the British Minister of Trade, Robert S. Hudson, during his visit to Stockholm in April 1939, that in the event of war Sweden would attempt to preserve its economic ties with both sides of the conflict. Dissatisfied, Hudson reported that this would only prolong the war.[2] Nevertheless, not long after the outbreak of the war the Swedes managed to regulate its commercial relations by means of relevant arrangements both with Great Britain (7 December 1939), and with Germany (22 December 1939).[3] These agreements formed the basis for trade that proved satisfactory for Sweden until the German attack on Denmark and Norway on 9 April 1940. At the time, the Polish government in Angers first and foremost hoped that orders for missiles for the destroyers *ORP Grom* and *ORP Błyskawica* would be completed in Sweden. Yet, attempts to initiate the discussions on this subject turned out to be fruitless.[4] The problem that Polish diplomatic services had to face right from the very first day of the war was securing the interests of Polish exporters, mainly those dealing in coal.

Sweden endeavoured to adapt to the new situation in Europe. Following the conclusion of the commercial agreements with the British and the Germans, in 1940 Sweden signed commercial arrangements with other countries: Turkey (28 February), Estonia (15 May), Greece (24 May), Norway (8 July and 17 December), Denmark (24 July), Hungary (31 July), Finland (7 September), the Soviet Union (7 September), the Netherlands (7 September), and Belgium (7

---

[1] G. Hägglöf, *Svensk...*, pp. 9-10.
[2] Ibidem, pp. 25-26.
[3] W. M. Carlgren, *Svensk utrikespolitik...*, pp. 29-35; G. Hägglöf, *Svensk...*, pp. 52-103.
[4] *Polska Marynarka Wojenna.*, p. 57.

September). The end of year was crowned with the renewal of the agreement with Germany (17 December), which controlled international trade in the occupied countries, and therefore in a considerable part of Europe.

Following 9 April 1940, Sweden was almost entirely reliant on the trade with Germany. In 1937 and 1938, 21 percent of Swedish imports came from Germany, in 1940 (including the occupied countries) this had risen to 50 percent and by 1941 as much as 70 percent.[5] It was from Germany that Sweden imported coal, coke, metal products, chemicals and artificial fertilizers. In addition, Sweden granted Germany a loan for 100 million crowns. From Sweden the Germans imported iron ore, wood, paper pulp and paper, as well as ball bearings. The Swedes also attempted to preserve the sea route to Great Britain through the Finnish port in Petsamo, but as of September 1940, following the tightening of the German blockade, exporting goods from there became impossible. In turn, following the outbreak of the German–Soviet war, on 22 June 1941, the British stopped using the route.[6] Commercial relations with the countries of Central Europe, the Balkans and Western Europe were also dependent on the transit route that ran through Germany.[7] The extraordinary solution of sea traffic to Gothenburg facilitated contacts with America. A special agreement with Great Britain and Germany on 9 September 1940, allowed the tanker *Sveadrott* to carry 13 tons of oil from New York. On 28 November 1940, the Swedes obtained the consent of Great Britain to send four merchant ships to and from the port for one month. The Germans accepted this on 7 February 1941, but as early as in 29 December 1940 the transatlantic liner *Gullmaren* reached Sweden with a cargo of food supplies. Over the next two months, and then from the summer until the end of 1941, and throughout 1942, the Swedes were, thanks to this agreement, in touch with the world outside territories controlled by the Germans.[8]

Cut off from Great Britain and non-European markets brought about an economic crisis, which Sweden battled throughout the war. Gradually, by 1943, Swedish foreign trade was reduced by 50–60 per cent, as compared to the years before the war.[9] Substitute production, for instance cellulose feed, was developed. Obviously, food was rationed. It was impossible to maintain high standards of living, and their decline could only be slowed down by

---

[5] G. Hägglöf, *Svensk...*, pp. 152–153.
[6] Ibidem, pp. 170–171, 185.
[7] Ibidem, p. 142.
[8] E. Boheman, *På vakt. Kabinettssekreterare...*, pp. 138–139; G. Hägglöf, *Svensk...*, pp. 179–181; H. Dahlberg, *I Sverige...*, pp. 149–153.
[9] K. Åmark, Sweden. Negotiated neutrality, [in:] R. Bosworth, J. Maiolo (eds.), Cambridge History of the Second World War, vol. 2: Politics and Ideology, Cambridge 2015, p. 254.

becoming part of the German system of economic dependence. The government in Stockholm chose to dodge between Berlin and Moscow whilst simultaneously maintaining minimum contacts with the global market (most importantly the USA).[10] The German pressure, especially in the initial years of the war, continuously worsened the situation. The Germans employed the tactic of selling their own products at inflated prices, whilst at the same time forcing their economic partners to lower the prices of goods they exported, and in several cases Sweden had to export goods from Germany. When coal transports from Great Britain and Poland became impossible, Germany became Sweden's sole supplier. Moreover, following the annexation of iron ore deposits in France, Belgium and Luxembourg, Germany reduced its dependence on Swedish supplies. In 1939, 41 per cent of the total German consumption of iron was imported from Sweden, in 1943, the figure was 27 per cent.[11] In 1939 Sweden was forced to conduct unprofitable trade with Germany, and, on top of that, needed to hire five hundred carriages for coal transport, lower the price of iron ore by several percent, increase the supplies of wood and accept the 20 percent increase in the prices of German coal. One solution was increasing trade, from 1940, with the Soviet Union, but this lasted only until June 1941, which was not long enough. In December 1940 the Polish Legation estimated that Sweden's trade with Germany continued to maintain forms of exchange like those it maintained by before the war, and it did not become entirely economically dependent on Germany.[12] A significant role in controlling the size of economic difficulties was played by the reserves of foreign currency and gold, collected in the period of the pre-war upturn in the economy.[13]

On 9 September 1939, Potworowski wanted to discuss with Hägglöf the situation following the Germans' possible takeover of the Polish coal mines and their intention to continue their operation and selling coal to Sweden. However, Hägglöf avoided granting him any declarations in this matter. He explained that Sweden, as a neutral country, would not take a hypothetical

---

[10] AAN, HI/I/10, letter by Envoy G. Potworowski to the Ministry of Foreign Affairs, Stockholm, 27 XII 1940.
[11] K. Åmark, Sweden. Negotiated neutrality, p. 255.
[12] AAN, HI/I/10, letter by Envoy G. Potworowski to the Ministry of Foreign Affairs, Stockholm, 27 XII 1940.
[13] AAN, HI/I/10, letter by Envoy G. Potworowski to the Ministry of Foreign Affairs, Stockholm, 28 XII 1940.

theoretical stance regarding the events that had not yet taken place.[14] When the Polish envoy returned to the issue from 21 September he was told the specific stance of the Swedish diplomacy. Potworowski was informed that it was impossible for the Swedish government to issue directives for private coal importers who were relishing the freedom of choosing suppliers. The same was the case with the yet to be finalized payments to the Polish coal companies. The Swedish Ministry of Foreign Affairs could nevertheless advise the envoy, without commitment, against the conclusion of contracts with the companies who had taken over the Polish coal mines. It was pointed out that it was all but impossible to check if German suppliers were selling coal from Germany or Poland at any particular moment.[15] When in July 1940 Potworowski was persistent in inquiring about the potential regulations of the Swedish–German commercial treaty concerning the Polish occupied territories, he again received evasive answers from Boheman or information which were in fact false:

> As far as coal is concerned, it is being brought mostly from Szczecin, and its actual origin is not revealed. Only small amounts of coal are obtained from Westphalia and from Silesia, since it is principally transported to Italy and Russia. Relations with the General Government? Clearing? He only knows that some quantities of sugar are obtained from there.[16]

It was nonetheless known that the coal from the Polish Upper Silesia would continue to be exported to Sweden. According to the pre-war statistics, approximately 2.5 million tons of coal annually originated from Poland, which constituted nearly 43 percent of the Swedish import of coal. Great Britain managed to provide almost 47 percent of the supplies as part of the relevant contracts, and Germany – nearly 10 percent. Following the outbreak of war, Swedish statistics reflected the import of Polish coal only in trace amounts, but it is known that the rapidly annexed coal mines were not destroyed and that the Germans were able to begin their operation. By the end of September, all but one of the coal mines resumed their usual operation. The coal output from the Polish coal mines in 1938 was 38.1 million tons, in 1940 up to 45.7

---

[14] RA, Handelsdepartementet, Huvudarkivet, Rapporter från UD, F II aa, vol. 210, memorandum by G. Hägglöf [?] concerning the import of coal from occupied Poland, Stockholm, 9 IX 1939.
[15] Ibidem, memorandum by G. Hägglöf [?] concerning the import of coal from Poland, Stockholm, 21 IX 1939.
[16] *Notes by Polish envoy to Stockholm G. Potworowski 1939–1942*, entry from 21 VII 1940.

million tons, and in 1943 up to 57.5 million tons.[17] Naturally, part of the annual supplies from Germany, approximately 4.2 million tons of coal, originated from the same coal mines and was sold by Poland to Sweden up until the outbreak of the war, and which were at that point taken over by the German entrepreneurs. According to the estimates of the Swedish negotiators who conducted the talks with the German delegation in September 1940, this amount was even to constitute the greater part of coal supplied by the German side, about 2.4 million tons. According to the findings of Swedish historian Sven-Olof Olsson as much as 66 percent of coal imported from Germany to Sweden was transported along the trunk route, which was constructed as early as in the period of the Second Polish Republic, and then loaded onto Swedish ships in Gdańsk and Gdynia.[18]

For the Polish authorities it was also important to secure the interests of their native shipping companies. The Transport Committee was founded in Paris, the task of which was to save the Polish ships moored in the ports of neutral states. The funds for the entire campaign were granted by the shipping companies. The government only granted a loan which was to be returned by the Polish companies. On 31 October, a new Transport Committee was established by the minister of industry and commerce, as an assisting, consultative, and executive authority for the operation of the Polish commercial fleet and the sea fishing sector. Its members were Engineer Leonard Możdżeński (officer for naval affairs at the Ministry of Industry and Commerce), Tadeusz Geppert (representative of the Ministry of Industry and Commerce at the Inter-Allied Committee of Maritime Transport) and Feliks Kollat (Geppert's deputy). In Stockholm, from September 1939, it was Władysław Potocki who acted on behalf of the former Transport Committee. The Polish ships moored in Swedish ports sailed to Great Britain having been insured by the local agencies. Potocki was sure that such actions were necessary to, 'show our good will to these people or companies who actually provided us with professional services, and to show them that their trouble is compensated by us in an appropriate way.'[19]

The Polish Legation in Stockholm immediately passed on handling the issues connected with the payments due by the Swedes to Polish companies.

---

[17] J. Jaros, *Historia górnictwa węglowego w Zagłębiu Górnośląskim w latach 1914–1945*, Katowice–Kraków 1969, pp. 227–228.

[18] S.-O. Olsson, *German coal and Swedish fuel 1939–1945*, Gothenburg 1975, pp. 68–69, 79, 82–83, 98–100, 147, 161, 177–178, 202–203.

[19] AAN, Ministry of Industry, Trade and Shipping (Paris), 708, letter by W. Potocki to F. Kollat, Stockholm, 21 X 1939, pp. 141–142.

Payments from the importers of the Polish coal were to be transferred to the account of the legation.[20] Potworowski requested powers to act on behalf of the Bank of Poland and to be given access to these sums based on the Polish foreign exchange legislation, to prevent the Germans seizing the amounts due to the Upper Silesian coal mining and metallurgical companies.[21] The accounts of Polish coal concerns in the Swedish banks held considerable funds acquired from the final coal deliveries prior to the war. On 12 September 1939 Potworowski still maintained that these funds, 'are not yet in great danger, because they can only be accessed upon the order of the account owner, after being marked with a stamp and relevant signatures, and importers would fear to risk making payments to unauthorized persons.' Nevertheless, the envoy proposed he be authorized by Polish coal concerns to access these funds, and even transfer them into the account of the Polish Legation. Three days later the matter became urgent, as it transpired that the Germans were acting to seize these accounts.[22] The Swedish banks were also holding sums owned by Polish banks: the Bank of Poland (Bank Polski), the American Bank (Bank Amerykański), the Commercial Bank (Bank Handlowy), the Western Bank (Bank Zachodni), the Common Credit Bank (Powszechny Bank Kredytowy), the Discount Bank (Bank Dyskontowy) and others.[23] Potworowski secured 50 thousand crowns for Bank of National Belongings (*Bank Gospodarstwa Krajowego*). Subsequently he accounted for the amounts due for the sale of scrap iron load that was intended for the Ostrowiec steelworks (*Zakłady Ostrowieckie*) and transported to Gdynia on the ship *Consul Korfitzon*. The remaining sum of 13 500 crowns was transferred by him to the Midland Bank. A similar thing happened with the payment for the load carried by the ship *Ulven*. The Minister of Treasury, Adam Koc, wanted to examine the sums held in the accounts of the Commercial Bank of Warsaw in the Swedish banks. The company's management authorized the government to unfreeze these sums.[24] Some Swedish companies settled their accounts by contacting

---

[20] AAN, HI/I/243, telegram by Deputy Minister of Foreign Affairs J. Szembek to Polish Legation in Stockholm, 12 IX 1939.
[21] AAN, HI/I/243, telegram by Polish Envoy to Stockholm G. Potworowski to the Ministry of Foreign Affairs, Stockholm, 13 IX 1939.
[22] AAN, the Polish Legation in Stockholm, 18, letter by Polish Envoy to Stockholm G. Potworowski to the Ministry of Foreign Affairs, Stockholm, 15 IX 1939. p. 53, 55.
[23] AAN, the Polish Legation in Stockholm, 20, letter by Polish Envoy to Stockholm G. Potworowski to the Polish Embassy in London, 22 IX 1939. pp. 38–39.
[24] AAN, HI/I/246, telegram by Polish Ambassador to Paris J. Łukasiewicz to the Polish Legation in Stockholm, 29 X 1939.

the foreign branches of Polish companies. In July 1940, the Johnson's concern transferred 1800 pounds sterling to the account of the Bank of National Belongings at the Bank of Lazarth Brothers for it to be allotted to the *Wspólne Biuro Sprzedaży Węgla i Koksu w Cieszynie* (Common Office of Coal and Coke Sales in Cieszyn).[25] *Łódzka Fabryka Pluszów i Dywanów* (The Łódź Plush and Carpet Factory) set out to recover the sum of over 10 thousand crowns from the Swedish company Mystrodt.[26] One of the Swedish companies owed nearly 50 thousand crowns to *Towarzystwo Żyrardowskie* (the Żyrardów Society) for supplies of linen. Others, in contrast, managed to import textile materials from Bielsko.[27] The legation assumed responsibility for the fate of the cargoes, which were already being prepared for transport to Poland on Swedish ships. This was the case too for the load of leather, wool, cotton and quebracho wood, most of which belonged to the Kugler Banking House (Dom Bankowy Kugler) in Gdynia. What was also accounted for was selling the goods in Sweden.[28]

On 9 October 1939 the Polish Legation sent out a letter to the Swedish companies which had earlier traded with Poland, pointing out to the Swedish businessmen that any payments made to the accounts of the Polish companies placed in German receivership would be considered invalid by the Polish government. In case of any disputes regarding this issue the Polish owners would have to enforce their rights before the Swedish courts. The payments were advised to be made to the account of the legation or deposited. Simultaneously, the legation emphasized that the purchase of goods in occupied Poland could bring about financial claims from the owners of Polish companies under German management.[29]

The activity of the Swedish–Polish Chamber of Commerce was not terminated, but this was only of symbolic significance. No meetings were held, nobody paraded about being a member of this organisation, and a portion of the Swedish companies decided to leave it, including almost all coal companies. Thanks to the membership fees, paid in by only a few companies, its

---

[25] AAN, HI/I/246, telegram by Polish Envoy to Stockholm G. Potworowski to the Ministry of Foreign Affairs, 25 VII 1940; AAN, HI/I/87, telegram by Polish Envoy to Stockholm G. Potworowski to the Ministry of Foreign Affairs, n.p., 10 VIII 1940.
[26] AAN, the Polish Legation in Stockholm, 18, letter by Polish Envoy to Stockholm G. Potworowski to the Ministry of Treasury, Stockholm, June 1941, pp. 1–2.
[27] AAN, the Polish Legation in Stockholm, 18, letter by Polish Consul to Malmö J. Głębocki to commercial counsellor to the Polish Legation in Stockholm T. Pilch, Malmö, 6 XI 1939, p. 27.
[28] AAN, the Polish Legation in Stockholm, 18, letter by commercial counsellor to the Polish Legation in Stockholm T. Pilch the Polish Embassy in London, 5 XII 1939. pp. 23–24.
[29] AAN, the Polish Legation in Stockholm, 18, circular by commercial counsellor to the Polish Legation in Stockholm T. Pilch, Stockholm, 9 X 1939.

business establishment continued to be rented, necessary expenses were covered, and even a financial reserve was established. In December 1941 the Chamber asked companies that were former members, to pay in their membership fees. Helge Norlander, the owner of Sveaexport company (a pre-war importer of coal from Poland), proposed that coal companies, which were formerly part of the Polish Coal Committee in Stockholm, but later left the Chamber, manifested their will to establish economic relations with Poland. This gave rise to a debate as counsellor Pilch opposed the initiatives that were with companies that, according to his view, had compromised themselves. This issue also had a deeper undercurrent, since the coal sales structure prior to 1939, according to the assessments of the officials of the Polish Legation, left much be desired.[30]

Poland's financial obligations towards Sweden at the end of 1939 included a debt relief. The conditions for its payment were established in the agreement of 14 March 1935, where it was stated that Poland was to pay instalments amounting to approximately 6.15 million crowns up until 1 January 1942. The sum due to be paid in 1940 amounted to 760 thousand crowns, payable in two instalments on 1 January and on 1 October. Another national debt of Poland to Sweden was the so-called match loan the repayment of which took place in half-yearly instalments of approximately 930 thousand dollars each. The 1 October instalment was not paid.[31] On 24 February 1940, the Polish Embassy in Paris informed the international committee of credit assistance that at that moment Poland was temporarily incapable of paying off the rest of the debts due to the current circumstances. At the same time, it declared that the negotiations concerning the repayment would be initiated on the first date available. On 15 March 1940, the Swedish government discussed the issue of the debt relief. It consented, as did the remaining creditor nations, to the debt's payment extension. The remaining part of Poland's debt was 1 293 600 crowns.[32]

On 15 December 1939, still before the signing of the Swedish–German economic arrangement, Potworowski met with Günther and Boheman to discuss the matter of further economic activity of Swedish companies in Poland. Seemingly, both diplomats were rather avoiding this subject. They

---

[30] AAN, the Ministry of Industry, Trade and Shipping (London), 88, letter by Polish Envoy to Stockholm G. Potworowski to the Ministry of Foreign Affairs, 23 XII 1941.
[31] AAN, the Polish Legation in Stockholm, 19, letter by Polish Envoy to Stockholm G. Potworowski to the Ministry of Foreign Affairs, Stockholm, 5 XII 1939. pp. 73–75.
[32] RA, Kabinettet/UD Huvudarkivet, Statsrådsprotokoll, serie A3A, vol. 108, Protokoll över Utrikesdepartementets ärende, Stockholm, 15 III 1940.

suggested that there were 'no hopes for the development of the Swedish capital in occupied Poland.'[33]

An important financial matter to be regulated by the diplomatic services were the Polish advances, paid to the Bofors company as part of orders the execution of which was made impossible by the war. Part of the sum, approximately 371 thousand crowns, was transferred to the account of the legation in December 1939. Envoy Potworowski left 325 thousand crowns in cash in Stockholm at the disposal of the Ministry of Finance, and approximately 46 thousand crowns were transferred to the Midland Bank.[34] In the spring of 1940 the commander of the Polish Navy, Rear-Admiral Jerzy Świrski, started demanding the return of the advance payment of 2 063 594 crowns. The Swedes countered, mentioning the sum of 2 773 172 crowns minus 192 335 crowns for unpaid bills, the sum as part of the letters of guarantee amounted to 4 842 788 crowns[35], whereas the remaining part of the sum allotted to the ammunition supplies and payments due for the army supplies were to be accounted for in the future.[36] By the end of May 1940, the Bofors company initially proposed to repay another 462 687 crowns under two contracts. In exchange it demanded the termination of these contracts, the returning the relevant letters of guarantee regarding the contracts executed prior to the war and the payment of 230 503 crowns for unpaid navy and army bills. The Polish side would receive 232 184 crowns that was to be returned by a third party. At the same time the Swedes did not yield to the Poles and did not provide drawings for 120 mm missiles.[37] Świrski accepted the proposed repayment of loans under two agreements, but he described the plan to repay the remaining advance payments by a third party as unlawful and dishonest.[38] It was on 4 July 1940 when, following long-term negotiations, an agreement was reached under which all orders placed with the

---

[33] *Notes by Polish envoy to Stockholm G. Potworowski 1939–1942*, entry of 15 XII 1939.
[34] AAN, HI/I/245, telegram by Polish Envoy to Stockholm G. Potworowski to the Ministry of Foreign Affairs, Stockholm, 21 XII 1939.
[35] PISM, MAR, A V 9/1, radiogram by Polish Naval Attaché to Stockholm Captain T. Podjazd-Morgenstern to head of the Polish Navy Command Rear-Admiral J. Świrski, Stockholm, 15 III 1940.
[36] PISM, MAR, A V 9/1, radiogram by head of the Polish Navy Command Rear-Admiral J. Świrski to Polish Naval Attaché to Stockholm Captain T. Podjazd-Morgenstern, Stockholm, 12 IV 1940.
[37] PISM, MAR, A V 9/1, radiogram by Polish Naval Attaché to Stockholm Captain T. Podjazd-Morgenstern to head of the Polish Navy Command Rear-Admiral J. Świrski, Stockholm, 27 V 1940.
[38] PISM, MAR, A V 9/1, radiogram by head of the Polish Navy Command Rear-Admiral J. Świrski to Polish Naval Attaché to Stockholm Captain T. Podjazd-Morgenstern, Stockholm, 27 V 1940.

Bofors company were cancelled due to the circumstances at the time, and the issue of returning the advance payments paid by the Polish party was regulated. Upon the request of the Swedes, the agreement was dated to 20 December 1939, which did not clash with the commercial treaty concluded with the Germans two days later. It was thanks to this agreement that the Polish government most importantly saved its due payments from German recovery. That is why the Polish negotiators, who wanted to avoid making the talks difficult, did not guarantee the transfer of the entire amount due and appropriate interest rate on the debt. The Swedes only accepted the interest rate for the period between 20 December 1939 and 4 July 1940.

As part of the repayment, on 6 July 1940, the Swedish side paid approximately 237 thousand crowns to the legation's account[39] and Envoy Potworowski informed the government that two agreements with the Bofors company had been terminated, that the accounts of the army and the Polish navy, 99 907.85 and 130 287.26 crowns respectively, had been settled, and that on 5 July the total sum of 516 276.49 crowns had been added to the account of the legation.[40] Obtaining subsequent payments turned out to be impossible. Only the letters of guarantee were successively prolonged. According to Pilch, this created favourable conditions for the systematic repayment of advance payments, although everyone was aware that obtaining this return would be dependent on the general political situation. From the point of view of the Polish side, the arrangement was also important as a beneficial precedent in the legation's process of payment recovery from other Swedish companies.[41] Nevertheless, the efforts towards the recognition of the right of the Polish companies to their own due payments or property drew on for months. In the summer of 1940 Potworowski informed London that the Swedes adopted the strategy of not recognising the claims of both the Polish companies and the German receivership management.[42] Taking action was made difficult due to the lack of the Polish diplomats' authorization by the Polish companies and the lack of communication with Western Europe, where the board members of these companies may have resided. Initially, the legation focused on the receivables of three Polish companies: *Robur, Polskie Biuro Sprzedaży Rur* (the Polish Office of Pipe Sales) and the *Zjednoczone*

---

[39] AAN, HI/I/87, copy of note by commercial counsellor to Polish Legation in Stockholm T. Pilch, 6 VII 1940.

[40] PISM, MAR, A V 9/1, radiogram by Polish Envoy to Stockholm G. Potworowski, Stockholm, 8 VII 1940.

[41] AAN, HI/I/87, letter by commercial counsellor to the Polish Legation in Stockholm T. Pilch to the Ministry of Foreign Affairs, Stockholm, 29 VII 1940.

[42] AAN, HI/I/87, letter by Polish Envoy to Stockholm G. Potworowski to the Ministry of Finance, n.p., 19 VIII 1940.

Fabryki Związków Azotowych (United Factories of Nitric Compounds). The results of the proceedings were to decide whether other cases would be considered.

At the outset of December 1939 Władysław Radziwiłł paid a visit to Sweden as a representative of the Committee of Property and International Debts Defence (*Komitet Obrony Mienia i Wierzytelności Zagranicznych*) with the intention to establish the Committee of Swedish Creditors of Poland (*Komitet Szwedzkich Wierzycieli Polski*). This initiative was to transform the so far one-sided procedure of securing Polish receivables in Sweden. Potworowski's feelings were mixed, as he believed that the procedure could lead to the implementation of a clearing procedure, which, given the passive pre-war balance of payments between Poland and Sweden, would result in blocking the process of recovery of Polish assets in Sweden. On the other hand, the so far one-sidedness had hindered contact with the Swedish company owners. The private initiative of Radziwiłł had therefore filled a gap and presented a good opportunity to enter talks with the leading local financiers about the future of Swedish property in the occupied territories. It was exactly owing to the talks with Norlander, Gunnar Bolander and Jacob Wallenberg that Potworowski became acquainted with the result of the Swedish–German negotiations on this matter. The Germans allegedly were to demand that the Swedes recognize the annexation of Poland in exchange for the protection of their financial interests in this territory, and especially for making the transfer of assets possible. Due to the negative attitude of the Swedes, an agreement was not reached. Potworowski discovered that, 'The Germans only agreed to allow the representatives of the Swedish companies to enter the territory of Poland to settle the economic affairs of these companies, on the condition that the Swedish industrial institutions would continue their activity in Poland and set about the necessary renovations or, alternatively, investments.' In connection with this, Potworowski proposed to wait for the unfolding of the situation and for the conclusion of the negotiations between Sweden and Germany and the simultaneous establishment of contacts with the Swedish creditors by the delegate of the Committee of Transport and Navy, Władysław Potocki, who agreed to become a temporary representative of the Committee of Property and International Liabilities Defence.[43] The Polish Ministry of Foreign Affairs maintained that the presence of foreign companies in the occupied territories would be useful, on the condition that

---

[43] AAN, the Polish Legation in Stockholm, 20, letter by Polish Envoy to Stockholm G. Potworowski to the Ministry of Foreign Affairs, Stockholm, 5 XII 1939. pp. 1–5.

they would be working for the benefit of civilians. The companies which were contributing to the increase of the military potential of Germany were evaluated negatively.[44]

Despite these multilateral actions, the process of recovery of due amounts from the Swedish companies was suspended. The legation watched over this matter but as time went by and the war continued it was decided in 1941 that no claims would be addressed towards the Swedish companies, in order to 'avoid provoking any counteractions from the Germans, on whom Sweden was currently to a large extent dependent.' The trade volume between Sweden and Germany increased over two times from 1939 to 1942. As Scandinavia was isolated from the rest of the world, its dependence on German supplies, especially coal, was obvious.[45] Taking more radical steps was avoided because Swedish companies were not transferring any assets to the accounts of the Polish companies which were placed under German receivership, and that the amounts due were placed on notary's deposit. In cases when the disputable issues were submitted to court, the latter always defended the interests of the former Polish owners of the companies which were seized by the Germans. The recovery took place only in individual cases, when a particularly favourable stance was presented by a relevant Swedish company or when the debtor decided to make a payment to the legations' account in exchange for receiving a certificate proving the settlement of his liabilities towards the Polish contracting party.[46]

In 1941, the Swedish Ministry of Foreign Affairs entered the next stage of the negotiations regarding the advances paid to the Bofors company. Of somewhat importance were the maintenance costs of the interned seamen and Polish vessels. At the time, the Ministry of Treasury authorized Envoy Potworowski to use 500 thousand crowns of the so-called 'Bofors sums' for the payment of the vessels' maintenance costs, as such a solution was perceived as an opportunity to unfreeze the advance payments.[47] However, it was only in June 1943, namely in the generally favourable political atmosphere, that a specific Swedish proposal was presented regarding making an advance payment to the Polish side, on the condition that part of it would be allocated

---

[44] AAN, the Polish Legation in Stockholm, 20, letter by commercial counsellor to the Polish Legation in Brussels L. Litwiński to the Polish Legation in Stockholm, 16 XI 1939, pp. 6.
[45] K. Wittmann, *Schwedens Wirtschaftsbeziehungen zum Dritten Reich 1933–1945*, München 1978, p. 197.
[46] AAN, the Polish Legation in Stockholm, 20, letter by the Polish Legation in Stockholm to the Ministry of Treasury, Stockholm, 13 VI 1941. p. 45.
[47] AAN, HI/I/271, telegram by the Ministry of Treasury to Polish Envoy to Stockholm G. Potworowski, 1 IX 1941.

to covering the costs of the internment. Sokolnicki was planning to use 1 million crowns to cover the costs and to transfer 1.5 million to the legation's account.[48] On 29 July 1943, the envoy sent a note to the Swedish Ministry of Foreign Affairs with a proposal of the final settlement of the issue of receivables from the Bofors company. Sokolnicki demanded that a sum of approximately 1.5 million crowns be paid to the account of the legation and 800 thousand crowns be used to cover the costs of the Polish submarines' maintenance. The payment due for the maintenance of the interned seamen was 2 million crowns. The envoy was unofficially informed that the Polish proposal would be accepted. The Swedish Ministry of Foreign Affairs was interested in this matter only on the condition that taking over the debt of the Bofors company would settle part of the state treasury's liabilities towards the armament manufacturer and would make the ministry obtain the advance payment for the maintenance of the interned seamen. The Swedes were nevertheless unwilling to pay the Poles the due sums in cash.[49] That is why there had been silence on this matter for many months and it was only on 28 February 1944 that Sokolnicki and Pilch were invited to the Ministry of Foreign Affairs to discuss the issue. The Bofors company offered to make a payment totalling 2.31 million crowns on the condition of a guarantee from the Swedish treasury. In turn, the state treasury officials expressed their readiness to grant a guarantee provided that the Swedish side submit 1.81 million crowns as an advance on the Polish government's liabilities from the costs of the maintenance of submarines and interned seamen. By the end of 1943 these liabilities amounted to approximately 2.25 million crowns. The remaining amount, approximately 500 thousand crowns, was to be paid to the legation. Sokolnicki wanted to begin negotiations about increasing the amount, which would be submitted in cash as an advance on the maintenance of the interned, but the Swedes declared their proposal final. Sokolnicki had no other choice but to accept.[50] The Ministry of Treasury advised the envoy that he did his utmost and negotiated the appropriate interest rates and a higher sum which was to be submitted in cash.[51] Eventually, Sokolnicki, during his negotiations with the Bofors company, only discussed the matter of the

---

[48] AAN, HI/I/305, copy of telegram by Polish Envoy to H. Sokolnicki to the Ministry of Foreign Affairs, Stockholm, 2 VI 1943. Sokolnicki was granted consent to such solution from the acting Minister of Foreign Affairs, E. Raczyński.

[49] AAN, HI/I/87, letter by the Polish Envoy to Stockholm H. Sokolnicki to the Ministry of Foreign Affairs, Stockholm, 12 VIII 1943.

[50] AAN, HI/I/88, letter by Polish Envoy to Stockholm H. Sokolnicki to the Ministry of Foreign Affairs, Stockholm, 1 III 1944.

[51] Ibidem, telegram by the Ministry of Treasury to Polish Legation in Stockholm, 31 III 1944.

interest rate on the sum due from the day of informing the Polish side about suspending the execution of orders for the Polish Navy, that is from mid-September 1939. The first person to comment on this, director Oscar Lindén, neither questioned the principle of using the interest rate nor its duration, but he pointed out that in such circumstances the Bofors company would also make financial claims due to the inability to execute the orders for Poland.[52] On 27 May 1944 Sokolnicki was surprised to receive a letter where Linden, on behalf of the supervisory board, without reason refused to settle the current liabilities. The only choice the Poles had was to intervene with the Swedish Ministry of Foreign Affairs. In a conversation with Grafström, on 9 June, Pilch highlighted that part of the payment from the Bofors company was to be allocated to the support for the refugees. According to Pilch, this argument was effective as Grafström promised to take care of this issue.[53] Pilch also proposed that 500 thousand crowns be paid in monthly instalments of 50 thousand crowns, and the issue of interest rates only be settled following the conclusion of the war.[54]

Swedish industrial and diplomatic circles attempted to adapt to the situation after the Polish defeat in September 1939. On 5 October a meeting was held in Stockholm, which was attended by the Envoy to the Polish government, Joen Lagerberg, Gunnar Hägglöf and Nils Ihre from the Ministry of Foreign Affairs, the famous banker, Jacob Wallenberg and the director of the *Sveriges Allmänna Exportförening* (Swedish Export Association or *SAE*), Gunnar Bolander. According to the surviving protocol, an informal discussion was held regarding commercial and financial relations with Poland, mostly with the forthcoming Swedish–German commercial negotiations in mind. The participants ruled out the introduction of the payment blockade in the relations between Sweden and the occupied territories, describing it as an unfavourable solution for the Swedish side, since the claims of the Polish companies were relatively small, and surely less than the value of the Swedish goods, which were already located in Poland, but not yet paid for. This solution was abandoned because of the expected difficulties of legal nature. It was decided that the SAE would carry out an inventory of the property of

---

[52] Ibidem, letter by T. Pilch, counsellor to the Polish Legation in Stockholm, to the Ministry of Treasury, Stockholm, 11 II 1944.
[53] Ibidem, letter by T. Pilch, counsellor to the Polish Legation in Stockholm, to the Ministry of Treasury, Stockholm, 17 VI 1944.
[54] Ibidem, note by T. Pilch, counsellor to the Polish Legation in Stockholm, to the Swedish Ministry of Foreign Affairs, Stockholm, 17 VI 1944.

the Swedish companies in the occupied territories. All securities, which constituted the basis for the claims towards the companies in Poland were to be transferred to the Stockholms Enskilda Bank, where their legitimacy would be verified and where it would be examined as to whether the Swedish banks were holding any company accounts of debtors. It was considered unnecessary to raise the issue of the separate treatment of the occupied territories during the negotiations regarding the trade with Germany. It was predicted that the settlement for the coal from the Polish mines would be nevertheless performed as part of the clearing procedure. The possible Swedish exports to Poland were to take place by means of an import organisation in Germany, from where all the goods would be transported to the Polish territory.[55] These preliminary considerations were to be verified in the reports of the Swedish diplomats and businessmen, who were observing the policy of the German occupation authorities in Poland.

The first news concerned the requisitions of goods in Gdynia and Gdańsk. The so-called *treuhänders* (trustees), who were taking control over the Polish companies, were not inclined to pay the amounts due (for the Swedish goods), which were not settled until the outbreak of the war. However, they insisted on the payments from the Swedes, in cases when they were not paid in to the accounts of the Polish contractors. Some of them resorted to blackmail. The non-settling of a debt by Swedish shipowners, it was threatened, would result in their vessels being confiscated soon after arriving at the German port. Consul Knud Lundberg predicted pessimistically that the Swedish companies could suffer losses by fulfilling their obligations, whereas the receivers of the Polish companies would evade theirs. Lundberg's last resort was to present the German authorities with the lists of goods that the Swedish companies claimed rights to.[56]

Sven Grafström, who returned to occupied Warsaw on 12 November 1939, was left with depressing impressions. In his diary he noted talks with German officials who did not hide that the General Government would be treated as a colony:

> The Germans are trying to exploit Poland as much as possible. The people are to be impoverished. The aim is to force everyone, especially the so-called intelligentsia, to perform physical labour for the Germans to stay alive. What follows from these assumptions is that contrary to the situation in the incorporated

---

[55] RA, UD 1920 års dossiersystem, HP 64, vol. 2735, memorandum by N. Ihre regarding Swedish-Polish commercial-payment relations, Stockholm, 6 X 1939.
[56] RA, Handelsdepartementet, Huvudarkivet, Rapporter från UD, F II aa, vol. 210, copies of letters by Consul K. Lundberg to the Ministry of Foreign Affairs, Gdańsk, 14 XI, 28 XI 1939.

parts of Poland, the Germans were making no efforts to launch the local economy. For instance, the banks have no right to make pay-outs from the accounts, this excluding only insignificant sums. Post, telephone and telegraph services will be re-launched only for German purposes. This to a large extent also concerns the railway sector. Jewish companies are being confiscated, Aryan companies are being deprived of material possibilities to operate.[57]

Grafström reported that the representatives of companies which were owned by the Swedes, were able, at least for the time being, to continue their operation in subdued Poland. The representatives of the *Monopol Zapałczany* (the Match Monopoly), Bank Amerykański and the ASEA company were already back in Warsaw. Leave permits were granted, although the bureaucratic procedure was protracted. This was dependent on whether the companies were to continue to function or become liquidated. Goods designated for sale were not confiscated by the Germans, but it was not advised that they be removed from the warehouses in Poland either. It was possible to take payment for goods in cash, in Polish or German currency, but transfer abroad was prohibited. As a result, Grafström advised the agents of the Swedish companies not to sell goods. An exception to this were transactions for the occupation authorities, performed on their request. It was feared that if such transactions were refused goods would be confiscated regardless. Communication problems, sending the goods back to Sweden, was also excluded. The situation of representative companies was particularly difficult, because most of them were managed by individuals of Jewish origin. Grafström highlighted that the Jews were subjected to consistent repressions and could be arrested at any time. He was hoping that the certificates he issued about employment in Swedish companies would protect them against forced labour for the Germans. Nevertheless, for the benefit of the goods which were held in the warehouses, Grafström advised that they were placed in 'Aryan hands.' Part of the goods disappeared or were, nevertheless, destroyed during the military operations. What was most reliable was the Swedish service, for which the Germans still felt a certain respect. When, in Radom, following the Germans' entry into Poland, the Swedish engineers from the L. M. Ericsson telephone factory, E. Rundström and K. Forsberg, went missing (on 7 September they headed off to Warsaw with a group of refugees and were found following the capitulation), the Polish employee Walenty Madajewski attempted to convince the German military and civil authorities that the confiscation and re-

---

[57] S. Grafström, *Anteckningar 1938–1944*, pp. 189–190.

quisition were inappropriate. It was only the emissary of the Swedish Legation in Berlin who guaranteed the factory's allegiance.[58] Grafström supported Bolander's proposal to create an information centre for the Swedish companies maintaining commercial contacts with Poland. Such an institution would have a great deal of work to do. Its responsibilities would include collecting debts and, where possible, their transfer to Sweden, carrying out inventories of submitted goods, which were eventually not paid for, breaking commercial relations and the simultaneous recruitment of representatives who were to develop contacts in favourable conditions. According to Grafström, it was impossible to exclude compensation for the goods which were lost by the Swedes, in the form of goods which were exported from the General Government and which were not interesting for the Germans, such as oak wood or zinc white.[59]

In reports to ASEA's authorities Sven Norrman described his attempt to recover a 1 million zloty loan granted to the power station in Włocławek. The German commandant would answer little could be done for now and that they should wait until the end of the war.[60] Continued management over the Swedish companies' property was significantly limited. It is beyond any doubt that the Swedish capital was facing the difficult task of maintaining its presence in the Polish territory, especially in the first months of the German occupation. The Germans intended to exploit the Polish industrial potential. Industrial equipment, means of transport and raw materials were to be taken to the Reich. Czesław Łuczak, expert in economic policy of the Third Reich in occupied Poland, claimed such actions were to 'plunder everything that could be of any value for the military economy of Germany, and also to dismantle and move industrial plants to Germany, this excluding small manufacturing companies, which were essential for satisfying the minimum needs of the local population.' The General Government was to become a farming region and a source of workforce. In mid-November 1939, Hitler changed his mind and consented to the launch of industrial companies. The dismantling of machinery continued, but the campaign was slowed considerably. The outbreak of the German–Soviet war in June 1941 created favourable conditions for various services, including repairs of defective devices and

---

[58] RA, UD 1920 års dossiersystem, R 20, vol. 565, copy of report by C. Petersén regarding the visit in Radom, Berlin, 25 X 1939.
[59] RA, Handelsdepartementet, Huvudarkivet, Rapporter från UD, F II aa, vol. 210, memorandum by S. Grafström regarding the Swedish interests in Poland following the conclusion of military activity, Warsaw, 23 XI 1939.
[60] S. Thorsell, Warszawasvenskarna. De som lät världen veta, Stockholm 2014, p. 45.

means of transport. Some of these repairs were performed in the General Government, being a natural back room of the Eastern Front.[61]

The confiscations and liquidations of companies included, in the first instance, those of other occupied countries, but the gradual takeover of companies with the neutral states' capital share was also planned. Jewish owners were fighting a losing battle and the remainder were usually placed into receivership. Łuczak claimed the friendly attitude towards the Third Reich ensured the economic activity of entrepreneurs representing the neutral states on their own account. One example he mentioned was the Swedish Nazi John Weibull, who owned shares in a factory producing tannins in Warsaw. In 1942 his company ownership rights were restored, and he was even granted a loan for its development.[62] Nevertheless, the Germans while maintaining the appearance of legitimacy, were trying to remove foreign owners from occupied Poland, including Swedes. Some cases became the subject of interest for Polish diplomats. One such example was a factory producing railway signal systems in Bydgoszcz, owned by the Gasaccumulator company in Stockholm. The Swedes presented the factory's *treuhänder* with documents proving their ownership of the factory, which they had purchased in 1938 from the Siemens company for approximately 1.12 million marks. It came to light that they had used simulated Polish co-owners to acquire the controlling share. In this situation the German receiver proposed paying the Gasaccumulator company 700 thousand marks for the factory. The Swedes concluded that it was of benefit to sell the factory, even at such a low price as its value under German receivership would continue to fall. The transaction, however, was not completed, as the Polish authorities filed a protest in Stockholm citing that there existed, previously fictional, Polish co-owners.[63]

The ASEA company made claims regarding payment for machines and the steam turbines distributed by its Warsaw daughter company. It was only at the outset of 1942 that the German *treuhänder* transferred the due funds to the account of Exportkreditbank AG in Berlin. It quickly transpired that a transfer to Sweden was impossible as the maximum transfer amount in Swedish–German relations for the given period had been reached. The funds were to be held in a special account until a later date. The only retribution the

---

[61] Cz. Łuczak, *Polityka ludnościowa i ekonomiczna hitlerowskich Niemiec w okupowanej Polsce*, Poznań 1979, pp. 32–33, 35–36.
[62] Ibidem, pp. 356–357.
[63] AAN, the Ministry of Industry, Trade and Shipping (London), 88, letter by Polish Envoy to Stockholm G. Potworowski to the Ministry of Finance, Industry and Trade, Stockholm, 17 XII 1941, p. 25; copy of letter by G. Dalen to commercial counsellor to the Polish Legation in Stockholm T. Pilch, Stockholm, 2 XII 1941, p. 26–27.

Swedes could use was a refusal to maintain the equipment that had not been paid for, but this did not have the desired effect.[64]

It was the Swedish Chamber of Commerce, with its registered office in Warsaw, and managed by Hilding Molander and Carl Herslow, that became the institution which provided information to Swedish companies interested in occupied Poland.[65] The organization, derived from the Polish–Swedish Chamber of Commerce, was established in 1930 and would operate in special conditions as an outpost for the Swedish economy in the territory of the General Government. Both Molander (in Warsaw) and Bolander (in Stockholm) independently reflected on the Chamber's future. Following the mutual consultations, the Swedish Chamber of Commerce together with the SAE watched over the interests of the Swedish companies in the General Government. Both these institutions were consulted by dozens of Swedish companies, which were engaged in trade with Poland and learned about the fate of their contractors as well as the goods which were sent but not yet paid for. Molander was also the basic source of information about German policy in Poland and the fate of the companies with Swedish capital. Together with the authorities of the SAE, Molander sought the best solution on the matter of Swedish goods that were still to be paid for or still yet to be sold by Polish agents. A proposal was presented in Stockholm to organize one central warehouse, controlled by the Chamber, to store the goods awaiting sale or being sent back to Sweden. It was also advised that when improving the operation of the Chamber, it would be worth establishing a permanent executive committee as well. A working committee was established and its members included the head of the American Bank, Harald Axell, the director of ASEA's daughter company, Sven Norrman, and Molander. Others who operated in the Chamber, besides Carl Herslow, were the head of Svea's daughter company and the former military attaché to Warsaw Colonel Axel von Arbin, the director of L. M. Ericsson Sigge Häggberg, and the director of SKF, Per Olof Silfverskiöld. This group also included businessmen Axel Bentzler, Nils Fernström and F. Sarnek. In January 1940 Molander highlighted in the letter to Bolander that nobody expected that the costs incurred during the process of gathering information about the fate of the assets would ever be retuned,

---

[64] RA, UD 1920 års dossiersystem, HP 64, vol. 2373, letter by S. Norrman to UD, Västerås, 24 IX 1942.
[65] RA-Arninge, Sveriges Allmänna Exportförening, E 1 a, vol. 814. The file contains voluminous correspondence between the Swedish Chamber of Commerce in Warsaw and the management of the SAE and, occasionally, the German authorities, in the period between November 1939 and May 1941.

unless they concerned great outlays on essential travel.⁶⁶ Nevertheless, Bolander began charging small amounts for the information activity of the Chamber. The establishment of the border between the General Government and the lands incorporated into the Reich simultaneously determined the scope of the Chamber's activity. In the territory of the Reich its members were virtually unable to fulfil their tasks. In the letter to Bolander, in February 1940, Molander explained that the controller of the company, or the *treuhänder*, risked a penalty for bringing outsiders in the company's warehouse. Nevertheless, despite great difficulties, part of the goods was successfully brought to Sweden. However, another part was lost without compensation. No definite German policy existed in this area, besides the tacit consent of the authorities in Berlin to the liquidation proceedings. Each case was considered on an individual basis. The Germans initially confiscated the property, and only then was it possible to enforce one's rights. According to Molander, foreign owners stood a better chance of receiving compensation than Polish or Polish-Jewish owners. In the case of the latter, there was no chance at all.

At the outset of 1940, Molander met with the authorities of the Warsaw district and proposed a re-launching of trade with Sweden involving cash sales of goods from the General Government or the exchange of Swedish raw materials for Polish goods. The idea attracted interest, but no commitment.

In September 1941, the Swedish industrialists in Warsaw imagined that the German occupation was short-term. They started to consider their own role in the rebuilding of Polish economy after the war. Harald Axell, in his conversations with the Poles in Stockholm, emphasised that he was 'against various German suggestions focused on exploiting the capital of the *Ceks* (the Swedes' code name) from the country and replacing it, as well as against investment projects adapted only to the current situation and convenient for the Germans.' In Warsaw he discussed the future of the Polish–Swedish relations and actions calculated for long-term cooperation with the former official at the Ministry of Foreign Affairs, Karol Bertoni.⁶⁷

---

⁶⁶ Ibidem. The report by the Chamber's official Halmstedt from such travel to Lublin in March 1941, whose purpose was to find the traces of the company J. Turkeltaub – an intermediary in the sales of the products of the Garphytte Bruk company from Garphyttan in Sweden.
⁶⁷ PISM, col. 25/17, general note from the talks with Samuel [Harald Axell] from 27 September and 2 October 1941. The author of the note was most probably M. Thugutt, who, on behalf of the Ministry of Internal Affairs, was managing communication between London and the General Government.

The German authorities tolerated the Chamber, which was the only Swedish institution to exist under the occupation, but they did not make its operation straightforward. The Chamber's account in the Bank Amerykański held funds of 55 thousand zlotys, the withdrawal of which was blocked in October 1939, and later rationed according to the binding principles under the occupation. Each withdrawal required prior application. Consent for the withdrawal was never given. This situation resulted in no cash for covering either the costs of the Chamber's operation or maintaining its members. Bolander managed to obtain a benefit of 5 thousand crowns from the Swedish government for the Chamber's activity; it was granted for the first time in December 1939 and half a year later another subsidy of 10 thousand crowns was announced. At least once, in May 1940, Molander asked Bolander for a small transport of basic food supplies with a total worth of 150 crowns), which he justified due to insufficient supplies and high prices on the black market. The correspondence between the Chamber and Sweden took place through the diplomatic courier service of the Swedish Legation in Berlin, and it was by means of this service that cash in dollar banknotes was delivered to Warsaw, outside the official channels. The principles of the functioning of the Swedish Chamber of Commerce constituted a foundation for the humanitarian activity and cooperation with the Polish underground movement, which was performed by the Swedes independently, but in line with the intentions of the Swedish financial leaders. Sven Norrman, the most distinguished Swedish courier of the Polish Underground State, many years later said that Marcus Wallenberg, who managed Stockholms Enskilda Banken (now Skandinaviska Enskilda Banken), namely an institution engaged in virtually all investments in Poland, advised the Swedish businessmen, who were trying to redeem their property in the General Government: 'we need to take actions which will let us return there after the war with our heads held high.'[68] The activity for the benefit of the underground movement and ordinary people in the need of help has already been described in detail by Józef Lewandowski. It may only be added that the arrests in July 1942 led to the suspension of the Chamber's activity in Warsaw.

At times the German officials in Kraków had doubts concerning the legality of such an institution. In 1941, in a memorandum to the authorities, Herslow explained that the existence of the Swedish Chamber of Commerce in Warsaw did not breach German regulations, and was also in their interest, because the Swedes were trying to initiate trade between Sweden and the

---

[68] J. Lewandowski, *Polska…*, pp. 15–16; J. Szymański, *Skandynawia–Polska…*, p. 208.

General Government. This was impossible at that point due to the lack of exports in the Polish territory, which would be subject to compensation required by the Swedish-German trade.[69]

The Germans also made efforts to establish direct trade between the General Government and Sweden. In December 1940, the German Chamber of Commerce in Sweden addressed a letter to *Sveriges utrikeshandels kompensations AB*, a company dealing with Swedish foreign trade compensation, where the exchange of fish for rock salt was proposed to the General Government, and the commercial headquarters in Kraków and Warsaw were to be parties in this transaction. Subsequently, at the request of the same Chamber, the seat of the Swedish Ministry of Foreign Affairs was visited by German businessman Imhof, who represented the R. Th. Möller & Co. company from Hamburg with a branch in Warsaw. He proposed the exchange of goods for compensation, instead of payments to settle accounts. What Sweden was to import from the General Government was salt, chlorinated lime, potassium chlorate, window panes, gin and vodka, whereas the Germans were counting on the import of cellulose, wood pulp, paper, mining stands, iron ore and herring. Imhof was sure that the consent of the German authorities in Berlin was not necessary, as 'commercially and politically the General Government needed to be treated as an independent entity.' Nils Ihre, who welcomed the German in UD, showed interest in importing the proposed goods as they were unavailable on the market, whereas he referred to Sweden's export capacity with reserve and only permitted the sale of herring. Imhof, encouraged by the favourable course of the conversation, was planning to complete the formalities related both with the German authorities and *Sveriges utrikeshandels kompensations AB*.[70] In May 1941 the *Maklerstwo Handlowe/Handelsmaklerei* from Lublin sent out its offer of intermediation in commercial contacts with the General Government to many Swedish companies. Referring to the permission from the German authorities for the purchase of an export calendar for 4 crowns, the representatives of the company argued that trade, even in the form of foreign exchange dealings, was possible. It was ob-

---

[69] RA, Handelsdepartementet, Huvudarkivet, Rapporter från UD, F II aa, vol. 230, copy of memorandum by C. Herslow about the activity of the Swedish Chamber of Commerce in Warsaw, 31 VII 1941.

[70] RA, UD 1920 års dossiersystem, HP 64, vol. 3735, letter by the Sveriges Utrikeshandels Kompensations AB to UD, Stockholm, 28 XII 1940 r.; Ibidem, memorandum by N. E. Ihre, Berlin, 30 XII 1940.

vious for Molander that such a sum could be neither evidence of a breakthrough nor a precedent in the commercial relations of the General Government with the rest of the world.

In October 1941 AB Karlstads Mekaniska Werkstad asked UD if any regulations existed on which pre-war relations with Poland could be terminated. Ihre replied that there was nothing that had occurred to date which could predict success in talks with the relevant authorities on settling outstanding Swedish debts in the General Government.[71]

In December 1942 the German company Heinrich Brand GmbH in Kraków requested the German authorities' permission to pay compensation for a purchase in Sweden of 200 tons of chromium salt in exchange for 125 tons of paraffin, worth 330 thousand crowns, to be sent to Sweden.[72] The German authorities agreed, on the condition that as part of the purchase the Swedish company ASEA would send replacement parts, worth 50 thousand crowns, for the turbines used in the General Government. The Swedish authorities had no objection. They established that the Germans' partner in this matter was the AB Hugo Mattssons Eftr. company from Stockholm.[73] The German authorities' claim made the issue even more complex, as it transpired that the partners had already made a deal. The Swedes purchased 125 tons of paraffin, reported the amount due, but did not pay it in cash, as they were planning to use the entire sum to purchase 200 tons of chromium salt in Portugal for the Germans; whereas ASEA agreed to supply the replacement parts, but demanded first the settlement of the debt by the new owners for the turbines, 158 955.18 crowns (where 1 zloty = 0.84 crowns), which the Polish owners of the salt mine in Wieliczka, the electrical plant in Zamość and the sugar factory in Strzyżów were unable settle before the war. *Statens handelskommission* (Sweden's board of trade) also added that after satisfying the financial claims of ASEA, 20 tons of paraffin should be sent as compensation for the claim regarding the machine replacement parts worth 50 thousand crowns. The German authorities in Kraków were inclined to cover these

---

[71] RA, UD 1920 års dossiersystem, HP 64, vol. 2735, letter by AB Karlstads Mekaniska Werkstad to the trade department of UD, Karlstad, 8 X 1941; Ibidem, letter by N. Ihre (trade department of UD) to AB Karlstads Mekaniska Werkstad, Stockholm, 11 X 1941.

[72] RA, UD 1920 års dossiersystem, HP 64, vol. 2735, letter by Attaché P. Zethelius from Swedish Legation in Berlin to N.E. Ihre, Berlin, 9 XII 1942.

[73] RA, UD 1920 års dossiersystem, HP 64, vol. 2735, letter by Sweden's board of trade to the trade department of UD, Stockholm, 22 XII 1942.

liabilities, but no such permission was granted by the Reich's Ministry of Economy.[74] The issue of the replacement parts was not settled.

At the outset of April, Garvamnes AB Weibull from Landskrona received a purchase order for 100 tons of calf skins, cow skins, ox skins and bull skins from one of the companies operating in the territory of the General Government. *Statens industrikommission* (Sweden's Board of Industry) requested detailed pricing for the types of skins to calculate the compensation.[75]

In May 1943, representatives of ASEA, the clearing committee and UD met. The Swedish authorities emphasized that payment for the supplies for the General Government could not be made as part of the Swedish–German clearing procedure as a matter of principle. On the question of the agreement between ASEA and the relevant the German authorities, regarding the supplies for the General Government as part of the settlement of ASEA's German foreign currency quota, the Swedish authorities made an unusual decision. These supplies would be settled as part of the Swedish–German clearing procedure. ASEA's Berlin daughter company had 100 thousand crowns in its account at *Exportkreditbank* in Berlin. The aim was to transfer this sum as part of the clearing procedure and to deliver replacement parts of an equal value to the General Government.[76]

The General Government was also receiving cream separators produced by the AB Separator company in exchange for feathers. In October 1943 the import of feathers and the trade were terminated due to the risk of animal disease.[77]

It is hard to determine the size of trade between Sweden and General Government. It was certainly not extensive, as the General Government offered little. Technical cooperation was necessary only to the extent that it allowed for increasing or at least not interrupting the economic exploitation of conquered Poland. The Swedes in turn, as time went by and as the prospect of the defeat of Germany and the conclusion of the war in Europe was becoming increasingly likely, had to respond to the statements of the governments of the Allied countries, including Poland, that any transactions by citizens from the neutral states with the occupied countries were unacceptable, and the legal acts of the

---

[74] RA, UD 1920 års dossiersystem, HP 64, vol. 2735, letter by N. E. Ihre to Attaché P. Zethelius from the Swedish Legation in Berlin, Stockholm, 28 XII 1942.

[75] RA, UD 1920 års dossiersystem, HP 64, vol. 2735, copy of Garvamnes AB Weibull's letter to UD, Landskrona, 9 IV 1943.

[76] RA, UD 1920 års dossiersystem, HP 64, vol. 2735, ASEA's letter to N. E. Ihre (the trade department of UD), Västerås, 21 V 1943.

[77] RA, UD 1920 års dossiersystem, HP 64, vol. 2735, letter by L. Belfrage (Sweden's board of trade) to the Trade Division of UD, Stockholm, 30 X 1943.

occupying forces – invalid, this including purchasing 'directly or indirectly of property, rights and interests of any kind' which belonged to the citizens of the occupied countries on the day of the aggression.[78]

Worse was the issue of the custody of Swedish property located in the part of Poland that was occupied by the Soviet Union. The members of the diplomatic circles of Moscow did not delude themselves that it was possible to recover the property of international companies, which had already been nationalized or confiscated. Neither did anybody expect any compensation.[79] In December 1939 Swedish Envoy to Moscow Wilhelm Winther informed Stockholm, that it was difficult to obtain credible information about the situation in eastern Poland.[80] Despite incorporating these territories into the Soviet Union, the regular passport control was maintained on the former borders. Foreigners were not authorized to enter the annexed territories. The only exception were diplomats, whose responsibilities forced them to visit the Borderlands. The commercial counsellor of the Italian consulate, which had been liquidated in Lviv, presented Winther with the report from his journey. He said that Lviv was overcrowded with refugees, that there were shortages of food and other essentials, and that prices were increasing every day. An intensive nationalization campaign was in progress, but in many cases the members of both staff and management of the companies decided not to leave their workplaces and keep their jobs. The receivers' oversight, nevertheless, was omnipresent. As early as on 20 September the Polish–Swedish match factory in Pińsk ran three shifts, the number of its industrial workers doubled, and production improved significantly. Several days earlier, Winther talked to the Vice-Commissioner for Foreign Affairs, Solomon Lozovsky, who announced the setting up of a special committee for foreign property legal affairs.[81]

* * *

---

[78] As early as on 30 November 1939, the Polish president enacted a decree on the invalidity of legal acts issued by the occupying forces (the Journal of Laws of the Republic of Poland, Angers, 2 XII 1939, no. 102, item 1006). On the works on the common statement of the Allied governments in this matter see *Protokoły posiedzeń Rady Ministrów Rzeczypospolitej Polskiej*, vol. 4, pp. 387, 405–408.
[79] RA, Handelsdepartementet, Huvudarkivet, Rapporter från UD, F II aa, vol. 210, memorandum regarding the attitude towards property rights in the territories of Poland annexed by the Soviet Russia, Stockholm, 10 XI 1939.
[80] RA, Handelsdepartementet, Huvudarkivet, Rapporter från UD, F II aa, vol. 210, copy of report by Swedish Envoy to Moscow W. Winther to UD, Moscow, 20 XII 1939.
[81] RA, Handelsdepartementet, Huvudarkivet, Rapporter från UD, F II aa, vol. 210, copy of letter by Swedish Envoy to Moscow W. Winther to UD, Moscow, 7 XII 1939.

During the war, just as prior to 1939, the most important natural resource imported by Sweden from Poland was hard coal (anthracite). Following the German annexation of Upper Silesia, coal mining increased, and exports continued. No statistics exist that show precisely how much German coal exported to Sweden came from Upper Silesia, that is from Polish coal mines. Historian Sven-Olof Olsson estimated nearly 6 million tons 1940–41 and 1942–43.[82] In January 1945, Pilch, acting Chargé d'affaires, on behalf of the eighteen Allied states, submitted a declaration to the Swedish Ministry of Foreign Affairs, concerning the non-recognition of the changes in proprietary relations, performed by the occupational authorities during the war.[83] On this occasion he reminded Ragnar Kumlin, Deputy Director of the Political department of UD, that as a commercial counsellor of the legation, together with Envoy Potworowski, he paid a visit to the head of the trade department of UD, Gunnar Hägglöf, in October 1939. At the time they indicated that the Polish government would not recognize the payments for the import of Polish goods to Sweden, which were made by Swedish companies before the war to the German receivership management. In addition, the Poles noticed that the Germans had launched the transports of coal from the Polish coal mines, and that the Swedish companies receiving this coal were risking that the moneys paid to the Germans for the delivered coal would be later recovered by the rightful Polish owners of the mines. An interesting commentary about the 1943 declaration of the Allied governments regarding the exploitation of the occupied territories, which was to warn the neutral states against participation in the robbery of property, was published on 15 January 1943 by *Trots Allt!*. It was suggested that following the war the Polish government would have the right to demand from the Swedish government the payment for the coal which was currently imported by the Germans from Poland.[84] The Polish authorities were aware that the Swedish companies often settled their pre-war liabilities towards the Polish companies in the form of agreements with the *treuhänder*, who were controlling individual companies in the General Government. The Polish Ministry of Finance even examined a possibility to make use of the information on this subject during the financial negotiations with Sweden after the war.[85] The Swedes' official stance,

---

[82] S.-O. Olsson, *Swedish-Polish…*, p. 32.
[83] AAN, HI/I/102, letter by Chargé d'affaires ad interim T. Pilch to the Ministry of Foreign Affairs together with attachments, Stockholm, January 1945.
[84] 'Skarp allierad varning för olaga statsaffärer. Hur går det med Sveriges tyska handel i Polens kol?', *Trots Allt!*, 15 I 1943.
[85] AAN, HI/I/285, telegram by Minister of Treasury H. Strasburger to Polish Envoy to Stockholm G. Potworowski, 18 VIII 1942.

however, was that they were not using the Polish coal reserves but importing coal from German coal mines.[86]

---

[86] AAN, HI/I/88, letter by counsellor to the Polish Legation in Stockholm T. Pilch to the Ministry of Foreign Affairs, Stockholm, 31 VIII 1944.

9. Plans of Polish–Swedish Post-War Economic Cooperation

At the turn of 1942 and 1943, when it was obvious that the Germans would lose the war, the Swedish authorities started to examine the possibility of launching talks with the Polish government in London on the rules for post-war trade. At the same time, they were constantly struggling in their negotiations with their partners from Germany, Great Britain and the USA, as far as the issue of regulation of the current trade was concerned. Together with the weakening of Germany's position in 1943, the Allies were pressing Sweden for gradually reducing the trade with the Germans. It was mostly about shrinking the export of iron ore, although the most sensitive issue was the sales of ball bearings. The Swedish government explained that it was impossible for it to completely quit cooperation with Hitler, as this would put the country at risk of occupation, and mostly at risk of becoming cut-off from coal supplies. In September 1943 Sweden concluded an arrangement with the USA and Great Britain, as part of which it committed itself to reducing the export of iron ore from 10 million tons every year to 7.5 thousand tons in 1944. As a compensation for the continuation of the existing policy regarding the sales of ball bearings to Germany, they offered to sell them also to the British. From 1944 onwards, five English motorboats with volunteer crews were fighting their way through the Skagerrak strait and collecting the precious cargo. It was known that the German supply sources would eventually run out and that no compromises with the Allies would be of any help.

In 1943 *Statens bränslekommission* (Swedish fuel) started to examine the possible post-war coal supply sources for Sweden. This most probably gave the impulse for the letter, which was written by the Polish-Swedish Chamber of Commerce to the Minister of Industry, Trade and Shipping, Jan Kwapiński, towards the end of 1942. Later, the exchange of correspondence between Kwapiński and Sweden's board of trade took place. It was obvious that the Swedes were mostly preoccupied with the coal supplies. In 1944 closer contacts with the Poles were re-initiated, although Stockholm was sceptical about the actual point of the talks due to the expected occupation of the territory of Poland by the Soviet armies and slim chances for the Polish government's return from exile. The Swedish diplomats, on establishing initial contacts with the PKWN in Moscow in November 1944, were aware that in the face of the lack of chances for importing coal from other countries only the Polish coal mines could become the possible supplier of this raw material. Envoy Sokolnicki maintained that preliminary economic negotiations should be initiated. Similar was the opinion of Kwapiński, although it was slowly becoming clear that the Swedes were interested in contacts with the Soviet side, which they started to consider as more competent in making decisions concerning Poland. Press Attaché Żaba was gathering information on this subject. This is what he heard from the famous journalist Arvid Fredborg at the end of 1943: 'Certain Swedish economic circles are of the opinion that post-war Russia would be a perfect destination market for Swedish goods and therefore they favour the option of cooperation with the Soviet Union, and they [are] even ready to support compromises at the expense of Russia's neighbours.' Peter Tennant, Press Attaché of the British Legation, also stated that 'for several months now the Swedish government has been conducting the policy, which need to be described as a pro-Moscow policy.' According to Tennant, such tendency was determined by economic considerations. In turn, the chief editor of *Svenska Dagbladet* daily, Otto Järte, admitted that the Swedish government was starting to conduct the same policy towards the Soviet Union as the one he conducted in the years 1940–1941 towards Germany. The overall situation was different, but, according to the eminent opinion journalist, one could expect that Sweden would avoid even 'the slightest appearances of anti-Soviet attitude.'[1] The stance of Swedish economic circles was evaluated slightly differently by the famous friend of Poland, Sven Norrman. He convinced the Naval Attaché of Poland, Commander Lieutenant Wolbek, that 'all Swedish industrialists would rather deal with Poland, for they strongly fear the Soviets.' He believed that the Polish government was not sufficiently protecting its interests and that the Soviet diplomats were much smarter, which resulted with the pressure from the Swedish economic circles on their own government to develop good relations with Moscow.[2]

---

[1] PISM, A 9, VI 21/1, note based on Żaba's reports to the Ministry of Internal Affairs, Stockholm, 30 XII 1943.
[2] PISM, MAR, A V 9/2, report by the Polish Naval Attaché to Stockholm, Commander M. Wolbek, to the head of the Intelligence Division of the Staff of Commander-in-Chief, n.p., 4 XI 1943. What is interesting is that opinion journalist Tadeusz Nowacki, in the Polish press in London, also criticised the passivity of the Polish government in its relations with the Swedish authorities about the subject of initiating economic and political cooperation: T. Norwid[-Nowacki], 'Na marginesie stosunków polsko-szwedzkich', *Dziennik Polski i Dziennik Żołnierza*, 28 XI 1944.

9. POLISH-SWEDISH ECONOMIC COOPERATION

The first voices supporting the initiation of international discussion about the plan of post-war economic development appeared in Sweden in the summer of 1942 and were raised by the members of the youth branch of the liberal party (*Folkpartiets ungdomförbund*). In January 1943 numerous proposals were submitted by the liberals to the parliament. Their intention was mostly to ensure that Sweden received imports of coal and coke, chemicals and food. It was assumed already then that Germany would become occupied and the goods that were purchased there by Sweden during the war would have to be sought elsewhere. Nobody expected generosity from the USA, which was perceived as a country whose evaluation of the Swedish policy of neutrality was negative.[3]

The Minister of Finance, Ernst Wigforss, proposed on 15 October 1943 to form a special commission for post-war economic planning with the budget of 10 million crowns allocated exclusively to economic issues and 100 million crowns allocated to rebuilding and humanitarian actions. Wigforss predicted that the support would be granted not only to the Nordic neighbours, but also to other European countries ruined by the war, and especially to those whose quickest possible revival was in the vital interest of Sweden.

The natural point of departure for the Polish side to the rebuilding of economic relations with Sweden was the presence of Swedish capital in Poland before the war. In 1937 it was ranked on the ninth place among all foreign capitals and amounted to 2.6 percent of the share.[4] The Swedes invested in electric and technical industry, chemical industry, woodworking industry, textile industry, metal industry and paper industry. The most renowned companies included: *Polska Akcyjna Spółka Telefoniczna w Warszawie* (the Polish Telephone Joint-Stock Company in Warsaw), *Polskie Towarzystwo Elektryczne ASEA* (the Polish Electric Association ASEA – most of its shares was owned by the ASEA company in Västerås), *Polski Monopol Zapałczany* (the Polish Match Monopoly, entirely owned by the Swedes). The Swedish capital was also represented by the companies: *Radocha* (producer of potassium, sodium chlorate and other chemicals), *Linoleum* and *Quebracho* (both representing the same segment as *Radocha*), *Wikander, Polski Przemysł Korkowy* (the Polish Cork Industry) and *Trak* (woodworking industry), *Stockholm AB Privat* (textile industry), *Mokwin* (paper industry), *Optimus* and *Gaz Akumulator* (metal industry). Apart from that there also operated three trading companies: *SKF Łożyska Kulkowe i Rolkowe* (SKF Ball and

---
[3] K.-R. Böhme, 'Handel och hjälp' [in:] *Nya fronter...*, pp. 351–353.
[4] AAN, HI/I/86, attachment to the report by the Polish Legation in Stockholm, Stockholm, 22 XII 1943.

Roller Bearings), *Svea* and *Inwestycje* (Investments). Moreover, most of the capital of Bank Amerykański was owned by the Swedes. The Swedish capital also provided the Polish government with issuance loans. Part of the 1927 stabilization loan was taken out in Sweden and through the agency of the Swedish match concern a loan in dollars was financed in 1930. Poland also owed Sweden part of the interest-free loan, which was provided to it directly following the First World War (the so-called relief loan), similarly to the loans granted by other countries (payment of the final instalment fell on 1 January 1942). The regional governments of Kalisz and Włocławek received from Sweden loans for the construction of urban power plants.[5]

First mentions about the future post-war Polish-Swedish economic co-operation started to appear in the reports of the Polish Legation in Stockholm in 1943. In the spring of 1944 one could already speak about a systematic submission of information about the economic situation of Sweden, which, according to Sokolnicki, was to constitute 'the point of departure which made the establishment of commercial relations between Poland and Sweden easier.'[6] Councillor Pilch emphasized from the very outset that Poland could find itself in a convenient position for the negotiations, provided it managed to deliver coal and coke following the conclusion of military operations.[7]

Gathering reliable information and preparing comparative studies was impossible without the cooperation of the Swedish industrial circles. Counsellor Pilch attempted to induce the renowned potentates to prepare reports about the Swedish trade and finance, but in 1944 the issue was not getting any easier than in the period when the Swedes feared the contacts with the legation due to the inconveniences from the Germans. When in August 1944 Pilch encouraged the famous merchant Waldemar Dahn to prepare an economic analysis for the purposes of the legation, he received his firm refusal. Dahn, just in case, communicated this fact to the security police and told them about his speculation that the task had been probably undertaken by director Axell.[8] This issue tells us much about the atmosphere of suspicion, which reigned in Sweden during the war, and about the attitude towards the contacts with the Poles, which were considered dangerous both because of

---

[5] J. Szymański, *Stosunki...*

[6] AAN, HI/I/51, report by Polish Envoy to Stockholm H. Sokolnicki to the Ministry of Foreign Affairs, Stockholm, 28 III 1944.

[7] AAN, HI/I/88, letter by counsellor to the Polish Legation in Stockholm T. Pilch to the Ministry of Foreign Affairs, Stockholm, 31 VIII 1944.

[8] RA-Arninge, SÄPO arkiv, P 201 Polish Legation, pro memoria, Stockholm, 22 IX 1944.

Germany (in the initial years of the war) and because of the Soviet Union (in the final period of the war).

At the outset of 1944 Sokolnicki noted a revival in the Swedish–Soviet commercial relations, which had to have an impact on the future trade with Poland. In March 1944 Żaba wrote to the Ministry of Foreign Affairs: 'An increased activity of the local Russian commercial representation has been noticeable lately. Talks have been initiated with the Swedish government on the subject of providing additional loans, and a special mission consisting of the representatives of the local Soviet Legation has been visiting individual Swedish industrial centres, taking interest in the capacity of the Swedish postwar production.'[9] Counsellor Pilch confirmed: 'the members of local economic circles are, so to speak, under the spell of the serious future transactions with Russia, which naturally also impacts the Swedish policy towards the Soviet Union, as well as the attitude of part of the local press towards the Russian problems. [...] What is more, the Swedish economic spheres are taking into their attention the fact that even prior to the conclusion of the war, in the case of Russia's annexation of the Baltic Sea coastline, or alternatively, following the conclusion of the Finnish-Russian war, the practical opportunities would open up for Sweden to communicate with Russia, and thereby, the opportunities for the increased Swedish-Russian trade right before the penetration of this market by the Western Allies.'[10]

Already in December 1942 the Polish-Swedish Chamber of Commerce in Stockholm asked the Minister of Industry, Trade and Shipping of the Polish government in exile, Jan Kwapiński, to raise the subject of revival of Poland's commercial relations with Sweden following the conclusion of the war. The authors of the memorandum, G. Klemming, the chair of the Chamber, and Przemysław Kowalewski, the director of the Chamber's office and a local delegate of the Polish Red Cross, were trying to found the future of the Polish–Swedish economic relations on the import of coal from Upper Silesia to Sweden and on the investments of Swedish capital in Poland. The then temporary head of the Polish Legation in Stockholm, T. Pilch, presented Kwapiński with a list of issues to discuss with the Swedes in the future: value of liabilities arising from trade up until the outbreak of the war, analysis of economic relations between Sweden and the General Government in terms of commitments which had arisen during that period, situation of the Swedish capital

---

[9] AAN, HI/I/51, report by Polish Envoy to Stockholm H. Sokolnicki to the Ministry of Foreign Affairs, Stockholm, 28 III 1944.
[10] PISM, col. 20/23, letter by counsellor to the Polish Legation in Stockholm T. Pilch to the Ministry of Foreign Affairs, Stockholm, 3 III 1944.

in the territory of Poland, analysis of the Swedish import and export market with particular focus on coal market, use of the Swedish commercial fleet in supplying goods to Poland and cooperation in the area of military defence (mainly with the Bofors company).[11] Kwapiński responded to this initiative by sending a letter on 20 January 1943 where he accepted the idea of preliminary talks regarding these issues.[12] Director Helge Norlander from AB Sveaexport forwarded Kwapiński's letter – which took the shape of a form containing specific questions – to the Swedish Ministry of Foreign Affairs.

Hägglöf, on thanking for the letter, pointed out that the character of many of the questions assumed the participation of Swedish authorities in discussing the subjects concerning the Polish-Swedish economic relations (or at least their approval). That is why the Swedish Ministry of Foreign Affairs reserved itself the right to participate in the discussions about the issues which would be raised by Kwapiński in the future.[13]

During his visit to Stockholm Kwapiński took more specific actions and on 1 May 1943 he submitted a written inquiry to Helge Norlander. In the document he communicated his needs. He also wanted to know whether it was possible to rely on the Swedish commercial fleet when it comes to the transport of goods imported by Poland.[14] The answer was mostly positive, which only strengthened the Polish conviction that 'Sweden, with its reliable, technically advanced industry developed already during the war [...] may play a quite important role at initial supplies to Poland.'[15] In connection with the fact that many other countries were interested in economic cooperation at the rebuilding of the destroyed infrastructure, this including the Soviet Union, Norway and the Netherlands, the Polish diplomats considered that it would be necessary to start, as quickly as possible, submitting orders requiring competitive down payments, and, in case of need, to place the goods, most importantly the machines, in warehouses.

On 6 May the Sveaexport company sent the answer to Kwapiński. Its representatives claimed that without the delivery of the materials (mainly

---

[11] AAN, HI/I/88, letter by Polish Chargé d'affaires to Stockholm T. Pilch to the Ministry of Industry, Trade and Shipping, Stockholm, 18 XII 1942.
[12] RA, UD 1920 års dossiersystem, HP 64, vol. 2735, copy of letter by the Minister of Industry, Trade and Shipping, J. Kwapiński, to the chair of the Polish-Swedish Chamber of Commerce in Stockholm, London, 20 I 1943.
[13] Ibidem, copy of letter by G. Hägglöf to director H. Norlander, Stockholm, 24 III 1943.
[14] Ibidem, letter by head of the AB Sveaexport company H. Norlander to G. Hägglöf (Ministry of Foreign Affairs) together with attachment, Stockholm, 15 X 1943.; AAN, HI/I/71, copy of the memorandum 'The Issue of future Polish-Swedish Trade', Stockholm, 6 V 1943.
[15] AAN, HI/I/71, copy of report by the Polish Legation in Stockholm, 9 V 1943.

metal sheets) the Swedish shipyard would not be able to sign any shipbuilding contracts. This meant that this would be impossible before the conclusion of the war. But it was possible to repurchase ships from the Swedish shipowners, and Norlander proposed that this was done with four units. It was possible to sell one of those ships right away, and the other three also, but on the condition that they would by flying the Swedish flag until the end of the war. The Svenska Orient Linien company also offered one ship for sale. The legation suggested that some other ship sale offers were sought for. It was only after considering all offers that an expert from London would make the purchase decision.[16]

The talks conducted by Minister Kwapiński during his visit to Stockholm were an important stage in the unfreezing of relations with the highest authorities of Sweden, also as far as economic issues were concerned. On 7 May 1943 Kwapiński sent a proposal to the Minister of Trade, Herman Eriksson, to discuss, through the Polish Legation in Stockholm, the issue of the future Polish-Swedish economic relations. A memorandum of the same content was sent also to the Swedish Ministry of Foreign Affairs. During the meeting with Eriksson, who received it several days later, Sokolnicki raised the issue of Polish-Swedish economic negotiations and the issue of Hägglöf's nomination as the representative of Sweden at the Polish government in London. The Swede was unwilling to make any commitments and used the excuse that he was to resign in the autumn, and said that the communication difficulties with Great Britain were virtually making it impossible to use the support of Hägglöf, who resided in London.[17] More promising was the answer that came on 27 May from the deputy head of UD's bureau for foreign trade, Rolf Sohlman. It expressed interest in the future commercial relations with Poland. According to Sokolnicki: 'As for [...] the local relations, and especially the tendencies of feigning strict neutrality by the local Ministry of Foreign Affairs, this letter needs to be considered as very positive.' Nevertheless, the Swedes requested that the issue was treated confidentially.[18] One day later Sohlman sent a letter to *Statens handelskommission* with the request that the Polish proposal was analysed.[19] The letter was passed on further to *Statens*

---

[16] Ibidem.
[17] AAN, HI/I/86, letter by Polish Envoy to Stockholm H. Sokolnicki to the Ministry of Foreign Affairs, Stockholm, 13 V 1943.
[18] AAN, Ministry of Industry, Trade and Shipping (London), 92, letter by counsellor to the Polish Legation in Stockholm T. Pilch to Minister of Industry, Trade and Shipping J. Kwapiński, Stockholm, 5 VI 1943, pp. 13–16.
[19] RA, UD 1920 års dossiersystem, HP 64, vol. 2735, copy of letter by R. *Statens handelskommission* (Sweden's board of trade), Stockholm, 28 V 1943.

industrikommission (Sweden's board of industry), *Statens livsmedelskommission* (Sweden's board of food), *Statens bränslekommission* (Swedish fuel) and *Statens trafikkommission* (Sweden's board of transport). A meeting between Sohlman and Pilch took place during which the expectations of both sides were initially determined together with the procedure of agreeing orders. It was the trade department of UD, directed by Hägglöf and Sohlman, that was to be the partner in these talks. The Swedes predicted difficulties in the eventual filling of the orders for the machines. They explained these difficulties as a lack of raw materials and rationing, but did not exclude securing special allocations for the Polish production. The Swedish companies would also expect large deposit payments and procurement specifications. During this time, the Polish diplomats established contacts on their own initiative with companies and banks regarding possible cooperation. It was known that the Swedes were most preoccupied with coal supplies. This information was used by Polish negotiators to their advantage. In one of the reports to London, the legation even suggested that the Swedes be promised a preference clause in this area.

Statens handelskommission (Sweden's board of trade) received two answers, on 13 September, from the State board of industry and on 16 September from Swedish fuel. Both analyses were sent to the Ministry of Foreign Affairs on 12 October. Sweden's board of industry emphasized in its analysis that the opinions listed in both Polish memoranda regarding the circumstances favouring the Polish–Swedish cooperation were shared by the experts there.[20] The need to settle satisfactory payment conditions was also pointed out at the very beginning was.

The first Polish–Swedish conference, with Envoy Sokolnicki, counsellor Pilch and Hägglöf in attendance, was held on 18 October 1943. The discussion took the shape of preliminary negotiations, which upon the request of the Swedes were to remain classified. During this meeting, Hägglöf underlined immediately Sweden's particular interest in supplies of Polish coal following the conclusion of the war, in light of the anticipated closure of the British and the German markets. His estimate of Swedish demand was 5.8 million tons of coal and 2 million tons of coke per annum. He suggested that the governments of Poland and Great Britain address the matter of parity of coal supplies to Sweden based on the agreement concluded before the outbreak of the war, when it was established that both sides, the British and the

---

[20] Ibidem, copy of confidential letter by R. Sohlman to *Statens handelskommission*, Stockholm, 12 VIII 1943.

Polish, would each supply the market with 47 percent of the material. The point was to free Poland from this commitment.

The Poles were very cautious in their evaluation of the possible post-war export opportunities for Poland. They noticed the need for making the Swedish rolling stock accessible and for the Swedes to participate in the rebuilding of Polish ports. The Poles also requested consent to purchase medicines in Sweden and their storage until the end of the war, when they would be sent to Poland. The cost of which was estimated to be 2.5 million crowns.[21] Hägglöf declared the intention to invest Swedish capital in Poland and organize supplies of iron ore. He expected difficulties in accessing various iron alloys, which were mentioned in the Polish memorandum. These were iron nickel and iron tungsten alloys, as well as graphite and carbon electrodes. As far as the machines were concerned, Hägglöf requested a detailed list, but saw no obstacle to the filling of orders for wooden barracks, seeds and livestock. He also suggested that Poland and Sweden had common interests in servicing Polish trade by means of the Swedish fleet. The Polish party put forward a draft for a loan, initially for 20 million crowns, which was to be granted as quickly as possible to the Polish government and which was to settle deposit payments for the orders. In exchange, the Poles offered to pay the loan off with coal supplies following the conclusion of military operations. The additional guarantee was the storage in the local warehouses, until the conclusion of military operations, of the goods purchased in Sweden. Hägglöf suggested that obtaining the guarantee from the British or American banks, or possibly, from international organisations dealing in economic support would be prudent. In the second meeting on 9 November, apart from addressing affairs connected with supplies of humanitarian aid from Sweden to the General Government, the participants re-addressed the matter of a trade loan for Poland. Hägglöf indicated that for Sweden it was very important that coal supplies were delivered during the first year following the conclusion of the war. That is the reason why he pressed forward on the issue of the priority for Sweden's in the Polish export. The Poles, on the other hand, wanted to use this argument as a bargaining chip in the future.[22]

Meanwhile, the Swedish experts on economy continued their work. Karl-Gustaf Ljungdahl, on behalf of the Swedish fuel, focused exclusively the

---

[21] Ibidem, letter by G. Hägglöf (UD) to the Materials Commission of the Medical Management Board (*Komisja Materiałowa Zarządu Medycznego*), Stockholm, 21 X 1943.

[22] AAN, Ministry of Industry, Trade and Shipping (London), 92, note regarding the current Polish-Swedish economic issues, Stockholm, 10 XI 1943, pp. 41–49.

question of coal and coke import. Sweden's board of transport (*Statens trafikkommission*) sent its analysis to Sweden's board of trade (*Statens handelskommission*) on 25 November,[23] whereas on 12 November a similar analysis was sent by Sweden's board of food.[24] The latter commission made the supplies to Poland dependent on the supply needs of Sweden as well as on the needs of its Nordic neighbours, who were to be prioritised over others. Expectations were low for exports to Poland in the initial period following the conclusion of the war. It was established that, later, exports to Poland of fish and fishery products, and initially, herring would be possible. The sale of a large number of pigs was also excluded. Whereas, it was predicted that the seeds of high-quality cereals (oats, rye and wheat) would be exported only in small amounts. On 11 December, the commission sent the memorandum concerning the seeds.[25]

Polish–Swedish contacts concerning economic planning were also being developed in London. On 7 June 1943, Envoy Prytz sent a memorandum from London to Stockholm regarding economic cooperation between Poland and Sweden, which he received four days earlier from the Polish government. The document highlighted the opportunity for making large Swedish investments in Poland, including electrification projects. The Polish side emphasized that it was necessary to continue the export of Polish coal to Sweden, more so that the export opportunities of Great Britain in this area were to be limited.[26] In the memorandum it was indicated that Sweden may, to some extent, replace Germany as Poland's economic partner, due to the destruction of German industry during Allied bombings. According to the Polish analysts, German export and import opportunities would decrease in the forthcoming years. The German occupational policy introduced a psychological element, namely, a Polish unwillingness to conduct any business with the Germans. What was mentioned were the numerous circumstances that would favour the development of Swedish–Polish economic contacts: the differences in the economic structure of both countries, the excess of capital in Sweden and a lack in Poland, the urgent need for the rebuilding of Polish infrastructure, agriculture and industry, the neighbourhood across the Baltic

---

[23] RA, UD 1920 års dossiersystem, HP 64, vol. 2735, copy of letter by A. Granholm (Sweden's board of transport) to the *Statens handelskommission* (Sweden's board of trade), Stockholm, 25 XI 1943.

[24] Ibidem, copy of memorandum by C. G. Widell (Sweden's board of food) regarding the possible export of food to Poland following the war, Stockholm, 12 XI 1943.

[25] Ibidem, memorandum by C. G. Widell regarding the export of seeds to Poland following the war, Stockholm, 11 XII 1943.

[26] Ibidem, letter by Swedish Envoy to London B. Prytz to UD, London, 7 IV 1943.

Sea, and the lack of political conflicts which could disrupt economic relations. Naturally coal was the strategic resource to be exported through Poland to Sweden. In addition to coal, zinc and zinc ash export would be of value. Agricultural products could also be taken into consideration. Poland needed machines and equipment of all kinds, as well as iron ore. The participation of Swedish companies in the electrification of Poland was counted on. The Swedish plan from 1935, regarding the construction of motorways was revisited. The Swedes were also offered the opportunity to partake in residential construction, mainly as instructors and qualified workers. The cooperation in the field of shipping was a separate issue.[27]

The Polish Legation in Stockholm started to be visited by the representatives of Swedish companies who were hoping to enter (or re-enter) the Polish market following the war. In November 1943, counsellor Pilch was visited by representatives of Svepolex (*Svensk-Polska sillexportföreningen*) – an association of companies which, before the war, were dealing with the export of fresh and frozen herring to Poland. Their share in this export at the time was over 80 percent. They informed Pilch that their company was still operating and that following the liberation of Poland it would be possible for them to organize the transport of fish from Sweden. On the condition of obtaining a guarantee for the transfer of part of the gains and tax advantages they were also willing to invest their capital in the foundation of a fish import and processing centre in Gdynia. Moreover, they offered to provide training to twenty Polish refugees in herring trade and fish processing (the initiator of the training was a Norwegian, Herman Mathiessen).[28] Initially, the legation prepared a list of twenty two candidates to take part in the training.[29] The Swedish companies showed good will, but the project faced difficulties from the authorities during implementation; during the war, for safety reasons, it was decided that foreigners were prohibited in port areas. As a result, it was all but impossible to acquaint the trainees with fish processing, as fish processing plants were usually located within port areas. Eventually, the training was completed by only three Poles.[30] Nevertheless, the management of Svepolex expected the subject of fish export to Poland to be taken up during

---

[27] Ibidem, copy of Polish pro memoria.
[28] AAN, HI/I/156, letter by T. Pilch, counsellor to the Polish Legation in Stockholm, to the Ministry of Industry, Trade and Shipping, Stockholm, 1 XII 1943.
[29] AAN, Polish Legation in Stockholm, 46, letter by Polish Envoy to Stockholm H. Sokolnicki to the Ministry of Industry, Trade and Shipping together with attachment, Stockholm, 12 II 1944, pp. 1–3.
[30] AAN, HI/I/156, letter by Polish Envoy to Stockholm H. Sokolnicki to the Ministry of Industry, Trade and Shipping, Stockholm, 3 III 1944; AAN, Polish Legation in Stockholm,

bilateral negotiations.³¹ One of the fish exporters, Algot Bergström, made direct contact with two Polish trainees and decided to obtain, as quickly as possible, a permit to trade in Gdynia and Gdańsk and to fish cod and herring in the Baltic Sea with modern fishing boats. The Swede planned to supply other countries as well as Poland, and the Polish ports would act as distribution centre for Central Europe.³²

In contrast, the company Geoprint AB from Stockholm submitted an offer to print maps and atlases. Counsellor Pilch announced the news that there was an option of printing books and manuals in Sweden, as Sweden had an unlimited amount of paper.³³ The ASEA company sent its catalogues to the Polish Legation. The latter, on the other hand, asked the Nohab company to send it its catalogue about the production of locomotives and freight wagons, which it was famous for before the war.³⁴

At the same time the Polish Red Cross in London turned to its branch office in Stockholm to request permission from the Swedish authorities to buy medicines to send to Poland in the near future. The director of the trade department of UD informed Sokolnicki that priority for purchasing the medicines was granted to the Nordic States, especially Norway. This information was passed on to the Swedish Ministry of Foreign Affairs by Doctor Nilsson from the Medical Management Board, which was responsible for the supply of medicines. As the supplies to the Nordic States were a priority, he advised against assuming any responsibilities towards the Poles.³⁵ As a result, the Swedish diplomats pointed to the importance of reaching an agreement with the Norwegian government in London to find out the country's demands for medicines. Eventually, they agreed to allocate sufficient quantities for Poland. For the legation it was important that the issue was concluded before the forthcoming economic negotiations with the Swedes. Pilch asked London for an immediate transfer of funds. He emphasized that the purchase represented the first practical result of the rebuilding of Polish-

---

46, letter by counsellor to the Polish Legation in Stockholm T. Pilch to the Ministry of Industry, Trade and Shipping, Stockholm, 8 IV 1944, p. 18.

³¹ RA, UD 1920 års dossiersystem, HP 64, vol. 2736, letter by C. E. Wallén (Svensk Sillexport) to UD, Gothenburg, 23 XII 1944.

³² Ibidem, copy of letter by A. Bergström to the Ministry of Trade in Warsaw, Gothenburg, 12 III 1945.

³³ AAN, HI/I/88, letter by T. Pilch, counsellor to the Polish Legation in Stockholm, to the Ministry of Industry, Trade and Shipping, Stockholm, 5 XI 1943.

³⁴ AAN, Polish Legation in Stockholm, 104, letter by counsellor to the Polish Legation in Stockholm T. Pilch to the Ministry of Industry, Trade and Shipping, Stockholm, 27 XI 1943, p. 1.

³⁵ RA, UD 1920 års dossiersystem, HP 64, vol. 2735, memorandum regarding the shipment of medicines to Poland after the war, Stockholm, 16 XI 1943.

Swedish economic relations.[36] In November 1943, the delegate of the Polish Red Cross, Przemysław Kowalewski, informed the Ministry of Labour and Social Welfare in London of the opportunity to purchase the medicines in Sweden. Earlier, Envoy Sokolnicki informed the Swedish Ministry of Foreign Affairs about the demand for 2.5 million crowns' worth of medicine. The Swedes answered that some vaccines, among other things, were available for purchase. Thus, Kowalewski turned to the largest pharmaceutical companies with a request to submit their offers.[37] At the same time, he warned the ministry in London against shipping the medicines to Poland due to the likelihood of their seizure by the German authorities. Minister Stańczyk, somewhat surprised by these reservations, explained that the transports of the International Red Cross, sent from Geneva, were reaching the Central Welfare Council (Rada Główna Opiekuńcza) in Kraków.[38] Meanwhile, on 10 March 1944, Pilch sent a letter to the Ministry of Industry, Trade and Shipping to brief them on his meeting with the representative of the NeoPharma company.[39]

The Polish Ministry of Foreign Affairs took some purchases in Sweden into consideration, including the medicines. The United Nations Relief and Rehabilitation Administration (UNRRA), the intention of which was to monopolize humanitarian aid in Europe following the conclusion of military operations, imposed restrictions that made it impossible to purchase goods for the post-war period without its participation. Nevertheless, there were attempts to evade these rules. Medicines were purchased whilst the war was in progress. Officially this was done to meet demand, but in reality they were deposited for use after the war.[40] Initially, the very possibility of talks between Envoy Sokolnicki and the Swedes on economic matters was rejected due to the international commitments of the government. One possible solution was talks through intermediaries.[41] Eventually, a different solution was found. The medicines were purchased and stored until the end of the war. The Polish

---

[36] AAN, HI/I/86, copy of letter by counsellor T. Pilch to the Ministry of Foreign Affairs, Stockholm, 19 XI 1943.
[37] Ibidem, copy of letter by delegate of Ministry of Labour and Social Welfare P. Kowalewski to the Ministry of Labour and Social Welfare, Stockholm, 22 XI 1943.
[38] Ibidem, letter by Minister of Labour and Social Welfare J. Stańczyk to the delegate of the Polish Red Cross in Stockholm, P. Kowalewski, London, 13 XI 1943.
[39] Ibidem, letter by counsellor T. Pilch to the Ministry of Industry, Trade and Shipping, Stockholm, 10 III 1944.
[40] Ibidem, letter by the Ministry of Foreign Affairs to the Ministry of Labour and Social Welfare, London, 15 XII 1943.
[41] AAN, HI/I/86, letter by Secretary-General of the Ministry of Foreign Affairs W. Babiński to the Ministry of Labour and Social Welfare, London, 18 XI 1943.

Legation in Stockholm received an offer for the construction of concrete barracks from the Gunnar Westholm AB. Nolander was the shareholder and director of this company, as well as one of the interviewees of minister Kwapiński during his stay in Stockholm in 1943.[42] At the start of November 1943, the offer was sent by counsellor Pilch to London, where it stirred up an unexpected reaction from the FO.[43] On 4 January, the British demanded explanations concerning the economic negotiations conducted in Stockholm. The Polish government clarified that the talks were not negotiations but more of an exchange of information.[44]

Towards the end of December 1943, Pilch submitted to the Ministry of Industry, Trade and Shipping the offer from the Sandvikens Jarnverks AB, which was interested in supplying Poland with cutting tools for metal and wood treatment and non-corrosive and acid-resistant steels among other items. Pilch emphasized that before the war the company had owned a saw factory in Warsaw.[45] In January 1944, Pilch reported that L. M. Ericsson, which invited him to visit its newest factory, proposed the renewal of its contacts with Poland.

Following the talks with the Swedish industrialists, Pilch was optimistic about further cooperation and so was the tone of his messages to London. Nevertheless, on this occasion he ignored the Soviet threat. Following his visit to the L. M. Ericsson factory he wrote:

> On this occasion I would like to point out that the local industrial circles, independently of our current political difficulties, are very optimistic about the result of our clash with Russia, and therefore our talks on the subject of the future development of economic relations with Sweden are currently unburdened of our political situation in this area. These circles believe the Polish–Soviet conflict is only part of the political difficulties of England and the USA on the one hand, and Russia's difficulties on the other, and it needs to be settled in the interest of the Anglo-Saxon powers at a suitable moment. During the recently recurring talks and contacts, it was additionally possible for me to state that the local industrial and economic spheres are adopting a very favourable

---

[42] Ibidem, copy of letter by T. Pilch, counsellor to the Polish Legation in Stockholm, to the Ministry of Industry, Trade and Shipping, Stockholm, 4 XI 1943.
[43] Ibidem, letter by the Ministry of Foreign Affairs to the Ministry of Industry, Trade and Shipping, London, 18 I 1944.
[44] Ibidem, letter by Secretary-General of the Ministry of Industry, Trade and Shipping J. Kożuchowski to the Ministry of Foreign Affairs, London, 27 I 1944.
[45] Ibidem, letter by T. Pilch, counsellor to the Polish Legation in Stockholm, to the Ministry of Industry, Trade and Shipping, Stockholm, 28 XII 1943.

approach towards increasing trade with Poland in the future and are willing to grant us more serious trade loans at the initial stage after the war.'[46]

The Swedes were also willing to assume the role of an intermediary in the commercial contacts between Poland and other Scandinavian countries. The focus was to import cod liver oil and insulin from Norway and medicines from Denmark.[47]

In February and March 1944, counsellor Pilch informed the Ministry of Foreign Affairs that he was working on offers concerning accommodation and hospital barracks. The Swedish government did not object regarding the plans to export prefabricated houses to Poland as part of future trade.[48] The Polish project assumed that the Swedes would build three border stations (with one hundred beds in each) with full hospital equipment. The Sveaexport company invited Pilch to visit the disinfection station in Stockholm, which provided shelter to the refugees from Finland. Pilch submitted a detailed description of its disinfecting devices adding, 'the licences to produce these devices were purchased by the Germans and the Finns, who are to use them on a large scale.'[49] In general, the information sounded encouraging:

> Without going into detail, I only want to point out that the devices are extremely easy to use, do not require any additional special equipment like, for instance, specially sealed rooms, they are easily portable (one piece of equipment weighs about 18 kg), and their operation is very cheap. These devices are produced in Sweden by a company the production capacity of which is 30 devices per month. However, this capacity may be considerably extended.

However, Pilch requested that an expert be sent from London, who, 'will be able to gain the best insight into the local opportunities and establish contact with numerous Swedish experts.'[50] At the same time, Pilch announced that he would help Tadeusz Olszowski, who was to arrive in Stockholm, make contact with a representative of one of the Swedish companies. Then, discussions could take place about the conditions for placing an order, through Sweden, for a ship from the Swedish shipyards for one of the Polish shipping lines.

---

[46] Ibidem, letter by counsellor to the Polish Legation in Stockholm T. Pilch to the Ministry of Industry, Trade and Shipping, Stockholm, 20 I 1944.
[47] Ibidem.
[48] AAN, HI/I/86, letter by T. Pilch to the Ministry of Industry, Trade and Shipping, Stockholm, 25 II 1944.
[49] Ibidem, letter by T. Pilch, counsellor to the Polish Legation in Stockholm, to the Ministry of Industry, Trade and Shipping, Stockholm, 23 III 1944.
[50] Ibidem.

The Swedish intermediary assured the counsellor that the order for a ship for Poland could be placed right away, on the condition that the official client would be a Swedish company, and that it would be delivered to Poland after the war. There were many indications that this was how the Germans ordered ships in Sweden.[51]

In April 1944, the Ministry of Industry, Trade and Shipping drafted the future Polish–Swedish agreement. In the initial part it was indicated that the provisions of the possible agreement could not interfere with the obligations imposed on Poland by the UNRRA or other international organisations. Poland was to declare its intention to meet the Swedish demand for coal, equal to that prior to the war, as soon as possible following the repair of the ports, with priority given to supplies for Sweden and using the Swedish commercial fleet. Sweden would commit to supplying iron ore and other minerals at prices no higher than those offered to other recipients or those calculated based on official stock exchange listings. Moreover, Sweden was to grant Poland an open loan, yet it not exceed the value of half of the annual coal supply. The agreement was for one year only, with the option of an automatic extension.[52] The plans regarding the agreement with Sweden would be communicated to the FO.[53] Meanwhile, in the report from 6 April 1944, the officials of the Polish Legation in Stockholm recounted the talks which had taken place in the British and American Legation. The British were interested in the Swedish Market and were unwilling to allow the establishment of specific Polish–Swedish talks regarding the issue of coal export. They preferred Sweden to accumulate the largest stocks of coal possible before the end of the war, thus allowing it manage during the period when supplies from Great Britain would be impossible. Similar opinions, unfavourable towards the Polish efforts to conclude the agreement with Sweden, were uttered by the British in London. The Poles relied on the support of the Americans, as it was important for them that trade between Sweden and Germany cease as quickly as possible.[54] The commercial counsellor of the legation of the USA, Christian M. Ravendale, informed Pilch in the conversation on 6 April 1944 that the negotiations with the Swedes about stopping exports to Germany were taking place. The Swedes justified exports with the explanation that coal

---

[51] AAN, HI/I/86, letter by T. Pilch, counsellor to the Polish Legation in Stockholm, to the Ministry of Industry, Trade and Shipping, Stockholm, 25 IV 1944.
[52] AAN, Ministry of Industry, Trade and Shipping (London), 92, draft of Polish-Swedish agreement, London, 7 IV 1944, pp. 74–77.
[53] Ibidem, draft of letter to the Foreign Office, London, 7 IV 1944, pp. 78–79.
[54] AAN, Ministry of Industry, Trade and Shipping (London), 92, note regarding Polish-Swedish economic relations, pp. 94–99.

and coke from Germany were indispensable for industry. Even in the event of a rapid end to the war, the Swedes were counting on the supplies from Great Britain and Poland. This argument was not altogether convincing for the Americans, who estimated that Swedish coal stocks were sufficient for at least 18 months, but even up to two and a half years. Although they shared the opinion of the Swedes and rejected greater supplies from the British mines, they did not consider coal supplies from the USA. Instead, the intention was to familiarise themselves with the opportunities for supplies from Poland. They were curious whether the Poles had established contacts with the Swedes on this issue. Pilch responded that the preliminary talks were ongoing, though their character was semi-official, emphasizing, 'It is nevertheless highly likely that from the small number of goods that Poland, devastated by the war, would be able to export relatively soon after the end of the war, coal should be given absolute priority.' Pilch considered the Swedish market to be the natural market for Poland and noted that the Swedes were very interested in procuring coal from Poland. At that moment it was impossible for the Polish side to commit to providing any supplies, but it was possible to consider certain warranty provisions. Based on the agreements concluded before the war, Poland secured its percentage share in coal supplies for Sweden. Any changes in this area could only be performed as part of the agreement with Sweden and Great Britain, which Pilch considered to be the issue of 'both loyalty as well as formal necessity.' He left the initiative in this respect to the government in London. He counted on the Swedish offers that would consider not only their own import demands but also 'facilitate and speed up investments and make it possible to put port transport and handling equipment in order', as well as consider the necessity to grant Poland a lease on rolling stock. Pilch added that when it came to Sweden Poland expected, as he put it, 'certain exceptional imports' in the shape of various industrial equipment and agricultural products necessary for the rapid rebuilding of the country. Pilch drew the attention of his superiors to the information on abundant Swedish coal stocks. He considered that this situation was not beneficial to Poland, as it weakened its negotiating position. Moreover, during the talks with the Allies, the Swedes made pessimistic evaluations of Poland's export opportunities. Pilch demanded that the Polish government adopt an active approach during the negotiations between the Allies and Sweden regarding coal:

> Since it is quite probable that Sweden would have to give way as a country being economically dependent on international commercial relations; what

we could also do is make it easier for both sides to reach a compromise, thereby obtaining some actual warranties regarding coal export from Poland to Sweden after the war.

The Swedes would be guaranteed coal supplies, and the Allies would speed up negotiations with Sweden. As far as Poland was concerned, Pilch claimed, 'for us, this would not only be a warranty concerning the future export of coal to Sweden. This would also represent our meaningful entry into further concrete economic negotiations with Sweden as well as strengthen our position regarding this issue.' Pilch considered it important that the Polish authorities in London attempt to establish contacts with the Swedish negotiator Gunnar Hägglöf (who was at the time staying in Great Britain) as he did not exclude that, 'on the occasion of the current talks between the Allies and Sweden certain decisions may be made without our participation, which would constitute a precedent not only to the export of our coal to Sweden, but also to the overall economic cooperation.' At the same time, he examined the ways of acquiring a loan in Sweden. He put forward an idea of using the funds blocked in the USA and Great Britain, for the orders of barracks and a ship in Sweden, which would require purchases in the country of the depositaries anyway.[55] A few days later, Pilch spoke with the commercial counsellor to the British Legation in Stockholm on a similar matter. The meeting confirmed his earlier conclusions, but the diplomat pointed out in his subsequent note that the entire issue needed to be conducted with great care. He also demanded that the government explain in detail what the possible repercussions of the Polish cooperation with the UNRRA (Poland's principal donor) could be on the talks with the Swedes. This was to be the principal source of the substantial part of goods donation assistance for the ruined country. He explained, 'This is all the more important as we may be asked questions on this subject by the Swedes, and we must be acquainted with the local Allied legations, which may reveal tendencies to introduce a certain degree of control over our talks with Sweden.'[56]

Because of these talks, as early as in April 1944, during the meeting with the Swedes, Envoy Sokolnicki planned to raise the matter of exporting Polish coal to Sweden. He believed that it would be possible to make use of the English–American pressures aimed at forcing the Swedes to reduce the

---

[55] AAN, HI/I/86, note by T. Pilch, counsellor to the Polish Legation in Stockholm, Stockholm, 6 IV 1944.
[56] Ibidem, note by T. Pilch, counsellor to the Polish Legation in Stockholm, Stockholm, 9 IV 1944.

supplies of iron ore and ball bearings to the Germans, since he assumed, the Swedes were justifying the necessity of maintaining commercial contacts with the Germans with the fact that they had no other coal and coke supplier. Sokolnicki argued, 'In this context certain compromises may be reached, which to some or other extent may consider the issue of Sweden's post-war supply of coal, in which we are naturally very much interested.'[57]

Sokolnicki agreed with Pilch that this was a good moment to contact Hägglöf in London to acquaint him with the issues of the future trade between Poland and Sweden. Moreover, Sokolnicki emphasized, 'The establishment of contact with Hägglöf may be of certain political benefit for us, as it may facilitate and speed up my efforts to appoint him minister plenipotentiary to the government of Poland.'

In May 1944, Ravendale, commercial counsellor to the legation of the USA in Stockholm, again turned to counsellor Pilch to ask whether the Poles had considered the issue of initiating talks with the Swedes about post-war Polish coal supplies. According to the American diplomat, 'this issue is currently mature enough for it to be discussed with the Swedish side and it could facilitate the American–British efforts to limit the ore transportation from Sweden to Germany.'[58]

The Minister of Industry, Trade and Shipping, Jan Kwapiński, supported the view of Sokolnicki and Pilch (and Ravendale) that at that point the Polish government should have already launched preliminary talks with the governments of other countries about future trade. In the letter to the Ministry of Foreign Affairs he explained:

> it is not about any specific steps regarding the conclusion of commercial contracts, but rather about considering the opportunities existing after the war, estimating the readiness of individual countries to provide some or other supplies (either not included or insufficiently included in the UNRRA programme), explaining the form of the future arrangements, becoming informed as to the import demands of individual countries and so on.'[59]

Eventually, at the inter-ministerial conference held on 15 June 1944, it was established that the negotiations with the Swedes should begin as soon as possible and conclude with an appropriate agreement for the post-war period. The

---

[57] Ibidem, letter by H. Sokolnicki, Polish Envoy to Stockholm, to the Ministry of Industry, Trade and Shipping, Stockholm, 12 III 1944.
[58] Ibidem, letter by Minister of Industry, Trade and Shipping J. Kwapiński to the Ministry of Foreign Affairs, London, 19 V 1944.
[59] Ibidem.

point of departure to the establishment of parity of coal supplies was to be the pre-war agreement granting the Polish side a 47 percent share of the import of the raw material to Sweden 'including the clause concerning a possible increase in the share depending on the results of the future talks with the English.' Besides, it was necessary to obtain a loan to fill the orders that were already being placed. The procedure of making payments for the supply of goods permitted a clearing procedure. On the pre-war trade, receivables would be omitted.[60] Reservations were voiced by the Ministry of Foreign Affairs and the Ministry of Finance regarding the idea of extending the instructions for Sokolnicki and Pilch from the very start by two options of payment for the Swedish goods: by means of foreign currency dealings and settlement. The Department of Economy and Sales was of another opinion, maintaining that what needed to be considered first were the short-term priorities:

> The Agreement needs to be of special character, concluded for a transitional period, which is most important for us, and its *main objective* [underlined in the original] is to obtain the necessary resources, machines and tools *at all costs* [underlined in the original]. The instruction should clearly indicate to Sokolnicki and Pilch that although it would be important for us to establish a loan and foreign exchange arrangement, which would be beneficial for us, this issue is nonetheless of *secondary* [underlined in the original] importance in relation to the principal target – obtaining goods from Sweden.'[61]

Pilch believed that speed in establishing mutual relations to beat the Soviets in bringing their resources to the Swedish market would prove to be important.[62] He soon sent the text of the article from *Affärsvärlden* magazine, where it was recounted that the following companies were present in Poland prior to the war: *Szwedzkie Towarzystwo Zapałczane* (the Swedish Match Company) (29 million dollars), the L. M. Ericsson telephone network with 140 thousand customers and the ASEA company factory that held shares in Polish power plants. According to the author of the article: 'All the Swedish businesses mentioned add up to a substantial amount.' At the same time, the author confirmed Pilch's apprehensions that the most important decisions would be made in Moscow, 'What will be Russia's position regarding the areas where Sweden conducted its business and which, as it may be assumed,

---

[60] AAN, Ministry of Industry, Trade and Shipping (London), 92, note from the conference devoted to Sweden held on 15 VI 1944 with Minister J. Kożuchowski, pp. 100–101.
[61] Ibidem, note by T. Łychowski regarding the instructions for the talks with Sweden, London, 6 VIII 1944, p. 151.
[62] AAN, HI/I/86, letter by T. Pilch, counsellor to the Polish Legation in Stockholm, to the Ministry of Industry, Trade and Shipping, Stockholm, 4 VIII 1944.

9. POLISH-SWEDISH ECONOMIC COOPERATION

would remain under Russian administration? This will become apparent in the future.'[63]

In June 1944, at the request of the Minister of Treasury, counsellor Pilch contacted Sohlman, deputy head of the trade department of UD, to discuss the matter of printing Polish zloty banknotes in Sweden. The Minister of Treasury anticipated the need to prepare a stock of banknotes totalling approximately 30 billion zlotys.[64] Sohlman showed interest in the Polish plans, but after consulting the Riksbank, returned a negative response. Pilch was told that Sweden would have no major reservations about the order, but that insurmountable technical difficulties existed.[65] The printing house, which satisfied the needs of the Swedish state, was too small to execute this particular task. No orders of this kind from abroad had ever been received before. Nevertheless, the Swedes wanted to avoid making a bad impression. Pilch pointed out, 'The Swedish Ministry of Foreign Affairs, wishing to present its best side to us, has agreed to provide a certain amount of the necessary special printing paper, on the condition that the printing process would take place in the territory of another country.'[66]

It was also necessary that the transport of the paper took place discreetly and be kept secret from the Germans. The Swedes maintained that the conclusion of agreement with the British would make it possible.

On 8 December 1943, the Swedish government established the National Reconstruction Board (*Statens återuppbyggnadsnämnd*) directed by Stig Sahlin and the *Svenska kommittén för internationell hjälpverksamhet* (Swedish Committee for International Assistance) chaired by the president of the Svea Court of Appeal Lars Birger Ekeberg. These institutions would deal with the planning and settlement of business connected with the Swedish participation in the post-war reconstruction of European countries. On 20 July 1944, UD sent a letter to the National Reconstruction Board, informing them of the goods that Poland was interested sourcing from Sweden. Relating to this, the board requested the State Industry Commission issue a statement. On 2 July 1944, Erik Grafström from the Foreign Trade Office at Sweden's board of industry replied that firstly the Poles would need a complete set of equipment for the paper mill. They also needed equipment for chemical and

---

[63] Ibidem, 'Szwedzkie interesy w Polsce' [translation of the article], Stockholm, 19 VIII 1944.
[64] Ibidem, letter by the Minister of Treasury to T. Pilch, commercial counsellor to the Polish Legation in Stockholm, London, 31 V 1944.
[65] Ibidem, letter by T. Pilch, counsellor to the Polish Legation in Stockholm, to the Ministry of Finance, Stockholm, 22 VI 1944.
[66] Ibidem.

mechanical production. The Karlstad Mekaniska Verkstad AB focused on the development of a detailed offer, which was to be ready on 1 September. It was impossible to carry out the feasibility study for the order until the Swedes had access to this analysis. Yet, the board was able to present preliminary information regarding the order and accepted its contents. It was emphasized that Polish–Swedish economic relations in the paper-making industry had existed before the war. In general, nothing should prevent the filling of the order.[67]

On 18 August the instruction regarding negotiations concerning the economic arrangement with Sweden was sent to Sokolnicki.[68] The document proposed opening negotiations for a loan of 26 million dollars for the first nine to twelve months after the war according to the demand for the goods based pre-war prices (considering the upsurge in prices – 34 million dollars). The Polish side intended to secure the quickest and most efficient way of supplying Swedish goods to Poland. In exchange it was ready to take on commitments concerning the supplies of Polish coal to Sweden. The agreement was to be based mostly on the loan granted to Poland, guaranteed by coal supplies, which, as it seemed, was not an issue for the Swedes. The Polish negotiators demanded that the loan be repaid over a long time, as long as ten years, due to the destruction of the country during the war. The basis for the mutual relations was still to be the treaty of commerce and navigation of 1924, whereas the trade quota arrangement of 1936 was treated as expired by the Polish side. The Poles were unwilling to raise the issue of the management of Swedish assets invested in Poland or other receivables from before the war. The position was voiced that these issues would be solved by a multilateral international agreement concluded after the war. In line with the instruction, any future arrangement was not to be a long term economic one, but a single, ad hoc agreement, meeting the needs of both parties. The basic postulate of Poland was a loan immediately following the signing of the agreement. The purpose was also to negotiate the best terms for repayment. The loan was to be sufficient to cover the purchase and transport of the goods included on the government list. The sum of 34 million dollars would allow for a free handling of foreign currency from coal sales. The limit for repayment was set at five years, and the annual interest rate could not exceed 3 percent. The repayments were to be based 'on mutual allocation of free exchange.' It was

---

[67] RA, UD 1920 års dossiersystem, HP 64, vol. 2736, copy of letter by E. Grafström from Sweden's board of industry to the National Reconstruction Board, Stockholm, 3 VII 1944.
[68] AAN, HI/I/86, instruction regarding the negotiations on the economic arrangement with Sweden, [August 1944].

assumed that Poland's future trade balance would be positive, and that is why it was necessary to avoid clauses on clearing exchange. The Polish government wanted to make purchases directly or through authorised companies. Sea transport, used for the exchange of goods, was to be provided by the Swedes, although the Polish government would reserve the right to use vessels that were either Polish or chartered by Poland. Envoy Sokolnicki was burdened with developing a preliminary draft of the agreement based on the obtained instruction. Finally, it was pointed out that it was important for the Polish government to sign the arrangement and begin the exchange of goods. The list of Swedish goods demanded by Poland, which were to be exported there during the first year after the war, included: raw materials (especially iron ore), high speed cutting steel, metal tools, measuring and workshop instruments, drilling tools, ball bearings, electric welders, machine tools, saw blades, excavators, road rollers, compressors with associated fittings, mixers, combustion engine pumps, power units, tractors, one- or two-cylinder engines, electrical equipment, cereal seeds, scythes, breeding cattle, horses, diary equipment. The government instruction also included a proposal that Sweden deliver equipment for two plants producing edible animal fat and plants producing insulating boards from wood pulp. In line with the pre-war Polish–English coal arrangement, Poland was entitled to meet 47 percent of Swedish coal demand. It was calculated that in the post-war period Sweden would demand approximately 6 million tons of coal annually, of which Poland would supply 2.785 million tons. According to the average price of 30–31 shillings per ton, the value of export of the Polish coal was estimated at 85 million shillings 17 million dollars (US).

In the instruction of 18 August, the Minister of Foreign Affairs Tadeusz Romer announced that Envoy Sokolnicki would decide on the form and moment for addressing the Swedish government to initiate talks on an economic arrangement 'without risking refusal.'[69] The minister emphasized, 'It is important for the Polish government to conduct the talks and, afterwards, to sign the arrangement as soon as possible so that there was certainty that the goods included on the import list would be delivered to Poland in the expected time frames.' In the face of economic negotiations with the USA, the Polish government wanted to find out to what extent it could count on the import from Sweden. The Polish side was keen to quickly reach agreement, even without signing, provided this would be possible at any moment. According to experts,

---

[69] Ibidem, letter by the Minister of Foreign Affairs to Polish Envoy to Stockholm H. Sokolnicki, 18 VIII 1944.

the rapid launch of industry was dependent on obtaining the supplies of goods from Sweden included on the list drawn up in London.[70] In addition, on awaiting talks with the Americans about future economic aid, the Polish government wanted to know what goods and in what amounts may be expected from Sweden,[71] since the Ministry of Foreign Affairs assumed that part of the relief aid for Poland would not be received from the UNRRA. As far as agricultural goods were concerned these included seeds (2 thousand tons), scythes (400 thousand tons), machines and tools for the processing of agricultural products, as well as special varieties of breeding livestock, including cows (500 thousand) and horses (100 thousand) from Sweden.[72]

On 31 August 1944, the Ministry of Foreign Affairs sent a letter to the Polish Legation in Stockholm with instructions for Engineer Borys Saryusz-Zaleski from the Department of Agriculture at the Ministry of Industry, Trade and Shipping, regarding the negotiations with Sweden. The Undersecretary of State, Kuźniarz, requested Saryusz-Zaleski to 'remain in close contact with the Polish Legation during the negotiations to provide professional explanations concerning the agricultural import to Poland and in to obtain the final decision whether and when the conditions necessary for conducting concrete talks with the Swedish experts in the form of orders, concluding transactions etcetera will be in place.'[73] The ministry offered to purchase 400 thousand scythes from the Odenberg and Olson company. It was pointed out that as part of the UNRRA supplies Sweden was put forward as the additional supplier of 1 million scythes, which would meet Polish demand. What is more, there was a plan to purchase 60 stallions and 60 mares of the *nordsvenska* breed. Just as in the case of scythes, however, as part of the agreed UNRRA supplies with Sweden specified as the seller, there was an intention to order an additional 100 stallions and 100 mares. The Ministry intended to purchase 1 thousand heifers and 100 lowland black-piebald bull calves, as well as 1 thousand tons of oats, 600 tons of rye and 400 tons of wheat. For the seeds, there was a proposal to renew relations with the Polish–Swedish seed production company Svalöf, but the Ministry of Defence was unable to provide the final quantities of the seeds. The demand for machines and dairy equipment also remained unspecified. There was an interest in 10

---

[70] Ibidem, note by W. Czyszkowski regarding Polish–Swedish commercial negotiations, London, 4 XII 1944.
[71] Ibidem.
[72] AAN, HI/I/86, note, 18 IX 1944.
[73] Ibidem, copy of letter by T. Kuźniarz, Undersecretary of State to the Ministry of Industry, Trade and Shipping, to B. Saryusz-Zaleski, London, 16 VIII 1944.

9. POLISH-SWEDISH ECONOMIC COOPERATION

sets of equipment for the collection and urban distribution of pasteurized milk with a daily processing capacity of 45 thousand litres and approximately 100–200 sets of devices for making butter (the daily capacity of which was processing 10–25 thousand litres of milk into butter). Towards the close of September, the Ministry of Industry, Trade and Shipping extended the demand list with 1 thousand arithmometres worth about 200 thousand dollars.[74] In exchange, Poland offered to sell Sweden sugar and salt.

The *Statens återuppbyggnadsnämnd* (National Reconstruction Board) accepted the Polish proposals. The export of the amount of grain determined by the Poles did not pose a problem. The same was true of horses and cattle. In contrast, the import of Polish sugar was excluded as the Swedes had the means to produce it on their own. The import of Polish salt became an issue, as prior to the war Sweden had imported it in small amounts from Poland. The Board left the issue open for Poland to determine the price and export options for the countries from which salt was currently purchased (Germany, the Soviet Union, Great Britain and the Netherlands).[75]

The Polish side was clearly striving to formalize the bilateral agreements. On 13 September 1944, Pilch, at a meeting with Sohlman, made an unofficial and preliminary declaration that the Polish government was willing to begin economic negotiations on bilateral relations following the conclusion of the war. He warned him that Sokolnicki was planning to hold a meeting on this matter with Minister Günther. They both informed the Swedish partners that they had obtained full powers from their government regarding this issue. According to the instruction from the government, Pilch highlighted that the basis for future relations should continue to be the Polish–Swedish treaty of 1924. Coal was to remain the main Polish export commodity (3 million tons annually). Poland counted on a long term loan of 35 million dollars, out of which 2–4 million dollars was expected as soon as possible. Sohlman requested that the Polish proposals were submitted in writing. For his part, he demonstrated interest, but at the same time pointed out, on examining the Polish proposal, that Sweden would also be forced to consider matters of general policy.[76]

---

[74] Ibidem, letter by J. Kożuchowski, Secretary-General to the Ministry of Industry, Trade and Shipping, to the Ministry of Foreign Affairs, [received on] 29 I 1944.
[75] RA, UD 1920 års dossiersystem, HP 64, vol. 2736, letter by S. Sahlin to UD, [received on] 15 VIII 1944.
[76] Ibidem, memorandum regarding Polish–Swedish post-war economic relations (T. Göransson), Stockholm, 13 IX 1944.

In another meeting on 3 October 1944, Sokolnicki presented the Swedes with the memorandum regarding future Polish–Swedish economic relations for the first twelve months after the war together with the list of goods Poland intended to buy from Sweden. As a preliminary remark, Sohlman pointed out that before taking any specific actions he would rather wait for the result of the Polish–Soviet talks in Moscow. Regarding Poland's idea of Gunnar Hägglöf's engagement in the Polish affairs, he expressed doubt whether he, considering his service as envoy to the Dutch and Belgian governments and service as plenipotentiary in the Swedish–American and Swedish–British negotiations, was the right person for the task. Talks with the Poles were of a general, preliminary, and non-mandatory character. According to Pilch, the reasons of personal importance could be of some significance here, as, allegedly, Sohlman's ambition was to conduct the talks with Poland on his own. The Polish diplomat clearly comforted himself and at the same time underestimated that the Swede was very much interested in the course of Prime Minister Mikołajczyk's visit to Moscow.[77] Perhaps this optimistic attitude was the result of Sohlman's discussion of the Polish memorandum with the Poles on the next day.[78]

The meeting on 4 October was attended by counsellor Pilch and T. Olszowski. Sohlman was accompanied by Tord Göransson, who recorded the minutes. The Swedes confirmed that they accepted Polish quota demands for cereal seeds, breeding cattle and horses, but did not plan to import salt and sugar from Poland, as they either had their own stocks (sugar) or planned to purchase supplies from other countries (salt). Sohlman pointed to the issue of the possible sanctions imposed by the Allies on the Swedish commercial fleet. He was not certain, however, whether the vessels would be involved in commercial relations with Poland. The Poles assured him that the Baltic Sea area was not subject to any limitations. The Swede mentioned that telephone equipment was not part of the Polish quota proposals and also expressed his dissatisfaction with the small amount of electrical equipment. The issue had to be expressed firmly, as Sokolnicki noted, 'we will lose support for our loan demands from our friends in Sweden.' Besides, the Swedes considered the *virement* clause (moving loans from one quota to another) hard to accept,

---

[77] E. Boheman made a rather accurate assessment of R. Sohlman's activity in his wartime memoires: 'his tolerance for the Soviet Union and its policy was often far beyond the boundaries of reason and therefore I considered it unacceptable.' E. Boheman, *På vakt. Kabinettssekreterare...*, p. 25.

[78] AAN, HI/I/86, letter by H. Sokolnicki, Polish Envoy to Stockholm, to the Ministry of Foreign Affairs, Stockholm, 14 X 1944.

whereas they agreed to replace the automatic *virement* clause by a *contrahendo* clause, namely a preliminary contract listing the goods and the prices that were to be covered by the future loan agreement. Sohlman also wanted Swedish companies, with branches in Poland, to receive special treatment. He reiterated that Polish partners constantly highlighted the loyalty of the Swedish capital. An important issue discussed during the meeting were the coal supplies for Sweden; Sohlman asked about the earliest possible date for beginning the transport. He mentioned six months from the end of the war and the Swedish order of 8 million tons of coal per year, of which Poland's contribution would be 3.76 million tons. Sokolnicki declined to commit to a time for the deliveries. In addition, instead of the arbitration agreement, the Poles proposed the establishment of government commissions the sessions of which were to be held quarterly. Points of contention were to be settled separately in each individual contract, although one commercial partner from the Polish side, namely the government commission for purchases, pointed to the practical value of developing a standard procedure for the resolution of disputes. The Swedes considered the Polish suggestion of a 3 percent interest rate to be too low. They referred to the example of Swedish national liabilities, for which the rate was set at 3.5 percent, and of a loan to the Soviet Union, the rate of which was higher still. Besides which, Sohlman inquired about the date of repayment of the earlier, outstanding loans.[79]

This first meeting made it possible for both sides to become acquainted with mutual expectations. Previously determined priorities were confirmed. The loan's interest rate, a contested issue, seemed not to pose problem.

Sokolnicki and Pilch had already decided beforehand to create an atmosphere for further economic negotiations thanks to having established closer contacts with the Swedish economic circles, with whom the relations during the war they described as 'rather loose.' The consent of the Ministry of Industry, Trade and Shipping to provide a small loan (50 pounds) for the promotion of Poland made a series of conferences and receptions possible, which were attended by representatives of companies operating in Poland prior to the war. In September meetings took place attended by Norrman (ASEA), Norlander (Sveaexport), Magnusson and Grounes (Sandviken), Raab and Jacobson (the Johnsons concern), Brolin (Karlstad Mekaniska Verkstad), Magnuson and Bylund (Defibrator), Hellstedt (Separator), Ström

---

[79] Ibidem, attachment no. 2 to confidential letter by the Polish Envoy to Stockholm H. Sokolnicki to the Ministry of Foreign Affairs, Stockholm, 14 X 1944; RA, UD 1920 års dossiersystem, HP 64, vol. 2736, memorandum regarding Polish–Swedish commercial relations, Stockholm, 4 X 1944.

and Kollberg (Sweden's board of coal), Vinell (Swedish Export Association), Calisendorf (Enskilda Banken) as well as representatives of other companies and institutions.[80] Whereas, the meeting of the board of the Swedish–Polish Chamber took place on 26 September. Following these meetings and talks the Polish diplomats thought that, 'The representatives of industrial and coal sector are most enthusiastic about our projects [...] The least enthusiastic are the representatives of banking sector.' At the same time, they highlighted that the investors were far kinder towards Poland than towards the Soviet Union, because, 'For the local economic spheres the very form of trade with the Russian market, which is alien to the capitalist system, is rather objectionable.' Hence the allure of the Polish market, which was smaller than that of Russia. In addition, the Poles received the news of the Swedish–Soviet negotiations, which the Swedes were disappoint by:

> It can also be expected that some preparatory works connected with the new Swedish–Russian credit agreement, which have been conducted for some time now by the local Soviet commercial representation, put off some representatives of Swedish industry due to the ruthlessness in putting forward various claims towards Swedish industry. The purpose is most probably to extend certain production departments, and thereby to intensify some deliveries to Russia.

The news was vague and unproven, but they strengthened the Polish Legation's hope talks regarding the Polish–Swedish economic arrangement. It was known from the industrialists that the Swedish Ministry of Foreign Affairs put pressure on them to accept Russian demands. In connection with this, Rolf Sohlman from the trade department of UD was accused of Russophilia, reinforced him being married to a Russian who sympathized with the Bolsheviks. To some extent it was anticipated that, 'Independently of our political situation we may most probably count on great sympathy especially from the local industrial spheres, and expect a certain cautiousness from the Swedish authorities.' It was hoped, however, that it would be possible to

---

[80] AAN, HI/I/86, attachment no. 3 to letter by Polish Envoy to Stockholm H. Sokolnicki to the Ministry of Foreign Affairs, Stockholm, 14 X 1944. The Ministry of Industry, Trade and Shipping at the request of Envoy Sokolnicki agreed that the Polish Legation in Stockholm used the 50 pounds – primarily allocated for the training of experts in sea fishing – to prepare materials for the commercial negotiations with Sweden and to cover the costs of representation, according to the request of Envoy Sokolnicki. See Ibidem, telegram by the Polish Envoy to Stockholm H. Sokolnicki to the Ministry of Foreign Affairs, Stockholm, 5 IX 1944; Ibidem, letter by the Ministry of Foreign Affairs to the Ministry of Industry, Trade and Shipping, 11 IX 1944; Ibidem, copy of letter by General Secretary of the Ministry of Industry, Trade and Shipping J. Kożuchowski to the Ministry of Foreign Affairs, 13 IX 1944.

return to the pre-war Polish coal supplies to Sweden, even more so that, according to the Poles' knowledge, the Swedes, during talks with Soviet representatives, were to be informed that they could expect coal supplies initiated by Russia, but that the coal would not necessarily be Russian. In the legation representatives of the Swedish coal companies started to appear who had been informed by the Legation of Great Britain that starting transports from the British Isles was unworkable. The companies that found themselves on the so-called black list were excluded from the cooperation. What was unclear was the future of the companies that had paid for coal and imported it before the war to the *treuhänder*. The adopted position was not outright. On 13 October Sokolnicki, informed the Ministry of Foreign Affairs that the Johnson company, one of the main coal importers, 'is ready to accept the first payment in pounds sterling and will provide the allocation of steel in exchange for being included in the future coal import.'[81] This position, which was beneficial for Poland, was conclusive for Sokolnicki: 'The company is currently going along with us, by facilitating our gaining orientation in some factories' production capacity as well as by showing its readiness to make it easier for us to place orders for the construction of ships at local shipyards.' The envoy nevertheless did not make a final decision and waited for the arrival of Julian Cybulski, director of the Department of Industry at the Ministry of Industry, Trade and Shipping, who was to conduct the final stage of the negotiations with the Swedes.

By preliminary talks the Polish side had to consider Swedish reservations mostly concerning the excessive quantity of raw materials and semi-finished products included in the list of Polish demands. The tone of the commentary indicated that the Poles acknowledged the Swedish point of view: 'our list seems to be too detailed and in practice it would undoubtedly have to be substantially altered.' It was also noticed: 'one cannot shake off an impression that the list may be of only theoretical importance.' According to the Swedish postulates, the telephone and electric equipment was included:

> The export of this equipment prior to the war from Sweden to Poland was one of the most important items of the Swedish export agenda. In the face of the damage of Polish telephone lines during the war, the absence of telephone equipment on the list of our future orders is unintelligible. On the contrary, a concern should be expressed that this may be caused by the competition, especially American. The same thing may be said about the ASEA company,

---

[81] Ibidem, telegram by the Polish Envoy H. Sokolnicki to the Ministry of Foreign Affairs, 13 X 1944.

which believes that the quantities of electrical equipment, included in our quota list, are disproportionately small.[82]

An argument in favour of considering the Swedish reservations was the conviction that, 'the support from the Ericsson and ASEA companies towards our claims regarding the loan is very important and we must have these companies support us, and not be against us, or alternatively, have them express their so-called *désintéressement*.' The Swedes warned that the UNRRA would be mostly expecting the deliveries of food (not installations) and that is why it was worth considering cooperation with Sweden around non-consumable goods. The Polish offer regarding orders in Sweden was passed on to *Statens industrikommission*, where a counter-proposal of the presented quota list was to be prepared. It seemed that the Swedes accepted the proposal of the economic arrangement. They only highlighted their fear that the trade in the hands of the Polish government commission would become centralized. A proposal was put forward that the companies who already had their representative offices in Poland would become the first to be granted the opportunity to conduct direct sales, outside the government commission. The Poles reassured the Swedes that a compromise on this matter was highly probable. For the Swedes it was also very important that the Poles try to obtain a private loan based on a state guarantee. Although in this case obtaining a long-term loan, which was important for the Polish side, was an uncertainty despite a state guarantee.

For the Poles, the initial talks were satisfactory, as the Swedes did not raise any political matters, giving the impression that they were not crucial for the progression of the negotiations. Nevertheless, a careful reading of the report would reveal signs of adverse developments: 'It is vital for the economic interests of Sweden that the talks be continued, but their pace may be slowed down due to the intention of waiting [for] explanations in the meantime [and] solving our political problems in relation to Russia.' It is therefore hard to understand the optimism of the Polish side on this issue, especially because 'one of the more serious representatives of the industry' explained that Sweden could not make any arrangements with the Polish government, which may be significantly reconstructed in the near future, or even based on 'the current representatives in the Lublin Committee.' Despite this, the Polish Legation tried to influence the Swedes to speed up negotiations. The incentive for which was another instruction from the Ministry of Industry, Trade

---

[82] Ibidem, attachment no. 3 to letter by the Polish Envoy to Stockholm H. Sokolnicki to the Ministry of Foreign Affairs, Stockholm, 14 X 1944.

and Shipping developed together with the Ministry of Foreign Affairs and the Ministry of Finance on 31 October, which was sent to Sokolnicki on 9 November. The government in London agreed to increase purchases of electrical and telephone equipment including equipment for telephone exchanges and railways among other things.

Work on the implementation of earlier commitments was still underway. The correspondence on the negotiations shows that Minister Kwapiński attributed a great importance to the fate of Ericsson's daughter company – the Polish Telephone Joint-Stock Company (*Polska Akcyjna Spółka Telefoniczna*, PAST). Referring to the pre-war concession, which was granted in 1922 for twenty-five years,[83] he drew attention to the limitations regarding the development of a state telephone industry, which were unfavourable for Poland. Considering the widespread devastation in many cities, Warsaw in particular, Kwapiński believed that the execution of the concession should only apply to the areas beyond the range of military operations. At that point it was difficult to determine the magnitude of destruction. The talks about potential loss and compensation for the Ericsson company were, therefore, considered by the Polish minister to be premature and he advised not raising the issue during the economic negotiations. The issue was quite complicated, as many years earlier, in exchange for obtaining the so-called match loan, Poland obliged itself to purchase a certain quantity of Ericsson telephone equipment.[84] The assessment of the quality of the Swedish telephone exchanges had to consider compatibility with other communication systems. In Poland, Ericsson's competitor, the English Strowger company operated and additional devices were necessary for their connection with Ericsson technology. This was the reason for the Poles position of non-commitment.[85]

The Polish party also attempted to persuade the Swedes that the transactions with international companies should be carried out by the Polish state apparatus, since many private owners had died during the war and documentation of many companies had been destroyed. What is more, the government intended to carry out reconstructions as part of its specific economic

---

[83] Ibidem, copy of note regarding the PAST concession. Telephone exchanges in Warsaw, Łódź, Lviv, Bydgoszcz, Lublin, Boryslav, Drohobych and Białystok fell under the concession which expired on 1 July 1947.

[84] Ibidem, copy of letter by the Minister of Industry, Trade and Shipping, J. Kwapiński to the Polish Envoy to Stockholm H. Sokolnicki, 4 XI 1944.

[85] Ibidem, note by W. Czyszkowski regarding Polish–Swedish commercial negotiations, London, 4 XII 1944.

plan and import was to be subjected to this, which, while maintaining the overall freedom of trade, required introducing certain restrictions.[86]

Yet, instead of successive reports from the talks with the Swedish negotiators, on 16 November counsellor Pilch sent an alarming letter to Deputy Minister Kożuchowski, where he highlighted, 'Our situation in relation to Sweden is becoming increasingly delicate.' He also suggested that, 'the lack of agreement with Russia sees us increasingly pushed aside. According to Pilch, the Swedes' position towards the Soviet Union was increasingly submissive, which he associated with the policy of isolation used against Stockholm by the Western Allies. It is worth noting the comparison of the current Swedish policy with that at the time of the Third Reich's prevalence in Europe:

> [Sweden] expects to settle its relations with Russia in its own capacity and by means of methods which were successfully applied during its relations with the Germans. Besides, Sweden is aware that for Russia, just like for Germany before, it may be important that it "calmly" encouraged its industry to a closer cooperation with Russia, which is heading more and more towards conducting an intensive policy of rebuilding war damage and increasing its industrial potential by turning it into a more multilateral direction, namely by focusing on the consumer goods production much more than before the war. For Russia it may be important, at least to a small extent, to become independent from the exclusive American supplies or the Anglo-Saxon supplies in general, and therefore Russia's interests are turning to a close cooperation with Sweden, which may be always politically pressured by it and blackmailed as it once was by Germany. Sweden on the other hand is under the spell of its successful actions during the on-going war with Germany, to whom she granted economic concessions for the price of being left alone and for the price of avoiding, as much as possible, political concessions, in order not to risk being accused of too drastic abandonment of its traditional policy of neutrality. What is characteristic for the Swedish society – extremely disciplined and suffering from an overall inferiority complex – is that such an approach towards the problem is generally convenient for it, more so that the fear [towards] Russia is common here.[87]

As a result, both the government spheres and the economic spheres started to yield to the Soviet demands: 'Criticism towards everything that is Russian is avoided, future commercial relations with Russia are discussed, and at the same time a lot of caution is being shown towards us, while emphasizing our

---

[86] Ibidem, letter by Minister of Foreign Affairs to Polish Envoy to Stockholm H. Sokolnicki, London, 9 XI 1944.
[87] Ibidem, copy of letter by T. Pilch, counsellor to the Polish Legation in Stockholm, to J. Kożuchowski, Stockholm, 16 XI 1944.

"strange obstinacy" and uncompromising attitude in reaching agreement with Russia.' Therefore, in the face of supply difficulties, Sweden:

> decided *nolens volens* to implement the policy from 1940 – under which it concluded the first serious commercial arrangement and provided Russia with loans – involving seeking compensation in Russia both in the sphere of export and, especially, in the sphere of import, for it is believed that Russia may supply Sweden with a certain amount of raw materials, or perhaps even coal, as Russia keeps moving further west and towards the annexation of the Silesian coal basin.

Sweden wanted coal. On 27 November, during his visit in London, Boheman commented on Sweden's economic needs in the upcoming months. He talked about the lack of coal and hoped that at least part of it would be from Poland, highlighting that the Swedes worried little about the source of coal, if their basic needs were satisfied.[88]

In practice, the Swedes began to avoid contact with the staff of the Polish Legation. The meeting on 4 October 1944 was the only official meeting that took place and where negotiations continued. Later, there would only be very detached, non-committal, private conversations. Pilch claimed, 'silence ensued.' Contact was denied using various excuses. The actual reason was the weakening political position of the Polish government in exile. The suspension of the negotiations with Pilch and Sokolnicki coincided with the fiasco of Prime Minister Mikołajczyk's visit to Moscow and the establishment of relations with the PKWN representative by Envoy Staffan Söderblom.

Pilch also drew attention to the increasingly efficient activity of the Union of Polish Patriots in Sweden (ZPP). At first, this activity centred on the circle of Polish refugees. Later, Jerzy Pański began to reach out to various Swedish companies interested in trade with Poland. He promised them intermediation and major facilitations. As Pilch noted: 'Even if major Swedish companies will not take these steps seriously, the result will be nevertheless even greater cautiousness towards us and pushing our issues aside.' Another issue was that following the conclusion of the war various Swedish entrepreneurs requested Polish consulates and the legation mediate in contracts with new or former, pre-war contracting parties. They were informed, however, that this was impossible, as the 'political situation in Poland, is, as we know, un-

---

[88] NA, FO, 371/43509, note from the conversation between D. Foot and E. Boheman, 27 XI 1944.

clear, and until its conclusion establishing any contacts with Polish manufacturers is not permitted.'[89] It also transpired that the character of the negotiations with the representatives of the Polish Legation could have been exclusively instrumental. One of Pilch's Swedish interlocutors stated frankly, 'what will be done today with the Polish government in London would certainly be accepted by Lublin if things went in that direction.'[90] What proved to be the most effective, according to Pilch, were Pański's efforts to obtain Swedish humanitarian aid for the people from the areas occupied by the Soviet army. Pilch summed up, saying, 'our political situation has currently weighted over our economic arrangements.' According to Pilch, it was coal that was the chief Polish asset in the negotiations with Sweden:

> This final argument was also the reason why I defined the coal-related issues in our draft of the arrangement right away in detail, without waiting, as one usually does, for further negotiations. My intention in doing so in this difficult moment for us was to withdraw our "visiting card", even though the opportunities it created for us were rather favourable.[91]

Towards the close of 1944, the Ministry of Foreign Affairs requested specific information about the possibility of supplies of accommodation and hospital barracks from Sweden. The Ministry of Labour and Social Welfare was prepared to delegate experts from London to conduct the negotiations on this matter.[92] In London there was confusion about the assessments provided by an UNRRA expert who estimated the Swedish production potential as far as the barracks were concerned to be much lower than the estimates of counsellor Pilch. The Polish Legation in Stockholm suggested a purchase of over 2.1 million square metres of barracks over six months, whereas the UNRRA estimated that the Swedes could deliver 500 thousand square metres. Consequently, the Ministry of Foreign Affairs asked Pilch for an explanation.[93]

---

[89] AAN, Polish Legation in Stockholm, 103, correspondence from May 1945 between Polish Consul to Malmö B. Żukowski and Swedish companies: Broderna Rejme – Boras, Oscar L. Wallin – Smålands Taberg, and letter to the Polish Legation in Stockholm regarding the contacts of A. Esklung with the Łódź Plush and Carpet Factory, pp. 3–9.
[90] AAN, HI/I/86, copy of letter by T. Pilch, counsellor to the Polish Legation in Stockholm, to J. Kożuchowski, Stockholm, 16 XI 1944.
[91] Ibidem.
[92] AAN, HI/I/86, telegram by the Ministry of Foreign Affairs to the Polish Legation in Stockholm, 15 XII 1944.
[93] Ibidem, letter by the Ministry of Labour and Social Welfare to the Ministry of Foreign Affairs, 25 XI 1944.

9. POLISH-SWEDISH ECONOMIC COOPERATION

At the outset of December, the Polish Legation became acquainted with the offer of SKF, which, prior to the war, had a large warehouse with its products in Warsaw. Per Olof Silfverskiöld, the current representative of SKF in Poland who, in the common view, compromised himself due to his pro-German sympathies, attempted to redeem himself and repeatedly emphasized his pro-Polish attitude. It was through him that SKF paid 10 thousand crowns to the account of the poverty-stricken children of Warsaw.[94] The ministerial list included 50 tons of ball bearings. Pilch argued that the offer by SKF (Swedish ball bearing factory AB), which included the delivery of over 257 tons of bearings in the first year after the war, was worth accepting. He noticed that this quantity covered Polish demand for a three-month period in the year 1939, this excluding the bearings for cars, aircraft and other specialist machinery and that accepting SKF's offer would grant Poland the support of this company, which was very influential in Sweden, at further negotiations.[95]

In response to the 14 October report by the Polish Legation in Stockholm, the Ministry of Industry, Trade and Shipping, ignoring the letter by counsellor Pilch of 16 November 1944, completed the instructions about further economic negotiations with Sweden. London considered it a wise tactic not to provoke Sweden until the negotiations were formally concluded. It was explained unofficially to the Swedes that the Polish government understood their cautiousness and was ready to continue talks in confidence. The Polish side agreed to postpone the signing of the contract until a time when the international situation had become clearer and Polish–Soviet relations were regulated. At the same time, the Poles saw no obstacles to agreements on issues regarding future Polish–Swedish trade, or even to drawing up the entire text for arrangements that could be only concluded later. The legation made the Swedes aware that the PKWN was far from representing Polish society, that its long-term existence was in doubt and that, naturally, none of its arrangements would be acknowledged by the legitimate Polish government. The ministry asked whether it would be advisable, despite the difficult position of the Polish government, to conclude certain current transactions by private Polish companies, for instance the Gdynia-Ameryka Line (GAL) joint-stock company order for 4 cargo ships, 6 fishing trawlers and 10 fishing cutters. The issue of the initial date for delivery of coal supplies to Sweden was put bluntly. It was stated in the instruction that it was mainly dependant

---
[94] Ibidem, letter by T. Pilch, counsellor to the Polish Legation in Stockholm, to the Ministry of Industry, Trade and Shipping, Stockholm, 2 XII 1944.
[95] Ibidem.

on two factors which were at that moment impossible to determine – the extent of damages in the coal mines and the condition of communication infrastructure between Silesia and the ports. Where damages were small, the plan was to begin deliveries within six months of the conclusion of the war. Further, it was explained that, according to the new Polish interpretation, the matter of the telephone equipment purchase was not included in the match agreement to which the Swedish negotiators referred. At the time, the Swedes forced Poland purchase additional products manufactured by L. M. Ericsson, but this was an ad hoc incident and not the subject of any larger financial arrangement. The demand list was to be completed by the order for a battery of accumulators for the submarines interned in Sweden – *ORP Sęp* and possibly *ORP Wilk*.[96]

The essential demand of the Polish side continued to be a loan in Sweden for goods, whereas its disbursement would occur immediately following the signing of economic arrangement to facilitate orders with Swedish companies at the close of 1944. The optimal sum for the loan was thought to be 34 million dollars. Within the time limit no shorter than five years and in annual instalments of approximately 8.5 million dollars, the loan would need to be repaid, together with the accrued interest. These repayments would represent half of the value of Polish coal supplied to Sweden. The second half would be the free exchange from the Swedish market. Naturally, the Polish–Swedish arrangement could not include the goods that were to be part of the UNRRA supplies for Poland, unless they were purchased in Sweden on the UNRRA's account. This, however, went beyond the Polish–Swedish negotiations. The greatest problem was the issue of handling former Polish liabilities towards Sweden. The Swedes expected that Poland would oblige itself to repay the amounts due by means of post-war export. For the Polish side such a solution was unacceptable as this would create a precedent for other creditors, who could require the payment of the debts in the most difficult period of the country's reconstruction. The Ministry of Treasury estimated Poland's debt to be approximately 100 million crowns. In December 1944, analyst Witold Czyszkowski supposed that the Swedes would not engage themselves

---

[96] AAN, HI/I/86, draft of letter by the Ministry of Industry, Trade and Shipping to the Ministry of Foreign Affairs regarding economic negotiations with Sweden, n.p., 1944. [no exact date provided]. The instructions, supporting the position of the negotiators in Stockholm, but not as detailed as their earlier drafts: AAN, Ministry of Industry, Trade and Shipping (London), 92, letter by J. Kożuchowski, Deputy Minister of Industry, Trade and Shipping, to T. Pilch, counsellor to the Polish Legation in Stockholm, 15 I 1945; Ibidem, letter by T. Łychowski, director of the Department of Economy and Trading to T. Pilch, counsellor to the Polish Legation in Stockholm, 17 I 1945, pp. 328–329.

in further talks on post-war deliveries for Poland if the issue remained unsettled. He, therefore, proposed a financial agreement postponing the payment of the former debts for about five years.[97]

These considerations nonetheless turned out to be pointless. Pilch was right. Some divergences in the negotiations did not have a decisive impact on the reserved attitude of the Swedish side. What prevented the Swedes from progressing with the negotiations was the uncertain political position of the Polish government. Hägglöf wrote to Envoy Prytz: 'No one can predict the fate of the Polish government in London. On attempting to guess, it should be noted that most probably the one to act in Warsaw after the announcement of ceasefire will not be the government.'[98]

It is hardly surprising then that the Polish government in exile was not a credible borrower, even more so because the support for the Polish government in London would be very much frowned upon in Moscow.[99] Nevertheless, the Swedes were unwilling to officially send the Poles away with nothing. Sokolnicki was assured of the good will of the Swedish government and of its interest, especially with the import of Polish coal, and at the same time they asked for more detailed information about the excavation prospects and the sea transport of coal to Sweden immediately following the liberation, which could turn out to be useful in the future. In his war memoirs, published in 1947, Jan Kwapiński wrote, not without reason, with disappointment, that the plan of concluding a trade agreement with Sweden, prepared by the Polish government in exile, was wilfully used during the negotiations with the Warsaw government.[100] It is possible that some details of the ongoing negotiations, were, already at their initial stage, forwarded to Moscow and to the PKWN by Staffan Söderblom, who, on finding out about, for example, the plan of creating five transit camps on Polish borders, asked for permission to consult with Stefan Jędrychowski and Commercial Attaché Wojciech Chabasiński on this matter.[101]

According to the Ministry of Industry, Trade and Shipping, the Polish Legation in Stockholm should nevertheless do everything it could to prevent the negotiations from being aborted. What was considered crucial was the

---

[97] AAN, HI/I/86, note by W. Czyszkowski regarding Polish-Swedish commercial negotiations, London, 4 XII 1944.
[98] RA, UD 1920 års dossiersystem, HP 64, vol. 2735, copy of letter by G. Hägglöf (UD) to B. Prytz, Swedish Envoy to London, Stockholm, 24 XI 1944.
[99] Ibidem.
[100] J. Kwapiński, 1939–1945 (kartki z pamiętnika), London 1947, p. 81.
[101] RA, UD 1920 års dossiersystem, HP 64, vol. 2736, letter by S. Söderblom, Swedish Envoy to Moscow to R. Sohlman, Moscow, 5 XII 1944.

GAL order for ships with simultaneous payment of advances on all receivables, which were to be settled following the signing of the Polish–Swedish treaty. It was believed that such transactions did not pose any risk, secured the delivery of goods necessary for Poland, and on top of that should contribute to the strengthening of Poland's position within Swedish economic circles. In addition, the ministry decided that, just as in the case of aid campaigns conducted by the UNRRA, consent would be granted for sending Swedish aid to part of the territory of Poland annexed by the Soviet armies: 'It would even seem politically beneficial if our legation in Stockholm, officially and out loud, communicated such an attitude, and even, if possible, actively participated in the organisation of such aid.' At the same time, it was advised that the efforts not be neglected and the attempts to organize such campaigns in the territories permanently controlled by the Germans were prioritized in circumstances when Sweden, apart from Switzerland, was the only country who could allow itself to do so.[102]

Nevertheless, on 7 December, counsellor Pilch again confirmed, 'In the meantime, these negotiations have not moved forward.' He explained that he was not urging the Swedes so as not to risk the response that the negotiations were postponed to the moment of resolving the political situation. At the same time, the Polish diplomatic mission maintained direct relations with Swedish economic circles, including the members of Sweden's board of industry, working on the list of demands prepared by the Polish side. Owing to these contacts, Pilch unofficially found out about the Swedes' reservations concerning both import and export goods. In his letter he provided a detailed analysis of the proposals for changes that were presented by Sweden's board of industry. In fact, at that point they were not submitted by the Swedes and could be changed by UD, but for Pilch it did not seem very probable.[103] The Swedes were to agree to the delivery of 1.2 million tons of iron ore as well as of 25 thousand tons of both cellulose and wood pulp. Other raw materials were provided in small amounts. There was no consent for any quantities of high-speed steel cutting tools, drills, cutters, saws (up to 30 percent of Polish demand), files (up to 50 percent). The quantity of other products was substantially reduced, especially for electrical hand drills and welders. The Swedes agreed to supply three-phase motors, but refused to supply electrical conductors. In most cases they did not object to supplies of chemical

---

[102] AAN, HI/I/86, copy of note for the Minister of Industry, Trade and Shipping regarding commercial negotiations with Sweden, London, 4 XII 1944.
[103] Ibidem, letter by T. Pilch, counsellor to the Polish Legation in Stockholm, to J. Kwapiński, Minister of Industry, Trade and Shipping, Stockholm, 7 XII 1944.

equipment. Similar was the case with agricultural goods, although the delivery of as many as 400 thousand scythes was excluded. On 15 January Pilch forwarded an additional detailed list of Polish import demands to the Swedish Ministry of Foreign Affairs, which became the condition for the continuation of the negotiations and the signing of the treaty. The Swedes, however, were procrastinating. The National Reconstruction Board pointed out in the letter to UD that, 'in the current circumstances there is no reason to raise the issue of regulating future trade and the issue of payment in the form of a treaty.' The only proposal was to prepare a report with the results of analyses carried out by various supply commissions dealing with the Polish proposals.[104] In contrast to the preliminary analyses from 1944, some items were challenged. The State Food Commission, referring to the poor harvests of 1944, disagreed with the export of 1000 tons of oats.[105] The State Industry Commission had nothing against the orders for machines manufactured in Sweden, but drew attention to the fact that some of the arithmometres were not used in Sweden. The same Commission highlighted that the export of telephone equipment and electrical machines could take place only through subsidiaries of L. M. Ericsson and ASEA. Also, part of the proposals concerning the equipment for post offices and railway lines were questioned.[106] Bearing in mind the detailed analyses prepared by the Swedes, perhaps Pilch was hoping that his talks with the delegation of trade department of UD would continue.

In mid-March 1945, following Pilch's visit to London, subsequent meetings took place. On 14 March, the counsellor talked to Sohlman and confirmed that he would submit the complete list of goods Poland was interested in importing. Pilch also renewed his contacts with the L. M. Ericsson and ASEA.[107] Following Pilch's assurances, the Swedes expected to receive within twelve months 5 million tons of Polish coal valued at 100 million crowns. At the same time, Poland could delivery other goods. The Poles expected payment to be made partially by a loan and partially through funds obtained

---

[104] RA, UD 1920 års dossiersystem, HP 64, vol. 2736, letter by S. Sahlin to the trade department of UD, Stockholm, 23 I 1945.

[105] Ibidem, copy of letter by C. G. Widell (Sweden's board of food – *Statens livskommission*) to the National Reconstruction Board (*Statens återuppbyggnadsnämnd*), Stockholm, 15 I 1945.

[106] Ibidem, copies of classified letters by E. Grafström (Sweden's Board of Industry – *Statens industrikommission*) to the National Reconstruction Board (*Statens återuppbyggnadsnämnd*), Stockholm, 11 I, 23 I 1945.

[107] IPMS, A 11, E/446, copy of letter by T. Pilch, counsellor to the Polish Legation in Stockholm, to Deputy Minister of Industry, Trade and Shipping, J. Kożuchowski, Stockholm, 7 IV 1945.

thanks to the export of coal. Pilch had no option but to accept the position of the Swedes, who in the current political situation were unwilling to assume any commitments, especially loans. He pointed out, however, that for the Polish authorities it was important to prepare the arrangement as quickly as possible so as not to lose time in the period when fundamental political issues would be clarified. Sohlman promised that as soon as Pilch provided detailed specifications for the goods, they would be studied carefully by competent services. He also highlighted the issue of political difficulties. Pilch arrived initially at the number of 1 thousand railway carriages for the transport of coal. He expected that Sweden would begin the transport of food at once. In connection with the planned Swedish humanitarian aid campaign in Poland, he expected that wooden houses worth 50 million crowns would be supplied. Sohlman confirmed that earlier arrangements were binding for the Swedish side, but that it was impossible for him to commit to supplying more houses. Finally, Pilch informed Sohlman confidentially that the Polish–British talks regarding the division of the coal market were in progress. It was initially settled that part of the supplies for Sweden would be handled by Poland, and a possible option would be to transport coal initially from Poland to Great Britain and only then to Sweden.[108] Shortly after this meeting, Pilch confirmed the intention to purchase emergency supplies (food and clothes) in Sweden for around 40 thousand dollars.[109] Sohlman prolonged negotiations, asking for a specific proposal, as well as information as to how and when such transport would be provided.[110]

Meanwhile, the Swedish press called for bolder talks to be held with the Polish communists and Stalin about the import of Upper Silesian coal. On 10 January 1945, the newly launched *Expressen* afternoon daily published an interview with the alleged Minister of Trade to the Polish Provisional Government, the so-called 'Petrowski.' From the article it followed that Sweden could count on the coal supplies from Poland. The text presented a vision where Poland was to be included in the economic system of Scandinavia, following the absorption of vast areas of the German territory.[111] One month later, in that very same daily it was argued that Swedish industry needed direct contact with Poland:

---

[108] RA, UD 1920 års dossiersystem, HP 64, vol. 2736, memorandum regarding Polish proposals, Stockholm, 14 III 1945.
[109] Ibidem, letter by Polish Envoy to Stockholm T. Pilch to R. Sohlman, Stockholm, 19 III 1945.
[110] Ibidem, letter by R. Sohlman to counsellor to the Polish Legation in Stockholm, T. Pilch, Stockholm, 29 III 1945.
[111] 'Lublin-polskt intresse för handeln med Sverige', *Expressen*, 10 I 1945.

9. POLISH-SWEDISH ECONOMIC COOPERATION

A certain well known entrepreneur stated in *Expressen* that to launch trade with Poland in the current circumstances it was crucially important to establish commercial relations as quickly as possible. The current political situation naturally hindered even the preliminary commercial negotiations – our source says – but despite all the difficulties a temporary solution must be devised in the shape of sending a representative and have him investigate the options of launching coal transports for Sweden.'[112]

The publication of the article almost coincided with the announcements of the imminent acquisition of control over Silesia and East Prussia by the Warsaw government and with the press mentioning the need to establish economic cooperation with Poland. Although, concerns were raised about the condition of coal mines and port facilities in Gdynia.[113] The Swedish government was criticised for granting recognition to the Polish government in exile and rhetorical questions were posed whether the Swedish Ministry of Foreign Affairs understood the crucial importance of Polish coal for Sweden.[114] On 11 April, several dailies published correspondence from London, the authors of which were convinced, referring to the Polish pro-Soviet opinion journalist Stefan Litauer, that Polish coal would soon be on its way to Sweden. Pański confirmed these rumours in an interview with the press. On 23 May, the opinion was voiced by *Dagens Nyheter* that even the misunderstandings between the powers 'on a long-term basis should not hinder the economic relations between the two countries, which have become very extensive before the war, especially when it comes to coal.'[115] Other dailies published articles concerning future trade between Poland and Sweden. At the close of April, news was announced that a Swedish delegation had been sent to Poland to begin economic talks.[116]

It was Staffan Söderblom who encouraged his government, as already mentioned, to undertake more courageous action in contacts with the Polish Provisional Government in Warsaw. In mid-March, he called for starting talks on trade, and most importantly, on the issue of coal and coke import by Sweden.[117] At the outset of April, ambassador Modzelewski officially turned

---

[112] 'Våra industrier behöver direkt-kontakt med Polen', *Expressen*, 6 II 1945.
[113] AAN, Norbert Żaba's collection, copy of report by N. Żaba to the Ministry of Information and Documentation, Stockholm, 3 III 1945.
[114] 'Polen i behov av svensk varukredit för inköp av maskiner och avelsdjur', *Expressen*, 29 III 1945.
[115] 'Svenska ombud till Warszawa för förhandling om kolinköp', *Dagens Nyheter*, 23 V 1945.
[116] 'Kontakt med Polen för handelsutbyte', *Expressen*, 31 V 1945.
[117] RA, UD 1920 års dossiersystem, HP 64, vol. 2736, letter by S. Söderblom, Swedish Envoy to Moscow, to R. Sohlman, Moscow, 16 III 1945.

to Söderblom to establish commercial relations. The Swedish Ministry of Foreign Affairs, on 14 April, presented its instruction requiring him to report the readiness of Sweden to send its delegate to Poland to examine the perspectives for the re-establishment of trade. Two days later, Modzelewski convinced Söderblom that in the face of Mikołajczyk's negotiations regarding the reconstruction of the government in Warsaw, the government's recognition by the Western Allies was only a matter of time and that nothing prevented the establishment of bilateral Polish–Swedish relations. At the same time, Modzelewski assured Söderblom that none of the Polish ports were destroyed and that it would soon be possible to use both for the shipment of goods. He also sent a representative of his government to Stockholm to agree the course of the Swedish humanitarian aid campaign in the territory of Poland.[118] In turn, on 22 April, during the accidental meeting of Söderblom, Modzelewski and Minister of Industry Hilary Minc (who had recently visited Moscow) in the Grand Theatre, the Polish ambassador stated that the Swedish delegate would receive a warm welcome in Warsaw. He guaranteed that many millions of tons of coal were waiting for Sweden in Poland. What Poland expected to receive as part of the settlement were trucks, iron ore and machinery. Minister Minc also anticipated that the Swedish side would make its trade fleet available to Poland. The Swedish Ministry of Foreign Affairs instructed Söderblom that the demands put forward by the Polish Provisional Government would be met on the condition that Poland organize the quick transport of coal. There were no objections to this being carried out with the support of the Swedish fleet.[119] In the Polish embassy, on 25 April, Söderblom officially proposed Modzelewski and Minc send Eng to Poland as a Swedish delegate at the Polish government in Warsaw. Modzelewski initially accepted this candidacy and announced detailed talks about the machinery, which were required by Poland, as well as payment methods. He also confirmed for Söderblom that the port in Gdańsk was in good condition. Söderblom, though, met with the Soviet Deputy People's Commissioner for Foreign Affairs, Vladimir Dekanozov, to secure the acceptance of his actions and preliminary permission for a transit visa for Eng.[120] Modzelewski referred to another of Molotov's deputies, Andrey Vyshinsky. For Söderblom, this

---

[118] Ibidem, memorandum regarding the establishment of relations with the Polish government in Warsaw, Stockholm, 24 IV 1945.
[119] Ibidem, memorandum regarding commercial relations with Poland, Stockholm, 25 IV 1945.
[120] Ibidem, memorandum regarding commercial relations with Poland, Stockholm, 28 IV 1945; Ibidem, letter by S. Söderblom, Swedish Envoy to Moscow, to Swedish Minister of Foreign Affairs Ch. Günther, Moscow, 30 IV 1945.

was proof that, 'the Poles were keen to open maritime and telegraphic links with Sweden and Europe at all costs.'[121]

The possible coal import from Poland was a subject of discussion in Swedish parliament. Fears about the political future of Scandinavia were mixed with concerns about Swedish coal supplies. During the closed session of the first chamber of the Swedish parliament, on 19 April, the Minister of Trade, Bertil Ohlin, was asked about the possibility of concluding an agreement with the new Polish authorities regarding coal supply. Ohlin explained that the Swedish government maintained contact with the government in Warsaw concerning the immediate exchange of goods between Poland and Sweden. The goods he mentioned included Polish coal and Swedish machinery, adding that the analysis of the opportunities for the transport of these goods was in progress. At the same time, he highlighted that this contact was not politically motivated. Ohlin also mentioned the Swedish humanitarian aid campaign in Poland, which was not directly connected with the discussions on trade, but the minister believed that it contributed to a favourable atmosphere.[122] In contrast, communist leader Sven Linderot claimed openly that one could not count exclusively on, as in the case of the Western Allies, commercial trade. The starting point would nevertheless have to be political issues. That is why Sweden could buy coal in Poland and gain other benefits.[123]

Meanwhile, Eng started to receive information from the Swedish companies about the interests conducted in Poland, for example with L. M. Ericsson, by *Svenska Tändsticks AB* (Swedish Match AB or *STAB*) and *Allmänna Svenska Elektriska AB* (General Swedish Electric Company or *ASEA*). There was a request for information about both the condition of the estate as well as the fate of the staff.[124] A study by Sven Norrman contained a detailed report about the future of ASEA's daughter company, *Polskie Towarzystwo Elektryczne S. A.* [the Polish Electrical Association Joint Stock Company], which following the September Campaign renewed its production, although on a smaller scale than before the war (before the German aggression it hired 400–450 labourers and from 1940 until the Warsaw Rising 150).

---

[121] Ibidem, telegram by S. Söderblom, Swedish Envoy to Moscow, to UD, Moscow, 29 V 1945.
[122] *Protokoll...*, p. 370.
[123] Ibidem, p. 361.
[124] RA, UD 1920 års dossiersystem, HP 64, vol. 2736, memorandum to the secretary of the legation B. Eng concerning the interests of L. M. Ericsson in Poland, Stockholm, 15 V 1945; Ibidem, memorandum regarding Stab's business matters in Poland, Jönköping, 15 V 1945; Ibidem, S. Norrman: Memorandum concerning the ASEA concern's business matters in Poland, Västerås, 16 V 1945.

The Swedish Export Association sent Eng a list of 43 companies, which in 1940 claimed the right to the debts of Polish companies totalling more than 100 thousand crowns. The Swedish companies demanded compensation of approximately 58.5 million crowns. Within a few years there were considerable changes, as part of the receivables of the Swedish side was taken over by the German banks and therefore in these cases it was Germany that became the addressee of the claims. The association also counted on additional income from the interest.[125]

Modzelewski was also contacted by Ruben Ljundberg, who was negotiating trade with the Soviet Union for a long time as director of a Swedish–Russian Commercial Enterprise (Svensk–Ryska Handelskammaren Service AB). On 8 February 1945, he sent a letter to the ambassador of the Polish Provisional Government in Moscow announcing Sweden's intention to buy 5 million tons of coal and 1 million tons of coke. One month later he sent a list of 13 Swedish companies interested in the import of Polish coal. He expanded the list further in the following month.[126] On 23 April 1945, Modzelewski responded firmly, 'The Polish government is ready to initiate the negotiations regarding coal supplies, but on the condition that normal diplomatic relations between Swedish and Polish governments are established.'[127] Ljundberg and Modzelewski, contrary to during the negotiations conducted by Söderblom, never discussed the issue of the leasing of Swedish locomotives or railway trucks. Yet, on his own initiative, the Swede offered to lend to the Polish side ten special harbour cranes. Following the initial insight, he concluded that only the reloading of coal from railway trucks on to the ships could present some difficulty. As far as he knew, the harbours, the mines and the railway lines were not significantly damaged. On 2 May 1945, Ljundberg informed the head of the State Fuel Commission that Polish partners were ready to send their representative to Stockholm and according to his estimates it would be possible to reach an agreement regarding the issue of coal import within eight days. As he learned, the shipment of Polish coal via the harbours of Gdańsk and Gdynia to Leningrad and to former harbours of the Baltic States was already in progress. The daily volume of reloading was

---

[125] Ibidem, letter by the SAE to B. Eng, Stockholm, 15 V 1945. See detailed specification: RA, UD 1920 års dossiersystem, HP 94, vol. 2373, list of liabilities of Swedish companies in the territories under German, Soviet and Lithuanian occupation (as of April 1940).

[126] RA, UD 1920 års dossiersystem, HP 64, vol. 2736, copies of letters by R. Ljundberg to the Polish Ambassador to Moscow Z. Modzelewski, 8 II, 7 III, 3 IV 1945 r. See AMSZ, issue 27, w. 4, vol. 55, letter by R. Ljundberg, 8 II 1945.

[127] RA, UD 1920 års dossiersystem, HP 64, vol. 2736, copy of telegram by the Polish Ambassador to Moscow Z. Modzelewski to R. Ljundberg, 23 IV 1945.

estimated by him to be 5 thousand tons, but he noticed an opportunity to double it. Ljundberg convinced his Swedish friends that finally there were no obstacles, not even from the Soviet authorities, to purchasing the coal from Poland. He was certain that the Polish Provisional Government would continue its mission and would be granted recognition from the Western Allies as soon as the Polish politicians from London became part of it. Sweden should therefore take the chance to provide itself, as quickly as possible, with a source of energy, indispensable for both industry and households. The board did not feel competent enough to settle complex issues in the field of international policy, but in the analysis prepared for UD it highlighted that guaranteeing the quickest possible coal import to Sweden was the issue of highest priority.[128]

The Swedish diplomacy treated the idea of granting recognition to the government in Warsaw with indifference. Söderblom was to explain in Moscow whether the Polish side was in fact insisting on the official establishment of diplomatic relations. In such a case sending a Swedish delegate to Poland would be pointless. On 18 May, Söderblom was told by Modzelewski, who had just been appointed vice minister of foreign affairs, that the supply of 1 million tons of coal, as early as in the summer of 1945, was highly likely. The Polish diplomat did not mention granting de iure recognition to the government in Warsaw. The meeting between the Swedish envoy and head of the Polish coal industry Topolski, his closest collaborator Biernacki and Attaché Chabasiński took place on 19 May. The Poles proposed that the coal negotiations between Eng and Minc be initiated in Warsaw in the near future.

They announced that during the forthcoming summer months the transport of 1 million tons of coal and 150–200 thousand tons of coke would be possible. The transport of coal from Upper Silesia to Gdańsk, Gdynia and Szczecin required 150 locomotives and 8–10 thousand carriages. Sweden was requested to supply some rolling stock, which was to be settled during the negotiations. The Poles emphasized that the more rolling stock that reached Poland, the quicker the completion of transport would be. They also expected to receive mine scaffolding, trucks, iron ore, machinery, electric motors and

---

[128] RA, UD 1920 års dossiersystem, HP 64, vol. 2736, V.P.M. by K.-G. Ljungdahl regarding information on the subject of Polish coal, Stockholm, 2 V 1945. Ljungberg most probably operated alone and served the interests of his own company. Anyway, no trace has been found of the authorisations from the Swedish government circles. Similar conclusions: A. Kłonczyński, *Stosunki...*, pp. 33–34.

telephones.¹²⁹ They submitted their suggestions in writing to Söderblom on 22 May.

Some Swedish companies began pressurizing their ministry of foreign affairs with letters requesting the Swedish diplomacy mediate in their commercial relations. The company of Oscar Hirsch wanted to purchase zinc, lead and scrap iron.¹³⁰ Companies dealing in fish sales were to make similar requests of the Swedish diplomacy. Utrikesdepartementet (UD) replied constantly that the delegation headed by Eng was to negotiate only the coal supplies and that extensive trade with Poland was surely a matter for the future, and that raising the subject at that moment seemed premature.¹³¹

The Polish Legation in Stockholm underestimated the matter of establishing relations between the Swedish government and the Polish Provisional Government in Warsaw in the economic sphere. On 26 April, Sokolnicki argued, 'the attempts to establish economic relations with us are gaining in momentum every day, more so because the Swedes are convinced that the agreement regarding the Polish matters, whose starting point is Yalta, would be reached.'¹³² At the outset of May, Sokolnicki tried to calm London down, 'The news of the intention to send a delegation only for the purpose of examining the issue of coal supplies is being confirmed.' The delegation was to consist of an expert and an official from the trade department of UD, which, according to Sokolnicki, lowered the rank of the enterprise.¹³³ Towards the close of May, Sokolnicki's tone was similar:

> E[ng], in a conversation with his source described his travel as an introduction to the recognition of the *Lublin* government. When this fact was communicated to Prime Minister [Hansson] he commented on E[ng]'s attitude harshly and announced that he would see him. The Prime Minister also stated that the purpose of E[ng]'s delegation is not only the resolution of the coal issue,

---

[129] RA, UD 1920 års dossiersystem, HP 64, vol. 2736, memorandum concerning coal import from Poland, Stockholm, 19 V, 22 V 1945.

[130] Ibidem, letter by O. Hirsch to UD, Stockholm, 23 V 1945.

[131] Ibidem, letter by I Secretary of UD, T. Göransson, to the company Mauritz Breijer, Stockholm, 30 V 1945.

[132] AAN, Ministry of Industry, Trade and Shipping (London), 92, letter by H. Sokolnicki, Polish Envoy to Stockholm, to the Ministry of Industry, Trade and Shipping, Stockholm, 26 IV 1945, pp. 397–399.

[133] PISM, A 11, E/1099, telegram by H. Sokolnicki, Polish Envoy to Stockholm, to the Ministry of Foreign Affairs, 5 V 1945.

9. POLISH–SWEDISH ECONOMIC COOPERATION

and that Sweden will keep granting recognition to the Polish government in London as long as it would be recognized by the Western Allies.'[134]

However, the British envoy, Victor Mallet, was of a different opinion. He stated that the needs of the Swedes on the matter of coal supply were so great that they were determined to send any representation to Poland if this would guarantee them coal supplies.[135]

---

[134] Ibidem, telegram by H. Sokolnicki, Polish Envoy to Stockholm, to the Ministry of Foreign Affairs, 26 V 1945.
[135] NA, FO, 371/48057, telegram by Envoy of Great Britain to Stockholm V. Mallet to FO, 17 V 1945.

10. The Mission of Brynolf Eng

The delay concerning the formation of the new Polish government following the conference in Yalta caused the Swedes to seek other solutions that would give them economic benefits without political concessions. Among such ideas was Eng's mission. When it was known that Eng would become the Swedish negotiator, Jerzy Pański visited him on 12 May and gave assurances that the output of coal in the Polish mines was increasing successively. The leader of Polish communists in Sweden also convinced Eng that the transport conditions were constantly improving, evidenced by the air connection between Gdańsk and Warsaw. In his opinion, the export of coal could begin immediately following the conclusion of the commercial arrangement and the Polish side would be able to supply Sweden with 5 million tons. He saw no risk in withholding the export from the Soviet authorities, saying, 'the access to coal in new Poland is so extensive, and the extraction – so efficient, that the Russians, due to the current transport opportunities, would not regard it as a breach of their interests.'[1]

The negotiations were to take place in Moscow. It was only following the signing of the coal agreement that Eng was to travel to Warsaw. This guaranteed that the significance of his presence in Poland would not be exclusively political.[2] Sokolnicki intervened with UD and informed the Ministry of Foreign Affairs in London that, 'the announcement made in connection with E[ng's] departure *contains* [underlined in the original] our wishes.'[3] However, when the Swedish dailies began to speculate that it was about more than coal negotiations, Pilch expressed the wish that the Ministry of Foreign Affairs issue another announcement, belying that Sweden wanted to establish diplomatic relations with Warsaw. Pilch's idea was rejected and he was told that the earlier announcement sufficed.[4]

---

[1] RA, UD 1920 års dossiersystem, HP 64, vol. 2736, memorandum by B. Eng, Stockholm, 14 V 1945.
[2] NA, FO, 371/48057, telegram by A. Clerk-Kerr, Ambassador of Great Britain to Moscow, to the FO, Moscow, date unknown.
[3] PISM, A 11, E/1099, telegram by H. Sokolnicki, Polish Envoy to Stockholm, to the Ministry of Foreign Affairs, Stockholm, 2 VI 1945.
[4] RA, UD 1920 års dossiersystem, HP 64, vol. 2736, memorandum regarding the conversation with the counsellor to the Polish Legation in Stockholm T. Pilch, Stockholm, 29 V 1945.

On 31 May, Eng flew to Moscow,[5] and on 6 June he was followed by coal experts Karl-Gustaf Ljungdahl and Ture Ström, which on this occasion was correctly interpreted by Sokolnicki as a sign of progress in the negotiations.[6] These assumptions were confirmed several days later when the Legation of Great Britain reported that the coal quota was initially settled at 1 million tons.[7] In the instruction for the Swedish delegation, which was prepared in the trade department of UD, and the content of which was confirmed with Minister of Trade Bertil Ohlin, it was pointed out that the aim was to conclude the preliminary commercial agreement as quickly as possible, at that point only for the period between 1 July and 30 September 1945 and with the possibility of its extension by another nine months. The Swedes were to find out immediately whether it would be possible to conclude such an agreement having taken the needs of the Polish market into account. From the Polish side, the delegation was to be given confirmation of the delivery of 1 million tons of coal and 150–200 thousand tons of coke within three months for no more than 30 crowns per ton with reference to the FOB clause. This meant that the Polish side was to cover the costs of delivering goods to the harbour and loading them on vessels. The Swedish delegates became familiar with the prices of zinc, zinc white, common salt, potassium salt and paraffin. The Swedish export offer included 300 thousand tons per year of low phosphorus iron ore, whereas in the next three months it was only possible to deliver 150 tons. There was an abundance of high phosphorus iron ore meaning supply was unlimited. From Sweden it was possible to transport 75 thousand square metres of mine scaffolding. Fulfilling the order for 2 thousand carriages was not a problem, on the condition that they each weighed no more than 3 tons and cost no more than 3 thousand crowns. Sweden also offered 200 railway carriages at 12 thousand crowns each. What is more, the Swedish railway would offer up to 1350 carriages and 20 locomotives. As part of the offer, a private owner provided 325 carriages and 5–7 locomotives, all of which came at a high cost (7.50 crowns per carriage per day). Locomotive rental (80 crowns per night) was permitted only in special cases. L. M. Ericsson committed itself to supply telephone equipment at a price of 1.1 million crowns. The Swedes expected detailed specifications of the demands for

---

[5] NA, FO, 371/48057, telegram by V. Mallet, Envoy of Great Britain to Stockholm, to the FO, Stockholm, 30 V 1945.
[6] PISM A 11, E/1099, telegram by H. Sokolnicki, Polish Envoy to Stockholm, to the Ministry of Foreign Affairs, Stockholm, 7 VI 1945.
[7] Ibidem, telegram by H. Sokolnicki, Polish Envoy to Stockholm, to the Ministry of Foreign Affairs, Stockholm, 15 VI 1945.

electrical equipment from the Polish side, although Eng's task was to initially assure the Poles that this issue should not pose any difficulties. At that point the Swedish authorities had not yet made a decision regarding the export of agricultural equipment, but Eng was to confirm the delivery of 100–200 tractors at 13–14 thousand crowns each, 100 harvesters at 11–12 thousand crowns each and 100 threshing machines at 8–9 thousand crowns each. The payments were to be made in Swedish crowns through the Bank of Sweden (*Sveriges Riksbank*), where a special account was to be opened for the Polish authorities. The delegation was to make sure that the provisions of the commercial contract were consistent with the policy of the Swedish government regarding the issue of granting recognition to the government which exercised authority in Poland, although Minister Ohlin claimed that it was not in Sweden's interest to hold on to the principle of not granting recognition to the government in Warsaw before the Western Allies.[8]

On 1 June, Eng and Söderblom (2 June according to Eng's report) visited Modzelewski in the Polish embassy. The Polish Deputy Minister, accompanied by Matwin, First Secretary of the Embassy, and Commercial Attaché Chabasiński, assured the interlocutor that Poland was ready to launch the air connection with Sweden. He confirmed that it was possible to perform a quick launch of coal transport across the sea to Sweden, but that this would only be by means of the Swedish trade fleet and railway. He saw no problem exporting coal and coke in the amount required by the Swedish side (1 million plus 200 thousand tons). He insisted that the Swedish delegation visit Warsaw and that a group of Polish economic experts be sent to Stockholm at the same time. Modzelewski suggested that the arrival of the Polish 'de facto representatives' may stoke unrest since a diplomatic mission of the London government was also operating in the capital. According to Eng's report, Söderblom went on to say that as far as he was concerned, there was no Polish envoy in Stockholm. Whereas Eng himself, according to the instruction from Stockholm, insisted that the initial agreement was signed already in Moscow. Regarding this he referred to communication difficulties, which would significantly delay the conclusion of the principal agreement, and both Swedish and Polish side were pressed for time. Modzelewski also raised the issue of interned submarines. Returning them to the government in Warsaw would

---

[8] RA, UD 1920 års dossiersystem, HP 64, vol. 2736, memorandum for the delegation travelling to Poland, Stockholm, 30 V 1945; Ibidem, notes from the conversation with Minister B. Ohlin, Stockholm, 30 V 1945; Ibidem, excerpt of the protocol of the government session, Stockholm, 8 VI 1945.

constitute a friendly gesture. Söderblom claimed that the issue was complicated and that the Swedish government was not yet prepared to make any settlements. He pointed out that the delegation to be sent to Poland would focus only on technical and economic issues, and therefore no political conditions should be made towards it. The Poles expressed their disappointment with Sweden's inability to supply the desired quantity of trucks of the required class to the Polish side. The Polish negotiators accepted the Swedish reservations concerning the hiring of locomotives with clear disapproval. As far as the coal trade was concerned, the Polish side would be represented by the state-run monopoly, and the Swedish side by individual import companies. The Polish side reserved its right not to maintain commercial relations with the companies which cooperated with Germany and with the Polish government in exile. Eng attempted to explain that the companies which had submitted offers to the government in London were only intending to re-launch their business in Poland and that these were not acts of political demonstration.[9] The Poles generally accepted Swedish proposals, both on import demands as well as the prices of goods which were to be sold to Poland, but the latter would be based on international market prices.

It is worth mentioning that the Ministry of Industry, Trade and Shipping in London produced an analysis showing that export perspectives for Poland were minimal at that point.[10] On 6 July 1945, in the Ministry of Industry, Trade and Shipping, the analytical work regarding the future trade treaty with Sweden was still in progress.[11] On that same day, Söderblom and Eng again held a meeting with Modzelewski and Chabasiński. During their conversation, the Swedish envoy raised the issue of rapid demining of the Baltic Sea routes, which should be conducted in agreement with the Soviet side. Modzelewski agreed to discuss this issue with competent authorities in Moscow. He referred to the issue of sending a commercial delegation from Warsaw to Stockholm, and to the inevitable, in his opinion, local conflict with the Polish Legation. He also suggested that Sweden place at least one cargo

---

[9] RA, UD 1920 års dossiersystem, HP 64, vol. 2736, telegram by S. Söderblom, Swedish Envoy to Moscow, to UD, Moscow, 3 VI 1945; Ibidem, memorandum regarding negotiations with Poland, Stockholm, 4 VI 1945; Ibidem, B. Eng: memorandum notes no. 1 and no. 2 concerning Swedish-Polish commercial talks, Moscow, 2 VI 1945.
[10] PISM, A 11, E/1099, telegram by T. Gwiazdoski to the Polish Legation in Stockholm, 7 VI 1945.
[11] PISM, col. 20/7, letter by T. Kuźniarz (Department of Agriculture at the Ministry of Industry, Trade and Shipping) to Agricultural Officer of the Polish Legation in Stockholm, B. Saryusz-Zaleski, 6 VI 1945.

ship at Polish disposal, which would be of remarkable psychological importance. He emphasized the significance of such gestures, underlining the Polish national character. Söderblom expressed his understanding for the issue of relations between the Swedish government and the representation of the London government at the time being raised by the Polish government in Warsaw. He promised to address both this issue and the proposal to hand over a commercial ship to Poland in Stockholm. Whereas Eng and Chabasiński were to continue 'the talks of technical nature.'[12] During the negotiations, Eng understated the number of carriages that were to be delivered to Poland to leave some room for concessions in the future.[13] He also informed his superiors in Stockholm that according to the UNRRA representative responsible for supplies of goods to Poland and Czechoslovakia, Colonel Cecil Cross, Chabasiński's promises regarding the unblocking of Polish harbours by 25 June 1945 were impossible to realize. In his opinion, this would be possible by mid-July at the earliest.[14]

Eventually, on 8 June, Eng, the first secretary of the Swedish Legation in Helsinki, was authorized by the Swedish government to sign the commercial agreement with the Polish Provisional Government.[15] Then, the coal experts Ljungdahl and Ström arrived in Moscow on 12 June to support Eng in his conversations with the Poles. Accompanied by Söderblom, they held a meeting in the presence of Molotov and Vyshynsky, on 14 June, with the highest authorities of the People's Republic of Poland in the Polish embassy in Moscow. President of the State National Council (KRN) Bolesław Bierut mentioned the earlier friendship between the Polish and Swedish nations and expressed a hope for the best possible the relations between the two countries in the future, which was eagerly confirmed by representatives of the Soviet authorities.[16]

On 16 June, Eng, clerk Arne Waldenström, typist Denise Eriksson and the coal experts departed on a special flight from Moscow to Warsaw, where they

---

[12] RA, UD 1920 års dossiersystem, HP 64, vol. 2736, memorandum no. 2 regarding negotiations with Poland, Stockholm, 8 VI 1945; Ibidem, B. Eng: memorandum no. 5 regarding Swedish-Polish commercial discussions, Moscow, 6 VI 1945.
[13] RA, UD 1920 års dossiersystem, HP 64, vol. 2736, B. Eng: memorandum no. 6 regarding Swedish–Polish commercial discussions, Moscow, 7 VI 1945.
[14] Ibidem, B. Eng: memorandum no. 7 regarding Swedish-Polish commercial discussions, Moscow, 9 VI 1945.
[15] RA, Kabinettet/UD Huvudarkivet, Statsrådsprotokoll, serie A3A, vol. 118, Protokoll över Utrikesdepartementets ärenden, Stockholm, 8 VI 1945.
[16] RA, UD 1920 års dossiersystem, HP 12, vol. 890, copy of report by S. Söderblom, Swedish Envoy to Moscow, to Minister of Foreign Affairs Ch. Günther, Moscow, 18 VI 1945.

stayed in Hotel Polonia.[17] Intensive negotiations took place 18–20 June. The Polish delegation was headed by Hilary Minc. An important role was played by E. Gorączko, head of the newly established Centre for Merchandising of Coal Industry Products (*Centrala Zbytu Produktów Przemysłu Węglowego*), an expert in coal-related issues who was earlier engaged in the trade with Swedish companies from Stockholm, Malmö and Gothenburg as a representative of the Giesche coal company. Within three days the agreement was concluded, under which Sweden was to obtain from Poland 1 million tons of coal and 200 thousand tons of coke. The deliveries would begin on 15 July and end within three months, with the option of a two-month extension. Prior to the signing of the arrangement, Eng travelled to Stockholm to consult with his government. He returned to Warsaw on 28 July, and initialled the agreement the next day. Sweden would be the first country to sign the agreement with the Provisional Government of National Unity.[18]

Thanks to the ad hoc agreement, the Swedes secured deliveries of the raw material that was indispensable for their economy. At the close of July in Stockholm other negotiations began on a long-term economic arrangement. According to the new agreement, Sweden was to obtain as much as 4 million tons of coal and 800 thousand tons of coke from Poland in the first nine months of 1946. The arrangement was signed on 20 August 1945. It soon transpired, however, that Poland was unable to fulfil these orders. In 1945 only 122 tons of the agreed upon 1 million tons were delivered to Sweden and in 1946 only 1642 million tons from the anticipated 4 million tons. The Polish negotiators had to be aware of the technical difficulties preventing the implementation of the provisions of bilateral agreements with Sweden. At the same time documents from the on-going talks proved that the Poles were making great efforts to meet Swedish demands. Both sides wanted to sign the

---

[17] RA, UD 1920 års dossiersystem, HP 64, vol. 2736, memorandum no. 8 concerning negotiations with Poland, Stockholm, 16 VI 1945.
[18] The agreement consisted of two parts – commercial arrangement and coal arrangement. The Swedes committed themselves to deliver various types of iron ore, although in some cases (iron-tungsten alloy, titanium-iron alloy, nickel-iron alloy) the quantities were much smaller than those demanded by the Polish side. In Sweden there was shortage of carbon electrodes and it was completely impossible to import them from there. The Swedish side also agreed to borrow (not give away) 1300 railway wagons at a unit price of 5 crowns per night. The Swedish delegation managed to avoid making commitments involving granting access to their locomotives. RA, UD 1920 års dossiersystem, HP 64, vol. 2736, letter by E. Grafström from Sweden's board of industry (*Statens industrikommission*) to B. Eng, Stockholm, 27 VI 1945; Ibidem, memorandum regarding the borrowing of railway wagons to Poland, Stockholm, 29 VI 1945. See also S.-O. Olsson, *Swedish-Polish...*, p. 36; A. Kłonczyński, *Stosunki...*, pp. 144–145.

agreement at all costs. It should be highlighted that in the initial years following the war, despite breaching contracts, Poland was Sweden's main coal and coke supplier (59 percent and 30 percent, 1945–48).[19]

Statistics on Swedish exports to Poland 1945–48 show that trade with Sweden was of vital importance for Poland. There was no other country that provided Poland with industrial products in comparable quantities. The exchange was important also for Sweden as there was no alternative to the Polish coal supplies. The situation in Germany continued to be uncertain, and the Western Allies had neither an option nor will to support a neutral state that was not enduring damages inflicted by the war. The opinion of the Swedish researcher Olsson was justified in that the Polish coal supplies, although smaller than those scheduled, fulfilled their task.[20] It would also be worth examining the sense of the Swedes' negotiations with the representatives of the Polish government in exile. At the beginning it was most probably thought that the reconstruction of the Polish government was possible while retaining the London politicians' influence on the shaping of relations between Warsaw and other countries. In addition, negotiations made it possible relatively early to gain orientation in the needs and demands of the Polish side as well as in what it could offer in return.

---

[19] S.-O. Olsson, *Swedish-Polish...*, p. 39.
[20] Ibidem.

PART 3
Humanitarian Mission of Sweden

11. The Fate of Polish Refugee

Until the outbreak of the Second World War the number of foreigners in Sweden was insignificant. They were admitted rather reluctantly, treated with distrust and there were no plans of a broader opening to them. Experts on this matter emphasized that the Swedes, just like the citizens of other European countries, considered themselves to be superior to other nations, which, reinforced by a belief in racial purity, bred nationalism, anti-Semitism and a general disapproval towards foreigners. This was coupled with a widespread fear of competition in the labour market.[1]

Nevertheless, in the 1930s, as Europe faced an increasing political refugee problem, some associations formed in Sweden, the task of which was to provide aid for people persecuted for their political beliefs. The oldest organisation of this sort was *Röda Hjälpen* (Red Aid), the Swedish branch of International Red Aid (MOPR) that was founded in Moscow in 1922 to provide support for communists being persecuted in various countries. The social-democratic circles set the tone for the humanitarian activity. After Hitler came to power, the social-democratic party, the Swedish Trade Union Confederation (LO) together with the Swedish Social Democratic Youth League, established an organisation which from 1936 was known by the name *Arbetarrörelsens flyktinghjälp* (translation: Labour Movement's Committee for Refugee Aid). It collaborated with many other similar organisations and, most of all, with state authorities.[2] It focused the supporters of asylum right liberalisation, and its opponents were associated with the right wing. These divisions became clear in the second half of 1930s, when the discussion on the amendment of the refugee act was in progress. Ethical reasons favoured the facilitation of the refugees' arrival in Sweden and the simplification of procedures for acquiring the right to permanent residence. Aversion was caused by the typical fears about the disruptions in the labour market and, generally, about the influx of foreigners. The Swedish government predicted that the prolonging political tensions in Europe would cause an increasing wave of immigration. Relating to this they preferred to introduce strict rules that would allow the control of the inflow of foreigners and at the same time

---

[1] H. Lindberg, *Svensk flyktingpolitik under internationellt tryck 1936–1941*, Stockholm 1973, pp. 37–38.
[2] Ibidem, pp. 42–44.

did not oblige the state authorities to accept all people who declared themselves as political refugees. This was to be the way to preserve a certain balance between two opposite attitudes towards the issue of migration. To preserve the freedom of actions in this area, Sweden did not ratify the refugee convention, which was put forward by the League of Nations at the outset of 1938, although the Swedish government did not generally reject the possibility of accepting a certain number of people. After all, the aim was to avoid a situation where a large group of refugees would arrive on a one-off basis, which it was believed posed a threat both from economic and socio-psychological point of view. In the diplomatic reports one could read, among others, the opinion that the inflow of a large group of Jews could spark a wave of anti-Semitism.[3] In 1937 the new act on foreigners came into force, the aim of which was to provide control over their arrival and residence. The issues of granting visas as well as residence and work permits or arrival of citizens of the countries with which Sweden signed the agreement on visa-free movement, were handed to the management of various specialized institutions. This decentralisation continued to raise fears about the irrepressible inflow of foreigners. It was especially the Swedish Ministry of Foreign Affairs that did not trust in the efficiency of the Swedish system of border control and it was mainly thanks to its diplomatic interventions that the wave was successfully held back.[4]

The Swedish authorities were responding to social pressure as 1938–39 saw protests in some circles against excessively liberal immigration law. These included associations of small entrepreneurs, textile traders, colonial goods retailers, shop assistants and restaurant musicians. In February 1939 pharmacists and students in various disciplines demonstrated against 'the import of Jewish physicians, dentists and pharmacists.' Most attention was devoted to the discussion organized by students of the Uppsala University on 17 February 1939. In the new tennis hall, a capacity-exceeding crowd composed a resolution to the king, expressing opposition towards the influx of foreigners. Nevertheless, at the same time in the *Riksdag*, where social democrats had the edge over committed opponents of immigration, an act was passed, allocating 500 thousand crowns for covering the refugees' cost of living and professional training. Following the German annexation of Austria and the Sudetes the head of the *Arbetarrörelsens Flyktinghjälp*, Axel Granath, pledged that Sweden could admit several hundred refugees from

---

[3] Ibidem, pp. 71–74, 77–118, 169.
[4] Ibidem. Following the Anschluss of Austria, the Swedes managed to revoke the agreement on the visa-free movement with Germany.

the annexed territories. The motivation to do so was financial aid, which was promised by the British government to cover the immigrants' cost of living. After 15 March 1939, and following the liquidation of Czechoslovakia, Granath began to contact the Polish authorities and the British refugee committee regarding the issue of the migration of a small group of refugees. He declared in Warsaw that it was possible for his organisation to take care of certain individuals 'due to their profession and other circumstances.' Eventually, a list of 94 people was drawn up, but the outbreak of the war prevented them from leaving. Only some of them reached Sweden. Because of the wave of refugees from the war-stricken areas, and due to other repressions, in 1939 the Bank of England eventually donated over 550 thousand crowns to the Swedish Ministry of Foreign Affairs. Most of this sum reached the account of the *Arbetarrörelsens flyktinghjälp*.[5]

Socialstyrelsens utlänningsbyrå (translation: National Board of Health and Welfare's agency for foreign nationals), established in 1938, was a small unit of the Office for Social Affairs – an agency of the Ministry of Social Welfare. Within five years, by 1 July 1944, the Office was transformed into *Statens utlänningskommission* or *SUK* (translation: national migration commission), which employed over six hundred people. The immigrants' affairs were usually dealt with by the Ministry of Foreign Affairs. In addition, from 1939 the *Nämnden för statens flyktingshjälp* (translation: Committee for National Refugee Aid) was in operation (known as the Government Board of Refugee Relief (*Statens flyktingsnämnd*) from 1 October). Its task was to provide arriving immigrants with financial security. The Swedish state provided funding for refugees mostly in agreement with the diplomatic missions of their countries of origin. These matters were also managed by non-governmental organisations. In 1944 there were sixteen such organisations. They cooperated with the Government Board of Refugee Relief. The Swedish government provided financial support for this organisation, covering up to 40 percent of the cost of benefits, and up to 70 percent in the case of children. Towards the close of 1944, the Polish Aid Committee was financed to an even larger extent by the Swedish authorities even.[6] Local humanitarian organisations were also operating, including *Polenhjälpen* (Aid for Poland), which

---

[5] H. Lindberg, *Svensk...*, pp. 119–122, 200–202, 208, 251, 257.
[6] L. Olsson, *Pa tröskeln till folkhemmet. Baltiska flyktingar och polska koncentrationslägerfångar som reservarbetskraft i skånskt jordbruk kring slutet av andra världskriget*, Lund 1995, pp. 45–46. See also: A. Berge, *Flyktpolitik i stormakts skugga. Sverige och de sovjetryska flyktingarna under andra världskriget*, Uppsala 1992, pp. 31–32.

operated in Malmö and Lund and earned a particularly good reputation for the collection of clothes and other items called.

In November 1938 Swedish offices estimated the number of refugees to be 1800–2300 people. By 10 January 1939, nearly 1800 people had applied for an arrival permit, but only 900 were approved.[7] In mid-1939, 4300–4800 foreigners resided in Sweden, including 400–500 political refugees and 2500 German citizens.

During the first years of the war, asylum seekers were held under strict control. By 22 August 1939, diplomatic and consular posts in Sweden were instructed to show as much restraint as possible in granting entry permits. After 1 September, border control was tightened. Foreigners without visas could not cross the border. Lennart Nylander, head of UD Passport Office, warned of the wave of refugees from Poland. He explained to his superiors, 'If Sweden adopts a favourable attitude towards the transit of these refugees, one would have to count on that some of them would remain here.' The Poles were treated like other nationalities. On evaluating the pre-war period and the first years following the outbreak of the war, one may agree with the Swedish researcher Hans Lindberg's point of view that the immigration policy conducted according to the individual national interests of Sweden was extremely cautious.[8] It changed, however, at the turn of 1943, when credible information about German crimes began to reach Stockholm.[9]

Poles and citizens of the Baltic States, and from 1940, Norwegians and Danes, affected by the German or Soviet occupation gradually started to flow into Sweden. Precise statistics for the numbers of refugees cannot be found. Official lists exist of foreigners who were granted permanent residency, however. These lists do not include children under the age of 16, as they were granted visas automatically with their parents. These lists neither include special cases, for instance the thousands of Finns who were evacuated following the conclusion of the Finnish–Soviet ceasefire in September 1944 nor the former German concentration camp prisoners, who were brought to Sweden from shortly before the conclusion of the war and several weeks after. Following the evacuation of the Jews to Denmark, in October 1943, 35 thousand refugees resided in Sweden. The largest group was composed of Norwegians (18 thousand), Danes (9 thousand), Germans (3 thousand), Estonian Swedes (2 thousand), Poles (800), Czechs (700), and Austrians

---

[7] H. Lindberg, *Svensk...*, p. 292.
[8] Ibidem, pp. 266, 293.
[9] P. A. Levine, *From indifference to activism. Swedish diplomacy and the Holocaust, 1938–1944*, Uppsala 1996, 134, passim.

(600). Finnish children constituted a separate group (12 thousand). At the turn of 1944, over 90 thousand refugees were already registered, caused by the wave of refugees from Finland and the Baltic States. In September and October 1944, about 50 thousand Finns (with approximately 30 thousand breeding animals) moved west and crossed the Swedish border in fear of repression both from the German army, which was retreating to Norway after the conclusion of the Finnish–Norwegian ceasefire, as well as from the Soviet army, which continued its offensive. At the turn of October and November these refugees began to return home, and by July 1945 all had left Sweden. Nearly 30 thousand refugees travelled to Sweden from the Baltic States, including many former soldiers who fought under German command. In Sweden there were still 30 thousand Norwegians, 15 thousand Danes and more than 5 thousand Germans.

According to official records, in Sweden 1940–44 there were 362–759 Poles, whereas in 1945 there were 3521. Even if the number of refugees from Poland was higher (900–1000 by spring 1945, according to expert estimates), as a proportion of all foreigners in 1940 (18 thousand) and 70 thousand in 1944, this was not a large group. The proportions changed only following the arrival of approximately 6500 Polish women from the concentration camps in April and May of 1945 and a further 9 thousand following the conclusion of the war. Yet, one needs to remember that at the time the total number of all refugees rose to 100 thousand.[10]

The Poles fled to Sweden throughout the war. Initially, in the autumn of 1939 and in the spring of 1940 a wave of refugees came in the immediate aftermath of the September defeat. Later, these were fugitives, personnel of the Todt Organisation in Norway or people who managed to escape occupied Poland on Swedish ships carrying coal, moving from Gdynia to Swedish harbours. Most of the refugees moved on to France and Great Britain to join the Polish army. The Poles, just like other foreigners, were placed in refugee camps. In May 1945, 24 transitional and 22 permanent camps already existed. In the transitional camps the refugees stayed for between three and six months. Thanks to such camps located in Sweden nearly 4 thousand Poles, 1942–45, joined the Polish Armed Forces in the West. The unemployed refugees were paid benefits of 170 crowns per month by the Polish Aid Committee. At the same time, the organisation tried to find them employment, but the possibilities were limited.[11] The demands of the local market saw the

---

[10] L. Olsson, *På tröskeln...*, pp. 22–28.
[11] Ibidem, pp. 43, 48.

Swedish authorities reach out to the refugees and allow them to carry out unpopular hard labour, especially in forests.

During the war, relating to serious difficulties caused by insufficient fuel and coal imports, the Swedish government determined the needs of industry and private households to be 63 million cubic metres of wood. To guarantee such a high volume, all men over twenty were mandated to work in the winter at the turn of 1942 and 1943. Anyone willing to take work in logging was welcomed, and many fugitives would come to choose it as their occupation. A majority of the candidates were Norwegians (20 thousand), who were used for the work involved. In March 1943, the Swedish authorities decided that logging, farming and peat-digging should not require a permit. To encourage the refugees to work in the forest, it was announced that workers had to stay a minimum of four months in such jobs before seeking other employment. Some of the Polish refugees also worked in logging. In 1943, thanks to the refugees, one fifth of the demand for wood was met.[12] One sawmill employed the last commander of the Border Protection Corps (KOP), General Wilhelm Orlik-Rückemann, who was stranded in Sweden on his way to France,[13] as well as Jerzy Pański, the Polish communist and deserter from the commercial ship.[14] Many refugees considered such occupations to be persecution and occasionally both Norwegians and Poles protested the working conditions.[15]

Following the German aggression of September 1939, thousands of Polish refugees, soldiers and civilians, attempted to move from the Baltic States to France via Sweden. Sandler promised Potworowski his 'utmost support' in the

---

[12] H. Dahlberg, *I Sverige...*, pp. 139–140.
[13] A. Kralisz, *Na straży wschodnich rubieży. Biografia ostatniego dowódcy KOP gen. bryg. Wilhelma Orlik-Rückemanna (1894–1986)*, Warszawa 1999, p. 126, fig. 19.
[14] J. Pański, *Wachta...*, pp. 101–107.
[15] L. Olsson, *På tröskeln...*, pp. 52–53. See the recollections of a former volunteer, in the Winter War, in defence of Finland from his work in the forest in Sweden: A. Bogusławski, *Pod Gwiazdą...*, pp. 124–125: 'Our work in the forest involved cutting down large trees so that the smaller ones could grow better, have more space and light. The branches of the fallen trees had to be cut off. Then the trunks were cut into parts of equal length which later, with the help of wedges and axes, were split into smaller logs. We had to find the right spot to place the wedge. The logs were arranged in piles of clearly defined size and we got paid for each "metre". This job was hard and difficult. Another type of work was cleaning the limbs and large branches and removing shoots with axes and saws. Afterwards, the wood was arranged in sharp angled racks. The thickest parts of wood were placed one on another until the rack reached the desired height. This was much easier, so as a novice I started my job with this task. My salary was meagre, far worse than what I was getting on the farm in Svartsjö. What took time was sharpening axes and saws and keeping the tools in good condition. But nobody forced us to do this work. Everybody earned as much as one was able to chop and cut up. I worked there for only a while, most probably for a little over a month. I was so tired after work that I took trip to a village nearby on a borrowed bike only once.

organisation of their transit.[16] At the turn of November and December of 1939, before the reconstruction of the government and Sandler's resignation, Potworowski was forced to intervene, however, to prevent Swedish diplomats from holding up the process of issuing visas.[17] After a few months, travel via Sweden to the west grew more difficult due to the reluctance of the Swedish authorities and the German conquests in northern and Eastern Europe. During that period, the Germans warned the Swedes that supporting Polish efforts to reach France and Great Britain was contrary to the principle of neutrality.[18] The Swedes were therefore subjected to pressure from Berlin, the aim of which was to prevent the transit, but they were also afraid that the refugees would stay in their country for good. Nearly 4100 people were denied entry to Sweden in 1940 and 1942–44, which was about 5 percent of people who applied for a Swedish visa. Only an small fraction of those individuals who were permitted to enter Sweden met the criteria to be granted political refugee status. One researcher pointed out that such inconsistent behaviour could be the result of concerns about an excessively large group of foreigners remaining permanently in Sweden. It was assumed that their stay should be temporary and that the emigrants would eventually return to their homes.[19]

Therefore, leaving Lithuania or Latvia was by no means easy. According to information passed on to Paris by the Polish Socialist Party (PPS) activist Maurycy Karniol at the beginning of 1940, only passengers under eighteen and over fifty years of age were admitted on to the flight bound for Stockholm.[20] This measure was coupled with the painstaking procedure of obtaining Swedish and French visas, where possession of the latter was a condition for securing the former. Also, starting in the summer of 1939, Swedish diplomats were banned from issuing visas to Jews. In general, most of the Poles entered Sweden illegally. Refugees started to flow in relatively early, prior to the conclusion of the military campaign in Poland. Five seamen, Edward Skrzypek, Michał Przepiórczyński, captains of commercial fleet Jerzy Lewandowski and

---

[16] AAN, HI/I/246, telegram by G. Potworowski, Polish Envoy to Stockholm, to the Ministry of Foreign Affairs, Stockholm, 5 IX 1939.
[17] AAN, HI/I/245, telegram by G. Potworowski, Polish Envoy to Stockholm, to the Ministry of Foreign Affairs, Stockholm, 15 XII 1939.
[18] RA, mf. F 035-3-32252, copy of memorandum by the head of the Political Department of UD S. Söderblom of his conversation with counsellor to the German Legation in Stockholm C. von Below from 27 X 1939.
[19] A. Berge, *Flyktingpolitik...*, p. 27.
[20] PISM, col. 133, vol. 283, postcard by M. Karniol to B. Wojciechowski, Kaunas, 12 I 1940; Ture Nerman in his book form 1942 delivers a number of 3 000 Poles in the Baltic States who were even refused to buy tickets for flight to Stockholm by Svenska Aerotransport. See T. Nerman, *Sverige i beredskap*, Stockholm 1942, p. 117.

Władysław Grabowski and mechanic Brunon Wyglądacz from Gdynia reached Karlskrona on the sailing boat *Olga*.[21]

The PPS activists, who managed to reach Paris following the defeat of the Polish army (or like Herman Lieberman who had been in France since the beginning of the 1930s), tried to make the journey from Lithuania to Sweden easier for a large group of Polish socialists. Adam Ciołkosz, through the minister for labour, Jan Stańczyk, sent the Swedish authorities a list of nine refugees and proposed preparing an aircraft from Stockholm, where the Swedes would 'order and send the aeroplane.'[22] Similar actions were taken by the Ministry of Foreign Affairs. At the same time, the Labour Movement's Committee of Refugee Aid (*Arbetarrörelsens flyktingshjälp*) in Stockholm received a request from a socialist Artur Salman (who after the war used the name Stefan Arski) for support in evacuating himself and his comrades from Lithuania.[23] At this request, Herman Lieberman wrote a letter to Zeth Höglund, the leading activist of Sweden's Social Democratic Workers' Party (SAP), as he expected that the Polish efforts to obtain visas for as many as thirteen people would be supported (Karniol's name was last on the list).[24] Nevertheless, he achieved little. Karl-Erik Jansson from the Labour Movement's Committee of Refugee Aid explained that when the Poles had obtained French visas, in line with procedure, nothing would prevent their Swedish transit visas being issued.[25] This explains why the evacuation action had come to a standstill and Karniol's immediate arrival in Stockholm, in March 1940, was an exception. Thanks to associates of Jan Masiak, a Polish socialist who had been living in Sweden for a long time, Karniol came to know many activists of the Swedish social democracy, including from the Labour Movement's Committee of Refugee Aid, who he desperately asked for a swift intervention. In the letter to Paris he reported:

> I pointed to the danger, which was facing our people who were still fighting, and that it is impossible to adopt a bureaucratic attitude towards the issue of aid, that when once every 30 years the PPS needed support from the Swedeso

---

[21] B. Chrzanowski, *Organizacja*..., p. 14.
[22] PISM, col. 133, vol. 283, copy of letter by A. Ciołkosz to J. Stańczyk, Paris, 1 II 1940.
[23] PISM, col. 133, vol. 283, postcard by M. Karniol and A. Salman to H. Lieberman, Kaunas, 6 II 1940.
[24] PISM, col. 133, vol. 283, copy of letter by H. Lieberman to Z. Höglund, Paris, 4 II 1940.
[25] PISM, col. 133, vol. 283, letter by K.-E. Jansson to H. Lieberman, Stockholm, 10 II 1940; Ibidem, letter by K.-E. Jansson to A. Ciołkosz, Stockholm, 10 II 1940.

for only a couple of units, the slogan 'working men of all countries, unite!' should be actually in force.'[26]

Because of these appeals, Emil Wallin provided substantial help in issuing visas to the Poles, whereas K.-E. Jansson, secretary of the Committee, proved to be a not-so-pleasant figure.[27] Rapid military developments on the western front in the spring of 1940 made the protracted issue of the French visas outdated. Most of the refugees left Lithuania and travelled by train to Vladivostok and on by ship to California. By July 1940 a couple of activists had reached Stockholm.[28]

What may seem surprising is that Polish refugees also attempted to reach Sweden legally, directly from German-occupied Pomerania. The German authorities planned to expel all Poles to the General Government. In October of 1939 Konstanty Jacynicz, former director of the GAL company (Gdynia-America Shipping Lines), who was a long-time collaborator of the Polish intelligence and commander of Civil Guard during the September fights for Gdynia,[29] asked Knud Lundberg, Swedish consul to Gdańsk, for permission to transport six hundred Polish refugees, women and children, mostly Polish seamen's families, to Sweden. Although he did not object to the project, Lundberg considered it unrealistic as every day he met the starving and oppressed wives of Polish seamen, who visited him asking for help. On the one hand, a ship from Sweden needed to be organized, and on the other, refugees from Sweden needed to be taken care of, as it was not known whether they would be granted entrance in to other countries. The German authorities allegedly promised Jacynicz that the evacuation of the families of Polish seamen deep into Poland would be postponed in anticipation of the Swedish ship. Lundberg communicated this to Richert[30] and on 30 October it was discussed by the government. Minister Sandler together with Minister Möller

---

[26] PISM, col. 133, vol. 160, letter by M. Karniol to A. Ciołkosz, Stockholm, 5 IV 1940.
[27] RA-Arninge, Sapo arkiv, P 1945 Maurycy Karniol, testimony by M. Karniol, n.d., n.p., pp. 67–68.
[28] D. Urzyńska, *Polski...*, p. 27.
[29] From the beginning of the occupation Jacynicz was engaged in the operation of the underground movement. He soon became the officer of the Home Army. See the biographies of: A. Gąsiorowski, Konstanty Jacynicz (1889–1970) [in:] *Zasłużeni Pomorzanie w latach II wojny światowej: szkice biograficzne*, Wrocław–Gdańsk 1984, pp. 102–107; R. Mielczarek, Jacynicz Konstanty Leon (1889–1970) [in:] *Słownik Biograficzny Pomorza Nadwiślańskiego*, ed. S. Gierszewski, vol. 2, Gdańsk 1994, pp. 256–258; B. Chrzanowski, A. Gąsiorowski, K. Steyer, *Polska Podziemna...*, pp. 600–601.
[30] RA, mf. F 035-3-32252, copy of letter by Consul K. Lundberg to the Swedish Envoy to Berlin A. Richert, Gdańsk, 18 X 1939.

supported the idea of bringing the wives of the Polish seamen to Sweden, but other members of the government voiced their doubts. Initially, consent was granted to look into the matter further.[31] On 15 November, the Swedish ship company offered its ship *Ragne* to carry the refugees (341 children and 397 adults) from Gdynia to Stockholm in two trips by the end of the month.[32] At the same time, Rederi AB Svea offered to transport 350 people from Riga on two ships for 55 thousand crowns.[33] In Stockholm preparations were made for the admittance of a large group of refugees from Gdynia. Possible accommodation and quarantine facilities were examined. Nevertheless, on 20 November, the decision was made to scrap the project. The plan of transporting a group of armed Polish soldiers was also rejected.[34] When the Lithuanian authorities put pressure on the Swedes regarding the admittance of 1 thousand Polish refugees from their territory, the head of the legal department of UD, Gösta Engzell, answered on 11 December that, 'due to the current extraordinary relations I see no possibility to respond favourably to the proposal.'[35] He then explained that the admittance of a much smaller number of Poles, approximately 700 wives and children of Polish seamen from Gdynia, was also evaluated negatively, as it was determined that this matter would require asking the *Riksdag* for 500 thousand crowns.[36] This distancing attitude from the idea of providing support for the Poles, was mostly the result of the ongoing Winter War and the plan to help the Finns. It is hard to find a definitive explanation for the news that Potworowski sent to the Polish Ministry of Foreign Affairs on 11 December 1939. The Polish envoy reported that he had negotiated permission to issue visas for 80 women and children from Gdynia, who remained following the German deportations.[37] The Swedes likely decided, discreetly, to admit a much smaller number of refugees that most likely included the wives of officers from the Polish submarines interned in Sweden.

The Swedes considered that the Germans should not delay the process of the seamen's wives and their children leaving Gdynia, as their deportation to

---

[31] K.G. Westman, *Politiska...*, pp. 43–44.
[32] RA, mf. F 035-3-32252, copy of letter by the Ministry of Foreign Affairs, Stockholm, 15 XI 1939.
[33] RA, mf. F 035-3-32252, copy of note by K. Bergström, Stockholm, 16 XI 1939.
[34] K.G. Westman, *Politiska...*, p. 52.
[35] RA, mf. F 035-3-32252, copy of letter by G. Engzell to the Swedish Legation in Kaunas, Stockholm, 11 XII 1939.
[36] RA, mf. F 035-3-32252, copy of letter by G. Engzell to Swedish chargé d'affaires in Kaunas C. Westring, Stockholm, 12 XII 1939.
[37] AAN, HI/I/245, telegram by G. Potworowski, Polish Envoy to Stockholm, to the Ministry of Foreign Affairs, Stockholm, 11 XII 1939.

the General Government had been ordered. It was only on 2 December that the German authorities agreed to issue the passports immediately after visas had been granted by the Swedish authorities. This became the practice that was enforced until the spring of 1940. Interventions by the Swedish authorities did not provoke disputes and Polish citizens in possession of such passports could leave the German-occupied territory mostly as stateless persons. The situation began to change in March 1940. On the pretext of spreading hostile propaganda (*Greuelgeschichten*) about the living conditions in Gdynia, the Germans started to deny the refugees the right to travel abroad. Consul Lundberg claimed that there was no point in asking the German authorities to issue passports at that time, as this would cause trouble for those seeking to leave. Besides which, the Swedish diplomat's permit to stay in Gdynia was no longer valid. He clarified for his colleagues from the Swedish Legation in Berlin that life in Pomerania was different to the relations that existed in Berlin. The Germans also treated the area of the former Free City of Danzig (Gdań as an occupied territory and the Gestapo was given power over it. The institutions that had previously maintained contact with the representatives of other countries were liquidated, and the officers of the Reich were brought into the city. Lundberg was under constant pressure due to the surveillance he was subjected to. The clearest sign of this was the officially recognised telephone tapping.[38] He proposed that the most appropriate solution would be an intervention by the central authorities of Germany in Berlin. This was arranged for the wife of a Polish seaman, Klotylda Winiarska, for instance, who had been refused a passport in Gdynia.[39] According to von Post, the Germans intended to seal their border, which was reflected in their overall policy of introducing restrictions in the movement between the Reich and the General Government. He did not consider it appropriate to go beyond the boundaries that had been imposed by the German authorities.[40]

Through the Swedish agency, the Polish government attempted to find out something about the Poles who came to be living under the Soviet occupation. The Swedes called on their German colleagues for information and permission for the Polish citizens to leave to the General Government. Such

---

[38] RA, UD avdelningar och byråarkiv 1864–1952, Andra B-avdelningen, vol. 362, copy of letter by the Swedish Consul to Gdańsk K. Lundberg to the counsellor to the Swedish Legation in Berlin E. von Post, Gdańsk, 28 III 1940.
[39] Ibidem, copy of letter by the Swedish Consul to Gdańsk K. Lundberg to the counsellor to the Swedish Legation in Berlin E. von Post, Gdańsk, 2 IV 1940.
[40] RA, UD avdelningar och byråarkiv 1864–1952, Andra B-avdelningen, vol. 362, letter by the counsellor to Swedish Legation in Berlin E. von Post to J. Lagerberg, Berlin, 4 IV 1940.

attempts met with resistance from the Soviet authorities. The Swedish Legation in Moscow informed Lagerberg that it would be extremely difficult to extricate the people living within the borders of the Soviet Union, and that only a miracle could save them, especially the prisoners of war.[41]

At the outset of January 1940, Envoy Potworowski informed the Swedish Ministry of Foreign Affairs that, together with envoy Lagerberg, he was seeking an organisation in Sweden that could rescue at least a group of several hundred Polish children. *Rädda Barnen* (Save the Children Sweden) was the organisation considered most. Engzell promised to examine the matter, but he took no further action.[42] It is worth mentioning that the representatives of the Transport Committee in Paris, who were tasked with recovering Polish ships located in neutral countries, made efforts in Sweden to bring from Poland the families of soldiers who were staying in France. The only condition for taking action in individual cases was an advance payment for the cost of travel and stay in Sweden (which was to be a transit point).[43] Władysław Potocki, a representative of the Committee in Stockholm, tried to gather information about the fate of people whose names were sent to him from London by Feliks Kollat. In January 1940 he claimed that 'it is easier to take people out via Italy.'[44]

Based on the surveillance of the Polish correspondence, the Swedish police concluded that these people were harmless. The attitude towards Sweden of over three hundred Poles, who found themselves mostly in Stockholm, was positive. They admired its culture and 'with tenderness noted the successes in many areas.' Criticism was rare and mostly focused on food, which was considered too sweet.[45] The letters mostly mentioned visa-related issues. Very rarely, the letters to the USA covered the situation in occupied Poland. Their senders preferred to remain anonymous, but based on other letters it was possible to establish their identity. The Swedes also turned their attention to the report that was sent to Chicago in November 1940, concerning the cooperation between Polish and Jewish socialists. The authors of the document

---

[41] RA, UD avdelningar och byråarkiv 1864–1952, Andra B-avdelningen, vol. 362, letter by counsellor to the Swedish Legation in Moscow L. Nylander to J. Lagerberg, Moscow, 30 XI 1940.

[42] RA, mf. F 035-3-32252, memorandum by G. Engzell, Stockholm, 10 I 1940.

[43] AAN, Ministry of Industry, Trade and Shipping (London), 708, letter by T. Geppert (Transport Committee) to P. Kowalewski together with attachment, n.p., 5 IV 1940, pp. 23–26. The list included the names of fifteen Polish sailors.

[44] AAN, Ministry of Industry, Trade and Shipping (London), 708, Letter by W. Potocki to F. Kollat, Stockholm, 3 I 1940, p. 81.

[45] RA-Arninge, SÄPO arkiv, P 201 Polish Legation, report 'Underground movement in Poland with branch in Sweden'.

called upon their colleagues in America to create a central unit for financing the activity of socialists in Poland. The senders of the letter, Władysław Malinowski, Artur Salman with his wife Halina Lauer, Wiktor Ehrenpreis and Bolesław Mendelsohn, were identified by the police. From further letters it followed that the Jewish socialists in Poland received financial support of 20 thousand crowns. The return letters contained reports from the Polish underground press. The Swedes suspected that the materials from Poland were reaching Sweden together with the refugees. What remained a puzzle was the method of money trafficking to the General Government.

Following the German attack on Denmark and Norway in April 1940, transit via Sweden to the West became virtually impossible. In the autumn of 1940, Military Attaché Major Brzeskwiński took care of 49 people who 'for some reason became stuck in Sweden and have a direct or indirect relation with the army.' By and large, there was no chance of evacuation. Brzeskwiński saw the only chance in leaving through the Soviet Union, but such journey involved great risk, and most importantly difficulties in obtaining transit visas.[46] At the outset of September 1941, 592 people remained in the custody of the Polish Aid Committee. Until mid-1942 when this number was reduced by approximately 50 people, who left for Great Britain or the USA.[47] From the beginning of the war to the end of 1941, 16 Polish illegal refugees arrived in Sweden.

An increasing number of Polish refugees reached Sweden through the green border from Norway. According to the findings of Andrzej Nils Uggla, the largest number of people escaping forced labour was reported in the summer and in the autumn of 1944, when the overall number grew by as many as hundred people. Not everyone escaped, however. The press reported that some Poles had been shot by the German guards or froze to death on their way through the mountains.[48] The refugees who reached the border were supported there by Doctor Einar Wallquist.[49]

The number of Polish fugitives trafficked on Swedish ships transporting coal from Gdynia or Szczecin to Sweden grew in 1943. According to Żaba, this was related to the growing disorganisation in Germany. According to the information of the Press Attaché, 'the refugees were mostly supported by the Swedish seamen who sympathised and made it a point of personal honour to

---

[46] PISM, A XII, 4/175, report by Polish Military Attaché to Stockholm Major F. Brzeskwiński for October 1940, 3 XI 1940.

[47] AAN, HI/I/448, annual report by the activity of the Polish Assistance Committee in Stockholm for the period between 1 IX 1941 and 3 VIII 1942, Stockholm, September 1942.

[48] 'Två polacker funna döda i fiskestuga. Dukade efter tapper ödemarkskamp', *Göteborgs Posten*, 30 X 1944.

[49] A. N. Uggla, *I nordlig hamn...*, pp. 32–34.

save the Poles.'[50] Special efforts were made by the crews of *Agne, Ultklippan, Gustaf, Ingrid* and *Beta VI*. As Żaba said, 'The crews never reveal anyone, but one needs to avoid the captains, as many are sympathetic to the Germans.'[51] Żaba was personally acquainted with the three seamen who purposefully sailed to Gdynia and Szczecin to transport Poles, mostly seamen. According to the reports of the fugitives, more people could have taken advantage of this opportunity, but all were concerned about the fate of their families back home. Some of the Swedish crews had to be bribed. In Sweden, the fugitives were treated cordially and hospitably, even by the police.[52] The Swedish press was keen to publish notes on the illegal arrival of the refugees, which posed a problem for the Polish mission, as this immediately led to a stepping up of German harbour controls. According to the reports by Żaba, all efforts to prevent the Swedish dailies from publishing information of this sort failed.[53]

As time went by the number of Poles grew, and the Polish Legation was the destination not only for refugees travelling on ships or escaping through the green border, but also for fugitives from German harbours who were travelling through Sweden. These were the Poles who were forced to join the *Wehrmacht*. Having deserted they turned themselves in to the Swedish authorities, and the Polish Legation made efforts to secure their release. In this way two groups of refugees found themselves in Sweden on 23 March and 2 April 1943. In total, 19 soldiers deserted, who, after Envoy Sokolnicki's intervention, were considered civilian political refugees and subsequently discharged.[54] As Żaba wrote in his report to London, 'It was a sensation when they were brought to the Polish Legation in two taxis wearing German uniforms.' He added, 'A year ago the Swedes would never have allowed this,

---

[50] AAN, Norbert Żaba's collection, 17 VIII 1943. See also Ibidem, note by N. Żaba regarding 7 people who were smuggled to Sweden in May 1943, place and date unknown.

[51] Ibidem, note by N. Żaba, place and date unknown.

[52] Ibidem, report by N. Żaba, Stockholm, 19 VIII 1943. A colourful description of the illegal trip by Swedish ship from Gdynia to Gotland (April 1943), then of return from Stockholm to occupied Poland via Stettin (June 1943) was given by Jan Nowak-Jeziorański in his memoirs. He appreciated the kindness of the Swedes: 'A year ago I knew them as dangerous enemies of Poland from the novel *Deluge* by Sienkiewicz. Now I felt like telling them that I will become a friend of Sweden and Swedes, especially seamen, by the end of my life – no matter I will live for a long or for a very short time.', J. Nowak, Kurier..., p. 111.

[53] Ibidem, report by N. Żaba, Stockholm, 19 VIII 1943. The reports about Poland already at the beginning of 1943 contained complaints on restrictions which were introduced by the Germans in harbours, since the Swedish seamen were prevented from disembarking in Gdynia. Visiting ships was also prohibited. See *Armia Krajowa w dokumentach 1939–1945*, vol. 6, doc. 1747, p. 296.

[54] AAN, Norbert Żaba's collection, letter by N. Żaba to M. Thugutt (Ministry of Internal Affairs), Stockholm, 9 IV 1943.

11. THE FATE OF THE POLISH REFUGEES

which also proves the change in their attitude.'[55] At that point the Swedish authorities even agreed to their evacuation to Great Britain.[56]

What was the fate of the Polish refugees? Although the authorities placed fugitives in special camps and employed them as loggers for meagre pay, Brzeskwiński emphasized that the attitude of the Swedes towards the refugees was generally good. The refugees could not leave the camps, which were in rural areas, without a special permission. It was noted that, 'The Swedes are trying to relieve their capital city of the immigrant community.' Such a strategy made it very difficult for Attaché Brzeskwiński to evacuate the Polish army volunteers to Great Britain.[57] In 1943, the Polish–Swedish agreement was signed, which laid out detailed rules for procedures regarding Polish citizens arriving in Sweden, for example, their stay in Stockholm was limited to ten days. During this time, the refugees were given clothes, verified in terms of grounds for granting them Polish passports, and subsequently given food stamps. The evacuation was drawn-out considerably by a lack of transport. It was not until the outset of 1945 that the Polish Legation would sign an agreement with AB Aerotransport (ABA), a Swedish government-owned airline, regarding the provision of an aeroplane. Carrying twenty passengers and at intervals of several days, the plane serviced the route from 2 February to 15 March 1945 and transported 146 volunteers to Great Britain in total, which according to Andrzej Nils Uggla was more than the total number of evacuees in the years 1942–44.[58]

The fate of the fugitives could have been worse. On two occasions the Swedes turned the refugees over to the Germans. On one occasion, a Polish seaman arrived in Sweden as crew on a German cargo ship. The Swedes denied his request for asylum. An intervention by Envoy Potworowski failed too. Minister Günther consequently explained that the general rules of conduct in such cases were never specified, and that each case was and would be considered separately.[59] The Polish seaman was refused the right of residence and later turned over to the Germans. In December 1941 Zygfryd Lipkowski,

---

[55] Ibidem, letter by N. Żaba to M. Thugutt (Ministry of Internal Affairs), Stockholm, 22 IV 1943. The issue was recorded by the Polish intelligence, see: *Armia Krajowa w dokumentach 1939–1945*, vol. 6, doc. 1764, p. 334 (here exact personal details of the escapees).
[56] AAN, HI/I/100, letter by Polish Envoy to Stockholm H. Sokolnicki to the Ministry of Foreign Affairs, Stockholm, 14 III 1943.
[57] IPMS, A XII, 4/175, letter by the director of the Stockholm evacuation facility Major F. Brzeskwiński to the head of the Staff of Commander-in-Chief, n.p., 6 V 1941.
[58] A. N. Uggla, *I nordlig hamn...*, pp. 37–41.
[59] *Notes by Polish envoy to Stockholm G. Potworowski 1939–1942*, entry from 21 I 1941.

who came to Sweden as a stowaway, was dealt with in the same way. Potworowski commented, 'the decisions of the Swedish authorities vary between genuine humanitarianism and reluctance to keep dubious foreign elements in Sweden.' In addition, before making a decision in each case, the Polish side was forced to provide material guarantees. Nevertheless, the Polish diplomat considered the most important factor to be the German pressure, especially in the situations where the fugitive was part of ship's crew. The compassion shown by the local police played a role. Several days after the incident, for instance, four stowaways from ships running between Gdańsk and Gothenburg were released from custody.[60]

Despite these rare incidents, in general Envoy Potworowski supported the opinion of Attaché Brzeskwiński. He claimed that the attitude of the Swedish authorities towards the Polish refugees was correct.[61] Residency permits in more than 60 cases were extended without complications, and the Swedes also supported them in finding work. Considerable financial and material help poured in to the Polish Aid Committee in Stockholm from various Swedish social and charity institutions. In May 1940, the Committee for the Support of the Nordic States, operating under the auspices of the heir to the Swedish throne, donated the modest amount of 10 thousand crowns for the refugees, with the promise of further donations. Obtaining visas for Poles wanting to leave the Baltic States annexed by the Soviet Union What was particularly difficult, however. The Swedish authorities stopped the inflow of refugees, most probably in fear of Soviet infiltration. In the spring of 1941, less optimistic news came in from Stockholm, regarding the intention of the Swedes to rid themselves of the Polish refugees by enthusiastically granting financial aid for their departure to America through the Soviet Union. It was emphasized, 'It is impossible to find any kind of work in Sweden, and the old foxes who have managed to find temporary jobs as specialists are being eradicated by competition and often end up in prison.'[62]

Following Hitler's aggression towards the Soviet Union, Finland joined the war and, because of pressure from Germany, demanded the Polish diplomatic mission in Helsinki be liquidated. Many Polish citizens, for fear of internment, fled to Sweden. The Swedish government agreed to accept them on the condition that they be placed in a special camp and that the costs be

---

[60] AAN, HI/I/448, letter by the Polish Envoy to Stockholm G. Potworowski to the Ministry of Foreign Affairs, Stockholm, 22 I 1942.
[61] PISM, A 12, 3/2, part 2, letter by Polish Envoy G. Potworowski to the Ministry of Foreign Affairs, Stockholm, 22 VII 1940, p. 538–539.
[62] AAN, HI/I/436, note: 'Wiadomości otrzymane ze Sztokholmu', n.p., 11 IV 1941.

11. THE FATE OF THE POLISH REFUGEES

covered by the Polish side. Although the number of Poles in the camp gradually fell due to being evacuated to Great Britain, expenses continued to rise due to inflation. The Swedes demanded the quickest possible settlement of all liabilities, and the legation maintained that timely payments were indispensable 'due to the influence they may have on the attitude of the relevant Swedish authorities towards the Polish refugees.'[63] When in 1944, together with a group of refugees from Finland, Sweden began welcoming immigrants, for example, Poles who had deserted the Todt Organisation and former soldiers who were forcibly conscripted into the Soviet Army, the Swedes posed no problem. Origins were not investigated and visas were granted, despite the delicacy of the matter concerning granting visas.[64]

It is worth mentioning at this point the cultural events which were organized by the Polish refugees in Sweden. A good example was the aforementioned Polish–Norwegian art exhibition held in Stockholm in November 1942. In January and February 1943 recitals by Polish singers Lucjan Prus-Bar and Antoni Frankowski took place in Stockholm.[65] In December 1944, Poles, together with Norwegians, Danes and Czechs, participated in a literary evening that was organized in Stockholm and devoted to the countries under German occupation.[66] Education constituted a separate activity for the Polish refugees.[67]

Relating to the gradual increase in the number of refugees, in 1943 the Refugee Support Office (*Biuro Opieki nad Uchodźcami*) was established in the Polish Legation in Stockholm.[68] Officially, custody of the refugees was

---

[63] AAN, HI/I/448, copy of letter by counsellor to the Polish Legation in Stockholm T. Pilch to the Ministry of Foreign Affairs, Stockholm, 9 VII 1942.
[64] AAN, HI/I/478, letter by the Polish Envoy to Stockholm H. Sokolnicki to the Ministry of Foreign Affairs, Stockholm, 6 X 1944. The Poles who were hired in the Todt Organisation and who escaped to Sweden are mentioned by: E. Denkiewicz-Szczepaniak, *Polska siła robocza w Organizacji Todta w Norwegii i Finlandii w latach 1941–1945*, Toruń 1999, pp. 234–237. See also W. Biegański, M. Juchniewicz, S. Okęcki, *Polacy w ruchu oporu narodów Europy 1939–1945*, Warszawa 1977, pp. 167–169. This book contains a description of an unsuccessful escape of the group of Poles from Norway (together with Witold Pławski, son of Captain E. Pławski). They were captured and shot dead.
[65] 'List ze Szwecji' ['Letter from Sweden'], *Wieści Polskie*, 28 II 1943.
[66] 'Wieczór literacki w Sztokholmie' [Literary evening in Stockholm], *Dziennik Polski i Dziennik Żołnierza*, 13 XII 1944.
[67] For extensive information on this subject see A. N. Uggla, *I nordlig hamn...* See also 'Jak się wiedzie Polakom w Szwecji?', *Dziennik Żołnierza*, 31 VII 1941; N. Ż[aba], 'Nauka polska w Szwecji w sprzyjających warunkach', *Dziennik Polski*, 23 VII 1942; T. Potworowski, 'Liceum Polskie w Sztokholmie', *Wiadomości Polskie*, 5 XII 1943.
[68] AAN, HI/I/469, justification of the budget estimates for the year 1944, Stockholm, 10 XI 1943.

taken over on 15 January 1944 by the delegation of the Ministry of Labour and Social Welfare.[69]

In February 1942, Potworowski again asked the Swedish authorities for a permission to bring children from Poland to Sweden. The Swedes, who were recognized for similar campaigns involving bringing children mainly from Finland, but also from France and Belgium, did not refuse, but on the account of the experiences of Norway, did not expect that the Germans would agree to such arrangements.[70] The issue of the evacuation of children from Warsaw to Sweden or to Switzerland was re-addressed during the session of the Polish government in London on 9 October 1944 at the request of Minister of Labour and Social Welfare Ludwik Grosfeld and Minister of Foreign Affairs Tadeusz Romer. Initially, Prime Minister Mikołajczyk was sceptical whether such operation could be carried out.[71] Nevertheless, during the session on 13 October the government adopted the authorization for the Minister of Foreign Affairs to initiate the negotiations with the governments of Switzerland and Sweden regarding the acceptance of children from Warsaw. The Polish government committed itself to bearing the cost of their support. The Ministry of Foreign Affairs was to seek support in this matter from the governments of the USA and Great Britain. At the same time, the Minister of National Defence pledged that he would ensure that the Polish Red Cross turn to the International Red Cross to request that Germany allow the children to leave to the neutral states.[72] In March 1945 Sokolnicki was asked by his government if he knew whether the Swedish government would agree to admit the evacuees from Warsaw to hospital for treatment. The Swedish side proposed a number it would be willing to accept. Minister Tarnowski guaranteed that the Germans had already agreed to the departure of the Polish women.[73] It was only at the outset of April 1945 that Sokolnicki confirmed Prime Minister Hansson's consent to accept 25 thousand Polish children 'on the condition of considering further [...] technical details [...] with the Swedish executive authorities, which

---

[69] PISM, A 11, E/508, letter by the Polish Envoy to Stockholm H. Sokolnicki to the Ministry of Labour and Social Welfare, Stockholm, 15 I 1944.
[70] AAN, HI/I/498, letter by G. Potworowski, Polish Envoy to Stockholm, to the Ministry of Foreign Affairs, Stockholm, February 1942.
[71] *Protokoły posiedzeń Rady Ministrów Rzeczypospolitej Polskiej*, vol. VII, p. 504.
[72] Ibidem, p. 517.
[73] AAN, HI/I/334, telegram by Minister of Foreign Affairs A. Tarnowski to Polish Envoy to Stockholm H. Sokolnicki, n.p., 22 III 1945.

may give rise to certain complications.' This number could include a certain group of people who were to take care of the children.[74]

Towards the end of April, events would alter the aforementioned plans. During the last weeks of the war, between March and May 1945, Sweden admitted several thousand former concentration camps prisoners, who were transported in dramatic circumstances connected with the so-called White Buses operation headed by Count Folke Bernadotte. Himmler, who was keen to establish contact with the Western Allies to begin peace negotiations, had made a gesture of good will and agreed to release all prisoners from the Scandinavian countries. Bernadotte, having talked to Heinrich Himmler and Joachim von Ribbentrop and managed the operation's logistics, prepared the transport of many more than the total number of Scandinavians (mainly Norwegians and Danes) in Germany. He also attempted to convince the Germans that they allow the Swedes to take prisoners of other nationalities, most importantly French women. This request was the consequence of talks with the authorities of an already liberated France. Himmler also agreed to release Jewish women from the women's camp in Ravensbrück. Though, he wanted to hide this from Hitler. This political game, further meetings and discussions, led to the release of about 7.5 thousand Polish women from the camp in Ravensbrück.[75]

These women were then cordially welcomed by the Swedes in Malmö.[76] They were accommodated at a castle, in the theatre, in a ballroom, tennis hall

---

[74] PISM, A 12, 53/40, telegram by Polish Envoy to Stockholm H. Sokolnicki to the Ministry of Foreign Affairs, n.p., 4 IV 1945.
[75] A. N. Uggla, *I nordlig hamn...*; S. Persson, 'Vi åker till Sverige'. *De vita bussarna 1945*, Rimbo 2003, pp. 347–363; K. Åmark, *Att bo granne med ondskan...*, pp. 598–613; L. Einhorn, Handelsresande i liv. Om vilja och vankelmod i krigets skugga, Stockholm 1999. See the reports of the participants: F. Bernadotte, Slutet. *Mina humanitära förhandlingar i Tyskland våren 1945 och deras politiska följder*, Stockholm 1945; S. Frykman, *Röda korsexpeditionen till Tyskland*, Stockholm 1945; N. Masur, *En jude talar med Himmler*, Stockholm 1945; F. Kersten, *Samtal med Himmler. Minnen från Tredje Riket 1939–1945*, Stockholm 1947. Folke Bernadotte, in his other book *Människor jag mött* (Stockholm 1947), tried to convince the reader that the reason for his request to Himmler, to take women from Ravensbrück camp, was a striking view of a group of prisoners he experienced on his trip to Berlin. The woman leading the group impressed him by holding herself with dignity (p. 14). Another impression was made by Polish princess Sapieha, the wife of a French nobleman, who was engaged in the resistance movement. She was imprisoned and suspected of the same crime as her husband. Bernadotte, on behalf of her Swedish relatives, asked the Germans for releasing the woman. She met her in Berlin and was impressed: 'Proud, brave, calm, she saved all these habits' (p. 90).
[76] PISM, PRM 175, telegram by M. Karniol to Prime Minister Arciszewski, 8 V 1945, pp. 183–185. See also article with expressive title: 'Nigdy Szwedom tego nie zapomnimy! 6120

and school buildings. Following quarantine, they were moved to refugee camps in southern Sweden. One large group of Poles was immediately transported to Ystad and, just like in Malmö, housed in formerly prepared lodgings, located mostly in schools. Others were placed at a castle, at a citadel near Landskrona and in school buildings in Lund.[77] Envoy Sokolnicki hoped that the expenses connected with the Poles' stay would be taken by the Swedes from a fund that was previously reserved for the arrival of Polish children.[78] In his correspondence to London he highlighted Bernadotte's efforts and individual cases, for example, the release of Princess Sapieha, the Skórzewski family and Consul Komierowski, who had been imprisoned in Berlin. In response to the telegram and with thanks from Prime Minister Arciszewski, Bernadotte wrote that he was 'happy that he could fulfil this task.'[79] On the day before the withdrawal of recognition towards the Polish government by Sweden, Envoy Sokolnicki decorated Bernadotte with the Polonia Restituta order. Earlier, on Gustaf V's birthday, President Raczkiewicz sent his best wishes and thanked the King for his hospitality, which had benefitted numerous Poles.[80]

Zbigniew Łakociński, lector at Lund University, collected testimonies about the everyday life in German concentration camps and founded the Polish Source Institute (Polski Instytut Źródłowy) in Lund. He asked the Swedish Institute of International Affairs (Utrikespolitiska institutet) in Stockholm for financial support and began interviewing former prisoners.[81] He and his colleagues interviewed over 500 individuals. The questionnaires were deposited at the Lund University Library. Similar work was undertaken by the Swedish professor and his wife, Einar and Gunhild Tegen. They interviewed women survivors and published a book shortly after based on

---

Polek z piekła niemieckiego do Szwecji', *Dziennik Polski i Dziennik Żołnierza*, 7 V 1945; W. Bogatic, Exilens dilemma. Att stanna eller att återvända..., pp. 170–172.

[77] L. Olsson, *På tröskeln...*, pp. 14–15; According to Inga Gottfarb, who took care of the former prisoners, the Polish women looked much worse than other nationalities: 'Short, lean, pale. Dirty shawls, untidy clothes, knocking wooden shoes and no stockings or stockings with holes in them. Many in prisoner's striped clothes.' See I. Gottfarb, Den livsfarliga glömskan, Stockholm 2006, p. 187.

[78] AAN, HI/I/508, letter by Polish Envoy to Stockholm H. Sokolnicki to the Ministry of Foreign Affairs, Stockholm, 28 III 1945.

[79] PISM, PRM 175, telegram by Count F. Bernadotte to Prime Minister T. Arciszewski, 16 V 1945.

[80] 'Prezydent RP do Króla Szwecji', *Dziennik Polski i Dziennik Żołnierza*, 18 VI 1945.

[81] E. S. Kruszewski, Polski Instytut Źrółowy w Lund (1939–1972). Zarys historii i dorobek, London–Copenhagen 2001.

the collected material.[82] Interest in these unique sources was only spiked at the beginning of the 21st century.[83]

The literature contains information that proves that clear distinctions existed between Polish and Jewish women prisoners, consolidated by mutual accusations of anti-Semitism and anti-Polonism. Sokolnicki estimated there to have been two thousand Jewish refugees. He communicated these conflicts to London:

> 'Unfortunately, various disputes were taken from Germany and the concentration camps and dragged into Sweden, and complaints are coming from both sides. Some of them are brought to light by foreign elements. I, however, have been doing everything I could from very beginning to relieve all frictions, and I gave everyone comprehensive instructions to counteract all impulses of this sort, which caused an unpleasant surprise here, and, at the same time to counteract the distribution of inaccurate and exaggerated news which were then used by the foreign propaganda to its benefit. The issue is nevertheless not so easy and I anticipate difficulties.'[84]

According to Sokolnicki, it was only in mid-May that Jewish organizations resigned from isolating Jewish women from Polish women and the conflicts died down:

> It seems that the issue of isolating the Jewish women has lost on its validity, and definitely on its severity. The initiative, which was undertaken by certain Jewish circles on charges of manifestation of anti-Semitism, was inhibited by the triviality of the accusations, by our action, by the fact that on the spot the delegation of the Association of Polish Jews became familiar with the important context and took our stand towards other Jews, and learned that isolating people who want to consume food ritually is neither popular nor appropriate etcetera.'[85]

On 11 May, the women were joined by 760 men. In total, in mid-May nearly 7300 Polish citizens, former concentration camps prisoners, were already

---
[82] G. & E. Tegen, *De dödsdömda vittna. Enquêtesvar och intervjuer*, Stockholm 1945.
[83] Eugeniusz Kruszewski published 20 questionnaires (*Mówią świadkowie Ravensbrück*, wybór wstęp i opracowanie E. S. Kruszewski, Copenhagen 2001), Artur Szulc chose some questionnaires and presented them with comments in order to show typical lots of prisoners (A. Szulc, *Röster som aldrig tystnar. Tredje rikets offer berättar*, Stockholm 2005). Pia-Kristina Garde was interested in the lot of the prisoners after 1945 (P-K. Garde, *De dödsdömda vittnar – 60 år senare*, Bromma 2004).
[84] AAN, HI/I/508, letter by Polish Envoy to Stockholm H. Sokolnicki to the Ministry of Foreign Affairs, Stockholm, 12 V 1945.
[85] Ibidem, letter by Polish Envoy to Stockholm H. Sokolnicki to the Ministry of Foreign Affairs, Stockholm, 18 V 1945.

residing in Sweden. They were placed in 19 transitory camps and 33 permanent camps in the Skåne and Småland provinces. The workers of the Polish Legation in Stockholm and the Polish consulate in Malmö collaborated with the Swedish authorities on camp management. They recorded the names of the evacuees and issued passports. This work was performed by the group of 16 interned officers and submarine seamen. Towards the end of May, successive transports arrived carrying a total of 5300 Polish former prisoners, who were sent to Sweden on the initiative of the UNRRA. In autumn 1945, a further 1300 Poles (former concentration camps prisoners) came to Sweden within the action of family reunification. Altogether, 13 800 Poles came to Sweden from Germany in 1945.[86] This brought the total number of Poles to 15 000.

According to the first secretary of the legation, Wiesław Patek, both the Swedish authorities and society 'viewed the newcomers favourably and were full of compassion.'[87] The head of the legal department of UD, Gösta Engzell, already during his first conversation with Patek, shortly after the arrival of the women prisoners, however, inquired about the date of their departure to Poland and whether they would be transported across the sea to Gdańsk or Gdynia. According to Sokolnicki, such interest proved 'that the Swedes considered the issue to be very important and that it could perhaps be necessary to discharge the groups of recently arrived refugees.'[88] Patek claimed that their quick departure to the West would prevent the Swedish authorities from establishing relations with the government in Warsaw. In the end, 5200 Poles left Sweden for Poland.

---

[86] A. N. Uggla, *I nordlig hamn...*, p. 173.

[87] The publications of the Polish press in Great Britain were dominated by the feeling of thankfulness towards the Swedes. The Polish women were telling the correspondents that: 'We feel just like in heaven'. See 'Opowiadania Polek w Szwecji o nieprawdopodobnych zbrodniach Niemców', *Dziennik Polski i Dziennik Żołnierza*, 16 V 1945; 'Opieka nad Polkami przybyłymi do Szwecji', *Dziennik Polski i Dziennik Żołnierza*, 15 V 1945 ('Organizacja pomocy władz szwedzkich przebiega bez zarzutu', 'Nastroje wśród Polek są znakomite'); 'Pozdrowienia od Polek w Szwecji', *Dziennik Polski i Dziennik Żołnierza*, 23 VI 1945; 'Sympatie Szwedów dla uchodźców Polskich', *Dziennik Polski i Dziennik Żołnierza*, 23 VI 1945.

[88] AAN, HI/I/508, report by W. Patek, Director of the Consular Department and First Secretary of the Polish Legation in Stockholm, to the Ministry of Foreign Affairs, Stockholm, 15 V 1945. On 9 July the Swedes started to persuade the Poles that they returned to their homeland: 'We would like to help you to regain health, to build up strength and to return home. However the resources at our disposal are limited. [...] Therefore we cannot help you as much as we would like to: it will not be possible to satisfy all your needs.' See the complete text of the appeal: 'Apel do Polaków radia szwedzkiego', *Dziennik Polski i Dziennik Żołnierza*, 12 VII 1945.

11. THE FATE OF THE POLISH REFUGEES

Yet, in the spring of 1946, about 8 thousand Poles resided in Sweden, and they did not intend to return to their homeland.[89] This is clearly why the Swedish government categorically refused to admit contingents of any size, containing former soldiers of the Polish Armed Forces in the West, when the British government made such a suggestion to Stockholm in April 1946.[90] One could notice that, after the war, the Swedish attitude towards the refugee issue was the result of a clash between two opposite tendencies: humanitarian reasons and political and social interests.

---

[89] A. N. Uggla, *I nordlig hamn...*, p. 233.
[90] NA, FO, 188/561, letter by the Swedish Ministry of Foreign Affairs to the Envoy of Great Britain to Stockholm, 23 IV 1946.

12. Swedish Humanitarian Aid for Poland

Humanitarian activity 1939–44

On 8 September 1939, on Envoy Potworowski's initiative, the Polish Aid Committee (*Polen Hjälpen*) was established in Sweden, with his wife Magdalena Potworowska as its head. The Committee, which had access to the legation's financial resources, to the subsidies of the local National Board of Health and Welfare (*Socialstyrelsen*) and of other Swedish charity institutions, tried to provide financial aid to the refugees.[1] Humanitarian efforts focusing on the Poles affected by war were needed on a much grander scale.

From the first day of the German aggression, representatives of the American Red Cross examined the possibility of sending medical supplies to Poland.[2] The Swedes, however, maintained that it would be better to wait until the conclusion of the fights. Meanwhile, on 16 September, the Americans informed Stockholm that the ship *Drottningholm* would start out from New York with a cargo of 10 thousand wide gauze bands, 5 thousand cotton bandages and 100 kilograms of cotton wool, intended for the Polish people. At the time, branches of the Swedish Red Cross all over Sweden began receiving gifts from Swedes, which were to be dispatched to Poland. Clothes were transferred to *Rädda Barnen*. Individual deposits were also made. Sister C. Wallengren of Tollarp (who requested anonymity), for instance, donated 10 thousand crowns to support the Polish refugees in the Balkan countries,[3] whereas J. Palmen offered her services as a nurse. On justifying her decision, she referred to the experiences she gathered during the First World War, her Polish origin and command of several foreign languages.[4] On 24 September, the head of the Swedish branch of Rotary International, the former consul to Russia during the First World War, Carl Harald Trolle, proposed organizing a collection of clothes and shoes for the Swedish Red Cross, which were to be

---

[1] See: A. N. Uggla, *I nordlig hamn...*, pp. 74–81. The Polish State Railways (*Polskie Koleje Państwowe*, PKP) were operating throughout the entire war.

[2] RA-Arninge, Svenska Röda Korset, Överstyrelsen, F I a, vol. 44, copy of letter by E. Stiernstedt to Sweden's board of trade in Stockholm, 18 IX 1939.

[3] RA-Arninge, Svenska Röda Korset, Överstyrelsen, F I a, vol. 44, letter by C. Wallengren to the Swedish Red Cross, Tollarp, 3 X 1939.

[4] RA-Arninge, Svenska Röda Korset, Överstyrelsen, F I a, vol. 44, letter by J. Palmén to the Swedish Red Cross, Stockholm, 14 X 1939.

sent the people in Poland. In the letter to Baron Stiernstedt from the management of the Swedish Red Cross, he emphasized, 'Poland was always popular in Sweden and its fight for freedom in the past we have always followed with sympathy. I am convinced that the appeal made by the Red Cross regarding this matter would meet with utmost understanding and would certainly bring great results.'[5] Initially, the option of taking action was examined. As early as September, the Swedish Red Cross transferred 20 thousand crowns to Geneva for the refugees in Lithuania, Latvia, Hungary and Romania, nearly half of which was sent to Lithuania. Nevertheless, shortly after, on 9 October 1939, the Management of the Swedish Red Cross, 'in connection with the uncertain political situation in Finland', decided not to participate in the collections to support the Polish refugees in the neighbouring countries.[6] In October, Sweden had planned to hold a great state collection for the Polish refugees, where the Swedish Red Cross were to participate. However, the project was abandoned because of the news about preparations for war on the Finnish–Soviet border. The intention then was to limit the aid campaign of the Swedish Red Cross to the Nordic States. Eventually, Prince Carl, chairman of the Board of the Swedish Red Cross 1906–1945, informed Envoy Potworowski in writing on 13 October 1939 that the Swedish Red Cross had allocated an insignificant sum of 10 thousand crowns for the refugees from Poland, including 6 thousand crowns for Lithuania, and 4 thousand for Hungary and Romania.[7] What therefore proved to be pointless and belated was the appeal for further aid for the Polish refugees in Lithuania, where the Lithuanian Red Cross found it impossible to support 30 thousand Poles, including 14 thousand soldiers. There were nearly 100 thousand refugees staying around Vilnius.[8] On 6 November, the management of the Swedish Red Cross refused to grant financial aid to the Lithuanian Red Cross.[9] Two days earlier, on 4 November 1939, however, the Swedish Red Cross had allocated another insignificant sum of 300 crowns to the activity of the Polish Aid Committee.[10]

---

[5] RA-Arninge, Svenska Röda Korset, Överstyrelsen, F I a, vol. 44, letter by C. H. Trolle to E. Stiernstedt, Kalmar, 24 IX 1939.
[6] RA-Arninge, Svenska Röda Korset, Överstyrelsen, F I a, vol. 44, copy of letter by Prince Charles to the members of the board, Stockholm, 25 XI 1939.
[7] RA-Arninge, Svenska Röda Korset, Överstyrelsen, F I a, vol. 44, copy of letter by Prince Charles to Polish Envoy to Stockholm G. Potworowski, Stockholm, 13 X 1939.
[8] RA-Arninge, Svenska Röda Korset, Överstyrelsen, F I a, vol. 44, copy of report 'Informacje Litewskiego Czerwonego Krzyża', Kaunas, 17 X 1939.
[9] RA-Arninge, Svenska Röda Korset, Överstyrelsen, F I a, vol. 44, copy of letter by Prince Charles to the Ministry of Foreign Affairs, Stockholm, 13 XI 1939.
[10] RA-Arninge, Svenska Röda Korset, Överstyrelsen, F I a, vol. 44, copy of letter by E. Stiernstedt to the Polish Aid Committee, Stockholm, 4 XI 1939.

What is more, three churches, in Balingsta, Hagby and Ramsta donated 105 crowns.[11] The outbreak of the Winter War held back the Swedish campaigns for occupied Poland. The Swedes were mostly focused on helping their Nordic neighbours. The war over their eastern border presented serious competition for humanitarian initiatives for Poland,[12] which became occasional activities at best.

When diplomat Sven Grafström travelled to Warsaw in November 1939, the Swedish Red Cross, most probably at his request, provided him with 1 thousand crowns that he was to allocate at his discretion. Prince Carl was also interested to know whether the Luftwaffe respected the symbols of the International Red Cross placed on hospital buildings during the September Campaign.[13] At the earliest opportunity, Potworowski transferred a considerable sum of money to Grafström and requested it be forwarded to one of the people from a list he had included. After reaching Warsaw, the Swedish diplomat handed the money to Prince Zdzisław Lubomirski, who was engaged in the activity of the Social Self-Help Committee of the Capital City of Warsaw (*Stołeczny Komitet Samopomocy Społecznej*).[14] Grafström tried to locate various people, to whom he was to send correspondence, money, or simply information about their friends and families who were outside the country. Grafström saw the city under the German terror, if only the first weeks of a cruel year-long occupation. He intervened with the Gestapo to release a Swedish woman who was a Polish citizen. He could see humiliation of Jews in the streets. However, as Klas Åmark underlined in his book, Grafström did not think about a possible way to make Poles or Polish Jews leave the country. It is one of the examples how much the Swedish policy towards refugees in the beginning of the war was restrictive.[15] A similar description to that made by Grafström, was included by Sven Norrman in reports to ASEA's authorities on his return to Warsaw in autumn 1939. Norrman wrote that the 'impression from Warsaw is depressing'. He esti-

---

[11] RA-Arninge, Svenska Röda Korset, Överstyrelsen, F I a, vol. 44, letter by J. Cullberg to the Swedish Red Cross, Balingsta, 23 XI 1939.
[12] Finland was a competition for Poland also in the context of assistance organized in the United States of America. See *Protokoły posiedzeń Rady Ministrów Rzeczypospolitej Polskiej*, vol. 1, p. 176.
[13] RA-Arninge, Svenska Röda Korset, Överstyrelsen, F I a, vol. 44, copy of letter by E. Stiernstedt to S. Grafström, Stockholm, 27 X 1939 r. S. Grafström described his mission in his diary: *Anteckningar 1938–1944, pp. 163–197.*
[14] RA, UD 1920 års dossiersystem, HP 39, vol. 1586, letter by S. Grafström to Z. Przybyszewski-Westrup, Warsaw, 24 XI 1939.
[15] K. Åmark, *Att bo granne med ondskan...*, p. 546.

mated that 70 percent of the city was destroyed by the German bombardments. He was shocked by the news that 'all Polish professors, teachers and priests were arrested and deported to the camps in East Prussia' and Jews were repressed in an extraordinary way. Norrman registered also that the Germans were robbing works of art.[16]

Alarming letters about the situation under the German occupation were flooding in from Gdańsk, from Vicar Sven Hellqvist, who was a chaplain for the seamen. The Swede not only reported the consequences of the bombings, but also the omnipresent poverty as well as shortages of food and fuel for the winter. On top of that the Germans launched a hurried displacement of the Poles, which included, according to Hellqvist's estimates, about two hundred people. Each Pole could leave with no more than 200 zlotys and only items they could carry. Then, they were all loaded onto trains and transported to the General Government, where they were left to their own devices. At the time the Germans did not allow any humanitarian aid from abroad. Hellqvist was never granted permission to enter the General Government. He purposely summed up his brief correspondence from 24 October, 'When reading between the lines it is possible to see the [true] picture of disease, exhaustion and cold, hunger and death.'[17] Carl Petersén, who managed the B Division of the Swedish Legation in Berlin, informed Minister Sandler of the threat of epidemics and starvation in the Polish territory. The Swedes felt obliged to take some steps relating to the agreement regarding the protection of the Polish citizens in Germany. However, the lack of a possibility to carry out the duties under this agreement justified the passive attitude of some of the diplomats. Petersén told the Swedish Red Cross that an efficient campaign in Poland would require at least 1 million crowns.[18] Initial discussions within the diplomatic circles about the possible organisation of humanitarian aid for Poland were begun in September 1939. On 22 September, the Chargé d'affaires to Kaunas, Claes Westring, inquired with the Ministry of Foreign Affairs in Stockholm whether it was possible to send aid to the Polish refugees in Lithuania. The plan was to send 1 thousand crowns, which was collected by the Polish–Swedish Association. However, two days later, when Westring spoke to Engzell and relayed the news that the British had rushed to help

---

[16] S. Thorsell, Warszawasvenskarna. De som lät världen veta, Stockholm 2014, pp. 46–51.
[17] RA-Arninge, Svenska Röda Korset, Överstyrelsen, F I a, vol. 44, letter by S. Hellqvist to E. Stiernstedt, Gdańsk, 24 X 1939.
[18] RA-Arninge, Svenska Röda Korset, Överstyrelsen, F I a, vol. 44, copy of letter by C. Petersén to Swedish Envoy to Berlin A. Richert, Berlin, 29 XI 1939.

12. SWEDISH HUMANITARIAN AID FOR POLAND

Poland, even this idea was abandoned.[19] At the outset of October, Westring repeated his request, but the issue had been forwarded to the management of the Swedish Red Cross.[20]

In mid-December 1939, the B Division informed Swedish Envoy to Berlin Richert, who was in Berlin, that Polish professors had been arrested in Kraków. The first to be mentioned was Professor Władysław Konopczyński, who was a member of various Swedish academic societies and one of only twelve foreign members of the Swedish Academy of Science. The authorities of the Academy pushed for an intervention in this matter, but in connection with the elimination of the mission to protect Polish interests in Germany, UD shirked from taking official steps.[21] In December 1939, Richert, Swedish Envoy to Berlin, announced that the Germans had nothing against the Swedes submitting gifts for the Poles through the German Red Cross.[22] On 5 January 1940, the German Red Cross planned to establish a special branch, which was to search for the Poles, both civilians and the prisoners of war, in the camps. Poles in the neutral countries now had an address to send their letters to. Those in the countries at war with Germany could only write to Geneva. The same procedure applied to money transfers.[23]

The Swedish Red Cross activity report for 1939 listed 10 thousand crowns, which was remitted to the Polish refugees in Lithuania and Latvia, as well as an additional 3 thousand crowns, allocated to the aid for the intellectuals. The aid for Poland did not go beyond routine activities undertaken on the national arena.[24] From the internal correspondence of the Swedish Red Cross, we know that these were individual donations and the foundation for the aid for the Poles. Sweden, as a neutral country, could continue its role as the centre for searching for persons missing since during the acts of war or as a result of politics conducted by the occupants. From Sweden it was also possible to send parcels with food and clothes to the Poles in the occupied territories.

---

[19] RA, mf. F 035-3-32252, note by G. Engzell, Stockholm, 24 IX 1939.
[20] RA, mf. F 035-3-32252, memorandum by G. Engzell regarding Polish refugees in Lithuania, Stockholm, 5 X 1939.
[21] RA, UD avdelningar och byråarkiv 1864–1952, Andra B-avdelningen, vol. 297, copy of letter by J. Beck-Friis to Swedish Envoy to Berlin A. Richert, Stockholm, 16 XII 1939.
[22] RA-Arninge, Svenska Röda Korset, Överstyrelsen, F I a, vol. 44, copy of letter by Swedish Envoy to Berlin A. Richert, Berlin, 21 XII 1939.
[23] RA-Arninge, Svenska Röda Korset, Överstyrelsen, F I a, vol. 44, copy of excerpt from letter by E. von Post to J. Beck-Friis, Stockholm, 22 XII 1939.
[24] Berättelse över Svenska Röda Korsets verksamhet under år 1939, Stockholm 1940, pp. 124–127.

On 3 January 1940, Hilding Molander, who represented the Swedish Chamber of Commerce (*Svenska Handelskammaren i Polen*), shared the content of his conversation with the Swedish Red Cross with the delegate of the Polish Red Cross, who requested aid for the Polish refugees in the Baltic States. News of aid donated by the Swedish and Dutch branches of the International Red Cross was gratefully received by the Polish Red Cross. The Poles also learned the delegate of the American Red Cross, Malcolm Davis, was to visit Stockholm and take with him 25 thousand dollars in aid for their compatriots. The Polish Red Cross requested that the information about the allocation of this sum be passed through Molander.[25] On 12 January Stiernstedt, responded that the Swedish Red Cross would send 20 thousand crowns for the refugees through Geneva. For financial reasons and the circumstances at the time, he was unable to offer more. Support from the USA, in the form of 20 thousand kilograms of cold-weather clothing, was on its way to Norway, then by rail on to Stockholm, and later to Lithuania and Latvia.[26]

The Swedish Red Cross did not send packages individually. Stiernstedt said that he had not considered sending clothes to Poland and regarded the money collected of greatest important.[27] In March 1940, the local authorities in Helsingborg requested the Swedish Red Cross mediate in the sending of packages to Poland, as there were so many.[28]

The issue was addressed in a letter from a resident of Gothenburg, who wanted to know if it would be possible for her to send a package to a relative in Lublin. The response to such inquiries was to confer with the Polish Aid Committee in Stockholm, which was likely preparing a larger transport for Poland, or with the Swedish Aid Committee for War Victims (*Hjälp Krigets Offer*).[29] Requests for packages be sent to specific people were refused, as well as to territories annexed by the Soviet Union. The message that it was only possible to send a letter or a postcard was constantly repeated.

The postal service operated in the occupied territories by the outset of October. Stiernstedt advised that anyone seeking information about their

---

[25] RA-Arninge, Svenska Röda Korset, Överstyrelsen, F I a, vol. 66, letter by H. Molander to the Swedish Red Cross, Warsaw, 3 I 1940.
[26] RA-Arninge, Svenska Röda Korset, Överstyrelsen, F I a, vol. 66, copy of letter by E. Stiernstedt to H. Molander, Stockholm, 12 I 1940.
[27] RA-Arninge, Svenska Röda Korset, Överstyrelsen, F I a, vol. 44, copy of letter by E. Stiernstedt to C.H. Trolle, Stockholm, 10 X 1939.
[28] RA-Arninge, Svenska Röda Korset, Överstyrelsen, F I a, vol. 66, copy of letter by E. Laurin to the Swedish Red Cross, Malmö district, Helsingborg, 21 III 1940.
[29] RA-Arninge, Svenska Röda Korset, Överstyrelsen, F I a, vol. 66, letter by Ch. Wanner to the Swedish Red Cross, Gothenburg, 20 III 1940; copy of letter by E. Stiernstedt to Ch. Wanner, Stockholm, 27 III 1940.

relatives send 'postcards with short inquiries in German' to the B Division.[30] On 30 January 1940, Envoy Richert informed the Swedish authorities that the Germans, just like the Soviet authorities, would resume their postal service between the Polish territories and abroad, on the condition that packages came from neutral countries and were addressed to residents in the former territory of Poland. In this way the agency of the German Red Cross, which had previously dealt with all correspondence, was lifted. According to Richert, language limitations were no longer an issue. To avoid delays, however, the envoy advised that letters be written in German, there content short and that only personal or trade-related matters be mentioned.[31] From October 1939, reminders regarding this issue arrived in large numbers in to the Swedish Red Cross, as part of every-day questions mostly from relatives or friends of people who remained in Poland. Folke and Estelle Bernadotte, who were members of the royal family, unexpectedly turned to the B Division for information about the fate of the Smoluchowski family. During a visit in the USA, the Bernadottes became acquainted with their relatives and agreed to help gather information about them.[32] In August 1940, Lagerberg handed a letter to UD secretary Stig Unger, which was obtained by Boheman from an acquaintance of the Krzysztoporski family from Lviv, who were deported to the Urals. Lagerberg believed that it would be possible to help the Poles through the German authorities. However, UD refused to grant its support.[33] In November 1939, Professor Gunnar Rudberg from Uppsala inquired about the fate of his colleague from Warsaw, Professor Tadeusz Zieliński.[34] Zbigniew Merdinger, counsellor of the Polish Embassy in London, via the Swedish Red Cross, attempted to send a letter and money to his wife, who lived near Warsaw.[35] In December 1939, the agency of the Swedish Red Cross made it possible for Milla Steinberg, who was staying in Paris, to obtain

---

[30] RA-Arninge, Svenska Röda Korset, Överstyrelsen, F I a, vol. 44, copy of letter by E. Stiernstedt to Consul J. Hüttner, Stockholm, 13 X 1939.
[31] RA-Arninge, Svenska Röda Korset, Överstyrelsen, F I a, vol. 66, copy of letter by Swedish Envoy to Berlin A. Richert to the Ministry of Foreign Affairs, Berlin, 30 I 1940.
[32] RA, UD avdelningar och byråarkiv 1864-1952, Andra B-avdelningen, vol. 358, letter by E. Bernadotte to J. Lagerberg, New York, 17 IX 1939.
[33] RA, mf. F 035-3-32252, copy of letter by J. Lagerberg to Secretary S. Unger, Stockholm, 19 VIII 1940. Unger's answer is dated to 18 IX 1940.
[34] RA-Arninge, Svenska Röda Korset, Överstyrelsen, F I a, vol. 44, letter by G. Rudberg to the Swedish Red Cross, Uppsala, 15 XI 1939.
[35] RA-Arninge, Svenska Röda Korset, Överstyrelsen, F I a, vol. 44, letter by attaché M. von Wachenfelt to E. Stiernstedt, London, 17 XI 1939. The Germans refused to deliver the package.

information about her mother Judyta Grynberg.[36] Franciszek Sokal sought the location of the prisoner camp where his son was being held.[37] The Polish Aid Committee and later the Swedish Red Cross received many similar letters with requests for help or searching for family members staying in the General Government.[38] In November 1940, the Swedish Red Cross received a letter from Mira Jarczyk from Katowice who was seeking information about her husband, who was taken prisoner by the Soviet armies. Adolf von Rosen from the Swedish Legation in Berlin sent a letter from Berlin to Stockholm with a clue that perhaps such information could be gathered through the Swedish–Soviet circle of doctors. At the same time, he asked for information, if not about the results or the action, then at least about making such an attempt. Stiernstedt explained that Stockholm referred such matters to Geneva.[39] A special task was locating the family of president in exile Władysław Raczkiewicz and presenting them with the letter and the money. By December 1939, contact was established and then discreetly maintained with assistance from Swedish entrepreneurs.[40] In later years, there were far fewer such attempts, but it is worth noting that in January 1944 Grafström used the Swedish Red Cross to acquire information about the sister of Janusz Kruszyński from the Polish Embassy in London, who once worked as a secretary in the Polish Legation in Stockholm,[41] whereas in December 1944 Carl Bergenström, director of the Polish Match Monopoly (*Polski Monopol Zapałczany*), sought information about her mother in law, Marianna Tarnowska, who lived in Otwock, Poland.[42] The Swedish industrialists, until the arrests of seven of them in summer 1942, willingly and selflessly helped private individuals find information regarding their loved ones. The director of the Polish Match Monopoly, Carl Herslow, while travelling to Warsaw in

---

[36] RA-Arninge, Svenska Röda Korset, Överstyrelsen, F I a, vol. 66, correspondence regarding this matter in the period between October and December 1939.
[37] RA-Arninge, Svenska Röda Korset, Överstyrelsen, F I a, vol. 66, letter by C. Ekman to the Swedsh Red Cross, Gothenburg, 8 III 1940.
[38] RA-Arninge, Svenska Röda Korset, Överstyrelsen, F I a, vol. 66, letter by the Polish Aid Committee to the Swedish Red Cross, Stockholm, 14 X 1940.
[39] RA-Arninge, Svenska Röda Korset, Överstyrelsen, F I a, vol. 66, letter by A. von Rosen to E. Stiernstedt, Berlin, 28 XI 1940; Copy of letter by E. Stiernstedt to A. von Rosen, Stockholm, 18 XII 1940.
[40] AAN, HI/I/245, telegram by Polish Envoy to Stockholm G. Potworowski to the Ministry of Foreign Affairs, Stockholm, 23 XII 1939; P. Jaworski, *Brev kring...*, pp. 287-293.
[41] RA-Arninge, Svenska Röda Korset, Överstyrelsen, F I a, vol. 180, letter by S. Grafström to E. Stiernstedt, Stockholm, 8 I 1944; copy of letter by E. Stiernstedt to S. Grafström, Stockholm, 12 I 1944.
[42] RA-Arninge, Svenska Röda Korset, Överstyrelsen, F I a, vol. 180, copy of letter by Swedish Envoy to Moscow S. Söderblom [sender unknown], Stockholm, 5 XII 1944.

1939, carried a letter from General Sikorski to his wife, who was staying in the capital.[43] Opportunities for this type of activity also existed later. For example, the former vice president of Kalisz, Mateusz Siwik, who was acquainted with Sven Norrman of the ASEA company, ended up in Palestine following the war. There, in November 1943, he visited the Swedish consulate and asked to be put in contact with Norrman, through whom he hoped to obtain some information about his family which resided in Warsaw under the German occupation. Norrman, lacking permission to enter Germany, was unable to contact Siwik's family personally, but thanks to the staff of ASEA, whose branch in Warsaw was not liquidated by the Germans, passed him news of his family's survival in May 1944.[44]

The management of the Swedish Red Cross expected that the Red Cross in Germany and in the Soviet Union would open special centres in the occupied territories, where it would be possible to make a direct request for help or information.[45] These were false hopes though, especially in the territory of Eastern Borderlands. The Swedes resigned from searching for people there. They referred those in need to the German Red Cross, which had 'direct contact with the Red Cross organisation in Soviet Russia'[46] or to the headquarters of the International Red Cross in Geneva.[47] It is difficult to evaluate the exact scale of the activity of searching for missing members of families and friends, but the extensive documentation of the letters submitted proves that it undoubtedly involved searches for thousands of people.

In mid-April 1940, for fear of the German aggression towards Sweden, the Polish Aid Committee persuaded the Swedish Red Cross to open a special account using a name that would not suggest that it belonged to the Poles. Press attaché Alf de Pomian-Hajdukiewicz and envoy Potworowski asked that the 10 thousand crowns, which was promised by the Swedes and allocated as aid for the Polish refugees in Sweden, was paid in to this account. The persons authorised to use the money in the account were Consul Pomian

---

[43] J. Lewandowski, *Knutpunkt Stockholm...*, p. 82–83.
[44] RA, UD avdelningar och byraarkiv 1864–1952, Andra B-avdelningen, vol. 363, letter by M. Siwik to the Swedish consulate in Jerusalem, November 1943; letter by S. Norrman to B. Johansson, Västerås, 13 V 1944.
[45] RA-Arninge, Svenska Röda Korset, Överstyrelsen, F I a, vol. 44, copy of letter by E. Stiernstedt to the Swedish Red Cross, branch in Gothenburg, 10 X 1939.
[46] RA-Arninge, Svenska Röda Korset, Överstyrelsen, F I a, vol. 66, copy of letter by E. Stiernstedt to I. Scharfstein, Stockholm, 29 III 1940.
[47] RA-Arninge, Svenska Röda Korset, Överstyrelsen, F I a, vol. 66, copy of letter by E. Stiernstedt to E. Sommerfeld, Stockholm, 2 IV 1940.

and Maria Ramstedt.[48] On the same day as the deposit was paid in to the *Hjälpkassan* (Help Fund) account in *Stockholms Enskilda Banken*. An identical sum was to be transferred through Geneva, and subsequently by means of a representative of the American Red Cross, to Poland, for the families of the Kraków professors who were imprisoned by the Germans in the Sachsenhausen concentration camp.[49] Initially, the Germans did not agree to the transfer of money to Poland.[50] Potworowski advised that the sum be distributed through the Aid Committee in Kraków which was managed by Archbishop Adam Sapieha.[51] In 1940, 20 thousand crowns in total was allocated for those in need, half of which for the families of the arrested Kraków professors and rest for people in Warsaw and Kraków. This campaign was carried out with the co-participation of the Polish Aid Committee in Stockholm and the Swedish Aid Committee for War Victims. The total weight of packages sent was 6300 kg with a total value of 10 thousand crowns. The money was transferred by UD to the German Red Cross which forwarded it on to the archbishop's committee in Kraków, which allocated the funds to the families of the scholars.[52]

On 23 April, the Polish Aid Committee produced a list of articles (822.5 kg in total), which were to be sent to the General Government, the prisoner camps in Germany and to the Polish refugees in Lithuania, together with a request for dispatch.[53] The first two batches of packages contained food, and

---

[48] RA-Arninge, Svenska Röda Korset, Överstyrelsen, F I a, vol. 66, letter by the Polish Assistance Committee to the Swedish Red Cross, Stockholm, 16 IV 1940.
[49] RA-Arninge, Svenska Röda Korset, Överstyrelsen, F I a, vol. 66, copy of letter by Prince Charles to P. Hallström [Swedish Academy], Stockholm, 5 V 1940.
[50] AAN, HI/I/246, telegram by Polish Envoy to Stockholm G. Potworowski to the Ministry of Foreign Affairs, n.p., 18 VII 1940.
[51] RA-Arninge, Svenska Röda Korset, Överstyrelsen, F I a, vol. 66, letter by Envoy G. Potworowski to E. Stiernstedt, Stockholm, 13 XII 1940.
[52] *Berättelse över Svenska Röda Korsets verksamhet under år 1940*, Stockholm 1941, pp. 145–146. In June 1941 Lagerberg returned to the issue of sending 10 thousand crowns to the families of Polish professors. Due to the difficulties that were posed by the German side during the transfer, he suggested that the entire sum be converted into German marks. The German authorities were to agree to this but on the condition that the official exchange rate was unfavourable to the recipients. It is not known whether this considered the non-executed transaction or another sum, or whether the Swedes wanted to make the unofficial transfer legal. See RA, UD avdelningar och byråarkiv 1864–1952, Andra B-avdelningen, vol. 297, copy of letter by commercial counsellor to the Swedish Legation in Berlin T. Vinell to the Swedish Red Cross, Berlin, 15 VII 1941.
[53] RA-Arninge, Svenska Röda Korset, Överstyrelsen, F I a, vol. 66, letter by the Polish Aid Committee (Polska Hjälpkommiten i Sverige) to the Swedish Red Cross, Stockholm, 23 IV 1940.

the last, to Lithuania, mostly clothing. The first transport to Poland was dispatched by rail on 16 July, the second, on 28 September, and the third, on 13 December 1940. On the second occasion, 182 kg of food was sent to Kraków, and 1367 kg to Warsaw, and the third time, 232 kg to Kraków and 1175 kg to Warsaw. The Swedish railway exempted the transport from fees, but this did not apply in the territory of Germany.[54] Not all boxes containing bacon and butter reached their destination.

In March 1941, the management of the Swedish Red Cross decided to donate a further 10 thousand crowns, half was to be allocated for the refugees and half for those deported from the Eastern Borderlands to the Soviet Union. Support for the Father Baudouin orphanage in Warsaw was also arranged in the shape of personal care products, which were sent by the resident of the German Red Cross in the General Government. In addition, the Polish prisoners in Germany were sent five-kilogram food packages, for which 3 thousand kilograms of food was used, which was earlier bought in South America and shipped to Gothenburg. The Swedish Red Cross was an intermediary in this initiative.[55]

In September 1941, the Polish government discussed purchasing grains in Sweden to sell in Poland, where food supplies were meagre. The Swedish Ministry of Foreign Affairs agreed to such sales following the approval of the project by Great Britain, payment in foreign currency and conducting negotiations with the Germans by the USA. Counsellor Pilch asked on this occasion, on behalf of the Polish government in London, whether it was possible to purchase rye and wheat in Sweden and then send grains and flour to the Polish territory under occupation. The Swedes doubted the possibility because of a poor harvest.[56]

In December 1941 grains totalling 200 thousand dollars were bought. The Swedes expected the Western Allies to agree, whilst ignoring blockade provisions, to send the transport to occupied Poland. Following the attack on Pearl Harbour, and Hitler's declaration of war on the USA by, the content of the talks between the Americans and the Germans proved no longer valid. Envoy Potworowski was tasked with assessing whether the Swedish authorities could assist in talks with the Germans, and later in the process of purchasing the goods, organizing transport and distribution. On this occasion, Boheman's stance was firmer. He considered that the purchase of grains in Sweden

---

[54] RA-Arninge, Svenska Röda Korset, Överstyrelsen, F I a, vol. 66, letter by N. Ahlberg (the Management of Royal Railways) to the Swedish Red Cross, Stockholm, 8 X 1940.
[55] *Berättelse över Svenska Röda Korsets verksamhet under år 1941*, Stockholm 1942, p. 124.
[56] RA, UD 1920 års dossiersystem, HP 64, vol. 2735, pro memoria, Stockholm, 26 IX 1941.

was impossible due to the poor harvest. Nevertheless, he did not exclude that the project could be implemented if the grains originated from outside the territory of the blockade, meaning not from Sweden.[57] The matter ended there.

In 1942, Potworowski attempted to organize a special medical mission to Poland to control the epidemic of typhoid fever. What made the Polish envoy propose this initiative was on the one hand reminders from London and on the other the promising results of research into vaccination against the disease, performed by the director of the Swedish State Institute of Bacteriology, Professor Carl Kling. Detailed information on this subject was provided to the Polish Legation by Doctor Bolesław Skarżyński, who had been working at Kling's laboratory for several years then. Prince Charles, fully supported this initiative as a head of the Swedish Red Cross, whereas Minister Günther pledged that he would try to convince the Germans to agree for the mission's arrival to Poland.[58] Potworowski claimed that this would make a good occasion to send a greater amount of different types of medicines to Poland. However, the answer of the president of the German Red Cross was negative.[59]

The budget of the Ministry of Social Welfare at the Polish government in exile also included funds for Poles residing in Sweden. At the end of December 1941, during the session of the Council of Ministers in the preliminary estimates of the department's expenditures for 1942, it was stated with satisfaction that 'social welfare in Sweden and Portugal poses no difficulties', which was naturally a consequence of the insignificant number of refugees in these territories and the friendliness of local authorities.[60] The Ministry of Social Welfare was planning to allocate 4 thousand pounds for parcels. For this purpose, a special list was produced, containing addresses of political and social activists, scholars, artists, writers and military families.[61] At the outset of 1942, the Ministry of Foreign Affairs inquired whether Envoy Potworowski had undertaken actions aimed at obtaining a declaration of providing aid for the

---

[57] AAN, HI/I/271, telegrams by Polish Envoy to Stockholm G. Potworowski to the Ministry of Foreign Affairs, Stockholm, 29 IX, 19 XII 1941; Ibidem, telegram by acting Minister of Foreign Affairs E. Raczyński to Polish Envoy to Stockholm G. Potworowski, 13 XII 1941.

[58] AAN, HI/I/498, letter by Polish Envoy to Stockholm G. Potworowski to the Ministry of Foreign Affairs, Stockholm, 2 IV 1942.

[59] Ibidem, letter by Chargé d'affaires of the Polish Legation in Stockholm T. Pilch to the Ministry of Foreign Affairs, Stockholm, 6 XI 1942. Copy of letter by Prince Charles Edward to Prince Charles, Berlin, 30 VII 1942; translation of letter by Prince Charles to Polish Envoy G. Potworowski, Stockholm, 1 IX 1942.

[60] *Protokoły posiedzeń Rady Ministrów Rzeczypospolitej Polskiej*, vol. IV, p. 51.

[61] AAN, HI/I/271, telegram by the Ministry of Social Welfare to P. Kowalewski, n.p., 2 XII 1941.

Polish population under occupation and, most importantly, for children. Among other things, of crucial importance were the typhoid vaccines. The Ministry of Foreign Affairs counted on the opportunity to send a neutral commission to Poland, the members of which would acquaint themselves with the situation and propose the character and scope of aid required.[62] Independently of the plans, Envoy Potworowski was also asked to organize the sending of fish oil to the children in Poland.[63] The branch of the Polish Red Cross dealt with sending packages, but Potworowski explained, 'It is completely out of question to provide aid on a larger scale by sending locally purchased food or clothing.' The funds that were available to the delegate were insufficient and they only allowed the sending of 500 packages a month to individuals and for intermediation in sending 250 packages by people residing in Sweden and Great Britain to their families and friends. According to the Swedish Red Cross activity report, until the close of 1941 the institution acted as a go-between in sending 3600 five-kilogram packages to the Polish prisoners of war. It also dispatched three carriages of goods for the Father Baudouin orphanage in Warsaw. Besides the financial issue, export laws were problematic as they restricted the dispatch of the packages by social welfare and charity institutions. Potworowski offered the import of food and clothing from Sweden to the USA, which could then be freely sent on to Poland. In relation to this, the Swedish Ministry of Foreign Affairs was asked to allocate part of the tonnage (3 tons or 1 thousand packages equivalent) to the goods for Poland, which were shipped from America to Gothenburg. The Swedish Red Cross accepted these parcels and dispatched them to individual addressees in occupied Poland. The parcels contained clothing, underwear, shoes and canned sardines. Moreover, in 1942 another 3 thousand similar parcels were successfully purchased in the Swedish market. Nevertheless, further dispatches were mainly dependant on supplies from America.[64] In the second half of 1942 and in 1943, 17 transports, 3 thousand kilos each, were transported from Sweden to Polish prisoners. In 1944, the next transports, of 10 thousand kilograms each, were prepared following the granting of permission. In total, 12 thousand parcels totalling 150 thousand crowns were successfully sent, which was supplemented by 120 thousand crowns worth of sardines purchased in Sweden. The Swedish Red

---

[62] AAN, HI/I/497, letter by director of the Ministry of Foreign Affairs K. Morawski to Polish Envoy to Stockholm G. Potworowski, London, 13 I 1942.
[63] Ibidem, letter by the Ministry of Foreign Affairs to the Ministry of Social Welfare, London, 13 I 1942.
[64] *Berättelse över Svenska Röda Korsets verksamhet under år 1942*, Stockholm 1943, pp. 132–133.

Cross continued to act as a go-between sending parcels to Poles residing in the General Government. In July 1943, parcels totalling 3 thousand kilograms were sent from the USA and, in September, further 7 thousand kilograms of clothing and shoes. In total, 5 thousand clothing parcels with a value of 300 thousand crowns were successfully delivered, as well as 25 thousand food parcels with a total value of 450 thousand crowns. Aid continued to be sent to the Father Baudouin orphanage, containing nappies, paper towels and medicines. The committee *Hjälp åt Europas Judar* (Help for the Jews in Europe) sent a carriage with duvets.[65] In the second half of 1944, aid for the prisoners was doubled thanks to the increase in sea transport from Argentina.[66]

Of greatest difficult when organising dispatches with food supplies, was convincing the British to transport the goods to Portugal and Sweden to send them on to Poland. In April 1942, the Ministry of Foreign Affairs informed other government departments, 'the British authorities have adopted a negative stance towards our postulate in this respect, pointing to, among other things, the fact that making an exception for us would naturally result in the allocation of similar quotas for other Allied governments.' Nevertheless, a way was found to evade the regulations concerning the blockade of Germany and the occupied countries. As the British authorities did not prohibit the transport of goods to Portugal and Sweden, they were sent in parcels to the prisoners of war from there. That is why the three-ton cargo of goods from America was allocated to the parcels for the prisoners, and only part of it was planned to be reserved for the parcels to Poland.[67] At occasion, spontaneous actions were undertaken depending on the circumstances. In October of 1942, counsellor Pilch asked the Ministry of Foreign Affairs for permission to dispatch 20 thousand cans of sardines to Poland, which according to standard procedure had not been agreed with the British authorities. In this case, however, the commercial counsellor of Great Britain, Jack Mitcheson, who was fond of Poland, was inclined to grant an exception without consulting London.[68] Mitcheson, who at the moment of the outbreak of the war acted as commercial counsellor in Warsaw, tried to support the Poles in their

---

[65] *Berättelse över Svenska Röda Korsets verksamhet under år 1943*, Stockholm 1944, pp. 136–137. See the mentions on the Swedish aid for the orphanage of Father Baudouin: A. Słomczyński, *Dom ks. Boudena 1939–1945*, Warszawa 1975, pp. 99, 126, 141.
[66] *Berättelse över Svenska Röda Korsets verksamhet under år 1944*, Stockholm 1945, p. 146.
[67] AAN, HI/I/497, copy of circular by the Ministry of Foreign Affairs, [April 1942].
[68] Ibidem, telegram by chargé d'affaires T. Pilch to the Ministry of Foreign Affairs, Stockholm, 20 X 1942. Ministry of Foreign Affairs and Ministry of Labour and Social Welfare gave their consent.

activities. He convinced his superiors on the appropriateness of the postulates regarding granting permission for sending goods to Poland despite regulations.[69] At the time, the parcel-sending action was directed by the delegate of the Polish Red Cross and the member of the Management Board of the Polish Aid Committee, Przemysław Kowalewski, who had over 200 Polish addresses, to which he was sending nearly 140 parcels a month. Chargé d'affaires Pilch, who managed the mission following Potworowski's expulsion from Sweden in 1942, considered this solution to be optimal:

> It seems that in the conditions of the current work here, where utmost caution is necessary to avoid putting individual people at risk and maintaining the operation of various posts, where this is only possible, there needs to be observed the principle of greatest possible simplification of the work and its concentration in the hands of one individual.

According to Pilch, Kowalewski was perfect for this role as he dedicated himself to this activity, unlike Maurycy Karniol, for instance, who was famous for his opinion journalism and propagandist activity, or Stanisław Kocan, who had maintained relations with the Polish Ministry of Internal Affairs.[70] In December of 1942, the Ministry of Foreign Affairs confirmed that it would allocate more funds (3 thousand pounds) to parcels for Poland and nappies for the Father Baudouin orphanage in Warsaw.[71]

The secretary general at the Ministry of Labour and Social Welfare, Ludwik Grosfeld, on 10 June 1943, presented a draft for expanding the aid campaign for the people in occupied Poland by increasing the number of parcels with food, medicines and clothing that were being sent from the neutral states. During a government session, he demanded that the funds which were to be transferred to Portugal and Sweden be increased and permission be obtained to send supplements, condensed milk and vitamins, tea and coffee.[72] Do the numbers provided in the Polish and Swedish statements mean that a considerable portion of aid for Poland was transferred through Sweden? Such an assessment is not easy due to the chaotic records. It is also hard to evaluate this from the perspective of an occupied country, where each parcel was gratefully received. From the perspective of the aid organizers, the

---

[69] AAN, HI/I/305, copy of telegram by Polish Envoy to Stockholm H. Sokolnicki to the Ministry of Foreign Affairs, Stockholm, 11 V 1943.
[70] AAN, HI/I/497, letter by Chargé d'affaires T. Pilch to the Ministry of Foreign Affairs, Stockholm, 6 XI 1942.
[71] Ibidem, telegram by the Ministry of Foreign Affairs to the delegate of the Polish Red Cross in Stockholm P. Kowalewski, London, 3 XII 1942.
[72] *Protokoły posiedzeń Rady Ministrów Rzeczypospolitej*, vol. 5, p. 475.

Swedish channel was not the most effective. Polish diplomat Stanisław Schimitzek, who evaluated the situation from the perspective of Lisbon, recorded in his memoirs that until the initiative of Minister Grosfeld, the shipment of parcels to Sweden and Turkey was small and it could not replace the mission in Portugal.[73] Schimitzek was not motivated by the intention to display his Portuguese post. This is demonstrated by the surviving annual programme of providing aid for Poland, drawn up in September 1943, included the plan to organize a monthly dispatch of 100 thousand 500-gram food parcels, 80 percent of which were to be dispatched from Portugal and only 20 percent from Sweden. What is more, Minister Grosfeld planned to buy, mostly in the USA, but also in the territory of Sweden, medicines, vitamins, bandages, and clothing. In total, the campaign of sending parcels totalled 2.169 million British pounds, out of which only 98 thousand was to be spent in Sweden.[74] On 3 April 1944, Grosfeld presented a request he had prepared in collaboration with the minister of the treasury, regarding the draft budget of the main charity institution of the Polish-American community, the Polish Relief Fund, for 1944. The draft included expenses amounting to approximately 7 million dollars. The plan was that 400 thousand dollars would be spent in Sweden on 2500 parcels, which would be sent to Poland by mail, as well as on six transports with nappies and swaddles for the Father Baudouin orphanage.[75]

Officially, however, many of the parcels had to be dispatched to the prisoner camps. In the summing up of the Swedish aid campaign for Poland, in November 1943, it was written that, 'All attempts of expanding this campaign to include civilians in Poland, or, possibly, political prisoners in

---

[73] S. Schimitzek, *Na krawędzi Europy. Wspomnienia portugalskie 1939–1946*, Warszawa 1970, p. 547.

[74] *Protokoły posiedzeń Rady Ministrów Rzeczypospolitej Polskiej*, vol. 6: September 1943–July 1944, scholarly editing by M. Zgórniak, compiled by W. Rojek in cooperation with A. Suchcitz, Kraków 2003, pp. 92–96. The parcels certainly did not satisfy the needs of the Polish community, but it is known from the surviving memoirs that the day of receiving a parcel was the day of a great celebration to each family. See M. Wojciechowski's foreword to the book by S. Schimitzek, *Na krawędzi...*, pp. 5–7. There was one tragic case when receiving a parcel by PPS activist Stanisław Dubois, who was held in the concentration camp in Oświęcim, led to his exposure and death. See: J. Garliński, *Oświęcim walczący*, London 1997, p. 118.

[75] *Protokoły posiedzeń Rady Ministrów Rzeczypospolitej Polskiej*, vol. 6, pp. 519–525. Already in 1943, the orphanage managed by Father Baudouin received two lots of parcels, firstly 227 parcels, mainly with nappies, totalling 12 thousand kilograms, and then 282 parcels totalling 14 thousand kilograms. See: AAN, HI/I/502, copies of certificates by Maria Wierzbowska, director of the orphanage of Father Baudouin, Warszaw, 19 III 1943, August 1943.

Germany, did not bring any results in spite of constant interventions and returning to this subject on every occasion.'[76] The British stubbornly upheld their objection towards violating the blockade rules. Towards the close of 1943, the English and American authorities accepted only the monthly dispatch of 300 tons of donated clothing. The Swedes on the other hand, agreed to increase the quota from 3 to 10 tons. Every month, the Father Baudouin orphanage received a carriage load of sheets, nappies and paper, to cover its needs. At the time, Kowalewski sent nearly 2500 parcels with food and clothing a month to Poland, whereas due to the laws that were in force, this was in secret thanks to the support of Swedish companies. The legation made use of this option and kept sending parcels to various institutions and private individuals from Great Britain. This was in addition to parcel dispatch by those individuals who had obtained permission from Swedish authorities. Poles residing in Great Britain used the opportunity to send their own private messages to families in Poland via Stockholm, thanks to Polish citizens who had reached Sweden in the first months of the war. The Swedish address of the sender acted as a good cover.[77]

The issue of expanding aid that was being sent to Poland from Stockholm was raised by Envoy Sokolnicki during his stay in London towards the close of 1943. In the British Ministry of Economic Warfare, he obtained permission to increase, by 500 thousand crowns, the quota of goods sent to the people under German occupation, with focus on children. Towards the close of 1943, Sokolnicki set out to obtain a permission from the Swedish authorities to buy medicines worth approximately 2.5 million crowns. They were held in storage until the end of the war and sent to Poland afterwards. The envoy expected the Swedish government to leave the clothes and the food, valued at 500 thousand crowns, at the disposal of the legation as soon as the Polish government was given permission by the Allied authorities.[78] The Swedish side agreed that the goods be sent while reserving its right to approve the list of articles accepted for dispatch.[79] The list, prepared by the Ministry of Labour and Social Welfare included sugar, marmalade, milk powder,

---

[76] AAN, HI/I/469, note by the Polish Legation in Stockholm regarding the Swedish aid campaign for Poland, n.p., 10 XI 1943.
[77] P. Cegielski, *Listy do okupowanego kraju. Nieznany epizod z działań sztokholmskiej Polonii w czasie II wojny światowej*, 'Acta Sueco-Polonica', nr 18 (2012), pp. 39–46.
[78] Ibidem.
[79] AAN, HI/I/502, letter by T. Pilch, counsellor to the Polish Legation in Stockholm, to the Ministry of Foreign Affairs, Stockholm, 1 XII 1943.

pasta, bouillon cubes, cheese, dried vegetables and secondhand clothes.[80] Minister Stańczyk pointed out that the majority of expenses connected with the purchase of these articles was to be covered from the funds collected by the organisation *Hjälp Polens Barn*. The Swedish activists of the committees of aid for Poland made efforts to make the members of parliament and ministers of various government departments interested in the needs of Polish society. Sigma Blanck intervened with the Swedish Ministry of Finance to procure a permanent subsidy for the Polish Aid Committee in Malmö, which she was head of. The approach towards the issue of sending nappies for the Warsaw Father Baudouin orphanage was different.[81] The bureaucratic procedure required several-months-long efforts to complete all formalities both in London, to secure the Allies' permission for the trade, which was incompatible with the blockade of Germany, and in Stockholm, in order to agree upon the export of a greater amount of goods necessary in the internal market.[82] The limiting of export licenses acted as a strong brake on the process of dispatching parcels from Sweden. The aid committees had substantial stocks of clothing, but they were unable to send them to Poland due to export restrictions.[83] Export from the countries which were located within the blockade limits, including Sweden, was treated not as rigorously as in the case of non-European countries, but making a decision to liberalise the regulations was complicated. This decision was affected by the bilateral agreements that regulated trade between Great Britain and other countries, and by whether the goods originated from an internal market or from the area outside the blockade, or whether they were purchased or donated, and in the case of purchases it was also important where funds originated. What was eventually considered was the goods' mode of transfer. The decision was made jointly by the British and American authorities, which lengthened the procedure further and made it more complicated.[84] Aid, however, was

---

[80] AAN, HI/I/502, letter by Minister of Labour and Social Welfare J. Stańczyk to the Ministry of Foreign Affairs, London, 30 XII 1943.
[81] AAN, HI/I/501, letter by Polish Envoy to Stockholm H. Sokolnicki to the Ministry of Foreign Affairs, Stockholm, 29 XI 1943; telegram by W. Babiński to the Polish Legation in Stockholm, London, 18 I 1944.
[82] AAN, HI/I/501, extensive correspondence regarding this matter between the Polish diplomatic post in Stockholm, Polish embassy in London, Ministry of Foreign Affairs and the Ministry of Labour and Social Welfare between January and March 1944.
[83] AAN, HI/I/501, letter by Polish Envoy to Stockholm H. Sokolnicki to the Ministry of Foreign Affairs, Stockholm, 31 III 1944.
[84] AAN, HI/I/501, note by counsellor to the Polish embassy in London J. Weytko from the conversation with W. A. Camps from the Ministry of Economic War on 17 III 1944, London, 21 III 1944.

gradually becoming more effective. The report by the Polish Aid Committee, 31 March 1943–13 March 1944, mentions a dispatch to Poland of 330 parcels, totalling approximately 1500 kilograms, and 447 parcels, totalling 4470 kilograms, for the prisoners.[85] At the outset of 1944, the British and American authorities initially agreed to increase the import quota from South America to Sweden from 3 to 10 tons, so that it was possible to dispatch food parcels that were still officially intended for Polish prisoners of war who were being kept in camps in Germany.[86]

The plans for providing post-war humanitarian aid

The Swedish side gradually began proposals to launch cooperation with Poland following the conclusion of the war. In January 1943, in Stockholm, on the initiative of Swedish students and researchers, a new organisation called *Studentförbundet för internationellt samhällstudium och uppbyggnadsarbete* (translation: The Student Union for International Society Study and Construction, or SISU) was established, the purpose of which was charitable work and the post-war rebuilding of Europe. On 13–14 June at a conference in Vigbyholm, the SISU organisation's work programme for the years ahead was presented.[87] According to the legation's official Ewa Zahorska, who was invited to take part in the meeting, the session was one of many signs that Swedish society was willing to take part in the rebuilding of Europe. The conference was attended by politicians, researchers and social activists, refugees from Norway, Germany, Austria and Czechoslovakia. Poland was represented by Zahorska. The Swedes announced the launch of special training courses, focusing on medical personnel initially, but also for other professions in readiness to travel to the countries destroyed by the war. There were also plans to organize language courses as well as meetings dedicated to the culture of the destination countries. Zahorska noted that the Swedes devoted much of their attention to the issue of the re-education of German society the switching to the democratic way of thinking. One of the Swedish speakers, editor Bo Enander, emphasized that Sweden lacked the economic resources of the USA, and help would, therefore, be limited to Norway in the

---

[85] AAN, HI/I/501, attachment to letter by Polish Envoy to Stockholm H. Sokolnicki to the Ministry of Foreign Affairs, Stockholm, 31 III 1944.
[86] AAN, HI/I/507, letter by T. Pilch, counsellor to the Polish Legation in Stockholm, to the Ministry of Foreign Affairs, Stockholm, 4 II 1944.
[87] AAN, HI/I/130, letter by Polish Envoy to Stockholm H. Sokolnicki with the report by E. Zahorska, Stockholm, 14 VIII 1943.

first instance, 'and when it comes to other countries, to Poland, which is closest to Sweden and with which Sweden is historically connected.' The chair of the meeting gave the floor to Zahorska, who spoke about Polish education before the war and about the underground struggle of the Polish youth during the war. He then highlighted, 'Poland is not only geographically close to Sweden, but is always close to Swedish hearts.'

It took no time for the representatives of the SISU organisation to contact the Polish Legation to glean information about the Allied plans to rebuild war-torn Europe. The British Legation's attitude towards the Swedes was reserved, whereas Norbert Żaba opined, 'the Swedish initiative was worthy of our support, all the more so that [the Swedes] are first of all keen to go to Poland' and argued:

> The arrival in Poland, after the war, of a certain number of people prepared to provide emergency aid to the occupied country undoubtedly lies in the interest of our propaganda, as this way it would be possible for us, to gain from amongst the younger Swedish elites, a group of people who know our country very well and whose attitude towards it is very positive.

Żaba then asked the Ministry of Information and Documentation to acquire appropriate letters approving the Swedish proposals and expressing the will for cooperation from the American institutions, Leath-Ross Committee and Lehman Commission, which were planning the post-war rebuilding of Europe.[88] In July, the Ministry of Foreign Affairs confirmed that in line with the guidelines sent to Envoy Sokolnicki already on 9 April, regarding the matter of fighting against the epidemics and hygiene-medical assistance, talks should be held in Poland with relevant Swedish circles, including the intellectuals. At the same time, it was highlighted that all campaigns conducted outside the UNRRA structures should take place with the knowledge and permission of this organisation to coordinate the assistance provided.[89] Sokolnicki, therefore, continued talks with the SISU organisation, and treated exchanges very seriously. To the legation's seat, he invited one of the main activists of the SISU organisation, Gunnar Rügheimer, who was a student of Stockholm University employed in the legation of the Netherlands. During this visit, Rügheimer mentioned that he was invited to Great Britain by the British Council to attend a six-month course in social welfare (Relief and

---

[88] AAN, HI/I/ 112, letter by N. Żaba to the Ministry of Information and Documentation, Stockholm, 30 VI 1943.
[89] Ibidem, letter by the Ministry of Foreign Affairs to Polish Envoy to Stockholm H. Sokolnicki, London, 27 VII 1943.

Social Welfare Course for Allied Nations) and that he was currently applying for a visa. At the same time, he pointed out that contrary to other Swedish organisations, which were focusing their interests on the Nordic States, the SISU organisation would like to 'also prepare the group of young Swedish intellectuals to help on the continent', especially Poland as, 'the country that was most devastated by the war.' This declaration was followed by Rügheimer presenting the plan of sending Swedish doctors and nurses to Poland, the Swedes' participation in international assistance commissions operating in the territory of Poland, and sending economic experts to Poland in agreement with the Swedish trade unions of qualified workers. The plans of assistance that was to be provided by Sweden to the occupied countries following the conclusion of the war, 'in the first place to Poland', were confirmed by the official message from the Health Office on 27 August. The message announced that qualified doctors would be provided. For this purpose, special courses were organized, preparing the medical staff for their visit to the continent. What was very important, according to Envoy Sokolnicki, was a favourable reception of the Swedish initiative by international organisations, in which Poland was represented. He highlighted,

> [this] will be an incentive to further organisational efforts in the local area and will constitute an argument for the Swedish parliament to implement appropriate loans for this purpose. On the other hand, it is necessary that the Ministry support Mr. Gunnar Rügheimer's efforts to obtain an entry visa to England [...]. Besides, it is desirable that Mr. Gunnar Rügheimer come to England some time before the start of the course, which was mentioned earlier, to contact our aid organisations and become familiar with our needs.[90]

The Polish Ministry of Foreign Affairs considered the readiness of the SISU organisation to become engaged in the rebuilding of Poland as an issue both important and worthy of support.[91] Towards the close of 1943, it intervened with the British authorities to provide Rügheimer with a visa.[92] An additional encouragement was the telegram from envoy Sokolnicki, who advised that the Swedish Minister of Finance, Ernst Wigforss, supported the SISU organisation's initiative and had a positive attitude towards both the of a special subsidy for the Health Office's training of doctors before their departure to

---

[90] AAN, HI/I/122, letter by Polish Envoy to Stockholm H. Sokolnicki to the Ministry of Foreign Affairs, Stockholm, 28 VIII 1943.
[91] AAN, HI/I/ 112, circular by the Ministry of Foreign Affairs, London, 13 IX 1943.
[92] Ibidem, letter by Second Secretary of the Polish Embassy in London to the Ministry of Foreign Affairs, n.p., 8 XI 1943; Ibidem, letter by general secretary of the Ministry of Foreign Affairs W. Babiński to the Polish Legation in Stockholm, London, 10 XI 1943.

Poland and for their remuneration in their destination, as well as towards the plan of allocating additional funds from the state treasury for qualified workers to be sent to Poland to help with its rebuilding.[93] The Ministry of Internal Affairs supported the position of the Ministry of Foreign Affairs. It was stated that:

> [Sweden] has brought the democratic model of government almost to perfection and its social structure is perhaps the most developed in entire Europe. Sweden is, moreover, more familiar with the relations across the continent than England and America, and therefore it will play an important role for us not only during the reconstruction of our economic life following the war, but also in the current circumstances.[94]

Nevertheless, in December 1943, in an official statement the Polish Ministry of Foreign Affairs considered the initiative to be premature, as the UNRRA conference devoted to the issue of post-war humanitarian aid was still in progress and the principles for providing this aid were not specified:

> The interested authorities are therefore assuming that although making greatest possible use of cooperation with Sweden is very much desired, it is nevertheless impossible to present any specific figures or demands. The failure to set specific figures or their periodical change could only create a bad impression here and that is why for the time being it would be most desirable to limit ourselves only to general conversations, registering specialists, supporting courses for doctors and medical practitioners and this way preparing the ground for cooperation in the post-war period.[95]

For this reason, the answer was not categorically negative. Counsellor Pilch, from the Polish Legation in Stockholm, according to the guidelines he received from the ministry, announced, 'As soon as the legation receives further detailed information about the decisions which have been made, You, Sirs, will be notified and then the delegate of the SISU organisation will be joyfully invited to establish direct contact with the Polish authorities in London.' He also claimed, 'The Polish Legation is always ready to assist the SISU organisation in supporting and organising training courses for individuals willing to go to Poland and is also ready to keep a register of specialists

---

[93] AAN, HI/I/122, letter by Polish Envoy to Stockholm H. Sokolnicki to the Ministry of Foreign Affairs, Stockholm, 7 X 1943.
[94] AAN, HI/I/112, letter by Minister of Internal Affairs W. Banaczyk to the Ministry of Foreign Affairs, London, 22 IX 1943.
[95] Ibidem, letter by general secretary of the Ministry of Foreign Affairs W. Babiński to the Polish Legation in Stockholm, London, 10 XI 1943.

interested taking part in such an expedition and make their names known to the Polish government.'[96] In his note from London, Żaba highlighted that the relations with the SISU organisation should not be neglected. He pointed out, 'the fact that such people are going to visit Poland must be considered as a chief asset for our propaganda, since my experience has taught me that our best and most active friends in Scandinavia are in the circle of people who have visited Poland and relate to Poland with the thread of personal relations.'[97]

Another kind of initiative which was to take place as part of the Swedish post-war assistance for Poland was the idea to organize a campaign to support the Polish institutions of higher education. In Uppsala, on 10 December 1944, a conference took place, which was attended by the rectors of the local university, Lund, Stockholm and Gothenburg, representatives from *Karolinska Institutet* of the Swedish Academy of Science, the Swedish Committee of International Aid and SISU. The result of this meeting was a memorandum, where a separate passage was devoted to Poland's cultural and intellectual losses. The situation of Polish science was described as catastrophic, and a decision was made to send laboratory equipment, tools, instruments, academic literature etcetera to Poland. Young Polish researchers were also to be offered places on courses held at Swedish universities.[98]

The Swedish plans of taking part in the post-war rebuilding of Europe were officially commented on by Prime Minister Hansson in a speech he delivered on Labour Day, 1 May 1944. Pilch quoted Hansson's words, who convinced the audience that, 'no interests of any kind but only the sense of general human solidarity makes us help those suffering and unhappy.' However, subsequent statements said that neutrality was not tantamount to isolation and keeping away from international cooperation in humanitarian campaigns gave these sort of actions political meaning.[99] The Minister of Finance, Ernst Wigforss, established that just as following the First World War, Sweden would provide help through the Swedish Red Cross and other private organisations in the shape of medicine and food to the prisoners of

---

[96] Ibidem, letter by T. Pilch, counsellor to the Polish Legation in Stockholm, to SISU, Stockholm, 21 XII 1943.
[97] AAN, the Ministry of Industry, Trade and Shipping (London), 413, note by Press Attaché of the Polish Legation in Stockholm N. Żaba, London, 3 I 1944.
[98] AAN, Polish Legation in Stockholm, 35, letter by commercial counsellor to the Polish Legation in Stockholm, T. Pilch, to the Ministry of Foreign Affairs, together with attachment, Stockholm, 16 XII 1944, pp. 1–6.
[99] AAN, HI/I/51, letter by counsellor to the Polish Legation in Stockholm T. Pilch to the Ministry of Foreign Affairs, 2 V 1944.

war, to the sick, and to children. Nevertheless, what he considered indispensable was the state's input in this activity. The Riksdag accepted his proposal to make financial gifts, intended as humanitarian aid and above 1 thousand crowns, tax deductible for every citizen. Initially, Count Folke Bernadotte, who was to manage the work of the Swedish Red Cross, did not seem to notice Poland on the list of the countries that were to receive Swedish aid. His proposal was to, in addition to neighbouring countries, focus on the Baltic States and Germany. He argued that these territories would receive least aid from Great Britain and the USA. In his opinion, Poland ought to be prioritized by the Allies as the war began there.[100] The *Svenska kommittén för internationell hjälpverksamhet* (Swedish Committee for International Assistance, SIH), contrary to the plans of Count Bernadotte, substantially extended the territorial range of its activity and included Poland. It ought to be highlighted that Sweden became engaged in mitigating the social impact of the Second World War in Europe. At the same time, it should be remembered that humanitarian campaigns were closely related to the Swedish policy regarding food supplies from other countries, and with the actions of the Swedish government in international trade.[101] Therefore, this is from the perspective that the change in decision regarding the issue of territorial range of the Swedish humanitarian aid needs to be evaluated.[102]

In the autumn of 1944, the Swedes established contact with the UNRRA to discuss their participation in supporting European countries after the conclusion of the military operations. Although the neutral countries were not invited to become part of this organisation, the material and territorial range of the Swedish humanitarian contribution needed to be decided. This was planned for during the Swedish Relief Committee's visit to London (the committee was composed of vice president of the Swedish Red Cross, Count Folke Bernadotte, Baron Erik Leijonhufvud and Ulf Nordwall). The visit of the Swedish delegation also served as an opportunity to analyse, together with the Polish authorities, the issue of providing the humanitarian aid to Poland. On 7 November 1944, Bernadotte met with the Minister of Foreign Affairs,

---

[100] K.-R. Böhme, 'Handel och hjälp' [in:] *Nya fronter...*, p. 367.
[101] Ibidem, p. 380.
[102] The Swedish plans of providing humanitarian aid for Poland were systematically communicated in the Polish press published in Great Britain: 'Szwedzi o pomocy dla zniszczonych krajów', *Dziennik Polski i Dziennik Żołnierza*, 26 VIII 1944; 'Młodzi Szwedzi chcą pomóc Polsce', *Dziennik Polski i Dziennik Żołnierza*, 20 IX 1944; 'Szwedzki Tydzień Dziecka Polskiego', *Dziennik Polski i Dziennik Żołnierza*, 20 IX 1944; 'Szwedzka ofiarność', *Dziennik Polski i Dziennik Żołnierza*, 17 X 1944; 'Ofiarność na pomoc Polsce w Szwecji', *Dziennik Polski i Dziennik Żołnierza*, 23 III 1945.

Tadeusz Romer, the Minister of Industry, Trade and Shipping, Jan Kwapiński, and Ambassador Edward Raczyński. He guaranteed that Sweden was not planning to send any missions to the territories controlled by the Soviets, but what was to be expected after the conclusion of the war was its direct support on a large scale. Two days later, a meeting took place in the Swedish Legation in London between the delegation of Bernadotte and the representatives of the Polish government headed by K. Załuski, the director of the Office for State Supplies (*Biuro Zaopatrzenia Kraju*) at the Ministry of Industry, Trade and Shipping. The Poles informed the Swedes of their expectations regarding humanitarian aid following the war. Following these talks, the Swedish side was presented with a memorandum where the Polish needs were outlined. Minister Kwapiński pointed out that the memorandum concerned humanitarian aid (*relief purposes*) only, 'Poland is very much interested in obtaining certain relief supplies from Sweden as the possibly closest source, to save time by securing the direct transport of goods to cover the most urgent needs.'[103]

For the Polish government the memorandum was a point of departure to more specific talks, the subject of which was presented in five points: hospital and residential barracks, layettes for infants and midwives, food, clothing and shoes and seeds.[104] In addition, the Polish government expected Swedish doctors and nurses to be sent in teams to Poland, as they lacked such personnel. The matter of Swedish aid to Polish agriculture was dealt with separately. Further conversations were to be conducted through the Polish Legation in Stockholm. Kwapiński finished his memorandum with a solemn appeal for initiating cooperation between Sweden and the Polish government.

A copy of the list that had been delivered to the UNRRA, of the necessary scientific and laboratory equipment, was also received by Count Bernadotte. Bernadotte highlighted that he could not yet declare the exact extent of Swedish aid to Poland, explaining that the humanitarian campaign would focus on the Nordic States in the first instance.[105] Sokolnicki informed London that the Swedish parliament had allocated 600 million crowns for humanitarian aid, out of which, he learned, nearly 10 percent was to reach Poland. Behind the scenes, the envoy also acted to increase this amount as

---

[103] RA, UD 1920 års dossiersystem, HP 39, vol. 1620, copy of memorandum by Minister of Industry, Trade and Shipping J. Kwapiński.

[104] RA, UD 1920 års dossiersystem, HP 39, vol. 1620, letter by E. Leijonhufvud from the Swedish Committee of International Help to R. Sohlman from UD, Stockholm, 7 XII 1944.

[105] AAN, HI/I/114, letter by the Ministry of Foreign Affairs to the Polish Legation in Stockholm, 22 XI 1944; Ibidem, notes by commercial counsellor to the Polish Embassy in London Z. Merdinger, 7 XI and 8 XI 1944.

much as possible. Initially, it was established that the liaison between the Polish Legation in Stockholm and Swedish humanitarian organisations would be Harald Axell, who before the war was the director of the *Bank Amerykański* in Warsaw and at that point the treasurer of the *Hjälp Polens Barn* committee.[106] Following the talks in London, the director of the Department of Social Reconstruction of the Ministry of Labour and Social Welfare, T. Nieduszyński, pointed out that after the war Sweden should become an important centre for providing aid to Poland, as it seemed destined to become due to its location in relation to Poland and its resources having remained untouched by the war, and due to the Swedes' positive attitude towards the action.[107] On 2 December 1944, the press reported that on the initiative of the Swedish Chamber of Commerce a central institution, Swedish Aid for Poland (*Svenska Polenhjälpen*), was established to deal with organising aid for Poland. Its launch was demanded by the Polish Legation as early as September 1944. *Polenhjälpen* was to coordinate the work of all aid committees. Its chair was Count F. Bernadotte and its secretary Henrik Beer. The new institution also included Marika Stiernstedt, representing the *Hjälp Polens Barn* organisation, Inger Bagger Jöback from *Rädda Barnen* (Save the Children Sweden), Baron Erik Stiernstedt from the Swedish Red Cross, Sigma Blanck representing the local committees dealing with aid for Poland, Brita Holmström from the *Inomeuropeisk Mission* organisation. The delegate of the Polish Red Cross, Przemysław Kowalewski, was to be invited to individual sessions.[108]

The mission of Sven Hellqvist in the General Government

The tragedy of the Polish people living in the occupied territories was made public to such an extent that in 1944 public appeals for current material aid for the Poles became more widespread. The press presented heart-breaking images of poverty and hunger in the General Government. Sigma Blanck, the diligent chair of the Aid Committee for Poland in Malmö, was giving repeated lectures and provided information to the press about the campaign of collecting funds. Mia Leche Löfgren, who associated with the Swedish Red

---

[106] Ibidem, telegram by Polish Envoy to Stockholm H. Sokolnicki, 28 IX 1944; Ibidem, letter by Polish Envoy to Stockholm H. Sokolnicki to the Ministry of Foreign Affairs, 17 X 1944.
[107] AAN, HI/I/114, note by Director of the Department of Social Reconstruction of the Ministry of Labour and Social Welfare T. Nieduszyński, 27 XI 1944.
[108] AAN, HI/I/501, letter by Polish Envoy to Stockholm H. Sokolnicki to the Ministry of Foreign Affairs, Stockholm, 2 XII 1944.

Cross, in the *Göteborgs Handels- och Sjöfarts-Tidning*, demonstrated the urgent need for humanitarian actions for Poland. She also quoted letters and reports proving how the Poles were grateful for the offered support, emphasizing, 'what we are doing for Poland is not only of material, but also symbolic dimension. We are paying tribute to the nation, which, through its martyrdom became a model for small nations.'[109] In the context of the reports from Warsaw, these appeals reached fertile ground.

Following the outbreak of the Warsaw Rising, Envoy Sokolnicki attempted to familiarize both *Utrikesdepartamentet* (UD) and other Swedish institutions with the tragic situation in the Pruszków camp.[110] A public collection for the people of Warsaw was instantly launched. At the same time, the press services of the legation informed the newspapers about the catastrophic situation of the inhabitants of the war-stricken capital of Poland. A discussion flared up in the press about organising a large humanitarian campaign.[111] The issue was publicized so effectively that the Swedish Ministry of Foreign Affairs started to admonish its legation in Berlin about the news on the opportunities of providing immediate material aid to the General Government. The Swedish Red Cross then asked Geneva to provide accurate information.[112]

Towards the close of September, the Swedish government awarded a 500 thousand crown grant to the Swedish Red Cross, which was intended for the Poles in the General Government. The money was spent on medicine, sanitary products and food. Clothing and shoes were to come from the USA. The materials were to be taken to Pruszków. The management of the Swedish Red Cross decided that the Swedish delegates should be present when the aid was distributed and only on this condition was the aid to be sent.[113] Prince Carl was convinced that the best candidate for supervising the Swedish transports would be the chaplain of Swedish seamen in Gdańsk, vicar Sven Hellqvist, who, 'on many occasions mediated and controlled the process of sending aid

---

[109] M. Leche, 'För Polen', *Göteborgs Handels- och Sjöfarts-Tidning*, 26 VI 1944.
[110] AAN, HI/I/503, telegram by Polish Envoy to Stockholm H. Sokolnicki to the Ministry of Foreign Affairs, Stockholm, 26 VIII 1944.
[111] 'Pruszków', *Morgon-Tidningen*, 29 VIII 1944.
[112] AAN, HI/I/503, telegram by Polish Envoy to Stockholm H. Sokolnicki to the Ministry of Foreign Affairs, Stockholm, 30 VIII 1944.
[113] RA-Arninge, Svenska Röda Korset, Överstyrelsen, F I a, vol. 180, memorandum by General Secretary E. Stiernstedt, Stockholm, 28 IX 1944.

from Sweden to Poland', and therefore 'the difficult and delicate mission supported by the Swedish government' would be placed in good hands.[114] The Prince convinced the German authorities that Swedish control was necessary, as the property belonged to the state, and was only formally handed over to the Swedish Red Cross. He asked that such an explanation be presented to Envoy Richert in Berlin.[115] The Swedish Red Cross contracted vicar Hellqvist, entitling him to remuneration as well as insurance. The contract would terminate on the vicar's return to Sweden.[116]

On 10 October 1944, a carriage laden with 245 boxes of tinned sardines and 30 boxes of underwear and stockings was sent from Stockholm to Pruszków near Warsaw, where the capital's inhabitants relocated following their expulsion by the German troops. One day later, the second transport set off with 15 tons of sugar and 10 boxes of clothing. On 21 October, 20 tons of crisp bread was sent. At the close of October 1944, Pilch informed London, 'The dispatch campaign is in full swing, and so far, it has not met any obstacles.'[117] A request was submitted to the Legation of the USA that the Americans agree to increase relief quotas from the territory of Sweden. Sweden's suspension of shipping to German ports led to transports sent by rail through Denmark to Kraków. There, they were handed over to a delegate of the German Red Cross. Further distribution was to be controlled by a delegate of the Swedish Red Cross. Most of the resources allocated came from the Swedish government, which had placed, as mentioned previously, 500 thousand crowns at the disposal of the Swedish Red Cross. The additional 100 thousand crowns came from the *Hjälp Polens Barn* organisation, 40 thousand crowns from the Swedish Aid Committee for Poland in Gothenburg, and 37 thousand crowns from the Swedish Aid Committees of Malmö, Uppsala and Borås. What is more, *Rädda Barnen* declared its intention to help evacuees from Warsaw. The total provided was 677 thousand crowns.

Following the talks at the German Ministry of Foreign Affairs and at the headquarters of the German Red Cross, Hellqvist expected that he would quickly be granted the necessary permission from Hans Frank and head off on a one-week expedition to the General Government. Nevertheless, Frank

---

[114] RA-Arninge, Svenska Röda Korset, Överstyrelsen, F I a, vol. 180, copy of letter by Prince Charles to King Gustaf V, Stockholm, 2 X 1944.

[115] RA-Arninge, Svenska Röda Korset, Överstyrelsen, F I a, vol. 180, copy of letter by Prince Charles to Swedish Envoy to Berlin A. Richert, Stockholm, 23 X 1944.

[116] RA-Arninge, Svenska Röda Korset, Överstyrelsen, F I a, vol. 180, contract between the board of the Swedish Red Cross and pastor S. Hellqvist, Stockholm, 1 XI 1944.

[117] AAN, HI/I/503, letter by T. Pilch, counsellor to the Polish Legation in Stockholm, to the Ministry of Foreign Affairs, Stockholm, 27 X 1944.

ignored the reminders of the Auswärtiges Amt and the interventions of the Swedish envoy.[118] It was not until 7 November that Hellqvist could leave Berlin. On 8 November, he met with the management of the Central Welfare Council (RGO) in Kraków. The chair of the Council, Konstanty Tchórznicki, informed him that 450 thousand evacuees, including 30 thousand children, from Warsaw, needed immediate assistance. The number of residents needing to leave the city was 700 thousand. Nobody, especially those who left Warsaw at the beginning of August, was thinking about the approaching winter. Many thought that it would be possible to return home beforehand, after the short-lived fighting had ended. People were, however, facing shortages of winter clothing. Those who were evacuated during the last stage of the rising were exhausted by the primitive living conditions they had suffered for several weeks. They dispersed throughout the General Government in search of shelter. Many people required immediate medical assistance, were wounded and burnt. In his reports, Hellqvist emphasized the devotion of the Polish doctors and nurses who brought relief to the sick gathering in overcrowded hospitals and hastily prepared rooms of the Jagiellonian University. The vicar also visited Częstochowa and Radomsko as well as several suburban towns around Warsaw: Pruszków, Piastów, Milanówek (where the Father Baudouin orphanage, regularly receiving material support from the Swedish Red Cross, was evacuated), Grodzisk and Tworki. Everywhere he saw members of all social groups united in a nation-wide suffering. He was surprised when he saw that the Kraków warehouses of the Central Welfare Council contained parcels of crisp bread, sent several days earlier from Sweden. The explanation for which was the need to save the stocks for the time when international aid would be suspended. In other towns and villages amounts of Swedish sugar and milk were stored together with coats. Hellqvist also suspected the Central Welfare Council of selling canned sardines on the black market, instead of distributing them, to raise money for buying cheaper products for a greater number of people. The vicar viewed these practices with mixed feelings. They were not in line with the intentions of the Swedish authorities, and he was aware of the specificity of the situation under the German occupation. He maintained that there was no control over the distribution. He could only instruct the Central Welfare Council on how to keep up-to-date and thorough records of donations.[119] In

---

[118] PISM, PRM 161A, note by Polish Envoy to Stockholm H. Sokolnicki 'Informacje uzyskane od pastora S. Hellqvista, delegata Szw[edzkiego] Czerwonego Krzyża w Krakówie', p. 26.
[119] RA-Arninge, Svenska Röda Korset, Överstyrelsen, F I a, vol. 180, S. Hellqvist: report from the travel to the General Government between 7 and 15 XI 1944, Berlin, 18 XI 1944; copy of

general, according to Hellqvist, the food situation 'was not disastrously bad.' The shoe and clothing situation was bad, but worst of all was the lack of detergents. There was also a dire shortage of duvets and blankets. Among the necessary items he also mentioned hospital equipment, soap, detergents, nappies, towels, tooth brushes, combs, buckets and mugs. He informed about an insufficient number of trucks and typewriters, which made it particularly difficult to organize the distribution in rural areas.[120]

After Hellqvist had submitted his first report about the difficult conditions in which he was forced to perform his humanitarian mission in the General Government, Stiernstedt continued to maintain the position of the Swedish government that the control of transports and distribution was necessary, and he reminded the vicar that this was state provided aid they were talking about. He showed appreciation for the finding of his aunt Mary Ciechanowiecka, to whom the vicar was to offer his help.[121] Several transports of tinned sardines, clothes, sugar, bread and salt had already arrived in Poland by that time. The last transport of clothing and food for Poland arrived in Lübeck on 5 December. Hellqvist was planning to set off on another expedition to Kraków and follow the transport, but he did not gain the relevant permission from the German authorities. Further monitoring of the aid from Sweden was impossible due to the approaching front. In December, the dispatch was suspended, since as it was stated in the official announcement of the Swedish authorities, 'the German authorities are making it difficult for the Swedish delegate to access the territory, where the submitted items are being distributed.' When the campaign was over, the chair of the Central Welfare Council in Kraków, Konstanty Tchórznicki, sent a telegram on 21 December 1944 to Prince Charles with thanks for the engagement of the Swedish Red Cross in helping the evacuated people of Warsaw.[122]

Sweden sent the total of 8 carriages with food products to Poland. These transports included 30 thousand tins of sardines, 15 tons of sugar, 2 tons of

---

letter by S. Hellqvist to S. Grafström, Berlin, 23 XI 1944; final report by S. Hellqvist from the journey between 7 and 15 XI 1944, Berlin, 5 XII 1944. Head of the SS and Police in Warsaw P. O. Geibel issued a permission for S. Hellqvist to travel across the ruined capital. The Germans even did not object to him taking photos of it. The vicar examined the building of the Swedish Legation, which survived together with all its equipment. In the piggery nearby Grodzisk he found the former staff member of the legation, Margit Vingqvist-Jelnicka.

[120] RA-Arninge, Svenska Röda Korset, Överstyrelsen, F I a, vol. 180, letter by S. Hellqvist to the board of the Swedish Red Cross, Berlin, 19 XI 1944.

[121] RA-Arninge, Svenska Röda Korset, Överstyrelsen, F I a, vol. 180, letter by general secretary of the Swedish Red Cross E. Stiernstedt to S. Hellqvist, Stockholm, 30 XI 1944.

[122] RA-Arninge, Svenska Röda Korset, Överstyrelsen, F I a, vol. 180, telegram by K. Tchórznicki to president of the Swedish Red Cross, Kraków, 21 XII 1944.

fish oil, 20 tons of milk powder, 20 tons fish preserves, 20 tons of peas, 20 tons dried vegetables, 20 tons of jam, 4 tons of vegetable stock cubes, 20 tons of meat preserves, 20 tons of crisp bread, 20 tons of flour, 50 tons of salted fish, 10 tons of clothes, 1 ton of socks, 2.5 tons of soap, 500 kilograms of vitamins, as well as 40 thousand crowns' worth of medicine, intended for 10 thousand people. The total value of aid that was sent to Poland is estimated at 300 thousand crowns. At the same time, the Swedish Red Cross acted as a go-between in the dispatch of parcels, with a total value of approximately 625 thousand crowns, from Polish aid organisations.[123]

Hellqvist made two short trips to the General Government over the period of two months; this included a visit to Kraków, to Warsaw and its nearby towns as well as to Kutno and Kielce. Following his return, he recounted his experiences not only to his superiors but also to the Polish Legation. In his view, the Polish people detested the Germans for the several cruel years of occupation, but at the same time they feared the approaching Soviets. The amount of supplies was not the worst, better than in the case of Germany. There was a shortage of clothing and the prices were high.

What needs to be highlighted is that the Swedish aid for the Poles living under German occupation was of considerable significance. It should be noted that the Ministry of Labour and Social Welfare continued to express regret in its reports that the British and American governments ignored the requests of the Polish government regarding the lifting of the blockade of the territories controlled by the Germans and permission for supplying food both to the occupied territories of Poland and to the neutral states, where, as it was initially established, 50 thousand Polish children were to be sent.[124]

Swedish transports of humanitarian aid to the Lublin Committee Poland

At the same time the Swedes, without much publicity, decided to send immediate humanitarian aid to Poland through Moscow. In December, while on his way back to Moscow from the consultations in Stockholm, Söderblom carried 212 kilograms of medicine on to the plane, with a total value of over 15 thousand crowns. This was the gift for Poland from the committee led by Marika Stiernstedt, which was delivered to Stefan Jędrychowski, the representative of the PKWN. In transpired that this was the first humanitarian aid

---
[123] *Berättelse över Svenska Röda Korsets verksamhet under år 1944*, pp. 146–147.
[124] PISM, PRM 161A, note regarding the aid for Poland in 1944, n.p., 16 XII 1944.

package sent to the Polish territory following the entrance of the Soviet armies. The representative of the PKWN announced that all items would be sent to Bolesław Drobner, who held the post of head of health department at the Lublin Committee. According to Söderblom, Jędrychowski was clearly familiar with the structures of the Swedish organisations of international aid. The Swedish diplomat attributed this knowledge to the efforts of Jerzy Pański. Söderblom clearly wanted to please his Polish interlocutor and expressed his personal view that appropriate aid would be granted by the Swedish state institutions as soon as the territory of Poland was liberated. Then, in line with the received instructions, he proposed that vice chair of the Swedish Red Cross, Count Folke Bernadotte, should come to Lublin as part of his visit to Moscow to help him to develop an opinion about the current situation in the territory of Poland. Jędrychowski declared his readiness to accept Count Bernadotte in Lublin, provided his visit to Moscow would take place and that the situation on the front allowed it. In addition, he promised to forward him the list of needs, which was drawn up for the UNRRA. Söderblom considered it necessary for the time being to continue small deliveries of humanitarian aid from private committees, before launching regular state deliveries. According to his information, the *Hjälp Polens Barn* organisation was to send 9 tons of clothing and shoes, some amount of food, sheets and paper towels, whereas other organizations in Sweden prepared amounts of pearl barley, peas and clothes.[125] Söderblom informed UD that the Poles were also interested in obtaining scientific and medical equipment, specialist literature (especially medical) for the Lublin University. In the near future, he was expecting to welcome Polish professors on this matter.[126] On 8 December, he was visited by director of the PKWN's science department Stanisław Skrzeszewski, director of the department of healthcare and Professor in Bacteriology Edward Grzegorzewski, together with two other professors, radiologist Murzyński and dean of the faculty of philosophy of the newly established Maria Curie-Skłodowska University in Lublin Konstanty Strawiński. He explained to Söderblom about the need for equipment and materials in the Polish laboratories and academic libraries. For Söderblom, this was another occasion for Sweden to show itself off in Poland in a way that was both relevant and immediately noticeable. He proposed, therefore, that the equipping of Polish research facilities be expanded to include not

---

[125] RA, UD 1920 års dossiersystem, HP 39, vol. 1620, letter by Swedish Envoy to Moscow S. Söderblom to Minister of Foreign Affairs Ch. Günther, Moscow, 5 XII 1944.

[126] Ibidem, memorandum regarding humanitarian aid for liberated Poland, Stockholm, 7 XII 1944.

only appropriate committees providing aid to Poland, but also individual Swedish higher education institutions. He informed that the American Red Cross, following the reception of the long-expected approval from the Soviet authorities, had already initiated the dispatch of aid to Poland via the Soviet Union, which, 'was allegedly accepted by the Polish government in London.' To acquaint himself with the attitude of the Soviet authorities towards the Swedish humanitarian campaign, Söderblom posed a question about this subject to vice commissary for foreign affairs Vladimir Dekanozov, who without hesitation answered, 'friendly'.[127] On 12 December, the Swedish envoy received a list of needs from the PKWN, which was submitted to the UNRRA for the Montreal conference.[128] Eventually the *Hjälp Polens Barn* committee was granted permission to dispatch approximately 22 tons of food and 5.5 tons of clothes and shoes to Poland. Commercial Attaché Wojciech Chabasiński explained to the Swedes that the dispatched supplies should pass through Leningrad, and from there they should be transported to Lublin. In connection with the lack of access to the port in Leningrad throughout the winter, Söderblom suggested that the aid for Poland be shipped to a Finnish port, and then by rail to Leningrad. He considered the coordination of the entire action extremely important. The Poles in Moscow were notified early enough about the date of the transport's arrival in Leningrad and given the option of taking over before its transport to Moscow and Lublin.[129]

At the outset of November 1944, when a two-way (focused also on the territories controlled by the Germans and the Soviet armies) aid transport for Poland was undertaken, unpleasant polemics took place. Marika Stiernstedt accused the actions of vicar Hellqvist of being ineffective due to the alleged German robberies, and argued that the aid should be sent to the areas controlled by the PKWN.[130] Envoy Sokolnicki rejected these arguments, maintaining, 'Aid should be sent to the places where the needs are the greatest, and to the places it can reach the quickest.'[131] In his report to London, he complained, 'The current situation has been caused by both neutrality and Sovietophilia, as

---

[127] Ibidem, letter by Swedish Envoy to Moscow S. Söderblom to Minister of Foreign Affairs Ch. Günther, Moscow, 12 XII 1944.
[128] Ibidem letter by Swedish Envoy to Moscow S. Söderblom to Minister of Foreign Affairs Ch. Günther, Moscow, 7 XII 1944.
[129] Ibidem, letter by Swedish Envoy to Moscow S. Söderblom to Minister of Foreign Affairs, Moscow, 12 XII 1944.
[130] AAN, HI/I/503, letter by Polish Envoy to Stockholm H. Sokolnicki to the Ministry of Foreign Affairs, Stockholm, 22 XII 1944.
[131] AAN, HI/I/501, note regarding the matter of sending material aid from Sweden to Poland occupied by the Soviet armies, London, 13 XII 1944. Cf. S. Jędrychowski, *Przedstawicielstwo...*, pp. 202–205.

well as by the intention to establish relations in advance with the part of Poland that has been liberated from the Germans (where some Swedish facilities are located, for example, the branch of the *Bank Amerykański* in Vilnius).' Pański's activities were of great importance. On behalf of the PKWN, he established relations with the Swedish industrialists, especially director Harald Axell (who was treasurer of the *Hjälp Polens Barn* committee), and the patronage of the Soviet Legation ('Mrs. Kollontai is casting a spell on Mrs. Stiernstedt'). The Swedish Ministry of Foreign Affairs was unwilling to officially become engaged in this dispute.[132] Meanwhile Pański, as a correspondent for the Polpress agency, presented an off-the-record interview with Stiernstedt as a radio announcement, where the Swedish writer argued the necessity of sending aid in cooperation with the PKWN. On 7 December 1944 in Gothenburg, at a meeting of the local *Polen Hjälpen* committee the writer attacked the campaign of sending parcels to the General Government. According to Stiernstedt, this initiative was undertaken only because the Polish diplomats in Stockholm wanted to give it a political tone. Vice Consul Borys Żukowski explained, 'The responsibility of this support and the ability to use the collected funds lies exclusively on the Swedes, who, undoubtedly have the right to offer this help in the form they consider most appropriate and to whom they consider most appropriate.' Żukowski described the writer's accusations as unfair and argued that the Polish Legation only played an advisory role. When reservations were raised about the action of sending aid by Moscow to Lublin, they concerned 'technical issues' meaning the Swedes could exercise control over its transport and distribution. Aid was expected to be delivered quickly by the Allies but the population of the occupied part of the Polish territory could not expect the same.[133] Eventually, Stiernstedt was persuaded that some of the help should be sent to the territories controlled by the Germans. Of the 180 bags of clothing, collected by the *Hjälp Polens Barn* committee, 100 bags were sent through Germany, whereas following the turn of the new year, 80 were to be sent to Lublin.[134] 15 thousand crowns worth of items were sent to the Soviet controlled Polish territories.[135] The Swedish authorities responsible for humanitarian aid, headed by the management of the Swedish Red Cross and the Swedish Committee of International Assistance, refrained from sending further aid to

---

[132] Ibidem, letter by Polish Envoy to Stockholm H. Sokolnicki to the Ministry of Foreign Affairs, Stockholm, 16 XI 1944.
[133] Ibidem, letter by Vice Consul B. Żukowski to the Polish Legation in Stockholm, Gothenburg, 7 XII 1944.
[134] Ibidem, letter by Polish Envoy to Stockholm H. Sokolnicki to the Ministry of Foreign Affairs, Stockholm, 16 XII 1944.
[135] *Berättelse över Svenska Röda Korsets verksamhet under år 1944*, p. 147.

Poland from state funds with help of or through the Soviet authorities and the PKWN until the political situation stabilized. In the short term, aid would originate from the stocks of the *Hjälp Polens Barn* committee. The Union of Polish Jews in Sweden, wanting to avoid contact with Pański due to the declared political neutrality, turned to this organisation to request aid be sent to Lublin.[136] Minister Tarnowski accepted Sokolnicki's decision that the campaign of sending aid to the territories controlled by the Soviet army was taken into consideration, and at the same time, efforts were continued to bring further transports to the German-controlled territories of Poland.[137] The Polish diplomats considered that the actions of Marika Stiernstedt were caused by the reaction of the Soviet Legation and Jerzy Pański to the propagandist success of the so-called Polish Week, a collection of money for the people of Warsaw, 15–22 September, which was organized to a large extent by the *Hjälp Polens Barn* committee.[138] It ought to be noted that the event, mostly associated with the rising's defeat, was planned in May 1944.[139]

In mid-February 1945, when virtually the entire territory of Poland fell under the control of the Soviet armies, the only option for the Polish government in exile was to send humanitarian aid to its homeland. Minister Tarnowski instructed Sokolnicki, 'Due to the immense needs of the people, it is important for us that the aid reach Poland by any route possible.' In December 1944 the branch of the Polish Red Cross in Stockholm was sent a hundred tents with heaters and equipment, which made them suitable for children. This was supplemented by 2 thousand parcels with a total value of 25 thousand crowns, which were to be handed out to the poorest Warsaw inhabitants. In March 1945, the Polish Red Cross received 17 tons of clothing and shoes, and in April an ambulance and four cars adapted for carrying the sick[140] For Tarnowski, it was important that the distribution was carried out by the Swedish Red Cross. This would ensure adequate control and allow for subsequent shipments without the risk of items being distributed against the

---

[136] AAN, HI/I/501, note regarding the matter of sending material aid from Sweden to Poland occupied by the Soviet armies, London, 13 XII 1944.
[137] Ibidem, telegram by Minister of Foreign Affairs A. Tarnowski to Polish Legation in Stockholm, London, 3 XII 1944.
[138] Ibidem, letter by Polish Envoy to Stockholm H. Sokolnicki to the Ministry of Foreign Affairs, Stockholm, 25 XI 1944.
[139] IPMS, A 11, E/508, letter by Polish Envoy to Stockholm H. Sokolnicki to the Ministry of Foreign Affairs, Stockholm, 27 V 1944.
[140] *Berättelse över Svenska Röda Korsets verksamhet under år 1945*, Stockholm 1946, pp. 133–134.

wishes of their donors.[141] This may explain why, at the outset of May 1945, the Ministry of Foreign Affairs suspended the dispatch of parcels to Poland. Food stocks that had been gathered for this purpose were allocated as aid to the Poles located in the territory of Germany.[142]

Final negotiations regarding humanitarian aid in the post-war period

In December 1944 and January 1945, counsellor Pilch met with the representatives of Swedish humanitarian organisations to convince them to talk with the Polish government in exile about the organisation of the post-war aid for Poland.[143] Pilch claimed that the talks with the Swedes were of great political significance. Insofar as the Swedish Ministry of Foreign Affairs avoided contact with Jerzy Pański, it did not prevent him contacting the Swedish relief authorities. Pilch argued, 'That is why an important issue was to present our political situation to these relief bodies as clearly as possible and convince them that our relief programme is the only programme that considers the entire issue together with the aid provided by the UNRRA' and was based on the will of the state representatives of the Polish government in London. He also emphasized that he had not established contact with the highest-level representatives of relief bodies, as their role was partial and more that of a figurehead, but with young people, who were committed solely to the activities of the relief body. On 29 January 1945, Pilch was permitted access to materials that were to be sent to the Swedish government and relief committees for final approval. These materials were, at most, preparatory works concerning sanitary and medical assistance, whereas the basis for the draft work programme was the Polish memorandum produced under the leadership of Doctor Nordwall. As part of Swedish aid campaign, provisional hospitals (barracks) were to be constructed, to house 3–4 thousand beds, at a cost of 15 million crowns. For a further 15 million crowns, the Swedes would also equip the hospitals and provide medicine and medical personnel for one year. A total of 30 million crowns then, including the costs, was donated by the Swedish government. It was estimated initially that 350 Swedish doctors and 200 nurses would be employed in Poland. Experience from the humanitarian

---

[141] AAN, HI/I/334, telegram by Minister of Foreign Affairs A. Tarnowski to Polish Envoy to Stockholm H. Sokolnicki, n.p., 19 II 1945.
[142] Ibidem, telegram by J. Kisielewski to S. Kocan, n.p., 2 V 1945.
[143] AAN, HI/I/115, letter by counsellor to Polish Legation in Stockholm T. Pilch to the Ministry of Foreign Affairs, Stockholm, 30 I 1945.

mission in the Soviet Russia at the beginning of 1920s proved that the activity in Poland should focus on certain counties (*powiaty*) and larger cities. Moreover, the Swedes planned to open orphanages. All these activities were to be managed directly by the Swedes. In addition, Pilch received a proposal from the *Internationella Arbetslag för Återuppbyggnad* organisation (translation: International team for reconstruction or *IAfÅ*) to set up a network of Finnish saunas, which would serve as sanitary stations. The cost of this initiative were to be divided between the Swedish and Polish sides. At the outset of 1945, the IAfÅ gathered a group of 43 individuals to perform humanitarian aid in Poland after completing special training acquainting them with the conditions of work and the basics of the Polish language.[144] The group was composed of mostly young representatives of various nationalities (mainly Swedes) including university students, craftsmen, engineers, mechanics, clerks and nurses of the Swedish Red Cross. The IAfÅ introduced a system of badges for those undergoing disinfection, which was to prevent excessive bureaucracy in the organisation of medical treatment.[145] Pilch was presented with a detailed description of the sauna installation, the cost of which was about 3 thousand crowns. The IAfÅ organisation encouraged the Polish authorities to buy the Finnish saunas, arguing 'there is no expert in the area of public healthcare who is familiar with the Finnish *bastu* [sauna], and who would not be glad to see the *bastu* introduced to the continent as an effective means of fighting all epidemics and taking public health to a higher level.'[146] There were fears that the Poles would be suspicious of the Swedish equipment and resist its introduction. Employing a Polish citizen to work at every sanitary group was to solve this. Swedish activists took into account that the *bastu* could have adverse health effects on the weak and sick. The argument for the saunas was that they were small stations managed by assistance teams and not medical centres. They were cheaper and for psychological reasons seemed to be a more convenient and beneficial solution as each person was treated individually and not as part of a group of patients.

Pilch was certain that the initiative to organize humanitarian aid for Poland was not a consequence of the belief that Poland most affected by the war. He claimed, 'Behind this there are naturally also the Swedish economic interests

---

[144] Ibidem.
[145] AAN, HI/I/115, complementary project of simplified sanitation control system, n.d., n.p.
[146] Ibidem, memorandum regarding the matter of *bastu* saunas, n.d., n.p.

and this is not only the hope to obtain coal from Poland, but also good experiences from the Polish-Swedish economic cooperation before the war.'[147]

On 19 January, Pilch submitted a memorandum to Sohlman, regarding the Swedish relief aid for Poland. Its content was in line with the document forwarded to Count Bernadotte in November 1944. This was the outcome of Pilch's meeting with Lars Birger Ekeberg, Stig Sahlin, Folke Bernadotte, Erik Lejionhufvud and Henrik Beer on 17 January, when the counsellor made the Swedes aware of the expectations of the Polish side.[148] On 30 January 1945, Pilch informed the Ministry of Labour and Social Welfare that Sweden was willing to grant Poland certain privileges regarding the shipments of barracks and prefabricated houses, if it received transports of coal and coke in a relatively soon.[149] In the spring of 1945, the Polish side began to formulate a list of specific demands. Poland expected Sweden to supply wooden barracks, 84 thousand blankets, artificial limbs, cooking pots, disinfection equipment, paper pallets used by the Swedish army, iron beds bunk beds, potato peelers and weighing scales.[150] In March 1945, social activists Alva Myrdal and Astrid Requel, who were in London at the time, were consulted on the printing Polish school and academic manuals in Sweden.[151] These conversations were problematic for the Swedes. On 22 May, Beer asked Sverker Åström from UD about what regarding reminders issued by Pilch, who scolded the Swedes for being slow to act and not arranging the meeting with president Ekeberg. Pilch expected that specific steps would be taken relating to the list of demands, which he had proposed previously. Beer asked what reply should be issued regarding the suggestions from UD to maintain the greatest possible caution in relations with the Polish Legation, which had been accomplished prudently so far, as no contact had been initiated. Åström advised that a method often used in UD be applied, namely only giving Pilch answers verbally.[152]

---

[147] Ibidem, letter by T. Pilch, counsellor to the Polish Legation in Stockholm, to the Ministry of Foreign Affairs, Stockholm, 23 XI 1944.
[148] AAN, HI/I/115, copy of letter by counsellor to the Polish Legation in Stockholm, T. Pilch, to R. Sohlman, Stockholm, 19 I 1945.
[149] AAN, HI/I/115, letter by counsellor to the Polish Legation in Stockholm T. Pilch to the Ministry of Labour and Social Welfare, Stockholm, 30 I 1945.
[150] Ibidem, letter by T. Pilch, counsellor to the Polish Legation in Stockholm, to the Ministry of Labour and Social Welfare, Stockholm, 13 IV 1945.
[151] AAN, HI/I/334, copy of telegram by Polish Envoy to Stockholm H. Sokolnicki to the Ministry of Foreign Affairs, Stockholm, 10 III 1945.
[152] RA, UD 1920 års dossiersystem, HP 39, vol. 1620, letter by H. Beer to S. Åström, Stockholm, 22 V 1945. The letter contains addressee's note with the instruction what was to be done.

12. SWEDISH HUMANITARIAN AID FOR POLAND

Throughout the war, Sweden primarily concentrated on granting humanitarian aid to its Nordic neighbours. Until 1940 Sweden provided humanitarian aid to Finland in various forms, totalling 145 million crowns, 105 million crowns of which was in cash.[153] In Sweden each year, Swedish families welcomed thousands of Finnish children, who took shelter from the Soviet bombings that plagued Finland.[154] Sweden or the International Red Cross also sent food aid to Greece, which was systematically transported on the Swedish ships from the outset of 1942 until 1944. In 1944, a similar aid campaign was organized for the Netherlands. In 1942, a special train brought several hundred Belgian children for treatment in Sweden.[155] Poland did not receive any priority treatment, and it was excluded from the initial plans for post-war aid. The decision to award Poland with a large government grant for the immediate support of people living in the General Government in the autumn of 1944 needs to be associated with Sweden's strong response to the tragedy of the Warsaw Rising and with the intention of importing coal from Poland as soon as the military activity ceased.

---

[153] S. Söderberg, *Svenska röda korset 1865–1965*, Stockholm 1965, pp. 277–279.
[154] H. Dahlberg, *I Sverige...*, p. 281.
[155] Ibidem, p. 317.

13. The Problems of Polish Soldiers Interned in Sweden

Submarine crews

In September 1939, under the Hague Convention of 1907, three Polish submarines, *Sęp*, *Ryś* and *Żbik*, were detained in Sweden.[1] The Swedes initiated internment before the twenty-four-hour limit for vessels lying in home ports, to which the Polish submarines were entitled to. Neither the crews nor Envoy Potworowski reacted to this. They most likely predicted that none of the units would be able to reach the Baltic Sea within twenty-four hours; the submarine *ORP Sęp* was badly damaged. All the vessels were moored around the Vaxholm fortress, within the limits of the Stockholm archipelago.

Other Polish vessels reached Sweden. On 2 October 1939, the cutter *Batory* carrying sixteen escapees from the Hel Peninsula (ten officers, three civilians and three customs agents) arrived on Gotland.[2] All were arrested and detained in Stockholm until the case was clarified. Several days later they were granted a two-week visa which was valid until their departure to Great Britain. The matter was publicized when the freed refugees from Poland complained to Envoy Potworowski about the conduct of Swedish policemen. Based on explanatory reports, the Swedish authorities rejected the complaint. One consequence of this report is that the allegations which were contained in the letter of complaint to the envoy had been raised by the Poles during their time in custody. A large majority of the focus fell on the statement of

---

[1] This issue has been numerously discussed in both Polish and Swedish historiography. See: A. N. Uggla, *I nordlig hamn...*, pp. 42–71; D. Nawrot, 'Internowanie i rehabilitacja załóg polskich okrętów podwodnych w Szwecji w latach II wojny światowej', *Przegląd Historyczno-Wojskowy* 2001, iss. 2, pp. 9–40; J. Pertek, *Mała flota wielka duchem*, Poznań 1989, chpt VIII: 'Na bocznym torze wojny', subchpt 1: 'Sześć lat internowania w Szwecji', pp. 447–461; Z. Wojciechowski, 'Internowanie polskich okrętów podwodnych w Szwecji', *Przegląd Morski* 1991, no. 11; E. Jarneberg, 'Internering av polska ubåtar med besättningar i Vaxholms fästning', *Vaxholms fästnings museum meddelande* 1981, pp. 41–60; U. Sobéus, 'SEP, RYS, ZBIK, de polska ubåtarna. Ett 60-årsminne', *Vaxholms fästnings museum årsbok* 1999, pp. 5–13.

[2] RA, mf. F 035-3-32252, police report, 5 X 1939. According to the Polish studies, on board of the *Batory* vessel there stayed six officers, four non-commissioned officers and seamen and two civil border guards. See: D. Nawrot, *Internowanie...*, p. 11.

one of the policemen, 'The Poles should be shot' or 'handed over to the Germans.'[3] Not all passengers were released by the Swedes. Six people were interned.

At the outbreak of war, the tall ship *Dar Pomorza* was berthed in Stockholm. Its young crew was not interned, but the ship remained in Sweden for six consecutive years. In March 1940, the idea of selling *Dar Pomorza* was considered, but the government decided to hold on to the ship for propaganda purposes. There were fears that the sale of a symbol of generosity from the residents of Pomerania could undermine morale (the ship was bought thanks to the public money collection in 1929).[4] Instead, the two fishing cutters were sold, *Marie Alice* and *Mir 9*, which had arrived in Gothenburg in August 1939, as part of an expedition organized by the Marine Fishing Institute in Gdynia.[5] A third cutter *Cecylia*, which also took part in the expedition, was captured by the Germans in April 1940 in Bergen, Norway. The maintenance costs of the *Dar Pomorza* and the *Batory* became a burden for the legation in later years.

During the war analyses were carried out to establish whether the Polish submarines fulfilled their objectives and if they left for Sweden prematurely. The naval commander's order of 14 September said that the military action against the Germans should be continued, and follow that the navy should move to Great Britain. The submarines were only to travel to neutral Sweden if this became impossible. There were doubts from the beginning whether the commanders, especially of *Ryś* and *Żbik*, had reasons to return the units to the hands of the Swedes.[6] In 1944, a commission was set up to examine the issue of the commanders of the submarines detained in Sweden. Its chair, Captain Czesław Petelenz, convinced Rear-Admiral Świrski that the orders of the Navy Command, where Sweden was called a partner and a friendly country, were of particular importance, although any specific arrangements were out of the question on the matter of a possible operational collaboration with the Swedish side: 'Constant pointing to Sweden could make the commanders presume that some possibilities existed only there and could undermine their spirit of initiative.'[7]

---

[3] RA, UD 1920 års dossiersystem, HP 39, vol. 1541, correspondence regarding this matter.
[4] *Protokoły posiedzeń Rady Ministrów Rzeczypospolitej Polskiej*, vol. 1, p. 260.
[5] AAN, HI/I/232, note by Polish Envoy to Stockholm G. Potworowski and counsellor to the Polish Legation in Stockholm T. Pilch, Stockholm, 30 VI 1940.
[6] D. Nawrot, *Internowanie...*, pp. 14–18.
[7] PISM, MAR, A V 9/5, letter by Com. Cz. Petelenz to head of the Polish Navy Command Rear-Admiral J. Świrski, Brighton, 12 XII 1944.

13. POLISH SOLDIERS INTERNED IN SWEDEN

From the beginning the submarines were of interest to the Polish supreme military authorities in exile. According to the head of the Polish Navy Command, Rear-Admiral Jerzy Świrski, to place the submarine crews under appropriate care it was necessary to know the stance of the naval attaché to Stockholm, even at the cost of eliminating the function of military attaché. Initially, Świrski proposed that commodore Czesław Petelenz, who at the time resided in Lithuania, assume the post of naval attaché. As Świrski informed General Sikorski:

> the crews of the three submarines interned in Sweden (*Ryś*, *Żbik* and *Sęp*) require permanent care from the officer with appropriate authority, who could exert a moral impact on them. The vessels themselves also require care. What is indispensable are constant talks with the Swedes regarding these matters and watching over the political fluctuations, which could at some point make it possible for the vessels to leave Sweden and move to England.[8]

Sikorski did not agree with the proposal and motivated his decision by the need to organize the evacuation of Poles from the Baltic States, which was to be decided by Attaché Brzeskwiński. Świrski insisted that the evacuation was a short-term task and, therefore, the office of naval attaché would be sufficient for Sweden. Eventually, independently of the military attaché's post, the post of naval attaché was also created. The person to assume the post, however, was not Petelenz, who was 60 years old and had retired before the war, but a serving officer, commodore Tadeusz Podjazd-Morgenstern.[9] The matter of *agrément* for Morgenstern was examined in greater detail. He arrived in Stockholm on 18 December 1939 and, regardless, had to settle all matters through a military attaché.[10]

On 1 December 1939, the Polish submarines became the subject of the session of the Swedish government. In response to the royal instructions of 20 October, a discussion took place about covering the costs of food and accommodation of the Polish crews, composed of 180 officers and seamen. Minister of Foreign Affairs Sandler proposed to conclude a special agreement in this matter with the Polish side.[11]

---

[8] PISM, MAR, A V 31/3, letter by head of the Polish Navy Command, Rear-Admiral J. Świrski to Minister of Military Affairs General W. Sikorski, Paris, 7 XI 1939.
[9] Ibidem, letters by head of the Polish Navy Command, Rear-Admiral J. Świrski to Minister of Military Affairs General W. Sikorski, Paris, 7 XI, 27 XI 1939.
[10] PISM, MAR, A V 9/3, letter by Com. T. Podjazd-Morgenstern to the Polish Navy Command, Stockholm, 3 II 1940.
[11] RA, Kabinettet/UD Huvudarkivet, Statsrådsprotokoll, serie A3A, vol. 106, Protokoll över utrikesdepartaments ärenden, Stockholm, 1 XII 1939.

Independently of the Swedish authorities' concern with financial issues, their attitude towards the Polish crews was 'very correct', as Commodore Ludwik Ziembicki put it, who with Bronisław Łątkiewicz visited the internment camp posing as alleged relatives of the interned seamen. Although, he quickly added that 'a strict adherence to the camp's internal regulations is necessary.' Nevertheless, he admitted, 'Rooms are decent, food is good.' All officers submitted an official written commitment to King Gustaf V, that they would not leave the camp for the next two months. Owing to this, they were permitted twenty-four hour's leave to visit Stockholm. The seamen arranged curfew with the guards, in exchange for payment.[12]

From the beginning, the command of the Polish navy considered liberating the submarines from internment. Acting Sub-Lieutenant Mieczysław Zygmunt Cedro, assistant of the Polish attaché to Stockholm, discussed the topic with Captain John R. Poland, who was assistant of the naval attaché of Great Britain in Stockholm and Lieutenant Lambert, who represented France. He assured them that the submarines were to be ready for operation by the end of the year. The attitude of the Swedish authorities was promising. They began to assist in the restoring of the vessels to operational condition, which was contrary to their attitude during the previous several weeks, when, posturing as strictly neutral, they simply allowed maintenance work to be performed.[13]

Meanwhile, at the outset of December, various sources reported on the German demand that the submarines be released to them when the Polish–German war was concluded. And so, on 30 November, the Germans requested the Swedish authorities release the submarines. The issue was discussed at the government level and the decision was that no official response would be given to the Germans. Nevertheless, an implication would be made that their demand was inappropriate and incompatible with the generally accepted rules of international law (from Article 6 of the Sea Convention), since Poland was at war.[14] At that point, and for the first time, the British Naval

---

[12] PISM, MAR, A V 31/2, report by Sub-Lieutenant B. Łątkiewicz about his visit to the internment camp for submarine crews in Sweden, n.p., 8 XII 1939. The visit took place around 15 November.

[13] NA, FO, 371/23709, note by Captain J. R. Poland for the Admiralty intelligence, n.p., 9 XII 1939, p. 229.

[14] G. Andolf, 'Militära interneringar i Sverige under de första krigsåren' [in:] *Vindkantring...*, p. 194; C.-A. Wangel, 'Neutralitetsrätt – regler och tillämpning' [in:] *Sveriges militära beredskap 1939–1945*, ed. C.-A. Wangel, Köping 1982, p. 66.

Attaché Captain Henry Denham advised the Poles that they should prepare to destroy the submarines if the Swedes attempted to seize them.[15]

For the Poles, it was important that the submarines were sea worthy. On 15 December, the Polish Naval Attaché to London, Captain Tadeusz Stoklasa, informed the British admiralty that Rear-Admiral Świrski had decided free the Polish vessels from Stockholm. *Ryś* and *Żbik* were to be ready to set sail on 20 December and *Sęp* on 25 December. Stoklasa asked the British to assist in the entire undertaking, and most importantly in provide information on activity in the Danish straits, about the minefields on the route to the North Sea and the rendezvous point with the British navy following the successful passage to the Baltic Sea. Rear-Admiral Świrski's reached the crews through the British naval attaché to Stockholm.[16] It caused embarrassment in the circle of the British Admiralty, which was reflected in the nervous written exchanges between the highest-ranking navy officers, as well as between the Admiralty and the Foreign Office (FO). The British were unable to solve the issue of assistance to the Poles without creating problems for the Swedes. Alan Ker from the Admiralty agreed that the action was too risky, but if the Poles decided to go through with it they should be provided with all the information that could help. The German demand that the submarines be released to them was additional motivation that the plan be executed. Seemingly against it, besides risk, was the prospect of employing the vessels in the future on the Baltic Sea, in the service of Finland or Sweden and the role that they would play in the British operations on the North Sea.[17] The FO maintained that the liberation of the Polish submarines could become a pretext for a German or Soviet campaign against Sweden, and should, therefore, be abandoned. Moreover, the Swedes were dissuaded from passing any information to the Poles which could facilitate their escape, as there was no trust in the loyalty of the command of the Polish navy and their ability to await approval from the British. According to the British plans, the Polish vessels were to cooperate with the Finnish navy in the Baltic Sea. The danger of releasing them to the Germans was trivialized by the British diplomacy, which did not believe that the Swedes would make such a concession.[18]

---

[15] NA, FO, 371/23709, telegram by Naval Attaché of Great Britain to Stockholm [H. Denham] to the Admiralty, 13 XII 1939, p. 231.
[16] Ibidem, letter by T. Stoklasa to R.H. Carter [Admiralty], 15 XII 1939, p. 228.
[17] Ibidem, A. Ker to D. W. Lascelles [Admiralty], 20 XII 1939, pp. 226–227.
[18] Ibidem, letter by the FO [head of the Northern Department of the FO L. Colliers?] to A. Ker [Admiralty], 21 XII 1939, pp. 232–233.

From the information reported by Polish Military Attaché to Helsinki, Colonel Władysław Łoś, Marshal Mannerheim proposed the Polish submarines fight in the Winter War against the Soviet navy. Morgenstern maintained that this would be an opportunity to liberate the vessels, considering the equipment and volunteers for the armed forces provided to Finland by Sweden. At the time, he learned that Polish pilots flying English aircraft, having reached Sweden en route to Finland, could enter Finnish airspace and fight on the Finnish–Soviet front. Nevertheless, in London there was a belief that if the Allies moved against the Soviet Union, Sweden would not discharge the vessels in fear of reprisals from the Germans, who were Stalin's ally at the time. The best, if unrealistic, solution from the Polish perspective seemed to be a joint campaign with the Swedish navy.[19]

On 2 January 1940, Captain Morgenstern sent a report to Świrski, where he described the political situation of Sweden and the condition of the Polish submarines. In his view, the circumstances forced Sweden to comply with the principles of neutrality. That is why he decided that the talks on the possible release of the vessels 'are not appropriate, and for the time being even seem inadvisable, as they could arouse concern among the Swedes and cause reaction in the shape of restrictions towards [...] the submarines and their crews, which would naturally make their [...] work difficult.'[20] Despite this, Morgenstern only considered the option of Sweden joining the war on the side of the Allies. Meanwhile, he was making plans to escape internment. The British were striving to settle the situation. Commander Poland noticed the excitement of the Polish crews after the submarine *Orzeł* managed to break through the Danish straits. According to the reports, which were sent to London, he advised against similar attempts by the vessels interned in Sweden. He claimed, 'it is almost impossible to break out of Vaxholm on your own.' Nobody was familiar with the area, which was fully guarded, and it was also difficult to progress to the North Sea. The British officer advised the crew to stay in Sweden and join the military operations on the Baltic Sea at a suitable moment, since he expected that in March 1940 the Germans and the Soviet Union would attack Scandinavia. Poland added that he considered two Polish officers to be incapable of commanding 'as their nerves were not

---

[19] IPMS, MAR, A V 9/3, report by Captain T. Podjazd-Morgenstern to head of the Polish Navy Command Rear-Admiral J. Świrski, Stockholm, 2 I 1940. note on the margin by J. Świrski from 16 I 1940.
[20] Ibidem.

strong enough.'[21] At the same time he was aware of the immense enthusiasm of the Poles, who were very eager to take actions. Nevertheless, he predicted that without help from the Swedes the submarines would be unable to escape. He also pointed to the fact that, with or without the help from the Swedes, the escape of the Polish submarines could trigger a German attack in retaliation for not keeping the internment restrictions. It was this issue that was a decisive factor in assessing the plan of escape. Poland argued:

> Sweden is in a very difficult situation at the moment, and it may end up in a state of war with Germany or Russia, or with both these countries at the same time, and therefore the presence of three additional excellent submarines on the Baltic Sea would be extremely valuable for the Allies. My French colleague agrees with me on this matter and that is why during today's meeting, among the three of us, we advised patience in waiting for the instructions from the Admiralty, preparation of the vessels as quickly as possible and not doing anything which would cause difficulties to the Swedes.[22]

However, for the proposition of any action to be conceivable, the submarines had to be technically sound. The report by Captain Morgenstern revealed that only the condition of the *ORP Sęp* submarine could be described as 'generally good.' The condition of *Żbik* was 'generally satisfactory', whereas the riskiest would be sending the damaged *Ryś* out to sea. The attaché informed that 'the Swedes […] have generally already agreed to carry out this repair', but they were neither rushing its launch nor did they adequately protect the vessels against winter. Another issue was the mental state of the crew members, which was mentioned by Commander Poland to the Polish attaché. His view was confirmed by Morgenstern, who noted that the commander of *Sęp*, Lieutenant-Commander Władysław Salamon, and the commander of *Ryś*, Lieutenant-Commander Aleksander Grochowski, 'seem to be mentally exhausted.' Other officers, according to his view, broke down during the military action. However, he had no objections towards the seamen: 'The mood among the crew members, despite the three-month stay in a closed camp, was not the worst, but constant action is required to keep up their spirits and faith that their fate would change in the near future and there is a constant search for inventive ways to keep them occupied.' The seamen

---

[21] Ibidem. See also: NA, FO, 371/23709, note by Captain J. R. Poland for the Admiralty intelligence, 9 XII 1939, p. 229.

[22] Ibidem, p. 230. See also: T. Skinder-Suchcitz, 'Próby uwolnienia okrętów podwodnych z internowania w Szwecji. Wrzesień 1939 – czerwiec 1940', *Zeszyty Historyczne* 1996, iss. 115, pp. 59–72.

helped with renovations and repairs, but were nevertheless burdened by concern for the fate of their families in the occupied country, from whom they received desperate letters.[23] Over time the seamen assumed the role of a transit channel for the letters and money sent by their colleagues from Great Britain to the families of the Polish seamen who were in Britain after September 1939. Morgenstern noted, 'large, in the current situation, sums of money are passing through their hands [...]. For instance [...] over two months nearly 4500 crowns from fellow British seamen were sent to Poland.'[24] Świrski only suspended sending money to Poland via interned soldiers by the end of April 1940.[25]

Protecting the Polish submarines became an urgent matter after the Soviet bombing of Sweden on 14 January 1940. Two days later, Attaché Brzeskwiński turned to the Swedish authorities and demanded the submarines be armed, refuelled and overhauled, to ensure they could be evacuated if called upon. The violation of the Swedish airspace was, therefore, used as a pretext to prepare the submarines' escape to Great Britain. This was one of the least likely of the developments that were presented by Morgenstern. The captain believed that the escape was 'exceptionally difficult and has minimal chance of success.' The submarines were carefully guarded by Swedish soldiers and located too far away from the open sea. A major obstacle between southern Sweden and northern Germany were the minefields, which prevented access to the Danish straits. A report produced in the Headquarters of the Navy Command, based on Morgenstern's reports, contained the analysis of the preparations for the escape. Some elements of the plan sounded incredible, 'he designed ways to dull the Swedes' and the Germans' vigilance', and, 'he designed ways to supply oil on the sea'. Moving the submarines further inland, however, which the Swedes planned to do, was considered to create favourable conditions for the action to be initiated. Both the British and the French opposed the escape and

---

[23] PISM, MAR, A V 9/3, report by Commodore T. Podjazd-Morgenstern to head of the Polish Navy Command Rear-Admiral J. Świrski, Stockholm, 2 I 1940. Seamen were sending small amounts of money home that they were receiving for their service on the ships.

[24] PISM, MAR, A V 31/3, report by Naval Attaché Commodore T. Podjazd-Morgenstern to head of the Polish Navy Command, Rear-Admiral J. Świrski, Stockholm, 24 III 1940 Morgenstern demanded that the process of sending money from Great Britain be suspended, mainly due to its influence on the morale of the crews who were paid less than the seamen living in Great Britain.

[25] PISM, MAR, A V 9/1, radiogram by head of the Polish Navy Command Rear-Admiral J. Świrski to Polish Naval Attaché to Stockholm T. Podjazd-Morgenstern, 28 IV 1940. The channel had to be efficient. This was mentioned by the then officer of the *ORP Wilk* – the warship which broke through to Great Britain in September 1939. See: B. Romanowski, *Torpeda w celu! Wspomnienia ze służby na okrętach podwodnych 1939–1945*, Gdańsk 1997, p. 85.

advised against the planning of it. They maintained that the submarines would prove more useful on the Baltic Sea and would cooperate with the Swedish navy on the side of the Allies. In the event of a threat from Germany or the Soviet Union, destroying the vessels and facilitating the escape of the crews was also considered. If alerted, the crews had prepared even explosives to be detonated.

In the short-term, however, the Polish high command pressed for the preparation of the submarines. In mid-February General Sikorski sent a telegraph to Attaché Morgenstern, ordering him to announce preparation for the escape. Morgenstern would disappoint the Commander-in-Chief on this occasion, as his answer fell in line with the advice from the British:

> The escape of the submarines without the permission of the Swedes is impossible now. From previous negotiations with the Swedes it follows that in the current political situation they would refuse to grant their consent to the escape. An intervention is currently inadvisable, because it would make further actions difficult. Now ice is blocking the straits. The Polish Navy Command is in possession of information about the critical situation and the submarines' operational readiness.[26]

While omitting the issue of a noticeable lack of communication between the Commander-in-Chief and the navy command, it should be noted that Morgenstern had adopted a British point of view, including the concern about the position of Sweden in the Baltic Sea region. Perhaps these were only appearances, as preparations for the action were proceeding, which may be evidenced by the plan for bringing Lieutenant Borys Karnicki to Sweden to take command of the submarine *Sęp*. Lieutenant Jerzy Rekner, appointed by Świrski, became the commander of the submarine *Ryś* and Lieutenant-Commander Michał Żebrowski continued to be commander of the *Żbik*. Officers performing inadequately in September 1939 were not assigned any posts.[27]

It was impossible to execute the escape plan as the submarines *Ryś* and *Żbik* were in poor condition. The Swedes, to prevent the escape, compromised the structure of the submarines and systematically checked that the Poles had not introduced any alterations. Morgenstern ordered the necessary parts in London, but the only way they could be delivered to Sweden was by diplomatic mail, the operation of which was beyond all Swedish control.[28] The

---

[26] PISM, MAR, A V 9/1, radiogram by head of the Polish Navy Command Rear-Admiral J. Świrski to Polish Naval Attaché to Stockholm Com. T. Podjazd-Morgenstern, 19 II 1940.
[27] Ibidem, radiogram by head of the Polish Navy Command Rear-Admiral J. Świrski to Polish Naval Attaché to Stockholm Com. T. Podjazd-Morgenstern, 19 II 1940.
[28] Ibidem, study on the subject of solving the issue of Polish ships interned in Sweden [the Polish Navy Command, March 1940].

Polish attaché feared exposure, which could bring restrictions from the Swedish authorities and render the escape impossible.[29] Świrski answered correctly that failure to deliver the essential parts for the submarines would nevertheless prevent any actions, so the risk was small. He also said, 'The only thing that may be harmful is [exposure] in general politics, which could have a negative impact on the opportunity of obtaining consent to escape.'[30] Eventually, Morgenstern did not accept the package, which raised suspicion among the Swedes.[31] The escape plans were additionally hindered by weather conditions, since the frozen Baltic Sea, as reported Morgenstern, 'excluded the option of sailing out to sea at least until the end of March.'[32]

What is more, the Swedes, for whom it was important that the Winter War was concluded as soon as possible, were trying to increase the protection over the submarines and prevent their preparation for going to the sea.[33] However, in the last days of the Winter War, the Finns were more interested in being ceded with Poland's orders for the supply of cannons and ammunition from the Bofors company than in the collaboration with the Polish submarines.[34] Świrski made efforts to make the Polish navy join the Finnish–Soviet conflict[35] and eventually appointed Lieutenant Bogusław Krawczyk to become *Sęp*'s commander. However, he came to Sweden towards the close of March, when the political and military circumstances were already completely different.[36]

The armistice between Finland and the Soviet Union was concluded on 12 March and 'the spirit of the *ORP* vessels' crews has visibly fallen at the moment.'[37] For Morgenstern this meant increasingly difficult working conditions: 'All the efforts of the Swedish policy are currently focusing on manoeuvring

---

[29] Ibidem, radiogram by Polish Naval Attaché to Stockholm Com. T. Podjazd-Morgenstern to head of the Polish Navy Command, Rear-Admiral J. Świrski, Stockholm, 27 II 1940.

[30] Ibidem, radiogram by head of the Polish Navy Command Rear-Admiral J. Świrski to Polish Naval Attaché to Stockholm Com. T. Podjazd-Morgenstern, 28 II 1940.

[31] Ibidem, radiogram by Polish Naval Attaché to Stockholm Com. T. Podjazd-Morgenstern to head of the Polish Navy Command, Rear-Admiral J. Świrski, Stockholm, 5 III 1940.

[32] Ibidem, radiogram by Polish Naval Attaché to Stockholm Commodore T. Podjazd-Morgenstern to head of the Polish Navy Command, Rear-Admiral J. Świrski, Stockholm, 21 II 1940.

[33] Ibidem, letter by Naval Attaché Commodore T. Podjazd-Morgenstern to head of the Polish Navy Command, Rear-Admiral J. Świrski, Stockholm, 27 II 1940.

[34] Ibidem, radiogram by Polish Naval Attaché to Stockholm Commodore T. Podjazd-Morgenstern to Commodore H. Pistel, 20 II 1940.

[35] Ibidem, radiogram by head of the Polish Navy Command Rear-Admiral J. Świrski to Commodore K. Korytowski, 22 II 1940.

[36] Ibidem.

[37] IPMS, MAR, A V 31/3, classified report by Polish Naval Attaché to Stockholm Commodore T. Podjazd-Morgenstern to head of the Polish Navy Command, Rear-Admiral J. Świrski, Stockholm, 24 III 1940.

between the Germans and the Allies, whereas the policy is more flexible and submissive towards the former, and more framed and firm towards the latter.'[38]

What did this mean for the Polish interests in Sweden? Morgenstern was exacting when he wrote in that same piece of correspondence: 'There is tacit tolerance towards Poland. There is no doubt that the existing good will or even kindliness comes up against certain limits. In the case, it touches on the risk of the Germans' dissatisfaction – it is, very diplomatically, withdrawn.'

The Polish Naval Attaché formulated his evaluation mostly based on the statements regarding the Swedish authorities' treatment of the Polish submarines. In March 1940 he wrote, 'All the matters which seemed to be already settled and decided, like the work of our non-commissioned officers with our torpedoes and docking of the submarine *Ryś* has been, for the time being, under various pretences, suspended, and all my new demands are meeting with courteous, but evasive answers.' According to Morgenstern, 'The fear against the great neighbour paralyses all good intentions.' The high-ranking officers of the Swedish navy told the attaché repeatedly that, 'The Germans are keeping a close watch […] on the interned submarines and all that is happening on them.' That is why he believed that the issue of putting the Polish warships out to sea would become valid only after a radical change to the political situation. The escape without the Swedes' consent owing to small chances of success had to be treated as the last resort.[39]

Moreover, the Bofors company completely withdrew from executing the orders. The company's representative offered to return the advance payments with compensation for the unpaid bills, to terminate the non-executed contracts and to return various letters of guarantee.[40] It seemed that the Swedish authorities, just in case, wanted to avoid being accused of providing the Polish army with more arms, and at the same time it was important for them that this did not make them lose out financially.[41]

The political situation changed radically after the Germans had attacked Denmark and Norway on 9 April 1940. At the time, the Minister of Foreign

---

[38] IPMS, MAR, A V 9/2, classified letter by Polish Naval Attaché to Stockholm Commodore T. Podjazd-Morgenstern to head of the Polish Navy Command, Rear-Admiral J. Świrski, Stockholm, 24 III 1940.
[39] Ibidem.
[40] PISM, MAR, A V 9/1, radiogram by Polish Naval Attaché to Stockholm Commodore T. Podjazd-Morgenstern to head of the Polish Navy Command, Rear-Admiral J. Świrski, Stockholm, 15 III 1940.
[41] Ibidem, radiogram by head of the Polish Navy Command Rear-Admiral J. Świrski to Polish Naval Attaché to Stockholm Commodore T. Podjazd-Morgenstern, 16 III 1940; Ibidem, radiogram by Polish Naval Attaché to Stockholm, Captain T. Podjazd-Morgenstern to head of the Polish Navy Command, Rear-Admiral J. Świrski, Stockholm, 4 IV 1940.

Affairs, August Zaleski, forwarded the Polish Legation in Stockholm the order of High Command, according to which the tall ship *Dar Pomorza*, which was moored at the Stockholm port, was to be scuttled, whereas the submarines were to use every occasion to attempt an escape to the approaching English navy.[42] The ideas, resulting from the anticipation of an inevitable German attack, were replaced with the request of the Poles that the vessels were hauled away to the centre of Stockholm, where they would be better protected from air raids thanks to the anti-aircraft defence, and where it would be possible to conduct the necessary repairs. From 15 and 16 April the crews were accommodated at the tall ship *Dar Pomorza*, whereas the refurbishment and rearming of the submarines was initiated. It seemed that the Swedes were expecting the German attack. On 16 April, Morgenstern reported that 'the Swedes are returning everything except for the mechanical parts.'[43] Two days later, General Sikorski ordered, 'In the face of the successful development of the war in the North, I expect You, Captain, to offer your full support in taking our submarines and the ship *Pomorze* [sic!] to the Baltic Sea.'[44] On the next day, Morgenstern reported that the Swedes 'are returning torpedoes, ammunition and oil.' They refrained from returning mechanical parts, cannon locks and torpedo detonators.[45] After only a couple of days the disappointed attaché informed the Polish Navy Command, 'In the face of [...] a somewhat relaxation of the political situation, as well as due to the slowness of the Swedes and excessive bureaucracy, it turned out to be impossible to keep up the efficient work speed and therefore the works have come to a temporary halt.' Nevertheless, he added, 'It is my intention to make an appropriate use of the current, exceptionally favourable attitude of the Swedes towards our matters by trying to do everything for which there may be later not enough time.'[46]

---

[42] AAN, HI/I/256, telegram by Minister of Foreign Affairs A. Zaleski to Polish Envoy to Stockholm G. Potworowski, 11 IV 1940.
[43] IPMS, MAR, A V 9/1, telegram by Polish Naval Attaché to Stockholm Captain T. Podjazd-Morgenstern to head of the Polish Navy Command, Rear-Admiral J. Świrski, Stockholm, 16 IV 1940.
[44] Ibidem, radiogram by Commander in Chief General W. Sikorski to Polish Naval Attaché in Stockholm Captain T. Podjazd-Morgenstern, 18 IV 1940.
[45] Ibidem, telegram by Polish Naval Attaché to Stockholm Commodore T. Podjazd-Morgenstern to head of the Polish Navy Command, Rear-Admiral J. Świrski, Stockholm, 19 IV 1940.
[46] IPMS, MAR, A V 31/3, letter by Polish Naval Attaché in Stockholm Commodore T. Podjazd-Morgenstern to head of the Polish Navy Command, Rear-Admiral J. Świrski, Stockholm, 25 IV 1940.

13. POLISH SOLDIERS INTERNED IN SWEDEN

On 26 April, at the government session, General Sikorski still optimistically reported on the progress of Sweden's preparations to join the war on the side of the Allies:

> Regarding the possibility of Sweden joining the war, there is hope that our interned submarines, which have been repaired by the Swedes, will be ready for action as soon as they receive cannon locks and torpedo point finders; a matter of seconds. It will be possible for them to fight efficiently in the Baltic Sea, which is greatly appreciated by the English. The relative potential of the Swedish navy, with which they would most probably cooperate, due to the extensive losses of the German navy, became relatively strong. [...] The Swedes on the other hand, are doing all they can to hinder the passage of the German vessels across the Swedish territorial waters. [...] Sweden is intensively preparing itself for the defence [...] Our envoy in Stockholm will receive instructions of the advance agreement with the Swedes; currently everything is being arranged there between our military representative and the English.[47]

The optimism of the Polish Prime Minister and the Commander-in-Chief General Sikorski turned out to be excessive. The refurbishments were progressing, but the torpedoes were never given to the Poles.[48] The crew maintained the installations, the Swedish labourers took care of the hull, and Morgenstern evaluated that the Swedes' work as very sound. The Polish attaché was not allowed to enter the shipyard, as the internment rules had to be observed, but all crew members were granted access to their submarines. Towards the close of April, the Swedes began to examine the possibility of moving the vessels further inland, which on the one hand would make it easier for them to keep an eye on the Poles, and on the other, constitute a valuable gesture towards the Germans. Morgenstern made every effort to fight against this idea with Admiral Claes Lindström, but he believed that the final decision would be dependent on the development of the situation on the western front. According to his estimates, 'So far, the Germans are very strong here.'[49] In mid-May 1940 Świrski, referring to the decision of the British admiralty, in a telegram to Morgenstern, considered three scenarios of the development of events.[50] If Sweden maintained its neutrality, the submarines were to remain where they were. If Sweden joined the war on the

---
[47] *Protokoły posiedzeń Rady Ministrów Rzeczypospolitej Polskiej*, vol. 1, p. 275.
[48] PISM, MAR, A V 31/3, report by Naval Attaché Commodore T. Podjazd-Morgenstern to head of the Polish Navy Command Rear-Admiral J. Świrski, Stockholm, 29 IV 1940.
[49] Ibidem.
[50] Discussion of British analyses, see: T. Skinder-Suchcitz, *Próby...*, pp. 68–69.

side of the Allies, the Polish submarines were to act as part of the Swedish navy and eventually become interned in Finland, 'provided this is safe, and that the Germans did not capture them.' The third solution was to destroy them. If Sweden yielded to the German demands, the submarines were to 'go out to sea and act as it was outlined in the second option, when the bases are taken away.' In other circumstances, 'Where the stance of the Swedes is wavering, the vessels will be lifted out to the sea, before any decision is made, and we shall see what is next.'[51] The instruction was equally imprecise as that of September 1939. Morgenstern was most likely focused on 'and we shall see what next', since eventually no actions were taken. The fate of the Polish submarines in Sweden was mostly decided by the French campaign which was lost by the Allies. The attaché reported, 'Everything seems to […] prove that recurring German interventions forced the Swedes to limit the current works only to those concerning maintenance and repairs, excluding new installations, which they nevertheless are unwilling to officially admit.'[52]

Between 4 and 7 July 1940 all the submarines were hauled away to Lake Mälaren. Over a dozen seamen were moved to central Sweden nearby Falun. Morgenstern characterized the situation as follows: 'the position of Germany in Sweden and the last English-Swedish clashes are not making the atmosphere pleasant.'[53]

In August of 1940, the Polish Navy Command intended to take actions leading to the release of four interned officers and two seamen. They were planning to make use of the circumstances which occurred relating to the decision of the Swedish authorities to release all the interned soldiers of both fighting parties of the Norwegian campaign.[54] Nevertheless, the Swedish authorities claimed that in the case of the crews interned in 1939, the release was out of question. Despite the unfavourable decision, the envoy accepted the Swedish statement with approval. He found it to be 'an indirect claim that the Swedish government did not consider the Polish war as concluded.'[55]

---

[51] PISM, MAR, A V 9/1, radiogram by head of the Polish Navy Command Rear-Admiral J. Świrski to Polish Naval Attaché to Stockholm Commodore T. Podjazd-Morgenstern, 15 V 1940.
[52] PISM, MAR, A V 31/3, report by Naval Attaché Commodore T. Podjazd-Morgenstern to head of the Polish Navy Command, Rear-Admiral J. Świrski, Stockholm, 21 VII 1940.
[53] Ibidem.
[54] AAN, HI/I/480, telegram by Minister of Foreign Affairs A. Zaleski to Polish Legation in Stockholm, 20 VIII 1940.
[55] Ibidem, letter by Polish Envoy to Stockholm G. Potworowski to the Ministry of Foreign Affairs, Stockholm, 29 VIII 1940.

13. POLISH SOLDIERS INTERNED IN SWEDEN

By mid-October 1940, the three submarines and their crews resided in Mariefred, a small town be Lake Mälaren.[56] The representative of the municipal authorities welcomed the Polish seamen warmly:

> We often think about how great our gratitude would be for the kindness shown to our fathers and sons if they came to share that very same unfortunate fate of being interned in a foreign country. We consider it to be our pleasant duty and our achievement in these painful times to show kindness to our Polish guests.[57]

The command of the Swedish navy was convinced that as the stay of the Poles in Sweden was prolonged it was necessary to offer a social programme, and at little cost, provide an opportunity for professional development. Thanks to the improvement of housing conditions, it was possible to maintain the positive atmosphere. A sightseeing tour of the surroundings was organized, as well as lessons in Swedish and weekly social meetings, during which films were screened and plays performed.[58]

More turbulence over the submarines was caused by the outbreak of the German–Soviet war on 22 June 1941. One day later the commandant of the internment camp, Captain von der Burg, ordered a special assembly and announced that the submarines would be separated from the crews and moved. He informed Captain Salamon that the Swedish authorities had discovered attempted sabotage by the Poles and were intending to repair it. Attaché Morgenstern intervened on 26 June with the head of the navy cabinet at the Ministry of Defence, Admiral Marc Giron. He referred to the hitherto impeccable and loyal behaviour of the crews. Giron expressed surprise with the situation, but confirmed that the Swedes were planning to move the submarines to Stockholm to carry out a technical inspection. Morgenstern was convinced that, 'The Swedes, due to some reason, which I am unfamiliar with, simply want to have the submarines in Stockholm.'[59] On seeing that he

---

[56] KA, Marinkommando Ost, Interneringsläger no. 2, series B I, Utgående skrivelse, vol. 1: 1940–1943, report by commander of HM Cerberus to the commander of the eastern coast, 16 XI 1941.
[57] Ibidem.
[58] The situation of the interned crews was often described in articles and notes of the Polish press in exile: 'Jasełka w Szwecji', *Dziennik Polski*, 10 I 1941; 'Internowani Polacy w Szwecji', *Dziennik Polski*, 17 I 1941; 'Jak żyją żołnierze polscy internowani w Szwajcarii i Szwecji', *Dziennik Polski*, 3 VI 1941; 'Polscy marynarze w Szwecji', *Wieści Polskie*, 11 VI 1943; 'Polacy internowani w Szwecji', *Dziennik Polski*, 3 XI 1943.
[59] PISM, MAR, A V 31/3, report by Naval Attaché Commodore T. Podjazd-Morgenstern to head of the Polish Navy Command, Rear-Admiral J. Świrski, Stockholm, 21 VII 1941.

would gain nothing in this matter, he only noted that it would be unacceptable to separate the crews from their submarines and that this 'would be a very serious issue of a highly political character, especially in the current circumstances.' Following another meeting and consultation with the Naval Attaché of Great Britain, Denham, he telephoned one of the Polish officers, to forewarn the crews about the Swedish plans and to order the removal of 'all, even the smallest traces that would prove that the submarines could have been prepared for destruction.' However, at that moment it was too late. Whilst Morgenstern was visiting Giron, the submarines were boarded by the Swedish seamen and hauled away to the base in Stockholm without the Polish crews on board. Only Captain Salamon fought his way onto the *Sęp* submarine without the consent from the Swedes, and refused to leave. The attaché communicated his objection to Giron, but Giron again answered that he knew nothing and would deal with the matter on the following day. The day after, Potworowski submitted a protest to Boheman against the action, which he described as sudden and treacherous. Boheman calmly explained that this was how the Swedish authorities reacted to the information about potential sabotage and denied the existence of plans where the submarines were to be handed over to the Germans. He justified himself by stating that he knew no details of the action and promised to discuss the possibility of allowing the Polish crews to return to the submarines with the navy command.[60] Boheman was also consulted on this matter by the Envoy of Great Britain, Mallet, who had heard the same news as Potworowski. Boheman emphasized that he had no evidence that sabotage had been planned, but 'in at present there is always risk that somebody could act too hastily.' He confirmed that the decision on occupying the vessels was made by the Swedish government, in the case the sabotage did take place, the Germans would accuse Sweden of breaching obligations under internment regulations, and could put forward claims. He assured that the Swedes would never hand over the property of the Polish government, the submarines, to the Germans, and that they would sooner destroy them. Moreover, Boheman admitted that the possibility of the Soviet arrival on the banks of Sweden meant that it was important to demonstrate that the Swedes' treatment of the interned would be tough, as 'the Swedish government would not trust Russian seamen, as it had trusted the Polish.'[61] The Polish government raised the issue of seizing

---

[60] PISM, A 12, 53/37J, telegram by Envoy G. Potworowski to the Ministry of Foreign Affairs, Stockholm, 27 VI 1941, p. 26.
[61] NA, FO, 371/29663, telegram by V. Mallet to the FO, 27 VI 1941.

the vessels at the session of 28 June 1941. There was an announcement that a protest would be carried out against this unexpected action.[62]

Morgenstern issued an order to break all outside-service relations that were maintained by the interned crews with the Swedish officers and seamen.[63] He unofficially learned that the action was inspired by the Swedish Ministry of Foreign Affairs and the General Staff of the Swedish Army, and that the staff of the navy most probably knew nothing about it, and therefore the outrage of Captain Giron was sincere. On 1 July, Söderblom suggested Potworowski visit the shipyard and see the vessels in the company of Admiral Lindström. On the following day, the envoy together with Attaché Morgenstern met with the admiral. Lindström stated that the submarines had been moved to Stockholm due to the threat of an air strike and for necessary renovation. The submarines were towed without crews on board, as the interned soldiers were banned from entering the Swedish capital. The admiral expressed his regret that the event had taken place and ordered that Polish flags be raised on masts of the submarines. This was met with a cutting remark from Envoy Potworowski to Lindström that despite the order for the Polish flags to be raised, they were not visible, which again proved that 'not everything happens in line with his orders.'[64] As it was impossible to force the admiral to compensate the crews or issue any declarations regarding the return of the crews to the submarines, in July Potworowski visited the headquarters of the Ministry of Foreign Affairs to meet with Söderblom. The Swedish diplomat stated that Admiral Lindström had failed to inform the envoy on the most important issue, namely that the search carried out on the vessels had failed to confirm suspicions of sabotage. In the evening of that very same day, the Swedes agreed that three technicians should be allowed on the submarines. The meeting in the Ministry of Defence, during which Attaché Morgenstern demanded that fifteen crew members be permitted to board each renovated vessel, took place on 5 July. On 9 July, Captain Dyrssen informed the Polish naval attaché that five men from each crew would be enough, and besides 'he expressed his hope that the submarines [...] would soon return to their former berthing place, as it seemed to him that the security conditions "were improved", and the renovation does not require a long period of standstill in the shipyard.' Eventually, by way of compromise, ten crew members per submarine was agreed. On 17 July, Potworowski

---

[62] *Protokoły posiedzeń Rady Ministrów Rzeczypospolitej Polskiej*, vol. 3, pp. 25–26.
[63] PISM, MAR, A V 31/3, report by Naval Attaché Commodore T. Podjazd-Morgenstern to head of the Polish Navy Command, Rear-Admiral J. Świrski, Stockholm, 21 VII 1941.
[64] Ibidem.

informed London that the intervention both with the Ministry of Foreign Affairs and with the navy command led to the Polish crews returning to the submarines. The Swedish side admitted that 'the examination of the submarines did not confirm any suspected sabotage' and expressed their regret. The envoy suspected that after completing the on-going renovations, the submarines would return to their former berthing place, which eventually took place at the beginning of September.[65] The British considered that the incident was explained satisfactorily.[66]

In his report to the Polish Navy Command, Attaché Morgenstern analysed the reasons why the Swedes hauled the Polish submarines away without the crews to another berthing place. He considered the official reasons to be untrue. Morgenstern was convinced that he was right:

> I consider it a certainty that the initiative of taking away the submarines started in the Ministry of Foreign Affairs, which, on the one hand, wanted to forestall any possible démarche [of Germany] in this matter, whereas Germany, relating to the outbreak of the Russian war, made demands towards Sweden. In such a case, the ministry's intention was to demonstrate that the Polish submarines were most certainly in Swedish hands. On the other hand, in the face of the emergence of a possibility of the Russian vessels' internment, the ministry perhaps thought that it was necessary to toughen up the regime towards the interned submarines, and thereby to facilitate the proceedings with the (perhaps even bigger) Russian vessels which could be interned [in the future].'[67]

According to the Poles, the rumours about the sabotage were to serve as a perfect excuse to take an action, which turned out to be misguided. Morgenstern highlighted the sympathetic attitude of the command of the Swedish navy, and he described the case of Admiral Lindström, who was in command of the eastern section of the Swedish coast and well-known for his strong pro-German sympathies, as isolated.

What was in fact the origin of the Swedish decision? The plans for destroying the submarines were forged in autumn of 1939, when the Germans began contact with the Swedish authorities regarding their release. With

---
[65] PISM, A 12, 53/37J, telegram by Envoy G. Potworowski to the Ministry of Foreign Affairs, Stockholm, 17 VII 1941, p. 29; AAN, HI/I/87, letter by Polish Envoy to Stockholm G. Potworowski to the Ministry of Foreign Affairs, Stockholm, 24 IX 1941.
[66] NA, FO, 371/29664, telegram by Naval Attaché of Great Britain to Stockholm Commodore H. Denham to Naval Intelligence, 17 VII 1941.
[67] PISM, MAR, A V 31/3, report by Polish Naval Attaché to Stockholm Commodore T. Podjazd-Morgenstern to head of the Polish Navy Command, Rear-Admiral J. Świrski, Stockholm, 21 VII 1941.

13. POLISH SOLDIERS INTERNED IN SWEDEN

every increase in the threat from Germany, these plans became more credible. In June 1941, the plans became of great interest to the British, who secretly, courtesy of the Poles, came into possession of plans for rendering the submarines inoperable without the need for explosives or scuttling in deep water. Bombing was inconceivable, as the submarines were a most difficult target for an aerial attack. The Polish specialists considered sinking the submarines in shallow waters, where they were located, by opening all hatches, doors, blockades, valves etcetera. Nevertheless, the engine rooms would be the target for most damage including short circuiting.[68] The British came in to possession of these plans only three weeks before Hitler's aggression against the Soviet Union, and the analyses were conducted in mid-June. In the internment camps, keeping secrets was no doubt impossible. The potential destruction of the submarines by the crews was treated seriously. Rumours of sabotage, as mentioned by Morgenstern in his report to London, took the form of specific plans. Doubts are cleared up by Admiral Lindström's letter to the commander of the navy, where he explained that he the report came from military intelligence. One of the officials of the Polish Legation allegedly initiated the preparations for sabotage on the submarines. Relating to this, he received the order to remove the crews from the submarines as quickly as possible, and to tow them away to Stockholm.[69]

From the Swedish police records we learn that on 22 May attaché Morgenstern requested the chauffeur of the Polish Legation, Krupski, purchase 10-litre petrol canister. On the same day, the captain took the canisters to Mariefred and ordered that they be kept on board the submarines or in other appropriate places and used to destroy them in the event of an attempted relocation. According to agent 'Kalle', the legation feared that the German demand for the submarines would be met. It was, therefore, preferable to destroy the submarines than to place them in the German hands.[70] Was Morgenstern really preparing for sabotage? Following the incident, the Polish naval attaché investigated the matter. He looked for a spy among the seamen, but in his own report to London he does not mention sabotage.[71] Many disparities in the reports mean it is hard to discover what truly happened. However, in the light of earlier preparations, from as early as the

---

[68] NA, ADM, 223/489, note by Campbell to the naval intelligence, 4 VI 1941 [together with the analysis from 12 VI 1941].
[69] RA, UD 1920 års dossiersystem, HP 22, vol. 1110, letter by C. Lindström to Admiral M. Giron, 4 VII 1941.
[70] RA-Arninge, SÄPO-arkiv, P 201 Polish Legation, memorandum by O. Danielsson, Stockholm, 10 VI 1941.
[71] Ibidem, memorandum, O. Danielsson, Stockholm, 5 VIII 1941.

autumn of 1939, the version confirming sabotage seems credible. Independently of whether Kalle's report was true, it spurred the intervention of the Swedish authorities.[72]

No similarly dramatic events would occur following this. In late autumn 1941, the Swedish commandant of the camp highlighted that the atmosphere around the Polish crews was quite good:

> In summing up, it may be stated that the seamen of the so-called internment camp for the Polish submarine crews, placed under the navy's command, have gained a good reputation among the town's population owing to their good behaviour during their work and following its conclusion. This means both the Swedes and the Poles. Both are being welcomed by various associations in Mariefred. The Poles especially deserve respect for the way they have been enduring their fate. After a year of my service as the internment camp's commandant, it is obvious to me that the humanitarian treatment of the interned is perhaps a seed which may bear fruit in the future, when international cooperation will be resumed.'[73]

Nevertheless, the crew were placed in various conditions. Officers and non-commissioned officers were accommodated at Ekbacken, a villa near Strängnäs, whereas the seamen were housed in two old barrack boats. This caused resentment among the seamen, as the living conditions on the vessels were dreadful.[74] Only in March 1942 would the Swedes allocate funds for the construction of new barracks, but the matter was not settled instantly. In September, at the request of the new Naval Attaché, Captain Eugeniusz

---

[72] In the files of the Swedish counter intelligence, it is highlighted that the observation of the submarines was initiated in connection with the information of the prepared sabotage, which was communicated to the police 11 June 1941. See: MUST arkiv, Försvarsstaben, Säkerhetsavdelningen, F VIII e, Underrättelsetjänst och sabotage, Polsk underrättelsetjänst, vol. 26, letter by Captain G. von Döbeln to head of the Security Department, 11 X 1941, pp. 115–116.

[73] KA, Marinkommando Ost, Interneringsläger nr 2, serie B I, Utgående skrivelse, vol. 1: 1940–1943, report by commander of HM Cerberus to the commander of the eastern coast, 16 XI 1941.

[74] There was a rumour spread among the seamen that the large sums of dollars allocated for the operation of the submarines (fuel, repairs) in the event of them being cut off from their home bases, were in fact used for private purposes by the officers. For more on this subject see: A. Staniszewski, *Na bocznym torze...*, pp. 58–59. A crew member of *Ryś*, Władysław Słoma, recalled the difficult housing conditions the crews had to endure, which were quite contrary to those offered to the privileged officers, and rumours about using official funds for private purposes of the commanders (based on the author's conversation with W. Słoma, 12 VII 2005). On the animosities between the officers and seamen also in England see: B. Romanowski, *Torpeda...*, pp. 75–76. Słoma published a memoir about the years of war that he spent in Sweden and where he stayed for good after 1945: W. Sloma, *En polsk ubåtsman i Mariefred*, Nyköping 2006.

13. POLISH SOLDIERS INTERNED IN SWEDEN

Pławski, Envoy Potworowski demanded that the Swedish authorities begin the construction of the new wooden barracks without delay. He agreed that the Polish government should bear the costs of the investment. Potworowski explained to the headquarters that he was forced to take decisive steps due to the ill health of the seamen and the cold time of the year.[75] On 17 December 1942, the Swedish government again discussed the issue of the interned Polish seamen. The discussion was sparked by the letter from the Polish Legation with a proposal that the Swedes granted a cash benefits to the crews of the submarines for the purchase of civilian clothes. In the letter it was argued that such benefits would by no means be at odds with the decision of the Swedish court from 1 December 1939, when the allocation of funding for clothing was to be made. The Polish side proposed donating 400 crowns benefit in the first year of internment and 250 crowns every subsequent year.[76] The seamen who were fed up with their continuous service on idle vessels demanded an option of civil employment outside the camp, partly to increase their modest income. Initially, the Swedish authorities' refused and the seamen, who had demanded the right to work, were either severely punished or moved to other camps. Nevertheless, 1942, just like 1941, was summed up by the camp being commanded in a manner which would benefit the Poles' 'Ability to adapt, conscientiousness and suitable behaviour – these are the characteristics of the interned, which were also shown by them in the preceding year.'[77] Not a single case of alcohol abuse was recorded.[78] Perhaps Naval Attaché Captain Eugeniusz Pławski claimed that the interned were treated badly due to their poor living conditions. It was not until the final period of his office, at the outset of 1943, that he would describe them as firstclass.' From the beginning he examined the possibility of Sweden joining the the Allies and the Polish submarines taking part in the military operations. Nevertheless, the vessels were showing signs of age and, in November 1942,

---

[75] AAN, HI/I/285, telegram by Envoy G. Potworowski to the Ministry of Foreign Affairs, Stockholm, 22 IX 1942; HI/I/488, letter by Rear-Admiral J. Świrski to the Ministry of Finance, 29 X 1942. The head of the Polish Navy Command highlighted that the Swedes were obliged to accommodate the interned in the conditions fulfilling the necessary health requirements, the costs of which were to be covered by the Polish side following the war.
[76] RA, Kabinettet/UD Huvudarkivet, Statsrådsprotokoll, serie A3A, vol. 114, Protokoll över utrikesdepartementsärenden, Stockholm, 17 XII 1942.
[77] KA, Marinkommando Ost, Interneringsläger nr 2, serie B I, Utgående skrivelse, vol. 1: 1940–1943, report by commander of HM Cerberus to the commander of the eastern coast, 5 I 1943.
[78] G. Andolf, Militära interneringar i Sverige under de första krigsåren [in:] *Vindkantring...*, p. 195.

only *Sęp* was considered a viable craft. The crews of the two remaining submarines were to be, on an appropriate occasion, transported to Great Britain or employed in the Swedish navy. Pławski verbosely dubbed his project 'the Baltic Flotilla.' On arranging the framework of actions, he wanted to prepare for the talks with the Swedes 'as a partner who knows what he wants' and who came 'not only to take their orders but also to bring orders from Admiral [Świrski].' In the conclusion of his letter he pointed out, 'All this is certainly very fluid, it may become subject to the most unexpected changes or it may never happen at all.'[79] The cooperation with the Swedes was very uncertain. Having concluded his mission, Pławski's assessment of relations with the Swedish military authorities, and especially the navy command, which held sway over the eastern section of the Swedish coast, was very negative. For this reason, he addressed UD on every matter in the first instance.[80]

At the beginning of April 1943, Commander Marian Wolbek, acting as a naval expert, visited Stockholm. The instructions of Rear-Admiral Świrski did not change from the autumn of 1939. He expected Wolbek to undertake efforts to make 'the submarines achieve full combat readiness as quickly as possible, both technical and that in terms of their crews, in the event of Sweden's involvement in the war.' He also claimed that, 'If the Swedes would like to remove the crew from one or more submarines, or, by other means, try to remove the submarines out of our sphere of influence, then the submarines would need to be destroyed and scuttled by us.' There was a further suggestion that the decision to destroy the vessels was to be made by Świrski, 'if the time comes to contact me'. If no such possibility arose, the decision was to be left to the naval attaché. What is more, Świrski forbade the employment of the seamen in any sort of intelligence activity.[81]

In his first report to Rear-Admiral Świrski, Wolbek recalled, 'What I came across was the courteous attitude of the Swedes.'[82] Despite this, one of the meetings took a bizarre turn. Count Folke Bernadotte raised the issue of an unpaid bill for shoes purchased for Acting Sub-Lieutenant Nowacki, which Wolbek claimed, had been lost by the Swedes. Bernadotte asked Wolbek to reimburse the 45 Swedish crowns, as otherwise it would need to be paid by

---

[79] PISM, MAR, A V 9/4, letter by Polish Naval Attaché to Stockholm Commodore E. Pławski to Rear-Admiral J. Świrski, Stockholm, 25 XI 1942.
[80] KA, Försvarsstabens marina avdelningens hemliga arkiv, F IV, Personliga anteckningar, vol. 2: 1940–1944, letter by Swedish Naval Attaché to London Captain J. G. Oxenstierna, n.p., 2 IV 1943.
[81] *Polska Marynarka Wojenna.*, pp. 206–207.
[82] PISM, MAR, A V 9/4, report by naval expert Commodore M. Wolbek to head of the Polish Navy Command (KMW) Rear-Admiral J. Świrski, Stockholm, 4 V 1943.

the commandant of the camp in Falun. When Wolbek visited the camp in Mariefred, the mood of the interned there was 'not too good'. Although, the documentation of the camp administration recorded only rare cases of insubordination or more serious incidents. For instance, in October 1940, Stanisław Zajączkowski was sentenced to 10 days imprisonment for beating assaulting colleague, and in March 1943, Karol Kowalik was sentenced to 14 days imprisonment for refusing to wash the dishes.[83] Among the recorded cases these were the most usual type. The seamen were thinking about the future and their internee status, which were unregulated by Polish laws. It seemed as if almost no one considered the option of military action in the crippled submarines. What also changed from the moment of the outbreak of war was the approach to underwater operations, meaning the seamen were not prepared for immediate deployment. According to Wolbek, sending 'the better ones to Great Britain' was the model solution and later, he reiterated that 'the finest should be sent first.' The principled stance of the Swedes posed an obstacle as they opposed releasing the interned. On occasion the Poles were reminded of the rules that limited their freedom. For instance, Wolbek was permitted to invite only a modest number of guests to a party in Marielund on 12 September 1943. A regulation was cited that only those who had 'official relations with the interned' could enter the camp.[84]

An unpleasant incident occurred on 24 May 1943, when Acting Sub-Lieutenant Kazimierz Sadowski, and Boatswain Franciszek Graczyk were arrested for using a radio in the internment camp. On discovering that they were monitoring news, the Swedes underestimated the incident. They did not find connections between this incident and the legation, which is why it did not jeopardise the relationship between Envoy Sokolnicki and the Swedish authorities[85] nor did it impact the living conditions in the camps.

In 1943, the matter of receivables from the Bofors company remained unsettled. In September 1943, Wolbek informed London, 'the Bofors case is constantly deferred.' The Polish side wanted the outstanding orders to be filled as soon as possible. Wolbek suspected the Swedes of deliberately delaying the process, as their intention was not to pay amounts due to the Poles: 'I do not know whether the behaviour of the Bofors company is sincere or

---

[83] KA, Marinkommando Ost, Interneringsläger no. 2, serie A, Förhörsprotokoll, vol. 1: 1940–1945.
[84] PISM, MAR, A V 9/4, letter by naval expert Commodore M. Wolbek to head of the Polish Navy Command (KMW) Rear-Admiral J. Świrski, Stockholm, 14 IX 1943.
[85] AAN, HI/I/489, letters by Polish Envoy to Stockholm H. Sokolnicki to the Ministry of Foreign Affairs, Stockholm, 5 VI, 11 VI 1943. Sadowski was sentenced to fifteen months and Graczyk to nine months in prison.

whether it is motivated by the want to protract the matter of returning the money as long as possible – until the end of the war, when the bills for the internment will be paid by us [...].'[86]

Until the close of 1942, the costs of internment reached 1.7 million crowns. The advance that was paid to the Bofors company could cover all the costs, but the company management withheld these sums to the Polish side. In 1944, the company objected to settling the matter in this way.[87]

Another issue raised by the Poles concerned the release of a small number of seamen from internment, while disregarding the formal basis for doing so in some of the cases. Six Polish officers (Lieutenant Ceceniowski, Lieutenant Korsak, Lieutenant Milisiewicz, Sub-Lieutenant Męczyński, Sub-Lieutenant Górski, Acting Sub-Lieutenant Tarczyński) and three seamen tried to obtain the fugitive status, as they had initially escaped from the Hel Peninsula on an unarmed, private boat and only boarded the patrol boat *Batory* once at sea. In February 1943, Attaché Brzeskwiński informed London that efforts to free them had failed. The Swedes justified their refusal by pointing out that the officers were subject to internment regulations, as they had not fled German bondage, but rather, left with the consent of the commander of the defence of the Polish coast, Admiral Józef Unrug, and departed prior to the Hel Peninsula falling in to German hands.[88] In May 1943, to re-examine the case, the Polish Legation in Stockholm employed professor Håkan Nial, from Stockholm University, who was a specialist in international law.[89] Re-addressing this issue relates to the visit of Minister Jan Kwapiński to Sweden at that time. On 2 May, Kwapiński, accompanied by Envoy Potworowski, Military Attaché Brzeskwiński, Lieutenant Konstanty Kowalski and Commander Wolbek visited the internment camp in Mariefred. According to Wolbek, 'The visit by the minister had a very positive impact on the moods of the officers and seamen, as he was able to sense their feelings and answer questions that concerned them.'[90] Following his return to London, during the

---

[86] PISM, MAR, A V 9/4, letter by Polish naval expert to Stockholm Commodore M. Wolbek to head of the Polish Navy Command Rear-Admiral J. Świrski, Stockholm, 14 IX 1943. Also the Tudor company, where the Poles ordered batteries for *Sęp*, did not propose its offer 'in spite of constant pressures from our side.'

[87] G. Andolf, Militära interneringar i Sverige under de första krigsåren [in:] Vindkantring..., pp. 194–195.

[88] PISM, A XII, 4/76, letter by director of the Main Evacuation Facility Stockholm (*Kierownicza Placówka Ewakuacyjna Sztokholm*) Major F. Brzeskwiński to head of the General Organisational Office of the Ministry of National Defense, 26 II 1943.

[89] PISM, MAR, A V 9/4, report by naval expert Commodore M. Wolbek to head of the Polish Navy Command Rear-Admiral J. Świrski, Sztokholm, 4 V 1943.

[90] Ibidem.

government session, Kwapiński asked the minister of defence, on behalf of the seamen, to grant them visitation by a priest and send books and cigarettes. He also emphasized that bringing the seamen from the boat *Batory* to Great Britain would be useful, as there they could be employed on Polish Merchant Navy vessels.[91]

At the outset of August 1943, the Swedish authorities released five officers and three seamen.[92] In September 1943 Minister of Foreign Affairs Romer suggested that Sokolnicki feel out the Swedish side, whether 'in the face of the changing moods in Sweden', it would be possible to release more seamen, who were not required for the maintaining of the submarines.[93] The matter was not simple, however.

In the telegram from the Polish Legation in Stockholm, it was stated, 'As the release of our officers is undoubtedly an act of politeness in light of a far-fetched interpretation of the internment regulations [...], the Swedish authorities continue to maintain their current view that these officers cannot leave Sweden on a Swedish aircraft.' This hindered greatly the evacuation, as the only other transport was an English single-passenger plane, running irregular flights from mid-1941.[94] Sending these seamen to Great Britain would help the progression towards the release of another group of the seamen. It was, therefore, important that the Polish side settle the issue of transport as soon as possible. Despite this, the evacuation caused problems until January 1945 when the legation was permitted to use a B-17 bomber as a Swedish passenger aeroplane.[95]

In the autumn of 1944, the Poles raised the issue of releasing the seamen again. They asked Professor Nial to provide a relevant legal assessment. The Swede did not hide the fact that the issue of releasing the Polish seamen was not legal, but political. On this occasion, Nial's and Pilch's efforts with UD brought success. In October of 1944, Pilch informed the Ministry of Foreign Affairs that the Swedish authorities had released three officers and seventeen

---

[91] *Protokoły posiedzeń Rady Ministrów Rzeczypospolitej Polskiej*, vol. 5, p. 439.
[92] PISM, A 11, E/508, letter by Polish Envoy to Stockholm H. Sokolnicki to the Ministry of Foreign Affairs, Stockholm, 6 VIII 1943.
[93] AAN, HI/I/305, copy of telegram by Minister of Foreign Affairs T. Romer to Polish Envoy to Stockholm, 4 IX 1943.
[94] H. Denham, *Inside...*, p. 42. Denham mentioned *Dakota*. Also the small *Mosquito* was flying on the route between Scotland and Sweden.
[95] AAN, HI/I/334, copy of telegram by Polish Envoy to Stockholm H. Sokolnicki to the Ministry of Foreign Affairs, Stockholm, 22 I 1945.

non-commissioned officers and seamen from the crews of the Polish submarines.[96] Nial did not expect the Swedish authorities to agree to further releases, but promised to continue his efforts. He justified his requests with humanitarian arguments, namely the adverse effects of long-term internment such as depression.[97]

The future of the Polish submarines were the subject of fitful diplomatic negotiations in 1945. Following the capitulation of Germany, the envoy of Great Britain requested that the Swedish government released the Allied soldiers and returned the military equipment. The Swedes did not object to this. The Poles issued a special request for British support in the efforts to release the interned submarines and the seamen of the Polish Navy.[98] The crews and the submarines were released from internment, but the release of the submarines was not straightforward.[99] The Bofors company's debts with Poland did not cover the total costs of the internment. Damage to the submarines also was so extensive that they had to be towed to Great Britain.[100] The British did not seem interested in the outdated vessels and advised they be sold.[101] Rear-Admiral Świrski asked the Polish Ministry of Foreign Affairs to initiate discreet talks with the Swedish authorities regarding the towing of the submarines to where they would be taken over by the British navy.[102] Nevertheless, the Swedes hesitated, as they feared the reaction of the Soviet authorities. This was even confirmed to the Polish naval attaché by Admiral Giron, who was described by Sokolnicki as 'the fictional custodian of the submarines.' Giron proposed that the submarines be kept temporarily in Sweden and that only their crews be evacuated.[103] Meanwhile, Minister Tarnowski demanded

---

[96] AAN, HI/I/490, letter by counsellor to the Polish Legation in Stockholm T. Pilch to the Ministry of Foreign Affairs, Stockholm, 27 X 1944.

[97] Ibidem, copy of letter by H. Nial to counsellor to Polish Legation in Stockholm, Nockeby, 10 X 1944. The Swede sent back the remuneration in the amount of 100 crowns, he described as 'modest input in the entire issue.' He requested that the money be submitted to the support fund for Polish children.

[98] NA, FO, 371/47796, letter by Northern Department of the FO the Legation of Great Britain in Stockholm, 15 V 1945.

[99] Ibidem, letter by the Legation of Great Britain in Stockholm to the Northern Department of the FO, 24 V 1945.

[100] PISM, A 11, E 81, telegram by Polish Envoy to Stockholm H. Sokolnicki to the Ministry of Foreign Affairs, 12 V 1945.

[101] Ibidem, telegram by Polish Envoy to Stockholm H. Sokolnicki to the Ministry of Foreign Affairs, 25 V 1945.

[102] Ibidem, letter by Polish Naval Attaché to London Captain T. Stoklasa to the Ministry of Foreign Affairs, 19 V 1945.

[103] Ibidem, telegram by Polish Envoy to Stockholm H. Sokolnicki to the Ministry of Foreign Affairs, 22 V 1945.

13. POLISH SOLDIERS INTERNED IN SWEDEN

that efforts continue to convince the Swedish authorities to agree to the moving of the submarines to Great Britain.[104] On 1 June, Sokolnicki announced that he had taken initial steps concerning the issue of returning the tall ship *Dar Pomorza* and the yacht *Kaparen*, which were to be moved to Gothenburg.[105] The British promised further support and assistance.[106] For security reasons, the possibility of navigating the vessels through the Göta Canal was considered.[107] On 26 June Minister, Tarnowski informed Sokolnicki that Captain Pławski would travel to Stockholm in connection with the submarines. The Swedes announced that the crews had been released and, as of 1 August, would be no longer supported by the Swedish government and that for the time being the submarines would not be able to leave their current location and that the Swedish side would be responsible for their restoration.[108]

The Foreign Office (FO) refused to grant official support to the efforts of the Polish government. The British only promised to consider supporting the Polish claims with the Swedes unofficially:

> The FO considers our special claims to be justified and unofficially advises us to continue our efforts with the Swedes along this line. If the Swedes were to refuse to place a collateral on the German property, then it would have to be stated that we consider the Swedes to be directly responsible and we demand compensation from them for all the losses.[109]

Several days later, both Great Britain and Sweden withdrew their recognition of the Polish government in exile, yet the submarines returned to Gdynia in October 1945.

---

[104] Ibidem, telegram by Minister of Foreign Affairs A. Tarnowski to Polish Envoy to Stockholm, 28 V 1945.
[105] PISM, A 11, E/1099, telegram by Polish Envoy to Stockholm H. Sokolnicki to the Ministry of Foreign Affairs, n.p., 1 VI 1945.
[106] Ibidem, telegram by the Ministry of Foreign Affairs to the Polish Legation in Stockholm, 9 VI 1945.
[107] Ibidem, telegram by the Ministry of Foreign Affairs to the Polish Legation in Stockholm, 19 VI 1945.
[108] Ibidem, telegram by Polish Envoy to Stockholm H. Sokolnicki to the Ministry of Foreign Affairs, 22 VI 1945.
[109] Ibidem, telegram by Minister of Foreign Affairs A. Tarnowski to Polish Legation in Stockholm, 28 VI 1945.

Aviators

During the Second World War, Sweden became the landing location, either due to emergency reasons or desertion, for 327 aircraft carrying nearly 1900 people (most of whom were the Americans, whose aircrews normally consisted of 9-10 people),[110] which included one Polish civilian aircraft, two bombers on a special mission to Poland and two bombers from the Bomber Squadron No. 300 of Great Britain, performing air strikes in Germany. These aircrafts brought twenty Polish pilots to Sweden, and apart from them two other pilots managed to break through into Sweden from Denmark, where they were shot down. The nationality of the crew members of the last aircraft from the Bomber Squadron No. 300, which landed in Sweden in the summer of 1944, is unknown. The identities of all the pilots are not known either.

The first Polish aircraft to land in Sweden following the outbreak of the war was the leisure aircraft RWD-13.[111] Acting Sub-Lieutenant Edmund Jereczek and Reserve Second Lieutenant Tadeusz Nowacki, started out from Gdynia on 13 September and reached Gotland three hours later.[112] There, Jereczek, wearing civil clothing, was released and by 2 October he had headed off to France, and later to Great Britain, where he served in the Royal Air Force. The case of Second Lieutenant Tadeusz Nowacki was unique. He was interned because he was caught wearing a military uniform. Towards the close of 1942, Nowacki engaged a lawyer, Hugon Lindberg, and turned to the court to question the legal basis for his internment, which took place, because at the time Sweden did not permit for the transit of soldiers representing any of the sides of the conflict. Nevertheless, in mid-1940, relating to the conclusion of the Swedish-German transit agreement, the regulations changed so that uniformed and unarmed soldiers from countries engaged in the war could be transported through Swedish territory. Towards the close of 1942, Nowacki began arguing that these regulations should be also applicable to the soldiers of other armies, including the Polish. From the point of view of international law then, such transit was acceptable and there were no grounds for the internment of Second Lieutenant Nowacki. Therefore, he should be released without delay. He obliged himself to leave the territory of

---

[110] B. Widfeldt, R. Wegmann, *Nödlandning. Främmande flyg i Sverige under andra världskriget*, Nässjö 1998, p. 183.
[111] Ibidem, p. 8.
[112] Nowacki was told to fly from Gdynia to Vilnius. He received the sum of 115 thousand zloty which was to be spent on the military families. In Gotland the Poles wanted to buy fuel and then continue their flight. Cf. T. Nowakowski, 'Polak, który wstrząsnął Szwecją – prozaik, publicysta, sowietolog Tadeusz Jan Nowacki (1902–1976)', *Archiwum Emigracji* 2001, issue 4, p. 280.

13. POLISH SOLDIERS INTERNED IN SWEDEN

Sweden as soon as he was freed. His efforts were supported by the Związek Armatorów Polskich (Baltic Exchange Chamber), which emphasized in a letter to Polish military authorities that Nowacki, who was a famous journalist and economist, would prove useful to the Polish commercial navy in Great Britain. However, the attitude of Commander Pławski towards this issue was negative. He convinced Rear-Admiral Jerzy Świrski that Nowacki 'did not represent any particular value as an officer, and his local reputation is average.' In addition, Pławski clarified that he was unfamiliar with Nowacki's achievements as an opinion journalist. He noted that he rather preferred officers engaged in active military service, who could be useful during armed combat.[113] In turn, Attaché Brzeskwiński was against releasing Nowacki if it would not lead to further releases of other officers (besides those serving on the interned submarines) for fear that morale could become undermined.[114] Following long discussions, the Polish Legation in Stockholm promised the Swedish authorities that it would facilitate Nowacki's departure from Sweden after he had fulfilled all the required formalities. The Poles declared that Nowacki was only soldier of the Polish army whose intention was to pass through Sweden, that his was an exceptional case and that it would not constitute a precedent as far as the remaining interned Polish soldiers were concerned.[115] Despite Nowacki winning the court case, the Swedes initially rejected his application.[116] It was only in April 1944 that the later co-author of the book *Land without Quisling* was released, granted a resident status and a work permit.[117]

The crew of the *Halifax* aircraft, which was on its way back from the special mission over the territory of Poland, composed of Colonel Roman Rudkowski, Lieutenant Tadeusz Jasiński, Lieutenant Stanisław Król, Sergeant Franciszek Sobkowiak, Sergeant Walenty Wasilewski, Sergeant Józef Chodyra, Sergeant Rudolf Mol and Sergeant Jerzy Sołtysiak, was forced to make an emergency landing on 8 November 1941 near to the city of Tomelilla

---

[113] PISM, A XII, 4/176, letter by Polish naval expert of the Polish Legation in Stockholm Commodore E. Pławski to the Polish Navy Command (KMW), 11 XII 1942.
[114] Ibidem, letter by Polish Military Attaché to Stockholm Major F. Brzeskwiński to Ministry of Military Affairs (MSWojsk), 11 XII 1942.
[115] RA, UD 1920 års dossiersystem, HP 22, vol. 1110, pro memoria, 12 II 1943.
[116] PISM, A XII, 4/76, letter by director of the Main Evacuation Facility (*Kierownicza Placówka Ewakuacyjna*) Major F. Brzeskwiński to head of the General Organisational Office of the Ministry of National Defence, 26 II 1943. Nowacki was able, based on the officer's word of honour, to periodically leave internment and stay in Stockholm, visit the interned Polish seamen and teach them foreign languages and economy. See: T. Nowakowski, *Polak...*, p. 281.
[117] G. Andolf, 'Militära interneringar i Sverige under de första krigsåren' [in:] *Vindkantring...*, pp. 193–194.

to the north east of Ystad. Attaché Brzeskwiński, as usual, made efforts to have the crew released from internment.[118] The VI Division of the Staff of Commander-in-Chief put pressure on the British authorities to evacuate the pilots from Sweden.[119] Rudkowski was released towards the end of November, whereas the rest of the crew had to wait until the beginning of January 1942.[120]

On the morning of 27 April 1942, another emergency landing was performed due to an engine failure in southern Sweden not far from Ystad by the Polish bomber plane *Wellington*, which was on its way back from the Rostock bombing. The entire crew composed of Lieutenant Czech Nowacki, Ensign Witold Bohuszewicz, Lieutenant Bernard Budnik, Seargant Zdzisław Taczalski, Platoon Bolesław Bestecki and Sergeant Krzysztof Grabowski survived and as per orders, destroyed the aircraft before the Swedish soldiers arrived. On the same day, an official of the Polish consulate in Malmö, Franciszek Mejor, and British Consul Castleton set off to Ystad to meet the crew of the bomber.[121] It transpired that three officers were accommodated in the Continental hotel, and three non-commissioned officers in military barracks. Vicar Daniel Cederberg, who had previously worked in the Swedish Seamen's Home in Gdynia, would also travel to meet the crew. Cederberg supplied the Polish pilots with books in English and item for shaving. He also contacted a Polish lector at Lund University, Zygmunt Łakociński, and encouraged him pay the pilots a visit.[122] Łakociński brought books in Polish. Cederberg was clearly trying to make the best possible impression. The pilots highlighted his helpfulness. In a conversation with Mejor, the vicar admitted that his former statements about the situation in Gdynia, unfavourable for Poles, 'could be used by the German propaganda.' Although, as it was reported by Cederberg, the Swedes were bearing a grudge towards the Polish pilots for destroying their machine, Łakociński highlighted in his report that the crew was surprised by the kindness expressed by the Swedish side, '[The non-commissioned officers] were healthy and happy, and they repeatedly emphasised

---

[118] PISM, Lot, A V, 1/43, letter by Polish Military Attaché to Stockholm Major F. Brzeskwiński to head of the Staff of Commander-in-Chief, 8 V 1942.
[119] PISM, A XII, 4/140, letter by head of the Division I of the Staff of Commander-in-Chief Colonel K. Glabisz to Polish Military Attaché to Stockholm Major F. Brzeskwiński, London, 19 XII 1941; Note by Colonel K. Glabisz to head of the Division VI of the Staff of Commander-in-Chief Colonel J. Smoleński, 19 XII 1941.
[120] B. Widfeldt, R. Wegmann, *Nödlandning...*, p. 31; G. Andolf, 'Militära interneringar i Sverige under de första krigsåren' [in:] *Vindkantring...*, p. 214.
[121] PISM, Lot, A V 1/43, letter by F. Mejor to the Polish Envoy to Stockholm, G. Potworowski, Malmö, 28 IV 1942.
[122] PISM, Lot, A V 143, report by Z. Łakociński, Lund, 13 V 1942. The document was published by E.S. Kruszewski in *Rocznik Instytutu Polsko-Skandynawskiego 2000–2001*, pp. 29–32.

the warm reception they were offered by all the Swedes. I purposefully asked about this matter, considering that the soldiers could include the Swedish Nazis. But nobody noticed any of them.' When it came to the officers:

> The general conversation was conducted in English and I may gladly say that the relations between the Poles and the Swedes were exceptionally cordial in all the cases. This was especially striking as I was familiar with many rumours about the Swedish officer corps. Our officers also told me that they never expected to be welcomed so warmly, and at the end of the day-long stay they also noticed no trace of aversion that could spring from the possible pro-Nazi orientation of any of the officers. [...] In Sweden they received everything they needed, and they liked the Swedish food far better than the English. [...] As I was saying my goodbye, they were all about to go for a walk together (the hotel is in the city centre).[123]

Mejor's attitude about the Swedish sincerity was more reserved. He found it to be the Swedes' technique for gather necessary information. It did not escape his attention when two Swedish officers kept asking Polish pilots about the technical details of the destroyed bomber. Mejor emphasized in his report that although the Poles 'realized right away what was going on and responded evasively,' he also pointed out, 'It would be desirable that prior to their departure from England the Polish pilots be reminded that in neutral states, where they are warmly welcomed, they should be cautious with their comments.'[124] Nowacki's crew was interned in a camp in Främby near Falun.[125] Łakociński predicted that the pilots would be released quickly from internment just like the crew, who had landed in Sweden in November 1941 and returned home a long time before. However, this time the Polish pilots remained in Sweden slightly longer. It was possible to establish that Nowacki and Bohuszewicz were released as late as on 15 February 1943 (they left

---

[123] Ibidem.
[124] PISM, Lot, A V 1/43, letter by F. Mejor to the Polish Envoy to Stockholm, G. Potworowski, Malmö, 28 IV 1942.
[125] B. Widfeldt, R. Wegmann, *Nödlandning...*, pp. 33–34. Łakociński mentioned in his report that the pilots were accommodated in the nearby guesthouse in Korsnäs. See also the recollections from the ill-fated flight: Cz. Nowacki, 'Śmierć dla U' [in:] *Czyż mogli dać więcej. Dzieje 13 Promocji Szkoły Podchorążych Lotnictwa w Dęblinie*, material collected by A. Dreja, prepared for printing by K. Łukaszewicz-Preihs, J. Preihs, London 1989, pp. 181–184.

Sweden on 21 February).[126] Bestecki returned to Great Britain on 31 March; and Taczalski together with Grabowski, on 3 April 1943.[127]

It is also interesting to note that Lieutenant Czech Nowacki force-landed in Sweden for the second time and was placed in the same camp.[128] His liberator (besides Nowacki, the crew composed of pilot Bronisław Hułas, navigator Mieczysław Malinowski, radiotelegraph operator Bolesław Woźniak, plane mechanic Witold Ruciński and gunners Stefan Miniakowski and Józef Dubiel) on 10 October 1943, on his return from a secret mission to Poland, had to land near Varberg in southern Sweden. Nowacki was the only Polish pilot to be interned twice in Sweden and one of two Allied pilots, except for an American, Lieutenant Leander Page.[129] According to Attaché Brzeskwiński, Nowacki and his crew enjoyed complete freedom. They were not guarded and they did not complain about the accommodation or food. The pilots were granted a small monthly remuneration and civilian clothing from the Legation of Great Britain.[130] In December of 1943, the Allies' register contained the names of seven Polish pilots interned in Sweden.[131] Lieutenant Nowacki and five members of his crew left Sweden between 11 and 17 June 1944, and two others (Miniakowski and Ruciński) followed by 9 September 1944.[132] According to the pilot release records of 1944, this group included twenty Poles. At the outset of 1945, there were no interned Polish pilots in Sweden.[133]

---

[126] RA, UD 1920 års dossiersystem, HP 22, vol. 1110, note regarding the Polish air force soldiers interned in Sweden, See: *Czyż mogli...*, p. 342. Nowacki wanted to steal one of the Swedish aircraft and escape internment as quickly as possible to Great Britain. The Swedish pilots were so sociable that they even showed him how to operate their *Junkers* aircraft. The escape was prevented due to the absolute ban from the representatives of both Polish and British diplomatic mission. They claimed that the chances for such an action were slim, and the escape attempt would only toughen the regime of the Swedes and make it worse for other interned soldiers (based on the conversation between the author and Cz. Nowacki, 18 XII 2000).

[127] PISM, MAR, A V 1/43, letter by Platoon B. Bestecki to the Commissariat Department, 11 V 1943.

[128] PISM, Lot, A IV I/37/15, record book: Second Lieutenant Nowacki Czech.

[129] B. Widfeldt, R. Wegmann, *Nödlandning...*, pp. 54, 87.

[130] PISM, Lot, A V, 1/43, letter by the Polish Military Attaché to Stockholm, Major F. Brzeskwiński, to the head of the Intelligence Division of the Staff of Commander-in-Chief, 20 X 1943.

[131] RA, UD 1920 års dossiersystem, HP 22, vol. 1110, telegram by Maycock to the Ministry of Aviation, 16 XII 1943.

[132] B. Widfeldt, R. Wegmann, *Nödlandning...*, p. 50.

[133] G. Andolf, 'Interneringen av britter och tyskar 1943–1944' [in:] *Vårstormar...*, pp. 235–236.

13. POLISH SOLDIERS INTERNED IN SWEDEN

Another case was Sergeant Tadeusz Miecznik, who made an emergency landing in Denmark on 17 September 1943, during which four crew members died and one died later from their wounds. Two others, including Miecznik, ended up in a German prison. Due to leg and arm injuries, Miecznik was taken to hospital from where, with the help of Danish staff, he managed to escape on 1 November. Several days later he reached Sweden by boat. Following a routine interrogation, during which the Polish pilot provided information on the course of flight training, the tactics of American aviation and the conducted operations, Miecznik was sent to Great Britain on 24 January 1944.[134]

Another Polish pilot would reach Sweden through Denmark. The crew of a Lancaster bomber, together with pilot Wasik was shot at by a German fighter aircraft on 30 August 1944 while heading towards the city of Szczecin. The bomber exploded and only Wasik survived. With the help of the Polish resistance movement, on 9 September he made it to Sweden, and two weeks later found himself in Great Britain.[135] On 30 August, another Polish Lancaster bomber from the Bomber Squadron No. 300 commanded by pilot Jones (according to Swedish documentation) landed in Sweden.[136] Its entire crew survived and, following a stay at an internment camp, they returned to Great Britain.

Release from internment was the subject of frequent discussions in UD, as the Hague Convention of 1907 completely ignored the pilots, leaving a lot of room for interpretation of the regulations applying to soldiers and seamen. In general, the Swedes adopted the principle of compensation. An equal number of pilots were to be released on both sides of the conflict. When it transpired that the number of Allied pilots who found themselves Sweden was greater than that of pilots from other countries, the Swedes, without passing on the news to the Germans, began to release groups of 10 pilots for every German machine that was forced to make an emergency landing in Sweden and yet, after repairs, resumed its flight.[137] The principle was also applied that pilots who broke through into Sweden, following their escape from prison or occupied territories, were released as civilians.

---

[134] B. Widfeldt, R. Wegmann, Nödlandning..., p. 47; A. Bielnicki, 'Lotnicy polscy w Danii w latach drugiej wojny światowej', *Zeszyty Historyczne* (Paris) 1981, iss. 56, pp. 201–203.
[135] A. Bielnicki, *Lotnicy...*, pp. 203–205.
[136] B. Widfeldt, R. Wegmann, *Nödlandning...*, p. 102.
[137] G. Andolf, 'Interneringen av britter och tyskar 1943–1944' [in:] *Vårstormar...*, pp. 224–225.

Soldiers of the 1940 Norwegian Campaign

The case of twelve privates from the Polish Independent Highland Rifle Brigade (*Samodzielna Brygada Strzelców Podhalańskich*) was unique. They crossed the Norwegian–Swedish border in May 1940. Initially, they were interned, but soon the Polish officers who contacted them informed the Swedish authorities that they were 'deserters, Jews and Ukrainians.'[138] The commandant of the camp advised his superiors to release the men to maintain camp discipline, and because the Polish Legation would not take responsibility for them.[139] The group of twelve was released in line with the rules applying to soldiers who had fought in the Norwegian Campaign, regardless of their nationality.[140] Eventually, ten of the twelve returned to occupied Poland and two wanted to travel to Great Britain and join the Polish army. At the time, they were found employment by the Swedish authorities, and most probably due to this they remained in Sweden.

This was a small group of approximately 4800 soldiers, mostly Norwegians, but also Britons and Germans, and one Portuguese, who were mostly interned due to the military actions which took place in Norway in the spring of 1940. For the Swedish authorities, it was important to unload such a large group of interned soldiers, which is why, as part of the agreements with the sides of the conflict, they were gradually released.

---

[138] RA, mf. F 035-3-32252, copy of pro memoria.
[139] G. Andolf, 'Militära interneringar i Sverige under de första krigsåren' [in:] *Vindkantring...*, pp. 199–200.
[140] PISM, A XII, 22/36, letter by the deputy head of the Division II of the Staff of the Commander-in-Chief, Lieutenant-Colonel S. Gano, to the head of the Staff of the Commander-in-Chief, London, 20 IX 1940.

Conclusion

Polish–Swedish relations during the Second World War is clearly divided into several stages. Following Hitler's aggression of September 1939, Sweden attempted, based on its experiences from the First World War, to maintain strict neutrality and to manoeuvre between the warring parties. At the beginning of the war, Poland became the main theatre of military operations, that is why Polish affairs were to a large extent dealt with by both the Swedish government and society. It should be noted that this was the period of the peak of a versatile interest in Poland, the course of the military campaign was described in Swedish newspapers in detail until the final Polish defeat. Comments were devoted to the Soviet aggression on September 17 and its consequences.

In 1939, the Swedish diplomacy fulfilled its obligations in representing Polish interests in Germany in line with the agreement of August 1939. After November, it suspended this mission under pressure from the Germans. Sweden began implementing a strategy of flexible neutrality. Swedish foreign policy was an unemotional policy of adaptation to the circumstances, which were coming into existence because of developments in the war. Its principal target was to prevent potential aggressors from occupying Sweden. As a result, the Swedes succumbed to the political and economic demands of Germany. At the time, Polish–Swedish relations were virtually limited to the meetings between Envoy Gustaw Potworowski and the heads of the Swedish diplomacy, whose purpose was to settle current affairs.

Following the Battle of Stalingrad, the Swedes gradually started meeting the expectations of the Allies. In 1943, they abandoned the policy of concessions towards Hitler and established a closer cooperation with Great Britain and the USA. The relations with the Polish government in exile improved only slightly. From the autumn of 1939 until the breakthrough in the war, the Swedes avoided, in favour of the Allies, official contact with the Polish government due to the Germans. From 1943 onwards, in relation to the confidential relations with the diplomats of other countries, the Swedish authorities started to treat political targets increasingly irreverently. What became noticeable about the Swedish policy was the fear about the dominance of the Soviet Union in the Baltic Sea region, whilst the Swedes were trying to maintain the best possible relations with Moscow. Poland could only be an obstacle for maintaining such relations. Regarding this, Stockholm quickly accepted the Soviet interpretations of the Katyń Massacre, the Polish–Soviet dispute over the border, and eventually the conflict around creating a new political representation of the Polish nation in Moscow in opposition to the Polish government in exile. And, therefore, the propagandist campaigns conducted by the Polish Legation in Stockholm were fruitless. Planned for raising compassion or even mercy for the Polish nation, they did not support the political actions. In this context the picture of Polish–Swedish relations during the war can be treated as bringing sometimes new views on the policy of Sweden in 1939–45.

Satirical pieces of literature from during the war stigmatized the cynicism of the heads of the Swedish diplomacy. Staffan Tjerneld wrote a text for a variety show staged in the *Nya Teatern*, where pointed out to the government that they were yielding to the political situation and were always 'true friends of those who are on top.'[1] Towards the close of the war, the best solution was rapprochement with Moscow. In the opinion of the Polish Naval Attaché to Stockholm, Commander Marian Wolbek, what was again given priority was 'cold calculation: how to struggle out of the difficult situation risking the least and achieving the greatest benefits.'[2]

The visit of Jan Kwapiński, Minister of Industry, Trade and Shipping, to Stockholm in April and May of 1943, and establishing direct relations with the social democrats who occupied the highest state positions (headed by Prime Minister Hansson), were not enough to overcome the Swedish fears about becoming involved with a partner whose relations with the Soviet Union were gradually worsening. This clearly shows that the issue of the Katyń Massacre (revealed in April 1943) was among other things a breakthrough in the Swedish–Polish relations. On taking a clear look on the development of the situation in Europe, it shows that the Swedes predicted quite early that the Polish government would never return to its homeland. In fact, they initiated the talks with the Polish Legation about coal import from Poland after the conclusion of military operations, but, as it turned out,

---

[1] H. Dahlberg, *I Sverige...*, p. 179.
[2] PISM, MAR, A V 9/2, report by the Polish Naval Attaché to Stockholm, Commander M. Wolbek to the head of the Intelligence Division of the Staff of Commander-in-Chief, 4 XI 1943. The methods of the Swedish diplomats were bluntly described in the summer of 1942 by the Finnish Minister of Foreign Affairs, Rolf Witting. He stated: 'in order to understand the Swedish policy one needs not to be a professor in oceanography but a professor in pathological anatomy' (quoted after W. M. Carlgren, *Svensk utrikespolitik...*). The reason for this view was most probably his disappointment with the excessively weak, in his opinion, Swedish support of Finland on the international arena.

they did this only to use the negotiations to gather precious knowledge about the intentions of the Allies on the issue of the neutral states' supplies and plans for the post-war reconstruction conducted by international organisations appointed for this purpose. Initially, it seemed that it would be precisely on the grounds of the renewal of economic relations that the common interests would be defined. However, when a suitable occasion came along, the Swedes changed their conversation partner and, in the fall of 1944, established relations with the representation of the PKWN in Moscow.

The Swedes did not accept the Polish arguments, both regarding the eastern and to the western border. They adopted a similar position to those western opinion journalists who maintained that Poland most naturally comprised of Warsaw and its surroundings, but further there lied 'only doubts.' It is worth noting that in the last years of the war, 1944 and 1945, Poland again started to appear on the front pages of Swedish newspapers. Despite the substantial efforts of the press attaché's office in Stockholm, many Swedish opinion journalists agreed with the slogans of the Soviet propaganda that the Eastern Borderlands were mostly inhabited by a non-Polish population and relating to this there were no grounds for them to be included in the Polish Republic. Towards the end of the war, the pro-German attitude was still very strong, but not associated with Nazism and close to the views of the supporters of European balance. The plans to award Poland with the entire territory of Silesia and Pomerania did not gain much support in Sweden and were perceived as hotbeds of new conflicts in the future.

However, towards the end of the war Poland could count on relatively extensive humanitarian aid, which, treated as an instrument of foreign policy, in the case of Poland was a gesture of good will at the outset of economic negotiations and a sign of acceptance for the deal created by Stalin in Central Europe. What was surely of great importance for making this decision was the tragedy of the Warsaw Rising. The Polish government in exile continued its efforts to prevent the neutral states from treating the Polish issue as closed. The aid campaign organized by the Swedish society for the citizens of Warsaw was a sign of support for the Polish aspirations for independence.

The Polish diplomats residing in Stockholm evaluated the position of Sweden with understanding. They did not excessively condemn the submissiveness towards Germany. With a far greater disappointment they reacted to the opportunism towards the Soviet Union. What was noticeable in this context were the interesting opinions about the Swedish policy in the Polish press in exile. In 1939–43, the policy of neutrality was criticised, as it was associated with supporting Hitler's aggression, and in 1944–45 there appeared acceptance for the cautiousness in the relations with the Soviet Union and the willingness to remain outside the Allied camp until the conclusion of the war. Thanks to the reports about the transports of Swedish humanitarian aid to the Polish territory and about good living conditions of the Poles, both the refugees and the interned, in Sweden, a positive picture of this country was consolidated in the minds of the Polish readership (although the descriptions of the Swedish prosperity could evoke mixed feelings).[3]

The Swedish politicians were, in general, unlikely to show their sentiments towards Poland. What needs to be emphasized is that the diplomats who had contacts with Poland looked on it favourably before the war. Not only were head of the Press department at Utrikesdepartementet Sven Grafström and Secretary-General Erik Boheman well oriented in the complex subject of Poland's relations with its neighbours, but they also understood the motives behind the actions of the government in exile. However, in general it would be difficult to speak of a Polish lobby in Sweden. One such small group was composed of several members of the diplomatic elite and discreetly operating industrialists. The Polish resistance movement collaborated with the Swedish industrialists who represented their own companies in Poland under the German occupation. Sven Norrman and Gösta Gustafsson, especially, contributed a great deal as couriers for the Polish Underground State and the Home Army. Many years later they never boasted about their activity in favour of Poland. Fears that the documentation would fall in to the hands of unauthorized persons were too strong.

For one thing, there was Polish heroism and dreams of independence because of the sacrifice and battle for a just cause, and for another, the Swedish opportunism and striving to reach compromise as a method of surviving the turmoil of war. According to the historian A. W. Johansson, compromise, also in the relations with other countries, was inseparably and naturally connected with the style of policy conducted by Prime Minister Per Albin Hansson. It is hard to evaluate this policy unequivocally, as its characteristic features were delay tactics, timidity and the anti-heroic attitude of an observer, whereas in reality it was prudent manoeuvring between the mutually exclusive aspirations

---

[3] Of interest was that the Polish or Swedish press recorded only three examples of the Polish–Swedish brotherhood of arms. A Swedish sailor's accidental participation in the defence of Gdynia in September 1939, a Swedish Royal Air Force pilot's control of a bomber carrying Polish crew and a Swedish construction company representative's joining Polish air force following the trauma he had suffered during an inspection of the occupied territories (M.S., 'Szwed z Oświęcimia', *Dziennik Żołnierza Armii Polskiej na Wschodzie*, 6 VIII 1944). To be honest, it is not certain whether any of the above examples is authentic.

of the powers.⁴ Using the term proposed by an American researcher Herbert R. Reginbogin: What was the Swedish face of neutrality as for the Polish matter during the war? The attitude towards the Polish matter is characterised by political pragmatism which is best described by Östen Unden, who held the office of the Swedish Minister of Foreign Affairs before and after the war, and government counsellor during the Second World War: 'small countries, just like ours, can seldom influence the course of events. Such countries also cannot help others in the event of war.'⁵ In this way the Swedish political elites denied all accusations of unethical conduct and absolved themselves from their lack of sense of responsibility for the situation in the Baltic Sea region. The newest interpretation of the policy of Sweden was proposed by Klas Åmark: "The negotiating policy also meant that the Swedish government accepted that the great powers had the right to make claims on Sweden and to start negotiations about these claims. The Swedish negotiators and the Swedish government understood negotiating was a risky business that involved unpleasant compromises, but it became the foremost method for the small state to protect itself against open violence and war".⁶

Sweden was not a strategic partner for Poland, and for Sweden relations with Poland were obviously subordinate to the relations with great powers. The course of military operations determined Sweden's role as an evacuation destination, a shelter for refugees, an important junction of communication with the occupied territories and, most notably, as a country that was not affected by the military operations. In the face of the looming downfall of the Third Reich, Sweden was considered a suitable partner in the process of economic restoration of Poland. In the eyes of Sweden, Poland was one of many Central European problems, which were to be followed carefully but not engaged in. As early as in the interwar period, it became clear that Swedish horizons of political thinking (despite the country's considerable engagement in the activity of the League of Nations) was limited to the Nordic States and, to a much narrower extent, the Baltic States, except Lithuania. During the Second World War, nothing changed in this respect. Consequently, the scope of shared Polish–Swedish interests could not be particularly broad. What was most noticeable were the issues of economic cooperation, or rather perspec-

---

⁴ A. W. Johansson, *Per Albin...*, p. 58.
⁵ Quoted after: P. Andrzejewski, 'Szwedzka neutralność – wizerunek poprzez Bałtyk' [in:] *Svea. Ze studiów nad szwedzką nauką i kulturą*, ed. B. Andrzejewski, Poznań 1990, p. 133.
⁶ Åmark K., *Sweden. Negotiated neutrality*, [in:] R. Bosworth, J. Maiolo (eds.), *Cambridge History of the Second World War, vol. 2: Politics and Ideology*, Cambridge 2015, p. 373.

tives of its renewal after the war. Political relations were practically non-existent. During the initial months of the war, Swedish diplomacy focused on representing Polish interests in Germany. Later, the Swedes observed Poland's fate closely and speculated about its future. Some degree of anxiety, but also opportunism, accompanied the observations of the initial phase of Soviet dominance of the Baltic Sea. Counting on satisfying Sweden's own interests, Swedish newspapers willingly repeated the slogan '*Vad angår oss polska affärer?*', which translates to 'Why should we care about Polish affairs?'

The Poles were expecting that their sovereignty would be defended and their territorial integrity maintained. Nevertheless, it turned out that such efforts were not among the priorities of European powers. The sacrifice made in combat with Germany was of little avail and political objectives of Poland, devoid of effective instruments of implementation, continued to remain merely a dream. No military attack was launched on Sweden and it maintained a consistent opportunistic policy of concessions towards the claims of the fighting powers, while preserving its main goal of non-involvement in the war. A part of this opportunistic strategy was diminishing the significance of Polish interests in the sphere of Swedish policy.

The lack of choices available to Poland ought to be noted. It was continuously faced with *faits accomplis*. Sweden, though, had a certain amount of room for manoeuvre in the diplomatic maze during the Second World War. Its concessions related to a sense of threat and limitation of sovereignty, but they were short-term in character and did not question Sweden's territorial integrity.

Bibliography

1. Archives and unpublished sources

Riksarkivet (Stockholm) – RA (National Archives of Sweden)
Handelsdepartementet
Kabinettet/UD Huvudarkivet
SÄPO arkiv
Svenska Röda Korset
Sveriges Allmäna Exportförening
UD avdelningar och byråarkiv 1864–1952
Utrikespepartementet (UD) 1920 års dossiersystem

Arbetarrörelsens arkiv och bibliotek – ARAB
(Swedish Labour Movement's Archive and Library, Stockholm)
Rickard Sandlers samling
SAP arkiv

Krigsarkivet (Stockholm) – KA (Military Archive in Stockholm)
Försvarsstaben, marinaavdelningens hemliga arkiv
Marinkommando Ost

Militära underrättelse- och säkerhetstjänstens arkiv (Stockholm) – MUST arkiv
Försvarstaben, Säkerhetsavdelningen

Carolina Rediviva (Uppsala), Handskriftsavdelning
Marika Stiernstedts samling

Archiwum Akt Nowych (Warsaw) – AAN
Maurycy Karniol collection
Norbert Żaba collection
Konsulat RP w Malmö
MPHiŻ (London)
MSZ (Instytut Hoovera)
MSZ 1918–1939
PKWN
Poselstwo RP w Sztokholmie
Związek Patriotów Polskich w Szwecji (ZPPwSZ)
Związek Patriotów Polskich w ZSRR (ZPPwZSRR)

Archiwum Ministerstwa Spraw Zagranicznych (Warsaw) – AMSZ
Ambasada RP w Moskwie (collection no. 27)
Departament Polityczny (collection no. 6)

Polish Institute and Sikorski Museum (London) – PISM
Ambasada RP w Londynie (A 12)
Kierownictwo Marynarki Wojennej (MAR)
Adam Ciołkosz collection (no. 133)
Władysław Sikorski collection (no. 1)
Jan Kwapiński collection (no. 20)
Wacław Gilewicz collection (no. 206)
Stanisław Kot collection (no. 25)
Stanisław Paprocki collection (no. 30)
Stanisław Stroński collection (no. 183)
Ministerstwo Informacji i Dokumentacji (A 10)
Ministerstwo Prac Kongresowych (A 21)
Ministerstwo Spraw Wewnętrznych (A 9)
Ministerstwo Spraw Zagranicznych (A 11)
Naczelne Władze Wojskowe (A XII)
Polskie Siły Powietrzne (Lot)
Prezydium Rady Ministrów (PRM)
Zbiór dokumentów różnych (B)

National Archives (London) – NA
Admiralty: History of Naval Intelligence and Naval Intelligence Department 1940–1945 (ADM 223)
Foreign Office (FO): Embassy and Consular Files (188), General Correspondence (371), Confidential Print (419)
Records of Special Operations Executive (HS)

Churchill Archives Centre (Churchill College, Cambridge)
Sir Victor Mallet: Memoir

Polish Underground Movement (1939–1945) Study Trust (London)
Skrzynie (Sk.)

Notes by Polish envoy to Stockholm Gustaw Potworowski 1939–1942
Copy in author's possession, given by Tomasz Potworowski (original document kept at Hoover Institution, USA)

2. Interviews

Czech Nowacki (Duszniki Zdrój, 16 December 2000)
Władysław Słoma (Mariefred, 12 July 2005)

3. Published sources

1. Documents

Armia Krajowa w dokumentach 1939-1945, t. 1: *wrzesień 1939 - czerwiec 1941*, T. Pełczynski (ed.), Wrocław 1990.
Armia Krajowa w dokumentach 1939-1945, t. 2: *czerwiec 1941 - kwiecień 1943*, T. Pełczynski (ed.), Wrocław 1990.
Armia Krajowa w dokumentach 1939-1945, t. 3: *kwiecień 1943 - lipiec 1944*, T. Pełczynski (ed.), Wrocław 1990.
Armia Krajowa w dokumentach 1939-1945, t. 4: *lipiec - październik 1944*, T. Pełczynski (ed.), Wrocław 1991.
Armia Krajowa w dokumentach 1939-1945, t. 5: *październik 1944 - lipiec 1945*, T. Pełczynski (ed.), Wrocław 1991.
Armia Krajowa w dokumentach 1939-1945, t. 6: *uzupełnienia*, T. Pełczynski (ed.), Wrocław 1991.
Berättelse över Svenska Röda Korsets verksamhet under år 1939, Stockholm 1940.
Berättelse över Svenska Röda Korsets verksamhet under år 1940, Stockholm 1941.
Berättelse över Svenska Röda Korsets verksamhet under år 1941, Stockholm 1942.
Berättelse över Svenska Röda Korsets verksamhet under år 1942, Stockholm 1943.
Berättelse över Svenska Röda Korsets verksamhet under år 1943, Stockholm 1944.
Berättelse över Svenska Röda Korsets verksamhet under år 1944, Stockholm 1945.
Berättelse över Svenska Röda Korsets verksamhet under år 1945, Stockholm 1946.
Documents on Polish-Soviet relations 1939-1945, t. 1: *1939-April 1943*, London-Melbourne-Toronto 1961.
Documents on Polish-Soviet relations 1939-1945, t. 2: *May 1943-1945*, London 1967.
Duraczyński E., Turkowski R., *O Polsce na uchodźstwie. Rada Narodowa Rzeczypospolitej Polskiej 1939-1945*, Warsaw 1997.
Hansson P. A., *Svensk hållning och handling*, Stockholm 1945.
Kumlin R., 'Småstatsdiplomati i stormaktskrig. Promemorior från krigsåren', *Historisk tidskrift* 1977, nr 4.
Mówią świadkowie Ravensbrück, wybór wstęp i opracowanie E. S. Kruszewski, Copenhagen 2001.
"My tu żyjemy jak w obozie warownym". Listy PPS-WRN Warszawa-Londyn 1940-1945, O. Zaremba-Blatonowa (ed.), L. Ciołkoszowa, W. Czapska-Jordan, London 1992.
Polska Marynarka Wojenna 1939-1947. Wybór dokumentów, t. 1, wybór i oprac. Z. Wojciechowski, Gdynia 1999.

Polska w polityce międzynarodowej (1939-1945). Zbiór dokumentów: 1939, oprac. W. T. Kowalski, Warsaw 1989.
Polskie dokumenty dyplomatyczne 1939 styczeń-sierpień, S. Żerko (ed.), współprac. P. Długołęcki, Warsaw 2005.
Polskie dokumenty dyplomatyczne 1939 wrzesień-grudzień, W. Rojek (ed.), Warsaw 2007.
Protokoll vid riksdagens hemliga sammanträden 1942-1945, L. Frykholm (ed.), Stockholm 1976.
Protokoły posiedzeń Rady Ministrów Rzeczypospolitej Polskiej, t. 1: *październik 1939 - czerwiec 1940*, nauk. M. Zgórniak (ed.), oprac. W. Rojek, współprac. A. Suchcitz, Kraków 1994.
Protokoły posiedzeń Rady Ministrów Rzeczypospolitej Polskiej, t. 2: *czerwiec 1940 - czerwiec 1941*, nauk. M. Zgórniak (ed.), oprac. W. Rojek, współprac. A. Suchcitz, Kraków 1995.
Protokoły posiedzeń Rady Ministrów Rzeczypospolitej Polskiej, t. 3: *czerwiec 1941 - grudzień 1941*, nauk. M. Zgórniak (ed.), oprac. W. Rojek, współprac. A. Suchcitz, Kraków 1996.
Protokoły posiedzeń Rady Ministrów Rzeczypospolitej Polskiej, t. 4: *grudzień 1941 - sierpień 1942*, nauk. M. Zgórniak (ed.), oprac. W. Rojek, współprac. A. Suchcitz, Kraków 1998.
Protokoły posiedzeń Rady Ministrów Rzeczypospolitej Polskiej, t. 5: *wrzesień 1942 - lipiec 1943*, nauk. M. Zgórniak (ed.), oprac. W. Rojek, współprac. A. Suchcitz, Kraków 2001.
Protokoły posiedzeń Rady Ministrów Rzeczypospolitej Polskiej, t. 6: *lipiec 1943 - kwiecień 1944*, nauk. M. Zgórniak (ed.), oprac. W. Rojek, współprac. A. Suchcitz, Kraków 2003.
Protokoły posiedzeń Rady Ministrów Rzeczypospolitej Polskiej, t. 7: *maj 1944 - listopad 1944*, nauk. M. Zgórniak (ed.), oprac. W. Rojek, współprac. A. Suchcitz, Kraków 2006.
Protokół obrad KC PPR w maju 1945 roku, oprac. A. Kochański, Warszawa 1992 (Dokumenty do dziejów PRL, p. 1).
Sprawa polska w czasie drugiej wojny światowej na arenie międzynarodowej. Zbiór dokumentów, S. Stanisławska (ed.), Warsaw 1965.
Svensk utrikespolitik under andra världskriget. Statsrådstal, riksdagsdebatter och kommunikéer, R. Lundström (ed.), S. Dahl, Stockholm 1946.

2. Diaries and memoirs

Assarsson V., *I skuggan av Stalin*, Stockholm 1963.
Bernadotte F., *Människor jag mött*, Stockholm 1947.
Bernadotte F., *Slutet. Mina humanitära förhandlingar i Tyskland våren 1945 och deras politiska följder*, Stockholm 1945.
Boheman E., *På vakt. Från attaché till sändebud. Minnesanteckningar*, Stockholm 1963.

BIBLIOGRAPHY

Boheman E., *På vakt. Kabinettssekreterare under andra världskriget*, Stockholm 1964.
Churchill W. S., *The Second World War, vol. 1: The Gathering Storm*, London 1985.
Churchill W. S, The *Second World War, vol. 2: Their finest hour*, London 1985
Dahlerus B., *Sista försöket. London-Berlin sommaren 1939*, Stockholm 1945.
Denham H., *Inside the Nazi Ring. A Naval Attaché in Sweden 1940-1945*, London 1984.
Diariusz i teki Jana Szembeka (1935-1945), t. 4, oprac. J. Zaranski, London 1972.
Dzienniki czynności Prezydenta RP Władysława Raczkiewicza 1939-1947, t. 1: *1939-1942*, t. 2: *1943-1947*, oprac. J. Piotrowski, Wrocław 2004.
Erlander T., *1901-1939*, Stockholm 1972.
Erlander T., *1940-1949*, Stockholm 1973.
Fredborg A., *Bakom stålvallen. Som svensk korrespondent i Berlin 1941-43*, Stockholm 1943.
Frykman S., *Röda korsexpeditionen till Tyskland*, Stockholm 1945.
Gistedt E., *Från operett till tragedi*, Stockholm 1946.
Goebbels J., *Tagebücher 1924-1945*, R. G. Reuth (ed.), t. 5: *1943-1945*, München-Zürich 2000.
Gottfarb I., *Den livsfarliga glömskan*, Stockholm 2006.
Grafström S., *Anteckningar 1938-1944*, S. Ekman (ed.), Stockholm 1989.
Grafström S., *Anteckningar 1945-1954*, S. Ekman (ed.), Stockholm 1989.
Hägglöf G., *Möte med Europa. Paris-London-Moskva-Genève-Berlin 1926-1940*, Stockholm 1971.
Henderson N., *Failure of a Mission. Berlin 1937-1939*, New York 1940.
Jędrychowski S., *Przedstawicielstwo PKWN w Moskwie*, Warszawa 1987.
Jones R. V., *Most Secret War*, Chatham 1997.
Kersten F., *Samtal med Himmler. Minnen från Tredje Riket 1939-1945*, Stockholm 1947.
Kochanowicz T., *Na wojennej emigracji. Wspomnienia z lat 1942-1944*, wyd. 2, Warsaw 1979.
Kollontai A., *Diplomaticeskie dnevniki 1922-1940*, vol. 2, Moscow 2001.
Kwapiński J., *1939-1945 (kartki z pamiętnika)*, London 1947.
Lipski J., *Diplomat in Berlin 1933-1939. Papers and Memoirs of Jozef Lipski, Ambassador of Poland*, W. Jędrzejewicz (ed.), New York-London 1968.
Macmillan H., *The Blast of War 1939-1945*, London 1967.
Mannerheim C. G., *Minnen*, vol. 1-2, Stockholm 1951-52.
Masur N., *En jude talar med Himmler*, Stockholm 1945.
Mikołajczyk S., *Polska zgwałcona*, Warsaw 2005.
Mitkiewicz L., *Wspomnienia kowienskie 1938-1939*, Warsaw-Wrocław 1989.
Müllern G., *Det har inte stått i tidningen. En svensk utlandsjournalists minnen från två krigsår*, Stockholm 1942.
Nagórski Z., *Wojna w Londynie*, Paryż 1966.
Nahlik S. E., *Przesiane przez pamięć*, vol. 2, Kraków 2002.
Nowak J. [Jezioranski Z.], *Kurier z Warszawy*, Kraków 1989.
Osóbka-Morawski E., *Dziennik polityczny 1943-1948*, Gdańsk 1981.

Pański J., *Wachta lewej burty*, Gdynia 1965.
Pański J., *Związek Patriotów Polskich w Szwecji*, "Z pola walki" 1964, nr 4.
Potworowski T., *Zapiski do pamiętnika: Sztokholm, wrzesień-grudzień 1939*, "Acta Sueco-Polonica" 2003-2005, nr 12-13.
Pragier A., *Czas przeszły dokonany*, London 1966.
Raczyński E., *W sojuszniczym Londynie. Dziennik ambasadora Edwarda Raczyńskiego 1939-1945*, wyd. 3, London 1997.
Romanowski B., *Torpeda w celu! Wspomnienia ze służby na okrętach podwodnych 1939-1945*, Gdańsk 1997.
Rudnicka-Jaroszynska L., *Mitt möte med Röda armén*, Malmö 1943.
Sapieha V., *Mitt liv i Polen*, Stockholm 1941.
[Schellenberg W.], *The labyrinth. Memoirs of Walter Schellenberg, Hitler's chief of counterintelligence*, 2000.
Schimitzek S., *Na krawędzi Europy. Wspomnienia portugalskie 1939-1946*, Warsaw 1970.
Skandynawia w oczach Polaków. Antologia, wybór, oprac. i wstęp Z. Ciesielski, Gdańsk 1974.
Sloma W., *En polsk ubåtsman i Mariefred*, Nyköping 2006.
Sokolnicki H., *In the service of Poland: memoirs of diplomatic and social life, chiefly before and during World War II, in Poland, the USSR and Scandinavia*, Helsinki 1973.
Sokolnicki M., *Ankarski dziennik*, London 1974.
Sokolnicki M., *Dziennik ankarski 1939-1943*, London 1965.
Szembek J., *Diariusz wrzesień – grudzień 1939*, oprac. B. Grzeloński, Warsaw 1989.
Tennant P., *Vid sidan av kriget. Diplomat i Sverige 1939-1945*, Stockholm 1989.
Wachowiak S., *Czasy, które przeżyłem*, Warsaw 1991.
Westman K. G., *Politiska anteckningar september 1939-mars 1943*, W. M. Carlgren (ed.), Stockholm 1981.
Westrup Z. P., *Jag har varit i Arkadien*, Stockholm 1975.
Winiewicz J., *Co pamiętam z długiej drogi życia*, Poznań 1985.
af Wirsén E., *Minnen från fred och krig*, Stockholm 1942.
af Wirsén E., *Från Balkan till Berlin*, Stockholm 1943.
Wrzesień 1939 r. w relacjach dyplomatów: Józefa Becka, Jana Szembeka, Anthon'yego Drexel-Biddl'ea, Leona Noëla i innych, wybór i oprac. A. Skrzypek, Warsaw 1989.
Wysocki A., *Na placówce dyplomatycznej w Sztokholmie 1924-1928. Wspomnienia*, wybór, oprac., przedm. P. Jaworski, Toruń 2004.
Zabiełło S., *Na posterunku we Francji*, Warsaw 1967.
Zagórski W., *Wolność w niewoli*, London 1971.

3. Newspapers 1939–1945

Swedish:
Affärsvärlden
Aftonbladet
Aftontidningen
Arbetaren
Arbetet
Barometern
Dagens Nyheter
Dagsposten
Expressen
Falu-Kuriren
Folkets Dagblad
Gefle Dagblad
Göteborgs Handels- och Sjöfarts-Tidning
Göteborgs Morgonpost
Göteborgs Posten
Göteborgs Tidningen
Gotlänningen
Hufvudstadsbladet
Jönköpings-Posten
Kalmar Läns Tidning
Karlshamns Allehanda
Mellanfolkligt Samarbete
Mellersta Skåne
Morgon-Tidningen
Nerikes Allehanda
Norrbottens-Kuriren
Norrköpings Tidningar
Nu
Ny Dag
Ny Tid
Nya Dagligt Allehanda
Örebro-Kuriren
Östgöta Correspondenten
Reformatorn
Skånska Socialdemokraten
Skaraborgaren
Social-Demokraten
Stockholms-Tidningen
Svensk Tidskrift
Svenska Dagbladet

Svenska Morgonbladet
Svensk underbefälstidning
Sydsvenska Dagbladet Snällposten
Trots Allt!
Upsala Nya Tidning
Västernorrlands Allehanda
Vestmanlands Läns Tidning
Ystads Allehanda

Polish (if not specified – London):
Dziennik Polski i Dziennik Żołnierza
Dziennik Polski
Dziennik Żołnierza APW (Middle East, Italy)
Dziennik Żołnierza
Myśl Polska
Nowa Polska
Orzeł Biały (USSR, Middle East, Italy, Great Britain)
Przedświt
Polska Walcząca
Robotnik Polski w Wielkiej Brytanii
Wiadomości Polskie
Wieści Polskie (Hungary)

4. Publications from the years 1939–1945

Almstedt G., *Dagligt liv i Polen*, Ängleholm 1944.
Almstedt G., Johnson E., *Warszawa!*, Stockholm 1944.
Bagiński H., *Wolność Polski na morzu*, Kirkcaldy 1942.
Binental L., *Chopin. Hans liv och konst*, Stockholm 1940.
Curie E., *Min mor Marie Sklodowska-Curie*, Stockholm 1941.
Detta hände i Europa. Härtagna länder 1938–1941, Stockholm 1945.
En polsk svart bok om den tyska „nyordningen" i Polen, Stockholm 1942.
ESWU [Adamek S.], *Folkens frihetskamp. Det nya världkriget*, Stockholm 1940.
Hansson P. A., *Vår neutralitetspolitik*, Stockholm 1942.
Hedlund-Nyström T., *Polens fjärde delning. Dess förhistoria och fullbordan*, Malmö 1940.
Höglund Z., *Alliansen Hitler–Stalin*, Stockholm 1939.
Justus, *Hur det skedde! Från Versailles till i dag*, Stockholm 1940.
Kända svenskar om Polen, Stockholm 1944.
Karski J., *Den hemliga staten*, Stockholm 1945.
Kentrschynskyj A., *Sanningen om Ukraina*, Helsingfors 1943.
Lundberg G., *Missnöjets missionärer. En vidräkning med de kommunistiska sabotörerna*, Stockholm 1940.

Nerman T., *Sverige i beredskap*, Stockholm 1942.
Norwid S. T., *Landet utan Quisling*, Stockholm 1944.
Olberg P., *Polens öde. Ett europeiskt kardinalproblem*, Stockholm 1944.
Pitjeta V., *Om Västukraina och Västvitryssland*, Stockholm 1945.
Polens martyrium. Förhållanden under tyska ockupationen belysta av Polska informationsministeriet, Stockholm 1942.
Emitjov W., *Ett land försvann. Ödesveckor i Polen*, Stockholm 1939. Szende S., *Den siste juden från Polen*, Stockholm 1944.
Thulstrup Å., *Den polska-ryska konflikten*, Stockholm 1944.
Vougt A., *Ur svensk synvinkel. Inlägg i den utrikespolitiska debatten*, Malmö 1943.
Vysocki A., *Ett polskt levnadsöde*, Stockholm 1944.
Walterson J., *Öster om Bug. Fakta kring de östpolska problemen*, Stockholm 1944.

4. Books and articles

Aalders G., Wiebes C., *Affärer till varje pris. Wallenbergs hemliga stöd till nazisterna*, Stockholm 1989.
Agrell W., *Fred och fruktan. Sveriges säkerhetspolitiska historia 1918–2000*, Lund 2000.
Åmark K., *Att bo granne med ondskan. Sveriges förhållande till nazismen, Nazityskland och Förintelsen*, Stockholm 2016 (1st edition 2011).
Åmark K., *Makt eller moral. Svensk offentlig debatt om internationell politik och svensk utrikes och försvarspolitik 1938–1939*, Stockholm 1973.
Åmark K., *Sweden. Negotiated neutrality*, [in:] R. Bosworth, J. Maiolo (eds.), *Cambridge History of the Second World War, vol. 2: Politics and Ideology*, Cambridge 2015.
Bartoszewicz H., *Polityka Związku Sowieckiego wobec państw Europy Środkowo-Wschodniej w latach 1944–1948*, Warsaw 1999.
Batowski H., *Agonia pokoju i początek wojny (sierpień–wrzesień 1939)*, wyd. 3, Poznań 1979.
Batowski H., *Rok 1940 w dyplomacji europejskiej*, Poznań 1981.
Batowski H., *Walka dyplomacji niemieckiej przeciw Polsce 1939–1945*, Kraków–Wrocław 1984.
Batowski H., *Z dziejów dyplomacji polskiej na obczyźnie (wrzesień 1939 – lipiec 1941)*, Kraków 1984.
Berge A., *Flyktingpolitik i stormakts skugga. Sverige och de sovjetryska flyktingarna under andra världskriget*, Uppsala 1992.
Berner Ö., *Svensk grannlandspolitik över seklen – exemplet Polen* [w:] *Utrikes ärenden. Sverker Åström 75 år*, G. Berg (ed.), P. Wästberg, Stockholm 1990.
Biegański W., Juchniewicz M., Okęcki S., *Polacy w ruchu oporu narodów Europy 1939–1945*, Warsaw 1977.
Bielnicki A., *Lotnicy polscy w Danii w latach drugiej wojny światowej*, "Zeszyty Historyczne" (Paris) 1981, p. 56.

Björkman L., *Säkerhetstjänstens egen berättelse om spionjakten krigsåren 1939–1942. Så gick det till när säkerhetstjänsten skapades*, Stockholm 2007.

Björkman L., *Sverige inför Operation Barbarossa. Svensk neutralitetspolitik 1940–1941*, Stockholm 1971.

Boëthius M.-P., *Heder och samvete. Sverige och andra världskriget*, Stockholm 2001.

Bogatic W., *Exilens dilemma. Att stanna eller att återvända – beslut i Sverige av polska kvinnor som överlevde KZ-lägret Ravensbrück och räddades till Sverige 1945–1947*, Växjö 2011.

Bogusławski A., *Pod Gwiazdą Polarną. Polacy w Finlandii 1939–1941*, Warszawa–Paryż 1997.

Borodziej W., *Od Poczdamu do Szklarskiej Poręby. Polska w stosunkach międzynarodowych 1945–1947*, London 1990.

Byström M., *Utmaningen. Den svenska välfärdsstatens mote med flyktingar i andra världskrigets tid*, Lund 2012.

Carlgren W. M., *Svensk underrättelsetjänst 1939–1945*, Stockholm 1985.

Carlgren W. M., *Svensk utrikespolitik 1939–1945*, Stockholm 1973.

Carlquist E., *Solidaritet på prov. Finlandshjälp under vinterkriget*, Stockholm 1971.

Chrzanowski B., *Ekspozytura "Północ" Oddziału II Sztabu Naczelnego Wodza na terenie Szwecji* [in:] *Polski wywiad wojskowy 1918–1945*, P. Kołakowski (ed.), A. Pepłonski, Toruń 2006.

Chrzanowski B., Gąsiorowski A., Steyer K., *Polska Podziemna na Pomorzu w latach 1939–1945*, Gdańsk 2005.

Chrzanowski B., *Organizacja sieci przerzutów droga morską z Polski do Szwecji w latach okupacji hitlerowskiej (1939–1945)*, "Zeszyty Muzeum" (Stutthof) 1984, nr 5.

Ciechanowski J. M., *Powstanie warszawskie. Zarys podłoża politycznego i dyplomatycznego*, Pułtusk 2004.

Ciećwierz M., *Próby neutralizacji propagandy antypolskiej na Zachodzie w latach 1944–1947*, "Kwartalnik Historii Prasy Polskiej" 1987, nr 4.

Cieślak T., *Zarys historii najnowszej krajów skandynawskich*, Warsaw 1978.

Cruickshank Ch., *SOE in Scandinavia*, Oxford–New York 1986.

Cygański M., *Publicystyka państw skandynawskich wobec agresji III Rzeszy na Polskę w 1939 roku*, "Przegląd Zachodniopomorski" 1983, p. 1–2.

Czubiński A., *Druga wojna światowa 1939–1945*, cz. 1: *Geneza konfliktu i działania wojenne do 1942 r.*, cz. 2: *Kontrofensywa państw antyfaszystowskich*, Poznań 1999.

Czyż mogli daç więcej. Dzieje 13 Promocji Szkoły Podchorążych Lotnictwa w Dęblinie, materiał zebrał A. Dreja, przyg. do druku K. Łukaszewicz-Preihs, J. Preihs, London 1989.

Dahlberg H., *I Sverige under 2:a världskriget*, Stockholm 1983.

Davies N., *Europa walczy 1939–1945. Nie takie proste zwycięstwo*, przekł. E. Tabakowska, Kraków 2008.

Denkiewicz-Szczepaniak E., *Polska siła robocza w Organizacji Todta w Norwegii i Finlandii w latach 1941–1945*, Toruń 1999.

Dębski S., *Między Berlinem a Moskwą. Stosunki niemiecko-sowieckie 1939–1941*, Warsaw 2003.

Długoborski W., *Polska a wojna zimowa 1939-1940* [w:] *Bałtowie. Przeszłość i teraźniejszość*, A. Kastory (ed.), A. Essen, Kraków 1993.
Dobrowolski S. W., *Dyplomacja Polski Ludowej 1944-1980. Organizacja i funkcjonowanie*, Warsaw 1981.
Dorniak J., *Stosunki polsko-szwedzkie w latach 1944-1974*, Słupsk 1978.
Drangel L., *Den kämpande demokratin. En studie i antinazistisk opinionsrörelse 1935-1945*, Stockholm 1976.
Dudek A., *Mechanizm i instrumenty propagandy zagranicznej Polski w latach 1946-1950*, Wrocław 2002.
Duraczyński E., *Generał Iwanow zaprasza: przywódcy podziemnego państwa polskiego przed sądem moskiewskim*, Warsaw 1989.
Duraczyński E., *Rząd polski na uchodźstwie 1939-1945. Organizacja. Personalia. Polityka*, Warsaw 1993.
Engblom G., *Himmlers fred. Tyska fredstrevare genom Sverige under andra världskriget*, Lund 2008.
Flemming M., *Jeńcy wojenni: studium prawno-historyczne*, Warsaw 2000.
Flyghed J., *Rättsstat i kris. Spioneri och sabotage i Sverige under andra världskriget*, Stockholm 1992.
Garde P-K., *De dödsdömda vittnar – 60 år senare*, Bromma 2004.
Gardner L. C., *Strefy wpływów. Wielkie mocarstwa i podział Europy. Od Monachium do Jałty*, Warsaw 1999.
Garliński J., *Oświęcim walczący*, wyd. 2, London 1997.
Garliński J., *Polska w drugiej wojnie światowej*, Warsaw 1994.
Gondek L., *Na tropach tajemnic III Rzeszy*, Warsaw 1987.
Hadenius S., Molin B., Wieslader H., *Sverige efter 1900. En modern politisk historia*, Stockholm 1988.
Hägglöf G., *Svensk krigshandelspolitik under andra världskriget*, Stockholm 1958.
Historia dyplomacji polskiej, t. 4: *1918-1939*, P. Łossowski (ed.), Warsaw 1995.
Historia dyplomacji polskiej, t. 5: *1939-1945*, W. Michowicz (ed.), Warsaw 1999.
Höjer T., *Svenska Dagbladet och det andra världskriget september 1939 – maj 1945*, Stockholm 1969.
Horisonten klarnar. 1945 – krigsslut, B. Huldt (ed.), K.-R. Böhme, Stockholm 2002.
I orkanens öga. 1941 – osäker neutralitet, B. Hugemark (ed.), Stockholm 2002.
Irving D., *Marszałek Rzeszy Hermann Göring 1893-1946. Biografia*, tłum. B. Zborski, Warsaw 2001.
Jałoszyński I., *Niektóre problemy dotyczące powstania i struktury organizacyjnej Związku Patriotów Polskich w ZSRR* [w:] *Najnowsze dzieje Polski: Materiały i studia z okresu 1914-1939*, t. 4: *1939-1945*, Warsaw 1962.
Jarneberg F., *Internering av polska u-båtar med besättningar i Vaxholms fästning*, "Vaxholms fästnings museum meddelande" 1981.
Jaros J., *Historia górnictwa węglowego w Zagłębiu Górnośląskim w latach 1914-1945*, Katowice-Kraków 1969.
Jaworski P., *Brev kring det ockuperade Warszawa (år 1942)*, "Acta Sueco-Polonica" 2003-2005, nr 12-13.

Jaworski P., *Maurycy Karniol – przedstawiciel Polskiej Partii Socjalistycznej w Szwecji w latach. 1940-1946* [w:] *Od Napoleona do Stalina. Studia z dziejów XIX i XX wieku*, T. Kulak (ed.), Toruń 2007.

Jaworski P., *Polish experiences with Scandinavian activity in the League of Nations*, "Scandinavian Journal of History", 2015, Vol. 40, No. 5.

Jaworski P., *Polska niepodległa wobec Skandynawii 1918-1939*, Wrocław 2001.

Jaworski P., *Problemy stosunków polsko-szwedzkich w latach od 1944 do 1948*, "Wrocławskie Studia z Polityki Zagranicznej" 2001, nr 1.

Jaworski P., *"Raporty" posła szwedzkiego w Warszawie Joena Lagerberga z września 1939 roku*, "Dzieje Najnowsze" 2006, nr 2.

Jaworski P., *"Rapporter" från det svenska sändebudet i Warszawa Joen Lagerberg i september1939*, "Acta Sueco-Polonica" 2003-2005, nr 12-13.

Jaworski P., *Z dziejów kształtowania polityki rządu RP na uchodźstwie wobec problemu bałtyckiego (1940-1944)*, "Slavica Ludensia", t. 23: *Skandinavien och Polen. Möten, relationer och ömsesidig påverkan*, B. Törnquist-Plewa (ed.), Lund 2007.

Jaworski P., *Związek Patriotów Polskich w Szwecji (1943-1947)*, "Pamięć i Sprawiedliwość" 2005, nr 1.

Johansson A. W., *Per Albin och kriget*, Stockholm 1984.

Karlsson R., *Så stoppades tysktågen. Den tyska transiteringstrafiken i svensk politik 1942-1943*, Stockholm 1974.

Karski J., *Great Powers and Poland 1919-1945. From Versaille to Yalta*, Lanham 2014.

Kastory A., *Złowrogie sąsiedztwo. Rosyjska polityka wobec europejskich państw ościennych w latach 1939-1940*, Kraków 1998.

Kersten K., *Jałta w polskiej perspektywie*, London-Warsaw 1989.

Kersten K., *Narodziny systemu władzy 1943-1948*, wyd. 2, Poznań 1990.

Kimball W.F., *Roosevelt, Churchill i II wojna światowa*, tłum. O. Zienkiewicz, Warsaw 1999.

Kisielewski T., *Federacja środkowo-europejska. Pertraktacje polsko-czechosłowackie 1939-1943*, Warsaw 1991.

Kliszewicz L., *Baza w Sztokholmie*, "Zeszyty Historyczne" (Paris) 1981, p. 58.

Kliszewicz L., *Placówki wojskowej łączności kraju z centralą w Londynie podczas II wojny światowej*, t. 5: *Baza w Sztokholmie*, Warsaw-London 2000.

Kłonczyński A., *Stosunki polsko-szwedzkie w latach 1945-1956*, Gdańsk 2007.

Konecki T., *Skandynawia w drugiej wojnie swiatowej. Od neutralności i pacyfizmu do militaryzmu i wyścigu zbrojeń*, Warsaw 2003.

Kornat M., *Polska 1939 roku wobec paktu Ribbentrop-Mołotow. Problem zbliżenia niemiecko-sowieckiego w polityce zagranicznej II Rzeczypospolitej*, Warsaw 2002.

Kowalski W. T., *Polityka zagraniczna RP 1944-1947*, Warsaw 1971.

Kowalski W. T., *Walka dyplomatyczna o miejsce Polski w Europie 1939-1945*, Warsaw 1979.

Kralisz A., *Na straży wschodnich rubieży. Biografia ostatniego dowódcy KOP gen. bryg. Wilhelma Orlik-Rückemanna (1894-1986)*, Warsaw 1999.

Kroll B., *Rada Główna Opiekuńcza 1939-1945*, Warsaw 1985.

Kruszewski E. S., *Akcja Kontynentalna w Skandynawii 1940-1945*, Copenhagen 1993.

Kruszewski E. S., *Polski Instytut Źródłowy w Lund (1939-1972). Zarys historii i dorobek*, London-Copenhagen 2001.
Kunert A. K., *Rzeczpospolita Walcząca. Powstanie Warszawskie 1944. Kalendarium*, Warsaw 1994.
Kunert A. K., *Rzeczpospolita Walcząca. Styczeń-grudzień 1940. Kalendarium*, Warsaw 1997.
Kunert A. K., *Rzeczpospolita Walcząca. Styczeń-grudzień 1941. Kalendarium*, Warsaw 2002.
Kunert A. K., *Rzeczpospolita Walcząca. Wrzesień-grudzień 1939. Kalendarium*, Warsaw 1993.
Leinwand A., *Przywódcy Polski Podziemnej przed sądem moskiewskim*, wyd. 2. popr. i uzup., Warsaw 1989.
Levine P. A., *From indifference to activism. Swedish diplomacy and the Holocaust, 1938-1944*, Uppsala 1996.
Lewandowski J., *Finowie i Polacy w 1944 roku*, "Zeszyty Historyczne" (Paris) 1994, vol. 107.
Lewandowski J., *Knutpunkt Stockholm: den polska motståndsrörelsens svenska förbindelser från september 1939 till juli 1942*, Stockholm 2006.
Lewandowski J., *Polski dziennik Svena Grafströma*, "Zeszyty Historyczne" (Paris) 1982, vol. 60.
Lewandowski J., *Raport Vendla. Próba mikro- i makroanalizy*, "Biuletyn Żydowskiego Instytutu Historycznego" 1992, nr 4.
Lewandowski J., *Swedish Contribution to the Polish Resistance Movement during World War Two, 1939-1942*, Uppsala 1977.
Lewandowski J., *Węzeł stockholmski. Szwedzkie koneksje polskiego podziemia IX 1939-VII 1942*, Uppsala 1999.
Lindal K., *Självcensur i stövelns skugga. Den svenska radions roll och hållning under andra världskriget*, Stockholm 1998.
Lindberg H., *Svensk flyktingpolitik under internationellt tryck 1936-1941*, Stockholm 1973.
Lindorm E., *Gustaf V och hans tid 1938-1947. En bokfilm*, Stockholm 1979.
Lööw H., *Nazismen i Sverige 1924-1979. Pionjärerna, partierna, propagandan*, Stockholm 2004.
Ludlow P. W., 'Scandinavia between the Great Powers. Attempts at Mediation in the First Year of the Second World War', *Historisk tidskrift* 1974, nr 1.
Łopuszański J., Matuszewicz H., *Kobiety w "sprawie szwedzkiej"* [w:] *Służba Polek na frontach II wojnie światowej*, cz. 4, M. Golon (ed.), K. Minczykowska, Toruń 2000.
Łuczak C., *Polityka ludnościowa i ekonomiczna hitlerowskich Niemiec w okupowanej Polsce*, Poznań 1979.
Łuczak C., *Polska i Polacy w drugiej wojnie światowej*, Poznań 1993.
Madajczyk C., *Dramat katyński*, Warsaw 1989.
Madajczyk C., *Polityka III Rzeszy w okupowanej Polsce*, t. 1-2, Warsaw 1970.
Materiały do dziejów polskiego uchodźstwa niepodległościowego, t. 1: *Władze RP na obczyźnie podczas II wojny światowej*, Z. Błażynski (ed.), London 1994.

Materski W., *Dyplomacja Polski "lubelskiej". Lipiec 1944 – marzec 1947*, Warsaw 2007.
Matuszewski S., *Ministerstwo Informacji i Propagandy*, "Zeszyty Prasoznawcze" 1984, nr 3.
Molin K., *Försvaret, folkhemmet och demokratin. Socialdemokratisk riksdagspolitik 1939–1945*, Stockholm 1974.
Molin K., Nissen H.S., Skodvin M., *Norden under andra världskriget*, Lund 1979.
Möller Y., *Östen Undén. En biografi*, Stockholm 1986.
Möller Y., *Rickard Sandler. Folkbildare. Utrikesminister*, Stockholm 1990.
Müssener H., *Exil in Schweden. Politische und kulturelle Emigration nach 1933*, München 1974.
Myślinski J., *Z działalności resortu informacji i propagandy PKWN w zakresie prasy i informacji prasowej*, "Rocznik Historii Czasopiśmiennictwa Polskiego" 1967, p. 1.
Najnowsze dzieje Polski: Materiały i studia z okresu 1914–1939, t. 6: *1939–1945*, C. Madajczyk (ed.), Warsaw 1962.
Nawrot D., *Internowanie i rehabilitacja załóg polskich okrętów podwodnych w Szwecji w latach II wojny światowej*, "Przegląd Historyczno-Wojskowy" 2001, nr 2.
Nevakivi J., *The appeal that was never made. The Allies, Scandinavia and the Finnish winter war 1939–1940*, London 1976.
Nowakowski T., *Polak, który wstrząsnął Szwecją – prozaik, publicysta, sowietolog Tadeusz Jan Nowacki (1902–1976)*, "Archiwum Emigracji" 2001, p. 4.
Nurek M., *Klimaty polityczne w rejonie Bałtyku przed i po wybuchu drugiej wojny światowej* [w:] *Bałtyk w polityce polskiej w tysiącleciu*, F. Nowiński (ed.), Gdańsk 2000.
Nya fronter? 1943 – spänd väntan, B. Hugemark (ed.), Stockholm 1994.
Nybom T., *Motstånd – anpassning – uppslutning. Linjer i svensk debatt om utrikespolitik och internationell politik 1940–1943*, Stockholm 1978.
Olsson L., *På tröskeln till folkhemmet. Baltiska flyktingar och polska koncentrationslägerfångar som reservarbetskraft i skånskt jordbruk kring slutet av andra världskriget*, Lund 1995.
Olsson S.-O., *German coal and Swedish fuel 1939–1945*, Gothenburg 1975.
Olsson S.-O., *Swedish-Polish Trade Negotiations at the End of the Second World War and Their Results*, "Scandinavian Economic History Review" 1988, nr 2.
Oredsson S., *Lunds universitet under andra världskriget. Motsättningar, debatter och hjälpinsatser*, Lund 1996.
Padfield P., *Himmler. Reichsführer SS*, London 1990.
Osborne P. R., *Operation Pike: Britain Versus the Soviet Union, 1939–1941*, Westport, CT, USA, 2000.
Pałyga E. J., *Dyplomacja Polski Ludowej 1944–1984 (kierunki – treści – mechanizmy)*, Warsaw 1986.
Partacz C., Łada K., *Polska wobec ukraińskich dążeń niepodległościowych w czasie II wojny światowej*, Toruń 2004.
Pepłoński A., *Wywiad Polskich Sił Zbrojnych na Zachodzie 1939–1945*, Warsaw 1995.
Persson S., *"Vi åker till Sverige". De vita bussarna 1945*, Rimbo 2003.

Pertek J., *Mała flota wielka duchem*, Poznań 1989.
Piotrowski B., *Propaganda III Rzeszy w Szwecji w okresie II wojny światowej*, "Komunikaty Instytutu Bałtyckiego" 1971, p. 14.
Piotrowski B., *Tradycje jedności Skandynawii. Od mitu wikińskiego do idei nordyckiej*, Poznań 2006.
Piotrowski B., *Wojna radziecko-fińska (zimowa) 1939–1940. Legendy, niedomówienia, realia*, Poznań 1997.
Pobóg-Malinowski W., *Najnowsza historia polityczna Polski 1864–1945*, t. 3: *1939–1945*, London 1960.
Polen fjärde delningen, Stockholm 1939.
Polityka morska państwa w 40-leciu PRL, Gdańsk 1986.
Polska–Szwecja 1919–1999, J. Szymanski (ed.), Gdańsk 2000.
Polsko-brytyjska współpraca wywiadowcza podczas II wojny światowej, t. 1: *Ustalenia Polsko-Brytyjskiej Komisji Historycznej*, T. Dubicki (ed.), D. Nałęcz, T. Stirling, Warsaw 2004.
Potocki S., *Uwagi o neutralności Szwecji i jej stosunku do Polski w czasie II wojny światowej*, "Komunikaty Instytutu Bałtyckiego" 1974, p. 21.
Potworowski T., *The Polish Legation's undiplomatic activities, Stockholm September 1939 –July 1942*, "Acta Sueco-Polonica" 2001–2002, nr 10–11.
Raack R. C., *Stalin's Drive to the West 1938–1945. The Origins of the Cold War*, Stanford 1995.
Raczyński E., Żenczykowski T., *Od Genewy do Jałty. Rozmowy radiowe*, Lublin–London 1991.
Radowitz S., *Schweden und das "Dritte Reich" 1939–1945. Die deutsch-schwedischen Beziehungen im Schatten des Zweiten Weltkriges*, Hamburg 2005.
Reginbogin H. R., *Faces of neutrality. A comparative Analysis of the Neutrality of Switzerland and other Neutral Nations during WWII*, Berlin 2009.
Richardson G., *Beundran och fruktan. Sverige inför Tyskland 1940–1942*, Stockholm 1996.
Rockberger N., *Göteborgstrafiken. Svensk lejdtrafik under andra världskriget*, Stockholm 1973.
Roth D. B., *Hitlers Brückenkopf in Schweden. Die deutsche Gesandtschaft in Stockholm 1933–1945*, Flensburg 2007.
Sawicki J. K., *Pod flagą komodora*, Gdańsk 1992.
Sawicki J. K., *Polska Marynarka Handlowa*, t. 1: *1939–1945*, Gdynia 1991.
Schwedische und Schweizerische Neutralität im Zweiten Weltkrieg, R. L. von Bindschedler (ed.), H. R. Kurz, W. M. Carlgren, S. Carlsson, Basel 1985.
Sjögren O., *Geografisk läsebok*, vol. 2: *Europa utom Norden*, Stockholm 1942.
Skarżynski B., *Motywy polskie w piśmiennictwie szwedzkim w czasie wojny*, "Nowa Polska" 1945, vol. 3.
Skarżynski B., *Motywy polskie w pismiennictwie szwedzkim w czasie wojny (ciag dalszy)*, "Nowa Polska" 1946, vol. 1.
Skinder-Suchcitz T., *Próby uwolnienia okrętów podwodnych z internowania w Szwecji. Wrzesień 1939 – czerwiec 1940*, "Zeszyty Historyczne" 1996, vol. 115.

Słomczyński A., *Dom ks. Boudena 1939–1945*, Warsaw 1975.
Sobéus U., *SEP, RYS, ZBIK, de polska ubåtarna. Ett 60-årsminne*, "Vaxholms fästnings museum årsbok" 1999.
Söderberg S., *Svenska röda korset 1865–1965*, Stockholm 1965.
Staniszewski A., *Na bocznym torze wojny, czyli sześć lat internowania polskich okrętów podwodnych w Szwecji* [w:] *Historia i polityka*, t. 5: *Myśl polityczna i dyplomacja w XX w.*, P. Tomaszewski (ed.), Toruń 2006.
Stormvarning. Sverige inför andra världskriget, (ed.) B. Hugemark, Luleå 2002.
Strzałka K., *Między przyjaźnią a wrogością. Z dziejów stosunków polsko-włoskich (1939–1945)*, Kraków 2001.
Suchcitz A., *Polska a wojna fińsko-sowiecka 1939–1940*, "Niepodległość" 1988.
Svea. Ze studiów nad szwedzką nauką i kulturą, pod B. Andrzejewskiego, Poznań 1990.
Sweden's relations with Nazism, Nazi Germany and the Holocaust, S. Ekman (ed.), K. Åmark, Stockholm 2003.
Sveriges militära beredskap 1939–1945, C.-A. Wangel (ed.), Köping 1982.
Szulc A., *Röster sam aldrig tystnar. Tredje rikets offer berättar*, Stockholm 2005.
Szwecja–Polska. Lata rywalizacji i przyjaźni. Polen och Sverige: År av rivalitet och vänskap, J. Niklasson-Młynarska (ed.), Stockholm 1999.
Szymański J., *Polsko-skandynawska współpraca w zakresie żeglugi w okresie międzywojennym (1919–1939)*, Gdańsk 1988.
Szymański J., *Problemy polityki Polski wobec Skandynawii w okresie międzywojennym (1919–1939)*, "Zapiski Historyczne" 1993, p. 1.
Szymański J., *Skandynawia–Polska 1918–1945–1989* [w:] *U progu niepodległości 1918–1989*, R. Wapinski (ed.), Gdańsk 1999.
Szymański J., *Stosunki gospodarcze Polski ze Szwecją w latach 1919–1939*, Gdańsk 1978.
Szymański J., *Wybrane aspekty kwestii rozbrojenia w stosunkach polsko-skandynawskich w okresie międzywojennym*, "Acta Universitatis Lodziensis", "Folia Historica" 1991, nr 42.
Szymański J., *Z genezy stosunków Polski ze Szwecją w latach 1919–1925*, "Zeszyty Naukowe Wydziału Humanistycznego UG", "Studia Scandinavica" 1978, nr 1.
Śląski K., *Tysiąclecie polsko-skandynawskich stosunków kulturalnych*, Wrocław 1977.
Tarka K., *Emigracyjna dyplomacja. Polityka zagraniczna rządu RP na uchodźstwie 1945–1990*, Warsaw 2003.
Tarka K., *Z Litwy do Finlandii? Polacy w wojnie sowiecko-fińskiej*, "Zeszyty Historyczne" (Paris) 1996, p. 115.
Tegen G. & E., *De dödsdömda vittna. Enquêtesvar och intervjuer*, Stockholm 1945.
Thorsell S., *I hans majestäts tjänst. En berättelse från Hitlers Berlin och Stalins Moskva*, Stockholm 2009.
Thorsell S. *Warszawasvenskarna. De som lät världen veta*, Stockholm 2014.
Torbacke J., *Dagens Nyheter och demokratins kris 1937–1946. Genom stormar till seger*, Stockholm 1972.
Törnbom, G. Zetterberg, *Chopin*, Stockholm 1943.

Uggla A. N., *Den svenska bilden av Katyńmorden. Från uppdagande till historisk tillrättaläggelse*, "Multiethnica" 2003, nr 29.
Uggla A. N., *Den svenska Polenbilden och polsk prosa i Sverige 1939-1960: två studier i reception*, Uppsala 1986.
Uggla A. N., *I nordlig hamn. Polacker i Sverige under andra världskriget*, Uppsala 1997.
Uggla A. N., *Polacy na południu Szwecji*, Stockholm 1993.
Uggla A. N., *Polacy w Szwecji w latach II wojny światowej*, Gdańsk 1997.
Uggla A. N., *Polen i svensk press under andra världskriget: en bibliografi*, Uppsala 1986.
Uggla A. N., *Szwedzkie spojrzenie na zbrodnię w Katyniu*, "Relacje" 2004, nr 5.
Uhlin Å., *Februari-krisen 1942. Svensk säkerhetspolitik och militär planering 1941-1942*, Stockholm 1972.
Urladdning. 1940 – blixtkrigens år, B. Hugemark (ed.), Luleå 2002.
Urzyńska D., *Polski ruch socjalistyczny na obczyźnie w latach 1939-1945*, Poznań 2000.
Utrikespolitik och historia. Studier tillägnade Wilhelm M. Carlgren den 6 maj 1987, Stockholm 1987.
Vindkantring. 1942 – politisk kursändring, B. Hugemark (ed.), Luleå 2002.
Widfeldt C., Wegmann R., *Nödlandning. Främmande flyg i Sverige under andra världskriget*, Nässjö 1998.
Wilhelmus W., *Jeszcze o działalności "warszawskich Szwedów"*, "Komunikaty Instytutu Bałtyckiego" 1976, p. 23.
Wilhelmus W., *Szwedzkie monopole w służbie polskiego rządu emigracyjnego? Przyczynek do losów "Szwedów warszawskich"*, "Komunikaty Instytutu Bałtyckiego" 1973, p. 18.
Wittmann K., *Schwedens Wirtschaftsbeziehungen zum Dritten Reich 1933-1945*, München 1978.
Wojciechowski Z., *Internowanie polskich okrętów podwodnych w Szwecji*, "Przegląd Morski" 1991, nr 11.
Wrzesiński W., *Polska a problem bałtycki. Ze studiów nad stanowiskiem polskim wobec Bałtyku w okresie drugiej wojny światowej*, "Przegląd Zachodni" 1990, nr 5-6.
Wyrwa T., *Szwedka o powstaniu warszawskim*, "Zeszyty Historyczne" (Paris) 2000, nr 134.
Zalewski B., *Polska morska myśl wojskowa 1918-1989*, Toruń 2001.
Zawodny J. K., *Katyń*, Lublin-Paryż 1989.
Zawodny J. K., *Powstanie Warszawskie w walce i dyplomacji*, Warsaw 1994.

4. Varia

Bellman C.M., *Fredmanowe pieśni i posłania*, tłum. L. Neuger, Kraków 1991.
Berberyusz E., *Anders spieszony*, London 1992.
Matuszewski I., *Wybór pism. Kulisy historii Polski (1941-1946)*, Rzeszów 1991.

Słownik Biograficzny Pomorza Nadwiślanskiego, S. Gierszewski (ed.), t. 2, Gdańsk 1994.
Stroński S., *Polityka rządu polskiego na uchodźstwie w latach 1939–1942*, t. 1–3, oprac. J. Piotrowski, New Sandec 2007.
"Warsaw concerto". Powstanie Warszawskie w poezji, wybór i oprac. A. K. Kunert, Warsaw 2004.
Zasłużeni Pomorzanie w latach II wojny światowej: szkice biograficzne, Wrocław–Gdańsk 1984.

Index

Adamek, Stanisław 106, 215, 308, 354
Adamkiewicz, Włodzimierz 89, 90, 91
Adlercreutz, Carlos 48, 154
Ahnlund, Nils 259, 304
Åkerberg, Harald 309
Åkerrén, Bengt 74, 75
Aleksandr I, Romanov 305
Allen, Edmund 52
Almstedt, Gunnar 263–264, 289, 291–292
Alter, Wiktor 212–213, 232
Altonen, Alexi 132
Åman, Walter 232
Anders, Władysław 225
Anderson, Ivar 105, 224
Andersson, Carl-Albert 309
Andersson, Kurt 194, 271, 300
Andolf, Göran 123, 516, 533, 536, 541–542, 544–546
Arbin, Axel von 182, 381
Arborén, Olof Carl 154
Arciszewski, Tomasz 307, 310–312, 314, 333, 335, 345, 354, 467–468
Armfelt, Józefa, 255, 347
Arrhén, Erik 128, 197, 304
Arski, Stefan, see Salman Artur
Assarsson, Vilhelm 78, 112, 161, 216, 218–219, 230, 252, 329
Åström, Sverker 216–218, 324, 510–511
Atlee, Clement 200
Axell, Harald 185, 293, 323, 381–382, 394, 498, 506
Babiński, Wacław 236, 403, 490, 493–494
Baliński, Antoni 157
Baliński, Stanisław 301

Banach I. 140
Banaczyk, Władysław 494
Bandura, Aleksy 272, 276, 281
Beck, Józef 11, 12, 13, 23, 30, 31, 72, 173
Beck-Friis, Hans 78
Beck-Friis, Johan 56, 77, 78, 80, 81, 82, 83, 341–342, 477
Beer, Henrik 498, 510–511
Belfrage, Leif 386
Bellman, Carl Michael 292
Below, Carl von 148, 455
Bentzler, Axel 381
Berent 84
Bergelin, Sune 45, 46, 47, 49, 66
Bergenström, Carl 480
Berglind, Nils 186
Bergström, Algot 402
Berling, Zygmunt 195, 252, 275, 320
Berman, Jakub 357–358
Bernadotte, Estelle 479
Bernadotte, Folke 319, 332–333, 467–468, 479, 496–498, 504, 510, 534
Berson, Jan Otmar 43, 118, 151, 177
Bertoni, Karol 382
Bertram, Hans 108
Bestecki, Bolesław 542–543
Bick, Józef 286
Biegański, W. 465
Biernacki, 435
Bierut, Bolesław 443
Birnbaum, Immanuel 259
Björklid, Erland 180
Björklund, 339
Blanck, Sigma 293, 490, 498

Bogomolov, Aleksandr 242
Bogs, Alexander 43, 126
Boheman, Erik 11–13, 23, 26, 34, 56, 116–117, 123, 125, 129, 133, 135, 137, 139, 140–145, 156–158, 164, 166, 168–170, 172, 187, 196, 229–230, 249–250, 279, 332, 338, 341–342, 364, 370, 416, 423, 479, 483, 528, 550
Böhm, Wilhelm 233
Bohuszewicz, Witold 542–543
Bolander, Gunnar 373, 376, 379, 381–383
Bolander, Knud 158, 183
Böök, Fredrik 134
Bór-Komorowski, Tadeusz 287, 298, 306, 315, 345
Borejsza, Jerzy 282
Borśniowski, Tadeusz 281
Brandt, Willy 232
Branting, Hjalmar 279
Bratt, Karl-Axel 51, 62, 63, 68
Brolin 418
Broniewski, Władysław 181
Brzeskwiński, Feliks 95, 122, 129–131, 135, 140, 145, 149, 154, 158, 159, 165, 223, 227, 263, 316, 328, 461, 463–464, 515, 520, 536, 541–542, 544
Brzeskwiński, G. 316
Budnik, Bernard 542
Burckhardt, Carl 31
Burg, von der 527
Bylund 418
Calisendorf 418
Campbell 531
Camps, W. A. 490
Carter, R. H. 517
Casparsson, Ragnar 132, 309
Castleton 542
Catherine, Jagiellon 202
Ceceniowski, Eligiusz 536
Cederberg, Daniel 293, 542

Cederschiöld, Gunnar 46
Cedro, Mieczysław Zygmunt 516
Chabasiński, Wojciech 319, 337–338, 427, 435, 441–443, 505
Chamberlain, Neville 33
Charles, Prince 474, 484, 499–500, 503
Charles, Edward, Prince 484
Chodyra, Józef 541
Chopin, Fryderyk 302
Chrzanowski, Bogdan 14, 456–457
Churchill, Winston 114, 127, 161, 247, 261, 317, 342
Ciechanowiecka, Mary (Maria) 322, 502
Ciechanowski, Jan 78, 79, 89, 90, 112
Cienciała, Andrzej 174, 175
Ciołkosz, Adam 17, 131, 132, 201, 256–257, 306–308, 336, 456–457
Clerk-Kerr, Alan 356, 439
Cnut 259
Colliers, Laurence 117, 517
Coote, E. O. 187
Cripps, Stafford 141,
Croneborg, Adolf 31, 317
Cross, Cecil 443
Crutzesco, Georges 94
Cullberg, J. 475
Curzon, Georg 215
Cybulski, Julian 419
Czapiński, Kazimierz 132
Czyszkowski, Witold 414, 421, 426–427
Dahlerus, Birger 32, 33, 34, 95, 96, 127
Dahn, Waldemar 323, 394
Dalen, G. 380
Danielsson, O. 531
Dankwort, Werner 217
Dardel, Gustaf von 58
Davis, Malcolm 478

Denham, Henry 250, 340, 517, 528, 530, 537
Dekanozov, Vladimir 432, 505
Dix 83
Dmowski, Roman 102
Döbeln, G. von 532
Dreja, Alojzy 543
Drobner, Bolesław 504
Dubiel, Józef 544
Dubois, Stanisław 488
Dyrssen 529
Edberg, Rolf 294
Eden, Anthony 12, 145, 161, 192–193, 228, 230, 236, 317, 332
Edgren, Folke 315
Egeland, Leif 249–250
Ehrenburg, Ilja 162
Ehrenpreis, Wiktor 461
Ehrensvärd, Albert 103
Ehrlich, Henryk 212–213, 232
Eidem, Erling 55, 56
Ekeberg, Lars Birger 411, 510
Ekman, C. 480
Ekstrand, Einar 320
Enander, Bo 352, 491
Enell, Harald 24
Eng, Brynolf 16, 344, 348, 356–358, 432–437, 439, 441–444
Engblom, G. 190
Engels, Friedrich 67
Englicht, Józef 28
Engzell, Gösta 458, 460, 470, 477
Eriksson, Denise 443
Eriksson, Herman 236, 397
Erlander, Tage 40, 45, 102
Errko, Eljas 26, 99
Esklung, Allan 424
Essén, Rütger 226, 312

Eugen, Prince 291
Facht, Stig 102
Fahlander, Nils 194
Fernström, Nils 381
Fierlinger, Zdeněk 251
Finkelstein, Leon 349
Folejewski, Zbigniew 109, 279, 308
Folkman, Adolf 263
Foot, Dingle 423
Forbes 33
Forsberg, K. 378
Forshell, Anders 24
Forster, Albert 31, 96
Frank, Hans 110, 500
Frankowski, Antoni 465
Frankowski, Feliks 255
Fredborg, Arvid 247, 392
Frösell, G. 352
Gano, Stanisław 230, 246, 277–284, 286, 321–323, 339, 546
Garter, John see Meurling, Per 64–65
Gaulle, Charles de 326, 340, 356
Geer, Jacob de 104, 223–225, 266
Geibel, Paul Otto 502
George VI, Windsor 127
Geppert, Tadeusz 367, 460
Gibson, George 152
Gie, Stephanus F. N. 228–229, 249
Gilewicz, Wacław 137, 186
Ginsbert, Julian 173
Giron, Marc 131, 527–530, 538
Gistedt-Kiltynowicz, Elna 295–297
Glabisz, Kazimierz 542
Głębocki, J. 369
Goebbels, Joseph 55, 103, 106, 219–220, 249, 355
Gołuchowski, Andrzej 286
Gorączko, E. 444

Göransson, Tord Ernst 416, 436
Göring, Hermann 32, 33, 34, 95, 96, 113, 127
Górka, Olgierd 151–152
Górniak, Franciszek 281
Górski, Alfons 536
Grabowski, Krzysztof 542–543
Grabowski, Władysław 456
Graczyk, Franciszek 535
Gradowska 87
Grafström, Erik 411–412, 429, 444
Grafström Sven 30, 31, 32, 72, 73, 91, 107, 116, 118, 133, 136, 154, 162, 163, 177, 189, 193, 197, 213, 229–230, 245, 317–318, 329, 333, 358–359, 376–379, 475, 480, 550
Graliński, Zygmunt 111
Granath, Axel 450–451
Granholm, A. 400
Greiser, Arthur 97
Grochowski, Aleksander 519
Grosfeld, Ludwik 466, 487–488
Grounes 418
Grynberg, Judyta 480
Grzegorzewski, Edward 504
Guarnaschelli, Giovanni Battista 340
Guldbrandsen, Jörgen N. 202
Gummerus, Herman 221
Gunnarsson, Gunnar 181, 294, 310
Günther, Christian 115–116, 118–119, 121, 123–124, 129, 139–140, 142, 147, 154–156, 159, 162, 164, 166, 167, 168, 178, 186, 188–189, 192–194, 196, 216, 218, 228, 251, 258, 315, 319, 337, 340, 346, 355, 357–358, 370, 415, 433, 443, 463, 485, 504–505
Günther-Schwarzburg, Władysław 342
Gustafsson, Gösta 185, 550
Gustaf V 28, 35, 39, 40, 123, 124, 127, 140, 144, 168, 189, 291, 318, 468, 500, 515

Gwiazdoski, Tadeusz 442
Gyllenkrok, Axel 44, 45, 65, 66
Gyllenram, R. 81
Haakon VII 121
Hácha, Emil 104
Hagberg, Knut 207–208, 294
Häggberg, Sigge 163, 381
Hägglöf, Gunnar 36, 41, 62, 99, 128, 196, 244, 363–366, 376, 388, 396–399, 408–409, 416, 427
Hägglöf, Ingemar 250–252, 267–268, 337–338, 344–345
Hahnewald, Edgar 232
Halifax, Edward 33, 47
Hallström, P. 482
Halmstedt 382
Hansen, Laurits 152
Hansson, Margit 181
Hansson, Per Albin 23, 27, 30, 32–33, 35–36, 39–41, 100, 114, 119, 122, 124, 139, 146, 150, 152, 171, 194, 196–197, 217, 231, 234–236, 238, 242–243, 250, 333–335, 436, 466, 495, 548, 550
Hansteen, Viggo 153
Hedin, Göran 55, 98
Hedin, Sven 96, 134, 242
Hedlund-Nyström, Torun 106
Hedström, Karl Olof 102, 103
Hellqvist, Sven 16, 476, 498–503, 505
Hellstedt 418
Hellstedt, Svante 185, 186
Henderson, Neville 34
Hennings, Einar 93, 94
Hercen, Aleksandr 305
Herslow, Carl 55, 66, 87, 162, 381, 384, 480
Hesselgren, Kerstin 295
Himmler, Heinrich 467
Hins Jan 273

INDEX

Hippler Fritz 108

Hirsch Oscar 436

Hitler, Adolf 23, 25–28, 30–31, 36, 39, 47, 57, 59–61, 63–64, 68–70, 82, 96, 99, 101, 103, 106–107, 114, 121, 127, 130, 134, 136, 142, 155, 160, 207, 213, 220, 222–223, 235, 248, 253, 263, 257, 303, 391, 449, 464, 467, 531, 547, 550

Hofbauer, Josef 258–259

Höglund, Zeth 59, 64, 101, 102, 107, 132, 456

Höjer, Torvald 123, 192, 212, 224

Holger, Hans Eric 41

Holmberg, N. 64

Holmström, Brita 498

Hornborg, Eirik 221

Huber, Max 97

Hudson, Robert S. 363

Hułas, Bronisław 544

Hultström, J. 171

Hüttner, J. 479

Ihre, Nils Edvard 376–377, 384–386

Imhof 384

Ironside, Edmund 106

Jacobson 418

Jacobsson, Emil (Jc) 314, 329, 352

Jacynicz, Konstanty 457

Jäderlund, Christer 57, 220

Jakerle, Jiří 232, 241

Jałowiecka, Halina 85, 87

Jałowiecki, Bogdan 76

Janecki, P. 173

Jansson, Karl-Erik 456–457

Jarczyk, Mira 480

Järte, Otto 212, 224, 392

Jasiński, Tadeusz 541

Jażdżewski, Antoni 154

Jędrychowski, Stefan 275, 286, 318–320, 324, 427, 504, 506

Jeka, Augustyn 273

Jensen, Johannes V. 193

Jereczek, Edmund 540

Jöback, Inger Bagger 498

Jobs, Anders 74

Johansson, Albin 237, 309

Johansson, Birger 78, 85, 87, 186, 481

John III, Sobieski 173

Johnson, Herschel 149

Johnson, Eyvind 291–293

Jones 545

Jones, R. V. 250

Josephson, Gunnar 323

Juhlin-Dannfelt, Curt 24, 25, 47, 51, 52, 55, 68, 97, 98,

Jung, Helge 325

Juryś, Roman 282

Kallio, Kyösti 100

Karlmark, Erik 217

Karlsson, E. 27, 65

Karnicki, Borys 521

Karniol, Maurycy 131–133, 138, 153, 161, 188, 190, 194, 198–199, 201, 203, 208, 210, 212, 231, 234–236–240, 248–249, 256–257, 262, 265–266, 268–269, 277–278, 287, 290–291, 304–309, 315–316, 321, 324, 331, 333–336, 336, 350–352, 355, 455–457, 467, 487

Karski, Jan 33, 352

Kellgren, Henry 227

Kemp-Welch, Anthony 19

Kennan, George 342

Kentrschynskyj, Bohdan 253–255

Ker, Alan 517

Kindgren 337–338

Kleen, Willi 169

Klemming, G. 395

Kling, Carl 484

Klintberg, C.-H. af 262

Koc, Adam 368
Kocan, Stanisław 487, 508
Koht, Halvdan 26, 121
Kollat, Feliks 367, 460
Kollberg 418
Kollontai, Aleksandra 26, 119, 141, 149, 162, 249, 280, 355, 506
Komierowski 468
Konopczyński, Władysław 477
Kopański, Stanisław 175
Kopeć, Norbert 281
Korniyczuk, Oleksandr 230
Korsak 536
Korsak, Konrad 79
Korytowski, Karol 172, 175, 522
Kot, Stanisław 112, 211, 216
Kowalewski, Przemysław 188, 321, 395, 403, 460, 484, 487, 489, 498
Kowalik, Karol 535
Kowalski, Konstanty 536
Kowalski, Włodzimierz T. 319
Kozłowski, Kazimierz 286
Kożuchowski, Józef 410, 415, 418, 422, 424, 426, 429
Kralisz, Andrzej 454
Krawczyk, Bogusław 522
Kreuger, Ivar 42
Kreuger, Torsten 42
Król, Stanisław 541
Krupski 531
Kruszyński, Janusz 480
Krzysztoporski (family) 479
Kučera, Vladimír 138
Kuczynski, Boguslav 197
Kulak, Teresa 19, 131
Kumlin, Ragnar 153, 160, 173, 188, 192, 195–196, 204, 388
Kuncewiczowa, Maria 181

Kutschera, Franz 262
Kuusinen, Otto 270, 303
Kuźniarz, T. 414, 442
Kwapiński, Jan 15, 17, 184, 231–242, 311, 333, 354, 391–392, 395–397, 404, 409, 421, 427–428, 497, 536–537, 548
Kyling, Folke 150
Lagerberg, Joen 30, 31, 32, 71, 72, 73, 81, 95, 111, 129, 185, 376, 459–460, 479, 482
Lambert 516
Lamming, G. N. 234, 338
Lancaster, O. 158
Landin, Sven 71
Larsson, Sam 150
Lascelles D. W. 517
Lauer Halina 461
Laurin E. 478
Laval, Erik de 28, 29, 30, 82, 87, 185, 186
Leche Löfgren, Mia 200, 498–499
Leifland, L. 247
Leijonhufvud Erik 496–497, 510
Lenin, Vladimir 59, 67, 305
Lewandowski, Jerzy 455
Lie, Trygve 250
Lieberman, Herman 133, 456
Lindberg 322
Lindberg, August 25, 132, 231, 236, 309
Lindberg, Hugo 540
Linde, Gunvor 274
Lindén, Oscar 376
Linderot, Sven 37
Lindh, Nils 300–301, 304–305
Lindquist, E. 290
Lindquist, Karl 37
Lindskog, Claes 266–267, 295
Lindström, Claes 525, 529–531
Lindström, Rickard 26, 131, 138, 231, 295, 308

Lipkowski, Zygfryd 463
Lipski, Józef 33, 34, 76, 81, 83, 84, 85, 86, 87, 89,
Lisiecki, A. 324
Lisiński, Michał 308
Litauer, Stefan 431
Litwiński, L. 374
Ljundberg, Ruben 339, 434–435
Ljungdahl, Karl-Gustaf 399, 435, 440, 443
Lorenc, Austin 273
Lubomirski, Stefan 88, 89, 90
Lubomirski, Zdzisław 475
Lundberg, Gunnar 109, 131, 132
Lundberg, Knud 31, 77, 96, 97, 377, 457, 459
Lundqvist, M. 276
Łakociński, Zygmunt 109, 468, 542–543
Łątkiewicz, Bronisław 516
Łoś, Władysław 518
Łossowski, Piotr 11
Łowczyński, Kajetan 275
Lozowski, Solomon 58, 387
Łubieński, Ludwik 31
Łukasiewicz, Juliusz 173, 368
Łychowski, Tadeusz 410, 426
Machiavelli, Niccolò 59
Maciejewski, Roman 177
MacInnes, Helen 309
Macmillan, Harold 116
Madajewski, Walenty 378
Magnuson 418
Magnusson 418
Maleszka, Franciszek 78, 79, 84, 85
Malinowski, Mieczysław 544
Malinowski, Władysław 461
Mallet, Philip 19

Mallet Victor 117, 119, 133, 144, 149, 180, 192–193, 229–230, 247, 250, 337–338, 340, 437, 440, 528
Mandel, Leon 281
Mannerheim, Carl Gustaf von 115, 518
Manuilsky, Dmitriy 37
Marecki, Andrzej 228
Martinson, Harry 294
Marx, Karl 59, 67
Masiak, Jan 321
Mathiessen, Herman 401
Matuszewski, Ignacy 172
Maycock, R. B. 544
Mayski, Ivan 146, 155, 216, 225
Męczyński, Tadeusz 536
Megerle, Karl 136
Mejor, Franciszek 542–543
Mellenthin, von 68
Melnyk, Andrij 254
Mendelsohn, Bolesław 461
Merdinger, Zbigniew 479, 497
Meurling, Per 64, 354–355
Mickiewicz, Adam 302
Miecznik, Tadeusz 545
Mikołajczyk, Stanisław 183–184, 187, 200, 247, 257, 265, 268–271, 301, 309, 315–317, 332–333, 343–344, 416, 423, 432, 466
Milczarek, Stanisław 283
Milisiewicz, Jerzy 536
Minc, Hilary 432, 435, 444
Miniakowski, Stefan 544
Mitcheson, Jack 486
Mitkiewicz, Leon 135, 145, 149
Modig, Einar 111
Modzelewski, Zygmunt 274, 336–337, 343–344, 348, 357, 359, 432–435, 441–442
Mohr, Hanna 281

Molander, Hilding 73, 87, 381–383, 385, 478
Möller, Gustav 132, 165, 190, 231, 334, 457
Möller, Yngve 100, 171, 172
Molotov, Vyacheslav 37, 58, 127, 224, 272, 318, 433, 443
Monson, Edmund 42, 47,
Montagu-Pollock, William H. 113, 149, 236
Możdżeński, Leonard 367
Müllern, Gunnar 109, 110, 312–313, 330
Munch, Peter 26
Munthe, Gustaf 295
Myrdal, Alva 295, 510
Myrdal, Robert 258
Nagórski, Zygmunt 72, 73
Nahlik, Stanisław Edward 112
Nerman, Ture 106, 178, 208, 295, 455
Neuman, Władysław 95
Nial, Håkan 90, 91, 536–538
Nieduszyński, T. 498
Niedziałkowski, Mieczysław 132, 138, 232, 237
Nilsson, Dr 402
Nilsson, Torsten 71, 132, 231, 238, 309
Nordwall, Ulf 496, 509
Norlander, Helge 369, 373, 396–397, 404, 418
Norrman, Sven 163, 185, 187, 295, 310, 379, 381, 383, 392, 417, 433, 475–476, 481, 550
Norwid-Neugebauer, Mieczysław 175
Nowacki (seaman) 534
Nowacki, Czech 542–544
Nowacki (-Norwid), Tadeusz 96, 173, 263, 310, 352, 392, 540–541
Nowak-Jeziorański, Jan 152, 462
Nybom, Thorsten 104, 121, 214, 225
Nylander, Lennart 452, 460

Ohde, Thorsten 237
Ohlin, Bertil 197, 433, 440–441
Olberg, Paul 107, 132, 133, 302–304
Oleynikov 277
Olivecrona, Karl 134
Olsson, S. 182
Olszowski, Tadeusz 405, 416
Orlik-Rückemann, Wilhelm 454
Örne, Anders 169
Osóbka-Morawski, Edward 285, 298, 313, 322, 331, 348, 357
Ostrowski, A. 320
Oterdahl, Jeanna 291, 295, 301
Otmar-Berson, Jan see Berson, Jan Otmar
Oxenstierna, Johan Gabriel 534
Paderewski, Ignacy 148
Page, Leander 544
Palmén, Janina 473
Palmstierna, Carl 177
Pański, Jerzy (a seaman) 272–286, 320–324, 338–340, 348, 423–424, 431, 439, 454, 506–508
Pański, Jerzy (literary critic) 282
Papuga, Jan 273
Parker, Ralph 329–330
Patejeruk, Sergiusz 273
Patek, Wiesław 141, 258, 321, 470
Paul I, Romanov 305
Paul, Ernst 236
Pauli, Ivan 183
Pawliszyn, Henryk 264
Penny, Martin 177
Persson, G. 154
Persson, Gösta 102
Persson, Per 300
Petander, Karl 168,
Petelenz, Czesław 514–515

Petersén, Carl 56, 77, 80, 82, 84, 87, 379, 476

Pfleging, Ernst 263

Piątkowski, Henryk 328

Pierkiel, Franciszek 286

Pihl, Gunnar Thorstenson 202, 346

Pilch, Tadeusz 91, 146, 188, 190–193, 195–196, 199, 203–204, 236–237, 241, 261, 315–316, 320–321, 332, 350–351, 369–370, 372, 375–376, 380, 388–389, 394–396, 398, 401–411, 415–417, 422–430, 439, 465, 483–484, 486–487, 489, 490, 494–495, 500, 508–511, 514, 537–538

Piłsudski, Józef 68, 102

Piskor, Aleksander 352

Pistel, Hugo 522

Pitjeta, Vladimir 305–306

Plater-Ankarhall, Ludwika 207, 255,

Pławski, Eugeniusz 156, 160–161, 194, 465, 532–534, 539, 541

Pławski, Witold 465

Podjazd-Morgenstern, Tadeusz 156, 160, 371, 515, 518–531

Poland, John R. 516, 519

Pomian-Hajdukiewicz, Alf de 101, 179, 212, 481

Post, Eric von 11, 80, 81, 91, 97, 162, 163, 270, 318–319, 459, 477

Potemkin, Vladimir 58

Potocki, Władysław 367, 373, 460

Potworowska, Magdalena 473

Potworowski, Gustaw 23, 28, 31–32, 43, 77, 79–87, 90, 95, 99, 101, 108–109, 111–112, 116, 118–119, 124–126, 128–130, 133–145, 147, 149–151, 153–160, 162, 164–172, 177–179, 182–183, 185–189, 195, 198–199, 206, 229, 365–366, 368–374, 380, 388, 454–455, 458, 460, 463–464, 466, 473–474, 480–485, 487, 513–514, 547, 524, 526, 528–530, 533, 536, 542–543

Potworowski, Tadeusz 182, 465

Potworowski, Tomasz 15, 18, 23, 43

Pragier, Adam 173, 303

Prigonikier, Ludwik 286

Prottas, Raja 273

Prus-Bar, Lucjan 465

Pruszyński Ksawery 181

Prytz, Björn 94, 112, 218, 228–229, 317, 332, 345–346, 400, 427

Przepiórczyński, Michał 455

Przybyszewski, Józef 288

Przybyszewski-Westrup, Zenon 36, 112, 148, 475

Quisling, Vidkun 104, 235, 269, 330–331

Raab 418

Rabanowski, Jan 319

Racięski, Z. 130

Raczkiewicz, Władysław 95, 144, 168, 188, 240, 468, 480

Raczyński, Edward 71, 94, 112, 154, 172, 183, 189, 205, 317, 375, 484, 497

Radziwiłł, Władysław 373

Ramstedt, Maria 482

Rappaport, Edmund 353

Rappaport, Leon 237

Rataj, Maciej 138

Ravendale, Christian M. 406, 409

Raykowski, J. 182

Razin, Vasiliy 279–281, 322, 324

Rekner, Jerzy 521

Remarque, Erich Maria 45

Requel, Astrid 510

Reuterswärd, Gustaf 43

Reybekiel, Wacław 182

Ribbentrop, Joachim von 58, 69, 127, 224, 272, 467

Richert, Arvid 31, 58, 73, 77, 80–87, 95, 97, 113, 118, 163–164, 185, 218, 228, 457, 476–477, 479, 500–501

Roberts, Frank K. 157

Rods, A. 182
Romanowski, Bolesław 520, 532
Romdahl, Axel L. 294
Romer, Adam 174, 413
Romer, Tadeusz 195–196, 216–217, 244–245, 275, 466, 497, 537
Roosevelt, Franklin Delano 228, 247
Rosen, Adolf von 87, 480
Rosenström, M. 276
Rowecki-Grot, Stefan 187, 306
Ruciński, Witold 544
Rudberg, Gunnar 479
Rudkowski, Roman 541–542
Rudnicka-Jaroszynska, Letta 107, 108
Rudnicki, Tadeusz 115, 137
Rügheimer, Gunnar 492–493
Rundström, E. 378
Sadowski, Kazimierz 535
Sahlin, Stig 99, 359, 415, 429, 510
Salamon, Władysław 519, 527–528
Salman, Artur (Stefan Arski) 456, 461
Sandler, Rickard 12, 23, 25, 26, 28, 32, 36, 41, 57, 58, 82, 94, 95, 98, 99, 100, 118, 130, 171, 178, 363, 454–455, 457, 476, 515
Sapieha, Adam 482
Sapieha, Princess 468
Sapieha, Virgilia 197
Saradjoglu, Sükrü 69
Sarnek, F. 381
Saryusz-Zaleski, Borys 414, 442
Sawczuk 281
Scharfstein, I. 481
Scheynius, Ignaz 257
Schreiber 154
Schück 323
Schulenburg 121
Schulz, Karin 208

Scott, John 353
Segerstedt, Torgny 104, 208, 224, 290, 295
Selter, Kaarel 69
Semenov, Vladimir 277
Semitjov, Wladimir (Volodja) 53, 54, 55, 103, 182
Shapiro, H. 298
Shirk, Elliot M. 344–345
Sikorski, Władysław 95, 114–115, 144–146, 155, 161–162, 167, 183–184, 187, 190, 193, 201, 205, 208, 214, 216, 219–220, 225, 228, 230, 247, 481, 515, 524–525
Silfverskiöld, Per Olof 73, 381, 425
Sillanpää, Frans Eemil 111
Silverstolpe, Gunnar Westin 220–221
Siwik, Mateusz 481
Sjögren, Otto 109
Skarżyński, Bolesław 109, 126, 202, 308, 310, 484
Sköld, Per Edvin 24, 128, 135, 150, 171
Skórzewski, (family) 468
Skrzeszewski, Stanisław 504
Skrzypek, Edward 455
Słoma, Władysław 532
Słowacki, Juliusz 302
Smoleński, Józef 542
Smoluchowski, (family) 479
Sobkowiak, Franciszek 541
Söderblom, Nathan
Söderblom, Staffan 31, 58, 73, 78, 94–95, 97, 147–148, 153, 163–164, 185, 193, 217–218, 228, 242, 249, 252, 270, 293, 317–319, 335–337, 342–344, 348–349, 356–357, 359, 423, 427, 431–433, 435, 455, 480, 504–505, 529
Sohlman, Rolf 315, 329, 357–358, 397–398, 411, 415–418, 427, 430, 432, 441–443, 510
Sokal, Franciszek 480

Sokolnicki, Henryk 90, 91, 92, 142, 188–189, 193–196, 206, 231–232, 236, 242–245, 253–255, 258, 260, 263, 267, 275, 277–278, 281, 286, 308–309, 315–316, 321, 328, 331–333, 338–339, 344–345, 351, 356, 358, 375–376, 392, 394–395, 397–398, 401–403, 408–410, 412–413, 415–423, 436–437, 439–440, 463, 465–470, 487, 489–494, 497–499, 501, 506, 508, 510, 535, 537–539

Sokolnicki, Michał 12, 41, 111, 112, 124

Sołtysiak, Jerzy 541

Sommerfeld, E. 481

Sommerstein, Emil 323

Sörmann, Py 202

Sosnkowski, Kazimierz 140, 261, 282, 288

Spała, Feliks 281

Spellman, Francis 214

Stalin, Josef 26, 27, 28, 31, 57, 58, 60, 61, 63, 64, 67, 68, 69, 70, 99, 100, 101, 107, 130, 190, 192, 205, 208, 213, 217–219, 224, 228, 235, 249, 251, 266–269, 274, 302–303, 315–319, 333, 342, 346–347, 353

Stańczyk, Jan 113, 133, 173, 403, 456, 489–490

Starzewski, Jan 174,

Steinberg, Mila 479

Stenbom, Adolf 132

Stiernstedt, Erik 473–476, 478–482, 498–499, 502

Stiernstedt, Georg 101

Stiernstedt, Marika 202, 208, 261–262, 291, 295, 309–311, 322–323, 498, 504–507

Stoklasa, Tadeusz 517, 538

Strasburger, Henryk 173, 388

Strasser, Otto 47

Strawiński, Konstanty 504–505

Strindberg, Axel 295

Ström, Fredrik 156, 355

Ström, Ture 418, 440, 443

Stroński, Stanisław 105, 152, 157, 183–184

Suvorow, Aleksandr 66

Svahnström, Bertil 38, 69, 70, 110

Szembek, Jan 23, 32, 71, 72, 367

Szende, Stefan 208, 262–263

Shkwarcew, Aleksander 58

Szymaniak, Witold 194–195

Szymański, Antoni 25

Szymański, Józef 110

Śmigły-Rydz, Edward 49, 94

Świętochowski, Henryk 286

Świrski, Jerzy 154, 175, 371, 514–515, 517–518, 520–527, 529–530, 533–536, 538, 541

Taczalski, Zdzisław 542–543

Tarczyński, Mieczysław 536

Tarnow, Fritz 232

Tarnowska, Marianna 480

Tarnowski, Adam 91, 92, 332–333, 356, 358, 466, 507–508, 538–539

Taub, Walter 282

Tchórznicki, Konstanty 501, 503

Tennant, Peter 108, 123, 211, 245, 392

Thorburn 290, 300

Thörnell, Olof 124, 131, 140,

Thugutt, Mieczysław 179–180, 183–184, 186–188, 206, 236, 241, 246, 382, 462–463

Thugutt, Stanisław 237

Thulstrup, Åke 302

Tigerstedt, Örnulf 220

Tilea, Viorel Virgil 173

Tillge-Rasmussen, Sven 57

Tingsten, Herbert 105

Tito-Broz, Josip 326

Tjerneld, Staffan 548

Tokarz, Tadeusz 147

Topolski 435

Torelius, Gösta 54, 65
Torén, Carl Axel 129
Tranmæl, Martin 132, 152, 232
Trębicki, Stefan 263, 308, 352
Tremtiaczy, Iwan 275–276, 281, 321
Trolle, Carl Harald 473–474, 478
Trypućko, Jerzy 109
Tunberg, Sven 183
Tworowski 84
Undén, Östen 135, 155, 172, 178, 551
Undén, Torsten 94
Unger, Stig 479
Unrug, Józef 536
Urbański, Edmund 39
Valentin, Hugo 199
Vanni, Mario 264–265, 289
Vendel, Karl Yngve 163
Vesterlund, Ivar 299
Vetrov, Mihail 277
Viklund, Daniel 183, 219–220, 271
Vinell, T. 418, 482
Vingqvist-Jelnicka, Margit 73, 502
Vougt, Allan 127, 131, 213, 238, 307, 309, 315, 331
Vrang, Carl Vilhelm Birger 27
Vuori, Eero 132, 152
Vyshinsky, Andrey 433, 443
Vysocki, Adolf 197
Wachenfelt, Miles von 479
Walden, Rudolf 115
Waldenström, Arne 443
Waligórski 84
Wallén, C. E. 402
Wallenberg, Jacob 373, 376
Wallenberg, Marcus 383
Wallenberg, Raoul 355
Wallengren, C. 473
Wallin, Emil 457

Wallquist, Einar 461
Walter, J. H. 340
Walterson, John 211–212, 259–260, 289, 302–305
Wangel, C.-A. 516
Wanner, Ch. 478
Warchałowski, Jerzy 76, 85
Wasik 545
Wasilewska, Wanda 195, 262, 268
Wasilewski, Walenty 541
Weibull, John 380
Wengelin, Ragnar Victor 315
Westman, Karl Gustaf 31, 82, 178, 458
Westring, Claes 476–477
Wettergren, Erik 294
Weygand, Maurice 41
Weytko, Józef 490
Wickman, Johannes 26, 27, 208, 210, 225, 248–249, 300, 341
Wickstrøm, Rolf 153
Widell, C. G. 400, 429
Wied, Victor zu 115, 126
Wierzbowska, Maria 488
Wierzyński, Kazimierz 181
Wifstrand, Naima 295
Wigforss, Ernst 393, 493, 495
Wilgress, Leolyn Dana 251
Wilkinson, Peter A. 187
Winiarska, Klotylda 87, 459
Winiarski, Witold 76
Winiewicz, Józef 207
Winther, Wilhelm 57, 58, 78, 98, 387
Wirsén, Einar af 109
Witting, Rolf 548
Wittlin, Józef 111
Wittmann, Klaus 374
Woermann, Ernst 80
Wojciechowski, B. 455

Wojciechowski, Zbigniew 100, 513
Wolbek, Marian 194, 267, 392, 534–536, 548
Woźniak, Bolesław 544
Wyglądacz, Brunon 456
Wysocki, Alfred 42
Żaba, Norbert 18, 152, 155, 157, 160, 179–181, 183–184, 193–194, 196, 200–203, 206–213, 223–226, 229, 231, 236, 240–244, 246, 248–249, 252–255, 257–258, 260–264, 266–267, 287–288, 290–292, 297–302, 309–312, 330–331, 340–341, 346–347, 351–355, 392, 395, 431, 461–463, 465, 492, 495
Zabiełło, Stanisław 113
Zahorska, Ewa 491–492
Zajączkowski, Stanisław 535
Zaleski, August 81, 85, 111, 112, 113, 140, 145, 154, 241, 524, 526
Załuski, K. 497
Zarański, Józef 23
Żebrowski, Michał 521
Żeligowski, Lucjan 255
Zethelius, P. 385–386
Zieliński, Tadeusz 479
Ziembicki, Ludwik 516
Żukowski, Borys 424, 506
Żymierski, Michał 267, 298, 313

Södertörn Academic Studies

1. Helmut Müssener & Frank-Michael Kirsch (eds.), *Nachbarn im Ostseeraum unter sich. Vorurteile, Klischees und Stereotypen in Texten*, 2000.
2. Jan Ekecrantz & Kerstin Olofsson (eds.), *Russian Reports: Studies in Post-Communist Transformation of Media and Journalism*, 2000.
3. Kekke Stadin (ed.), *Society, Towns and Masculinity: Aspects on Early Modern Society in the Baltic Area*, 2000.
4. Bernd Henningsen et al. (eds.), *Die Inszenierte Stadt. Zur Praxis und Theorie kultureller Konstruktionen*, 2001.
5. Michal Bron (ed.), *Jews and Christians in Dialogue*, ii: *Identity, Tolerance, Understanding*, 2001
6. Frank-Michael Kirsch et al. (eds.), *Nachbarn im Ostseeraum übwer einander. Wandel der Bilder, Vorurteile und Stereotypen?*, 2001.
7. Birgitta Almgren, *Illusion und Wirklichkeit. Individuelle und kollektive Denkmusterin nationalsozialistischer Kulturpolitik und Germanistik in Schweden 1928–1945*, 2001.
8. Denny Vågerö (ed.), *The Unknown Sorokin: His Life in Russia and the Essay on Suicide*, 2002.
9. Kerstin W. Shands (ed.), *Collusion and Resistance: Women Writing in English*, 2002.
10. Elfar Loftsson & Yonhyok Choe (eds.), *Political Representation and Participation in Transitional Democracies: Estonia, Latvia and Lithuania*, 2003.
11. Birgitta Almgren (eds.), *Bilder des Nordens in der Germanistik 1929–1945: Wissenschaftliche Integrität oder politische Anpassung?*, 2002.
12. Christine Frisch, *Von Powerfrauen und Superweibern: Frauenpopulärliteratur der 90er Jahre in Deutschland und Schweden*, 2003.
13. Hans Ruin & Nicholas Smith (eds.), *Hermeneutik och tradition. Gadamer och den grekiska filosofin*, 2003.
14. Mikael Lönnborg et al. (eds.), *Money and Finance in Transition: Research in Contemporary and Historical Finance*, 2003.
15. Kerstin Shands et al. (eds.), *Notions of America: Swedish Perspectives*, 2004.

16. Karl-Olov Arnstberg & Thomas Borén (eds.), *Everyday Economy in Russia, Poland and Latvia*, 2003.
17. Johan Rönnby (ed.), *By the Water. Archeological Perspectives on Human Strategies around the Baltic Sea*, 2003.
18. Baiba Metuzale-Kangere (ed.), *The Ethnic Dimension in Politics and Culture in the Baltic Countries 1920–1945*, 2004.
19. Ulla Birgegård & Irina Sandomirskaja (eds.), *In Search of an Order: Mutual Representations in Sweden and Russia during the Early Age of Reason*, 2004.
20. Ebba Witt-Brattström (ed.), *The New Woman and the Aesthetic Opening: Unlocking Gender in Twentieth-Century Texts*, 2004.
21. Michael Karlsson, *Transnational Relations in the Baltic Sea Region*, 2004.
22. Ali Hajighasemi, *The Transformation of the Swedish Welfare System: Fact or Fiction? Globalisation, Institutions and Welfare State Change in a Social Democratic Regime*, 2004.
23. Erik A. Borg (ed.), *Globalization, Nations and Markets: Challenging Issues in Current Research on Globalization*, 2005.
24. Stina Bengtsson & Lars Lundgren, *The Don Quixote of Youth Culture: Media Use and Cultural Preferences Among Students in Estonia and Sweden*, 2005.
25. Hans Ruin, *Kommentar till Heideggers Varat och tiden*, 2005.
26. Ludmila Ferm, *Variativnoe bespredložnoe glagol'noe upravlenie v russkom jazyke XVIII veka* [Variation in non-prepositional verbal government in eighteenth-century Russian], 2005.
27. Christine Frisch, *Modernes Aschenputtel und Anti-James-Bond: Gender-Konzepte in deutschsprachigen Rezeptionstexten zu Liza Marklund und Henning Mankell*, 2005.
28. Ursula Naeve-Bucher, *Die Neue Frau tanzt: Die Rolle der tanzenden Frau in deutschen und schwedischen literarischen Texten aus der ersten Hälfte des 20. Jahrhunderts*, 2005.
29. Göran Bolin et al. (eds.), *The Challenge of the Baltic Sea Region: Culture, Ecosystems, Democracy*, 2005.
30. Marcia Sá Cavalcante Schuback & Hans Ruin (eds.), *The Past's Presence: Essays on the Historicity of Philosophical Thought*, 2006.
31. María Borgström & Katrin Goldstein-Kyaga (ed.), *Gränsöverskridande identiteter i globaliseringens tid: Ungdomar, migration och kampen för fred*, 2006.

32. Janusz Korek (ed.), *From Sovietology to Postcoloniality: Poland and Ukraine from a Postcolonial Perspective*, 2007.
33. Jonna Bornemark (ed.), *Det främmande i det egna: filosofiska essäer om bildning och person*, 2007.
34. Sofia Johansson, *Reading Tabloids: Tabloid Newspapers and Their Readers*, 2007.
35. Patrik Åker, *Symboliska platser i kunskapssamhället: Internet, högre lärosäten och den gynnade geografin*, 2008.
36. Kerstin W. Shands (ed.), *Neither East Nor West: Postcolonial Essays on Literature, Culture and Religion*, 2008.
37. Rebecka Lettevall & My Klockar Linder (eds.), *The Idea of Kosmopolis: History, philosophy and politics of world citizenship*, 2008.
38. Karl Gratzer & Dieter Stiefel (eds.), *History of Insolvency and Bankruptcy from an International Perspective*, 2008.
39. Katrin Goldstein-Kyaga & María Borgström, *Den tredje identiteten: Ungdomar och deras familjer i det mångkulturella, globala rummet*, 2009.
40. Christine Farhan, *Frühling für Mütter in der Literatur?: Mutterschaftskonzepte in deutschsprachiger und schwedischer Gegenwartsliteratur*, 2009.
41. Marcia Sá Cavalcante Schuback (ed.), *Att tänka smärtan*, 2009.
42. Heiko Droste (ed.), *Connecting the Baltic Area: The Swedish Postal System in the Seventeenth Century*, 2011.
43. Aleksandr Nemtsov, *A Contemporary History of Alcohol in Russia*, 2011.
44. Cecilia von Feilitzen & Peter Petrov (eds.), *Use and Views of Media in Russia and Sweden: A Comparative Study of Media in St. Petersburg and Stockholm*, 2011.
45. Sven Lilja (ed.), *Fiske, jordbruk och klimat i Östersjöregionen under förmodern tid*, 2012.
46. Leif Dahlberg & Hans Ruin (eds.), *Fenomenologi, teknik och medialitet*, 2012.
47. Samuel Edquist, *I Ruriks fotspår: Om forntida svenska österledsfärder i modern historieskrivning*, 2012.
48. Jonna Bornemark (ed.), *Phenomenology of Eros*, 2012.
49. Jonna Bornemark & Hans Ruin (eds.), *Ambiguity of the Sacred: Phenomenology, Politics, Aesthetics*, 2012.
50. Håkan Nilsson, *Placing Art in the Public Realm*, 2012.

51. Per Bolin, *Between National and Academic Agendas: Ethnic Policies and 'National Disciplines' at Latvia's University, 1919–1940*, 2012.
52. Lars Kleberg & Aleksei Semenenko (eds.), *Aksenov and the Environs/Aksenov iokrestnosti*, 2012.
53. Sven-Olov Wallenstein & Brian Manning Delaney (eds.), *Translating Hegel: The Phenomenology of Spirit and Modern Philosophy*, 2012.
54. Sven-Olov Wallenstein and Jakob Nilsson (eds.), *Foucault, Biopolitics, and Governmentality*, 2013.
55. Jan Patočka, *Inledning till fenomenologisk filosofi*, 2013.
56. Jonathan Adams & Johan Rönnby (eds.), *Interpreting Shipwrecks: Maritime Archaeological Approaches*, 2013.
57. Charlotte Bydler, *Mondiality/Regionality: Perspectives on Art, Aesthetics and Globalization*, 2014.
58. Andrej Kotljarchuk, *In the Forge of Stalin: Swedish Colonists of Ukraine in Totalitarian Experiments of the Twentieth Century*, 2014.
59. Samuel Edquist & Janne Holmén, *Islands of Identity: History-writing and identity formation in five island regions in the Baltic Sea*, 2014.
60. Norbert Götz (ed.), *The Sea of Identities: A Century of Baltic and East European Experiences with Nationality, Class, and Gender*, 2015.
61. Klaus Misgeld, Karl Molin & Paweł Jaworski, *Solidaritet och diplomati: Svenskt fackligt och diplomatiskt stöd till Polens demokratisering under 1980-talet*, 2015.
62. Jonna Bornemark & Sven-Olov Wallenstein (eds.), *Madness, Religion, and the Limits of Reason*, 2015.
63. Mirja Arnshav & Anna McWilliams, *Stalins ubåtar: en arkeologisk undersökning av vraken efter S7 och SC-305*, 2015.
64. Carl-Gustaf Scott, *Swedish Social Democracy and the Vietnam War*, 2017.
65. Jonna Bornemark & Nicolas Smith (eds.), *Phenomenology of Pregnancy*, 2016.
66. Ulrika Dahl, Marianne Liljeström & Ulla Manns, *The Geopolitics of Nordic and Russian Gender Research 1975–2005*, 2016.
67. Annika Öhrner (ed.), *Art in Transfer in the Era of Pop*, 2017.
68. Jan Öhrming, *Allt görs liksom baklänges: verksamheten vid Nya Karolinska Solna*, 2017.
69. Piotr Wawrzeniuk, *Med osäker utgång*, (forthcoming)

70. Niklas Eriksson, *Riksäpplet: Arkeologiska perspektiv på ett bortglömt regalskepp*, 2017.
71. Christine Bladh, *Hennes snilles styrka – Kvinnliga grosshandlare i Stockholm och Åbo 1750–1820*, 2018.
72. Andrej Kotljarchuk & Olle Sundström (eds.), *Ethnic and Religious Minorities in Stalin's Soviet Union: New Dimensions of Research*, 2017.
73. Pawel Jaworski, *Dreamers and Opportunists*, 2019.

www.ingramcontent.com/pod-product-compliance
Lightning Source LLC
Chambersburg PA
CBHW020826160426
43192CB00007B/535